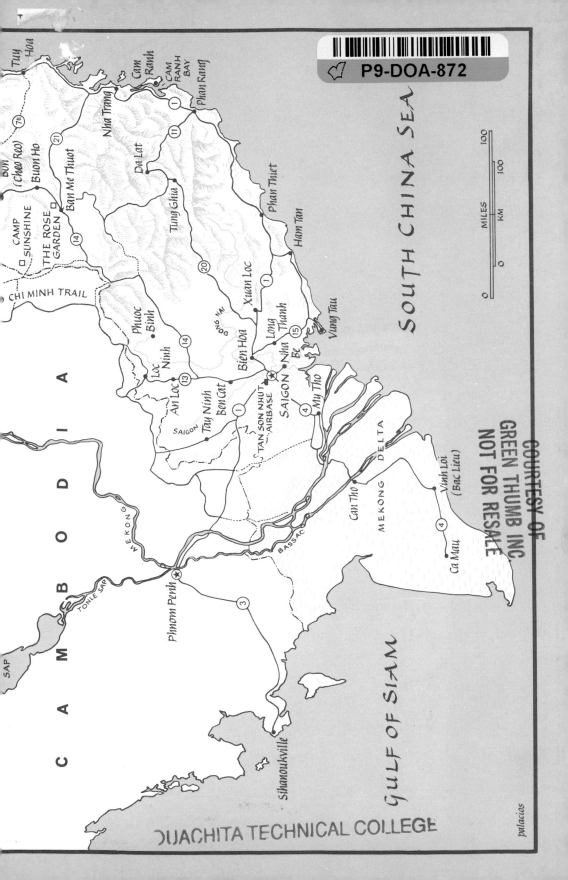

OUACHITA TECHNICAL COLLEGE

P9-DOA-872

SOUTH CHINA SEA

GULF OF SIAM

CAMBODIA

MEKONG DELTA

TONLE SAP

SAP

Phnom Penh

Sihanoukville

3

BASSAC

MEKONG

Ca Mau

Vinh Loi (Bac Lieu)

4

Can Tho

My Tho

4

SAIGON

Nha Be

TAN SON NHUT AIRBASE

Bien Hoa

Long Thanh

15

Vung Tau

Ben Cat

Tay Ninh

SAIGON

1

An Loc

Loc Ninh

13

14

Phuoc Binh

DONG NAI

20

Xuan Loc

1

Ham Tan

Phan Thiet

Vung Tau

CHI MINH TRAIL

THE ROSE GARDEN

CAMP SUNSHINE

Ban Me Thuot

14

Tung Ghia

Da Lat

11

Nha Trang

Cam Ranh

CAM RANH BAY

Phan Rang

1

Buon Ho

Buon (Cheo Reo)

21

7B

Tuy Hoa

MILES

KM

0   100   100   100

palacios

THE
FALL
OF
SAIGON

SCENES FROM THE SUDDEN
END OF A LONG WAR

DAVID BUTLER

Simon and Schuster
New York

Portions of the text centered on Graham Martin, Alan Carter and Ken Moorefield in the final three days of April appeared in slightly different form in *Playboy*.

Material from General Van Tien Dung's *Our Great Spring Victory* copyright © 1977 by Cora Weiss. Reprinted by permission of Monthly Review Foundation.

Library of Congress Cataloging in Publication Data
Butler, David —date.
The fall of Saigon.
Includes index.
1. Vietnamese Conflict, 1961-1975—Vietnam—Ho Chi
Minh City.   2. Ho Chi Minh City—History.   I. Title.
DS559.9.S24B87   1985   959.704′332   85-1788

ISBN: 0-671-46675-5

for
My parents
John Butler
and
Blanche Butler, née Blanche Madeleine Dufault

Acknowledgments

I am of course indebted to everyone who spoke to me for publication. The section titled "Sources" following the text indicates who many of those people are. Some of them had reason to harbor some mistrust of journalists. They spoke to me on the chance that I was out to get it right. I thank them for that leap of faith.

Joyce Barnathan, Germaine Swanson and Jackie Bong Wright were especially helpful when I first moved to Washington to work full time on this book in 1982.

The Historical Research Foundation, in New York City, generously underwrote a two-month reporting trip to France and England in the summer of 1983. That trip also led to an article for *National Review* about Dr. Nguyen Van Hao. I am grateful to the foundation for its grant, which was supported by William F. Buckley, Jr. I thank Mr. Buckley for that, and for the thousand other kindnesses he has shown me through the last fifteen years.

Additional financial support was provided by my parents; and by Dr. and Mrs. Paul Butler, Mr. David G. Dawley, Ms. M. Louise du-Fault, Rev. Omer L. Dufault, Dr. and Mrs. Steven R. Geary, Mrs. Elizabeth Butler Heath, Mr. Peter Roundy and Ms. Margareta Mussachia, and Mr. and Mrs. Steven Strasser.

All of them either lent or gave me money that allowed me to continue writing, uninterrupted by the demands of a job, after I had run through my publisher's advance. For their faith in the value of this book, they have my heartfelt thanks.

Generous financial and moral support also came from Arthur Kretchmer at *Playboy*.

I must acknowledge a special debt to Peter Roundy, whom I met in 1961, when I was twenty, and working as the attendant in the locker room of a New Hampshire golf resort during a college summer vacation. Peter was a couple of years younger than I, and an assistant pastry chef at the same resort. He was then and is now the possessor of one of the three most lively and subtle minds I have ever encountered. Night after night, in telephone conversations between Washington, D.C., and south Florida, where Peter now teaches American young people—white, black, Vietnamese and other—how to make a sentence, a paragraph, an essay, he has acted as patient sounding board, gentle critic and stern coach. Until the next project, I will miss the constant goading, and encouragement.

Finally, through the two and a half years of researching and writing that went into this book, Mr. Nguyen Hung Vuong was my (unpaid) master teacher in countless matters, many but not all of them Vietnamese. It was Mr. Vuong, for example, who tried to teach me the importance of the Second Internationale in the history of Vietnamese communism. He never succeeded, but the failure was mine, not his. Mr. Vuong is absolved of any blame for whatever misinterpretations of Vietnamese attitudes, customs or history appear in the text. He is largely responsible for whatever I happened to get right in such areas. For scores of hours of guidance and encouragement, I express my deep and abiding gratitude.

CONTENTS

DOWNTOWN SAIGON

1 ▪ THE MARINE STATUE
2 ▪ BUTLER'S APARTMENT BUILDING
3 ▪ THE CONTINENTAL PALACE HOTEL
4 ▪ THE NATIONAL ASSEMBLY BUILDING
5 ▪ THE CARAVELLE HOTEL
6 ▪ THE MAJESTIC HOTEL
7 ▪ THE CENTRAL PALACE HOTEL
8 ▪ THE HOTEL CATINAT,
   (home of the PINK NIGHT CLUB)
9 ▪ CITY HALL

10 ▪ THE CENTRAL MARKET
11 ▪ THE CERCLE SPORTIF
12 ▪ THE PRESIDENTIAL PALACE
13 ▪ THE basilica of OUR LADY OF PEACE
14 ▪ P.T.T.
15 ▪ THE FRENCH EMBASSY
16 ▪ THE AMERICAN EMBASSY

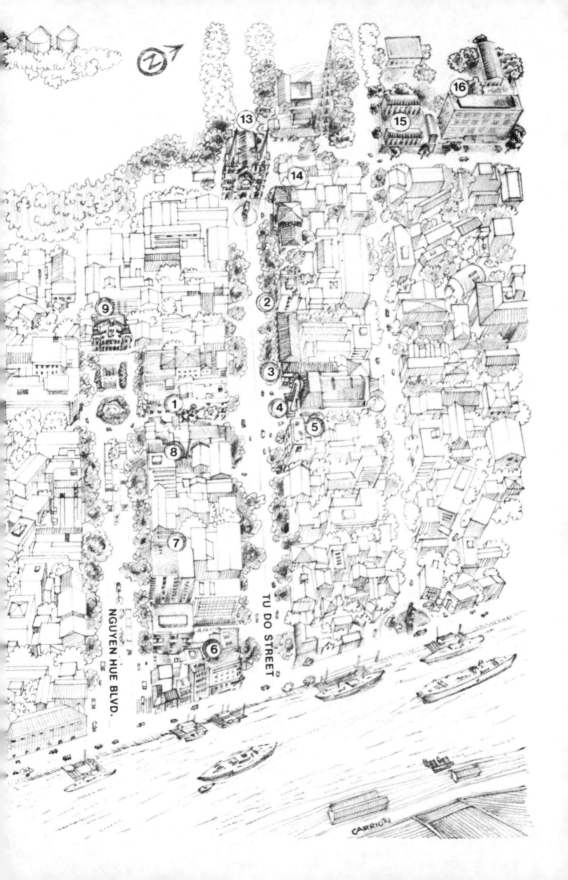

NGUYEN HUE BLVD.

TU DO STREET

CARRION

Author's Note

This account of events in Vietnam in the spring of 1975 is a collection of shards, the broken vessel being the reality of the lives that were lived and lost there in a terrible and climactic nine weeks. But these shards, in all of their particulars, are as near to the truth as almost ten years of reflection on my own experience and more than two years of intensive research, interviewing and checking can make them.

The great preponderance of the material is based on personal experience or was gathered in more than a hundred interviews conducted between the spring of 1982 and the fall of 1984. "Sources," following the text, is a guide to the previously published material on which 5 or 10 percent of the text is based.

Careful readers will note that when I wrote I was unsure whether the American Century ended on November 22, 1963, or April 28, 1975. I remain so. And once in a great while, I entertain the thought that it might get rolling again.

DAVID BUTLER
Washington, D.C.
December 1984

PART 1

APRIL 28, 1975

"Sparrows are wheeling in the sky . . ."

1

A violent storm swept through the city that afternoon. It was not the first rain of the monsoon season, but the first with thunder and lightning.

Hot gusts of wind boiled up dirt and debris from the streets; then thunder and the crack of lightning like the discharge of an artillery piece, and blowing curtains of rain; and now, at six-fifteen, low golden light on the washed pastels of the old French buildings of downtown Saigon, and a welcome coolness.

I sat out the end of it in a hotel lobby, then mounted my Honda and headed up Nguyen Hue* Boulevard toward the NBC office. In the course of the short ride I caught up with Don Harris, one of several correspondents the network had sent in to bolster its coverage in the last few weeks.

Harris looked like a cowboy. He was much too tall to fit under the strung ponchos and outsized umbrellas that shielded the sidewalk vendors from storms and shaded them from the sun, and was now striding up Nguyen Hue in the street, between the traffic and the parked cars.

During the storm, in a long televised ceremony, General Duong Van Minh† had become the third president of Vietnam in the last

* Pronounced Nwen Whay.
† Zuong Van Ming.

eight days. The French especially, and in the last few days even the Americans, had prodded the National Assembly to transfer power to Minh. He was the only political figure in the South with whom the communists might negotiate.

Harris had walked through the hotel lobby as the ceremony was drawing to a close and had seen me watching it on the lobby television set.

"So what did he say?" he asked now.

"The bartender said it's the same as Huong:* 'Fight fight, talk talk.' "

The office was so close that it was pointless to offer Harris a lift on the back of the motorcycle. "See you there," I said as we parted. I toed the machine into second gear and slowly accelerated away from Harris.

Then the firing began.

For a wild moment I thought that the machine under me was exploding between my legs. I braced my back and buttocks for a fall as I bumped over the curb and the low protective hoops around the small plot of grass and concrete that held the massive, pockmarked Marines Statue in the very heart of the foreigners' Saigon, skidded the motorcycle to a stop, crouched at the rear base of the statue and dug in my shoulder bag for my tape recorder.

I'm at the Marines. . . . Five, four, three, two, one. . . . I'm at the Marines Statue in downtown Saigon. It is twenty minutes after six, Saigon time. President Minh has just been inaugurated. For some reason, there is antiaircraft fire and the sound of small-arms fire right here in the heart of the city. I'm not certain where it's coming from. It seems to be coming from the area of the Presidential Palace. The palace is closely guarded. I have no idea why troops there would be firing in the air at this time. People are running in the streets. Yes, there's a plane in the air. And we have antiaircraft . . . [Bap bap bap bap bap bap bap bap] This is heavy fire now, tracers rising from positions on all sides of me, streaking up from behind the buildings. We are half an hour after a thunderstorm. The sky is gray and sparrows are wheeling. Sparrows are wheeling in the sky, and the tracers, the red tracers, arc through them. It's extraordinary. The war has come to Saigon. [Bap bap bap bap bap bap bap bap] Incredible barrage of antiaircraft fire now, aimed at a plane I can see. . . . It looks to be a four-engine. . . . It's a darker gray in the gray sky. . . . I'd say it's at about seventy-five hundred feet. It's maneuvering, I know it's maneuvering wildly, but from this distance it seems slow, clumsy, and I can't imagine why it hasn't been hit yet.

* Minh succeeded Tran Van Huong, who was president for seven days after the resignation of Nguyen Van Thieu.

The sparrows keep wheeling in the air. People have run for the
safety of buildings. It's extraordinary to witness this, standing behind
the famous Marines Statue, which has been photographed hundreds
of times by American TV crews, when correspondents did their com-
mentaries here. I'm in sight of the National Assembly Building. The
new president of South Vietnam was sworn in less than an hour
ago. . . . There must be . . . we . . . pardon me for being so in-
articulate. . . . I just . . . [Brrrrrrrrrrap! Brrrap! Bap bap bap bap]
I just was walking down the street and heard what sounded like in-
coming rounds, perhaps bombs, and all of a sudden we get this huge
barrage of antiaircraft fire, with some small-arms fire, close by; it
must be within just a few blocks. . . . I can see a cameraman now
on the roof of the Caravelle. Traffic is still moving. People ride by on
their motorcycles or scooters, everyone crouched low over the handle-
bars as if they were in a race, trying to keep their heads down. . . .
[Brrrrrrrrr, brrrrrrrrr, brrrrrrrrrr] *Everyone is running, quickly, and*
crouching . . . We've seen one small accident already. . . .
[Brrrrrrrrr, brrrrrrrrrr, brrrrrrrrrrrrrrrrrrrrrrrrr]
Then very fast: *"David-Butler-NBC-News-Saigon."*

II

Mike Marriott, a stocky young Australian cameraman for CBS News,
had paid little attention to the telecast of Big Minh's inauguration, except to ask a Vietnamese reporter who watched it if Minh was surrendering. "Fight and talk," the reporter said, repeating and then
mocking the familiar communist slogan: "Fight fight, talk talk."

Marriott was planning to stay on in Saigon through what virtually
everyone now agreed would be a full-scale American evacuation. The
bureau was under orders from headquarters in New York that all
staffers were to leave once the signal came from the embassy. But
Marriott and Ed Bradley, one of the several CBS correspondents who
had returned to Saigon for the climax of the war, decided privately
that they would manage to miss the evacuation and stay for whatever
followed.

When the firing started, Marriott grabbed a camera and ran down
the flight of stairs from the CBS office in the Caravelle Hotel to the
street. He got as far as La Pagode, a café two blocks up Tu Do toward
the basilica, where the chaotic traffic was blocked. One of the city's
fleet of ancient blue-and-yellow Renault taxis had stopped dead in the
middle of the road. The driver, at its open hood, was engaged in a
furious exchange with a South Vietnamese Army captain accompanied
by two MPs. The captain could not seem to believe that the man was
not going to move the car until he had located the source of the trou-

ble and fixed it. The officer waved his .45 at the driver, shouted what Marriott assumed was "Move the goddamned thing!" one more time, and then jabbed the gun into the front seat of the empty, tiny vehicle and fired.

Marriott started filming. *Blam!* The captain looked at the driver for his reaction, shouted something else and fired again. *Blam! Blam! Blam!* Now the driver, his arms waving wildly in the air, was screaming at the captain, whose face looked as if it was about to break into the laughter of the insane. *Blam! Blam!*

Then the officer turned and saw Marriott and his camera. He loaded a new magazine into the pistol, took three steps to Marriott's side—Marriott already backing and turning away—raised the gun and pulled the trigger.

The gun jammed. The captain flipped it and slashed Marriott's temple with the butt, three blows, opening Marriott's scalp and sending him to the pavement. As the blows came, Mike Marriott decided that he was not staying on to see more history made in Saigon after all.

III

We are talking now of the electric dusk of Monday, April 28, 1975, when the door slammed shut on what was to have been the American Century.

North Vietnamese pilots in captured American warplanes are bombing Saigon's Tan Son Nhut airport, which lies less than four miles north of the Marines Statue. In the previous seven weeks, an entire society built on the ideals, strategies, money and blood of the United States has all but collapsed. Now the equivalent of sixteen North Vietnamese divisions—140,000 men—are ranged around Saigon, their lead elements in Saigon itself, to the north and east no more than five miles away from the Marines Statue. The capital's 60,000 defenders this night have not broken; they wait at their posts, as Big Minh ordered them to do in the inaugural address. If there is to be a battle for Saigon, most of them will die.

IV

For many Americans, the sudden reappearance on their television sets of violent images from Vietnam—fighting, but more than that, night after night of fleeing South Vietnamese troops and civilians—was like the recurrence of a nightmare. The years of upheaval that began with the assassination of John F. Kennedy in 1963 had, it seemed, finally come to an end eight months earlier, with the resignation of Richard

Nixon. And America's direct combat role in Vietnam had ended more than two years earlier, with the signing of the Paris Peace Accords, the withdrawal of the last troops and the release of 591 prisoners of war—all they had, Hanoi claimed.

But the war wasn't over. The war hadn't stopped even for an hour at eight o'clock on the morning of January 28, 1973, the moment when the cease-fire was supposed to go into effect. Now, two years and three months later, there were still about 1,100 Americans left in Saigon, including an American ambassador who that night expected to be in Vietnam for months or at least weeks acting as the American presence in negotiations between Big Minh and the communists.

There were also tens of thousands of Vietnamese in Saigon who had been personally assured by American officials that they, the Americans, would never leave Vietnam without their Vietnamese friends and employees.

The city was frightened, but quiet. The South Vietnamese troops in and around Saigon were bitterly angry with their own commanders, and with the Americans, but there was no repeat in Saigon of the horror that had swept Da Nang in its final days just a month before, when the army had broken, spreading chaos.

The calmness had several causes. Among them was Graham Anderson Martin, of Thomasville, North Carolina, U.S. Ambassador to the Republic of Vietnam. For weeks, Martin had been performing an extraordinary tightrope act. Under enormous pressure from the American military establishment and eventually from the White House itself, he had drastically drawn down the number of Americans in Saigon, and permitted the evacuation of thousands of Vietnamese, while at the same time maintaining the fiction that all was normal.

Martin had many goals. Supreme among them was arranging for the safety of the Americans in his charge. After that he hoped to see to it that the manner of our leaving did not add a final horror to the thousands of mistakes Americans had already made in Vietnam.

And if what had happened in Da Nang recurred in Saigon, it would be ghastly indeed: U.S. Marines killing South Vietnamese soldiers to get the Americans out.

v

Ken Moorefield, Joseph McBride and a few other young American Embassy officials were working that afternoon in a complex of barracks and recreational facilities—a gym, a swimming pool, tennis courts—called Dodge City at Tan Son Nhut air base. The facilities were for the use of Americans. But no one had swum in the pool or played on the tennis courts or in the gym for weeks. Since mid-April, Dodge City had been the processing center for the evacuation of people from Saigon; the great majority of the evacuees were Vietnamese, all of whom had a claim—firm, tenuous or false—on America.

The first string of explosions was distant. But the old wooden building, which stood on stilts, shook with the second string. A fluorescent lighting fixture fell from the ceiling onto McBride's desk. Moorefield, a blond young veteran of two combat tours in Vietnam, jumped up from his desk in the little corner office where he had been dealing with the borderline cases—draft-age men, for example—and ran into the main processing room. With the second string of explosions, the fifteen or twenty Vietnamese in the room broke from their lines. Women were screaming. McBride was brushing the debris from his desk and sitting down to resume work. Moorefield rushed past him and down the open front staircase to the ground.

Antiaircraft fire had opened up over the airport and the sky was filled with blossoming puffs of gray and black smoke. It was also filled with planes. Moorefield picked out two jets lazily twisting into a dive. He suddenly felt naked. "Gotta get these people under cover," he thought.

Back upstairs, the women were still screaming and babies bawled as their parents crouched with them under the folding tables and against the walls. McBride and two other consular officers were still trying to work. Moorefield shouted orders. In less than five minutes, he and the few other embassy and military officers in the compound shepherded eighty or a hundred Vietnamese into an abandoned barracks across the road from the processing center. The barracks was more substantial, set on the ground, and they were able to get everyone to crouch or lie against the walls in the long hallways.

As soon as that job was done and Moorefield had a moment to think, he realized that he had left his consular stamp on his desk. With that stamp and the forms lying around the office, anyone could approve himself for entry into the United States. Moorefield jogged back to the office and got that stamp and a couple of others.

Back in the barracks, he listened to the last explosions, which seemed to be over on the part of the base occupied by the Vietnamese Air Force. The attack itself lasted only about fifteen minutes, although the antiaircraft fire continued for at least another twenty minutes.

Moorefield had known when he had first seen them that the attacking planes were light U.S.-built fighter-bombers. He had assumed at the same moment that these were *not* disaffected South Vietnamese pilots, but North Vietnamese pilots flying captured planes. He had further assumed that their target was the evacuation itself, his evacuation—him. Now in the barracks, when he had a moment to reflect, he thought of the dozens of times he had called in helicopter gunships and tactical air support against Viet Cong positions.

Now he was the target. All that stood between him and extinction was the skill of communist pilots he would never see. And if he went, it would be an American bomb dropped from an American plane that got him.

VI

Downtown, French Ambassador Jean-Marie Mérillon was holding a security meeting for about thirty leaders of the French community. In the middle of April, a few weeks earlier than usual, Mérillon had quietly closed the *lycées;* but there were still about fifteen thousand French citizens in South Vietnam. If there was a battle for Saigon, all of them, along with tens of thousands of Vietnamese with claims to French citizenship, would seek asylum in the embassy, or at least look to it for protection. And Mérillon's modest security force had been augmented by only twelve additional gendarmes.

The staff had stockpiled some food, and there were reserve water and fuel tanks against the wall that separated the French compound from that of the Americans. Mérillon knew that those provisions would not last long if there was chaos in the city.

His guests were a mix of doctors, teachers, planters and, especially, Saigon businessmen. Each would be contacted through the coming days, as they had been off and on in the last few weeks, and would in turn contact five to ten others, who would in turn have others to call or see with news and instructions.

The meeting was not entirely grim. It was also a quiet celebration of the transfer of power to Duong Van Minh, the brooding general nicknamed Big Minh in the three languages of Saigon not for his power or intellect but for his size. In the last few weeks, the installation of Big Minh as the president of the Republic of Vietnam had become a major foreign-policy objective of the French government. It was a gamble, and a desperate one. If only the stupid Americans hadn't clung to Thieu in 1971, when there were elections and at least the chance of some kind of accommodation with Hanoi.

But now Minh was in. And if the communists acted intelligently and let Minh head up a procommunist but independent government in the South—if they didn't stupidly go for it all—then once again the French would play their rightful role as the dominant Western power

in South Vietnam. Which is why Mérillon, along with Pierre Brochand, his young political officer, had done as much as any two men in
Saigon to bring the policy to success.

Mérillon was a thin man of slightly less than middle height, with a
shock of brushed-back hair that made him look ten years younger than
the French president, Giscard d'Estaing, his classmate at L'Ecole Poly-
technique.

The ambassador did not look quite so youthful as usual that evening. He had been two nights without more than snatches of sleep in
his office. And through the weeks of crisis he had been fortifying himself with a viciously American drink: bourbon and Coke with three or
four aspirins popped in, velvet for the hammer blows.

Most of the guests drank champagne.

Mérillon's assistant, Pierre Brochand, was uncannily boyish-looking
for a man who in the last few days had helped engineer a major and
only crudely constitutional change of government in a country at the
center of world attention. (Brochand had also seen to it, without
bothering to worry his ambassador with such business, that the network whose leading members were there that early evening had among
them a quantity of arms.) He was in fact only thirty-four; more than
that, his neat small features in a square face under light-brown hair
that would have qualified as a crew cut if it were half an inch shorter
made him look more American than many men in their thirties in the
American Embassy next door, and younger than all of them.

With the first distant thuds, Brochand moved to a window. He had
good eyes. He saw four A-37s—the right identification, instantly—arc-
ing for their second pass on Tan Son Nhut, four miles to the northwest, and an American C-130 transport climbing at an extraordinarily
steep angle for such a large aircraft.

"Ky," Brochand said to himself.

But a quick telephone call revealed it wasn't Air Marshal Nguyen
Cao Ky or his friends in the first stage of a coup attempt. It was a communist attack in captured American jets.

The gathering broke up, with dignity but in some haste. If events
continued like this, there might very well be use for the weapons
Brochand had had the foresight to distribute.

VII

George Randall* was on the top floor of the American Embassy in
downtown Saigon when the planes hit Tan Son Nhut. Like most of
his CIA colleagues, Randall went out to the hallway and crouched.
As the distant bombing and close-by firing continued, a Marine below

* A pseudonym.

them yelled: "They're coming up the stairs! They're coming up the stairs!"

Randall—who was visiting Saigon from his post in the Mekong delta—asked a secretary with him if she knew of any guns on that floor. She directed him to one of the offices, and Randall found a handgun where she had said it would be. But it was unloaded, and if there was any ammunition for it in that office Randall couldn't find it.

The panicky Marine was wrong. No communist troops were storming up the stairwells of the fortresslike embassy. But there was action in the courtyard below.

Three men, of the hundreds of Vietnamese and American men, women, and children in the embassy compound late that afternoon:

Wolfgang Lehmann, fifty-two, deputy chief of mission, at this moment striding around the swimming pool in the middle of the compound to untangle the latest snafu, remembering what it was like to be a young officer in a war in which people knew what the hell they were doing.

Robert L. Frain, twenty, of Philadelphia, sergeant, United States Marine Corps, eleven months in Saigon, exhausted like the sixty other Marines in the embassy security detachment.

Donald S. Hays, twenty-seven, number-two budget officer in the two-man finance office, the lowest-paid Foreign Service Officer in the embassy, a piece of slightly discouraging intelligence that came with the job.

Hays was aglow with clean exhaustion, and the hamburger and Coke in front of him looked beautiful. Four days earlier the ambassador had finally authorized the evacuation of embassy Vietnamese staff. Through those four days, Hays had slept little and eaten less. He worked almost around the clock, first to discharge his duties in the finance office, and then, from midafternoon until after midnight, to shepherd Vietnamese employees of the United States Agency for International Development (USAID) into and through the evacuation procedure at Tan Son Nhut.

Late that afternoon, Hays and a friend had been relieved at the airport by two other embassy staffers. Hays had been driven in a white embassy Chevrolet to his apartment a few blocks from the embassy. He showered and packed a small bag, which he placed next to the apartment door, and then made it through the two South Vietnamese militia checkpoint roadblocks between the apartment building and the embassy, and into the clean, cool, quiet familiar restaurant of the Combined Recreation Association quadrant in the rear of the embassy compound.

The hamburger looked fine and the fresh clothes felt clean against his fresh exhausted body. This was like '68 and '69 and '70, when he was a sergeant with the 101st Airborne outside Da Nang and they were *working* for a living, the first real meal after seven or ten or fourteen days in the boonies.

He took a bite. As he chewed, he heard the jets come in, the distant explosions.

Hays and then the other young Americans in the restaurant quickly turned over tables and got close to the ground. Hays turned on the walkie-talkie the embassy's security officer had issued him a week before and determined that Tan Son Nhut was under attack.

Sergeant Frain also hit the deck with the first explosions. With the louder explosions he scrambled for the safety of the chancery, the main embassy building.

A couple of Frain's superiors decided that the first order of business was to get the deputy chief of mission under some sort of cover. "For Christ's sake, it's four miles away," Lehmann protested. "You know, in World War Two . . ." The Marines hustled him to the doors to the restaurant.

Lehmann stood with the doors opening out behind him. "What are you guys doing?" he asked Hays and the others. "There's nothing to be worried about. . . ."

At that moment, the second string of explosions, the one that sent Sergeant Frain scrambling to the chancery, knocked the doors inward, pitching Lehmann onto the restaurant floor.

He picked himself up. Now the antiaircraft fire had started, and not all of it arced high in the air. Some sounded as if it was screaming just over the compound. But Lehmann was quickly in possession of himself. Speaking fast and low in colloquial English, he told Hays and the two or three other Americans with walkie-talkies to turn the damned things off: The Vietnamese were not supposed to be eavesdropping on this traffic.

Lehmann left the restaurant and started back to the chancery, thinking that you got personally involved when the damned incoming was right on top of you, or right next door, but when it was four miles away it was an intellectual exercise. The air was filled with firing.

As Lehmann walked through the parking lot behind the chancery, he passed a tamarind tree that rose half the height of the building. A Seabee was swinging away at the tree with an ax. Lehmann knew that the ambassador did not want the tree down, the signal to all of Saigon that the Americans were preparing to cut and run, making a helicopter landing zone in their parking lot.

The chancery lobby was crowded. Lehmann found Marvin Garrett, the mission's security officer, and said, "Marvin, there's a guy out there trying to chop down the damned tree. With an ax. At the rate he's going, he might get it done in three days. Tell him to cease and desist. Bring in some power saws and hold them in abeyance.

"Do nothing about that f - - - - - - tree until I give the word."

2

Now, with the combination of the thunderstorm during Big Minh's speech and the bombing that so quickly followed, now the fear ran everywhere, like the relayed barking of the city's dogs in the cordite-laced dusk.

Doan Van Toai's* parents had moved to Saigon after their house in the Mekong delta was destroyed during the Tet offensive of 1968.

---

* Doan, the family name, rhymes with tone. Toai is more difficult: pronounced Twhoy. But as a rule there is no reason to be put off by Vietnamese names. They consist of monosyllables that more often than not are pronounced more or less as they appear to a native English speaker. I use footnotes for the exceptions. Nguyen, the most common family name, is pronounced Nwen.

Forms of address and the role of the family name are quite different from Western practice. The family name appears in conversation less frequently than in the West. A hypothetical Professor Nguyen Van Tai, for example, would be known to his students not as Professor Nguyen but as Professor Tai (Professor Bob as opposed to Professor Smith), and to his friends as Tai. In discussing him, one would normally use all three names only if it were necessary to distinguish him from another Tai, or Professor Tai. At the same time, he would be known variously throughout his life as younger brother, older brother, uncle, father-in-law, grandfather, etc., with or without the Tai and not necessarily depending on any blood relationship. Any close friend of one's parents would normally be called uncle or aunt, for example, as is sometimes the case in the West. They're all just people—which is to say that they are all human beings, touched with divinity.

They lived with their elder son, Doan Trung, in an apartment on Hong Thap Tu Street, behind the Presidential Palace. Toai and his family—he had three small sons—lived in the same building. A daughter, a teacher, lived nearby. They met in Trung's large apartment, and talked excitedly in low voices of the terrible omen and the stark reality of the bombing.

Through the many contacts he had as a business consultant, Trung had arranged space for the whole family on a freighter leaving for Singapore the next day. He argued that they all should go, with the logic of any nonpolitical Vietnamese who would much prefer to live in his own country but was also determined to survive: "If the communists are good people, they will let us come back. But if we stay and the situation is bad then maybe we won't be able to leave."

His father waved his hand in dismissal. "Your mother and I are too old to start a new life," he said. "We will stay here."

Trung turned to his younger brother.

"It's too dangerous," Toai said. "Someone will attack the freighter, either the Saigon troops or the communists."

"It's more dangerous for you to stay," Trung said. "You're too active for them, too independent."

Toai was twenty-nine. He was an officer in a Saigon bank, a former student activist and, as his family knew, a middle-level agent for the communists.

He was only a little surprised that when escape suddenly became a possibility his first instinct had been to consider it, and to weigh the risks. He looked at his wife and the three boys, babies still.

But he had made up his mind. He began to recite the political and patriotic reasons for staying. Trung cut him off. "Don't talk to me about their ten-point program, younger brother," he said. "You don't have any idea what they are going to do."

"I know," Toai said. "I want to see."

II

That evening General Van Tien Dung* and two other men made a decision. Dung was the gruff, square-faced general who commanded the 140,000 communist soldiers on the outskirts of Saigon. On that perfervid evening in Saigon, General Dung was thirty miles north of the capital—his lifelong goal—at what had been an abandoned camp in the light, pretty forest that lay between the town of Ben Cat and the big Michelin rubber plantation to the west.

General Dung had arrived at the camp two days earlier. Years before, it had been a base for a communist commando unit that lived and

* Zung.

worked in Saigon and repaired there to plan terrorist raids into the city. It was "a group of modest thatched huts, with the wind blowing in from all sides."

Dung and his staff had been joined by Pham Hung, the fourth-ranking member of the Politburo in Hanoi and the senior communist in the South throughout the war; and by Le Duc Tho, who, with Henry Kissinger, shared the 1973 Nobel Peace Prize for negotiating the Paris Peace Accords.

They were elated.

[That afternoon] Saigon's quisling administration [had] played out the final act of the drama. After much controversy, posturing, and bargaining, and under pressure from his foreign guiding mandarins, Tran Van Huong resigned, yielding the presidential chair to Duong Van Minh. The new president immediately called on the Saigon army: "Protect our territory," and "Do not lay down your weapons." At headquarters meanwhile, as we were listening to a report from Kim Tuan, deputy commander of the Third Army Corps, on the results of the preparations for the attack on Dong Du, a combat operations cadre entered, his face radiant. He reported that at 15:40 a flight of five A-37s piloted by our comrades, with Nguyen Thanh* Trung leading the way, had taken off from Thanh Son airfield [near Phan Rang, a "liberated" city two hundred miles up the coast] to strike Tan Son Nhut.

It was magnificent coordination, the most-perfect combined-forces strike ever by our troops, at an extremely important time which would have a great effect on the development of the campaign.

[That night, we] saw that the enemy were completely confused, their command in an uproar, and the III Corps command at Bien Hoa† gradually disintegrating. In the first two days and nights of the campaign, all wings of our troops had completely implemented the plans, so we issued orders for a general offensive on the whole front for the morning of April 29, to advance into Saigon.‡

III

Nguyen Van Hao§ went directly from Big Minh's inauguration at the palace to a meeting of the senior staff of the several ministries he controlled as deputy prime minister in charge of economic development.

---

* Thanh is pronounced Thahng. Twenty days earlier, this man, who was a pilot in the South Vietnamese Air Force, had pulled out of formation on a routine bombing run and bombed the Presidential Palace. President Thieu was unhurt. Lieutenant Trung flew to a hero's welcome in communist-held territory.
† Bin Wah.
‡ All quotations from General Dung are from *Our Great Spring Victory*, by Dung, Monthly Review Press, New York and London, 1977.
§ How.

He was only thirty-six, and normally wore the ease of a man who had won high position young, on the strength of sheer talent. But that afternoon he was excited. Putting his trust in Mérillon's assurances that the communists would negotiate with Big Minh, Hao had played a role in convincing the National Assembly to transfer power to Minh. The war was coming to an end. Vietnam was to have peace at last, an honorable peace under French protection.

Hao knew that the panic that had swept through Saigon in the last few weeks had reached high into his ministries. Some of the men and women at this meeting were still in Vietnam only because he had gone on television a few nights earlier to appeal for calm, pledging that no matter what happened, he and his family would not flee.

Now he told his people that with the installation of the new government he released them from his order not to leave their posts. As of this afternoon's ceremony, he was only an acting deputy prime minister. Personally, he still thought they all should stay, for the country. But they could go if they wished. He added that it would be against his principles to intercede with his contacts at the American Embassy to help those of them who wanted to flee.

"Is there going to be a political solution?" one of the officials asked.

"I think so," Hao said, "but nothing is sure."

The meeting broke up when, after the first bombs, the guns at the palace nearby and then everywhere around them opened up.

"Ky and his friends," Hao told his officials. "It must be."

It was not until he reached home that he realized from a few hurried phone calls that it wasn't Ky. Less than twenty minutes had passed between the end of the inaugural ceremony and the bombing. Hao knew that a step as important as hitting Tan Son Nhut would have been planned for days. It probably was only a coincidence that it came so close to the ceremony. But it meant that all the political maneuvering of the week just ended was futile.

Hao's wife was an accomplished and politically sophisticated woman. For days she had been urging Hao to get them and the children out. But after his television speech, she kept her silence. Tonight, Hao also became silent. In a time of crisis, one must be calm. He stopped making or receiving phone calls, sat in a hard-backed chair at the kitchen table, his hands flat on the table, and thought. His wife said nothing. But she packed.

IV

Late that afternoon, a few Vietnamese were being evacuated from the compound of the United States Information Service, which lay about half a mile away from the embassy proper. About 150 people had spent the last few nights in the compound. Some were local USIS staffers and their families. Others were Vietnamese businessmen, intellectuals or government officials for whom the agency had been given responsibility.

When the rolling fusillades of antiaircraft and small-arms fire shattered the dusk, one bus of would-be evacuees was leaving the gates of the compound, another waiting inside it. Alan Carter, the USIS chief, ordered the departing bus back in and the gates locked. He and his assistants herded everyone against the wall of the compound away from the greatest swells of firing, and then, in a lull, into the three main buildings of the compound, urging them to crouch clear of the windows. Carter checked that emergency provisions he had laid by in another crisis a few weeks earlier were still there, in case they were in for a siege.

The agency had sent a small contingent of its Vietnamese employees and their dependents—about thirty people in all—to the evacuation center at Tan Son Nhut the day before. That was very late in an evacuation that had moved into high gear ten days before because Carter was adhering to the letter of embassy directives. He alone among the agency chiefs was not bending the rules, which still insisted that draft-age males and (so Carter thought) parents of local employees could not be evacuated. In the last few days, he had seen grown men fall to their knees in his office when he told them that they could go, with their wives and their younger children, but they would have to leave their parents, or an eighteen-year-old son.

Carter did not know that almost every other official in Vietnam— that is to say, some but not all Vietnamese officials, and every other senior American official except himself—was bending the rules, because he was not in the know. And because he was not in the know, he was more Catholic than the pope. And in this there was irony.

The last American ambassador to Saigon was a man of deep commitment to his ideals, and of infinite cunning in his pursuit both of those ideals and of his own standing in the corridors of power. He needed the cunning, because his supreme self-righteousness tended to make him dangerously outspoken. He was a maverick who was cunning enough to recognize a fellow maverick as soon as one arrived on the scene; and to cut him dead.

In Saigon, the fellow maverick was Carter, the gregarious, goateed chief of the United States Information Service. As of that last Monday night in April 1975, Ambassador Graham Martin had been on the job for almost two years. Carter had arrived just eight months before. Within weeks, he had been effectively shut out of the place in the senior councils of the mission that normally would have come with his position. For the ambassador, Alan Carter was flawed and dangerous: He was not the ambassador's man. Worse, he actually *liked* some of the shallow young journalists who, in the ambassador's mind, were fighting America's interests in Vietnam.

In the final days, a man in the embassy with the title of Special Assistant for Press Affairs conspired—at the instigation of Henry Kissinger and with the grudging approval of the ambassador—with a producer from CBS News to fly dozens of Vietnamese employees of U.S. news agencies and their dependents, hundreds of people in all, out of Vietnam. And Alan Carter, while he had a rough idea that lots of people were leaving, had no idea that they were leaving in a coordinated plan with embassy approval.

He told his own USIS staffers that they had to stay until the last moment, when they would be seen to. And, as instructed, he passed along to the remote embassy list after list of persons who should be included in the evacuation, with the principal name and why he or she should go; and under each principal name five or ten or thirty relatives.

After the firing subsided, Carter and Ken Jackson, his deputy, circulated among the Vietnamese, assuring them that no matter what happened the Americans were still there and would take care of them.

Later, as the Vietnamese bedded down for the night on mats or blankets, Carter was driven north a couple of blocks to the villa that came with the job, bachelor digs for him these last eight months. He showered and ate whatever the cook served up and then the driver took him to the embassy for an emergency midnight meeting.

v

At first glance, it seemed that everyone left in Saigon who worked for NBC was in the bureau. The two correspondents, Don Harris and Don Oliver, were both typing. The room was littered with equipment. The crews—two Frenchmen, a Korean, a Japanese, a recently arrived black cameraman from the States named Aaron Fears—exchanged confused information in low voices as they emptied and loaded film and checked cable connections and battery levels.

Don Harris was leaving, with Fears. I asked where they were going. "To the roof of the hotel," Harris said. I got fresh cassettes and batteries from my desk and left with them.

I was down to just a few cigarettes. The nearby firing had stopped and the cigarette lady had set up her stand again in the crowded lobby of the Eden Building. But she didn't have change for my smallest bill. I caught up with Harris and Fears beyond the statue, thinking they would change the note and I'd be able to buy a pack before we reached the nondescript high-rise hotel on Nguyen Hue where Harris and the other NBC reinforcements were staying. But the streets were deserted.

The bar on the hotel's penthouse floor was closed. Harris led our small party down a flight of stairs to what the hotel called its rooftop restaurant. The room's manager and a few waiters stood at windows facing north over the city, toward Tan Son Nhut. Harris explained that we had to get on the roof and we needed drinks and sandwiches. The manager was distraught. "Maybe not open *here,*" he said to the room. "Maybe close everything. All foreigners go." He was not hostile as he repeated the staff gossip.

Harris said that we would pay the waiters for their trouble. "We *really* have to get up on that roof," he drawled, producing first one and then, after a moment, a second ten-dollar bill.

We set up on a corner of the roof behind a four-foot wall, and ordered beers and vodka tonics and sandwiches.

Over the next hour, we were joined by a German TV crew and a few other journalists. A changing half-dozen members of the hotel staff also were with us. Harris did what he could to get the young waiters to crouch so their white shirts weren't visible from the street, sixteen floors below. After the rain, clouds on the horizon between Cholon and the airport were rose and pale yellow, a subdued sunset; clean; bright; until the sky blued and deepened into darkness.

The signal for a general attack on Saigon and the start of a round-the-clock curfew was three thirty-second blasts on the city's sirens. It didn't come until late in the evening. But there was almost no one on the streets. The people of Saigon had declared their own curfew, which Harris had sensed as soon as we had arrived on the roof; it was a night to stay hidden from view.

We managed to get together a variety of chairs and boxes from the storerooms just under us, and sat on the roof watching the horizon explode. Twice we thought there were rockets into the city itself, so close were the explosions. But except for a small fire in the Navy headquarters behind us, on the river, all the action was off where land and sky met, a horizon we would not have been able to see except for the fires. The shelling was out at Bien Hoa, fifteen miles to the northeast. Flashes, sometimes in a row and sometimes singly, and then light rumbling so much later that the sound had little relation to the flashes. Nothing was evident from that distance except that either the city or the great air base at Bien Hoa—and to judge from the spread of the fires probably both—was being destroyed in the night.

Sometime in the last few days, walkie-talkies had suddenly materialized in the office. Arthur Lord, who had flown in from Houston in the middle of the offensive to act as a producer, was out at Tan Son Nhut, waiting to leave Vietnam. He had one of the radios, and so did Don Harris. Eventually, from Arthur Lord's calls back to the office and from the snatches of conversation around me, I finally understood that many bombs had been dropped on Tan Son Nhut, and people might have been killed.

Harris never volunteered anything. In response to my direct questions, he ticked off what he thought had been hit: some Air America planes, a building on the Vietnamese Air Force side of the field, an unknown number of planes on the flight line.

I looked again at the pulsating phosphorescent horizon, measured the twelve miles, such a small arc, from Bien Hoa to Tan Son Nhut.

"Close now," I thought, in Vietnamese.

I ordered another vodka tonic and asked Harris for the walkie-talkie. "Listen, Jack," I said, "can I talk to Arthur on this thing?"

Jack Critchfield, who had taken over Arthur Lord's duties, said it would be better if I went through him. "Okay," I said. "Tell Arthur I've got some friends, Vietnamese type, who may still be out there, I don't know. He'll know who I mean, that band I've got a crush on. Ask him if there's any chance anyone in the evacuation process got hurt."

The walkie-talkie squawked. "Lord says all those people are okay, far as he knows," Critchfield said.

"Good deal," I said. "Thank him for checking."

I looked out again at the fire on the rim of the world. "They are indeed close now," I said to myself in clear English.

3

Ambassador Martin was suffering from bronchitis and pneumonia, which made him gray and hoarse behind the cigarette smoke. But Martin was incapable of appearing weak. He wore his suit coat, and his tie was still knotted at his neck, when Wolf Lehmann was summoned to the office at about midnight.

After the bombing, the ambassador had put James Devine, his political-military counselor, and George Jacobson, a retired U.S. Army colonel who had been in Vietnam for years, in charge of planning for the movement of ten thousand evacuees the next day.

"I think you and I both ought to go home and get some sleep," the ambassador said in a voice just above a whisper. "We'll need to be rested in the morning. I have an idea that we're going to have to make some life-and-death decisions."

"Yes, sir," Lehmann said.

Colonel Jacobson, whose title that spring was Special Assistant for Field Operations, chaired the midnight meeting in the big conference room on the third floor of the embassy building. But attention focused on a political officer named Shep Lowman, who had emerged during the month as the central repository for lists of evacuees.

Through the preceding twenty-eight days of April, at a constantly accelerating rate, 43,479 people had been flown out of Saigon on Air Force planes or civilian chartered aircraft. About five thousand were Americans. The rest were orphans and bar girls, wives and children of Americans, the families of military and police officers, employees of some U.S. businesses in South Vietnam and some but not many Vietnamese employees of the embassy. The ambassador resisted attempts to evacuate U.S. mission employees, out of fear that doing so might trigger the panic in Saigon that he feared above all. (The military men at the Defense Attaché's Office, out at Tan Son Nhut, had direct access to the planes and got out the Vietnamese they wanted to without caring much what the ambassador thought about it. And the CIA ran its own evacuation throughout the month.)

Especially in the last ten days, the heads of various mission components had been feeding into the embassy lists of people they thought should be evacuated. Half of Saigon, it seemed, was on those lists. But now the end was drawing near, and the ten thousand who left tomorrow should be the ones who really deserved to go, not the cooks and chauffeurs. Lowman looked at Alan Carter and told him that he would have to produce a list of his "priority contacts."

"You son of a bitch, Shep!" Carter said. "I've been giving you lists for days! What are you talking about? Where did those other lists go?"

"They're all screwed up," Lowman said. "We've gotta start from scratch."

Denny Ellerman sat quietly through the long meeting. Ellerman had been in Saigon this time for only a couple of months. But he had served recently as an economist at the Defense Attaché's Office out at Tan Son Nhut, and his current position as the ambassador's economics counselor was a senior one.

Ellerman was fascinated that when the nuts and bolts of moving people were discussed, the meeting was dominated by grizzled old bushwhackers he had never before seen in Saigon. He assumed that they were spooks.

II

As that meeting was under way, three Americans who were the keepers of the most ambitious evacuation plan of all relaxed over drinks in the penthouse bar of a hotel on the northern bank of the Saigon River. Earlier in the evening, they had checked the radios one last time. Everything was in order. Operating from rooms on one of the upper floors of the hotel, they could reach the embassy, the DAO, and their contacts in each of the other agencies outside the embassy itself.

The hotel was leased by the United States Agency for International Development. It faced a bridge over the river leading to the docks of a southern district of Saigon called Khanh Hoi.

Two of the Americans were Mel Chatman and Russell Mott, young USAID officers who—with all of their colleagues—had escaped unharmed in the chaotic evacuation of Da Nang a month earlier. The third was a free-lance adventurer named Robert Schwab.

Only a select handful of the men at the midnight meeting in the embassy knew of the operation Chatman headed. He and Mott reported to James Devine, the ambassador's plump, chain-smoking political-military counselor.

The plan envisioned the worst-case scenario: the runways at Tan Son Nhut unusable and spreading disorder in Saigon. It envisioned for Saigon the nightmare that Da Nang had been in its final two days.

As the disorder spread, Chatman and his colleagues, with the help of six trusted Vietnamese interpreters, most of them from the Army, would, when the word to go came from Devine or the ambassador, man the radio net. And thirty to forty thousand Vietnamese would be marshaled down Vo Di Nguy Street and across the bridge to the docks, where barges would be waiting to receive them.

It would require at least a battalion of U.S. Marines. And the few men who knew of the plan knew that, even given the Marines, it would almost certainly be a bloody mess.

III

When the shooting finally died away at Tan Son Nhut, Ken Moorefield called the embassy and checked with the few military officers in Dodge City, where he and more than three thousand Vietnamese now seemed trapped. The assumption seemed to be that the evacuation would get going again within a few hours.

Moorefield was not so sure. Even before the bombing, the platoon of Marines deployed around Dodge City for the last two days had had trouble with South Vietnamese Rangers billeted near Dodge City who were trying to force their way into the evacuation. Moorefield felt that he was on an island—Dodge City—within an island—the air base—that itself lay inside the obviously tightening ring of the North Vietnamese Army. If they bombed you at six, why not bomb you again at midnight? Why not open up with their 122-mm. artillery pieces, some of which were known to have Tan Son Nhut within range? Moorefield also considered it entirely possible that the base would come under ground attack overnight.

During the eight days that Moorefield had been at Tan Son Nhut helping to process a few hundred Americans and a few thousand Vietnamese every day for evacuation on Air Force transport planes that came in from the Philippines, no one had given much thought to feeding the evacuees. They always managed to clear the processing center by nightfall. Some of the outgoing people might spend the night or even another day in Dodge City waiting their turn for a flight. They managed to fend for themselves.

Now, in part to do *something*, and also because he had little confidence that the evacuees would be enjoying a meal in the Philippines or on Guam in the foreseeable future, Moorefield organized a feeding. He raided a small warehouse, loaded up a jeep with flour and beans and rice and anything else that looked edible, broke into an abandoned mess hall and called for volunteer cooks from among the ranks of evacuees and official Americans. It took three hours to move everyone through.

That job done, Moorefield started thinking about getting back to Saigon. Don Hays and another officer had arrived with a station wagon full of sandwiches, of all things. Hays told Moorefield that the government had declared an around-the-clock curfew. This cleared the streets of civilians, but meant that there were many more roadblock checkpoints between the airport and downtown. Moorefield sensed that it was time to get to his apartment and put together his getaway bag.

About ten, he decided to make a last check of the perimeter.

You could tell the Marines were green because they were so white. They didn't even have sunburns, let alone tans. And they were tense. Dodge City wasn't all that big: the bowling alley, the gym, half a dozen or so other buildings like the abandoned mess hall and the building on stilts they had used as the processing center. But it was thirty or forty of them against—what? In the Marines' minds, probably a whole country.

Two of them were out on the narrow road running into the compound from the only access gate. Moorefield approached them, making a note of how exposed they were there, how isolated from their buddies.

A Vietnamese called urgently to him in English from the gate, which was guarded by a few Vietnamese soldiers. In a hurried exchange, Moorefield learned that there was a group of about forty Vietnamese there, in a ditch that they had lain or squatted in since the bombing.

Moorefield returned to the two young Marines and introduced himself. He explained that he was the embassy officer in charge of this part of the evacuation. One of the Marines was from Massachusetts, the other from Iowa. They answered in soft voices, volunteering only what Moorefield asked for, their eyes constantly flicking away from him to the darkness.

"Okay, look, we've got a problem," Moorefield said. "Things are tense. We don't know what's going to happen tonight. That guy I just talked to has got a group of people who belong on our side of the perimeter. I'm afraid that if there's any combat around here tonight, you could have sappers coming in through those people in the ditch, or they could just get wiped out in the cross fire. I want to get them inside."

"Okay, sir," one of them said.

The guards at the gate knew Moorefield's face and he had a little Vietnamese and a couple of packs of Ruby Queens he carried for moments like this. He got the people from the ditch inside and told them where to go without bothering to look at their papers and was glad he had gone to the trouble.

IV

Saigon was almost precisely halfway around the world from the eastern United States. At about ten-thirty that night, when Ken Moorefield was talking to the two young Marines, it was ten-thirty in the morning in Woburn, Massachusetts. Edna McMahon within the hour had picked up and read a postcard from her son Charlie, who had left Woburn for Vietnam just eight days before, after an unexpected home leave. "Hawaii's great," the scrawl read. "Stopped for an hour—12 hours of flying to go." It was postmarked April 22.

V

In the confusion, no one got word from Dodge City to the embassy that Moorefield had organized a chow line for the evacuees. Through the evening, Don Hays, the junior finance officer, helped the manager of the embassy restaurant load a station wagon full of sandwiches for the evacuees.

Halfway out to Tan Son Nhut, they were stopped at an ARVN* checkpoint. The officer in charge was specifically interested in the sandwiches. Hays turned on the radio in his embassy car and made it clear to the man that their conversation was being monitored. They were allowed to pass, and got through two more checkpoints without incident. Then, at the gate into Dodge City, a young U.S. Marine stuck a .45 almost into Hays's eye.

Hays carefully extracted himself from the car and showed the Marine his diplomatic identification.

* Army of the Republic of Vietnam, pronounced Arvin.

"Oh, sorry, sir," the Marine said. "Why didn't you just tell me? You didn't have to get out of the car."

"I make it a point never to argue with a forty-five," Hays said.

The very final stage of the evacuation—the boarding of the aircraft—was controlled by U.S. Air Force men from the Philippines who spoke no Vietnamese. Hays had rigged up a baggage-tag system for the evacuees, tags fixed to buttonholes, with each planeload of evacuees lined up in exact numerical order. Hays always cautioned them (in his limited Vietnamese): "If you get out of order, you'll be left behind."

At eight o'clock that night, just two hours after the bombing, the military men who controlled the evacuation decided that it could resume. But the estimated time for the arrival of the first planes kept slipping. It seemed to Don Hays that the waiting in the darkness was interminable. Three strings of 180 persons each had been lined up for hours. Finally, between three and three-thirty in the morning, three C-130s landed. All carried high explosives, including fifteen-thousand-pound bombs, and had to be unloaded in an ordnance staging area north of the runways.

They got one plane loaded. The second was at the loading area, awaiting its passengers. The third was taxiing slowly toward the other two.

It was five minutes before 4 A.M. on April 29, 1975. At 0400 precisely, Saigon's final agony would begin.

The Marines Statue. "I'm at the Marines Statue in downtown Saigon. It's twenty minutes after six, Saigon time. . . ." (Dirck Halstead/Gamma-Liaison)

Saigon, looking north. Cholon lies off to the west. The docks of Khanh Hoi are at the left. The Victorian-style City Hall (upper center) lies at the head of Nguyen Hue Boulevard and the Basilica of Our Lady of Peace, to the right of that, at the head of Tu Do Street.

The terrace of the Continental Palace Hotel on a slow afternoon. (The setting for a key early scene in Graham Greene's The Quiet American.) (David Butler)

Saigon, a city of one-legged men. (Dirck Halstead/Gamma-Liaison)

Saigon at sunset, looking northwest from the roof of the Caravelle Hotel. The Eden Building is prominent in the foreground. The NBC and AP offices were directly below the Sanyo billboard. The Marines Statue is faintly visible at ground level below the same billboard. (Neal Ulevich)

Above: General Van Tien Dung, chief of staff of the North Vietnamese Army and commander of the final offensive. (Vietnamese News Agency (VNA)/courtesy John Spragens, Jr.)

Above: General Duong Van ("Big") Minh on April 28, 1975, as he became South Vietnam's third president in a week. (Dirck Halstead/ Gamma-Liaison)

Above: Air Marshal Nguyen Cao Ky. "What can they do over there to make a living except become servants for the rich people?" (AP/Wide World Photos)

Right: Graham Anderson Martin, of Thomasville, North Carolina, the last American ambassador to Saigon. "No one ever outstared him." (David Hume Kennerly/Gamma-Liaison)

From left to right, Ambassador Martin with Army Chief of Staff Frederick C. Weyand, Secretary of State Henry Kissinger and President Gerald Ford on March 25, 1975. General Weyand headed the last "fact-finding mission" to Vietnam. (David Hume Kennerly/Gamma-Liaison)

From left to right, Deputy Assistant Defense Secretary Eric Von Marbod, General Weyand and Ambassador Martin with President Nguyen Van Thieu. At Thieu's left, their backs to the camera, are Vice-President Tran Van Huong (right) and Prime Minister Tran Thiem Khiem. (David Hume Kennerly/Gamma-Liaison)

Kissinger, Ford and Weyand in Palm Springs, California. The President accepted Weyand's recommendation that he ask Congress for $722 million in emergency aid for the faltering South Vietnamese army. (David Hume Kennerly/Gamma-Liaison)

From left to right, Thomas Polgar, last CIA station chief in Saigon; Colonel George Jacobson, special assistant to the ambassador; Congressman Pete McCloskey (R.-Cal.), a member of one of the last Congressional delegations to visit South Vietnam; and Wolfgang Lehmann, deputy chief of mission. (courtesy John Murray)

General Murray (left) with General Ngo Quang Truong, last commander of Military Region 1. The Americans thought Truong was the best commander the South Vietnamese had. But faced with confused orders from President Thieu, Truong was unable to hold the north, and salvaged only a fraction of his men and equipment. (courtesy John Murray)

General Nguyen Van Toan, commander of the military region that surrounded Saigon at the end. Toan was relieved for corruption in the fall of 1974, but reinstated as a corps commander in part as a result of Ambassador Martin's pressure. (courtesy John Murray)

Don Harris of NBC (foreground) and other journalists on the roof of the Central Palace Hotel, early evening, April 28, 1975. (Dirck Halstead/Gamma-Liaison)

Fuel or ammunition dumps north of Saigon burning on the evening of April 28. (Dirck Halstead/Gamma-Liaison)

From left to right, Khanh Ha, Anh Tu and Thuy An. "Anyone who took
one look at Anh Tu knew instantly he was made to sing pop music, not
to carry a pack."

Major Hien (left) and Captain Anh at one of
their afternoon press briefings on Tu Do
Street. (David Butler)

Above: Charlie Benoit
with an instant street
friend; this happened
dozens of times a day
when he traveled, though
somewhat less frequently
in Saigon. (David Butler)

Mr. Khi, the NBC office manager. (David
Butler)

Doan Van Toai in 1969, when he was a young student antiwar activist in Saigon.

Jay Scarborough, Vienna, 1977. Scarborough's blond good looks masked an inner strength.

Dennis Troute, Phnom Penh, 1971.

Carolyn Paine Miller and LuAnne in Ban Me Thuot, 1974. (courtesy Carolyn and John Miller)

March 15. South Vietnamese Air Force officers arrive in Nha Trang from Pleiku. "Uncle, where are they from? Where do the soldiers come from?" (David Butler)

Fleeing South Vietnamese officers unload their motorbikes. (David Butler)

The last plane out of Da Nang—mobbed by elite South Vietnamese troops—lands in Saigon. Visible at right, at least one pair of feet; at least one soldier tried to ride south in the undercarriage and was crushed. (AP/Wide World Photos)

Albert A. Francis, U.S. consul-general in Da Nang (waving, with black beard), is spotted by President Ford's photographer. Francis worked frantically to get people out of Da Nang as it dissolved in chaos around him. (David Hume Kennerly/Gamma-Liaison)

U.S. Agency for International Development officer—and student of Vietnamese culture—Mel Chatman. (Russell Mott)

Russell Mott. "Mott did carry it to something of an extreme, among those four or five hundred Americans during the course of the whole adventure who actually enjoyed eating raw pork once or twice a day." (Mel Chatman/Russell Mott)

The photograph below and the four that follow are previously unpublished photos of the helter-skelter, murderous sea evacuation of Da Nang.

Da Nang harbor, Easter weekend. The white building at the right was the U.S. consulate. Note the name of the tugboat at center. (Russell Mott)

Refugees in small fishing boats approach a jammed barge in Da Nang harbor. This barge has tall sandbag walls. (Russell Mott)

Night transfer of refugees from the barges, across the tug Oseola and, here, up onto a merchant ship called the Saigon Singapore. Infants were trampled to death at the base of the gangplank. (Russell Mott)

Opposite page, bottom: Vietnamese boats of all descriptions, many commandeered by armed troops, crowd the flanks of the Pioneer Contender, a U.S. merchant ship which the same troops would soon terrorize. (Russell Mott)

Debris left on the barge the Americans called "Big Blue" after the Vietnamese who covered every square inch of it had been transferred to larger ships. (Russell Mott)

PART 2

MARCH 6–APRIL 5

"Phao kich!"

4

Eight weeks earlier, Vietnam was not much in the news in the United States. In the first ten days of March, the front page of *The New York Times* included several dispatches from Phnom Penh reporting growing pessimism that the U.S.-supported government of Cambodia could survive that year's communist offensive. And Secretary of State Henry Kissinger left for his latest round of shuttle diplomacy in the Middle East. But generally the stories focused inward, on domestic concerns: energy, inflation, the complicated financial arrangements necessary to save New York's thirty-five-cent subway fare. Most Americans realized that the war in Vietnam had not ended. But for more than two years, the fighting had been only between the Vietnamese themselves.

Among Americans, only an interested party, such as General Homer Smith, the logistician who headed the U.S. Defense Attaché's Office in Saigon, would realize or care that the Yom Kippur War in October 1973, with the attendant fourfold increase in the price of oil, automatically reduced the value of U.S. aid to Vietnam for oil products—a significant portion of the aid—by seventy-five percent. Or that the Pentagon, under irresistibly enormous pressure not to reveal the extent of the Israeli losses in that war, used money and matériel that had been specifically earmarked for Vietnam to secretly restore the U.S. components in NATO stockpiles that had been poured into Israel.

Likewise, only specialists, including members of Congress and the young activists who lobbied their staffs, would take particular note of the fact that within days of President Nixon's resignation in the summer of 1974 an assertive Congress cut $300 million from the Administration's request for military aid to South Vietnam for the coming year.

The will of the American people to be done with Vietnam, a desire made perfectly clear in congressional appropriations, was fully understood in Hanoi. And it was understood by General Van Tien Dung, at fifty-eight the youngest member of the Politburo and chief of staff of the Vietnam People's Army.

On March 6, 1975, a Thursday, General Dung was issuing orders from his jungle headquarters west of the South Vietnamese mountain town of Ban Me Thuot.*

> We were in a green jungle next to a forest of *khooc* trees, whose dry fallen leaves covered the ground like a golden carpet. Whenever someone stepped on them, the leaves under their feet sounded like crisp rice crackers shattering, causing a commotion all through that part of the forest. Here the smallest spark could start a forest fire. This meant that those working hardest were the communications fighters: Whenever there was a fire and communications lines were broken, they went out to fix them and came back black as coal miners. Another problem was the elephants, which traveled in herds of forty or fifty, and would pull down and break the networks of communications lines even when they were quite high in the trees.

General Dung in the last few weeks had traveled by plane, boat and car from Hanoi. As he moved south on the Ho Chi Minh Trail, which in the last two years had been transformed into a network of two-lane roads, many of them paved, reaching to within thirty miles of Saigon itself, Tet came and went. Very few of the thousands of troops and Vanguard Youth workers whom he passed had any idea who he was. But they knew from the license plate of his battered field car that he was a senior official. As Tet presents, he passed out plastic combs to women along the way, cigarettes to the men.

For General Dung, it was the Tay Nguyen, the western highlands. The Americans called it the Central Highlands; the French, the Hauts Plateaux. It ran five hundred miles north to south, from the southern reaches of North Vietnam to within a hundred miles of Saigon, rising from the thin strip of cultivable land along the bulging coast of central Vietnam to the snaking barrier of the Annamite Chain of mountains

* Pronounced Bahn Me To-it.

that marked the border with Laos. Parts of the plateau could be made fertile. Jean-Marie Mérillon thought that with peace the plateau could become Vietnam's California.

In their day, the French chose the small city of Ban Me Thuot, the communications center of the southern reaches of the plateau, for the headquarters of the region's defense. When the Americans took over, their strategy of air mobility—the lavish use of planes and helicopters for the movement of men and supplies—led them to move the regional headquarters almost a hundred miles north, to Pleiku, which was closer to the geographic heart of the highlands. And yet all through the war, American officers knew and told each other and so informed their allies and Washington that South Vietnam's jugular, the point to strike to cut the country in half, was at Ban Me Thuot.

II

The Vietnamese had fun with Nguyen Cao Ky's name. It could mean either chess master or high-flying banner.* Ky had lost at the chess game of Vietnamese politics, coming to power too young—prime minister at thirty-four—and then being outmaneuvered by Nguyen Van Thieu on three counts. Thieu was an Army general in what was essentially a land war; Ky was Air Force. Thieu was from central Vietnam; Ky was from the North. Thieu was older, less flamboyant. He won not so much the mandate of heaven but what passed for the same thing in the mid-1960s, the mandate of the Americans.†

Ky was always a little too independent for the Americans. His own surface Americanness repelled them, finally: the fly-boy image, and the stunningly attractive Air Vietnam hostess named Mai‡ whom he married and who went ahead and Westernized her features, the two of them in their matching black jump suits.

Thieu prevailed, but he could not ground Ky altogether. Ky had too much support in the Air Force—in which he had been the first Vietnamese squadron leader when the French created an independent Vietnamese military—and among the many other northern-born commanders in the South. He kept his villa at Air Force headquarters inside Tan Son Nhut, and the two helicopters General William West-

* The second meaning was almost uncannily apt: Ky was one of South Vietnam's first fliers, and certainly its best known. He also enjoyed drinking, and a Vietnamese saying has it that a man without alcohol is like a flag without wind.
† Ellsworth Bunker, the patrician American businessman-turned-diplomat who was seventy-three when he became ambassador to Saigon in 1967, quickly decided that Thieu was the more stable man.
‡ My.

moreland had given him in exchange for permission for the Americans to use a soccer field on the air base, the single bit of "corruption" Ky ever admitted to.

Ky divided his time between the villa at Tan Son Nhut and a ranch. The ranch was in Khanh Hoa province, just south of Route 21, the road that wound from the coast up into the highlands and across to Ban Me Thuot.

In the middle of the day on Thursday, March 6, the Khanh Hoa province chief came to see Ky at the ranch. He said that what he thought to be a small communist force had cut the road west of the ranch, toward Ban Me Thuot. Sappers had blown two bridges, and then troops had overrun a territorial outpost. Like all province chiefs, the man was an Army colonel. He said that in a day and a half of trying, his men had still not been able to clear the road.

When Ky had gone into his ambiguous semi-retirement, the Americans had given him a powerful radio. It took only a few calls to learn that the communists had simultaneously launched even stronger attacks on Route 19, which ran roughly parallel to Route 21 seventy-five miles north, from Qui Nhon on the coast to Pleiku. In twenty-four hours, they had isolated the entire Central Highlands from ground resupply.

Ky got in the helicopter he had come up in and flew to Saigon. He landed in the soccer field, which had reverted to Vietnamese use, and was driven across the base to the headquarters of the South Vietnamese Joint General Staff. He met with Cao Van Vien, the chairman of the JGS.

Vien presented no argument when Ky said that the highlands were about to come under a major attack, and that the target might be Ban Me Thuot. In fact, Vien told Ky that at a meeting at the Presidential Palace the previous week President Thieu had specifically warned General Pham Van Phu, the commander in the highlands, that there was strong evidence that the North Vietnamese Army's 320th Division, which for years had operated north of Pleiku, had slipped down toward Ban Me Thuot. Phu had said that he was aware of all developments.

"But he still thinks the main target will be Pleiku," Vien said.

"Has he reinforced Ban Me Thuot at all?" Ky asked.

"Four hundred men."

"It's crazy," Ky said. "Why don't you do something?"

"You know as well as I do, Marshal," Vien said. "I can't order Phu to do anything. And now, more than ever, Thieu makes all the decisions."

That night, Ky asked his friend Charlie Timmes to come to the villa.

Major General Charles J. Timmes (U.S. Army, retired) had commanded one of the airborne battalions that spearheaded the landings at Normandy. He was at one time in the early 1960s the senior American military officer in Vietnam, but was eased out when the American commitment mushroomed. Then, when he retired from the Army in 1967, someone realized that an American hero who had known men like Cao Van Vien and Nguyen Van Thieu when they were division commanders or less might be useful in an effort that appeared to be more prolonged than originally envisioned. Timmes returned to Saigon under CIA contract, and was the embassy's main link to the South Vietnamese military commanders.

Timmes had seen General Phu at his headquarters in Pleiku in late January and again in early February. Phu, who was small even for a Vietnamese, had established a reasonably good reputation as a division commander in Military Region 1, the northernmost part of the country. He had been named commander of Military Region 2, which encompassed all of the Central Highlands, just four months before when Thieu, in the face of an anticorruption campaign led by a Redemptorist priest, had relieved three of the four regional commanders. Phu took over from an obese general named Nguyen Van Toan, whose corruption centered on control of the lucrative trade in cinnamon from Quang Ngai province.

Phu was still convinced that the target was Pleiku, Timmes told Ky. His main objective—he had repeated this at both meetings—was to keep Highway 19 to Qui Nhon, the main resupply road into the region, open. He was building up a sixty-day supply of fuel and ammunition for Pleiku.

At the second meeting, Phu told Timmes that two regiments of North Vietnamese troops that had detrucked west of Ban Me Thuot inside Cambodia might be from the communists' 10th Division, which was normally based even farther north than the 320th. And he said that his people had recently captured a sergeant from the 320th who said that his entire division was redeploying north of Ban Me Thuot. Phu had finally gone ahead and issued an order moving the balance of his 23d Division to Ban Me Thuot to reinforce the regiment that was already there. But he had countermanded the order when he learned that the 320th was broadcasting radio messages from the site of its old area of operations north of Pleiku.

"Fake," Ky said. "So easy. You see what it is, General."

"I see what it is if it is a fake, Marshal," Timmes said.

"Such an easy trick," Ky said, sprawled on the sofa, his low, gleaming boots propped on the coffee table. "A few radio messages. Three men. Two men. The right transmitter and a little generator. And then, so easy. In Ban Me Thuot: two divisions against a regiment."

III

The small collection of Westerners in Ban Me Thuot was roughly typical of South Vietnam as a whole, if overrepresented by committed Christians. There were the French planters, virtually indigenous by now, and above the fray in the sense that their government was represented in both Hanoi and Saigon and they themselves often paid taxes to both sides. There was a small delegation of Indonesians and Iranians, representing the International Commission of Control and Supervision of the peace accords, which controlled nothing and was bankrolled by the U.S. government.*

The U.S. government itself was represented by Paul Struharik, a thirty-four-year-old former Army lieutenant who was typical of many of the young American officials who lingered on in Vietnam in that he had married a pretty local girl.†

And then there were the missionaries—a Canadian couple and six Americans, including a couple with a five-year-old daughter.

On that same Thursday, word that something was wrong reached the missionaries. John and Carolyn Miller, the American couple with the five-year-old daughter, were working with two young Bru assistants in a house on the property of The Christian and Missionary Alliance in Ban Me Thuot where the Millers had lived as guests for five months. John Miller had been in Vietnam for fifteen years, Carolyn for fourteen. During those years, as missionaries for the Wycliffe Bible Translators, they had learned the Bru language, devised a system of writing it and nearly completed the work of translating the New Testament into the language. That afternoon, they were cross-checking the accuracy of certain key Greek words and phrases, the last step before their manuscript would be shipped to Saigon and published.

Carolyn Miller looked up to see Dick Phillips, their C&MA host, at

* The ICCS group in Ban Me Thuot should have included some Poles and Hungarians, representing the communists. But the night before the cease-fire was supposed to have gone into effect in late January 1973, the Viet Cong destroyed a Catholic village near Ban Me Thuot. When the helicopter carrying the Poles and Hungarians set down in a football field the next day, it was met by a crowd of several thousand Catholics, and the passengers were beaten. They fled to Saigon and never returned.

† She was the daughter of a judge in the dominant Rhade (Rah-day) tribe around Ban Me Thuot; that spring she and their infant daughter were living in what the U.S. government called "safe-haven" status, in Bangkok.

the door. Phillips had collapsed with what a local doctor diagnosed as nervous exhaustion a week before, and Carolyn was surprised to see him out of bed.

"I wondered if you knew Route 21 has been cut?" Phillips asked.

"No," John Miller said, "when did that happen?"

"The day before yesterday," Phillips said. "Apparently the communists are holding one of the mountain passes between here and the coast."

"I guess that means no more gasoline until the government opens the road again," John Miller said.

"No more fish or market supplies from the coast either," his wife added.

After Phillips left, the Millers discussed the news, without alarm. The road to the coast passed through stretches of isolated, rugged terrain, and it was not uncommon for traffic to be suspended when bridges were blown or government convoys were ambushed. Still, they were always uncomfortable when the fighting reminded them of their separation from their three older children, at school in Nha Trang, on the coast.

IV

On Saturday, March 8, Wolfgang Lehmann, the deputy chief of mission at the U.S. Embassy, made a note in his appointments calendar: "Major NVA* ops resume."

Before dawn that day, the North Vietnamese launched a strong series of jabs at government outposts in the two northernmost provinces of South Vietnam. As Lehmann wrote, fifty thousand people in Quang Tri, the province immediately below the demilitarized zone between the two Vietnams, were fleeing south. Quang Tri had been leveled to rubble in the last major offensive, in the spring of 1972.

"Cynical bastards," Lehmann said to himself. Through the last few weeks, there had been a battlefield lull, neatly coinciding with a staggered series of visits to Vietnam by several congressional delegations. These latest in a very long series of "fact-finding" missions had been promoted by the Administration, and lavishly attended to by the embassy in Saigon, in hopes that enough minds could be changed to win passage for the Administration's request for $300 million in emergency supplemental military aid for South Vietnam.

But few minds had been changed, which was one reason why Ambassador Graham Martin earlier that week had suddenly announced that he was returning to Washington with the largest delegation. He

* North Vietnamese Army.

hoped to do some last-minute lobbying on the plane, as well as on Capitol Hill; and while he was in the States he also hoped to be able to find the time for some long overdue dental work.

v

In Ban Me Thuot that evening, Dick Phillips called John Miller and Norman Johnson, one of the Canadian missionaries, to his home in the C&MA compound to share some ominous news. Phillips had just been visited by a Vietnamese government official who was also an evangelical Christian. The man said that the North Vietnamese had recently inserted two entire divisions into the area, reinforcing the units the government knew to have been there for years. The official was getting his wife and children to Saigon and advised the missionaries to leave.

But word was that the Air Vietnam flights out of Ban Me Thuot were booked for weeks ahead. The Millers decided that when Paul Struharik returned from Saigon the next day, they would ask for seats on the next U.S. Embassy courier plane, which was due on Tuesday.

On Sunday, March 9, the Millers packed four suitcases, in order of priority. In the first they put their manuscript and language notes. If they could take only one bag, that would be the one. The second bag contained tapes, a tape recorder and radio, toilet articles, money, mementos and their best clothes. In the last two cases they packed more clothing, books, tools, dishes, tennis rackets and balls—and Carolyn's portable sewing machine.

In the evening, Dick Phillips and Norm Johnson finally made contact with Struharik. They stopped by the Millers' house to say that Struharik had checked with the Vietnamese commanders in Ban Me Thuot and been told that they expected some fighting but were confident they could handle it. Struharik added that if any of the missionaries wanted to stay in his house, which was more strongly built than theirs, they would be welcome.

The missionaries decided not to impose themselves on Struharik. They knew that he already had one guest—an official of the Australian Broadcasting Commission who had decided to visit Ban Me Thuot as a break from his duties as an adviser to hill tribes' radio operations in northern Thailand.

The bedtime evasion tactics of five-year-old LuAnne Miller lasted longer than usual that night. She was keyed up by the packing, with its prospects of a visit to her brothers and sister in Nha Trang. But the adults' concerns had not been lost on her.

"Mommy, can't I sleep in your room?" she asked when Carolyn

Miller put her to bed on the living-room couch. "What if the fighting comes here?"

"If there's any fighting, we'll come and get you," her mother told her. Carolyn Miller then read until midnight, when she joined her husband under the mosquito net in their bedroom, careful not to wake him.

VI

Jay Scarborough was one of those young American civilians with no particular ideology who couldn't seem to put Vietnam behind them. He was twenty-nine that spring, and tall, with short curly blond hair and delicate good looks.

Scarborough came to Vietnam from Cornell with an organization called International Voluntary Services, a vehicle the U.S. government used to insert a Peace Corps contingent into a country where it was waging war.* For the government, IVS backfired. Before its Vietnam program disintegrated, many of its former volunteers had become point men for the antiwar movement. But for Scarborough, there were no politics in Vietnam, only friendships, and the yearning to capture something.

He was there for six years, teaching in high school for four years, then selling tickets for Pan Am and finally winning a year as a Fulbright lecturer in Da Lat, the pretty resort town in the mountains that formed the southeastern corner of the plateau. Many of his students were Chams, remnants of the people the Vietnamese had nearly extinguished in their long drive south out of China.

In 1973, Scarborough returned to Cornell to enter law school. But he was back in Vietnam the following summer on a fairly esoteric pursuit: He set out to photograph thousands of pages of old Cham manuscripts, with their Arabic-looking script. Early in 1975, in the midst of his second year at law school, he received a Ford Foundation grant to complete the work on the manuscripts. He took a leave of absence and returned to Vietnam.

When the bulk film carrier that was essential to his work was stolen on a bus, Scarborough came down to Saigon from the Cham enclaves on the coast to order another one. It was a waste of time, he thought, to sit around the noisy capital, which had never been his Vietnam. On Sunday, March 9, he flew to Ban Me Thuot to visit former students, some of whom he had been helping to support for years and some of whom were now themselves teachers.

---

* IVS was and is a private voluntary organization operating in a number of countries, normally under private sponsorship. But in Vietnam and Laos, it was funded entirely by the U.S. government.

Scarborough had heard in Saigon that Route 21 had been cut, but roads were always being cut and reopened in Vietnam. However, after taking the bus from the airport to the Air Vietnam office downtown and finding the office mobbed, he decided it might be prudent to get a ticket on the next available flight out. In part because he was fluent in Vietnamese, but also simply because he was a tall, polite American, he was able to work his way through the unqueued crowd at the counter and get a return ticket for the following day. (All flights out of Ban Me Thuot may have been booked for weeks, as Carolyn Miller believed, but Scarborough had a genuine charm that got things done.) On the way out of the office, a Vietnamese offered him twice what he had just paid. Scarborough kept the ticket.

He got around as he almost always did in Vietnam, paying the equivalent of twenty-five or fifty cents for a young man to take him where he wanted to go on the back of a motorcycle. He had originally thought to stay with friends at the outlying Ban Me Thuot teacher-training school. There was no panic in the little city. But the crowd at the Air Vietnam office convinced him it might be wiser to stay with another friend, a teacher at the highlanders' technical high school, in town.

His friend was worried. *"Chao anh,"* he said. "Greetings, older brother. There are VC two kilometers outside of town." Scarborough liked the man, and normally trusted his intelligence. But he simply could not believe the Viet Cong could be so close. And in more than six years in Vietnam, he had seen little fighting. Beyond that, there was little he could do about it. He did telephone a friend in Saigon, a fellow Cornell graduate student who was scheduled to fly to Ban Me Thuot the next day, and told her to stay where she was.

VII

On the night of March 9 [General Van Tien Dung] sat at head-quarters and continued to follow the situation and wait for "H" hour. None of the staff cadres sitting around could hide their joy and excitement as the momentous hour grew near. For a soldier in battle, the night spent waiting for "H" hour is like waiting for mid-night on New Year's Eve. From the highest ranks to the lowest, we had been waiting years for this New Year's Eve. Although this night in the Truong Son mountains was peaceful, tens of thousands of people were moving toward their objectives. Every commander had someone standing over him, their hair falling together on the maps as they checked their plans one final time. And on this night, too, the quislings from Saigon to the Tay Nguyen surely had not yet been able to guess where we would act or imagined our strength;

they had been led by us from one error to another, making us confident that when "H" hour began we would enjoy a great advantage.

Nguyen Cao Ky had been wrong when he bemoaned the possibility that the communists had positioned two divisions against a regiment at Ban Me Thuot. In one of the greatest strategic successes of thirty years of war, Dung had in fact assembled the equivalent of three divisions around the lightly manned little city.

VIII

"Phao kich! Phao kich!"*

His friend was shaking Scarborough's shoulder roughly, rudely. The breach of etiquette as much as the words—"Incoming! Incoming!"—brought Scarborough fully awake and told him that this was real, and urgent. He looked at his watch. It was three o'clock in the morning. He heard an explosion, but it seemed distant. "Where?" he said, pulling on chinos and a shirt. "At the airport, I think," his friend said. "Quick, downstairs."

The room was on the second floor of an old ramshackle wooden building. As Scarborough made his way downstairs, the shower sandals of the students slapping on the boards, a few of the small figures brushing past him in the dark like forest creatures, a string of shells blammed in the night, close.

His friend tugged at Scarborough to join him and half a dozen of the students on the concrete slab under the veranda of the building farthest away from where the rounds were landing. Scarborough crawled into the space and pressed his face into his arms as the night shook every thirty or forty-five or sixty seconds with explosions, sometimes just one, sometimes two or three. Scarborough assumed that the incoming rounds were all rockets, which were notoriously inaccurate. He was filled with a fear he had never known, the prolonged minute-after-minute fear that he would be blown to death. He could hear the rounds just before they landed—not a whistling, but a brief sucking in the air, less than a second, and then the crack, deeper and more muffled than the loudest crack of a thunderbolt, which travels straight through the ether to the ear, but loud.

It was like that for fifteen minutes, and then his shaking stopped. Scarborough listened to the talk of his companions, and came to think that the rounds were 122-mm. artillery shells, not rockets. The target was clearly the headquarters of the ARVN 23d Division, which the school abutted. It was too bad that the target was so close, but knowing

---

* Fow kick! Fow kick!

that there was a perfectly logical military target, and believing that the incoming was artillery, helped. And adrenaline is a hormone after all. Like sex, terror manifests itself in waves. Scarborough returned to something like normal. But he did not sleep.

The shelling stopped at 7:03 by Scarborough's watch, once he realized it had been silent so long that the attack might have stopped and he looked at his watch. He and the others crawled out into the fresh new morning. The air was still cool. The Army base was hung with dust.

IX

The Millers awoke with the first thudding explosions. Carolyn awakened LuAnne, dressed her and led her to the hallway, where there were no windows or outside walls. John brought the blanket and pillow from the couch; instantly, half cradled in her mother's arms on the concrete floor, the child was again asleep. She woke up only once, briefly, during the night, when Carolyn eased herself up and groped her way to the bathroom. "Mommy! Where are you?" LuAnne called.

"I'm right here, darling," her mother answered. "I'll be back in a minute."

Some of the rounds landed close enough to throw dirt on the roof of the house. Many rattled the windows and caused bits of plaster to fall from the ceilings. John Miller left the house twice during the night. Early on, he checked with the Phillipses and Betty Mitchell, another missionary in the compound. They agreed with him that it was best to wait until morning. And shortly before dawn, he took the suitcases out to the Land Rover. "Thank God the night is ending at last," Carolyn thought.

"John," she asked her husband, "do you think we should try to go now?"

"Yes," he said. "Maybe this is all we'll get this time. But if there should be a ground attack, we don't want to be here."

Carolyn knew what he meant. A few yards from the house were the grave site and memorial for six missionaries who had been killed by communist troops fighting their way into Ban Me Thuot in the 1968 Tet offensive.

The Rhade church pastor stood by the Land Rover as the Phillipses and Betty Mitchell loaded their suitcases into it. He promised to send someone down the hill to inform the Johnsons—the Canadians—who had their own vehicle, where the Americans were going.

The street leading into the city was deserted except for clusters of soldiers at intersections, and tanks at the gate to the province headquarters. Carolyn hunched over LuAnne as they drove past the tanks.

But the soldiers manning them simply stared in surprise at the Westerners.

John Miller honked the horn at the gate to the American compound. A Vietnamese guard pulled it open. As the missionaries got out of the Land Rover, Paul Struharik emerged from his one-story office building and told them to get into the house. He seemed not at all surprised to see them. "Take your things upstairs and make yourselves comfortable," he said. "I'll be up shortly. I'm trying to find out what's going on."

X

At the technical school, Jay Scarborough was still not aware of the scale of the attack. They had no radio, no way of knowing if places other than the ARVN headquarters had been shelled. Laborers who were doing some construction work at the school showed up, as did the teachers; in Vietnam, an artillery attack was not necessarily grounds for failing to go to work.

Because he did not know what was happening, Scarborough decided to get into the center of town. He wanted to find the ICCS compound, where, with luck, there might be some Hungarians or Poles. But the teacher who offered him a lift on his Honda also didn't know where the international delegation was housed. He knew the USAID compound. "Okay," Scarborough said, "with the Americans then."

He arrived a few minutes after the missionaries. Now there were twenty people in the compound, including Struharik: half a dozen local USAID employees; another Vietnamese man with his wife and two children; the missionaries; Peter Whitlock, the visiting Australian Broadcasting Commission official; Ike Tolentino, a Filipino agricultural expert under contract to USAID; and Scarborough.

When Struharik came up to the second-floor living room from his office, the missionaries asked him how serious it was. "I don't really know," he said. "No one seems to have a very clear picture of the overall situation."

John Miller was very concerned that the Canadian missionary couple still had not arrived. The next time Struharik passed through the room, Miller said that he thought he should drive out to their house. Struharik shook his head. "You'd never make it. The radio says there's heavy fighting right outside the province headquarters. Better just hope they got out."

A staccato burst of firing that Carolyn Miller couldn't identify—like short spurts of machine-gun fire, but much louder—rang in the air.

"What on earth is that?" she asked Struharik. "An antiaircraft weapon," he said. "And it sounds as if it's been set up right down the street from here." Then a series of explosions shook the house. Struharik decided to shepherd his guests down to his bedroom.

The house had once been occupied by the CIA, and the bedroom was a windowless twelve-by-twelve-foot bunker of reinforced concrete on the ground floor. Struharik lit a candle on the dresser by the door.

Dick Phillips had survived the morning's exertions, but he stretched out gratefully on Struharik's bed, his wife beside him, and Betty Mitchell beside her. The others sprawled in chairs or on pillows propped against the walls and spread on the floor.

Before noon, Struharik and his Vietnamese employees saw tanks lumber into the street, and young North Vietnamese soldiers take up positions along it. Struharik came down to the bedroom to tell his guests that he thought they should try to keep silent.

5

"David Butler, NBC News, *Sai-Gon*," George Esper intoned in a better radio voice than mine when I entered the Associated Press office on Monday morning. "Got the biggie?" The AP office was in a corner of the hulking Eden Building on the square that held the Marines Statue. The NBC bureau was directly above the AP's, and on my way to work I routinely stopped in to see Esper, the bureau chief, and to find out what the wire service was reporting. Esper had only glanced up from a piece of copy he was editing. The phone was ringing.

"I just got up," I said.

Esper pushed himself up from his torn gray swivel chair and crossed to the teletype room. "David Butler, NBC News, Saigon," he repeated on the way. "And today we've got a genuine biggie, folks."

I moved to the table that held the clipboards and picked up the one for outgoing Vietnam stories.

URGENT

VIETNAM

SAIGON (AP)—NORTH VIETNAMESE FORCES ATTACKED THE PROVIN-
CIAL CAPITAL OF BAN ME THUOT IN THE LOWER CENTRAL HIGHLANDS

BEFORE DAWN MONDAY AND LAID SIEGE TO THE SOUTHERN SECTION
OF THE CITY, THE SAIGON COMMAND SAID.

There was much more, some of it background and some of it repetitive as Esper constantly updated the top of the story. But much was also hard news, including the fact that military spokesmen in Saigon said that North Vietnamese tanks had been spotted three miles northwest of Ban Me Thuot.

"Jesus," I said to no one. *"Tanks?"*

That night, I had beers and a sandwich with someone on the terrace of the Continental Palace Hotel and then, fighting off the urge to walk a few blocks down Tu Do Street to the only nightclub I went to, made my way back to the AP office.

Esper's Indochina wrap-up repeated the news that eight Americans trapped in Ban Me Thuot were "all right," according to the embassy in Saigon, and that fighting had also broken out on "the so-called Street Without Joy, on the central coast northeast of Hue, where the French suffered heavy losses in the first Indochina War." It included this new paragraph:

WESTERN MILITARY ANALYSTS STOPPED SHORT OF CALLING IT AN
OFFENSIVE, SINCE LITTLE MAJOR FIGHTING WAS REPORTED IN THE
SOUTHERN HALF OF SOUTH VIETNAM, INCLUDING THE SAIGON REGION
AND THE MEKONG DELTA, BUT THEY SAID THE ATTACKS IN THE HIGH-
LANDS AND ALONG THE NORTHERN COAST MARKED THE BEGINNING OF
A "HIGH POINT" OF NORTH VIETNAMESE AND VIET CONG ACTIVITY.

Upstairs in the NBC office, I surprised the overnight teletype operator, who was preparing to sleep with a girl friend on the couch in the room with the machine. I apologized and left.

I had time before the curfew for a couple of drinks on the terrace of the Continental. None of the customers at the few occupied tables were journalists, so I sat alone at the short rattan bar under the eaves at the back wall. I seldom ventured into that quarter, where there were often prostitutes, some of ambiguous gender; but not this night. I ordered a double Scotch.

The bartender brought the drink and then moved to the end of the bar to fill a waiter's order. He did so slowly, prolonging a discussion through which he slowly shook his head. When the waiter left, the bartender slipped a chit with an elegantly crafted 1,700, the seven stroked, under a heavy ceramic Air France ashtray in front of me. He was one of the few Vietnamese men in middle age who had gone nearly bald. The yellow wall lights gave his face a dark pallor touched with earth red. His remaining hair and his eyebrows, eyes and nostrils were black. His face was unsmiling but intelligent, and he glanced at me as if he would welcome talk. We started in Vietnamese.

"How are you feeling, uncle?"

"I have a son in Ban Me Thuot. We haven't heard from him today, and I know he would have tried to call me here."

"He is in the Army?"

"Yes. He has a wife and two children."

"Where are they?"

"With him."

"Don't worry," I said. "Thieu will have to send in reinforcements. He can't let them take Ban Me Thuot." I'd had to pause and give "reinforcements" in English.

The man shook his head again. It could have meant either that he didn't understand me or that what I had said was small encouragement, which I realized it was.

He asked if I spoke French. I shrugged. "Better than Vietnamese," I said.

"He calls me every Sunday, here at the hotel," the man said in French, "just to say a few words. He called . . . *yesterday* . . . and said everything was fine. He has a younger brother at Tan Son Nhut. The younger brother tried to call, through the Air Force telephone. But they said they were too busy."

I tried hard to think of what to say next. The best I could come up with was "I hope you get good news soon, uncle," which I managed in Vietnamese. The bartender said, "Thank you, sir," and retreated into silent glass polishing.

Until the summer before, I had been an editor at *Playboy*. I had made two brief trips to Vietnam, one a four-month leave of absence in the early 1970s, the other my 1973 three-week vacation. I had come late to the war, thinking I was coming to a war. But something beyond the war had captured me. After the three-week trip, I began the process, which lasted almost a year, of disentangling myself from the magazine and leaving the woman—my wife—whom I frequently referred to without irony as the most beautiful woman of her generation in the Upper Midwest.

When I returned to Saigon—for good, I thought (to live there, for years)—in August 1974, I hoped that I could make a living as a magazine writer.

But the story was dead in late 1974. I realized quickly that I could not make a living as a free-lance writer, and gladly accepted Dennis Troute's offer to let me sit in as the only American in the NBC bureau while Troute and his French-Vietnamese girl friend went off to Indonesia for a ten-day vacation. I wasn't even insulted when Troute said: "It's funny—this must be the first time in ten years that there's been only one American free lancer in town."

Dennis Troute bore an uncanny resemblance to Dick Cavett. Like Cavett, he was quick. Even after years in Vietnam, years that had begun as a young officer in the Phoenix program, he walked faster on the sidewalks than anyone else I knew.

I also knew, from the previous trips and from the six months of close association with him now just ended, that Troute was as good as any of them. I wondered vaguely at the back bar on the terrace of the Continental Palace Hotel why Troute didn't quite seem to be included at the best dinner parties of the grave young men who made up the cream of the resident American press corps and, more important, why NBC didn't realize how good he was. Maybe it was because they had hired him (as a radio stringer, which I now was) in-country, and stupidly assumed that he could do only Vietnam. In any case, NBC never made Dennis Troute a staff correspondent. They always offered a yearly contract. When the last one ran out, in February, Troute brought the issue to a head; he was offered a raise, but still the same old contract. He packed his bags and left for Paris with his girl friend.

One night a few weeks earlier, as this major decision in Troute's life was forming, he told me: "You know, David, I should have quit two years ago, when the American troops pulled out and it became fairly clear that they weren't going to make me staff, that first contract when I was the only American in the office, bureau chief on yearly hire. But I couldn't get myself to leave. I always wanted to be here for the end."

I certainly did not think it was the end. But I knew that Vietnam was going to be in the news for a few weeks, until the government recaptured Ban Me Thuot. I was going to make enough to buy a motorcycle, and maybe enough to move up to the back penthouse apartment in my building.

And in the crazy event that it turned out to be the end, I was there, thank God.

"Poor Dennis," I thought. "Four days off the mark."

II

Once an hour, the attention of everyone in the bedroom focused on an olive-green battery-operated field radio. "Any Air America station, any Air America station," Struharik repeated each time. "This is fox-trot, over." All morning, the reply was static. Then in the early afternoon the weak signal was picked up by a plane circling high overhead.

Struharik listed the people in the house and reported their situation as he was able to gauge it from the roof.

The voice on the radio said that they had two helicopters standing by in Nha Trang for a rescue attempt. "Can you get somewhere where you can be picked up?"

A sizable concrete slab for drying coffee beans lay behind the house next door. It would have made a good landing pad. But the pilot couldn't locate it, even after Struharik put a brightly painted sheet of plywood on the roof of his house.

The plane stayed within range through the afternoon, and Struharik talked with the pilot every hour. Finally the man said, "We're going back to Nha Trang, but we'll be back at oh-six-hundred tomorrow."

The Vietnamese with the two young children nearly panicked. "Aren't they coming in to get us?" he asked. "They can't," Struharik said. "If the pilot knew exactly where to go, he could come straight in without circling and go straight back up. That's the only way he could even hope to make it. But from that altitude they can't identify the house. And I can't give them the street coordinates because the NVA is undoubtedly picking us up."

"But this is our last chance!" the man said, his eyes filled with fear.

III

The streets and avenues of Saigon were hung with propaganda banners, long horizontal strips of yellow cloth with bold red lettering, the national colors, over the noisome traffic.

Some of the most faded banners still carried Nguyen Van Thieu's "Four No's" from the time of the signing of the Paris Peace Accords more than two years earlier. The first No was: "No square inch of the national territory is to be abandoned to the communists."*

In compliance with that dictum, two of the best divisions in the armed forces, the paratroopers and the Marines, which should have been held in strategic reserve, were pinned down in territorial defense in the north. During those two years, a few of Thieu's aides, as well as a former commander of Australian forces in Vietnam named Ted Serong, who had returned as an unofficial adviser to the president, presented the case for withdrawal to a smaller, more defensible South Vietnam, with shorter supply lines. Thieu had always resisted. He had three letters from Nixon assuring him that if there was a major attack by the North, the United States would come to his aid. The letters were delivered in December 1972 and January 1973, when the Amer-

---

* The other three: no negotiating with the enemy; no communist activity in the South; no coalition government.

icans were bringing enormous pressure on Thieu to go along with the Paris Peace Accords. During the same period, Henry Kissinger personally assured Thieu that the American response in the face of a major communist violation of the accords would be "both swift and brutal."

But Thieu finally realized that Kissinger didn't count. Ford didn't count. Only the damned politicians in Congress mattered.

The Nixon Administration's original request for military and economic assistance to South Vietnam for 1975 was $1.45 billion. After Congress was finished with it, including the cuts it made within days of Nixon's resignation, the final appropriation was less than half of what the Administration had asked for: $700 million.

In early January, the communists had overrun and held all the government outposts and then the capital of Phuoc Long province, which lay just eighty miles north of Saigon. Phuoc Long was of little strategic or economic importance, but it was the first province in South Vietnam to fall to the communists since the last major offensive, in 1972.

Three weeks after the communists took Phuoc Long, the Ford Administration went back to Congress with a request for $300 million in supplemental military aid. Thieu sent Tran Van Lam, the president of the Senate, to Washington to lobby for the aid. Senate majority leader Mike Mansfield refused to see Lam, who returned to Saigon and told Thieu that they would not only not get the $300 million, there was a very good chance that in 1976 they would get nothing at all.

The Administration in Washington then arranged a series of congressional visits to South Vietnam and Cambodia.

They had been coming for weeks now. The last group had insulted Thieu at the dinner he gave for them at the palace, shouting out their stupid questions about "political prisoners" and "corruption." Some of them hadn't even bothered to go out to the Joint General Staff headquarters to see the weapons that had been captured since the communists took Phuoc Long.

The Americans were crazy. Women. There was the fat one with the hats who talked too much, and the one who smoked a pipe. No, the money probably would not come. It certainly wouldn't come if the Americans weren't made to see just how bad things were.

On Tuesday, the day after the attack on Ban Me Thuot, Thieu called on his three senior aides to join him for breakfast. When the servants had left, he abandoned the first No.

His guests were Prime Minister Tran Thien Khiem; Cao Van Vien, chairman of the Joint General Staff; and Thieu's national security adviser, Dang Van Quang.

All four of the men at the table were generals. None of them were surviving solely on a soldier's pay. But Quang, a fat man who giggled so often that the Americans called him "Laughing Boy," was thought by his fellow countrymen to be the most corrupt man in South Vietnam. No one ever proved that Quang was the country's major drug smuggler, or the front man for Thieu in all the other varieties of corruption that permeated the government. But both charges were assumed to be true.

Over the coffee service on the white linen tablecloth, Thieu propped a small map of South Vietnam. He briefly reviewed the situation, with which the three others were completely familiar. Then he said matter-of-factly: "Given our present strength and capabilities, we certainly cannot hold and defend all the territory we want."

He looked at the three men. They were silent. The government would keep the "rice bowl," Thieu went on—all of Military Region 4, the Mekong delta—and all of Military Region 3, which surrounded Saigon. It would drive the communists out of the relatively few areas in Military Regions 3 and 4 that they now held. And of course the Navy would protect the territorial waters, with their recently discovered oil. After all, this was the economic heart of the country: its rice, its rubber, its industries, as well as the great majority of the population.

As he gestured farther north, he seemed less sure of himself. Ban Me Thuot had to be retaken. Strategically and economically, it was more important than Pleiku and Kontum together. And the coastal provinces, especially those close to the continental shelf, where some of the oil had been found, would have to be held.

In Military Region 1, it would be a matter of holding what they could. He drew a series of dipping horizontal lines through MR 1 and the northernmost provinces of MR 2. If they were strong enough, he said, they would hold the territory up to Hue, or Da Nang. If not, they would have to redeploy south: "Here," Thieu said, pointing to one curve on the map; "or maybe here," his hand dropping to another line; "or possibly even as far south as here."

Cao Van Vien was the first to speak. He said that the plan was necessary, and one that he had embraced for some time. He had not pressed it on the president, he said, because it conflicted with national policy and could be taken as a sign of defeatism.

What he refrained from adding was that he thought it was too late to work.

IV

As far as one knows, David Sciacchitano was the only twenty-eight-year-old, six-foot-two-inch, red-haired, blue-eyed Italian-American in Vietnam that spring. He was a junior Foreign Service Officer in the consulate in Can Tho, ninety miles southwest of Saigon in the heart of the Mekong delta.*

That Tuesday, he happened to be visiting Saigon. A friend who worked for the United States Information Service said of the attack on Ban Me Thuot: "This is it. The whole thing's going to go."

Sciacchitano was not completely convinced that the USIS man was right. But he felt an odd kind of relief. He had been in Vietnam—up north, close to the DMZ—for nineteen months in the late 1960s as an enlisted man in the Air Force. He considered himself lucky to have survived that tour and a half, and strongly resisted when the State Department had insisted that his first posting as a Foreign Service Officer be in Vietnam. He resisted, but the department did indeed insist.

When he returned to Vietnam on February 1, 1975—a little more than a month ago—Sciacchitano assumed that South Vietnam would collapse around him right at the end of his scheduled eighteen-month tour. He also had a detached but deep and powerful hunch, which he respected, that he wouldn't be getting out alive. He was pleased now that the whole thing was starting early—that he wouldn't have to wait out the eighteen months.

V

During Tuesday afternoon, Paul Struharik held a meeting. He said that he thought they had two options. They could try to make their way to a pickup point outside of town, or they could stay in the house and await capture. Option one was not promising. They still were not sure about the direction of the attack. There seemed to be sporadic small-arms fire in all directions.

"Chances are we wouldn't get much farther than the front gate," John Miller said.

"If we're caught trying to get out of the area," Struharik said, "I think it's more likely that we'd be shot immediately than if we're discovered here in the house after the battle's over."

* South Vietnam was divided into four military regions, numbered 1 through 4, north to south. Each had an American consulate. With one exception, the consulates were in the same city as the military headquarters. The exception was in Military Region 2, which encompassed all of the Central Highlands. There, the military headquarters was at Pleiku, in the highlands, and the consulate in Nha Trang, on the coast. The other three consulates were at Da Nang (MR 1); Bien Hoa, close to Saigon (MR 3); and Can Tho, in the delta (MR 4).

The group lapsed into a silent consensus. Later in the afternoon, Struharik took one of the white pillowcases from his bed and tied it to a bamboo pole. He stood the makeshift flag next to the front door, inside. And he also had one of his employees letter a big sign reading: "Don't shoot! In here are foreigners who have taken refuge from the fighting." The banner was not visible from the street but would greet anyone coming into the compound.

Upstairs, Jay Scarborough got halfway through Gore Vidal's *Burr*, which he had found in Struharik's bookshelves. Occasionally he glanced out a window. All day, he had watched the residents of Ban Me Thuot leaving the city in small convoys of vehicles or on foot, heading west toward what were clearly the main enemy lines, flying white flags of surrender.

At eight-thirty on Wednesday morning, Struharik came into the bedroom, closed the door tightly, snuffed out his cigarette and squatted at the radio. Contact was re-established, but the conversation didn't last long. The pilot had nothing new to report. Struharik said that at their end the immediate area was quiet. "It looks as if Ban Me Thuot has been liberated," he said dryly.

"Who's in control?" the Air America pilot asked, apparently surprised.

"The guys with the red stars on their caps," Struharik said.

He signed off, and then suggested to the group that it would be a good idea to make an inventory of the food and water supplies in the house. Carolyn Miller was delighted to have a reason to get out of the bedroom.

Before noon, the wife of the agitated Vietnamese man produced a pot of freshly cooked rice. They fed the children rice with a little tuna fish. The adults reheated the beans and ham they had cooked the night before and ate that with the rice.

There was one last radio contact. Struharik reported that they had enough food and water to last for ten days. "Plan to spend one more night," the voice from the sky said.

Struharik was upstairs when he heard the old gate screech open. They must have cut the chain lock. He rushed downstairs and whispered urgent instructions that resulted in the several weapons in the house, as well as about two million piasters, being quickly shoved behind staircases and deep into cluttered closets. While that was being done, Struharik grabbed the pole with the white flag, and signaled for Jay Scarborough, the best Vietnamese speaker among the Westerners, to join him. Then he opened the front door.

VI

Despite the shelling of the advance command post of the 23d Division that woke Scarborough and the Millers—and the rest of the city, which lay in terrified darkness, all power out—the base remained operative until late Monday afternoon. Colonel Vu The Quang, the division's deputy commander, reported by radio to Pleiku that his men were "fighting with good spirit" and "we are in good shape." Then the base was struck by a string of bombs dropped by high-flying Saigon Air Force planes. The strike cut all the defenders' communications and disrupted any further defense from that quarter.

Against overwhelming odds, one Ranger unit managed to fight its way from the little town of Buon Ho, on Route 14, which ran from Pleiku south to Ban Me Thuot, into the edge of the city. The communists were still not strong on the ground inside Ban Me Thuot, holding back out of fear of the bombing.

General Le Trung Tuong, the 23d Division's commander, was in his helicopter above the city. His wife and children were in their villa on the base. General Tuong worked the radio furiously to get his family to a training center southeast of town, gave a direct order for the Rangers to circle around to secure the training center, and when all that was accomplished, he swooped down and picked up his family. When the Rangers turned back toward Ban Me Thuot, the communists had sealed it off.

Except for a few elite units, the wives and children of most ARVN soldiers lived with them or in a city nearby. In theory and often in practice in the past, this meant that the troops would fight to protect their families. But General Dung in his attack on Ban Me Thuot adopted a new tactic, bypassing outer defense posts and striking directly into the heart of the city. Many of the military dependents in the city fled east.

On Monday and Tuesday, badgered by President Thieu to reoccupy Ban Me Thuot "at all costs," General Pham Van Phu, at his Pleiku headquarters for all of Military Region 2, began to airlift other elements of the 23d Division into Phuoc An, about twenty miles east of Ban Me Thuot on Route 21.

He would do it just as the Americans had done: Drop the infantry in, and follow them quickly with artillery and armor. But there weren't enough helicopters for the guns and tanks. When the infantrymen left Pleiku they were ready to fight. When they landed on Route 21 and saw their families straggling out of the city, many disguised themselves as civilians and tried to lead their women and children to the coast.

And at Phuoc An, General Tuong took himself out of the action. A machine-gun round found his helicopter, and a piece of metal grazed his cheek. It left a surface wound requiring only a dressing. But Tuong flew to Nha Trang and had himself hospitalized, thus avoiding direct responsibility for the defeat of the division.

VII

The jungle was strung with wires. Wires stretched from Hanoi south to the Ho Chi Minh Trail, down the trail across five-thousand-foot chasms and into the jungle to General Van Tien Dung's headquarters in a misty valley west of Ban Me Thuot, and out from the headquarters to his field commanders.

The wires were a major element in Dung's extraordinary feat of military deception. They allowed him to keep real, as opposed to diversionary, radio communications to a minimum. He communicated up through Defense Minister Vo Nguyen Giap to the Politburo and down to his commanders almost entirely by telegraph or telephone. And at noon on Wednesday, just before the Westerners huddled in Struharik's house heard the screeching of the gate, the phones suddenly went dead.

> [Normally] the phones rang incessantly. The person answering, much as he tried to be calm and collected, could not stifle his joyful laughter as he received reports of victories from everywhere. Those serving at headquarters did their work quietly, walking softly and affectionately bringing cigarettes sent from the rear to the staff cadres answering the telephones.
>
> It was early spring. The *khooc* forests of the Tay Nguyen had not yet put out new leaves, and the noon heat was all the more sultry. The sounds of all kinds of insects and the cries of the peacocks beside the building blended with cannon fire echoing in the distance, the thrumming of [Saigon's] OV-10 reconnaissance planes hanging overhead searching for targets, and the "Hello! This is ZA-25!" from command headquarters.
>
> Then, at noon on March 12, when the enemy counterattack was at its most intense, all telephone lines to headquarters were suddenly broken off. We had heard no bomb explosion, no sound of any airplane. We called here and there to the outside, but got no answer. All commanders stopped working, shook their heads and looked at one another in silence. The communications cadre started, then raced out of the bunker to find the cause. At the same time there came the trumpeting of a herd of elephants, gradually growing louder, about 300 meters from headquarters.

Disturbed by the bombs and shells of the battlefield, a herd of elephants started "evacuating" past our headquarters, headed for the Vietnam-Cambodia border. The headquarters guard unit was sent out immediately to block these wild elephants who had such a "low level of political consciousness." But they were ordered not to open fire and kill the elephants, to follow the regulations on protecting valuable wild animals, and to avoid making them angry, so they wouldn't trample our headquarters. Everyone was ordered to go down into the reinforced Bunker A to escape if necessary, because "there's nothing wrong with running from elephants."*

Saigon would not admit it for days, but General Dung's forces had been in control of Ban Me Thuot since midday on Tuesday, the day before the elephant stampede. Dung's plans had called for the capture of Ban Me Thuot after seven to ten days of fighting. Instead, the communists had it after less than a day and a half.

The map at Dung's headquarters was dotted with circled red Xs indicating targets they had taken; red arrows showed his troops' advances; green arrows, blocked or fleeing into the forest, marked the South Vietnamese units.

A little more than two months earlier, at the end of an extraordinary three-week conference in Hanoi, the Politburo had resolved on a two-year strategic plan.

In 1975 [as Dung recounted it later], we would strike unexpectedly with large, widespread offensives, and create conditions to carry out a general offensive and uprising in 1976. In 1976 we would launch the general offensive and uprising to liberate the South completely.

Besides the basic two-year strategic plan, the Political Bureau had foreseen another tendency and included in the 1975 plan another essential course of action: *If the opportune moment presents itself at the beginning or the end of 1975, we will immediately liberate the South in 1975.*†

On Wednesday, communist party chief Le Duan remarked to officers in Hanoi's General Military Staff that they should consider whether the battle of Ban Me Thuot might mark the beginning of the full offensive to liberate the South.

VIII

The moment Struharik opened the door, his sixty-pound half-Doberman bolted from the house. Struharik's heart leaped to his throat. The dog didn't like Vietnamese much and certainly didn't like strangers.

* A Vietnamese saying.
† Dung's italics.

He called after her—and to his vast relief she came running back to him.

For security reasons, the front door of the very secure house did not face either of the gates into the compound. With Jay Scarborough two or three steps behind him, Struharik edged to the corner of the house, from which he could look into the front yard.

There were three of them, two civilians and an officer. All three were peering intently at the several vehicles in the compound—away from the corner of the house.

Struharik believed that the North Vietnamese, starting in about 1970, had realized that Western prisoners were more useful alive than dead. So he thought that everything depended on the first fifteen or thirty seconds. If you made it through those moments of danger, you would probably get out alive.

The three of them kept staring at the vehicles. The young man in uniform even had the Scouts and Land Rovers and the rest of them covered with his pistol.

Struharik cleared his throat and said: *"Ong! Ong!"** But not loud. The three of them turned. The soldier's eyes grew as large as duck's eggs. But he didn't fire. In fact, if he had pulled the trigger, he would have shot one of the vehicles, because the pistol was still pointed that way.

They approached. The soldier barked out his questions: "Who are you?" "What do you do?" "How many people are in the house?"

Jay Scarborough addressed him as *"ong."* After a few exchanges, the young man—he seemed about nineteen or twenty—began to address Scarborough as "older brother." Scarborough also sensed from the first moments that whatever happened next he was almost certainly going to survive.

Struharik concentrated to be accurate about the number of people in the house. "Eighteen," he said finally. Then they let him go back into it.

"We are to walk out in single file and go out into the street," Struharik said. "We are permitted to take one small bag apiece. The keys to all the vehicles are to be turned over to them."

After the two days of semidarkness, Carolyn Miller's eyes were dazzled by the light of day. When her vision cleared, she saw a soldier in the courtyard, his gun held ready. "So this is what a North Vietnamese soldier looks like," she thought, taking in the red star on the pith helmet, the youthful but suspicious face, the plain green uniform and green canvas boots. She was surprised at her feeling of detachment. It was as if part of her were a spectator at a play, or a dream.

* Ohm! Ohm!—"Sir! Sir!"

Betty Mitchell and Carolyn Miller were given permission to go back into the house for a few things. Soldiers were already at work in it. The contents of Struharik's dresser drawers and of most of the suitcases they had left behind were strewn on the floor.

Struharik had to tie up the big dog, who looked at him with deeply mournful eyes.

It took some time for Struharik to match up keys with vehicles, and for the soldiers to back them out into the street. The Caucasians were ordered into the Millers' Land Rover. Scarborough made it clear that Ike Tolentino was a Filipino employed by the U.S. government, but the soldiers insisted that he stay with the Vietnamese.

A civilian drove, with a soldier beside him in the front seat. The driver seemed unsure where he was to go, and they stopped once to ask directions of another civilian in the street. The few residential blocks they passed were virtually deserted, and showed no signs of battle.

The Land Rover pulled off the road and stopped. They were just three or four kilometers northeast of Ban Me Thuot, in a field by a stream. Other vehicles were grouped nearby, and camouflaged by tree branches. The Westerners were told to get out and take everything with them. This proved difficult. In addition to the small bags each had brought, they had to take the lowest-priority suitcases, which the missionaries had left in the Land Rover, including the bag containing the Millers' sewing machine.

They crossed the field, which was planted in manioc, to the edge of a heavily wooded ravine, where they were told to sit down. Scarborough felt safer than ever. The hillside swarmed with soldiers, and was cut with fresh trenches, which made him think it had been a staging area for the attack. But the tree cover was the best protection they could hope for against the only thing he still feared, bombing by the Saigon Air Force.

Some of the soldiers pressed close around the first Westerners most of them had ever seen. Carolyn Miller was strangely comforted when, at first, they ignored an officer's order to stand back. The mild insubordination made them familiar, human. But they frightened LuAnne, and she began to cry. The officer spoke to the men again, and sent one of them for a can of South Vietnamese military-issue sweetened condensed milk and North Vietnamese combat rations—a dry, biscuitlike substance pressed into a bar and wrapped in plastic. The officer stooped and spoke kindly to the child and gave her the things and she quieted.

Then he spoke to the adults. He told them in Vietnamese that they were guests of the liberation armed forces, and that they would be treated humanely so long as they did exactly what they were told.

Even the American pilots, who were guilty of grave crimes against the Vietnamese people, had been released.

He wanted to know how many other Americans there were in Ban Me Thuot, and was incredulous when they told him there were none. "We know there are twenty-four thousand American military men in Vietnam masquerading as civilians," he said. Through Scarborough, Struharik repeated that while he did not know about the rest of the country, as far as he was aware, all the Americans in Ban Me Thuot were here with him.

LuAnne was confused. "Mommy," she asked, "are these men keeping us so we won't be captured?"

Carolyn Miller decided to tell the truth. "No, honey," she said. "We *are* captured. But the man told us not to worry, because they will let us go back to our families. Besides, we know that God is with us and will take care of us."

A second officer came to them and began the gradual divestiture from the group of articles the communists considered threatening. They took the cameras, film and all the maps in their possession, including a couple of cards from the International Protestant Church in Saigon, which included a small diagram showing its location. Paul Struharik had a few anxious moments when he reached into his backpack and pulled out a bag of 9-mm. ammunition. The soldiers accepted it without comment. They were especially interested in confiscating anything that could produce a light, and mirrors. The Westerners gave the officer a pillowcase in which to put the things, and he carefully lettered out an itemized receipt.

A few minutes later, as they were quietly talking among themselves, a soldier came to them and told them that they must speak only in Vietnamese. Scarborough said: "Okay, if you insist. But the little girl and this man from Australia won't be able to understand anything."

"Then you will have to be quiet," the man said. "You should behave meekly, as prisoners." An uncomfortable stillness settled over them. But as the afternoon wore on, they discovered that if they kept their eyes out for the grouchy soldier, the rule could be broken.

They too were given the dry bars, which were so extraordinarily dry that they produced a great thirst. (Later, Struharik would think that the thirst, which lasted for several days, was dehydration caused by anxiety.) Scarborough noted that the rations were from China.

At sunset, they were told that they were going to be moved to a new location. With no idea what would come next, they trundled everything back across the manioc field to the Land Rover.

6

One of the traits that helped keep Nguyen Van Thieu at the top of Vietnamese politics for close to ten years was a remarkable ability to do nothing. This propensity for inaction and delay served many purposes. Most important, it meant that he very seldom surprised the Americans. For years, the last thing in the world Thieu wanted to do was surprise and therefore upset his sponsors. But with the shock of Ban Me Thuot, he all but gave up on the Americans, and acted.

On Thursday, two days after the breakfast meeting at the palace, he called for General Ngo Quang Truong, the commander of Military Region 1, encompassing the northernmost provinces, to fly to Saigon for a meeting. Even before the attack in the highlands, Thieu had told Truong that he planned to move the Airborne Division down to the capital. Now he outlined the larger plan to "lighten the top so as to keep the bottom." The strategy applied not only to the country as a whole but also to MR 1. Thieu told Truong that he would have to give up most of the region. He was to redeploy his forces so as to defend only Da Nang, with its seaport, and the immediately surrounding area.

On the same day, Thieu was trying to arrange a meeting with General Phu, his commander in the highlands. Thieu wanted to see Phu in Pleiku, at Phu's headquarters. But Pleiku and especially its airfield were coming under sporadic shelling—just enough to keep Phu convinced that Pleiku was still the main target, Ban Me Thuot the diversion. Phu suggested that the meeting take place the next day at Cam Ranh Bay.

In secret, without aides, Thieu and the three men he had told of his new strategy on Tuesday morning boarded the old but comfortably refurbished presidential DC-6 at Tan Son Nhut on Friday morning. Thieu told the pilot to take them to Cam Ranh.

The meeting began at 11 A.M. in a handsome white homey building on a sandspit, overlooking the sea, for the breeze. It was a place befitting presidents: The U.S. government had erected it for Lyndon Johnson's brief visit to South Vietnam in 1967.

It began routinely, with Phu briefing the president on the situation in the highlands. He was grave, and pessimistic. The equivalent of four NVA divisions were in the region, massed against no more than a division and a half. Both major routes into the highlands, as well as the road south from Pleiku to Ban Me Thuot, were firmly blocked.

When the general finished, Thieu asked the single question he cared about: Could Phu retake Ban Me Thuot?

"If I have reinforcements," Phu said. "Men, armor, artillery, air support . . ."

Wearily, for he certainly knew the answer, Thieu turned to Cao Van Vien, the chairman of the Joint General Staff, and said: "Yes, General. And what do we have in reserve for General Phu?"

"Nothing," Vien said.

Thieu lifted himself from his chair and walked to Phu's briefing map. Again gesturing with his arm, he outlined coastal enclaves to be protected, and insisted that Ban Me Thuot was more important than Pleiku and Kontum taken together. It had to be retaken.

Pham Van Phu, like Thieu, had received his training in the French Army. When Thieu became president, he rewarded his old friend with a series of field commands. The Americans considered Phu one of the best division commanders in the Army. But even Phu himself expressed doubts about his aptitude for command of an entire region. He was not a "headquarters man," he said.*

* Phu was given command of MR 2 in the fall of 1974, when Thieu replaced three of his four regional commanders. At the same time, he fired four of his ministers and demoted hundreds of military officers. They were the victims of an anti-corruption movement headed by a Redemptorist priest, Father Tran Huu Thanh. The anti-corruption forces published a bill of particulars against Thieu and his wife called "Indictment No. 1." It was thought in Saigon that much of the detailed information in the indictment originated with Thieu's own prime minister, Tran Thien Khiem.

Further, Phu had been in the French garrison that was defeated and captured at Dien Bien Phu in 1954. He spent several weeks in a prison camp, where he contracted tuberculosis and, his detractors later said, an overriding fear of being surrounded by communists. These factors could have led him to acquiesce in Thieu's vague orders. Instead, according to some accounts, he angrily told the president that if his men were told to retreat from Pleiku and Kontum before the battle had been joined they would feel bitterly betrayed.

There were just the four of them gathered in the living-room-like reception room, the light sea breezes augmented by the ceiling fans set low, to *moins vite*. The ghost of the big American who would have sprawled on the couch, swung his boots to the coffee table, slapped little Phu on the back and told him to pin the coonskin to the wall did not appear.

They met for an hour and a half. At the end of it, four main decisions had been reached: (1) All regular forces were to be withdrawn from Pleiku and Kontum and moved to the coast, with the aim of retaking Ban Me Thuot; (2) the Regional Forces and Popular Forces— the "Ruff-Puffs," as the Americans called them, the militia, who were overwhelmingly Montagnards—were not to be told of the retreat; they would screen it; (3) the redeployment was to be implemented secretly, and in a matter of days; and (4) the route of retreat would be a long-abandoned logging road that had been heavily mined over the years by the communists and by the South Vietnamese and their South Korean allies.

During the French war against the Viet Minh, the French Groupe Mobile 100 was slaughtered in an ambush on Route 19, the main road from Pleiku to the coast. One still does not know whether when Cao Van Vien brought up the fate of the Groupe Mobile 100 he was putting forth the old logging road as the only alternative, which was what General Phu maintained in a brief investigation of the ensuing disaster by a colonel of Saigon's military intelligence, or whether, as General Vien claims, he was reminding Phu of the "bloody and tragic lessons that any commander in the treacherous Central Highlands should have kept in mind" in trying to withdraw on "the very same type of terrain and road" as Interprovincial Route 7-B, which Phu had chosen because this was the only route out of the plateau the communists would not expect them to take.

One does not know if it is true, as Phu later told a colleague, that he "didn't have a choice—the president said I had only two days in which to accomplish the withdrawal."

In any case, the retreat from the highlands was the worst military mistake of a very long war, and set in train all that followed. It also cost tens of thousands of Vietnamese their lives.*

II

Thomas Polgar, the CIA station chief in Saigon, struck some of his colleagues as coarse. He was built like a small keg of beer, with pudgy features under a nearly bald dome, and was given to off-color jokes delivered in an accent derived from his birth in Hungary and years of German tutoring as a child. Everything unpolished in his style was highlighted by its contrast with the southern bearing of his ambassador. In fact, the face Polgar presented to the world—a cross between Edward G. Robinson and Henry Kissinger—masked a sharp analytical mind that carried a young man from Hungary through a steady rise in American military and civilian intelligence.

Polgar by and large deferred to Ambassador Graham Martin's insistence that he, the ambassador, controlled every official American agency in Vietnam, including both the military contingent at DAO† and the CIA. But on the late afternoon of March 14, with the ambassador out of the country, Polgar the professional looked at the reports crossing his desk and composed a cable to Washington.

The reports were concerned not only with events in the Central Highlands but also with the sharp upsurge of attacks in Military Region 1. The civilian flight from Quang Tri as well as the fall of Ban Me Thuot and the obviously precarious situation in Pleiku and Kontum were all in his mind when Polgar produced this concise, prescient cable:

SOUTH VIETNAM IS CONFRONTED WITH ITS BIGGEST MILITARY AND PSYCHOLOGICAL CRISIS. NOT COMPARABLE WITH 1972, BECAUSE AT THAT TIME SOUTH VIETNAM HAD U.S. MILITARY SUPPORT. NORTH VIETNAMESE CAN TODAY ACHIEVE MORE WITH LESS, BUT IN FACT THEY

* In the aftermath of disaster, the memories of the men who move armies are sometimes colored. There were only the five. Phu's testimony is sketchy, Vien's detailed. Until the president or his prime minister or his giggling national security adviser in Quebec chooses to speak, one can with any certainty claim only the above, with an acknowledgment that one is guessing that the fans were set at *moins vite*. They may have been set at *vite* or *plus vite*. For that matter, the place may still have been air-conditioned. But air conditioners were very valuable pieces of equipment that late in the war, and movable.
† DAO—the Defense Attaché's Office—consisted of several hundred Americans and several thousand Vietnamese, and was overwhelmingly concerned with logistics and maintenance of aircraft, radar sites and other paraphernalia of war. It occupied the same sprawling complex of offices on Tan Son Nhut air base that had, before the Paris Peace Accords in January 1973, been known as MACV (pronounced Mac-vee), which stood for Military Assistance Command, Vietnam.

ARE ACHIEVING MORE WITH MORE. NORTH VIETNAMESE ADVANCES FASTER AND MORE IMPRESSIVE THAN AT ANY TIME IN 1972.

GENERAL BINH* SAID NORTH VIETNAMESE CONTROL OF HIGHLANDS INEVITABLE. HE DID NOT THINK THAT PRESIDENT THIEU OR GVN† AS PRESENTLY CONSTITUTED COULD DIGEST THAT KIND OF LOSS. PSYCHOLOGICAL AND POLITICAL IMPACT WOULD LEAD TO GENERAL DEMORALIZATION.

FIRST WEEK OF GENERAL OFFENSIVE HAS UPSET AMMUNITION AND FUEL CONSERVATION PLANS. AMMUNITION RESERVES WILL RUN OUT WELL BEFORE END OF FISCAL YEAR.

IMPLICATIONS OF CURRENT CONGRESSIONAL SITUATION ON SOUTH VIETNAMESE MORALE ARE OBVIOUS. HOWEVER, IT IS NOT THE LEVEL OF MORALE WHICH WILL MAKE THE DIFFERENCE, BUT SIMPLY THE LEVEL OF MILITARY POWER WHICH EACH SIDE CAN BRING TO BEAR.

SOUTH VIETNAM IS IN DEEP TROUBLE BECAUSE OF THE INTERACTION OF NORTH VIETNAMESE DETERMINATION TO BRING ABOUT A MILITARY SOLUTION AND THE CONGRESSIONAL ATTITUDE TO UNILATERALLY TERMINATE OR LIMIT ASSISTANCE TO SOUTH VIETNAM REGARDLESS OF WHAT THE COMMUNISTS ARE DOING. ULTIMATE OUTCOME HARDLY IN DOUBT, BECAUSE SOUTH VIETNAM CANNOT SURVIVE WITHOUT U.S. MILITARY AID AS LONG AS NORTH VIETNAM'S WAR-MAKING CAPACITY IS UNIMPAIRED AND SUPPORTED BY SOVIET UNION AND CHINA. COS‡

III

Sometime in that first week of the offensive, a young South Vietnamese woman made a terrible mistake.

Her name was Tuyet,§ and she lived with her four-year-old daughter, Tam, in Gia Dinh, Saigon's only suburb, which lay to the north and east of the city. Tuyet made a decent salary as a secretary for a Japanese export-import company. She had come to the Japanese firm from USAID, where she had perfected her English and her secretarial skills.

It was also through USAID that she had met Tam's father, Charlie Benoit.‖ But she and Benoit had become estranged even before the girl was born.

Benoit made sure that his daughter—whom he called Tammy—never lacked for anything important. Beyond that, he had done what he could to assure her future, which he always hoped would be with

---

* General Nguyen Khac Binh, concurrently the chief of the National Police and director of the Central Intelligence Organization, Saigon's counterpart to the CIA. He was a prime CIA intelligence source.
† Government of (South) Vietnam.
‡ Chief of Station.
§ Twet.
‖ B'noyt.

him in a peaceful Vietnam. He had a medium-sized fruit orchard on the Saigon River, so close to the city that you could see planes making their final descent into Tan Son Nhut in the distance. Tammy stayed with her mother during the week, but spent almost every weekend at the orchard, which was in her name.

That spring Benoit was the Ford Foundation representative in Saigon. He had helped Jay Scarborough get the grant to complete the work on the Cham documents. Unlike Scarborough, Benoit was political. In his eight years in Vietnam, he had gone from being an enthusiastic USAID official through deepening disillusionment with American and South Vietnamese policies to the point where Ambassador Martin now placed him high on his list of the "Saigon chapter of the worldwide society of disaffected intellectuals."

Benoit was not ideologically procommunist. He was deeply pro-Vietnamese, thought that the sooner the war ended the better and knew which side would never give up.

He was thirty-three and baby-faced, the features made more baby-like by the fact that he was prematurely bald and had the build of a Yale guard, which he had been. The features were slightly comic on Benoit, adorable on Tammy.

Tuyet was a bright woman. But when it came to Tammy, she was, Benoit thought, not entirely in possession of her reason. When Benoit's brother had visited Saigon in the fall, Tuyet had suddenly withdrawn Benoit's access to their daughter. As nearly as Benoit could figure out, she thought that if the brother visited with Tammy—which he finally did—he might somehow escape from Vietnam with her.

Tuyet herself, even before the offensive began, wanted to leave Vietnam for the United States. She explored the possibilities with her former colleagues and bosses at USAID. But out of spite, or wounded feelings, or fears that if she cooperated with Benoit he would retain control of Tammy when they were in the United States, she refused to take the simple steps, with Benoit, that could have led to her and the child eventually emigrating to the States.

Benoit for his part had no intention of ever leaving Vietnam until he was forced to do so.

There was one possible outcome for a postwar Vietnam that Benoit would do everything in his power to prevent: that was a situation in which he was forced to leave Vietnam and Tammy was left behind. He knew that half-American children after this war were not going to fare well. Further, he simply loved her.

He tried to reason with Tuyet. But as in many broken love affairs, one of the parties would not listen to reason.

Benoit was never clear later as to the day that Tuyet acted, whether it was in the middle of the week or as late as Saturday, when he went to the bungalow in Gia Dinh to pick up Tammy for the weekend and found it empty. But some day that week Tuyet saw very clearly, and acted: "Now," she must have thought, "it will all tumble down, and he will steal her from me." She attempted to go into hiding with Tam.

Benoit was so fluent in Vietnamese that if he wanted to make an overseas telephone call quickly, he had to remember to book it in English. Otherwise the operators would assume he was Vietnamese and bump him back behind the American callers. He had hundreds of Vietnamese contacts, including friends and relatives of Tuyet's whom he had met over the years, and made it a point to be nice to.

Tuyet never had a chance. That is, she had a chance if she had chosen reason. But she didn't see reason until it was too late.

IV

Shortly before the attack on Ban Me Thuot, Jean-Louis Arnaud flew to Bangkok for what he thought would be two weeks of vacation. Arnaud was the bureau chief at Agence France-Presse. He went with some misgivings about leaving the bureau in the hands of Paul Leandri, its only other French correspondent. It wasn't that Arnaud didn't like the younger man. But he had not been able to convince himself entirely that Leandri had the judgment to function without not necessarily an editor, really, but just a more experienced hand to check that Leandri wasn't making too much of a small tip, say.

Actually, Leandri had matured, Arnaud thought, in the thirteen months since he had come out from Paris as a staff correspondent. Arnaud had opposed the appointment at first. The reports that filtered among the AFP network of foreign correspondents made Leandri sound a little difficult. Apparently he had a temper.

Leandri arrived, with a young German wife, and was not difficult at all. Arnaud seldom saw the temper. Perhaps the young man had simply needed a wife to settle himself. Nevertheless, something about Leandri always struck Arnaud as odd. He was a Corsican, and the other Corsicans in Saigon were a special breed in the French community: restaurateurs, hotel owners, landlords, merchants, some of the planters. Some of them were ancient, some second or third generation in Vietnam. All had secrets. And Leandri had some special tie to Vietnam. His Corsican father had served there. Sometimes Arnaud wondered idly if Leandri had a touch of Vietnamese blood. He never asked the man about it, and went to Bangkok with his misgivings.

On Thursday night of that first week of the offensive, Leandri filed a story quoting an unnamed Vietnamese Catholic priest as saying that partisans of an old Montagnard separatist group called FULRO* had guided the attacking communist troops to the approaches to Ban Me Thuot and joined with them in the fighting.

A Major Mai from the Immigration Department, which was a branch of the National Police, arrived at the bureau shortly before noon on Friday. He conferred privately with Leandri for five minutes. At three-thirty, a second major arrived, insisting in halting French that Leandri must reveal the identity of the priest. "I don't have to reveal my sources," Leandri told the man. "I am willing to bear the consequences of my story."

The official asked Leandri to come with him to the headquarters of the Immigration Department. Leandri insisted that he was needed in the office until six and would come then. He signed a slip of paper committing himself to the appointment.

Leandri had been through this before. At Christmas, his visa had been held up for a few days as a result of a few lines he had written about open police payoffs on the streets. Still, he was concerned enough to call a few colleagues before he left the office to tell them where he was going. And on the way to the Immigration Department, which he traveled to in the office Peugeot with the office driver, he stopped off at the Cercle Hippique, the city's small riding club, and spoke with other friends. They said later that they thought he was nervous. But Leandri also remarked to one of them that it might make his life easier if he were expelled. Hansi was expecting their first child. Maybe it would be a good idea to have it in civilization.

The immigration office was at the western end of Vo Tanh Street near the point where Saigon melded into Cholon. The office buildings and barracks of the National Police lay in a large compound across the street.

Between seven and seven-thirty, Leandri made a series of calls from the office to the bureau. He asked the Vietnamese staff to let Hansi know that he would be late, and to call the embassy and tell Ambassador Mérillon and the consul general what was going on. "I am being held prisoner here," he said in one of the calls.

Leandri was thirty-seven. He was a large man, with black hair and chiseled good looks partially obscured by the big lenses of dark sunglasses. He was open, emotional, Mediterranean, with a large sense of humor and in fact a larger temper.

He and Major Mai, who seemed to be the senior officer in the place, were stalemated, Mai insisting that Leandri provide the name of the priest and Leandri refusing. Leandri asked to speak to Major Mai's commander. A Colonel Pham Kim Quy, who was the director of some-

* Front Unifié pour la Libération des Races Opprimées.

thing called the Judicial Police, was mentioned, but Mai did not know when Leandri might see him.

In fact, at about seven, Colonel Quy telephoned Patrice Le Caruyer De Beauvais, the French consul general, to say that "several ministries" had complained to him about Leandri's refusal to name his source. He did not tell De Beauvais that Leandri was being detained.

And at seven-thirty a French-Vietnamese man named Morgan, who worked for De Beauvais, arrived at the immigration office. He and Leandri and Major Mai conferred in the front yard of the building. Leandri told Morgan to go back to De Beauvais and tell him that he was being held prisoner. According to Hung, the AFP driver, Leandri "spoke very loudly and seemed to be angry."

Leandri was in the early stage of what quickly developed into a full-blooded Corsican rage. When half an hour had passed and neither Colonel Quy nor De Beauvais had arrived, Leandri broke, screaming obscenities at Major Mai and smashing a chair and a desk lamp against a wall.

That was enough for Mai. Hung, the driver, was summoned to drive Leandri, Mai and two of his officers the fifty meters down Vo Tanh Street from the immigration office to the National Police compound.

It all might have gone differently, Jean-Louis Arnaud thought later, if De Beauvais had been a little quicker. As it was, the French consul general arrived at the immigration office very soon after Leandri had been moved. The officers left behind told him in a "desultory" manner that Leandri had "left, in his car." No, they had no way to contact Major Mai, or Colonel Quy, or any other responsible officer.

De Beauvais returned to his office and between nine-fifteen and nine-thirty made a series of phone calls, including one to the interior minister and another to the wife of the president of the French chamber of commerce. The chamber of commerce man or his wife, De Beauvais thought, could get in touch with Colonel Quy's household to locate him.

So far as one knows, Leandri knew nothing of this—the social relations among his consul general and the president of the chamber of commerce and Colonel Quy, whoever he was, their ways of doing business. One knows that he had a set of keys to the Peugeot, which was parked within sight at a front corner of the building to which he had been taken, a hundred meters inside the entrance to the compound, where numerous low office buildings and barracks lay off a network of alleys. Leandri could see that no barrier had been rolled across the main entrance to the compound. But he probably did not realize that a stretch of Vo Tanh Street encompassing the immigration headquarters and the police compound was routinely blocked off at some point in the middle of the evening.

For a man who in the last twenty-four hours had both written an extremely demoralizing dispatch for a major wire service and destroyed South Vietnamese government property, Leandri was guarded loosely. Between nine and nine-thirty, Hung, the driver, watched the correspondent pace between one nearly deserted office building and another, his arms crossed on his chest, muttering.

It is not difficult to imagine what went on in his mind. No Colonel Quy. No De Beauvais. Nothing happening, and no great prospect of anything happening. The open gate, the car sitting there, the keys in his pocket.

Hung sees the car dig back a few feet, roar forward. Hung runs, never reaching it. Eight or ten policemen do, clutching at the door handles until its speed forces them to let go. Shouts in the night. The car turns out of sight, accelerating, leaning into the turn with its roaring acceleration. Three shots.

It came up against a wall on Vo T anh Street. The official report said that the policeman at the guard post who fired the shots aimed at the tires. Maybe he did. He heard *"Stop him! Escape!"* and saw the car leaning as it accelerated out of the entranceway and he fired.

Whatever the man's intention, one of the three bullets went through the window on the driver's side and straight into Leandri's temple. The window must have greatly slowed its flight, because the round was lodged there in Leandri's head when they did the autopsy.

After midnight, De Beauvais and a few of Leandri's colleagues, French and Vietnamese, gathered at the Grall Hospital in central Saigon where the official French autopsy would be done.

When Hansi Leandri saw the blood-caked face, she howled like a wolf.

7

NBC virtually missed the first few weeks of the offensive. The tall, fat young man the network sent in to replace Dennis Troute had been in Vietnam as a stringer years before, but was unprepared to cover what was turning into the major world story. Just before the attack on Ban Me Thuot, he flatly turned down a request from regional headquarters in Hong Kong to relieve the correspondent in Phnom Penh for a couple of weeks. "I told them in New York," he told me, "I didn't come out here to get my ass shot off." Beyond that, he wanted to edit my radio scripts.

So it was with pleasure that I sat under a thatched umbrella in the garden of a French-style hotel in the pretty seaside city of Nha Trang on the night of Friday, March 14, enjoying a steak and several Scotches with an Air America pilot. It hadn't been easy to find the man, or to get him to agree to a meeting. On Wednesday, at just about the time the Westerners in Ban Me Thuot were being captured, NBC Saigon realized that the consulate in Nha Trang was considering a rescue mission. I flew up on Thursday morning, the Vietnamese camera crew following in the office van. I chased down addresses Dennis Troute had left, loitered at the Air America office on the airfield and killed hours at the hotel while the operator tried to put me through to

Saigon for calls the new man insisted he wanted even if there was nothing to report. Now, finally, as the pilot sipped from the top of his third double Scotch, I got some news.

"Deep background," the man said, "right?"

"Right," I said. "I've forgotten your name already. I just need some guidance, whether to stay or go."

"Well, if I were you I'd get back to Saigon," he said. "There isn't any story here anymore. We ain't going to see those Americans for a long, long time. If ever."

II

Very early on Saturday morning, March 15, the phone on Thomas Polgar's bedside table rang. It was General Nguyen Khac Binh, head of South Vietnam's Central Intelligence Organization and chief of the National Police. Binh may not have been on the Americans' payroll, but like all men with similar titles in client states of the United States, he worked very closely with the CIA station chief.

"Something terrible has happened," Binh said. "You have to come see me right away."

"General Binh," Polgar said, "it's seven o'clock in the morning. It's seven o'clock *Saturday* morning."

"I know," Binh said. "This is an emergency."

In his office at police headquarters, Binh was distraught. "It was a terrible mistake," he said more than once. "There was no reason to kill him. Oh, there is going to be terrible trouble from this. The French ambassador . . . the journalists . . . Mr. Polgar, you must help me. We have to write a communiqué that doesn't offend anyone: the French, the journalists, the government, the president . . ."

"That isn't going to be easy," Polgar said.

Polgar helped with the communiqué. Then he drove to the office. He knew that it was going to be some time before they would be back on a normal weekend schedule. He picked up the first message to come in from headquarters overnight. It directed him and everyone else at the embassy to have nothing whatever to do with or say about the Leandri affair.

III

The crew dropped me at the Nha Trang airport and headed south.

A small mob of Vietnamese, many of them women with even more than the usual paper bags and loose cloth bundles of goods, massed at the ticket window. One of the women was to fly with a pretty wicker basket crowded with a dozen live ducks. I squeezed between the crowd and a row of long wooden benches, knocked on a door and let myself in the office behind the ticket window. The officials' expressions indicated both that I had broken a rule and that they weren't all that surprised that I had. I spoke to the traffic manager, in English. The flight from Da Nang was delayed; it would be at least an hour until it arrived. Yes, my seat was confirmed.

In the air-conditioned snack bar at the other end of the building, I ordered a coffee and orange juice, and got instant coffee and Tang. The only other customer was an American. I joined him. He was a small man in khaki pants and a sports shirt from some PX. He said he worked for the Federal Electric Corporation and had been eight years in the country, "setting up radio and telephone systems in every damned province in Vietnam." With a mix of pleasure at the prospect of a major contract and skepticism that it would ever materialize, he said that the government seemed finally to be working up to the decision to tie into a telecommunications satellite.

All the years in the sun had left him with only a permanent sunburn. And he'd never learned the language. "I never was able to carry a tune," he said. "So I don't know how they expect me to know the difference between *maa, maa* and *maa.*" He used three of the seven tones, and I told him the accent was fine.

"Yeah, but I can't *hear* it," he said. "Besides, I never thought I'd be here this long."

One or the other of us checked at the office every half hour. The plane finally landed a little before three. The contractor knew from experience that it would be on the ground for at least half an hour. I ordered a large *bah mii bah** and two glasses.

Turning to the sound, we watched a VNAF† Huey bellying in on a descent that seemed at first as though it would carry it directly into the snack bar. Then it hovered, and settled about thirty yards in front of us. Over the noise, I said, "If this is the Americans from Ban Me Thuot, there are people in Saigon and Hong Kong and New York who are going to want my tail."

The doors were pulled back and a couple of young airmen jumped to the tarmac. They leaned back into the machine and accepted a big Yamaha that someone inside jockeyed out to them. A tall Air Force officer followed the motorcycle. He turned and lifted out a girl of nine or ten and then took the hand of a pretty woman who must have been his wife. The two of them, with the woman's hair blowing wild in the rotor wash, helped a fat old lady in a white blouse and voluminous black silk pajama pants gingerly to the ground. They were followed by

* Common corrupt pronunciation of the Vietnamese words for "33," the locally brewed French beer.
† South Vietnamese Air Force, pronounced V-Naf.

someone's teen-age son in civilian clothes and two other officers, one of them with another pretty, stylishly dressed young woman. I asked the contractor if he knew what was going on.

"Beats me," the man said.

"Why the motorcycle?" I said. "It's crazy."

Then a second one came in. I asked the man to watch my things and went out onto the field with my Pentax. At first, I shot from close to the building. A guard sat in a folding chair in the shade of the passenger entranceway. What was now a straggling line of people from the helicopters moved to a gate in the fence that ran away from the terminal. I walked past the guard leisurely, without looking at him, and shot three more exposures when the head of the column was ten yards away. The officer with the little girl had the mustache that many of them affected in imitation of Nguyen Cao Ky. He was young, and happened to look very much like Ky. He had the girl by her elbow and a Samsonite suitcase in the other hand. He kept walking, looking only briefly at me. I was now bolder, moving up so that I could get small family groups filling the frame. I checked behind me. The guard was moving toward me. An officer with a free hand motioned me to stop shooting and seconds later a young man set himself and aimed an M-16 at my head. I spread my arms and dangled the camera from its strap.

"Okay," I said, "gotcha," although the words couldn't cut through the roar. But some of the people passing were in range. "Where are you from?" I shouted in Vietnamese. "Ban Me Thuot? Ban Me Thuot?" The few who heard the question all shook their heads. Then the guard was on me, with his pistol drawn.

"Okay," I said. "I go back. Don't want to make trouble. Uncle, where are they from? Where do the soldiers come from? Ban Me Thuot?"

"I don't know," the guard said.

I switched to English and started babbling: "Jesus, they *must* be from Ban Me Thuot. They're whole families. And they're taking out their *Hondas*. What the hell is going on around here?" I engaged the man's eyes as we walked, and made elaborate expressions of confusion, the whole exercise an attempt to keep the man from asking for the film.

Whether or not the stream of words was necessary, the guard stayed outside and simply watched until I was in the terminal. My bag and tape recorder were gone from the snack bar, but the contractor had them at the end of the line at the checkpoint out to the flight to Saigon. I took them and again opened the door into the traffic office. "Sir," I asked, "do you know where the choppers are from?"

The manager looked up from a manifest and said, "You should get on the plane now." He rose from his desk and undid the snap on his holster.

"Yes, sir," I said. "Take care."

IV

For most of the last twenty years, the Americans had run the war. After the advent of the Paris Peace Accords in late January 1973, the level of direct American involvement dropped sharply. But they still expected to be informed.

On Friday afternoon, General Homer Smith drove from the Defense Attaché's Office in Tan Son Nhut around to General Cao Van Vien's office in the adjacent compound of the Joint General Staff. The two men discussed the situation in Ban Me Thuot and the effect it would have on the Army's logistical problems. Cao Van Vien did not mention that he had just come back from Cam Ranh Bay, or hint at the decisions that had been made there.

The first word to reach the embassy that something was going on in Pleiku came in the form of a cable from a CIA agent in Pleiku to Polgar shortly before ten o'clock on Saturday morning, a few hours after Polgar's urgent summons to police headquarters. The agent reported that there were rumors that the entire headquarters command for Military Region 2 was moving from Pleiku to Nha Trang. Whether or not the rumor was true, the agent said, people were packing and moving, soldiers and civilians alike.

The rumor was true. The night before, General Phu had met with four of his staff officers and sketched out a four-day plan for the withdrawal. As Thieu had ordered, even the province chiefs were not to be told of the plan. As for the militia forces, Phu said: "Let them find out about it later. They're *moi*.* Let them return to their mountains."

The next morning—Saturday—he flew to Nha Trang, leaving the worst-planned retreat in thirty years of war to his subordinates.

V

Ambassador Martin was still out of the country. Having returned to Washington with the last big congressional delegation to lobby for the $300 million supplemental military appropriation, he also planned to promote a much more ambitious idea.

Graham Martin understood very well that the American people would not support Saigon indefinitely. He also was convinced that South Vietnam was close to the threshold of economic self-sufficiency.

* Savages, the common Vietnamese word for the Montagnards.

This belief rested on certain assumptions. One was that the assurances contained in the letters from President Nixon and a similar letter from President Ford to Thieu—promising quick and sufficient American military aid in the event of a North Vietnamese offensive—were of course known in Hanoi and might be enough to deter such an offensive.* Another was that Nguyen Van Thieu was one of the best politicians in Asia, and certainly the best in South Vietnam. Finally—and this was not a supposition but a fact—there was oil offshore in quantities that could spark and sustain an economic boom.

This mix of factors had generated an idea, and over the past few weeks the ambassador had encouraged his newly arrived economics counselor to produce statistics to buttress it: Congress would vote a one-shot, three-year military and economic aid package for South Vietnam in the range of five billion dollars. Then America would get out of the business of supporting the country.

Shortly after Martin arrived in Washington, Senator Frank Church of the Senate Foreign Relations Committee told him that the idea had absolutely no chance of passage. The ambassador left for Buies Creek, North Carolina, where a cousin operated on his jaw to relieve an impacted tooth and abscessed sinuses that had required treatment for months. After the surgery, he traveled to Winston-Salem to convalesce with his oldest daughter.

Martin did not return to Saigon until March 28. He spoke with Wolfgang Lehmann, the deputy chief of mission, on several occasions. But he was not in Saigon for the first two and a half weeks of the crisis. At one point that month the White House called Saigon asking to speak with the ambassador, only to be informed that he wasn't there, he was back in the States, didn't *they* know where he was?

In Saigon on that Saturday morning, most of the ambassador's troops were still on a normal weekend schedule. Lehmann himself had asked for and been granted a nine o'clock meeting with Thieu. Not from anything specific the president said, but from the tenor of his remarks, Lehmann guessed that a major military action might be imminent; nevertheless, he decided to go ahead and keep an appointment with *his* dentist. Josiah Bennett, the political counselor, was shopping.

Polgar sent kindly old Charlie Timmes out to the Joint General Staff compound to talk to Cao Van Vien, and another operative to the

* In fact, Congress had totally undercut the Nixon promises more than a year before he was forced to resign. On July 1, 1973, an amendment to the Cooper-Church Amendment prohibited American combat support in Cambodia, Laos and North and South Vietnam. The amendment meant that the Seventh U.S. Air Force, based in Thailand, and the Seventh Fleet, in the Philippines, were legally no longer available to the South Vietnamese.

palace to see General Quang. Vien was not even in his office. Timmes met instead with the only senior officer he could find, the colonel who was the JGS operations officer. Both the colonel at JGS and Quang said that if anything was happening in Pleiku they had no idea what it was.

Quang undoubtedly was following President Thieu's orders that the operations in the highlands were to be kept in the strictest secrecy, as Cao Van Vien had acted the day before when he had met with Homer Smith. But when the reality of what was happening in Pleiku emerged in the days that followed, it was the inactivity at the JGS headquarters that convinced Polgar that Phu had, on his own, set in motion the withdrawal much more precipitately than anyone had expected. An operation of the magnitude of the one that got under way that day in Pleiku would normally generate feverish activity and reams of paper work at JGS. Instead, the Vietnamese high command in Saigon were also giving themselves a routine Saturday.

Soon after he read the report from his man in Pleiku, Polgar was on the phone to Moncrieff Spear, who as consul general in Nha Trang was the senior American official in Military Region 2. Polgar told Spear that he was arranging to remove his American assets in Pleiku and urged Spear to order the evacuation of all other American officials from the city.

"Is that an order?" Spear asked.

"Of course it isn't," Polgar said. "You know as well as I do that I'm not in your chain of command. But Lehmann's at the damned dentist's. I'm just saying that if I were you I'd get my people out of there. The Army's bugging out, and the bad guys could open up on the airfield anytime they want to. Hell, they're doing it already. You want to have another Struharik?"

Lehmann returned to the embassy about noon. The deputy chief of mission knew his boss well, and knew that in the same situation the ambassador's greatest fear would be that a premature withdrawal of the official American community from Pleiku might trigger panic among the local Vietnamese military commanders and then in the civilian population. But after a series of phone calls and meetings with Polgar, he acted.

Lehmann cabled the State Department and the White House, with a note to the situation room that they should pass the message along to the ambassador ("Eyes Only"):

IN LIGHT OF THE RAPIDLY DEVELOPING MILITARY SITUATION IN PLEIKU
AND KONTUM PROVINCES AND THE DECISION OF GVN* TO RELOCATE

* Government of (South) Vietnam.

THE COMMANDER AND STAFF OF II CORPS FROM PLEIKU TO . . . NHA
TRANG, I HAVE DIRECTED THE CONSUL GENERAL IN NHA TRANG TO RE-
MOVE AMERICAN PERSONNEL FROM KONTUM, PLEIKU AND QUANG DUC.
THESE PERSONNEL WILL BE MOVED TO NHA TRANG BY THE END OF
THIS AFTERNOON. LEHMANN.

They were caught off guard by their allies, and the ambassador was
away. But the second line of defense performed well: Within an hour
after I saw the Huey bellying in at the Nha Trang airfield, the officers trundling out their motorcycles, the word had gone out from the
Saigon nerve center to the Americans in the highlands: Run. It was
the order of the day.

VI

The new correspondent and a sound man and Mr. Khi, the office manager, were waiting for me at Tan Son Nhut. The new man started to
complain as if it were my fault that the plane was late. I interrupted
him to describe what I had just seen.

"S - - -," he said. "And you'd already sent the crew away?"

"Yeah," I said. "But what does it mean?"

"I don't know," he said. He was poring over the cameraman's shot
sheet, brief scribbled descriptions in pidgin English of what was on
the television film, which I had carried with me. "Some of the refugees
Vo Huynh shot had motorcycles. Maybe it doesn't matter."

The new man was absorbed in the notes now, constructing the story
he would write to the film. He sat down at his Olivetti in the waiting
room and tapped out a story. Then he and the sound man went off to
the car, where they would close the windows and tape the voice-over.
Much as I disliked him, I admitted to myself that he had written the
story faster than I would have been able to.

"Schiller* almost had a fight with the Air Vietnam people," Mr.
Khi said. "They wouldn't tell us when the flight would arrive. He
kept shouting, shouting very loud."

"Maybe somebody will shoot him," I said.

We got the mesh bag with the film and tape and scripts on the
Hong Kong flight a few minutes before it took off and headed back
into the city. "Six f - - - - - - hours at Tan Son Nhut," Schiller said. "I
haven't even had lunch yet. Come on, Minh, *drive*. Run over the little
f - - - ers if they don't get out of the way."

I was in the back seat with Mr. Khi and the sound man. I took a
deep breath to calm myself and leaned forward with my arms on the
top of the seat behind Schiller. "David," I said, "do me a favor and

* A pseudonym.

don't talk like that when I'm around. You're a damned fool to do it with Mr. Khi and the others here. But just don't do it anymore when I'm around."

"Oh, f - - - you," Schiller said, without turning. "If you don't like my style, I'll get another radio *stringer*. Look at the little . . . If the . . . If they'd just stay in their lanes like they're supposed to, we'd be at the building by now."

"That's a good boy," I said to myself. I leaned back into the seat and closed my eyes for the rest of the ride.

At the Eden Building, Schiller's door stuck. The car was a ten-year-old shock-sprung Pontiac that wallowed through Saigon's traffic like an obese matron skating skitterish and dainty through a hockey game, acre upon acre of skinny little players flying around her. Schiller tried the door over and over again and started bellowing. "God*damn*it! Goddamn this f - - - ing car! Goddamn this f - - - ing country!"

He jerked up a knee to begin the foot stomping, but the knee slammed into the low dashboard. Then the cries were inarticulate, a little softer, grimaces now that promised tears. I was slowly letting myself out of the car, a tricky proposition because traffic continued to scoot by on that side. The driver had opened his door, knocking over a motorcycle parked at the curb.

Finally the stream of *cyclo-pousses,* bicycles, motorcycles and cars on my side broke. I got out, opened Schiller's door and went about the business of getting the gear out. Even with his open door blocking traffic now, the horns starting, Schiller allowed himself a few seconds of what I guessed was an attempt to put himself back together. Then he lifted himself out of the car, slammed the offending door shut and headed through the crowd into the entrance of the building.

I made myself a coffee and took it down to the AP office, which was as tense and busy as it had been five days before, when the communists had attacked Ban Me Thuot. Carl Robinson, who covered Vietnamese politics, and George Esper were both on phones, Esper typing as he listened. A Vietnamese I had never seen was at a normally empty desk. Two others huddled with Neal Ulevich, the bureau's American photographer, over a light box in the photo office. I went to the table with the clipboards and learned that a new "tactical" forward command for Military Region 2 was being established in Nha Trang, amid rumors that President Thieu had decided to abandon the entire Central Highlands.

In the photo office, I tapped Ulevich on the shoulder and said, "Neal, excuse me. I was in Nha Trang this afternoon. I shot half a roll of film of officers getting off choppers, with their families and possessions. With their f - - - - -' *Hondas.*"

"Get it," Ulevich said.

Mr. Khi was still at the Telex machine, sending the afternoon's script and the waybill number for the shipment to Hong Kong. Schiller sat facing his typewriter and drinking Scotch. I rewound the film in my camera as I entered the office that the correspondent shared with Mr. Khi and the Telex machine.

"I think I'm going to quit, David," Schiller said. There was something of an apology in the tone and the use of my name and in the otherwise dead cast to his big features that made me go light on the remark that instantly formed: "You can't quit until tomorrow. It looks like Thieu has abandoned Kontum and Pleiku and what's left of Darlac, the whole Central Highlands. Those guys I saw this afternoon were the f - - - - -' headquarters staff of Two Corps, which is being moved to Nha Trang. I told Vo Huynh to call when they got to Phan Thiet or wherever they put in for the night. If he gets through, you've got to tell them to go back to Nha Trang."

"Too bad we didn't keep them there for a few more hours," Schiller said without rancor, reaching for his glass.

"I'll brief Mr. Khi and do radio," I said. "I think you ought to go down and read the AP."

"Yeah," Schiller said. He got up with a slight spark of energy, as if the nightmare receded a little when someone told him what to do.

VII

Before setting out on Wednesday at dusk for their new location, a soldier told the Millers and the other Westerners: "Keep all windows closed and be very quiet. If people are aware of your presence, they might seek to do you harm."

"But we've never done anything to hurt anyone," Carolyn Miller thought. "Who is going to try to harm us?"

John Miller had to show the young soldier who would drive the Land Rover how to turn on the headlights and shift into four-wheel drive. Asphalt gave way to grass and then they were in what seemed to be virgin jungle. While there was still light, the passengers in the back saw soldiers piling up branches and rocks at streams they had just forded, apparently for following trucks.

Shots rang out, the signal that there was a plane in the sky. The driver quickly braked to a stop and turned off the headlights. In the stillness, Struharik identified the sound of a cargo plane outfitted with mini-guns—"Puff the Magic Dragon" they had called one version during the war—laying down its blattering carpet of fire somewhere in the distance.

There were checkpoints. At one of them, soldiers crowded close around the vehicle. One of them pointed and said: "Look, *thang My*"—"those Americans"—a pejorative equivalent to referring to a person as "it."

LuAnne was sleeping in her mother's arms. Another soldier pushed open a window, reached in and stroked the girl's hair. Carolyn Miller's chest froze. The officer traveling with them was quickly out of the Land Rover, restoring discipline. The hand withdrew, they inched forward and Carolyn breathed again.

They would learn later that the second camp was only ten or twelve miles northeast of Ban Me Thuot. But it took them until close to midnight to reach it. Most of the group stretched out on a nylon tarp that Paul Struharik found in a survival kit someone had given him. Scarborough lay on the bare ground. Before he fell asleep, a North Vietnamese soldier knelt beside him and gave him a plastic sheet.

Carolyn Miller looked up at a wash of stars so brilliant they seemed part of a great banner flung across the tops of the trees towering above her. She fell asleep to the muffled footfalls of people being led past them in the darkness.

They awoke to find themselves part of a crowd of thousands, most of them men, civilian and military. An open trench latrine had been dug in a burned-over field near where the Westerners clustered. But it was soon full, and then the men squatted anywhere in the field. The Westerners decided to call their new home the Rose Garden.

None of the communist soldiers wore badges of rank, but some carried themselves like officers; and the group soon realized that most officers wore small black or brown plastic bags at their hips, hung from shoulder straps. On the first day, an officer approached them with forms to fill out. He was accompanied by a young soldier who was to act as interpreter. But Scarborough's Vietnamese was better than the soldier's English, so Scarborough again translated. The officer told them to answer all questions completely and honestly. "Don't think you can lie about anything," he said, "because the revolution knows everything, and you will certainly be exposed."

Scarborough realized by this time that the young man who barked out the questions at him the day before—it already seemed like a week—may not have been so startled as he first seemed: They all barked.

A very relieved Ike Tolentino joined them that afternoon. He had walked with South Vietnamese soldiers from Ban Me Thuot, which was how they got the fix on the camp's location. Tolentino had been allowed to keep his shoes. The South Vietnamese soldiers' boots were confiscated, and they marched barefoot. There were other reunions.

Struharik walked off to say hello to French planters he knew, Scarborough to see students from the technical school.

They were given rice and a can of chopped pork, and they whittled chopsticks from bamboo, found the wherewithal for boiling water. They began the routine of living almost at a subsistence level.

By the third day, the clearing that constituted the camp—really a clearinghouse for the population and defenders of Ban Me Thuot—was jammed with people. Soldiers were led away into the jungle under guard, but others continued to arrive. The stench from the latrine field was almost overpowering when the wind came from that direction.

A young officer arrived to photograph the disheveled group. Struharik was very displeased when the man posed him in front of a group of Montagnards and then seemed to focus on Struharik's Montagnard bracelet, the tableau apparently calculated to make him appear the leader of a commando squad. But the Westerners hoped that if the photographs were disseminated they would provide reassurance to their families.

Late in the afternoon, they were told that they would be moved again. They were crammed into an open truck with high wood-slatted sides—a captured GMC deuce-and-a-half—with at least sixty South Vietnamese prisoners, all of them tied together except for little LuAnne Miller in her mother's arms. Carolyn Miller was tied to Ike Tolentino but had been allowed to keep one arm free.

"Would you mind if I sat on this bag behind you?" a Vietnamese man behind her asked politely. "Of course not, please do," she said, and turned to see the man who until a few days ago had been the province chief. As the sun set, the truck bounced across the latrine area and set off on a track across the plateau. Carolyn Miller looked at the bag shoved against her knees, and lowered LuAnne onto it.

"God," she prayed, "the Darlac province chief—a man I would normally never meet—is sitting on one of my suitcases behind me, a prisoner. My daughter, also a prisoner, is sitting on another suitcase here. It contains the stupid sewing machine. They won't let us throw anything away. It will be dark soon, and we don't know where we are going. Hold us in your hand now. Above all, hold LuAnne. John and I will be okay."

VIII

From the day after he discovered that Tammy's mother had gone into hiding with her, Charlie Benoit knew where they were. Because from that day until the end, he had her tailed. His accomplices picked her up as she left her office and followed her to the home of one of her friends, in an alley off one of the streets running from Saigon into Cholon.

Over the next few days, Benoit made a few phone calls, speaking low, always calm, always making it clear when he spoke to someone whom he knew would relay his message to Tuyet that he was fully prepared to try to get her out of Vietnam with Tammy if that was what she wanted. Some of her friends and relatives did not have telephones, and so he drove here and there, in the city and its outskirts, stopping in for tea if it was offered, or simply passing along his message and picking up what he could from quiet questions in that extraordinarily fluent Vietnamese.

By the end of the week, he had heard nothing from Tuyet directly, but was confident that lines of communication had been established. Now he must reason with her, through intermediaries. And now he must begin to plan the terrible thing he would have to do if reason failed.

8

On Sunday, the government in Saigon finally sounded out the U.S. Embassy on Thieu's five-day-old decision to make vast territorial concessions to the communists. It did so at an odd level, and at a routine meeting arranged by the American principal.

The two principals were economists holding posts that normally would be held by men fifteen years their seniors.

Although he was just thirty-six, Nguyen Van Hao for the last few months had been the government's deputy prime minister for economic development, a portfolio that gave him control of several important ministries. (There were two other deputy prime ministers.) Hao was a trim tennis player, and dressed stylishly; he had what may have been a broken nose under exceptionally alert eyes that would have made him appear wary if he did not smile so often. Hao also had a reputation for total honesty, and the matter-of-fact ease of a man early used to power, won on sheer brains. But he was still young enough to be somewhat excitable, a talker.

His visitor that Sunday afternoon was Denny Ellerman, the embassy's economics counselor. In most American embassies, and certainly in the largest American embassy in the world, the economics counselor was normally at or very near the height of his career. Ellerman was a tall blond who had turned thirty-four shortly before he arrived in Vietnam for this, his third, tour.

He was there as a Marine Corps captain in the mid-1960s, in intelligence. He returned to the States and got a degree in economics from Harvard. In the spring of 1973, Ellerman was looking for a job and the Defense Attaché's Office in Saigon was looking for an economist. It hired the former Marine captain. Like his boss, General John Murray, and like Ambassador Martin, who arrived that summer, Ellerman could write. Because he could write, he caught Martin's eye. After a year, Ellerman returned to the U.S. for a job on the very small Indochina desk at the National Security Council.

When Ellerman came out to Saigon in the fall of 1974 on an NSC reporting trip to Phnom Penh and Saigon, Ambassador Martin offered him the job of economics counselor. The post had been vacant since Martin arrived. Because Ellerman was so junior, the State Department resisted Martin's request. Typically, Martin at one point told the man in the personnel office at State who was fighting the appointment: "To hell with you. I've been asking for an economics counselor for eighteen months. Now you can damned well send out the man I want."

Ellerman arrived in Saigon a few days before the attack on Ban Me Thuot. And now, ten days later, he was calling at the modest villa of Deputy Prime Minister Nguyen Van Hao to present his credentials.

To Ellerman's considerable surprise, what he had thought would be a courtesy call turned into a meeting of import. Over the tea and soft drinks, Nguyen Van Hao outlined a plan to abandon the northern half of South Vietnam.

Ellerman was a newcomer as economics counselor. But he knew enough about the situation to understand the military and economic rationales for drawing back to enclaves along the central coast, with unyielding defense of the capital and the rice bowl, the Mekong delta. What was new to him was Hao's analysis as to why the strategy made sense for southern Vietnamese regional reasons.

The peasants in the South, Hao said, thought of the war as a quarrel between northerners: the communists and the numerous northern-born commanders on the Saigon side, such as Nguyen Cao Ky. With a drastically truncated South Vietnam—the region around the capital and delta—the latent nationalism of the South Vietnamese would finally surface.

Ellerman went from the meeting with Hao to the embassy, where Wolfgang Lehmann was at his desk.

Lehmann said something to the effect that the people around Thieu, and especially that Australian, whatshisname—Serong—had been kicking around this idea for at least a couple of years, certainly since the Paris Peace Accords. But he asked Ellerman to work up a detailed account of what Hao had suggested, and sent Ellerman's report to Washington, flagging Washington to make certain that Ambassador Martin saw it.

II

As Dr. Hao and Denny Ellerman spoke, the regular ground forces in Pleiku were snaking out of the city in jeeps, trucks, tanks and armored personnel carriers.

Most of the Air Force had fled in the last thirty-six hours, some pilots demanding huge bribes to carry civilians to safety. And while the Air Force men and their families all escaped, they left behind more than sixty operational aircraft.

On Saturday and Sunday, military trucks equipped with loudspeakers roamed the city telling civilians that an attack was imminent: They should store provisions, dig bunkers and stay in their homes.

Police covered the military withdrawal, which first headed south on Highway 14. When the last of the military vehicles had left the city, the police and their families fell in behind.

During their ten years in Vietnam, the Americans had turned Pleiku from a small highlands settlement into a gigantic base, ringed with radar dishes and towering radio antennas. Even two years after the Americans had left, the civilian population of Pleiku were mostly camp followers: merchants, servants and prostitutes.

When the police turned their weapons and joined the exodus, the civilians—and the thousands of soldiers, with their dependents, who had not learned of the retreat in time to be in the organized head of the convoy—followed. They fled in every conceivable conveyance, from cars to Hondas and bicycles and oxcarts. Thousands were on foot. By nightfall, fuel and ammunition depots and other installations in the city were ablaze, the fire at the main ammo dump adding the terrifying noise of exploding shells and bombs to the infernal scene.

That night, as the head of the convoy branched off Highway 14 and headed southeast toward Phu Bon on Route 7-B, the old logging road, a North Vietnamese Army observation post flashed word of the retreat to General Van Tien Dung, who was still at his command post west of Ban Me Thuot.

Dung's jungle headquarters came alive. Maps of the highlands were spread on the table, and examined again with magnifying glasses under the illumination of flashlights. How long would it take the closest liberation units to get to Route 7-B? Where could the puppet troops be blocked and attacked?

Dung was quietly furious. "Many times" before the attack on Ban Me Thuot he had asked Kim Tuan, then the commander of the 320th Division, about this old Route 7-B. Each time he was told that it was abandoned, bridges were out, there were no ferries, the enemy could not possibly use it. Just two days earlier, on Friday, he had again asked about the road only to be given the same answer.

Now the enemy was retreating along Route 7-B; Tuan's forces still had no hold on it, and were not in pursuit.

> I picked up the telephone and talked directly with Kim Tuan. . . . I emphasized twice: "This is a shortcoming, negligence that deserves a reprimand. At this moment, if you waver just a bit, are just a bit negligent, hesitate just a bit, are just a bit late, you have botched the job. If the enemy escape it will be a big crime, and you will have to bear responsibility for it."
>
> At such times I do not want my subordinates to present excuses for trying less, I just want them to carry out their missions most strictly and completely. . . .
>
> [General Dung realized that] if the order to pull the Second Army Corps out had been issued by the central government in Saigon, then the matter had surpassed the bounds of this campaign and had reached strategic proportions. For the first time in the Indochina War, within the bounds of a campaign an enemy army corps with modern equipment had had to abandon an important strategic area and flee. This situation would lead to other important developments, and might lead to our quickly and victoriously concluding the war. But this would not be an easy thing for the enemy to swallow. It would cause a military and political chain reaction that would reach even to America. Even the United States, however, could not set this chaos straight.
>
> Our big opportunity had begun. If we wanted to grasp that opportunity firmly, the first thing we had to do was wipe out the fleeing enemy troops if possible, destroying them right here on the Tay Nguyen battlefield, and not letting them escape to the plains.

Through the night, Dung and his staff issued orders to the 320th Division and to other units in striking range of Route 7-B. A second division was ordered to advance quickly to Pleiku so as to be able to harass the fleeing column from the rear. And an engineering division was sent in to assume the administration of Kontum and Pleiku, put out the fires, "lead the people to safe places"—and take over whatever weapons of war the enemy had left behind.

III

The exodus continues this morning under a scorching sun on the first day of the week. Thousands of civilians and military vehicles in a long row roll on Highway 14 with Phu Bon as their destination. Many overloaded vehicles are seen parked on the roadsides. The military were ordered to pull out under the direction of Brig.-Gen. Tat . . . and they carried out the general's instructions properly.*

It's a pity to look at those people who could not afford to ride on cars or trucks or whatever vehicles were available. They are the miserable ones who can only use their feet and they are the majority—women, children, elders, walking as rapidly as they can, but not having even a drop of water to quench their thirst. . . .

A respected Vietnamese intellectual and journalist in his late fifties named Nguyen Tu happened to be in Pleiku when the exodus began. He stayed with it, filing dispatches for *Chinh Luan*, a serious popular Saigon newspaper, through four of the ten days until remnants of the columns began to reach the coast. His stories, which he sent out with helicopters that occasionally set down among the fleeing troops and civilians—one of which extracted him—seemed palpably to change the mood in Saigon, affecting it with a deep sadness and above all a bitter anger at Thieu.

A few days after they first appeared in *Chinh Luan*, some of the stories were excerpted in the English-language Saigon *Post*.

Nobody knows whether they can reach Phu Bon tonight with their feet [Nguyen Tu continued]. Perhaps many will collapse and die on the long road. On the way to Phu Bon, along Highway 14, villages, hamlets and *buon* [Montagnard villages] appear deserted. The desolation of this highway gives me an impression I find hard to express in words. . . .

The exodus actually began at 8 P.M. last night.

The vehicles, already loaded with belongings—furniture, vases, antiques, goods of all kinds—begin moving on Highway 14 towards Hau Bon, the capital of Phu Bon province, 60 miles to the southeast. The convoy, made up of thousands of vehicles bumper to bumper, is scores of kilometers long. . . .

. . . Explosions are heard, an indication that ammo dumps in Pleiku are being destroyed. Columns of smoke spiral skyward, signaling that fuel tanks have also been demolished. Everything is set afire. Many sections of Pleiku were destroyed by unidentified peo-

---

* This sentence may have been added by a censor in Saigon. But the fact that so much of the bitterness in these dispatches was allowed to appear at all demonstrates the contempt in which Thieu was now being held.

ple. The hardest hit were the homes of those who are taking part in the exodus. . . .

Not a single doctor, either civilian or military, was to be found in the city. . . . A number of patients in both the military and civilian hospitals at Pleiku have been abandoned to their fate. These poor people of course don't know how to react to the situation except to stay there on the sickbed and wait until death slowly sets on them.

I too, with a knapsack on my back, joined the exodus at about 10:30 Sunday night. . . . It was a beautiful night and the sky over Pleiku is scintillating with thousands of glittering stars. . . .

If I had a friend by my side, I would tell him: Dear friend, the sky has as many stars as there are sorrows in my heart.

Up to now, I still don't know where the order to make Pleiku and Kontum open cities has come. There was no explanation whatsoever of the move to the population. No organization of any kind was set for the mass evacuation. Aren't the military leaders supposed to work out such a plan for an exodus like this?

No support of any kind was given to the people, particularly the poor ones who have to walk. Since 1954 I have witnessed many evacuations. But the exodus from Pleiku-Kontum has filled me with such disgust that I find the slight hope I have been nursing in my inner-self since 1954 has disappeared. . . .

IV

Late on Monday morning, Colonel William Le Gro, who was the senior American military intelligence officer in Saigon, placed a call to Mike Marriott, the Australian cameraman in the CBS bureau.

Marriott was only thirty-one, but he had been in Indochina for nearly ten years, and had cultivated more sources than most cameramen.

Le Gro asked Marriott if he knew what was happening in Pleiku and Kontum. No, Marriott said.

"Well, it looks like they're bugging out," Le Gro said. "All of the regular forces and most of the population. Without a fight."

"Jesus," Marriott said, a name he invoked often. "Can we get up there?"

"I don't know," Le Gro said. "Call me back in ten minutes."

Marriott briefed Brian Ellis, a recently arrived CBS correspondent who acted as a producer through the next few weeks, and Peter Collins, one of the correspondents, and then called Le Gro back.

The trip was on. Le Gro gave Marriott the number of the Air America* plane that was waiting to fly them up the coast.

---

* At that time, the largest of the CIA-funded airlines. It served all agencies in the U.S. mission. In fact, Thomas Polgar had succeeded in persuading the ICCS—with its two communist delegations—to charter Air America for its travel in Vietnam.

"Why are you doing this?" Marriott asked Le Gro.

"We need the help," Le Gro said. "We're forbidden to go out into the field. And we don't want to lose any more people."

As they approached the head of the column toiling out of the highlands, the two journalists, Marriott and Collins, marveled. Even from their vantage several hundred feet above the ground in an Air America helicopter, the column stretched back, northwest, toward Pleiku, as far as they could see, in its farthest reaches just a curtain of dust rising in the air. Marriott asked the pilot to pass from side to side at the head of the column, and to move a kilometer along it, while he filmed.

Then the pilot turned and dropped them beyond the head of the convoy. He said he was going to gas up and would be back in forty minutes. He gave them flares and a radio tuned to his frequency and quick but precise instructions about selecting a pickup point a good half mile off the route of retreat.

Collins moved with his microphone interviewing anyone who spoke English. Quickly, he and Marriott realized it was a good idea to keep moving back along the column, because what had started as amazement that two Americans had just dropped among them turned into hostility. "This is all America's fault" was a remark they heard more than once.

Marriott was struck at how intact everyone and everything was. No wounded. No signs of combat. Just soldiers—some armed and some not, some dressed half in uniform and half in civilian clothes—and all their fresh-looking equipment: armored personnel carriers strung with baskets of chickens and ducks; military vehicles of all kinds, even motorized 155-mm. artillery pieces. And the wives, and the children, and the old grandmothers, and the chickens and the pigs. A whole society, not in retreat from battle but from—what?

Collins found a colonel, a regimental commander, the kind of man who would have to supply whatever backbone the Army had. "Phu didn't even tell us," the colonel said. "We found out yesterday that he has run away to Nha Trang, secretly. So we have to make the retreat ourselves."

"Was there fighting?"

"Some shelling."

"But did you have orders to retreat?"

"No," the colonel said. "But how can the Army fight when the commander runs away?"

Forty minutes later they moved off the road. When the helicopter came into view, they popped their flares. It was dusk. They weren't rushed. But the pilot wasn't taking any chances. His skids didn't touch the ground as Collins and Marriott scrambled aboard.

They were in Saigon less than two hours later. This was news. "This could be the day South Vietnam lost the war," Marriott thought.

V

That afternoon, Homer Smith was back in Cao Van Vien's office at the headquarters of the Joint General Staff. Smith asked bluntly what was going on in the highlands. This time, the JGS chairman told the American everything he knew.

Smith came from Texas, and looked like one's first impressions of Barry Goldwater, one of those men with the American West in their faces. He was the senior American military officer in the only war going and, like most of his predecessors, no fool.

"Why didn't you level with me on Friday, General?" he asked Vien now.

"President Thieu said it was a matter of the utmost secrecy," Vien said. "He said we were not to discuss it with anyone at all."

Smith took a breath. "Well," he said, "when we finally figured out that something was going on, yesterday, we started to follow it pretty closely. And it looks to me as if you may have a real debacle shaping up. Do you understand that word, General?"

"Yes, fully," General Vien said.

"It looks to me as if the withdrawal is going to develop into total chaos. And that's going to have repercussions down the line. Elsewhere."

"I know," Vien said. "I think you may very well be right. I see now that perhaps I should have told you on Friday. But you understand, General, that the decision wasn't mine. The order was given directly to General Phu by the president."

"Yes," Homer Smith said. "That's the problem. That's one of the problems. And you've got plenty of problems now, General."

"I know," Vien said.

VI

When he arrived at his desk early on the morning of Tuesday, March 18, Wolfgang Lehmann read his ambassador's response to the concept advanced by Nguyen Van Hao at his Sunday meeting with Denny Ellerman.

It was a classic Graham Martin offering, implying but not giving his imprimatur to a course of action; at the same time urging the action and distancing his government and himself from it; *yin* and *yang*, yes and no. The cable said, in effect: We recognize the logic, and the dramatic nature of the proposal. We see no flaws in the thinking. This is a weighty decision politically. I do not wish to comment on whether it is a good idea or not. Whatever you choose to do, do it well. The world will judge your success.

Lehmann called in Denny Ellerman and instructed him to relay the gist of the cable to Nguyen Van Hao.

Hao listened to Ellerman impassively. Then he said: "Mr. Ellerman, do you have any idea why my government chose to send this scenario—this possible course of action—through you?"

"No," Ellerman said quite honestly. This was all a bit above an economics counselor who had arrived less than two weeks earlier.

"Well," Hao said, "you just came from the White House. We wonder if the idea was discussed there."

Ellerman's heart sank. He realized suddenly that senior figures in the government of Nguyen Van Thieu, probably including Thieu himself, were under the bizarre impression that he—Ellerman, at the age of thirty-four—conferred hourly with President Ford about whether or not Saigon should draw back to defensible borders.

It was a sad joke. He decided not to spell out for Hao how pathetically junior, and shunned, he and his few colleagues on the Indochina desk of the NSC staff were.

VII

After two days on Highway 14 and then on Route 7-B, the part of the convoy out of Pleiku and Kontum that included the journalist Nguyen Tu reached Hau Bon,* the capital of Phu Bon province.

Tu wrote on the eighteenth:

> On the heels of refugees evacuating Pleiku and Kontum, the people of Hau Bon are also leaving their city.
>
> Refugees from Pleiku and Kontum who reached Hau Bon in small groups made the long journey in two days. The majority are still far behind, dragging their feet on the dirty road under a scorching sun by day and chilled by night in the forests.
>
> It was not possible to say how many children fell during the walk, how many helpless old people were standing along the road unable to move, how many others were suffering from thirst and hunger during the walk to freedom and democracy.
>
> A Ranger officer told me: "This time, I can never look straight to my people again."
>
> A private said: "Damnit, we got away without any fighting. I prefer to fight and run away if we lose. I will accept that."
>
> An Air Force captain said: "It is sad, very sad, especially when we

* Often referred to as Cheo Reo, its former name, or as Phu Bon City.

look back at Pleiku, a deserted city now. We can see only fires and fires. I am very sad."

"I am stunned. . . . Look at these people, the young ones. Isn't this miserable?" another soldier added. . . .

The people at Hau Bon today followed en masse the flow of refugees from Pleiku and Kontum.

Women, children, youngsters, and the elderly—all in small groups with their belongings either on their backs or in their hands—rushed out of their houses as they saw the convoy approaching. The same scenes of plundering and ransacking of the homes by unidentified people reappeared. . . .

Many sections of the town were set afire. . . . Phu Bon has capitulated not to the enemy but by its own. . . .

After Kontum and Pleiku on Sunday, Hau Bon became a lost town on Tuesday.

VIII

There were at least 100,000 people in what Nguyen Tu had begun calling the "Convoy of Tears" out of the Central Highlands. And before nightfall on Tuesday, the eighteenth, when lead elements in the column had pushed only a few miles east of Hau Bon, the convoy of tears became a convoy of death.

The head of the convoy was blocked at a downed bridge. And now elements from the division whose commander General Dung had lashed out at on Sunday night had set themselves up in high ground all around the convoy. They flailed it like a mongoose flailing a snake.

Nguyen Tu wrote on Wednesday, the nineteenth:

The leading part of our convoy got through the ambush point under a screen of supporting fire. But the tail end had to leave the road and pass through the jungle.

I was in the tail end.

Rebel mountain tribesmen armed with our (American) weapons and Communist B-41 rockets and AK-47 rifles shot into the convoy, while Communist artillery struck from all directions.

Many trucks were hit by shells and burst into flames and exploded.

The trucks were crammed with soldiers, children, old people. They fell everywhere.

Those who walked fell to machine-gun bullets. Their blood flowed in tiny streams.

The roaring artillery, crackling small arms, screams of the dying and crying of the children combined into a single voice from hell.

The Rangers resisted all night, permitting the tail end of the convoy to flee into the jungle.

At last, 200 of us succeeded in climbing up Chu Del hill, about six miles from Cheo Reo, 210 miles north of Saigon.

Helicopters contacted us and moved in for rescue. The operation was difficult, because Chu Del is a narrow and steep hill.

Finally, in an operation that evening and the next morning, 200 persons were lifted out and rescued.

That *Chinh Luan* felt free to publish that dispatch less than a week after Paul Leandri was killed as a consequence of writing a story that implicated the Montagnards in the attack on Ban Me Thuot was the first clear indication that Saigon had decided that Nguyen Van Thieu had lost the mandate of heaven.

IX

On Wednesday afternoon, I got on the last Air Vietnam flight to Nha Trang. All scheduled flights out of Nha Trang were booked, so the office arranged a charter for Thursday morning.

From Mike Marriott, who had come back up the coast, I pieced together what turned out to be an accurate idea of the size and location of the convoy and what was happening to it. I was principally a courier on this trip, but wrote three spots I would phone to New York as soon as I got back to Saigon.

That night, I ate with the crew on the open deck of a restaurant on the beach. The lobsters and clams and squid were simpler and better and much cheaper than the same fare at the hotel, but for the first few minutes I wished I were back in the hotel garden, where waiters brought moist facecloths and used, knowing, conspiratorial girls did not try to sit on my lap.

The next morning, from nine thousand feet up and a mile or two off the coast, the land was a dull smudge of green and brown. At that angle, most of the settlements were shielded by trees. "New Hampshire," I thought. "Maine." Here and there, inland, thin clouds of gray or white smoke twisted slowly in the sky. I realized that I did not know whether the smoke marked combat or burning farmers' fields.

As we came in north over the huge airfield at Bien Hoa, I could see Tan Son Nhut twelve miles ahead. When the bored, middle-aged Franco-Vietnamese pilot had learned that I had a hundred hours in the plane, he had let me fly it down the coast. Now I gave the controls back to the man and turned my full attention to Bien Hoa, and the divided highway that connected the air base to the capital, the American- and Japanese-built factories in industrial zones along the highway, asphalt and steel flung across rice paddies. I was untroubled by forebodings. The outskirts of Bangkok would look much the same, only more industrialized, less militarized. I stared down in simple boyish fascination. There was nowhere else I would willingly be.

X

Some night that week, as the highlands were being abandoned, a correspondent for the Hong Kong-based *Far Eastern Economic Review* attended a reception at which French Ambassador Mérillon made an appearance. The correspondent was a young round-faced Indian named Nayan Chanda. He understood Mérillon's emphatic French: *"Non! Kissinger ne pas se permettre de voir les chars de Giap defiller sur Tu Do! Jamais! Jamais!"**

* "No! Kissinger can*not* permit himself to see Giap's tanks roll down Tu Do! Never! Never!"

9

The first mortars landed about nine o'clock at night. Cuong's family, with many of their neighbors, took cover in a grove of tall bamboo that ran behind their homes. Cuong was fourteen. His oldest brother, a soldier on the Saigon side, had been sent far south, to the Mekong delta, several years before. An older brother and sister and a younger sister were still at home. The six of them ran and huddled on the ground in the bamboo when the first mortars were followed by close gunfire. It was chilly. The youngest child wandered back to the house in search of a blanket, and her face and chest were burned when a mortar made a direct hit on the house, setting it on fire. For hours, Cuong's father and mother hovered over her, trying to ease her suffering with wet towels. Neither Cuong's father nor his uncle had ever joined the local defense forces. Like millions of other Vietnamese, they went as many years as they could without taking up a gun for either side. But sometime after midnight the uncle finally decided to join the hamlet's dwindling number of defenders. He was given two M-1 carbines, one of which he shoved at Cuong's father. "I don't want you to have a gun," his wife whispered. "I'm not going to fight anybody," Cuong's father said. "This is to escape." The family from the house next door, who throughout the years of quasi peace had been vocally supportive of the Viet Cong, tied their hands together with string and set off in the direction of the only possible route of escape, west toward the provincial capital. Before they were a hundred yards out of the bamboo, a single round killed three of the five: the mother and two children.

Cuong's father tied the five of them together, he and the older boy struggling to carry the dying girl. In less than a mile they were free of the village, stumbling through a rice paddy. Before they set out, Cuong's mother hissed out her objections to traveling with the weapon. "Brother Vuong wasn't carrying any gun and what good did it do him?" Cuong's father said. "Brother Vuong, the great patriot."

When they could carry the girl no longer, Cuong's father untied himself from them and announced that he would stay with her. He spoke not to his wife but to the older boy: "I will stay here with Mai for a while," he said. "When she doesn't need me anymore, I will get away. Now you are the father. Go."

They stumbled on in the cold, wet-underfoot darkness, but there were no clouds that night and they knew the stars and could keep a westerly course. But the fighting was always close, and first the older brother was hit and they cut him loose to die and then the older sister was hit and they cut her loose to die and then there were only Cuong and his mother and Cuong was only fourteen and now suddenly the nightmare had made him the father.

His mother was hit near a loud stream. She untied him and told him to hurry on alone. Cuong moved up and down the stream until dawn, afraid to step into it. Finally he no longer knew where his mother was.

When the sun rose, twelve or fifteen Viet Cong were eating breakfast and looking out at the stream directly across from him. Cuong snuck north in the bushes but was captured by men he knew to be local Viet Cong two hours later. They walked him to a group of about three hundred villagers they were holding in a clearing nearby. Cuong looked about quickly for his mother or father in the crowd of prisoners who squatted or lay on the ground, their hands tied behind them and their eyes blindfolded. He didn't see them, and hoped that meant that they had found a way to escape. Then they blindfolded him and tied his hands. He squatted for a while, rolled softly onto his side, and slept.

It was more than eleven years in the past now, but Captain Do Duc Cuong still dreamed of it some nights, the night his world exploded, November 5, 1963. He would never forget the date. A few months after the attack, when he was working as a houseboy and gardener for a rich family in Saigon, he tattooed the numerals—5.11.63*—along the bottom tip of the calf muscle of his right leg. Further, it was three days after a major event in the short history of the Republic of Vietnam, which for the next eleven years celebrated the anniversary of the event as its National Day: the overthrow and assassination of Ngo Dinh Diem.

Cuong's family had lived in a strategic hamlet, villagers gathered together both for self-defense and to isolate the guerrillas from the populace. The communists had renewed the struggle in the South in 1958, calling on former Viet Minh who had stayed behind to rally to the patriotic side, and mounting sporadic raids on government installations and occasionally on the strategic hamlets, which they hated. But for young Cuong, the years under Diem were the only peaceful ones he was to know in Vietnam. On weekends, he and his friends could go off on excursions to the mountains or to the nearby seashore. After the coup, the generals who took over the country tore down the strategic hamlets. Cuong never understood why.

Now, in mid-March 1975, Cuong was a captain in the Military Security Service, a branch of military intelligence concerned primarily with neutralizing the enemy's intelligence operations. Cuong was assigned to the ARVN 1st Division, which was based in Da Nang with a forward command in Hue. And again Cuong could not understand what the generals were doing.

He was twenty-six, and as hipless and wiry as a whippet. His small features were arranged neatly under a bright, straight-ahead gaze that suggested eager curiosity as much as a natural intensity. Southerners often said that most of Vietnam's revolutionary leaders came from the narrow strip of fertile land between the highlands and the sea in central Vietnam because it was easier to argue politics than to grow rice there.

Cuong and his commanders had taken the fall of Phuoc Long province in the first week of January as a signal. Operations had been stepped up; in fact, they were successful, and until a few weeks earlier, the government's control of outposts and roads in the northern provinces was stronger than it had been the year before. After the fall of Phuoc Long, the 1st Division's new commander, General Nguyen Van Diem, asked his staff to prepare estimates as to how long the division could hold Hue if it were cut off from its supplies. He ordered extra shipments of rice into the city, and soldiers at the division forward headquarters, seven miles south of Hue, a site abandoned by the

* In the European manner, the Vietnamese date notations run day/month/year.

Americans, spent part of each day stooping over to pick up the unspent bullets with which the Americans in their profligacy had strewn the ground. General Diem himself was from Hue, as were most of his troops. Cuong thought that there might be an attack on the city that spring. He was sure the South would hold it. The Hue soldiers would fight to defend their families.

Cuong was an intelligence officer, and intelligent. He was reasonably well informed. He listened to the BBC and VOA Vietnamese-language broadcasts, and had access to weekly intelligence reports on world—and especially American—opinion prepared for limited distribution in the Army by Saigon. He knew, for example, that if there was a full-scale communist offensive that year, the B-52s would not return to the skies. American aid sufficient to make a difference in the face of a major offensive would not be forthcoming until after the next American congressional elections, if ever.

Cuong's intelligence gathering was focused on the 1st Division's limited area of operations. The communists' capture of Ban Me Thuot and President Thieu's decision to abandon the highlands were distant, affecting only another theater, Cuong thought.

But things had started to go wrong in the last few days. For some reason, General Ngo Quang Truong, the thin, quiet-mannered commander of MR 1, whom Cuong along with most of his comrades held in respect, seemed suddenly never to be at headquarters in Da Nang anymore. Orders were coming from his deputy, and they were confused.

On Tuesday, March 18, there were rumors that the Airborne Division, the best in the Army, was being moved south, out of the region.

As usual in times of crisis, Cuong turned to his immediate superior for guidance. Late that afternoon, Cuong asked Colonel Le Quang Nhon if it was true that the paratroopers were being sent south.

"Yes," Colonel Nhon said.

"But it's crazy. The offensive is just beginning here," Cuong said. "How can we stop them without the paratroopers?"

"I don't know," Colonel Nhon said. "There is some talk that we will get three Ranger battalions to replace them."

"But the paratroopers are the best," Cuong said. "Why are they being moved?"

"Officially, they're supposed to help General Phu retake Ban Me Thuot," Colonel Nhon said. "But the Army—the Army and the people too—are angry about the decision to get out of Pleiku and Kontum without a fight. So now the man in the palace has to be thinking about a coup. Air Marshal Ky must be talking to the other generals already. I would be surprised if he wasn't."

Cuong was a correct young officer. He kept his thoughts to himself. But his thoughts were bleak. A coup? Move the paratroopers out of MR 1 just for a coup? Didn't the president know what he was risking? Of course he couldn't give up Da Nang. But would he give up Hue—*Hue!*—just to have the paratroopers in Saigon to ward off a coup? No. Thieu was a general before he was president. He couldn't do that. But why was everything so crazy all of a sudden? Why wasn't General Truong here to tell them what was going on?

II

Actually, General Truong was at his Da Nang headquarters that Tuesday. He was conferring with Prime Minister Tran Thien Khiem, who had flown up to see how Truong was carrying out Thieu's orders to redeploy his forces.

When Thieu had told Truong earlier that he was planning to pull the paratroopers to Saigon, he had promised to replace one of the division's three brigades with a newly formed Marine brigade. Now Khiem told Truong that he would be getting no additional forces; the new brigade would remain in the defense of the capital.

Khiem also told Truong that one of the Airborne brigades had been split off at Nha Trang to block the North Vietnamese forces barreling down Highway 21 from Ban Me Thuot toward the coast. A second brigade was already on its way to Saigon, while the third was still in Da Nang, preparing to ship out.

The only good news the prime minister brought from Saigon was slim: He promised to send Truong and the mayor of Da Nang a staff of senior officials from the several ministries involved to deal with the tens of thousands of refugees pouring into Da Nang every day from both north and south.

En route to Da Nang, Khiem had stopped to see General Phu in Nha Trang. He found the man cringing in his office and nearly incoherent.

III

Truong was summoned to Saigon the next morning, Wednesday, March 19, for an eleven o'clock meeting with Thieu. As he had with Khiem the day before, Truong outlined his preparations for an orderly withdrawal.

Highway 1 was now so clogged with refugees streaming into Da Nang that it had become nearly impossible to move men and equipment on it. Truong told Thieu and the few others present that he was drawing back his forces to three coastal enclaves: Da Nang, Hue to the north and Chu Lai to the south. If necessary, he said, the men in Hue and Chu Lai could be shipped to Da Nang.

Truong had also heard rumors that the Marines were to be moved south to Military Region 3. He asked if the rumors were true.

Thieu was vague in his reply. He told Truong to hold whatever territory he could with the forces presently available to him, including the Marines. He ignored Truong's withdrawal plan altogether, instead turning to Quang, the national security adviser, and telling him to prepare a speech in which he would tell the people that the Army would defend Hue at all costs.

Truong was back in Da Nang by six that afternoon. As soon as he landed, his deputy called from Hue to say that 130-mm. artillery shells were pounding his headquarters area, and armored communist units were pouring across the line between North and South Vietnam.* The overt, massed offensive in the north had begun.

General Truong called the Joint General Staff in Saigon and pleaded to be allowed to keep the 1st Airborne Brigade—the only one of the three brigades left in Da Nang. Thieu of course had to be consulted. He told Truong he could keep the brigade, but it was to be used as a morale booster only, and could not be sent into combat.

That night, all the government forces in Quang Tri province fled south before the North Vietnamese tanks clanking down the sandy coastal plain. The Saigon forces regrouped and set up a new defensive line along the southern bank of the My Chanh River, which separated Quang Tri from Thua Thien province. Thua Thien was the province that contained Hue, the former imperial capital and for several centuries the intellectual and cultural heart of all Vietnam.

IV

On that same Wednesday, Thomas Polgar, the CIA station chief in Saigon, cabled headquarters in McLean, Virginia, that the situation in Military Region 1 was "unraveling with dramatic speed. . . ."

The unraveling in the north logically followed events in the highlands, Polgar wrote. He added:

NORTH VIETNAMESE OFFENSIVE HAS RADICALLY ALTERED THE SITUATION WITH RESPECT TO GVN-CONTROLLED SOUTH VIETNAM. GEOGRAPHIC CONCEPT OF THE REPUBLIC OF SOUTH VIETNAM WHICH

---

* The 17th parallel, which had been the demarcation line set by the Geneva Accords of 1954, lay a few miles north. The communists had occupied the territory between the parallel line and the river since their last major offensive, in the spring of 1972.

EMERGED FROM GENEVA ACCORDS AND WHICH KEPT ALIVE, IF NOT IN-
TACT, THROUGH MASSIVE AMERICAN SUPPORT, IS NO MORE.

He ended with a very blunt appeal for decisive American action:

SURVIVAL OF INDEPENDENT SOUTH VIETNAM DEPENDS IN LARGE
MEASURE ON U.S. ACTIONS. THERE IS NO DOUBT THAT A LACK OF U.S.
DETERMINATION IN THE VIETNAM CONTEXT WILL KILL THE NATION
WHICH EARLIER U.S. EFFORTS HAVE HELPED TO CREATE.

V

Early the next morning, General Truong flew to the My Chanh line
and met with his commanders in northern MR 1. Together they discussed a plan for the defense of Hue. South of the city, this meant
turning around tanks and artillery pieces that Truong under his previous instructions had thought he was supposed to remove. Moving
them back toward Hue against the civilian refugee flow would be difficult but not impossible.

In fact, the situation that Thursday morning did not seem hopeless.
Regular forces and territorial units were still possessed of good discipline; morale seemed high. Quang Tri had been abandoned, yes; but
most of the population had already evacuated, and the bulk of the
Marine Division had withdrawn to Hue.

On his way back to Da Nang, Truong stopped in Hue. Again, morale among the city's defenders seemed good. And it seemed to be
given a boost when President Thieu's well-modulated and now impas-
sioned voice was heard on radios everywhere ordering the troops in
Hue to hold the city.

Truong arrived back at his Da Nang headquarters late in the afternoon. And there he was handed a secret message from the president,
relayed through JGS, that contradicted what Thieu had told him the
day before and was now telling the people of South Vietnam in the
radio address, which was rebroadcast not only that day but through
the following several days. The new orders said that Truong was now
free, depending on battlefield developments, to redeploy his forces for
the defense of Da Nang only. Further, Thieu ordered that the last
Airborne brigade was to proceed immediately to Saigon. It shipped
out before midnight.

The orders were always couched ambiguously, so that Thieu could
deny that he had flatly ordered that Hue be abandoned. Truong was
furious, and close to despair. He interpreted the orders to mean what
Thieu had in fact said at his first meeting at the palace days after the
attack on Ban Me Thuot: Withdraw to an enclave around Da Nang,

and be prepared to get as much matériel and as many men out of Da Nang as possible.

VI

Early in the evening that day, which was the day I had returned to Saigon from the quick overnight in Nha Trang, I stopped as usual in one of the Eden Building's crowded entrances to buy a pack of cigarettes from an old woman who displayed them on a narrow folding tray. My mind was full of work. The mayor of Hue had urged the city's people to flee south to Da Nang, although Thieu and the military were insisting that they would hold it. Colonel Hien had announced at the afternoon briefing that the beginning of the overnight curfew in Saigon was being moved back two hours, from midnight to ten. And the bureau had two new Americans. Al Chambers, the young executive who ran NBC's Asian operations out of Hong Kong, would stay for a few days. Arthur Lord would stay indefinitely, not as a correspondent but as a producer. Lord had already taken over the desk I would always think of as belonging to Dennis Troute, relegating Schiller to the outer office.

Lord was a New Yorker on loan from the Houston bureau, a man in his mid-thirties with the face of a young Walter Matthau and an easy New York banter lightening an air of matter-of-fact competence. It seemed as if I had known him for weeks, as if the Schiller interregnum had been a mildly disturbing dream to be shrugged away.

As I turned out onto the sidewalk, crowded with people on urgent twilight business compressed by the new curfew, a teen-age female mute beggar who had lost a hand and half a lower arm to leprosy and who usually worked farther down Tu Do brushed her stump against my bare arm. She grinned at me when I flinched. And just before I got to the clutch of motorcycle taxis at the corner, an old woman with a baby in her lap jabbed her upturned conical hat against my leg. In each case, the physical contact was new. I made a mental note to do a spot the next day on the mood of the city.

VII

Thomas Polgar's Wednesday cable predicting the death of South Vietnam if the United States did not act must have elicited a suggestion that the agency mount some sort of propaganda campaign. On Friday, Polgar shot back:

PROPAGANDA IN FAVOR OF SOUTH VIETNAM WILL NOT MAKE ANY DIFFERENCE. NORTH VIETNAMESE CANNOT BE STOPPED WITH WORDS, ONLY WITH ANTITANK WEAPONS AND AIRCRAFT. FAILURE OF U.S. TO

HINDER ALL-OUT NORTH VIETNAMESE EFFORT WILL INEVITABLY TER-
MINATE EXISTENCE OF AN INDEPENDENT NONCOMMUNIST SOUTH
VIETNAM. NO AMOUNT OF WORDS WILL CHANGE THAT.

It is unlikely that a cable that blunt, predicting a full communist victory if the United States did not intervene heavily in the war, would have left the embassy had the ambassador been in Saigon.

VIII

Albert A. Francis, the American consul general in Da Nang, was in his early forties that spring. He was a protégé of Graham Martin's—and an ambitious, zealously hardworking bureaucrat who was also an exceptionally good manager.

Francis spent most of February and March in Washington recovering from a severe thyroid condition. When he arrived back in Da Nang, on Saturday, March 22, the city was filling with refugees, and the communists were increasing their pressure on Hue.

In addition to his many other problems, Francis found himself with more journalists on his hands than he could accommodate. On his first day back, as he was asking Saigon for all the help he could get, he called Alan Carter and asked for someone to help him with public relations.

Carter dispatched one of his deputies, a big, black-haired man named John Swenson. Swenson arrived on Sunday. One of his first stops was at Da Nang's city hall, where he advised the mayor how to deal with the press.

At the riverside consulate later that afternoon, Swenson asked Francis how long he thought he should plan on being in Da Nang.

"At least a month, I think," Francis said.

Swenson had flown to Da Nang with Colonel Charles Wahle, the Army attaché in the Defense Attaché's Office. The two visitors from Saigon and senior officials in the consulate were guests of Al Francis at the consul general's residence that evening. During the course of the meal, General Ngo Quang Truong, the commander of Military Region 1—comprising the five northernmost provinces of South Vietnam—presented himself at the house. Francis and Wahle retired with Truong for a brief conference. Even that late in the war, years after Vietnamization, it was routine for regional commanders—men who commanded several divisions, each with about ten thousand men—to confer frequently with the senior American in the region, even if the senior American was a career Foreign Service Officer with little military background.

IX

On Sunday, March 23, communist gunners began to bombard Hue. The shelling continued throughout the day. It was sparse, and militarily ineffectual. But it terrorized the civilians who were still trapped in the city. And that day they became nearly completely trapped. The communists cut all road links into the capital, in the process shelling the column of refugees streaming south from Hue toward the beautiful Hai Van Pass just north of Da Nang.

In the last offensive, three years before, when the North Vietnamese had barreled across the demilitarized zone and into Quang Tri province, they had been stopped at the My Chanh River, the province's southern border.

On Sunday, with the division of Marines in Quang Tri pulled south to replace the departing Airborne Division, local defense forces on the My Chanh broke and bolted for Hue, setting off a chain reaction that swept up some regular units in its path.

The cause of the panic was not fear of attack but an overwhelming desire among troops with families in Hue to see to their safety. With rumors washing through the ranks every day as to whether Thieu, or Truong—or anyone—would abandon Hue or fight for it, Captain Cuong's theory about the soldiers' motivation was stood on its head.

In a world where whole regions, such as the northern part of the Central Highlands, could be written off without a battle, the Army instead of fighting to defend its dependents broke ranks to find them and flee, fighting their own comrades, if necessary, to get their families to safety.*

---

* General Bruce Palmer, Jr., wrote in *The 25-Year War: America's Military Role in Vietnam* (Lexington: University Press of Kentucky, 1984):

> President Thieu once told Ambassador [Ellsworth] Bunker that the Vietnamese placed the safety and welfare of their families ahead of the security of their country, and that this factor could critically influence how well South Vietnamese troops would fight. Indeed, this had proved to be a decisive factor in [MRs 1 and 2], where South Vietnamese forces became intermingled with their own families in the battle area, as well as in [MR 3], where, conversely, the 18th Division and other ARVN units whose families were relatively secure in areas to the rear fought tenaciously and bravely.
>
> Upon reflection, I conclude that South Vietnamese troops are probably not much different in this respect from the soldiers of any other country. During the American Civil War, for example, Confederate soldiers often left their units because they were needed at home for spring planting. Southern leaders tried to discourage the tendency, but it worsened as the war grew longer; unit commanders wisely considered the offense to be simply taking a temporary, unauthorized leave of absence, rather than desertion. Only a nation engaged in a

X

Meanwhile, elements of the convoy of tears out of the Central Highlands were gradually approaching the coast, and becoming more ac-
cessible to journalists. On Sunday, a photographer for United Press
International named Lim Thanh Van talked himself on board a Huey
helicopter in Tuy Hoa. The helicopter was flown by a Captain Huynh
My Phuong, who was under orders to stick to his mission—to destroy
communists—and not to set down to pick up refugees.

Phuong disobeyed orders. At the same steep hill from which *Chinh
Luan*'s Nguyen Tu had been extracted four days earlier, Captain
Phuong hovered, picked up a load of refugees and gunned his engine
to rise.

An old man and a woman in their seventies, the old man holding a
small child, clung to the skids. When their feet were twelve or fifteen
feet above the ground, they released their grips and fell. The old
grandparents and the child lay there crying, and the photographer and
the pilot quickly learned that the child's mother had made it in the
mad scramble to board the helicopter.

Lim Thanh Van wrote later for the news agency:

> Phuong, tears in his eyes, tried to swing his helicopter around and
> pick up the abandoned child. He could not, because he already had
> so many aboard.
>
> We dropped this load of refugees at the province capital of **Tuy
> Hoa** and flew back, Phuong urging his helicopter on in an attempt
> to pick up the ones left behind.
>
> When we got there, they had gone. . . .
>
> Communist artillery, attacks by mountain tribesmen and dissident
> troops, the heat, the sheer struggle, the hardships have killed—who
> knows how many have died?
>
> Vehicles lie along Highway 7-B, route of retreat from the Central
> Highlands provinces of Pleiku, Kontum and Phu Bon. So do the
> dead children, women and old men.
>
> For miles and miles, people look up at us, falling to their knees,
> begging for rescue.
>
> Phuong saw a communist mortar team firing at one group of per-

---

war on its own soil, rather than in the enemy's homeland, can appreciate what
this means. The American South knew full well what it meant, as did the
South Vietnamese. Today the U.S. Seventh Army in Germany faces a somewhat similar situation in that the military families live on the potential battle-
grounds. More than one American on duty in Germany has asked himself the
question, "What would I do if war broke out suddenly and my wife and
children were in danger?"

sons in the convoy. He and his following gunships furiously attacked. The mortars stopped.

It is against Phuong's orders to land to pick up people, but he said he must.

The door gunners ran out to pick up children, old people. Others, including government Rangers, ran for the helicopters.

I fell down and had ten persons on my back. I didn't even feel any pain, worrying only that the children wouldn't get on the chopper.

In the helicopter, I was pinned down by people. I couldn't even click my camera.

No one knows how many have died in this most incredible convoy down Highway 7-B. No one likely ever will.

Babies are born on the route. More die.

The sheer incomprehensible terror is not only on Highway 7-B.

At Pleiku last Sunday, the last planes took off before the town was abandoned to the communists.

Old Mrs. Khien told me the huge crowd trying to get on the last three C-130 transports looked like a huge dragon dance, pushing, shoving, up and down, back and forth.

People grabbed for the tail, falling off as the plane taxied. Just as the last one took off, a small baby fell out of the aircraft, killed instantly as it hit the tarmac, she said.

And at Tuy Hoa sits Major Le Van Phuc, generally recognized as the best field information officer in the South Vietnamese Army.

Phuc was away at a training school when Pleiku was evacuated.

His wife and eight children are somewhere between Pleiku and Tuy Hoa on the convoy of death.

XI

On the fourth Monday in March, the twenty-fourth, the offensive was just fourteen days old. And that day at least half a million South Vietnamese were fleeing.

Richard Blystone, who flew into Saigon from his posting in Bangkok to augment the Associated Press bureau, reached Tuy Hoa, the coastal goal of the column out of the highlands, over the weekend. He reported:

The helicopters spill out weeping women and children limping on bare feet and soldiers in blood-caked camouflage fatigues. Some carry satchels and straw baskets, some have nothing but their lives.

An Army major, hoping his family has made the 150-mile march from Pleiku, watches each incoming helicopter intently.

An old woman drops down on the grass near the helicopter pad. "Now I know I am alive," she says. She has been on the road a week.

"It was such a misery I cannot describe it," says a mother after frantically searching for her ten children and finding they are all there.

Two children arrive alone. Their father put them aboard a helicopter thinking their pregnant mother was on board. But she was not.

A schoolteacher says his family walked through the jungle to avoid North Vietnamese shellfire and thought their luck had changed when they were able to climb aboard a truck. But later they realized that their five-year-old child was missing in the scramble.

The refugees are flown to this coastal province headquarters about 240 miles northeast of Saigon from a stalled refugee column that ends 15 miles to the southwest. Outgoing choppers carry ammunition, rice and bread—some of which the helicopter pilots pay for out of their own pockets.

Flying from Tuy Hoa toward the column, the reasons why the refugees cannot move soon become evident. Six miles from the city, a blackened armored truck sits in the road beside a flattened burned-out hamlet. This is as far as relatives of refugees hoping to meet their loved ones dare to go. . . .

The retreating soldiers at the head of the column have set up several camps beside the road. Farther on, cars, trucks and buses are clustered in a bizarre traffic jam in the middle of nowhere.

Other vehicles are backed up at a half-completed sand bridge across a river. Viet Cong shells have been hitting near the river crossing, killing and wounding many persons, refugees say.

Earlier in the week, they say, more than 100 persons, mostly civilians, were killed by shellfire near Cong Son, ten miles back.

The column trails out of sight into the foothills where a cloud of gray smoke rises; officers say there are about 35,000 refugees near [that fire] and another 30,000 stretching back to Cong Son, where a Ranger group harassed by communist fire brings up the rear.

How many hundreds are left behind along the rest of the more than 150 miles to the abandoned Central Highlands capitals of Pleiku and Kontum no one knows.

According to Colonel William Le Gro, the senior U.S. Army intelligence officer in Vietnam, about sixty thousand refugees from the highlands eventually straggled into Tuy Hoa and from there to Nha Trang. But he believed that "at least 100,000 [others] remained stranded in western Phu Yen province without food, water or medical assistance."

On that same Monday, Paul Vogle of United Press International was in a place called Nam-O, six miles north of Da Nang, watching thousands of refugees snake their way down from the Hai Van Pass to the bridge at Nam-O and the "dubious refuge of a sports stadium, a jam-packed building or a quiet alley" in Da Nang beyond.

He looked out on a six-mile traffic jam. "The incredible convoy contains cars, jeeps, trucks, buses, motorbikes, bicycles, pushcarts, *cyclo-pousses*—literally anything that can roll," Vogle wrote.

Those lucky enough to find rides in motorized vehicles were being charged about $135 for the trip from Hue—the equivalent of about three months' salary for a middle-level bureaucrat.

> Across the highway on a hillock stands a 60-foot-high Buddha erected by grateful refugees from the 1968 Hue holocaust [Vogle went on].
>
> The Buddha smiles down serenely on a quarter million heartbreaks—the pain, the tears, the panic, the anger.
>
> White rocks etched up to the green lawn at the foot of the statue pick out the final irony:
>
> "Welcome travelers."

XII

During Al Francis' absence as consul general in Da Nang, the senior American in the region, the consulate was run by his deputy, Theresa Tull. The province rep* in Quang Ngai, the southernmost of the five provinces that comprised Military Region 1, was also away on home leave that March. Shortly after the offensive began in the north, Tull sent Melvin Chatman down to Quang Ngai.

Chatman had served three years in the infantry in Vietnam in the late 1960s. When he quit the Army to join USAID, he was on the list for promotion to major. But he was in the early stages of a deep emotional and intellectual engagement with Vietnam, and decided he would prefer to do something for the people other than fight communists.

He was thirty-four, a solid two-hundred-pounder with the thighs of a football lineman. When the question came up, he identified himself, easily, as a black. The question came up because in his colloquial English there was little specifically black slang—Chatman had grown up in Michigan—and because his features were Polynesian. He could have been a native Hawaiian.

He was a savvy, tough American who had been in Vietnam for eight years. They couldn't have picked a better man to send down to Quang Ngai when things started to get a little flaky.

---

* Nearly all of South Vietnam's forty-four provinces had an American province representative. After the signing of the Paris agreements, these were all USAID officials, like Paul Struharik.

Quang Ngai province, where it was easier to talk politics than to grow rice, had seen more fighting and fostered more hard men than most of the provinces in South Vietnam. Among its sons were North Vietnamese Prime Minister Pham Van Dong, Viet Cong General Tran Van Tra and Captain Do Duc Cuong of the military security section in the ARVN 1st Division. In March 1968, a platoon of the Americal Division led by Lieutenant William Calley massacred approximately four hundred civilians in a hamlet called My Lai near Quang Ngai City.

Things got crazy fast. The communists, North Vietnamese and Viet Cong, took an important hill overlooking Highway 1, and the South Vietnamese lost hundreds of men in repeated unsuccessful attempts to retake it.

Chatman was there for two weeks. From the beginning, he felt an urgency among the population. They began to do everything at double time, trotting when they normally would have walked. He urged the Vietnamese who worked for his government—many of them guards at the few American facilities in the province—to evacuate to Da Nang. All of those who wanted to flee got out, most by road until the road north was cut.

He was less successful with Earl Martin, the young head of a Mennonite relief operation in the province. In the final week, Chatman and a colleague visited Martin every couple of days, to brief him on the worsening situation and urge him to leave. Martin eventually sent his wife and children to Da Nang. But he had what he thought were good contacts with the local communists, and elected to stay.

Finally, on Monday, March 24, there was no one left for Chatman to evacuate but himself and the handful of people with him: Charles Currier, another USAID officer; a Filipino community development worker under contract to USAID; and the final three or four Vietnamese, including the ARVN interpreters all of them had. A chopper was sent down from Da Nang. The airport was closed. Chatman rode to the improvised landing zone on the back of someone's Honda. As he and the others trotted to the helicopter, mortar rounds popped around them.

Chatman and his companions left Quang Ngai in the late afternoon. That morning, before dawn, following a two-hour artillery attack, all government resistance in Quang Tin, the next province north, had dissolved. Regular forces and militiamen and the province chief and police fled north to Da Nang or south to the port of Chu Lai, which offered the prospect of escape by sea. And that evening, hours after Chatman quit Quang Ngai, the South Vietnamese military in Quang Ngai likewise collapsed. As former Baltimore *Sun* correspondent Arnold R. Isaacs has observed in *Without Honor,* his scathing account of the agonies of Laos, Cambodia and Vietnam after the Paris Peace Accords, in both Quang Tin and Quang Ngai all levels of the Saigon government, "as if by telepathy," chose to run rather than to fight.

And in Quang Tin and Quang Ngai the flight of the government forces was so sudden that the population had little or no chance to join in the retreat. On that one Monday, the communists found themselves with an additional 1.3 million people under their control—as many as they had absorbed in the preceding two weeks of the offensive.

XIII

Some people found Russell Mott* a little crazy. He was the product of very good prep schools, Wesleyan and the Marine Corps (a somewhat rare combination) when he arrived in Vietnam in late 1968 with USAID. He was a fleshy Jack Nicholson. Curly black hair, receding fast from a square skull, and beetle brows, bushy upward-curling black eyebrows over a square nose and a wide mouth and good teeth, that mouth breaking once or twice an hour into the slightly crazed Nicholson grin. A chain smoker, and a drinker; a man of large appetites.

He was the kind of USAID official who managed to get himself kicked out of a couple of jobs, but never quite kicked out of the country. When John Paul Vann† was alive, Mott had a protector in Vann, one renegade protecting another. After Vann went down with his chopper, Mott lived by his wits, not really giving much of a s--- if the bureaucrats succeeded in getting rid of him. He had a couple of rules: He wouldn't take a city larger than fifty thousand people, and he had to be the only American in the district. He wasn't interested in running a province. Even toward the end, if you were the senior province rep you had to put up with too many Americans in coats and

---

* Russell Mott was born Russell Mott. His mother remarried and there was an adoption and he became Robert Lanigan until he was forty, in 1980, when he made the legal change back to Russell Mott. All the time he was in Vietnam—from late 1968 until the end of April 1975—he was known as Robert Lanigan. In what follows, this interesting man of somewhat conflicted identity will be referred to as Russell Mott.

† Vann served as a colonel in the Mekong delta in the early 1960s. His candor about the limitations of the South Vietnamese military and the government of Ngo Dinh Diem led to his retirement. He returned to Vietnam as a civilian, was the senior American in the Mekong delta and later the Central Highlands, and became a somewhat more conventional advocate of the embassy optimism. He died when his helicopter crashed near Pleiku in 1972.

ties. Mott dressed for the weather: black pajamas and a white cowboy hat over the fierce eyebrows.

Like Chatman, whom he was quite like, and liked, Mott was not unique. There were others. But Mott did carry it to something of an extreme, among those four or five hundred Americans during the course of the whole adventure who actually enjoyed eating raw pork once or twice a day. It wasn't just that he went native, and nailed down the lingo, and wore the crazy black clothes; he did things he wasn't commissioned to do. He slept in villages the spooks said belonged to the bad guys, and he was around when the South Vietnamese set up some ambushes, even after the Paris Peace Accords, when American officials weren't supposed to be involved in that kind of thing. Mott did it. And Mott discovered that he really liked killing commies. It disturbed him, the way he liked it. But he kept doing it.

Mott never wanted a province, but as the number of USAID officials in MR 1 was drastically reduced in March, he wound up in charge of two of them—Quang Nam, which surrounded Da Nang, and Quang Tin, the next province south. He found himself in Tam Ky, the capital of Quang Tin, on the afternoon of Sunday, March 23, visiting the province chief, an ARVN colonel.

The colonel asked Mott if he played tennis. Mott said that he did. So they left the radios with their reports of positions being overrun and abandoned and played a few hard games.

When he was ready to quit, the colonel said: "Thanks. I always like to play tennis when I have to think. Now I know what to do."

Mott stayed through the evening, monitoring Vietnamese and American radio nets that made it clear that the citizens of Hue were fleeing south.

What the province chief did, early the next day, after a predawn artillery attack on Tam Ky, was flee.

XIV

Despite the French cast to her name, Elizabeth Montagne—everyone called her Liz—was a pretty little Irish-American. She harbored ambitions to be more than a secretary, but nevertheless enjoyed most of her six months in Da Nang, South Vietnam's second-largest city.

There was a new culture to learn about. She had her own apartment, with a maid. And the size of the American consulate—eighty staffers, about a dozen of them American—was congenial: small enough to know everyone socially, large enough so that everyone didn't get on one another's nerves.

On Monday of that last full week in March, the twenty-fourth,

Montagne was asked to take dictation from a visiting American general from Saigon.

At the beginning of the session, the general said: "You understand, Miss Montagne, that this is classified."

"Of course."

Then he stood at a map and said, among many other more technical and more qualified things: "Da Nang has got a week, at the most."

Just a day or two ago, *Stars and Stripes* had reported that Hue had fallen, when it had not. Sure, there were a lot of refugees in Da Nang. But the routine in the embassy went on as usual, and no one had said anything about evacuation. Liz Montagne thought the general was off his rocker.

XV

Well before I was due at Ramuntcho's for dinner with Al Chambers, Arthur Lord and a new correspondent who had come in that morning from Tokyo, I stopped for a couple of drinks on the terrace of the Continental, which I was coming to think of as a refuge from the office and—not from the war, I had seen almost nothing of the war—from the war's effects on the Vietnamese I cared about. The terrace reminded me of my earlier trips, and of the first months of this one, when all had still been potential. I was amused by the theatrical commercial intercourse of the place. The mostly foreign customers eyed the street life a few open steps below them, and the Vietnamese as they passed watched their audience. Shoeshine boys darted furtively among the tables, shooed off by the waiters if they lingered without getting work. All day, a boy in his late teens or early twenties moved from table to table with a stack of paperbacks (frequently replenished from a sizable inventory on the sidewalk) stacked up one arm. Occasionally during the afternoon and early evening a thin Chinese palm reader of exquisite elderly poise drifted through the terrace, his features never breaking from their serenity as drinker after drinker glanced at him and shook their heads. I never saw him read a palm. Peddlers with bad watercolors in foldout portfolios and lacquer-ware panels etched with similar landscapes of low mountains and tiny temples under bird-crowded skies competed with fake Buddhist nuns in gray offering the chance to win merit by contributing to nonexistent orphanages. Child beggars reached up to anyone foolish enough to have taken a table at one of the two low walls along the sidewalks. (One gang of children who often loitered at the steps of the Tu Do sidewalk entrance was led by a girl of perhaps thirteen who spoke nothing but street Vietnamese and looked for all the world to be one hundred percent Caucasian. I knew that I would never interview her, not in the face of the mocking and desperate hostility with which she propositioned all Western men who had the misfortune to walk through her gang.)

It all had been little changed by the offensive, although the paperback boy's cache was larger than ever, and I changed tables before the first drink came when I realized that the first table would keep me constantly in sight of the bartender with the son in Ban Me Thuot.

Leaving the terrace, I was held at the curb by a pack of traffic released by the light at the Caravelle Hotel corner—first the motorcycles and then the cars and trucks and slower scooters and finally the bicycles. I tensed to dart in front of two boys at the end of the stream, but decided it was too hot to run. They could have been sixteen and fourteen. The smaller one straddled the bar that ran from the seat to the handlebars, his sandaled feet perched on the yoke. I wondered again how they did it without bruising themselves.

The older boy, pedaling, looked at me and waved his arm in a great sweep. In the dusk, I could just make out the precocious zeal in his face. "Go home," the boy cried. "All Americans go home now, go home."

10

Early in the afternoon on Tuesday, March 25, five principals with a few aides met in the Oval Office of the White House.

As the meeting got under way, David Kennerly, the young photojournalist whom Gerald Ford had taken on as his personal photographer, moved quietly around the office shooting the principals: the President; Secretary of State Henry Kissinger; Brent Scowcroft, the national security adviser; General Frederick Weyand, the Army Chief of Staff; and Graham Anderson Martin, America's ambassador to Vietnam. Martin had been called back to Washington from Winston-Salem, North Carolina, where he was still recovering from dental surgery.

Kissinger had been back in Washington for less than forty-eight hours following the collapse of his latest round of shuttle diplomacy aimed at bringing an agreement between Egypt and Israel, a mission on which he had embarked three days before the communist attack on Ban Me Thuot.

Now, two and a half weeks later, Indochina again assumed first place in American day-to-day foreign-policy attention, a place it had not occupied since the signing of the Paris Peace Accords in late January 1973.

Kissinger was of course well briefed. And Martin, who was a voracious, insomniac reader, had digested virtually all of the reporting from Saigon that had come in from Lehmann and Polgar and the rest of them.

Conspicuously absent was James Schlesinger, the Secretary of Defense. One of the first things Kissinger discovered on his return from the Mideast was that Schlesinger was out of step with the State Department/White House policy toward Indochina. That policy was still taking shape—but Schlesinger was not in tune even with its outlines. Just the day before, the Secretary of Defense had told a congressional committee that the loss of Southeast Asia to the communists would not significantly alter the world military balance. Whatever policy emerged from this meeting and from the fact-finding trip to Vietnam that Kissinger already knew General Weyand would be making, it would not include writing off the importance of the theater when the outcome was still uncertain.

For the next few weeks, the Secretary of State used his considerable resources to try to freeze Schlesinger out of Vietnam decision making, a campaign in which he largely succeeded.

But at that meeting even Kissinger and Scowcroft acknowledged that Cambodia's days were numbered. That Tuesday afternoon, the United States gave up on the government it had supported in that small, doomed nation. The Administration would cease pressing its case for additional aid for Cambodia.

For Vietnam, the Administration had originally requested $1.45 billion for the current fiscal year. Congress had authorized $1 billion, but appropriated only $700 million. For months, the Administration had been pushing a supplemental aid package to shake loose the missing $300 million. Now the question was whether to continue that effort or to ask for a great deal more in light of the rapid communist advances.

The discussion might have left Martin in something of a quandary. On the one hand, his instincts told him that the intelligence coming from his embassy in his absence was probably unduly pessimistic. On the other, he was not about to argue against less aid, when he could quite easily, without notes, tell the group how the government in Saigon would have spent every dollar in the original $1.45 billion request. Martin argued that if the executive branch made an all-out effort to explain the realities in Vietnam to Congress and the American people, and if that led to a major boost in aid, the Saigon government and its armed forces would at least have a chance of stopping the communists.

Two major decisions came out of the meeting. The President would order U.S. naval ships to assist in the evacuation of troops and civilians from north to south in Vietnam, an evacuation in which U.S. merchant ships were already taking part under contract to the U.S. government. By ordering the naval forces to remain outside South Vietnam's three-mile territorial limit and by consultation with Congress, the President assumed he could avoid invoking the War Powers Act.

Ford also decided to send General Weyand to Saigon on a one-week fact-finding mission. Weyand was the last commander of MACV, before it became the Defense Attaché's Office with the signing of the Paris Peace Accords. He knew Nguyen Van Thieu and the other senior Vietnamese generals as well as anyone in the U.S. military. Ford would decide on what level of aid to request from Congress when Weyand returned. He was to go as soon as possible, which turned out to be at dawn the next day.

As the meeting drew to a close, Kissinger attempted a joke. "I'm glad you're going back out there, Graham," he said, tilting his head and peering through his thick glasses at a man who was never outstared. "When it all goes down and the American people ask 'Who lost Vietnam?' Phil Habib* will have someone to point to."

David Hume Kennerly was twenty-eight that spring. He was a slight, good-looking wise guy who was starting to go bald but sported the first beard that had been seen in the White House since presidents had them. He had also won a Pulitzer Prize for his photographs for UPI and Time-Life in Vietnam during a two-year stint there that began in the spring of 1971 and ended shortly after the signing of the Paris accords.

Vietnam was not yet out of Kennerly's system. And it is a measure of the closeness of his relationship with Ford that after the photo session Kennerly retired to a chair and was not asked to leave.

When the great men who shape our affairs had left, Kennerly told Ford with the small quotient of *gravitas* one can muster at twenty-eight that he wanted to be included in the mission.

Ford thought for a few moments. Finally he said: "Okay, David, I understand. And I'll be interested to hear your views of what's going on when you get back."

Kennerly hung a sign on his office door that read: "Gone to Vietnam, back in a week or so."

Then he discovered that the banks were closed.

Later that night, he went to say goodbye to the President and Mrs. Ford in the family rooms at the White House.

* Assistant Secretary of State for East Asia, and one of Martin's many enemies in the bureaucracy.

"Do you have everything you need, David?" the President asked as Kennerly turned to leave.

"Well, as a matter of fact, I don't have any cash," Kennerly said. "The banks are closed and we're leaving at sunrise. Do you have a few bucks you could lend me?"

The President of the United States fished out his wallet. It contained forty-seven dollars. "Don't spend it all in one place," he said as he gave it to the photographer.

"Thank you, sir," Kennerly said. Again he turned to leave, accepting a light hug from Mrs. Ford.

"Hey, Kennerly," Gerald Ford said, and Kennerly grinned as his President flipped him a quarter. "You might as well clean me out."

Kennerly caught the quarter. Then the President put an arm around his shoulder. "Listen, David," the older man said, "take care of yourself over there."

II

Russell Mott was able to drive down to his home in the town of Hoi An, just south of Da Nang, for a couple of days after the collapse of the government defenses in all the rest of Quang Tin province farther south. On Wednesday, he shut up the house and released the geese he kept to guard it. Mott and many others in Vietnam kept watch geese. They slept more lightly than most dogs, and honked furiously at the intrusion of any stranger.* He then drove back to Da Nang with Hai, his driver/bodyguard.

III

As the White House meeting was taking place, halfway around the world in Vietnam it was 3 and 4 and 5 A.M. on Wednesday, March 26, and the men of the ARVN 1st Division and all the other defenders of Hue were packed together on a rocky beach and port east of Hue called Tan My. General Truong had given the final orders for the abandonment of the former imperial capital at 6 P.M. on Tuesday.

The retreat had been disorderly, and Captain Do Duc Cuong was confused and angry. The sea was rough, and in any case there didn't seem to be enough ships to pick up the more than two thousand men that crowded the beach. Squads of armed men set out north and south from the beach to look for fishing boats. During the long sleepless

---

* The obvious virtues of watch geese were so apparent that some American rather late in the war convinced the U.S. government to give every ARVN unit money to buy enough geese to guard its permanent installations. Unfortunately, it was late enough in the war to come in that period when ARVN salaries were not quite enough to eat on. Either the geese were bought and cooked or the unexpected cash went for other food.

night, Cuong had heard sporadic outbursts of shouting and firing. The stranded remnant of the division was not being attacked. Men were fighting among themselves for food and money and boats.

Cuong was an officer in military intelligence. He never wore a uniform, and ran agents. After midnight, the man in his section who dealt most often with their two best agents told Cuong that a woman had been sent to find him with a message from one of them. The communists would move into Hue the next night, and the man wanted to see Cuong at their normal meeting place in the city.

When the rising sun had turned the sky and sea a dull gray, a dozen artillery shells landed on the beach in twenty minutes. Cuong crouched and ran with the others away from the nearest explosions and cries and groans, away from the water into the edge of salt marshes. Three of his men were with him. The shelling stopped, but then the fighting among the men began again.

A single helicopter set down in a space cleared for it next to the enclave at one end of the beach where General Nguyen Van Diem, the 1st Division commander, and his senior staff had barricaded themselves through the night. Cuong watched nine men, including Diem, crouch and run to it.

"This is a bad place now," Cuong said to his lieutenant. "Get the others and meet me there, just inside the tip of that tree line. We will go back to Hue. If the communists come in, we can find a boat there easier than here."

And so it was that Captain Do Duc Cuong and all seven of the men subordinate to him in the section walked the five miles through salt marshes and rice fields and then over roads to an almost deserted Hue late in the morning on Wednesday, March 26, eighteen hours after their superiors had abandoned it.

They were not fools. They left a mob of men who were being shelled for a city they knew to be almost empty, and uncontested, a city with a river on which people had lived in houseboats, some of whom had left the houseboats behind when Highway 1 was still open.

Cuong and his men carried pistols, and Cuong and his lieutenant both carried small encoding devices. But they were dressed as farmers. It was odd for eight young farmers to be trudging through that landscape, but not wholly odd. Neither Hue nor the landscape was wholly deserted. A few people always stayed behind: the old, the infirm—and the communists.

Cuong trusted his best agent, who had a rank with the Viet Cong that was roughly equivalent to lieutenant. The communists would not arrive until the evening, and Cuong would find a way to get himself and his men out. Cuong also hoped to make contact with the other agent, a younger man who was a squad leader with the communists.

But there was this that was illogical, or emotional, in Cuong's return to Hue: His government had spent the lives of two thousand men to recapture Hue after the communists held it for more than a month in the great Tet offensive of 1968. It had sacrificed almost as many lives four years later, in the communists' spring offensive of 1972, to recapture the rubble of Quang Tri City farther north. Cuong still could not believe that the men who claimed to control his fate would give up Hue without a fight. If they were going to do so, he would see it happen. And he would find out what his agents could tell him now, and wanted of him; he would determine what he could give them, his tormented brothers.

Cuong set up a little headquarters in one of the offices of the university, near the Huong Giang River.* He sent his men to explore the city, posting two of them to the different pagodas where they normally rendezvoused with the agents.

As he waited alone in the abandoned office, Cuong entertained the possibility that the senior agent's message was a trick—that he would appear with a company of his comrades to capture or kill him. The possibility was slight, he thought, but he acknowledged its existence and felt a moment of fear.

The younger agent came in first, in midafternoon. "Where is my family?" he asked. "Where is everybody? How could the Saigon side give up Hue—*Hue!*—without a fight?"

"Everyone ran away," Cuong said.

"It's crazy," the young man hissed, as if unseen ears listened. "Think of *Tet mau than*.† Think of the spring offensive of '72. You fought. You died. Friends of mine died."

"I know," Cuong said. "I know. But now everything is broken."

Early in the evening, Cuong and the agent and three of Cuong's men were sitting in the dark office. They were eating a soup they had concocted from vegetables they took from an abandoned shop. A fourth member of the unit joined them. A few minutes later, the older agent called Cuong's name softly from a window at the back of the room.

"When are the communists coming?" Cuong asked.

"Soon," the man said. He remained in the shadow of the lawn sloping away to the river.

* Perfume River.
† Tet '68.

"How did you find me?"

"I followed the man who just came here. What are you doing? Why is there no one else here?"

"Everyone ran away," Cuong said. "And this morning they started shelling the beach, so we came back here. What are you going to do?"

"I don't know," the agent said. "Who is here with you?"

"A few of my men. One other agent, but he's not from your division."

"What's his name?"

Cuong told him.

"Okay," the older man said, and joined them. "We have to get out of Hue," he said.

Cuong knew he was right. But his heart was still unable to accept the truth that the communists would walk into Hue unopposed. If he didn't see it, it would be like a dream.

He sent two of his men to the river with orders to find a houseboat. They were back in less than an hour. And in a ten-minute period straddling midnight on Cuong's watch, his last three sentries arrived with news that the communists were in the city. The lead unit was the 312th Special Forces battalion, as the older agent and Cuong thought it would be. They were clearing vehicles and sidewalk stalls from the main streets to prepare the way for trucks or tanks.

The ten slipped down the lawn to the waiting boat, started it and throttled back the engine until it was a low gurgle with just enough power to inch them forward. Cuong's men and his agents crowded into the living quarters. Cuong himself lay in the stern, operating the engine and rudder and straining to find activity in the streets of the city slowly wheeling off to port. He saw a short column of armed men moving at a trot along the riverfront road toward the university. Twenty minutes later, before the houseboat cleared the city and headed out to sea, he saw two GMC trucks emptying dozens of country people into the market in front of the bus station. Among them, they carried half a dozen flags. In the moonlight Cuong could not make out the colors, but clearly saw the pattern of two of them and filled in the colors in his mind's eye: top half red, bottom half blue, the golden star in the middle.

Voices reached him faintly, none of them directed at the crawling houseboat. There had not been a single shot.

Cuong crept forward and told his communications man to find a ship. About two hours later they climbed onto a small coastal patrol boat of the Saigon Navy.

"Why are you so far north?" the captain asked.

"We just left Hue," Cuong said. "The communists came in."

"We thought they were there this afternoon."

"This afternoon it was empty," Cuong said. "Our generals gave it to the dogs and the chickens." He spat the dust of Hue from his mouth and looked for a place to lie down.

IV

Before I left the office, I sat down at the tinny European typewriter with the very light touch I had early on appropriated as my own and tapped out a letter to my wife:

Wed./March 26

DEAREST ONE—

I'll probably be in Bangkok when you get this. As you know, I have to get out of the country by the end of this month to avoid slipping over into resident status. Choice was a couple of days in Phnom Penh, or Bangkok. I throttled the urge to see Phnom Penh before it goes on the theory that I might have got stuck there for a week or so. And with the offensive rolling the way it is here, I think I'm getting six to eight spots a day on the air. I haven't come anywhere close to it yet, but am thinking there's an outside chance I'll hit $1,000 this week.

Well, it's a hell of an offensive. Thank God CBS has guys who know what the f--- they're doing and have been able to get film of the refugees trying to get out of the Central Highlands and Hue.

The old lady beggars are starting to jab you with their begging hats. And I've had two variations of "Yankee go home" from strangers on the street in the last few days. The people are ashamed of the retreat, bitter. There isn't a real wave of anti-Americanism yet, but it may come. I think the real anger is toward Thieu, not the Americans.

Even in Saigon, you can get a taste of what's happening. The nice old guy who watches the Telex at night had a son in the convoy from Pleiku. I was here last night when he got a call from Don Oliver, the third correspondent, who's up on the coast. Oliver was there when the son and his family were helicoptered into Tuy Hoa, safe and sound. The night man turned to me and said, "Thank God, thank God," in English, and then called his wife.

On the lighter side, I was at the radio station a couple of days ago—sometimes I have to feed from there—and overheard a conversation between some southern American in the States and his Vietnamese wife or girl friend. (The Vietnamese blithely listen to all the overseas calls; you can't help but eavesdrop on them as you wait for yours to be put through.)

American: Now listen, honey, it looks like it's gettin' pretty serious over there, and I want you to get out.

Wife/girl friend, in incredibly weak little-girl voice: It's okay. If I can just stay until the day on the ticket, I can take the buffies.*

American: Now listen, darlin', the 6th is too late. I want you to get on Pam Am flight 842 on the 25th. Now: It's Sunday there, right?

Girl: Riiiight . . .

American: Okay, so the plane is on Tuesday. Now I want you to go out to Tan Son Nhut, and you have them change the ticket. It's all confirmed and everything. And, honey, when you get to San Francisco, you're going to have to have some money for a hotel. That'll be about twenty-five or thirty dollars. So you go to Gillion and you tell him you have to borrow fifty dollars, and I'll pay him back, I'll send him a check for it, you understand?

Girl: But I already paid for all the buffies.

American: Listen, honey, to *hell* with the buffies. I don't *care* about the damned buffies. I just care about you.

Girl: Gee, I don't know . . .

Obviously, the girl had bought a dozen or more of the ceramic elephants called buffies that every military type who was ever here brought home for souvenirs, and she wasn't going to be able to take them if she went on Tuesday. It went on and on, all about the elephants. Maybe she thinks she's going to start a business with them over there. Maybe the truth is that she actually doesn't want to go. Well: One story I'll never get the kicker to.

Saigon of course is not going to fall. It *absolutely* isn't going to fall this year, and in my opinion will never fall. What five American presidents have not understood is that Hanoi doesn't want to take the South by force. It wants to force a political settlement that will give the PRG† a share of power and then there'll be a long process (five years?) of accommodation until the gov't is communist-dominated. The South Vietnamese don't want communism and they don't want any more war. And the North knows that. If Hanoi comes into Saigon with tanks, it will mean that their whole strategy failed.

It's been a good life. I missed two of them, but I'm here for the big one. And I managed to have one of the great women of my generation fall in love with me. And it's all going to get even better.

Love,
DAVID

v

There was a sweet kid down in the delta named Cary Kassebaum. Kass, as he was usually known, was quiet, and slight—a former Peace Corps volunteer. From 1969 until just before Christmas 1974, he served as deputy province rep and then province representative in An Xuyen, the southernmost province of Vietnam.

---

* For Big Ugly F - - - - - - Elephants.
† Provisional Revolutionary Government.

Kass took pictures. Years later, he would flash a slide of a school on a wall and say: "That's the school I built five times. Built it once. They blew it up. Built it again. They blew it up again. . . ."

Kassebaum would also say: "You have to realize that the South Vietnamese had no government, on the civilian side. We did everything—public health, the roads, refugee resettlement . . ."

That overstates the case. But it makes sense of the fact that until that last Wednesday in March, the consular office in Can Tho was open only on Wednesdays. That is, what one would normally think of as the work of a consulate—examining or vetting marriage and adoption papers, issuing visas and passports—was routinely handled by one officer one day a week. All the other officers were busy helping a society function and—at the very least—closely following how the allied armed forces were doing.

That Wednesday it was David Sciacchitano's turn as consular officer. And from that day forward, there was enough business so that the consular office was open every day, and Sciacchitano had a full-time job. They started pulling American officials in from the province capitals, and advising Americans of all types with common-law wives and children to get their papers in order. Quite suddenly, there was great urgency about correct documentation.

VI

Captain Cuong's rescuers put ashore at naval headquarters north of Da Nang at nine o'clock in the morning on Thursday, the twenty-seventh, a few hours after they had picked up the occupants of the houseboat. Cuong had slept fitfully in the few hours before dawn. He still carried his pistol and the code machine but nothing else. He had been in the same clothes for two days and nights. He was not a good sailor, and turned down the soup they were offered; he spent the morning moving down the coast both hungry and slightly sick and tired above all. It was not good preparation for what he found in Da Nang.

In normal wartime, Da Nang held about a million people, many of them refugees. In the last few weeks and days, at least another million refugees had crowded into the city, and most of them were trying to get away—refugees and Da Nang people and soldiers alike.

Four of Cuong's men left him at the naval base. The rest of them squeezed into two jeeps already crowded with Marines who were going to try to make a run to the huge air base that stretched almost the length of the city itself to the west of it.

A Marine in the front of Cuong's jeep sat on the back of his seat sweeping his M-16 ahead of him and firing in the air to inform the jeeps and trucks and motorcycles and cars and people on foot and dogs and pigs and chickens in front of them of their presence.

The Marines shouted as if they were drunk, but their faces weren't red and Cuong smelled no liquor on their breath. He asked the man jammed next to him why they were going to the air base, and the Marine answered: "Maybe some planes come from Saigon."

As they toiled through the heat and dust and crowds closer to the city, Cuong realized that the chaos derived not only from the numbers of people but also from the absence of control. If there were any police left in Da Nang they were no longer in uniform. As they were stuck in one particularly bad tangle of vehicles and people, Cuong calculated whether it would be faster to walk the remaining few kilometers to the MR 1 headquarters near the air base. He saw a band of men from his own division commandeering beer and cigarettes at rifle point from a sidewalk stall. He decided it was safer in the jeep with the Marines than on the sidewalks. But it was during that wait that the subordinate with him in that jeep jumped out of it. Cuong called after him. The man stopped and turned. "I have to look for my family," he said. "F - - - military security. But good luck, Captain. Get out of here. Go south. I will too. I'll look for you at number nine Nguyen Binh Kheim."*

Cuong never saw any of the seven again. But the two agents were still with him when they got to the headquarters compound. On the houseboat leaving Hue, they had told Cuong that they would stay with him until he led them to his superiors, for a discussion of the future, and at least one more payday.

The main gate into the big compound was unguarded and many of the offices were obviously abandoned. As they crossed the expanse of dirt toward the military security offices, that open ground so still compared to the chaos of the streets, Cuong wondered briefly, suddenly frightened, if all his commanders had left.

He asked the agents what they planned to do. "Look for my family," the older man said. "I don't want to run. Everyone with guns. The communists would be better than this."

The younger man said: "Older brother is right. This side is like a dog with rabies now."

Cuong knocked on the door of Colonel Le Quang Nhon, the commander of the security sections for the three divisions in the region. Nhon said, "Come in," and Cuong entered, alone.

Nhon sat at his desk with his head in his hands. He looked up.

* The street address in Saigon of the branch of military intelligence for which they worked.

"Cuong, where have you been? You're the first one. No one from the Second Division, no one from the Third."

Cuong explained where he had been. He admired Colonel Nhon, an honest officer. He told Nhon about the two waiting agents, and didn't raise his voice much when he asked why they had given up Hue without a fight.

"That *stupid* Thieu," Nhon said. "He is throwing the country away. He takes the paratroopers. He takes the Marines. They say it's for the highlands, but some of them go all the way to Saigon." He gestured. "This panic, all around us, he brought on our heads, and he is worried about a coup."

When he had calmed himself, he told Cuong to get some food and clothes. "Take an airline bag or a little suitcase from one of the empty offices," he said. "We may have to leave."

"No," Cuong said.

"Yes," Colonel Nhon said. "Don't expect a miracle. Come back in an hour. Now you are my whole staff."

As he left the office, it occurred to Cuong that he might not see the agents again. He shook hands with both of them, wishing them luck. He held the older man's eyes for a moment. "Last night, I wondered if you sent for me to kill me," Cuong said, smiling.

"For a long time I worked for two governments," the man said. "Last night I worked only for myself and my family."

"I hope they are okay," Cuong said.

"Yes," the man said. "You should get out of here now."

There were still a few workers and soldiers in the mess hall, and Cuong was able to eat. At the quartermaster's office, he put on green pants and a short-sleeved khaki shirt and looped a green T-shirt through his belt, leaving his civilian clothes on the floor. It was the first uniform he had worn in six years, but ill matched and unmarked with insignia. He could easily have been a civilian who had stolen it. To that extent, he anticipated further flight. But he didn't look anywhere for an overnight bag.

General Diem, the 1st Division commander, was in the compound. He called a meeting of what was left of his staff, and Cuong attended as Colonel Nhon's aide.

"The stupid government is killing the people," Diem said. "How long will it take to recapture Hue this time? Five weeks at *Tet mau than*. How many weeks this time? How many men? I tell you now: I'm not going anywhere. I stay here. All my troops stay here."

With a colonel and a general to give him orders, a bit of sanity was restored to Cuong's universe. Back in his own office, Colonel Nhon told Cuong that many of the disturbances in the city were being flamed by communist infiltrators. On a map of the city, he told Cuong where he thought they were, and suggested that Cuong set out to see if he could pinpoint some of them.

In the course of that briefing, Colonel Nhon identified the moment when the chaos had blossomed. "Yesterday I was having lunch, alone, here, near the market," he said, using his briefer's pointer. "When I sat down, everything was normal. When I paid and went outside, all the police were gone. The children were playing with the traffic signals, and the streets started to fill up with people with guns. That's when everyone started just taking what they wanted."

Cuong did not stay in the streets long. But at one point in his brief foray into the city, he climbed to the top of a six-story hotel. He watched the people below surge like fish in one direction and then another. Sometimes, he knew, they chased rumors. Other times he was able to see the object they chased: always a tank or some other vehicle still flying the yellow flag with three horizontal red stripes of the Saigon side.

To the north, a great crowd seeped slowly around a barricade across the gate on the road that led to the civilian docks at Trinh Minh The and the naval base beyond it. The barricade consisted of the big metal shipping crates called Conex containers stacked three boxes high. When Cuong asked Colonel Nhon about it later, Nhon said that the Marines, running first, had thrown it up behind them to keep civilians from reaching the docks.

Late that afternoon, General Diem established a new light headquarters for himself at My Khe,* a beach seven miles south of the city where the first American Marines—the first regular U.S. troops in Vietnam—had landed ten years before.

At dusk, General Diem was helicoptered north to the Da Nang naval base, where Cuong had put ashore that morning. General Truong was now using the base as the principal embarkation point for the forces left to him. About an hour after Diem left, communist artillery and rocket fire started pounding the naval base and the other points where Truong was trying to salvage his troops.

But no shells were coming in at My Khe, and the small group of them left behind at that beach had tents. Captain Cuong left the war for a while to sleep.

---

* My Khe means beautiful brook. The standard word for America and Americans in Vietnamese is *My,* pronounced me—beautiful. It refers to America's natural beauty.

VII

Mel Chatman had little to do in his first few days back in Da Nang. The feeling was that he had handled the evacuation of Quang Ngai well and could use a rest.

Al Francis, the consul general, had returned from his home leave. And he suddenly had a new deputy. Someone in Saigon had decided to replace Theresa Tull with Brunson McKinley, Graham Martin's well-polished personal aide.

Through the week, Chatman watched the city fill with refugees. They camped everywhere: in schoolyards and temples and the thin strips of public land along the river. And they started to trot on their errands. They surged in the streets on Wednesday morning when more than a dozen 122-mm. shells landed in scattered locations throughout the jammed city.

And on Wednesday the first flight by World Airways into Da Nang to extract refugees and others removed Liz Montagne and most of the rest of the consulate staff. Montagne was on the first plane, which loaded without incident. But with the second flight in it became increasingly difficult for the Americans and the military police units that were still intact to maintain order.

Chatman had an American friend who was in Saigon, looking for work. The friend had a Vietnamese wife and a three-year-old daughter in Da Nang. The friend contacted Chatman, who assured him that he would do everything possible to get the wife and daughter to safety.

He saw her for the last time in Da Nang on Thursday, the twenty-seventh. "Come to my house tonight," he said. "We may get a barge in to the consulate tonight. I can get you on it." But all of Da Nang knew that people had died on barges making the short trip from Hue to Da Nang. The woman's face constricted with fear.

On Tuesday of that last week in March, the government announced that President Thieu had instructed Prime Minister Tran Thien Khiem to form a "war cabinet" to "meet the urgent requirements of national defense, of relief and resettlement of war victims, to stabilize the economy in the rear areas, to increase production to support the front lines, to mobilize the anticommunist spirit and to defeat the communist aggressors."

The next day, Thieu's police rounded up a dozen opposition figures, some of them close to Nguyen Cao Ky. The arrested men had "plotted to overthrow the constitutional and legal regime to satisfy their personal ambitions," according to a brief announcement from the Interior Ministry.

VIII

On Tuesday, so late at night that he reached most of the journalists in their hotel-room beds, John Swenson at Al Francis' behest called all the foreign journalists in Da Nang to the consulate. Francis told them that he could no longer assure their safety. He was too busy to worry about them, he said, and strongly urged them all to fly out of Da Nang the next day.

On Wednesday, Swenson himself went to the airport to leave. The remaining dependents of Americans in the consulate were leaving that day, along with some of the consulate staff, such as Liz Montagne.

As Swenson waited for his flight, refugees rushed a plane. Security officers had to fire in the air to restore order. It made for good film—and Swenson was convinced that an ABC correspondent had in fact instigated it. Several other journalists were still at the airport, and Swenson decided to stay overnight. He found a crate to curl up on at the airport warehouse, and fell asleep with the sound of distant artillery in his ears.

In the morning, Swenson called Al Francis to report on the fracas of the evening before. Then he boarded an Air America Volpar and flew to Saigon, less than four days after Francis had told him he should plan on being in Da Nang for at least a month.

11

According to one of the senior CIA officials on the plane that brought the ambassador back to Saigon, Graham Martin had difficulty grasping the seriousness of the situation. At one point in the long Washington-to-Saigon run, Martin interrupted General Weyand to point to the map between them and say: "You mean that division is no longer here?"

"The division is nowhere, Graham," Weyand said. "It no longer exists."

"But that doesn't happen," Martin said.

"It does; it has," either Weyand or the senior spook said.

Shortly thereafter, Weyand went one on one with the ambassador. The CIA man could not overhear their conversation. But he saw the towering general briefly shaking Martin's shoulder, surely the only time since he was a boy that anyone had laid a hand on Graham Martin.

Like so many of the men who rise to dominance in American corporate life or public affairs, Martin himself was tall, although not so tall as Army Chief of Staff Frederick Weyand. Martin dressed conservatively, even for an ambassador, and spoke courteously. And he was feared in that Saigon embassy as none of his predecessors had been. Life was war. In the smaller war of the bureaucrats, the prize was turf. The ambassador's basic management strategy for the smaller war was to divide and conquer. He had been at it for forty-two years now, and would quite casually, courteously, inform subordinates who were lacking a piece of information he needed that in all those decades of public service, he had never once attended a meeting at which he was not the best-prepared participant. As he did so, his head would tilt slightly; and the well-modulated North Carolina phrases emerged from under unblinking gray eyes locked on the victim. No one ever out-stared him.

Junior staffers, whom he sometimes telephoned without identifying himself, called him "the gray ghost." He worked late, both in the embassy and in the residence a few short blocks away on a quiet street perpendicular to the back wall of the embassy compound. Sometimes young Ken Moorefield—who saw him every day and wouldn't dream of calling him the gray ghost—had to slip him notes reading, "Today is Memorial Day," or "No one else left in the embassy."

That was early on, when Moorefield was still the ambassador's personal aide. But the ambassador never took Moorefield into his confidence; Moorefield felt that he was doing nothing but passing along cables, watching the appointments calendar—secretary's work. Knowing that the request could easily result in a ticket on the next flight home, he asked for another posting. Generously, because Moorefield was not a Foreign Service Officer, the ambassador found a slot for him in the small political-military section of the consulate in Nha Trang.

Moorefield was a West Pointer who had served with distinction—and been wounded—in Vietnam as a battalion adviser in the mid-1960s. Back in the United States, he left the Army and was studying international relations at Georgetown University in Washington when he happened to become friends with the only surviving son of the man who was about to be named the next ambassador to Saigon. The ambassador-designate took a liking to Moorefield, and wanted to do a favor for his son.

In Moorefield's routine security clearance, he admitted that he had, in the past, occasionally smoked marijuana. Somebody at the State Department tried to block the appointment. The ambassador told the official that he would rather have an assistant who told the truth than a liar. When that didn't work, he upped the ante: "Fine," he told the man. "You tell the President that I take Moorefield or he can find another ambassador."

Ambassador Graham Anderson Martin did not need the posting to

Saigon. In fact, he spent several months after it was offered saying the diplomatic equivalent of "Hell, no, I won't go." (He was the second choice for the job. Henry Kissinger's deputy, William Sullivan, who would shortly become ambassador to Manila, turned down the Saigon job.) After his tour as ambassador to Rome, Martin and his wife, Dorothy, were planning to retire to a farm they had bought in the hills of Tuscany. Alexander Haig ultimately got him with an appeal to duty, saying that if he refused to do something the President of the United States had asked him to do he would be denying his whole life.

It had been a full life. He was born in Mars Hill, near Thomasville, North Carolina, the son of an itinerant Baptist preacher who taught him among other things to tell the truth; it was easier that way—you didn't have to try to keep the lies straight. Oddly, because the younger Martin went on to become an avid student of history, his father also told him to forget the past and look to the future, which would be the lame excuse Martin would offer in 1983 when he was asked why he would not write his memoirs.

The preacher's son studied history and the classics at Wake Forest College,* graduating in 1932, deep in the Depression. He worked as a newspaper reporter in North Carolina and later, when he was briefly a congressional aide in Washington, wrote dispatches for a string of southern papers. With the election of Franklin Roosevelt, Martin landed a job as an assistant to Averell Harriman, then deputy administrator of the National Recovery Administration. Harriman sent him to New York, where Martin helped establish one of the regional headquarters of the Social Security system. There he met and occasionally drank with another North Carolinian—the novelist Thomas Wolfe. When Wolfe died in 1938, at the age of thirty-eight, Martin traveled to Asheville for the funeral.

In the meantime, in 1936, Martin had joined the Army Reserves, as an intelligence officer. (Years later, he would say with a straight face that the compelling attraction of the job was that it let him ride horses free.) And so it was that early in World War II, more than thirty years before the spring of 1975, Graham Martin found himself frequently briefing General George Marshall and occasionally briefing Secretary of War Henry L. Stimson on the section of the globe he had been assigned to monitor: Southeast Asia.

He never met Stalin or Hitler, but there were not a great many Americans in their early thirties who came as close as Martin did to having the kind of World War II that Herman Wouk's fictional Pug

---

* Then still in Wake Forest, North Carolina, years before the R. J. Reynolds fortune lured it to Winston-Salem.

Henry had. He spent most of the war as an intelligence officer in the Air Transport Command, shuttling between his headquarters in West Palm Beach, Florida, and Cairo, the forward command base of the theater.

At the very end of the war, he was shifted to the Pacific. When the Soviet Union joined the struggle against Japan in the closing days of the war, Martin was assigned to fly to Vladivostok to escort a senior Russian general to Allied-occupied China. The general didn't want to fly at night. Martin said politely that if the brave Red Air Force chose not to fly at night that was its business, but he would adhere to his orders. Reluctantly, the general agreed. But first there must be a lavish dinner, with many toasts. It was the old trick, vodka for the Americans and water for the hosts. Martin matched them toast for toast. Then he repaired to the quarters they had given him, forced himself to vomit, returned to the Russian party and got them out on schedule. A few weeks later, he was on the third U.S. plane to land in Japan. He snuck himself onto the *Missouri* for the surrender ceremony.

There are others like him, although not a legion—men who in the middle decades of this century knew every great name of the republic's affairs. Ask him how he liked President Kennedy, who made him U.S. deputy coordinator of the Alliance for Progress, and he says, "I liked him; I liked them all; I liked Joe, Junior, especially; the parties at that house on P Street when JFK was in the Senate. . . ."

Henry Luce called it the American Century. It lasted twenty-one years, eleven months and fifteen days, Pearl Harbor to Lee Harvey Oswald. It formed a generation. America was right and the enemy was wholly evil. But Martin was no jingoist. We are talking of a man whose two greatest heroes in the American Century were David Bruce and Adlai Stevenson; we are talking of a very sophisticated North Carolina New Deal Democrat who saw it as his duty to accept what he certainly understood might be a suicide mission, if certain nightmarish scenarios came true.

Like his father's, Martin's life was peripatetic. Eight years in Paris, from 1947 to 1955, constituted the longest stay in one place. He had a variety of official assignments there, including assistant chief of mission and administrative counselor,* which meant that he was intimately involved in plans for the evacuation of Americans and hun-

---

* Most career diplomats who become ambassadors rise through the political sections of a series of embassies. Martin was an exception. A colleague recalled that when Martin was administrative counselor to Ambassador Douglas Dillon in Paris, the embassy ran like a well-oiled machine. Nothing ever went awry. No visiting congressman ever complained. Martin mastered every nook and cranny of the mission.

dreds of thousands of Europeans if the Soviets chose to roll across the plains of Germany. (Every U.S. Embassy does routine contingency planning for the evacuation not only of itself and of all Americans in its purview, but also of all foreigners who would be threatened in the event of an American withdrawal. These latter are called KIPs—key indigenous personnel, a phrase that refers centrally but not exclusively to foreign intelligence assets.) Martin was also during this period a member of the U.S. delegation to the Laos Conference. And of course he closely followed the course and conclusion of the French war against the Viet Minh. He and his wife, Dorothy, also in their years in Paris began to assemble a fine collection of old French maps.

In addition to his open duties, Martin helped run a very quiet intelligence network, an operation that was eventually taken over by the Central Intelligence Agency.

After a stint as a faculty adviser at the Air War College, where he tried to insert into the curriculum some discussion of the kind of war the French had just lost in Indochina, Martin moved from one senior assignment in the State Department to another, including the job in President Kennedy's Alliance for Progress. In 1963 he was promoted to the permanent rank of career minister and named ambassador to Thailand.

Even Martin's most severe critics admit that he performed masterfully in Bangkok, both officially and personally. In a four-year battle with the U.S. military, he succeeded in keeping U.S. ground forces out of Thailand. Maybe eighteen-year-old American troops could tell the difference between a good Vietnamese and a bad one, he was inclined to say, but he doubted it; and he was damned certain they couldn't tell the difference between a good Thai and a bad one. And as long as he was ambassador they weren't going to get the chance to try. "It's a funny thing," he would also say, "from what I hear about the war in Vietnam, you don't see any white faces on the other side."

At the same time, Martin succeeded in negotiating a series of agreements with the Thais that permitted the U.S. to build or upgrade both a port and seven major air bases from which American planes spied on and bombed its enemies in Laos and Vietnam. Thailand is the only country in Southeast Asia that was never colonized, a fact of which the Thais are rightly proud. They guard their sovereignty jealously. Martin was able to get the facilities his government needed by treaty language that made it absolutely clear that the bases belonged to and were commanded by the Thais, and by throwing in a network of modern highways connecting the widely scattered bases. Even in 1984, travelers on certain stretches of long, level road in Thailand can see the faded markers for emergency runways. In Thailand, Martin did not put in only eight military installations supporting his government's wars; he put in Thailand's modern communications infrastructure.

Of course the morality of the goal—miles of concrete on Thai soil to support B-52s taking off to rain death on the Ho Chi Minh Trail—is open to debate. But when Lyndon Johnson decided that those facilities were what was required, he had an ambassador in Bangkok who knew how to get them.

Martin's personal success in Bangkok was partly a matter of luck. At a state dinner for visiting Vice President Hubert Humphrey, after the prime minister of Thailand gave the toast to the President of the United States, Humphrey rose to reciprocate with the toast to the King of Thailand. Martin interceded, and gave the toast himself. After the dinner, he explained both to Humphrey and to a visiting Pepsi-Cola executive that President Kennedy had committed the long-accepted understanding to language: The ambassador was the President's personal representative to the country to which he was assigned, senior there not only to the Secretary of State but even to the Vice President. No ambassador ever guarded that prerogative more fiercely. Martin emphasized the point both with Humphrey and with the Pepsi-Cola executive, Richard Nixon. "If you become President yourself some day, Mr. Vice President," he told both, "you can be sure that I will guard your interests as closely as I did President Johnson's to-night."

Bangkok was a triumph. But in 1966 an adopted son was killed in the Central Highlands of Vietnam when a .50-caliber round ripped through the helicopter he was piloting.* That may or may not have been the turning point. But somewhere along the line, the New Deal liberal hardened into an eccentric anticommunist—the kind who imagines that a Jane Fonda can pervert the broad will of the American people, the kind Martin was when he arrived seven years later in Saigon.

In 1967, the pungency of the language in his cables to Washington about the ongoing effort to keep the military out of Thailand finally was too much for Secretary of State Dean Rusk, and Martin was relieved.

One year later, Richard Nixon was elected President. Graham Martin was rehabilitated and named ambassador to Rome. There he gathered around him some of the men whom he would later bring with him to Saigon. He also took over control of the slush funds with which Washington attempted to influence Italian politics, a function that in most embassies is the domain of the CIA. During his three years in Rome,

---

* Another son was killed on the day he graduated from college in the sports car Martin had given him as a graduation present.

for example, Martin helped finance that moderate faction of the Italian Socialist Party headed by Bettino Craxi, who would become Italy's first socialist prime minister, in 1983.

Martin was sworn in as ambassador to the Republic of Vietnam on June 24, 1973. The nightmare scenarios started to unfold less than a year later, with the charges, denials, hearings and revelations that culminated in the resignation of Richard Nixon on August 9, 1974. The American agony was covered in full in the Vietnamese press and on the national TV system the Americans had given South Vietnam. Few Vietnamese could understand how the leader of their powerful ally could be brought down by what seemed to them very minor political chicanery.

About two weeks later, the U.S. Senate by a margin of just two votes rejected a resolution that would have cut off all further U.S. military aid to South Vietnam. The Vietnamese high command, using accounting techniques the Americans had taught them, had estimated that they needed $1.45 billion for fiscal year 1975. In the end, Congress appropriated less than half that amount, $700 million.

Further, the Yom Kippur War of the previous fall had led quickly to the Arab oil embargo and eventually to the quadrupling of the cost of all petroleum products. In the United States, the embargo meant the Sunday closing of gas stations, and long lines on the other days of the week. It was during this period that a visiting three-star general told Thomas Polgar, the CIA station chief, "I'll be goddamned if the U.S. government should be sending money to Saigon to buy gasoline so these f - - - - -' cowboys can ride around Saigon on their Hondas while my wife has to wait in line for an hour to get a tankful of gas."

In fact, except for the U.S. military men still in Vietnam, in the Defense Attaché's Office, the U.S. military itself joined Congress and the many other forces in American society working to cut aid to Saigon. In 1973, the Pentagon adopted a new way of allocating its military assistance programs to friendly countries. The new system—called MASF, for Military Assistance Service Funded—meant that appropriations to the South Vietnamese Air Force, for example, came directly out of the U.S. Air Force budget, rather than from the Pentagon appropriation as a whole. And the U.S. forces were no longer *in* Vietnam. All of a sudden the Pentagon computer in Indiantown Gap, Pennsylvania, started kicking back requisitions for fuel, weapons and ammunition that the mission in Saigon had every reason to think should already have been on their way to the South Vietnamese. In a matter of fifteen months, running from the Yom Kippur War to the end of 1974, Saigon found itself having to fight a poor man's war.

General Homer Smith and Ambassador Martin had to plead with Cao
Van Vien, the chairman of the Joint General Staff, and President
Thieu himself, to order commanders in the field to cut their expendi-
ture of ammunition. South Vietnamese soldiers spent part of each day
stooping over in the dirt to pick up unspent rounds. In 1974, after
these cutbacks had gone into effect, a visiting Pentagon delegation determined that South Vietnamese forces in combat were expending ten
percent of the ammunition expended by comparable U.S. forces in
static, defensive operations.

And there was a further factor in the scaffolding of South Vietnam's
fate, a factor that genuinely surprised Graham Martin, who does not
easily admit to being surprised by anything. The committed antiwar
left in the United States never gave up. Naïvely, Martin thought that
with the signing of the Paris Peace Accords and the return of the
American prisoners of war, the antiwar movement would fade to in-
significance. The fact that Martin thought that the Jane Fondas or the
activists in the Indochina Resource Center, the most effective of the
congressional lobbying groups, cared more about the POWs than they
did about political prisoners in Nguyen Van Thieu's jails or the continued American financing of South Vietnam's struggle against the
North is a measure of his removal from the rhythms of American
opinion.

It is possible that a day went by during Graham Martin's tour as
ambassador to South Vietnam when he did not find occasion to refer
to the "Saigon chapter of the worldwide society of disaffected intellectuals," but not likely. Later, the preferred formulation was to call
them "Lluies"—"Lenin's league of useful idiots," which referred to a
passage in Lenin's writings to the effect that communists didn't have
to worry: When the going got tough, capitalism's intelligentsia and
opinion makers, such as journalists—its "useful idiots"—would do communism's work for it.

Now, with South Vietnam's final agony eighteen days old, Martin was
coming back. There had been a delay somewhere along the line. The
well-appointed plane from the fleet of them at Andrews Air Force
Base that collectively comprised Air Force One slid over the coast of
Vietnam in the blackness of 2:30 A.M., March 28.

At one of the seats, cigarette smoke lazed in a cone of light. A handsome gray-haired man made prematurely elderly by the damned cigarettes was reading cables. There was little else to do on the plane, except to talk to men who did not know as much as he did. His duty was
to learn even more. As routinely and unthinkingly as he smoked, he
did his duty. Forty years on, habits are set.

II

As the plane carrying Graham Martin and the Weyand mission approached Vietnam, Russell Mott was at an American hotel in Da Nang called the Alamo. He got word from Mel Chatman, who was at a dock near the riverside consulate, to bring his convoy of trucks and other vehicles filled with Vietnamese and a few Americans to the dock. A barge that would take them out to the harbor was pulling in.

Mott got in the lead jeep and led the convoy down Revolution Street, past the city hall—and then ran up against a roadblock of drums and concertina wire manned by one lone ARVN trooper.

Mott got out to talk to the man. It was three-thirty in the morning. The young soldier had orders that no one was to pass this checkpoint. He held his rifle, pointed in the air. Mott talked reason, but the man had his orders.

Mott had a young ARVN lieutenant with him in the jeep, a friend of a friend. The lieutenant had been useful in the last few days, and Mott had promised to get him out. He called for him now. Mott was fluent in Vietnamese, but he thought the young soldier might listen more earnestly to a Vietnamese officer.

Mott held a 9-mm. Chinese handgun loose behind his hip. "If you can't get him to take the barrels down and let us through, I'm going to execute him," Mott said. "But don't threaten him unless you have to. He looks kind of jumpy."

"The war's over, younger brother," the lieutenant said to the boy. "We have refugees here, people who worked for the Americans. We're going to Saigon. You have to let us pass."

Mott watched as the boy lowered his weapon, inch by inch. And as the gun slowly lowered, the boy started to cry.

"It's okay, nephew," Mott said as the lieutenant accepted the rifle. "Go home and get your family and come down to the dock at the American Consulate and we'll take you out."

The young soldier helped them dismantle the barricade and slipped away into the night.

They realized as soon as it was turned over that the weapon didn't have a clip in it. "I was ready to waste the kid," Mott thought to himself. "And he wasn't even armed."

12

Wolfgang Lehmann met the plane carrying the Weyand mission
and the ambassador at three o'clock in the morning on Friday, March
28. He traveled in Martin's limousine to the ambassador's residence,
where he stayed until four-thirty. In his briefing, Lehmann concentrated on the rapidly deteriorating situation in Da Nang. The ambassador said that maybe he'd get a few hours' sleep and fly up to see the
situation in Da Nang for himself.

Lehmann said that he didn't think that was a very good idea at all.

II

As Lehmann and the ambassador were talking, the barge was being
tugged to a dock at the riverside U.S. Consulate in Da Nang. The
final maneuver—at precisely four-thirty—was so skillfully done that
Vietnamese sleeping on the dock didn't awake.

Things did not remain silent and peaceful for long, although the
loading of most of the remaining consulate staff, including Vietnamese employees and their families, went smoothly at the beginning.

Mel Chatman and his colleagues also managed to load a company
of ARVN engineers, who had helped provide security. The engineers
and their families had arrived in dump trucks that were normally
used to haul gravel.

Both ends of the street in front of the consulate had been closed off. But with the withdrawal of the engineers, the consulate's normal security detail was unable to prevent troops and civilians from pouring through the consulate grounds and down to the dock.

The deck of the barge was seven feet above the pier. Americans on the barge had jerry-rigged a gangplank, and had been able to maintain order there. But now people started clambering up the tires that hung from the side of the barge, in some cases hauling up their Hondas and stereo sets with them. A civilian logistician who worked for DAO named Ernest Hey had arrived in Da Nang earlier in the week to help arrange the removal of critical matériel. On Thursday, Hey had recommended to Al Francis that they start moving people instead of weapons and ammunition. Francis had agreed. Hey was on the barge now, and among his other chores grabbed a motorcycle whenever he saw one and wrestled it overboard.

Then people started tossing small children from the pier up onto the barge. Some missed, the children falling into the black water between the dock and the barge, which rolled with the wakes of other traffic on the river and the surges of the several thousand people on board.

At five-thirty, there was a rush of ARVN troops. From the shore, Francis ordered the barge to depart.

But Ernie Hey and the other Americans on board were unable to free a thick rope that ran from a bitt on the barge down to the dock. And the Vietnamese mob on the dock was not about to free the cable at that end. In fact, lithe young men used it to scramble up onto the barge.

Without realizing what he was doing, the captain of the tug let the barge drift back into the dock. The men scrambling up the rope like monkeys were crushed. The tug strained to break the rope. More young men and boys clambered up the rope. The barge swung back to the pier and they were killed. Hey could see it all, but there was nothing he could do, no way to get in touch with the captain of the tug. The ghastly scenario was played out twice more and then something finally gave way and they were free and that particular roundelay of death ended.

III

When the barge was loaded and gone, Chatman caught a couple of hours of sleep in the consulate building.

In the morning, before setting off in an Air America helicopter to confer with General Truong and to check conditions at the city's two airports and above all to try to find more ships, Consul General Al

Francis told Chatman that they still had some people at the nearby USAID hotel called the Alamo. Could he go over there and try to keep them calm? "Tell them that we're doing everything we can to try to get them out," Francis said.

Chatman had a van, and his walkie-talkie. As he made his way from the consulate to the hotel, he thought that he was the last American official on the ground in Da Nang. That was not true; there were a few others elsewhere. But Chatman was alone, and for the hours through midday when he succeeded in restoring some order at the hotel, he was the only American there.

People rushed by him in the streets, many of them carrying furniture or office furnishings from some place they had looted. In the midst of the rushing Vietnamese, Chatman was struck by a Westerner in a pinstriped suit, neat and cool as a pin, adjusting his tie. Chatman assumed he was a Frenchman or some other European.

When he got to the Alamo, he discovered at least one source of the booty: Vietnamese streamed from it like ants with everything light enough to carry. Some of the looters had worked in the hotel.

The object of Francis' concern was a group of about six hundred people—sixty or seventy U.S. mission guards and their families.

"Why the hell don't you do something?" Chatman said to one of the leaders of the guards. "Mr. Francis is flying all over Da Nang trying to find a way to get you out of here, and you're letting people loot our property. Jesus."

In frustration, he then did a very uncharacteristic thing, wrenching his body around and letting fly with the side of his foot at the backside of a fat woman jogging out of the hotel with a chair on her head. The woman kept going, the chair tottering but safely hers, and Chatman lurched: "Sprained ankle," he thought as he put some weight on the kicking foot.

For several minutes, he walked about with the aid of one of the guards. Then they found a dry mop that he was able to use as a crutch.

Chatman discovered quickly that the guards were immobilized not only by their fear that they would be left behind—and if so, why not join in the looting?—but also by an armed ARVN soldier who seemed to be on the verge of a bellicose frenzy in his threats against the guards and their families.

"This is buffalo s - - -," Chatman said in Vietnamese. "He's one and you're ten. Tell him to *di di** outta here."

"He's crazy," the guards said.

Chatman carried a .38 Smith & Wesson. He put his hand around the butt of it in his pocket, an obvious signal, and had a few words

* *Di*, pronounced dee, is the verb to go.

with the man. "I'm trying to get these people out of here," he said. "If you can stop making trouble, maybe I can help you too." With that, the soldier calmed himself.

IV

That same Friday afternoon, Ed Daly, the founder and president of World Airways, bullied and cursed his way into the dim, spacious ambassador's office on the third floor of the American Embassy in Saigon. He had raised such hell getting in that an embassy Marine accompanied him.

World Airways at that time was a charter airline. With several others, it made plenty of money that spring shuttling weapons and rice into Phnom Penh from Saigon. For the past three days, since Wednesday, Daly had diverted his 727s to Da Nang, under embassy contract, to fly out Americans and refugees.

The ambassador permitted himself the slight indignity of standing. "Give the gun to the Marine if you want to talk to me," he said.

Daly removed the pistol from the bulging shoulder holster under his loose Hawaiian sports shirt and handed it over to the Marine. His belligerence remained intact.

"What are those bastards at Tan Son Nhut going to do if I take off without their goddamned clearance?" he asked.

"I imagine they'll shoot you down," the ambassador replied.

"And then what will you do?"

"Applaud," the ambassador said.

V

It was hot when Al Francis set down in his helicopter next to the Alamo in midafternoon. He trotted under the rotor wash and then walked quickly, eyes down, to Chatman. "Don't ask me a lot of questions," he said. "I've got to get you out of here. It's gone. Walk over to the chopper and get on and don't raise a fuss."

"What do I tell these people?"

"Tell them we're still trying," Francis said. "But make it short, Mel."

"You got an extra radio for me?"

"Sure."

Chatman gave one of the leaders his walkie-talkie, and told them in quick Vietnamese that either he would be back or he would find a boat for them and let them know on the radio where to go to meet the boat.

He and Francis were retreating as calmly as they could to the helicopter. The guards were suspicious, but in control of themselves.

Then, at the last moment, as Chatman, following Francis, backed up into the helicopter, a Vietnamese woman in early middle age simply barreled through him and onto the aircraft.

She was of average size for a Vietnamese woman in her thirties, about the same size as a skinny American boy of medium height at fourteen or fifteen. And there wasn't a chance in the world that she wasn't going to get past Chatman. He glanced at Francis. The decision was instantaneous. Lift-off, with an unexpected passenger who crouched like an adolescent tiger, a hundred pounds (maximum) of survival instinct in full flower.

That helicopter took Chatman to one of the sets of docks on the sea and Francis left him there to continue his search for ships. Chatman got in a Vietnamese Navy patrol boat that transferred him to a slightly larger Navy ship.

Chatman had never seen so many ships of all sizes steaming about in a patch of sea. It was the harbor equivalent of the crazed traffic in the streets of Da Nang, tugboats and barges and merchant ships of half a dozen countries and the Vietnamese Navy and sampans and fishing boats all crowded with people trying to escape, and bodies bobbing in the light grayish swells.

He rested for twenty minutes, orienting himself, gathering his strength as the afternoon light faded.

There was a young ARVN officer on board, not the captain but an Army man temporarily assigned to that small ship. In good English, he explained calmly to Chatman that he had sent his family south to Saigon but he was from Da Nang and would not run and would die there if it came to that.

As Chatman talked further to the young officer, it occurred to him that he might be able to get some Vietnamese Navy ships to rescue the six hundred people at the Alamo. He raised Francis on his radio, and learned that the consul general himself had been pleading with personal contacts in the Navy to arrange something for their remaining people, without luck.

Francis told Chatman that if he could find someone to get him to the naval headquarters he—Chatman—might be able to get some ships to help them.

One of the many Western and Japanese contracting companies that did business there during the war was called Alaska Barge and Transport.* Alaska Barge and Transport among its assets had a speedboat

* Alaska Barge and Transport was set up by Ted Serong, the retired Australian officer who was among those who had advised Thieu to withdraw to more defensible lines long before the offensive.

so powerful and swift it might have been a hydroplane—Chatman was never sure about that. At the moment, that boat happened to be idling next to the ship carrying Mel Chatman. It was piloted by a grinning young American with long, dirty-blond hair.

Chatman spoke to the guy. Then he radioed back to the Vietnamese at the hotel and told them to make their way as inconspicuously as possible to the docks Chatman had left from. "I'm going to try something," he told the guards.

Chatman had no idea where the Vietnamese naval headquarters in Da Nang was. The young Alaska Barge and Transport man knew. He took Chatman to the protected cove that held the headquarters and put him ashore.

Because of his ankle, Chatman still needed help. He flagged down a young Vietnamese with a Honda, and the young man took him the few hundred yards to the headquarters building.

VI

Now the communists closed quickly. From the north, the North Vietnamese Army's 324B and 325C Divisions advanced along Elephant Valley and were enveloping the entire western flank of the city. To the south, the 711th and 304th Divisions, augmented by other units, pressed along the Thu Bon River and attacked the district towns of Duc Duc* and Dai Loc. Da Nang was now within range of enemy artillery.

At noon, a message from the intelligence branch of JGS informed Truong that Da Nang would be attacked overnight. He was instructed to fly all remaining helicopters and jets south to Phan Rang and another base still in Saigon's control.

By two in the afternoon, Saigon's control of all the hamlets and villages around Da Nang had collapsed. All regular and militia troops had either fled to Da Nang or melted into the people. In Da Nang itself, neither the main ammunition or fuel dump was functioning; the men who ran them had fled.

Dusk has just set in when the communists opened up on the MR 1 headquarters, the naval base and numerous other military installations from their positions in Elephant Valley. The fire quickly became accurate, as it was adjusted by observers in the city.

Truong called Thieu and recommended immediate evacuation by

---

* In the early 1950s, when the United States was bankrolling the entire cost of the French war against the Viet Minh, an irate member of Congress asked at a committee meeting what in the name of God the fate of a place named Duc Duc had to do with America's national security.

sea. But Thieu was incapable of committing himself to any clear-cut order. He did not tell Truong whether to withdraw or to hold and fight. He simply asked how many troops could be extricated to safety in case of a withdrawal.

Minutes after that conversation ended, an artillery round found its target at a relay station and all ARVN communications with Saigon ceased.

VII

In his first five minutes at the naval headquarters, Mel Chatman determined that the South Vietnamese Navy had no assets to spare to rescue his six hundred people. Polite refusals changed to brusque, panicky refusals when the shells started landing.

The young Vietnamese with the Honda was waiting for him—waiting for his fare. And the young American with the speedboat was waiting for him as well, grinning nervously now and ready to do what was required in a crisis, within reason.

Chatman gave him the name of the one dock area he knew, where he thought his people would be waiting. The young man knew it. But as they approached it, he cut the engine to idle.

It was late dusk. Chatman could make out the faces of some of the guards and their wives and children. "Closer!" he shouted to the young man. "I've got to talk to these people!"

"This is close enough, man," the young man said, standing at the controls and eyeing the eager thousands on the docks with the mature wariness of a young man with a speedboat facing thousands of desperate people on shore while artillery shells landed here and there in the gloom.

The boat was rocking in the water now, thirty yards off from the docks, the faces still clearly visible in the fast-fading light.

Chatman stood, legs wide for balance, pain still in that ankle, and cupped his hands to his mouth. Then he realized that one hand still held the little radio. He formed a miniature megaphone with one hand, held the radio two feet away in the other, pressed it on.

"Get away!" he shouted in Vietnamese. "Find whatever boats you can, from here or some other place! Get into the harbor! We will try to find you! But don't wait here for me! I don't have any ships! I have nothing! You must get out on your own!"

The younger man with the speedboat let him shout, then gunned the engines and dipped into a turn away from the docks. Chatman sank heavily into a padded corner of the small deck, the walkie-talkie held loosely between his thighs, and sobbed.

VIII

With Thieu's refusal to give a clear order and the break in communications with Saigon, Truong decided it was time to salvage as many men as he could from Da Nang. He discussed the evacuation with Admiral Ho Van Ky Thoai, the naval commander for the region, and then met with his remaining subordinate commanders, ordering the displacement of all units during the night toward three embarkation points—the end of the Hai Van Pass; the foot of Marble Mountain, just south of the city; and the mouth of the river.

Before dawn on Saturday, a thick fog set in along the coast. All available naval ships were at the rendezvous points as planned, but the tide was low and the ships could not beach. Thousands of men waded into the surf and swam to the closest small ships. Among them was General Ngo Quang Truong, who was not a good swimmer, and had to be supported by aides as they struggled to reach the nearest landing craft.

IX

Truong was out but much of his disintegrating army was not. About an hour after the MR 1 commander left shore, Captain Cuong talked his way onto a helicopter flying north to the naval headquarters.

General Nguyen Van Diem's helicopter sat smoldering on its skids in a soccer field strewn with corpses. Knots of soldiers in and out of uniform clustered for shelter in the headquarters buildings. They explained to Cuong that most of the crowd the night before had run back toward the city when the shelling started. Some had tried to swim in the darkness to the lights of the ships offshore. No one Cuong talked to had seen what had happened to General Diem's helicopter, but one man said he was sure it had come in before the shelling. "I was down near the water, but I heard it come in," he said. "Right after it landed there were shots. Many, for a long time. In every crowd now, there are many communist soldiers, dressed like us."

"Yes," Cuong said.

He did not find General Diem, the commander of his division, among the dead. Many of them had been burned. He did not want to stay with them long because they stank, and the shells were still landing here and there. But as Cuong turned to leave, the sun touched a bright spot at his feet. He reached down to the shred of a shirt with a brass star sewn to it.

On the grounds of the Navy base, Cuong finally did pick up an airline bag, so he could carry his pistol and code machine out of sight.

Then he walked back into the city, where there was much less shelling.

The day before, the people had been frightened and disorderly, but the violence was kept in check. Soldiers took what they wanted with threats. Now the chaos was mixed with violence, the short blatter of an M-1 in the next block and people suddenly scattering. Armed bands of militiamen and regular soldiers and Marines—and the Marines the worst of all, some of them now truly drunk—moved toward the water or the air base, shooting civilians in their way, the pop-pop-pop of gunfire always nearby.

And yet even that day, off the main streets, there were some quiet streets, and the few open shops of those who had decided not to flee. As he made his slow, careful way to the headquarters compound near the air base, Captain Cuong stopped for a morning bowl of *pho,** again for a cup of tea and again for lunch. He said nothing, and listened carefully. Most of those who would stay had decided simply not to fight the armed men for the places on the ships. But it was clear also from the whispered conversations around him and even the occasional bold speech that now in Da Nang in every block, every shop, there were people willing to reveal themselves as communists.

The communists had stopped shelling the MR 1 headquarters compound. And, remarkably, Colonel Nhon was still in his office. Cuong quickly told him what he had seen and heard in the city, at the end producing the bit of cloth with the brass star.

Colonel Nhon puffed out his cheeks and expelled a stream of breath. He was silent for a few moments, working his mouth as if to force out whatever was in his chest with great lungfuls of air.

"He was a good man, nephew," he said finally. "It's too bad we did not have a few more like him."

"Yes," Cuong said.

If Colonel Nhon knew that General Truong had already left firm ground, he did not tell Cuong. In fact Truong was issuing orders from the larger naval ship to which he had been transferred.

"Now we have to run away," Nhon said.

Colonel Nhon had a transmitter, and after many tries succeeded in reaching the captain of a patrol boat—a friend—who agreed to come for them at midnight off the docks of the Navy base.

He and Cuong melted into the crowds and made their way to the base, where they found a room in which to hide. At some point during the long evening wait, Cuong remembered the two agents. Colonel Nhon said that he had given each of them three months' pay. "Maybe

* Fuh. A wonderful soup of noodles and scallions and bean sprouts with beef, pork or chicken, eaten any time of day but especially in the morning.

they got out," he said. "But I think both of them will stay with this side." Cuong thought the colonel was right. In any case, he never saw either of them again.

The shelling had eased off that afternoon and evening. But it began again in earnest at about eleven. Only a few landed nearby. They heard the others whistling overhead toward the sea. Still they waited. And when they swam for ten minutes toward the signal of the boat that had come for them, they heard the shells splashing into the water around them. They clambered onto the darkened ship and the engines roared.

X

Every agency and congressional committee in Washington that had anything to do with Vietnam tried to have someone in the Weyand mission. Ken Quinn, who had spent years in the Mekong delta working with the Hoa Hao* as a Foreign Service Officer, in 1975 was on the staff of the National Security Council. He made the plane. Soon after the group arrived, Quinn drove out to the consulate in Bien Hoa, which lay just fifteen miles northeast of the capital on Highway 1.

Quinn looked up Charles Lahiguera, an old friend who was then the number-two man in the consulate, which was responsible for all the provinces around Saigon. He asked Lahiguera how long South Vietnam would last.

"We've probably got until August," Lahiguera answered.

---

* A religious sect, pronounced Wah How.

13

Arthur Lord of NBC was up until three in the morning in the penthouse bar of the Caravelle Hotel trying to find out if Ed Daly was planning to make another flight into Da Nang on Saturday. On Friday, when the last flight was mobbed and the embassy first lost radio contact with Al Francis, the embassy terminated the contract. USAID officials told Daly that if he tried to fly again on Saturday, they would move to cancel his license.

At three in the morning, the founder and president of World Airways was drunk and loud, but still ambiguous about whether he would fly in the morning. Arthur Lord gave up.

Mike Marriott had been in the group earlier. He liked Daly—liked his crudeness, his drinking and his defiance of authority.

When Marriott got to the office that Saturday morning, an hour or two after General Truong waded into the surf off Da Nang, Brian Ellis, his producer, suggested that Bruce Dunning, Marriott and a sound man named Mai Van Duc go out to Tan Son Nhut and see what Daly might be up to.

Daly was at the airport. Marriott walked up to him and said, "Hey, Ed, what are you going to do?"

"I'm going to Da Nang," Daly said.

Marriott laughed. "What the f --- are you talking about, mate? They'll pull your license."

"They're my planes," Daly said.

"When are you flying?"

"Now."

"Can we come with you?"

"Hey," Daly said, "the more the merrier."

At that moment, Tom Aspell, a cameraman for the London-based Independent Television News, wandered over and asked Marriott what was going on. ITN had a cooperative arrangement with ABC News in the U.S. and was therefore a competitor of CBS. But Aspell was a New Zealander, and Marriott had known him for years; further, what was going on was rapidly becoming obvious. Paul Vogle, a thin United Press International correspondent who had first come to Vietnam eighteen years earlier as an instructor at the University of Hue, had come to Tan Son Nhut earlier with the World crew.

Daly had two 727s in Saigon. He was going to send both up, but with the second taking off half an hour later. He and his crew—Ken Healy, his chief pilot; a copilot; and a stewardess—and the five journalists boarded the first plane.

They were not interfered with on takeoff. Daly had laid on a small bar. Marriott allowed himself one drink on the forty-five-minute flight up the coast.

When they reached Da Nang, they circled the air base—two long parallel runways—several times at twelve to fourteen thousand feet. Then they swooped down for a pass at five hundred feet, climbed out of it. Marriott, Dunning and Daly had joined Healy and the copilot in the cockpit. They were amazed at the calmness of the scene. It was midmorning on a beautiful day. The air base lay seemingly deserted under bright blue skies. The night before, Marriott and Daly had listened to embassy officers telling them that the airport would be under artillery and rocket attack, and, if not, swarming with refugees. But beneath them all was still, and empty.

Daly turned to Marriott and Dunning. "You guys have had combat experience," he said. "What does it look like to you?"

"Well, it doesn't look like a city under attack to me," Marriott said. "Where are the refugees? It looks *too* quiet."

"What do you want to do?" Daly asked, as if the CBS newsmen were coconspirators in this venture—which was exactly the way Marriott took the question.

"Hang on, Ed," he said. "It's not a question of what *we* want to do. Remember, we asked you if we could come along on a refugee rescue mission that you're carrying out against the American government's advice. We're along for the ride. What are *you* going to do?"

Ever since they arrived over the base, the copilot had been trying to raise the control tower, with no success. Daly turned to Healy and asked what he thought they should do.

"It looks quiet," Healy said. "I think we can go in. Let's make another pass, even lower, and I'll wave the wings to show we're friendly."

But at that moment the control tower came up. "It's okay, we're here," the voice said in English. "You're cleared for landing, World."

Healy made a normal approach, landed, turned off the runway toward the terminal.

And then they poured out from the concrete revetments where F-5s and the other VNAF aircraft had been sheltered before they were flown south. They poured out in jeeps and trucks and armored personnel carriers and even in an old bulbous-nosed black Citroën taxi from the late 1940s; and running—women and children among them but overwhelmingly they were armed Marines and infantrymen, in a crowd of at least two thousand and perhaps four.

It must have taken enormous ruthless discipline after word reached them from Saigon that the two planes were on the way. Now all discipline collapsed. No; the mob still had vestiges of integrity. Two APCs* on either side of the plane and other military vehicles shepherded it down a taxiway toward the revetments, allowed it to turn.

Aspell and Marriott had a quick conference. "When they lower the ramp, I'm going to jump off, get the reverse shot," the ITN man said.

"Bulls - - -," Marriott said. "You want the film; they're desperate for their lives. You'd have to fight your way back on, alone."

Now Daly was lowering the stairs at the tail of the aircraft. And Aspell was going to go ahead and get off the plane.

"If you get stuck," Marriott said to him, "if you get stranded out there, go to the very southern end of the runways; you understand what I'm saying, mate? Still on the base, but the farthest away from the terminal you can get. Okay?"

"Right," Aspell said. Halfway down the stairs, he jumped to the tarmac, swung his camera to his shoulder.

Then there were three of them from the plane on the stairs, Daly closest to the ground, Paul Vogle shouting something in Vietnamese and Marriott behind Vogle. Daly had a pistol that he fired in the air, and swung at some of the soldiers. He was trying to drag the women and children into the line of men rushing by him. But the men were armed. They shot women and children to reach the point of the crowd

* Armored personnel carriers.

that pushed past Daly up the flimsy stairs. The ramp started to bend off to one side. They shot each other, and Marriott saw the bodies on the tarmac. As the men rushed past him, smoke curled from some of their M-16s, all of which were cocked. Marriott looked at the safeties on the M-16s and thought, "My God, I'm in an airliner half filled with JP-4 fuel . . ."

Eventually there would be 285 passengers on board, all but a handful of them soldiers. Most of them were Hac Bao—Black Panthers—from the toughest, most elite unit in the 1st Division. When about 150 of them had made it on board, Daly pulled himself back up to the top of the stairs and reached for the intercom. "Captain, let's get out of here," he said. His arms were clawed and bleeding and his pants had been pulled down to the tops of his thighs, exposing his boxer shorts.

They still kept coming as the plane began its roll, more than a hundred of them making it on even after it started rolling. In that final last rush, the thirty or forty seconds before the speed of the plane was too much, it was truly the survival of the fittest, and the killers.

Early in the roll, Tom Aspell jogged alongside the bent ramp, passed his camera to Marriott and cried "Grab me!"

Marriott passed Aspell's camera and then his own back to Duc, his sound man. He reached for Aspell's hands and got them. But now Vietnamese were clutching at Aspell as their skyhook, their passage out, and with their weight and the accelerating speed he slipped from Marriott's grasp and disappeared.

Now Vogle was back in the plane. Duc had anchored an audio-visual cable somewhere inside the plane and looped it around himself and then Marriott, and Marriott held on to Ed Daly's belt, and the three of them were being pulled toward the wrong end of the stairway, which was now roughly parallel with the ground, and Marriott figured they were going through sixty, seventy, eighty miles an hour, and still there were twenty or more hard-core Black Panthers clustered on the stairs, inching toward them. Eighty, ninety, a hundred miles an hour, and the weakest peeled off, their fingers giving way, and they dropped and rolled on the taxiway. Marriott heard the explosion of a hand grenade. Then another, which sounded as if it did damage. Shooting.

He glanced off to the runway and saw that it was blocked by vehicles. Still they picked up speed. He suddenly realized that Healy was going to take off from the taxiway, felt the nose lift. In seconds, as Daly and Marriott and Duc hauled themselves back into the plane, the undercarriage tore through a concertina-wire fence; the wire trailed off two hundred feet behind the plane. And then, it seemed, everyone was off the ramp.

The plane was lurching, pushing and shoving as it strained to gain altitude.

The stewardess worked the lever that might, conceivably, have closed the bent staircase. Daly and Marriott realized at the same time that a man who looked to be ninety-eight was caught between the fuselage and the stairs. "S - - -," they said simultaneously.

They leaned into the nearly upright but still open ramp, grabbed the old man by his arms, and signaled to the stewardess to inch the thing down. They pulled him into the plane. His chest was crushed. Marriott was sure most of his ribs were broken. In Saigon, he walked off the plane.

They never did get the ramp fully closed. But that was a minor problem.

They could see out the back that they were leaking fuel. But only a thin stream. Daly and Marriott went back up to the cockpit. The flaps were locked open. They made the flight south nose up, for altitude, stretching what should have been a forty-five-minute flight to an agonizing two hours.

Agonizing for two main reasons. When they tried to retract the landing gear, they got a green light on the nose wheel but the other two lights, for the main undercarriage, stayed red. The copilot then set the gear for landing, but those lights wouldn't go green either. So they were faced with the possibility of a belly landing.

Twenty minutes down the coast, the backup plane flew under them. They radioed: "You look okay; we can see you're leaking fuel and the flaps are locked, and there's a hole in the underside of your right wing." (The grenade that hit, locking the flaps.) Then: "Also, I can see something hanging from your undercarriage, and it sure looks like a body."

The other reason the flight was agonizing, at least for the first hour, was that there were about 280 soldiers back there with cocked M-16s and hand grenades, some of them with the pins pulled out.

When Daly had satisfied himself as best he could as to the airworthiness of the plane and the possibilities of a safe landing, he and Marriott moved back into the cabin. They saw Vogle working his way toward them while accumulating an armful of weapons and ammunition from the soldiers. Daly still had his pistol. Marriott was a large Australian, but unarmed. They reached out their hands to the men in the front rows. Silently, meekly, the men surrendered their weapons.

While Daly was conferring with Healy about the damage, Mike Marriott conferred with the copilot about Tom Aspell. Marriott was well plugged in at Air America, and knew the right frequencies. A little more than an hour after the World 727 left Da Nang, an Air America helicopter successfully extracted Aspell from the air base.

When the loaded 727 landed at Saigon and the undercarriage held rigid, not collapsing up into the plane as they had feared it might, the crew and the few journalists in the backup plane cheered. Several crossed themselves.

South Vietnamese MPs led the Black Panthers and the other troops off to waiting black trucks for their transfer to military jails.

A detail of the MPs was assigned the chore of extracting the mangled bodies of soldiers in the undercarriage who had been crushed to death when the copilot attempted to retract the gear.

Vietnam was wired for sound. All the major news-gathering organizations in Saigon, for example, had contacts at Tan Son Nhut. And there were journalists on both planes. As word reached the control tower at Tan Son Nhut of the possible emergency landing, Brian Ellis realized that he might have a major story on his hands. He checked. Only Mike Marriott, as it turned out, had a valid exit visa.

Ellis got Marriott's passport from the office secretary and went to the airport.

Marriott and Duc were detained for twenty minutes by a Vietnamese police colonel. When the colonel turned his back, Marriott and the sound man slipped away.

Marriott told Ellis what he had. Ellis said, "Mike, you're not going to like this [Marriott had a lovely Vietnamese wife and a small boy in Saigon], but there's a plane leaving for Hong Kong in an hour, and you've got to be on it, with the film."

"S - - -," Marriott said.

They satellited from Hong Kong that night. Because of the time difference, the film made the Saturday CBS news in the States. And Marriott later heard, from a friend, that Gerald Ford saw the film, turned to the friend, and said, "That's it. It's time to pull the plug. Vietnam is gone."

Other UPI reporters debriefed an emotionally devastated Paul Vogle and filed UPI's first reports of the flight. Several hours later, Vogle himself was sufficiently recovered to write what his bureau chief, Alan Dawson, has rightly called the single most memorable news story of the 1975 offensive:*

* Vogle's story differs in some minor particulars from the account above, which is based on Mike Marriott's recollections of events that day. Taken together, the two give as complete an account of the last flight from Da Nang as we are likely to get, since Ed Daly died in 1984, and Ken Healy spent all his time in the cockpit.

Da Nang, March 29 (UPI)—Only the fastest, the strongest and the meanest of a huge mob got a ride on the last plane from Da Nang Saturday.

People died trying to get aboard and others died when they fell thousands of feet into the sea because even desperation could no longer keep their fingers welded to the undercarriage.

It was a flight into hell, and only a good tough American pilot and a lot of prayers got us back to Tan Son Nhut air base alive—with the Boeing 727 flaps jammed and the wheels fully extended.

It all started simply enough. I asked World Airways Vice President Charles Patterson if he had anything going to Da Nang. He said, "Get on that truck and you've got yourself a ride."

It was a ride I'll never forget.

World Airways President Ed Daly was aboard. He was angry and tired. Daly said he'd been up all night arguing with American and Vietnamese officials for permission to fly into besieged Da Nang to get some more refugees out.

Daly finally said to hell with paper work, clearances, and caution, and we were on our way.

It seemed peaceful enough as we touched down at the airport 370 miles northeast of Saigon.

Over a thousand people had been waiting around a Quonset hut several hundred yards away from where we touched down.

Suddenly, it was a mob in motion. They roared across the tarmac on motorbikes, jeeps, Lambretta scooters, and on legs speeded by sheer desperation and panic.

Ed Daly and I stood near the bottom of the 727's tail ramp. Daly held out his arms while I shouted in Vietnamese, "One at a time, one at a time. There's room for everybody."

There wasn't room for everybody and everybody knew damn well there wasn't.

Daly and I were knocked aside and backward.

If Ed Daly thought he'd get some women and children out of Da Nang, he was wrong. The plane was jammed in an instant with troops of the 1st Division's meanest unit, the Hac Bao (Black Panthers).

They literally ripped the clothes right off Daly along with some of his skin. I saw one of them kick an old woman in the face to get aboard.

In the movies somebody would have shot the bastard and helped the lady on the plane. This was no movie. The bastard flew and the old lady was tumbling down the tarmac, her fingers clawing toward a plane that was already rolling.

A British television cameraman who flew up with us made the mistake of getting off the plane when we landed, to shoot the loading.

He could not get back aboard in the pandemonium. In the very best tradition of the business he threw his camera with its precious film into the closing door and stood there and watched the plane take off.

We heard later that an Air America helicopter picked him up and carried him to safety.

As we started rolling, insanity gripped those who had missed the last chance. Somebody lobbed a hand grenade towards the wing. The explosion jammed the flaps full open and the undercarriage in full extension.

Communist rockets began exploding at a distance.

Our pilot, Ken Healy, 52, of Oakland, Calif., slammed the throttles open and lurched into the air from the taxiway. There was no way we could have survived the gunfire and got onto the main runway.

A backup 727 had flown behind us but had been ordered not to land when the panic broke out. He radioed that he could see the legs of people hanging down from the undercarriage of our plane.

UPI photographer Lien Huong, who was in the cockpit of that backup plane, saw at least one person lose his grip on life and plummet into the South China Sea below.

There were 268 or more people jammed into the cabin of the little 727 limping down the coast.

Only two women and one baby [were] among them. The rest were soldiers, toughest of the tough, meanest of the mean. They proved it today. They were out. They said nothing. They didn't talk to each other or us. They looked at the floor.

I saw one of them had a clip of ammunition and asked him to give it to me. He handed it over. As I walked up the aisle with the clip, other soldiers started loading my arms with clips of ammunition, pistols, hand grenades. They didn't need them anymore. In the cockpit we wrapped the weapons and ammo in electrical tape.

There was no more fight left in the Black Panthers this day.

They had gone from humans to animals and now they were vegetables.

We flew down the coast, the backup plane behind us all the way. Healy circled Phan Rang air base 165 miles northeast of Saigon, hoping to put down for an emergency landing.

On the backup plane, Lien Huong served as interpreter, radioing Phan Rang control tower that the Boeing had to land there in an emergency. The reply came back that there was no fire-fighting equipment at Phan Rang so Healy aimed the plane for Tan Son Nhut.

I heard Healy on the radio, telling Tan Son Nhut, "I've got control problems." The backup plane was shepherding us in.

Huong, in the cockpit of the backup plane, told me later when we touched down safe the pilot and cabin crew on his plane pulled off their headphones, some of them crossed themselves, and all thanked God for a small miracle delivered this Easter weekend.

When we touched down the troops who had stormed us were off-loaded and put under arrest. They deserved it.

A mangled body of one soldier, M-16 rifle still strapped to his shoulder, was retrieved from the undercarriage. He got his ride to Saigon, but being dead in Saigon is just the same as being dead in Da Nang.

Over a score of others came out of the baggage compartment, cold but alive. Somebody told me that four others crawled out of the wheel wells alive. One [subsequently] died.

The last plane from Da Nang was one hell of a ride. For me. For Ed Daly. For Ken Healy. For the Black Panthers. And for two women and a baby.

But the face that remains is that of the old woman lying flat on the tarmac seeing hope, seeing life itself, just off the end of her fingertips and rolling the other way.

All over the world, Vogle's story, and photographs showing the dead infantrymen's* feet protruding from the undercarriage, made the front pages of the Easter Sunday papers.

II

Remarkably, Consul General Al Francis was still on the ground in Da Nang that Saturday afternoon. As Daly's plane was being mobbed, Francis was at a smaller airport, closer to the sea, called Marble Mountain. It had been a base for U.S. Marines after they arrived in Vietnam in March 1965, precisely ten years earlier.

Earlier in the day, before communications were cut, Wolf Lehmann had told Francis that Daly was coming up. "S - - -," Francis had said.

Now he was at Marble Mountain trying to get an Air America C-47 off the ground. Vietnamese were piled in it like cordwood. But the plane could not take off because crazy South Vietnamese military men—Francis didn't know if they were Marines or ARVNs or Ruff-Puffs, they were half in and half out of uniforms—were hanging on to the ailerons and flaps of the wings and the elevators of the tail. "The crazy bastards must think they can fly to Saigon on the wings," Francis thought.

He asked them, politely but firmly, to let go. When that didn't work, he started pulling them off the plane. Then they turned on him. Francis didn't give much resistance as the soldiers beat him up. In their frenzy, they let go of the plane and it finally was able to taxi away.

As it sped off, the soldiers gave up on Francis, who suffered only a few bruises.

* It seems clear from those photographs that there were at least two bodies in the undercarriage.

III

Mel Chatman and Russell Mott spent that Easter weekend on a tug-boat trolling in great circles in Da Nang harbor with a series of barges strung out behind it.

On Friday, after Chatman had shouted to the people on the docks that there was nothing he could do for them, he cried hard for at least five minutes, letting it all flow away from him, as the speedboat took him back out to sea.

He composed himself by the time they reached the Vietnamese ship. Then, using the walkie-talkie, he discovered that Mott was on a nearby tugboat captained by a New Zealander.

Early the next morning Chatman found someone to transfer him from the Vietnamese ship to the tug. As he approached it, shortly after sunrise, he saw that its flanks were hung with television sets, stereo systems, Hondas—all the good things of life that the Vietnamese troops and civilians were, in theory, going to stand and fight for rather than be stripped of by the communists.

The commander of the tug was a young, black-haired man from Auckland named Peter Scott. The tug was called the *Oseola,* but despite the Japanese name, it belonged to the Alaska Barge and Transport Company, the Ted Serong charter outfit with lucrative contracts in the waters in and around Vietnam.

There were several other Americans on board the *Oseola* besides Chatman and Mott, among them the CIA base chief for MR 1. As the tug steamed in circles in Da Nang harbor that weekend, the man refused to answer the frequent attempts by Saigon to raise him by radio. Saigon wanted its senior intelligence officer in Da Nang out of there. But so long as Consul General Al Francis was still operating in and out of the city, with a helicopter, and refugees were reaching the string of barges behind them, the intelligence man—a seasoned officer in late middle age—chose to ignore orders. Further, for three days no ship reached them that could begin off-loading refugees.

Every fifteen or thirty minutes, another small boat loaded with Vietnamese approached the tug. Mott or Chatman shouted at the approaching boats that they would have to go back and get their passengers on one of the barges. When the approaching boats persisted, Scott took his Swedish K and swept a line of fire—*Brrr-r-r-a-a-aaaaap!*—in the sea just forward of their bows. That worked.

They considered steaming out of the harbor. But the largest barge, the first in the string, was a huge, flat-bottomed platform with no sides or railings above the deck. It was at least a hundred yards long, Mott guessed, and jammed with people. There wasn't even room enough for people to maneuver to the edge of the deck to relieve themselves. They squatted in their own excrement. And when people died, they were thrown overboard. Dozens—or hundreds—surely would drown if there was any serious weather in open seas.

A lot of killing went on in the harbor. Armed thugs, most of them soldiers and Marines, darted in commandeered fishing boats among the other boats toiling to reach the barges or other larger ships. The renegades were looking for gold and other valuables.

Mott and the rest of them, including many of the five to ten thousand people on "Big Blue," which was what the Americans called the huge barge immediately behind them, watched in fascination as one of the boats commandeered by the soldiers crept up on another fishing boat tied alongside Big Blue.

As the two vessels bumped, a man on the boat tied to Big Blue leaped up with his hands in the air. The soldiers—they were still in uniform—on the second boat shot him and threw him overboard. There was no one to stop them from taking whatever they wanted.

In the middle of the second day, when it was getting hot, Peter Scott and the Americans—and thousands of Vietnamese in the same two or three minutes, as a listless crowd can do—all noticed a little brown dog about two hundred yards away from the *Oseola,* swimming toward it.

Scott cut himself loose from the convoy and rescued the dog. As they pulled it from the water, the Vietnamese—many of whom had lost their homes, parts of their families, their ability now to care for the ancestral graves—gave out a great cheer.

There was plenty of water on board the *Oseola* for Scott and his crew and the Americans, but not for tens of thousands of refugees. That night, Chatman and Mott were talking in the cockpit, the coolest place to be on the tug, when they heard a strange ululating sound. They looked out to a sea of white cloths—handkerchiefs, shirts, blouses—that the Vietnamese were waving, as they chanted *"Nuu-u-u-oc! Nuu-u-u-oc!"** over and over, off and on for hours.

They had reported earlier in the day that the refugees were dying of thirst. That night, the U.S. Air Force flew a C-147 to them, and Peter Scott turned on a powerful spotlight that illuminated some of the barges. The plane flew low and dropped a series of big white plastic containers, all full of water. All exploded on impact. One landed on the *Oseola* and knocked out its antennas. (A resourceful CIA radioman on board had them back in communication within an hour.)

* "Water! Water!"

Russell Mott thought the plan might have worked if they had had the brains to send the containers half full instead of topped off.

Early the next morning, Monday, March 31, they received word that a Vietnamese freighter was on its way to them with water. With that, they ran a hose out to Big Blue. And then, mercifully, it began to rain.

Russell Mott borrowed a camera from Peter Scott and ventured onto Big Blue. After he had moved about ten yards into it, and had seen a Honda, and a tuba, and ten to twenty corpses, he decided he had seen enough.

The *Oseola* finally made radio contact with the SS *Pioneer Contender,* a civilian American freighter on charter to Military Sealift Command.

The transfer of people from the barges to the freighter was difficult. When the tug stopped in the water, it was easy enough for people to move from barge to barge and eventually to the tug. But there was a twenty-foot drop from the deck of the freighter to the tug, and swelling seas in darkness. The gangplank up which at least fifteen thousand people eventually moved over the course of several hours became twisted. Chatman saw no one drop from it into the sea, but he sensed that there was an evil subdued shoving panic at the foot of it.

Sometimes it took a show of the Swedish K or Chatman's .38 to make the point, but all of them save one young man accepted the fact that they were not going to be allowed to try to wrestle their motorcycles or even to carry their TVs and stereos up that gangplank.

The one exception scurried about the tugboat and the lead barge amassing a small fortune in TVs. He was obviously drunk on the thought of what fifteen to twenty Japanese and American television sets would bring him in Cam Ranh Bay or Saigon.

Finally Chatman asked Peter Scott for his Swedish K. And in colloquial Vietnamese that included the phrase "you who f --- your mother," he talked the young man away from his treasure and up the gangplank.

As Big Blue finally emptied, Chatman walked onto it, as Mott had earlier. There were bodies everywhere, under blankets. Seven babies were lined up side by side. A blanket almost covered them, only their faces staring unprotected up into the blackness.

Then later, the last of the fifteen thousand or more were pulling themselves up the gangplank. Chatman was there. A woman pushed her way down the gangplank against the very last of them. And then

Chatman saw three infants dead at the foot of the gangplank, trampled to death.

The woman reached down and lifted one of them. The night sounded with her keening wail.

The American crew on the *Pioneer Contender* was holed up in the superstructure amidships. The decks were under the control of the ARVNs. If there were any officers among them, they had stripped their insignia from their uniforms. Gradually, during the day, Mel Chatman came to understand that a tough ARVN sergeant was in charge.

Chatman ventured out of the superstructure, his .38 in his pocket, but making no effort to signal that he was armed. Nor did he let on that he understood the language.

Gradually, during the afternoon, he came to understand that a fear gripped the ship. Boys of a certain age—it was specific, sixteen to eighteen—were being rounded up by the sergeant's men. The fear was so great that late in the afternoon Chatman heard instances of boys jumping overboard to their certain deaths.

Chatman remained out on the decks, listening. A Vietnamese crewman saw some of the executions that night, down in the hull. At dawn, Chatman's best intelligence was that the sergeant and his hard men had killed seventeen or eighteen boys. He also was given to understand by that crewman and the conversations he listened to all day and night on the decks that this was not quite madness; there was reason in it: The tough guys truly believed that they had been infiltrated.

The *Pioneer Contender* put in at Cam Ranh Bay the next day, Tuesday, April 1. In the morning, before the freighter reached Cam Ranh, an Air America helicopter came in and began to circle low overhead. Chatman had no idea what it was doing. It dropped nothing; it was as if the chopper was there simply to see what was going on.

After it had hovered above them for a minute or two, the helicopter irritated some of the ARVNs. They shot a few rounds up in its direction and it quickly rose and darted off.

In the chopper, which he had ordered up in Cam Ranh Bay to shoot pictures of the evacuation, David Kennerly was slightly shaken up. Getting shot at by the good guys was something new for him.

Chatman and Mott were on the ground for only a couple of hours. The embassy sent up an Air America plane. As Chatman jogged to it, he was keenly aware of the battalions of ARVNs and South Vietnamese Marines who crowded around the airfield. Most of them by now had thrown away their weapons, and all of them had stripped themselves of badges of rank. But even if they were unarmed and in flight, Chatman was glad to get away from them for a while.

Cam Ranh to Saigon was a short flight, thirty to forty minutes, depending on the winds and the traffic. But it was long enough for Chatman to begin to contemplate the possibilities: Da Nang in Saigon; the *Pioneer Contender* nightmare in Saigon.

"Hostages," Chatman thought. "So easy. All of us. Hostages of the army we made."

IV

When they had left the water that was taking shells and Captain Do Duc Cuong's ears adjusted to the noise of the engines and the sea, he realized that somewhere on the small ship a baby was crying. He found it, a boy about a year old. He asked a sailor what the child was doing there. The man said they had been at sea four days and nights ferrying people to larger ships out of range of the communist guns. "Earlier tonight, two big fishing boats reached us at the same time. After we got everyone off and were turning around, we realized the baby had been left behind. I could even hear a woman calling out to us. First she called to her husband, and when he said he didn't have it she called to us. But then the two ships were moving apart. We would have had to chase them." He looked at Cuong and added: "I don't know how many more trips we can make. But the baby is crying all the time. Someone should take him."

"Okay," Cuong said.

Less than an hour later, they were transferred to a naval repair ship. It was already badly overcrowded, but it stayed in the area until dawn to accept a few more people. The decks were so full that only about one out of ten persons could crawl into some narrow shelf or under the suspended lifeboats to sleep. Cuong slept even less than most of the others, because when he did wait for one of the precious plots and lay down, the child usually cried. The child cried a great deal. But he was able to sleep in Cuong's arms sometimes. And although water was very scarce, Cuong found a few women willing to nurse the boy. He cried, Cuong knew, not so much because he was tired or hungry or thirsty, but because he was filthy, and terrified.

Late in the morning on the second day, the ship's captain received an order from General Truong in an invisible helicopter somewhere. All ships within a certain radius of Quang Ngai, a little less than a hundred miles south of Da Nang, were to put in at an island off Quang Ngai and disembark their Army and Air Force officers. Everyone on the ship knew of the order five minutes after it was received, by which time the ship had turned west for the island. "Not us," Colonel Nhon said softly to Cuong. "Now we take orders only from Saigon."

"Okay," Cuong said. There were at least 1,500 people on the ship, more than half of them soldiers and officers. Ten or twelve officers left the ship at the island.

They took on water there, but it wasn't enough. Children started dying on the third day out. The bodies were piled in a few of the sleeping places. By sunrise of the fourth day, there were eight or nine of them in the quarter of the ship Cuong covered in his shuffling between the sleeping places and the toilet and the drooping chain railing.

Cuong secured a place at the rail for him and the baby in the middle of the fourth day. The breeze and the openness helped, but the sun was like the tongue of a great beast in the sky, lapping the skull. Cuong thanked God for his hair, and piled the T-shirt he had kept looped to his waist on the baby's head.

A man behind him asked Cuong if he smoked. The man's face was very close to his when Cuong turned his head. The man looked to be about thirty; he smiled, but the smile was full of a crazy fear or despair. Cuong was struck as much by the man's terrible baldness as by his crazy smile. The baldness was terrible both because it was not natural for a Vietnamese that young to be that bald—Cuong had seen enough Americans and Australians to know that it happened to some of them, but with Vietnamese it usually meant the man had some disease on his scalp—and because it was ugly, the grayish smooth skin beaded with great dollops of sweat.

Cuong smoked. He hoped he wouldn't have to share his few remaining cigarettes.

"Yes," he said.

"Here," the man said. They were all too tightly packed for him easily to reach between Cuong and the man next to Cuong at the rail. He reached over Cuong's shoulder and felt with his hand until he could safely drop a half-crushed package of Ruby Queens into the crevice between the baby's turbaned head and Cuong's chest.

"No," Cuong said. "I have plenty. I only smoke Marlboros."

"It's okay," the man said. "Give them to someone else. Here, I have about two thousand piasters I want to give you."

"No," Cuong said. "Why are you giving me money? We're almost at Cam Ranh. Everyone says we'll reach it tonight." But the hand was waving softly in front of his chest again, tucking the money next to the cigarette package. It happened quickly.

"You're a good man," the man said. "I know the child isn't yours. His mother will bless you, even if she is in the other world." As he spoke he was shoving, wedging between them, pushing harder against the man next to Cuong than at Cuong, but also wedging his hip in there against Cuong's, and then the hip found and strained the chain and he twisted his head to say, "Good luck, brother," to Cuong and tipped into the sea.

"Oh, God," Cuong said to himself as the green-uniformed legs and torso and the now-black head, only the briefest glimpse of the head, sped away and disappeared in the bright foam-flaked wake, Cuong appealing to his father's Christian God, who performed miracles, "help it end now quickly; it's too much now," clutching the suddenly silent infant to his breast as if the child might too suddenly jump to his death.

Cuong cried for the first time since the end of those first few months as a houseboy in Saigon, remembering that he had cried for the last time the night he finished putting the numbers on his leg, and the man next to him at the rail took him in his arms like a mother or a wife until the child cried and they separated, suddenly ashamed.

The closest Cuong came to crying again happened quickly, in the first few daylight hours of the next morning, when they finally did reach Cam Ranh Bay. There, on the gigantic steel-and-concrete docks left by the Americans, were a thousand small children, dead, with fish eyes and stacked like charcoal.

A thousand? Years later, Cuong would say "thousands" in English. Maybe, in truth, there were only 175, or 275. But the docks were long, and still the children were stacked like fish, or sticks of charcoal, and in fact Cuong put an *s* on the word "thousand," and whether there were 175 or 2,175 corpses of children on the long concrete piers of Cam Ranh Bay on the morning of April 3, 1975, there were many. Maybe only 125. (But then why were they stacked like that, such long lines of them, several lines, all stacked?)

They had died floating south. There wasn't enough water. There were few infants; infants could be fed at the breast. They ranged in age from about three to eleven, twelve. If the old grandmothers and grandfathers had died also in this exodus, as surely they must have, someone had taken them elsewhere. These docks had become the place to stack the children.

They had eyes like fish, Cuong thought at first, because when they were dying of thirst their guardians had given them salt water to drink. But perhaps it was just what the sun did to them after they died, puffing them up in the heat of the concrete docks. Their eyes bulged from the sockets like gray, dead light bulbs, or hung oozing from the sockets. A very old Catholic priest in a dirty soutane shuffled with decrepit slowness down a line of them with his cross in front of him, doing his magic. Cuong thought he was Vietnamese. But he was so old and wrinkled and bent that he could have been a shriveled old Frenchman. He had joined the raceless elderly.

The child still with him, Cuong made his way into the small city. With the very last of his own money, he bought a canteen and filled it with water at a café. Still with the child, he walked back to the docks. But he was too late. The old priest had died at the feet of the children. Already, death had started to smooth the wrinkles of his face. He had gone to the foreign religion, but he was of the central Vietnam people, like Cuong, now Cuong was sure. He tipped a little water onto the old man's lips, a small gift for the passage to the other side. Then he hurried away from the death stench.

As he walked back into Cam Ranh, which was full of refugees but still possessed of order, a young woman waiting along the road from the docks rushed to him and claimed her child. Cuong had never seen the baby before he found it on the small ship, but he knew the woman. She was the wife of a friend of his who was also an officer in the 1st Division.

He spent three days in Cam Ranh, living at first like a refugee. Colonel Nhon, who was now very angry with his superiors, set off south ahead of him, urging Cuong to stay behind. But Cuong had no role to play in Cam Ranh. The other remnants of the division, such as his friend who had waited for news of his child, were either talking or bribing or forcing their way onto ships going south or taking their chances on Highway 1.

The first night, Cuong was too tired and dispirited to find some military unit that would let him lie on a floor. He slept by a roadside. At midnight, a rumor or actual fighting, Cuong was never sure, caused a rush from the city. People running past and even over him woke him. Cuong listened for shelling or firing. When he heard none, he went back to sleep.

In the morning, he ate bread and little cakes that people had dropped in their flight. By then he was rested enough to find officers who would accept his account of who he was, which he verified with his military identification card, and he lived as a guest of a Cam Ranh intelligence unit.

Laurie Stark. "The receptacle of
all her mother's feisty Irish
genes, . . . who was starting to
beat the old man at tennis."

Dr. Meritt W. Stark and Laurie.
"He was a decent American."

Alan Carter, the last United States Information Service chief in Saigon,
receiving an award for his work as director of the Indiantown Gap
(Pa.) refugee camp after the war.

Charles McMahon, Jr., Corporal,
U.S. Marine Corps.

Sgt. Robert L. Frain,
U.S. Marine Corps.
(courtesy Timothy
Creighton)

Top: South Vietnamese helicopters settling on Highway 1 east of the embattled city of Xuan Loc were rushed by troops and civilians. (Dirck Halstead/Gamma-Liaison)

Bottom: A TV camera crew at Xuan Loc turns from a missed flight. The choppers were the only way out. (Dirck Halstead/Gamma-Liaison)

President Thieu resigned in a rambling, emotional nationwide television address on April 21. "Kissinger did not see that the Paris Peace Accords led the South Vietnamese people to death. Everyone sees it and Kissinger does not see it." (Dirck Halstead/Gamma-Liaison)

Tran Van Huong, the aged and infirm vice-president, lasted as president for a week. (Dirck Halstead/Gamma-Liaison)

Under pressure from the French and finally even from the Americans, Huong yielded to General Duong Van ("Big") Minh. Here Minh is deep in thought moments before being inaugurated as president. Less than forty-eight hours after he was sworn in, Minh surrendered to the communists. (Dirck Halstead/Gamma-Liaison)

Captain Do Duc Cuong, of the ARVN 1st Division; in California, 1984.

Bottom left: Nguyen Van Hao, deputy prime minister for economic development. Hao urged people not to flee, pledging that no matter what happened he and his family would stay.

Bottom right: Tung Giang on the afternoon that he crashed the evacuation. "I propped the Sony's microphone on an empty Coke bottle. . . ." (David Butler)

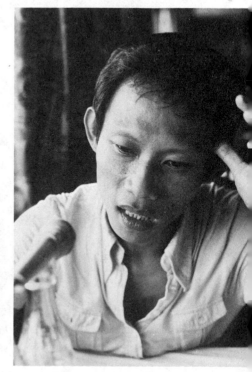

Four a.m., April 29, 1975. The artillery and rocket bombardment of Tan Son Nhut air base as seen from the roof of the Central Palace Hotel in downtown Saigon. (David Butler)

Secretary of State Kissinger briefs President Ford as the decision is made to go to Option 4—the helicopter evacuation of Saigon. (David Hume Kennerly/Gamma-Liaison)

General Homer Smith (seated), the commander of the Defense Attaché's Office, on the morning of April 29, the last full day of the war. ". . . one of those men with the American West in their faces." (courtesy E. F. Pelosky)

A Marine in his element as the helicopter evacuation from Tan Son Nhut gets under way. (Dirck Halstead/ Gamma-Liaison)

"Run!" Vietnamese and Americans dash for a helicopter at Tan Son Nhut. (Dirck Halstead/Gamma-Liaison)

At the U.S. embassy, mid-afternoon, April 29. There was a steady seepage of Vietnamese into the compound. (Nik Wheeler/Black Star)

A Marine at the front gate of the embassy levels his rifle at a South Vietnamese coming over the top. (Nik Wheeler/Black Star)

Marines guarding an embassy sidegate. (Nik Wheeler/Black Star)

The Vietnamese were frisked
for weapons, which were then
thrown into the embassy pool.
(Nik Wheeler/Black Star)

The remains of the
tamarind tree being
towed away.

The first CH-54 to land
in the embassy com-
pound. The embassy fire
station is at lower left.

Late in the afternoon, the Marine helicopters finally started to arrive. (Air America choppers had been ferrying small loads from the roof all day.) (Nik Wheeler/Black Star)

Marines hustle Vietnamese and Westerners into one of the big CH-54s that set down in the parking lot—behind the chancery—the lot from which the tamarind tree had been cleared. (Nik Wheeler/Black Star)

Vietnamese board barges at Khanh Hoi—one of Saigon's river ports—late on the afternoon of the 29th. (Nik Wheeler/Black Star)

The barges left with room for at least another eight thousand Vietnamese. But Mel Chatman's radio network had broken down as senior Americans in outlying installations around Saigon withdrew to the embassy. In many cases they abandoned their Vietnamese staffers, most of whom never heard about the barges. (Nik Wheeler/Black Star)

Terry McNamara, consul-general in MR-4 and, on April 29, 1975, "Commodore of the Can Tho Yacht Club." (courtesy Cary Kassebaum)

Terry and the pirates head down the Bassac River toward the open sea, with close to three hundred Vietnamese, on the afternoon of the 29th. (courtesy Cary Kassebaum)

After they were stopped by South Vietnamese riverine forces, McNamara sent for a real commodore, named Thang, who decided to take the American's word for it that there were no draft-age males or military officers in the convoy. (courtesy Cary Kassebaum)

At the center, an old man leaving Vietnam with McNamara stoops to embrace his son, who is in the navy and staying behind. (courtesy Cary Kassebaum)

Camouflaged North Vietnamese Army trucks. Moving south, as always.
(Vietnamese News Agency (VNA)/courtesy John Spragens, Jr.)

"Giai Phong!"—"Liberation!" An NVA flying the biggest Viet Cong flag
Neal Davis had ever seen crashes through the front gate of the Presidential
Palace. (VNA/courtesy John Spragens, Jr.)

Bo dois and Saigonese crowd the
front of the Presidential Palace in
downtown Saigon on the afternoon
of April 30, 1975. (VNA/courtesy
John Spragens, Jr.)

Bo dois occupy the abandoned
South Vietnamese National Police
Headquarters compound in Saigon.
(VNA/courtesy John Spragens,
Jr.)

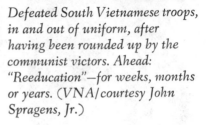

Defeated South Vietnamese troops, in and out of uniform, after having been rounded up by the communist victors. Ahead: "Reeducation"—for weeks, months or years. (VNA/courtesy John Spragens, Jr.)

Children were sent to gather weapons the South Vietnamese had abandoned as they shed their uniforms. (Paul Quinn-Judge)

Ambassador Martin arrives on board the USS Okinawa at five a.m., April 30, 1975. (David Butler)

Colonel George Jacobson, who had been in Vietnam forever, came out with Martin. (David Butler)

A loaded barge heads toward the 7th Fleet. (Dirck Halstead/Gamma-Liaison)

The author on the USS Okinawa. (Neal Ulevich)

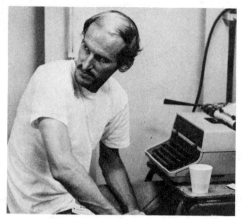

On the Okinawa, looking back. Fini, bye-bye Vietnam. (David Butler)

PART 3

MARCH 26-APRIL 24

WE HAVE JUST COMPLETED AN INTERAGENCY REVIEW OF THE STATE OF PLAY IN SOUTH VIETNAM. YOU SHOULD KNOW THAT AT THE WSAG MEETING TODAY THERE WAS ALMOST NO SUPPORT FOR THE EVACUATION OF VIETNAMESE, AND FOR THE USE OF AMERICAN FORCE TO HELP PROTECT ANY EVACUATION. THE SENTIMENT OF OUR MILITARY, DOD AND CIA COLLEAGUES WAS TO GET OUT FAST AND NOW. . . .

—*Kissinger to Martin, April 17*

14

Meritt W. Stark, M.D., spent the last six days of March traveling in three provinces on the central coast of South Vietnam, trying to anticipate the resettlement and health problems of thousands of refugees from the Central Highlands and the north. During the six days, the enormity of the task started to become clear to him. What did not occur to him was the idea that all his planning might be futile.

With a colleague from the Vietnamese Ministry of Health, Dr. Stark boarded an Air America plane on Wednesday, March 26, and flew to Nha Trang. Dr. Stark's companion briefed provincial health and refugee officials about the airlift from Da Nang to Cam Ranh Bay scheduled to get under way the next day.

That afternoon, at about four o'clock, the first of the refugees from the highlands began to trickle into Nha Trang. Someone at the U.S. Consulate advised Dr. Stark to stay in the American compound that night: The refugees were bitter, he said—against Thieu and against the Americans. Dr. Stark politely took the advice under consideration and went on with his round of meetings.

As usual, he scrawled entries in a notebook that his secretary would decipher when he returned to Saigon.

On Thursday morning, he was driven thirty miles down the coast to Cam Ranh, where he sat in on a meeting with the province chief and other officials. "The Army 5th Logistics Command at Cam Ranh Bay will receive all refugees," he noted, "provide medical services and arrange for ongoing transportation. There are six doctors and a 400-bed convalescent center. . . ."

Back in Nha Trang that afternoon: "Met [USAID official] Dennis Wood, who had just returned from Da Nang. He reports great unrest among the citizens and difficulties getting the evacuation planes properly boarded."

28 March

Met with Dr. Luc, who is overwhelmed by the enormity of the refugee problem and the limited number of personnel. He assigned Mr. Loc to accompany us on a tour of several of the refugee sites. The large camp at Ru Ri presently has about 13,000 refugees. There are now twenty-three separate sites on the base. . . . The chief problem is a shortage of water. The camp is so large, the distribution of water is difficult. No latrines have been constructed. The sidings of many of the buildings are being torn down for firewood. Several of the sites have been appropriated by the military and we were cautioned to stay away from these sites. . . .

Australian living in town roughed up and relieved of wallet and watch and received superficial scalp wound from gunshot. Rangers and ARVN causing some unrest and the scheduled visits to the refugee camps with [two consulate officials] canceled. . . .

To airport at 2030 hours to meet four choppers and a C-47—the last planes out of Da Nang. . . . Everyone arriving from Da Nang is visibly shaken.

On the next day, Saturday, the twenty-ninth, Dr. Stark helicoptered down to Cam Ranh to meet the first of the large ships to arrive from Da Nang. The ship sat outside the harbor for three hours because the captain of the harbor happened to be in Nha Trang. Finally someone decided that a tugboat could bring it in without him.

Dr. Stark was never certain of the name of that ship. It was overcrowded, and it took close to five hours for the six thousand persons on board to disembark. They were dehydrated, and rushed for eight metal drums of water in which Dr. Stark kept dropping salt tablets. But this was not one of the ships he heard about later on which people died. Of the six thousand, only forty to fifty needed medical attention.

Early on Sunday morning, Dr. Stark and Dr. William Oldham, USAID's director of public health, picked up Dr. Huynh Van Hoan, the government's recently appointed minister of health, who had arrived in Nha Trang the day before, and drove to Nha Trang's provincial hospital. There they had a brief unscheduled meeting with a Dr.

Minh, the government's chief medical officer in Binh Dinh province, more than a hundred miles north.

Dr. Minh had driven south from Qui Nhon, the province capital, to plead for the evacuation of the patients from the province hospital. All the doctors and staff had fled, he said.

Drs. Stark and Oldham drove back to the consulate and called Saigon to find out what could be done for the patients in Qui Nhon. Eventually they were told that all evacuations in MR 2 were being handled by the South Vietnamese authorities in the region. More phone calls determined that there were no ships or planes available for Qui Nhon.

Dr. Stark also learned that morning that the government had ordered its forces in Nha Trang to move out of the province as many as possible of the refugees and military units from other provinces. Obviously, the only place they could go was south. So Stark and Oldham headed south themselves, driving more than fifty miles to Phan Rang, the next town on the coast after Cam Ranh.

The senior medical officer in Phan Rang briefed the American doctors on the seven sites in the province selected to receive refugees. Each could accommodate ten thousand refugees. Stark and Oldham visited one of the three main receiving areas from which the refugees would be fed to the seven camps.

"The two wells at the site have been soiled with oil," Dr. Stark noted. "[But] there are two cement reservoirs that could be cleaned and used. The river is only about twenty-five meters from the edge of the camp, so water is easily obtainable. The deputy district chief . . . agreed to provide money to pay persons to clean the wells and reservoirs, procure pumps and purchase water drums. . . ."

Late in the afternoon, Stark and Oldham stopped in at two of the three main refugee camps in Cam Ranh. One was a former camp for ARVN dependents, and already had about eight thousand refugees. The other was a former Korean Army camp, with twenty thousand refugees. Neither camp had water.

> The people, except for the children, are all very solemn [Dr. Stark noted], but no unpleasant incidents occurred—no visible anti-American feeling.
>
> We departed Cam Ranh [heading north] about 6:15. The road was more heavily traveled [than earlier in the day] with refugees heading south—loaded to capacity with motorbikes, bicycles, household possessions and many people.
>
> Arrived Nha Trang about 7:30 and learned curfew has been changed to 8 P.M. Also, nonessential personnel are to be airlifted tomorrow.

. . .

Dr. Stark was among those leaving Nha Trang the next day, on what proved to be the last fixed-wing aircraft out of the city. On that last day in March, he was a couple of months short of his fifty-ninth birthday. For the last six years, he had been deeply concerned with the cleanliness of the water supply for South Vietnamese civilian hospitals, refugee camps and orphanages. He had been deeply concerned with many other things as well—all things touching on the physical well-being of South Vietnamese, as on everything touching on the safety of his family. He was also knowledgeable about a great many things, from pediatrics to the Vietnamese veneration for education, to give just two examples.

He was a decent American.

He stood five feet eleven inches tall, but there was a gut under his chest and he had a way of tilting his generous nose skyward when he spoke that made him appear to be a strapping woodsman.

At Yale, where he interned in pediatrics, he met a cute little five-footer from Woburn, Massachusetts, who had had six years of elocution at a Catholic girls' day school.

They made a perfect couple, the pretty little thing with the mock-British theatrical accent and the antiestablishment tilt in her character, and the big young pediatrician from Denver who was not exactly inarticulate but who found it difficult to frame a sentence that did not begin with or at least include a *gee,* a *golly* or a *gosh.*

Dorothy Stark almost botched her career as a nursing student. She was suddenly called to assist at a spontaneous abortion. It was late in the pregnancy. The thing came tumbling out with its tiny arms and legs and Dorothy nearly followed it into the pan she was holding. She would faint twice in her life. That was the first time.

In the mid-1960s Meritt had a big practice in pediatrics and they had a big house on Cheesman Park in Denver. They needed the big, comfortable house because they had six children, two boys and four girls. And the children out of the blue sucked their parents into the war in Vietnam.

It started with Tom, the firstborn. Early in 1966, he came home one day to announce that he had enlisted in the Marine Corps.

Meritt Stark was not the kind of father who goaded or guided his sons into the Marine Corps. But the two boys certainly knew that their father's grandfather had been a volunteer in the Civil War, that their father's father had been a volunteer in the Spanish-American War, and that their father and all three of his brothers had volunteered and served in World War II. So it was not a total surprise that Tom would volunteer for the war in progress when he came of age.

What Meritt Stark found more difficult to understand was that the next two eldest children, Ellen and Laurie, were vehemently opposed to the war. It not only puzzled him, it disturbed him. He assumed that the antiwar activists were making whatever the military was trying to do over in Vietnam more difficult. But he was not about to tell his daughters that they could not have their own ideas.

In that summer of 1966, when Tom was at boot camp in San Diego, Laurie attended a short course in the techniques of resistance to the war given by Quakers in Wisconsin. After the course, she was sent to spread the word in Oregon: going door to door, speaking at churches, getting on radio and television shows if she could.

When parishioners at one of the churches learned that she had a brother in boot camp, they took up a collection and bought her a ticket for the trip south.

Tom was out on maneuvers when Laurie got to the camp. One of his drill instructors invited Laurie to wait in his home while her brother was being sent for. Laurie was only seventeen that summer. But she was feisty. When she had finished proselytizing the drill instructor and Tom finally arrived for the reunion, the DI went off to report the encounter to the commanding officer of the base, who eventually sent for Tom.

"Do you realize what your sister is up to, Stark?" the man asked.

"Yes, sir."

"How do you explain it?"

"Do you have any daughters, sir?"

"No, as a matter of fact, I don't."

"Well, I don't know, sir," young Stark said, "but at least in my family it seems like the girls have got their own ideas."

Toward the end of Tom's thirteen-month tour with the 5th Marine Division, Meritt Stark at the age of fifty-one decided to see for himself about this war—this strange, far-off place—that had split his family. He signed up for an American Medical Association program called Volunteer Physicians to Vietnam.

He was in Vietnam for only two months on that first trip. He was assigned to Bac Lieu, a peaceful little city close to the South China Sea in the southern reaches of the Mekong delta. He flew up to Da Nang for a quiet, enjoyable reunion with Tom—who served his tour in Vietnam, received a Purple Heart, went home, started a family and put Vietnam behind him.

Bac Lieu was pleasant. After work, Dr. Stark would sit at a sidewalk stall, order a beer and watch the Vietnamese take their leisure in the cool of the evening. The work itself was a challenge, treating some childhood diseases he had only read about in the States and on the other hand trying to convince the Vietnamese—and their U.S. advisers—to fund and implement the most fundamental improvements in sanitation.

Back in Denver, he found himself giving a few talks about his experiences in Vietnam at the service clubs to which he belonged. As a result of one of those talks, a Denver colleague volunteered for the same program Dr. Stark had joined. That man arrived in Saigon in the middle of the Tet offensive of 1968.

That was the year that the war in Vietnam almost tore America apart. The shocks came one after another: Lyndon Johnson's announcement that he wouldn't run again; the assassinations of Martin Luther King and of Robert Kennedy; the Democratic Convention in Mayor Daley's Chicago.

Dorothy Stark sensed that something was wrong with her husband. One day late that year she said, "Meritt, if you were to give up the practice and do whatever you wanted, what would it be?"

Dr. Stark thought for a minute and then said, "Gee, you know, I think I'd go back to Vietnam."

At that point, Amy, the youngest child, was in fourth grade. Ann was a sophomore in high school. Laurie and Ellen and Mike were all in college. Among the five children old enough to have an opinion in this major shift in the Stark family lives, only Tom, the veteran, said: "Dad, I think you're making a mistake."

Drs. Stark and Oldham were met at the airport and driven to USAID headquarters on that Monday, March 31. Dr. Stark gave his notes to his secretary, and busied himself for a few hours with phone calls and paper work. Then he called for a car and was driven through the thick twilight traffic to the apartment on Phan Van Dat. His wife and two of his daughters, Laurie and Ann, would be there. Something was ending—what was it? Then he remembered: Ann would be leaving Saigon tomorrow as an escort on one of the flights taking orphans to the States.

Under the constant prodding of Rosemary Taylor, the director of Friends for All Children, the embassy and Washington were finally expediting the airlift of fairly large numbers of orphans from Vietnam to the States. And in the dehydrating atmosphere of the planes, every two or three children would need an adult to see to their needs. So a planeful of infants and young children required several dozen escorts, and Ann would be one tomorrow. The way things were going they had to assume that Ann was leaving Vietnam for good.

That thought was hard to digest, especially as the faces of some of the hundreds of children he had seen in the last five days crowded in on him. None of those children would be boarding a plane tomorrow morning for a flight to the United States of America.

Faced with the choice of worrying about whether the deputy district chief would actually go ahead and clean up the oil-soiled wells at the refugee clearinghouse at Co Mong in Phan Rang province or of remembering the party they had held at Number 3 Phan Van Dat a few months before, Dr. Stark yielded to memory.

Gee, what a nice party that was. Each member of the family had invited his or her Vietnamese friends. He invited a few colleagues from the ministries of health and refugee affairs. Dorothy invited friends she taught with at the embassy's Phoenix School and the Vietnamese woman who ran the small English-language school in her own home where Dorothy also taught part time. The two of them, Dr. and Mrs. Stark, also happened to know socially a justice of the South Vietnamese Supreme Court, and he was there with his wife.

Ann had her friends, musicians most of them.

And then there was Laurie, dear bright pretty Laurie, the antiwar activist. She had her French-speaking teacher friends from the Madame Curie school. And yes, of course, that was the night Laurie's friend Sister Koverman . . .

Sister Koverman was a young American nun who worked to improve the nutrition in Saigon orphanages and day-care centers. She came that night in "civilian" clothes, her long brown hair cascading down her back. Dr. Stark smiled at the memory, wondered at the naïve mischievousness of a beautiful young nun coming to a party looking that way, remembered the pretty girl saying over and over again to the young American and Vietnamese suitors, "I'm sorry, thank you, I'd love to really, but I can't, my work won't let me. . . ."

Laurie would have put her up to it, of course. Laurie—the receptacle of all her mother's feisty Irish genes. Laurie—who was starting to beat the old man at tennis. Laurie, who arrived in Saigon and was almost fluent after six months and then went out and started befriending street boys—shoeshine boys, purse snatchers. The justice of the Supreme Court had retained his composure as he circulated quietly, modestly, among the twenty-five or thirty Vietnamese guests at this strange party, a dozen of whom were runny-nosed twelve-to-fifteen-year-old boys eyeing his gold watch.

"I've never been at a party quite like this, Mrs. Stark," he said. "We Vietnamese would not think to do it. And I don't think any other American would dare to do it."

Laurie. And of course there was the young Vietnamese woman with whom Laurie just six months ago had started the Mother Hubbard preschool. . . .

Now they were at the apartment. Dr. Stark hauled himself out of the comfortable white car, overstuffed overnight bag in one hand, overstuffed briefcase in the other, and said good night to his driver in his pidgin Vietnamese. He pressed the button on the cage to the old French elevator on the off chance that the thing was working, began the five-floor trudge to the apartment, his mind filled with other remembrances of that wonderful party, filled above all with love for the spirit of that one, the third-born, the Irish one who was starting to beat him at tennis.

As he climbed in the near-darkness, he wondered, "What the *hell* are we gonna do if we get a *million* people from the north?"

Meritt Stark was closing in on fifty-nine. He smoked thirty cigarettes a day, and, as a medical doctor, had a fairly clear idea what thirty cigarettes a day were doing to him.

When he finally reached the fifth-floor hallway, he was breathing hard.

He took a breath, allowed himself one final blurred vision of all the faces of the last five days—the last six years—took a few steps, set down his bags, and knocked on the door of his huge, love-filled apartment.

Something horrible was coming, and he was guilty. Something beautiful would die.

But Tom—his son, the ex-Marine—was wrong. The evil came from elsewhere. His beautiful wife and two beautiful daughters were on the other side of that door. And there was nowhere else in the world where they, or he, should be.

II

In Saigon on the first night of April, a Tuesday night, the news of the fall of Da Nang just reaching the capital, just after sunset, two men whom most Vietnamese would assume were bitter enemies met to plot their country's future. The host was Thich Tri Quang, a Buddhist monk and political master. His guest was Dr. Tran Kim Tuyen, who during most of the presidency of Ngo Dinh Diem had been the director of the secret police.

Thich is the Vietnamese title of respect for a monk, but "venerable," the standard translation, conveys the wrong impression of Thich Tri Quang. He was a muscular man of about fifty who bore a strong resemblance to Yul Brynner, and not just because he shaved his head. When he spoke to Western journalists, as he had done rarely in recent years, and not for attribution, he sat cross-legged at a low table with one or two texts on it, constantly daubing his nostrils with Tiger Balm, spinning out in a mesmerizing whisper his dreams of a Vietnam at peace. One walked from his cell in Saigon's An Quang pagoda (down a winding staircase and across a narrow courtyard filled with low chanting and sunlight streaming through drying saffron robes hung like banners) convinced that one had approached the heart of the Orient at last, certain that the man one had left could have commanded armies.

For the past three years, Thich Tri Quang had been virtually silent. The silence was politically expedient both because it kept him safe and because it was widely understood by South Vietnam's Buddhists as the monk's expression of contempt for Thieu.

The president was a Catholic, although he was thought not to be as devout as his wife. Nevertheless, he depended on the support of South Vietnam's fiercely anticommunist Catholics, while large segments of the predominant Buddhist populace, especially those who looked to the An Quang pagoda for guidance, favored some kind of accommodation with the communists, and above all an end to the fighting.

Thich Tri Quang had not always been so silent. He was the chief strategist and orator of the Buddhist uprising against Diem in 1963. And it was during that crisis that he first met Tuyen. The monk at that time worked in Hue. The secret-police chief, who reported not to Diem but to his brother Ngo Dinh Nhu, was meeting every day with the only Buddhist contacts he had, those in Saigon, to try to defuse the crisis. Thich Tri Quang traveled to the capital to inform Tuyen that he, not the southerners, was the leader of the Buddhists.

Subsequently, working through an intermediary, Tuyen and the Buddhist activist in fact worked out an accommodation between the palace and the Buddhists—only to see it denounced by Nhu's beautiful, naïve and politically ambitious young wife. Had she not interfered, there is at least a possibility that the Buddhists would have been placated and the generals would not have felt compelled to mount the coup in which both Diem and Nhu were assassinated.

On that first day of April 1975, Tran Kim Tuyen was just fifty. He was a highly unlikely figure for a man who had not only run Diem's secret police but also, with the Americans, set up South Vietnam's first intelligence network targeted against the North.

Even the Vietnamese marveled at Dr. Tuyen's shortness. He was not conventionally small; his legs and arms seemed proportionately shorter than his torso, as if he might have a touch of dwarfism. But he was not unattractive; he was one of those northern Vietnamese with extraordinarily high cheekbones and bright black eyes and pixieish splayed nostrils above a pixie mouth. He had a way when he wanted to say something that demonstrated the profound stupidity of other men of tilting his large head, cocking one eyebrow and rolling his tongue in his cheek that would have been charming in a favorite schoolteacher or uncle, but curdled the blood when it came from someone with his power.

Toward the end of the Diem years, Dr. Tuyen—he had trained as both a lawyer and a medical doctor in Hanoi before coming to Diem's attention—joined a premature coup attempt, and was demoted to consul general in Egypt. He spent little time in Cairo, instead waiting in Hong Kong for events to sort themselves out in Vietnam. After Diem's assassination in November 1963, Dr. Tuyen made the mistake of listening to a couple of American journalists who said they were sure he would be safe in Saigon. Instead, under the various generals who ran South Vietnam after 1963, Tuyen spent several years on the prison island of Con Son and in Chi Hoa prison in Saigon. Even now, two or three policemen always stood watch over Dr. Tuyen's comings and goings, and those of his guests, at his home in Saigon.

With the signing of the Paris Peace Accords in early 1973, Tuyen and many of his friends assumed that Henry Kissinger's "decent interval," during which the United States would continue to support South Vietnam, was just two years. This was *le secret de Polichinelle*— the secret everyone knew. It was clear to Dr. Tuyen that the country must prepare for the possibility of a cutoff in American aid by 1975. This would require major reforms both in military strategy and tactics, and in politics. Dr. Tuyen had clear and detailed ideas as to what those reforms should be. He also had a means to make his ideas known, to the reading public at large and therefore of course to the palace. Under a pseudonym that also fooled no one who cared, he wrote regularly for *Chinh Luan*, the largest serious newspaper in Saigon.

By the first week of April, the time for setting out reforms was past. Now it was time to act. One day late in March, Dr. Tuyen had asked Dr. Truong Khue Quan, idly it seemed, what Dr. Quan thought Thich Tri Quang might be thinking. Dr. Quan was the director of the school for the children of dead soldiers. He was also a true Buddhist, and disciple of Thich Tri Quang, and the intermediary in the negotiations of 1963.

"He is fed up with politics," Dr. Quan said. "But I am sure he is not as leftist as most people think. You should try to see him in private. Maybe you two can do something good for the country."

A few days later, Dr. Quan came to see Tuyen. "Will you go to see him?"

"It is very dangerous," Tuyen said. "Is he ready to see me?"

"Yes," Quan said. "Go at night, secretly, by the back door."

And so it was that the tiny former secret-police chief slipped into the alleys leading to the back gate of the darkened pagoda of the silent monk well after sunset on the night of April 1. Now the time had come again to plot.

15

Jay Scarborough, Carolyn and John Miller, and the other Westerners
who had been captured in Ban Me Thuot spent five weeks straddling
March and April in a place they called Camp Sunshine.

They reached it after a bone-wrenching, enervating ride in the
GMC deuce-and-a-half in which they had set out from the Rose Garden. It was crowded in the back of the truck, all of them tied together
and the truck rolling and bucking over a deeply rutted trail deep into
the western reaches of Darlac province, near the Cambodian border.
Carolyn Miller feared that the truck would overturn and LuAnne
would be crushed. She reached for a purchase on the slats. Immediately the guard with them shone his flashlight on her hand and told
her to pull it down. Earlier, as they were setting out, one of the
ARVN prisoners grumbled that there would be more room for everyone if some people didn't have so many possessions. There was no
question whom he meant; Carolyn Miller wished that they had left
most of what they were carrying back in Ban Me Thuot.

They arrived at the new camp after midnight, were led someplace,
quickly spread out some thatch and slept.

In the morning, they discovered that their new home was a nine-
by-twelve-foot shelter of leaves and bamboo built by other prisoners. It
lay inside a stockade about the length of a football field and a bit

wider, enclosed by a fence of interwoven bamboo poles. Their fellow prisoners were about a thousand ARVN soldiers, a number that would double as the weeks slipped by.

In the first few days, they adjusted to camp life, which meant work details for the ARVN prisoners but demanded very little of the Westerners. They were allowed out of the stockade once a day to bathe and wash their clothes in a nearby stream. The guards and the other prisoners by and large respected the women's privacy, although the kitchen crews nonchalantly washed pots and pans in the stream even if the women and LuAnne were there. In midmorning, and again in the afternoon, after the traditional hour of rest after noon, they were given rice and a saltwater soup with, occasionally, a few leaves or powdered fish or bits of canned pork in it. Jay Scarborough was used to a Vietnamese diet, and routinely finished off five bowls of rice at a meal. He never had any trouble with his weight or his health in general. Some of the other Westerners, including both Carolyn and John Miller, could not eat as much rice and suffered especially from a vitamin deficiency, to which Scarborough seemed immune.

At the same time, the ARVN prisoners were allotted half a bowl of rice each meal, and many were seriously weakened. The Westerners were strictly prohibited from sharing their unlimited rations with the captured soldiers.

On the first full day in camp, nearly everything they had except their clothing and the small items they would need in camp were taken from them. They were given receipts for the confiscated articles, which included watches, money, pocketknives, passports, wedding rings, the Millers' Bru New Testament manuscript and the hated sewing machine.

"You can keep these," the officer in charge said, holding out a pair of tennis rackets.

"But why?" Carolyn Miller asked in surprise.

"You might want to use them," the man answered with a straight face.

At noon on Wednesday, March 19, four days after their arrival in Camp Sunshine, Carolyn Miller and the other women were making their way up the muddy track from the river to the camp when they passed a line of dusty new arrivals trudging down to the river. New prisoners arrived every day, and this group did not attract Carolyn Miller's attention until she recognized Norman and Joan Johnson, the Canadian missionaries they had not seen since the night of the attack. "We'll talk to you when we get back up," Norm Johnson said hurriedly. "Right now, I can hardly wait to get in that river."

Like the rest of them, the Johnsons had intended to get to Stru-harik's house that Monday morning. But when they emerged from their house—where they had spent the night in the shower stall—a series of rocket or mortar rounds, they didn't know which, popped down the street. They took quick cover in a neighbor's underground bunker.

They heard the communist troops advancing down the street "like a football team," Norm Johnson said. They heard them going from room to room in the house they had just left; heard one of the soldiers speak the word "Canada." He must have just come across the Canadian flag pinned to one wall in the living room.

"The eeriest part," Joan added, "was when one of them began to play our piano. I couldn't believe it. Sounds of fighting all around and this guy was playing the piano!"

When a soldier fired a round into the ground near the bunker, the Johnsons emerged and surrendered. During the days that the others were holed up in Struharik's house, they were moved from place to place in Ban Me Thuot, including areas that were being bombed by the South Vietnamese Air Force. Then they spent a few days at the Rose Garden. They didn't know it by that name. But that was where they first learned that their friends were captured, and safe.

An Indonesian and an Iranian delegate to the ICCS were in the same group. Struharik recognized the Indonesian, who came over to have a few words with them. As they were offering to let the man share their shelter, a camp official arrived and took both him and the Iranian away. The Westerners never saw them again. But they heard a few weeks later that they had been passed to Loc Ninh—the communists' command city in the South—and released from there to Saigon. The Westerners hoped that their few minutes of contact would lead to word to their families that they were alive and as well as could be expected under the circumstances.

They attended a few political lectures. And after Scarborough translated *giai phong* (liberation) and *de quoc My* (American imperialists) and the words for capitalism, socialism and revolution, even Carolyn Miller, whose Vietnamese was limited to what she needed to get around and to shop, could follow the drift of the proceedings. After it was decided that the foreigners need not attend the lectures, they still overheard them. They were, of course, unrelentingly anti-American. The Millers discussed how simple it would be for their captors to turn the ARVN prisoners against them. In fact, at the first lecture, the speaker had referred to the thousands of military advisers disguised as civilians that the Americans had left in Vietnam after the signing of the Paris Peace Accords, and pointed to the Ban Me Thuot group. Scarborough immediately rose to object, and the accusation was withdrawn.

Paul Struharik was struck at the similarities between the political meetings and church services. "Get everyone in the right mood with a few songs," he mused, "then the moral exhortation and pep talk, and finally a few more songs to finish it off. And here I am with a bunch of missionaries."

Despite the indoctrination sessions and the fact that the Westerners were being treated so much better than the captured soldiers, none of their fellow prisoners ever threatened them or even showed any resentment toward them.

Still, there were frictions, between the Westerners and the Vietnamese prisoners, and among the Westerners themselves.

Little things started disappearing: pens, cups, needles and thread—all of which they at first willingly loaned to the ARVN prisoners, until they realized that they were seldom returned. A last bit of cheese they were saving for Peter Whitlock's wedding anniversary was nowhere to be found when the day arrived. (Whitlock was called out for interrogation that day—they were called "work sessions"—and after he returned, the group made a special meal of rice, greens and fish.) Scarborough's multicolored Japanese-made shower sandals—his only footgear—were taken at the river as he was bathing, and his tarp disappeared after the first rain. Scarborough shrugged: "Someone must have needed them more than I did." The others were less philosophical.

One man in particular, whom they nicknamed "the moocher," irked them. Whenever the Ban Me Thuot group made a fire, he came over to heat something on it, and he routinely walked off with a few sticks of their firewood without asking for them.

The group had been given several cans of powdered milk. They discovered a variety of uses for the empty cans. One day the moocher borrowed one of the cans. The next day he returned with a canteen cup and offered to trade it for the can. While the missionaries were debating the trade, Scarborough said, "I can't speak for the others, but as far as I'm concerned you can *have* the can," and walked away.

Carolyn Miller and the other missionaries knew that it was not particularly easy for Scarborough, Struharik and Whitlock to spend hour after hour every day in the company of seven missionaries and a five-year-old girl who simply couldn't sleep or lie still as the adults did in the rest hour when the sun was at its highest. Indeed, Scarborough was spending more and more time each day with the ARVN soldiers, a group he had never before had occasion to know.

The missionaries had little choice but to let the moocher have the can without surrendering the canteen cup. Some of them grumbled at the way Scarborough had put them in a bad light. Carolyn Miller, who was particularly sensitive to the strains that were growing among them, knew that they could be eased only if they were talked about.

She found Scarborough sitting on a fallen log near the camp's front entrance. He looked up when she put her hand lightly on his shoulder. "Jay," she said, "please don't give up on us. I know we've got a long way to go, but we're trying. You're right, we have been pretty self-centered. But try to be patient with us and pray for us because God isn't through working on us."

Scarborough was what he would later call "a Catholic, for what it's worth," with the self-deprecation so common among nonpracticing Catholics. "Carolyn," he said now, "I just don't understand it. You people are supposed to be missionaries here, but sometimes I get the feeling you don't even *like* the Vietnamese."

Carolyn Miller was just a few years older than Scarborough. She said that he had to understand that while she and the others were missionaries they were also ordinary people, with the same "hang-ups and failures" as others. As for not liking the Vietnamese, she said that she had lived fourteen years in Vietnam and felt that she had never gotten to know them. "Our involvement has been almost entirely with the Bru," she said, "and they're completely different from the Vietnamese in both language and culture. With the Bru I feel completely at home. They are generally open and straightforward. They say exactly what they think and feel. But I've always felt the Vietnamese operate on two levels. The Bru say of them, 'The Vietnamese have two gall bladders.' "

Jay Scarborough was not given to lecturing people. He did not tell Carolyn Miller that she was the latest in a very long tradition: generation after generation of Frenchmen and then Americans—the Special Forces were a prime example—assigned to the highlands who then identified with the Montagnards against their traditional enemies, the lowland Vietnamese. What is remarkable is that Scarborough himself, with his affection for the Montagnards and the Chams, was now willing to befriend the South Vietnamese prisoners. Instead he said simply, "I think if you ever got a chance to know the Vietnamese in a rural community setting, you'd really like them."

"You're probably right," Carolyn agreed. "I wish I'd had the opportunity."

They sat in silence on the log for a few minutes. Then Carolyn said, "Jay, I'm concerned that we have harmony and unity as a group. We're a mixed bag in terms of backgrounds and personalities. But I'm praying that God will give us love and understanding toward each other."

"That's all very well," Scarborough replied, "but what about *them*," with a sweep of his arm that took in the whole compound. "There are a thousand people in this camp, all of them worse off than we are. We at least have the hope that some day we'll get out of here and go back to a country where there's freedom. These men don't even have that hope. One of them saw his wife and all his children killed in the fighting. Most of the others have no idea where their families are, or whether they'll see them again."

He paused, and then went on: "The way I see it, these may be the last weeks of my life. I'd like to spend them in a way that would do someone some good. These people are being fed a constant diet of anti-American propaganda. Maybe in some way I can counteract that by showing them that some Americans really care about them."

In that camp, the "work sessions" for the Westerners consisted only of interrogations. Ike Tolentino and all the missionaries had enough Vietnamese to function at the questionings with the help of the Vietnamese interpreter. Jay Scarborough had to interpret for Peter Whitlock, the visiting Australian, and also for Paul Struharik, the U.S. Agency for International Development man who had functioned as his government's Darlac province representative.

On Easter Sunday, the Westerners and Tolentino delayed their Easter service while Struharik underwent a particularly difficult interrogation. His questioners were eager that Struharik give them a complete list of the Vietnamese and Montagnards who had worked for him.

"I would feel very uncomfortable giving you that information," Struharik said.

"Why?"

"Those people were not only my employees, they were friends," Struharik said. "Do you think I want them to end up in a place like this?"

"Well," the official said, "you must realize that your attitude toward the revolution will be an important factor in determining when you will be released."

The discussion was not heated. But Struharik and Scarborough came away from it distressed at the threatening language.

When they returned to the group, the bamboo-and-thatch shelter in which they had been sleeping was being torn down to complete a new one in a quieter location out of the main traffic flow in the camp. Best of all, the new hut had a bamboo sleeping platform two feet off the ground. This was a blessing, because it was in Camp Sunshine that the rains began, and more than once in the last few weeks they had awakened on their mats on the ground to find themselves in cold rain and mud.

When the officials interrogated Jay Scarborough, they quickly realized that he liked Vietnamese and had made a number of close friendships over the years. They pressed him for the names of his closest friends. Like Struharik, Scarborough resisted. When they persisted, he hit on an ingenious way out. Through the first three days in April, he made a list.

Then he presented it to the authorities: a list of 653 Vietnamese, Cham and Montagnard names, as near as he could remember, every student he had ever taught. He guessed that he had remembered at least eighty percent of them.

II

A brief black storm shook Da Lat on Tuesday afternoon, the first day of April.

A Foreign Service Officer named Lamar ("Mac") Prosser, whose first experience in Vietnam had been a full thirty years earlier, waited out the storm in the largest Catholic church in the small mountain resort city. The previous bishop of Da Lat had been assassinated two years before. Recently, Rome had named his successor and the man, a Vietnamese, was coming now from Saigon to be invested.

Between the airport and the church, the bishop-to-be and his party ran into a small ambush. No one was hurt, but with the ambush and the storm he arrived two hours late. When he finally did arrive, the storm ended as suddenly as it had blown up, and sunlight streamed from the heavens as the ceremony got under way.

Years before, the Americans had given the university in Da Lat a small atomic reactor that was used for agricultural and medical research. In the closing days of March, Wolf Lehmann became extremely concerned that the fifty-seven fuel rods in the reactor—each in its own lead-lined barrel in a four-story-deep well of water—be removed from Vietnam. A Dr. Long directed the research institute, but neither he nor anyone else in Vietnam, American or Vietnamese, was qualified to disarm the reactor.

The night before the bishop's investiture, two C-130s arrived from Johnston Island, in the mid-Pacific. On board were a handful of MPs and two technicians from the Atomic Energy Commission. On the first night, the technicians sat down with Dr. Long and discussed what would have to be done to shut down the reactor.

They got it done and the barrels out through the next two nights. Prosser had already lined up heavy trucks to transport the barrels from the reactor to the airport.

The U.S. military plan was that the barrels would go on one plane while the other circled overhead. If anything happened to the first plane as it was being loaded, the second would land and get the cargo, security conditions permitting.

Mac Prosser went on the assumption that everything would go smoothly. Many of the residents of Da Lat had fled, but there was no communist pressure on the city.

Prosser had 125 people he wanted to get out. His own Vietnamese employees. Dr. Long, of course. Several other faculty members, all with their families. And Prosser had promised the French consul general in Saigon that he would see to the safety of the French nuns of the Eau de Vie order.*

The military at DAO were adamant that the pilots in Da Lat adhere to their orders: All the barrels were to go on one plane, if possible, and then both planes were to proceed directly back to Johnston Island.

Prosser wanted to use the backup plane to get his people to Saigon. And the recently returned ambassador agreed with Prosser.

In the first few days of April, the dispute escalated up to and beyond Secretary of Defense James Schlesinger, who still said no, the second plane could not be diverted to Saigon.

Martin then did a characteristic thing. He informed the White House that the plane sitting at the airport in Da Lat and now loaded with the fuel rods would be denied clearance to take off until Prosser's people were on the second plane and it was cleared for Saigon.

Faced with the ultimatum, Washington yielded.

III

General Weyand and Ambassador Martin had met with President Thieu on Friday, the first day of the Weyand mission. All three men had their principal aides with them.

Eric Von Marbod, an Assistant Secretary of Defense who was the Pentagon's top expert in logistics for the war, was stunned when Thieu raised the possibility that B-52s would reappear over the battlefields of South Vietnam. He and Weyand assured Thieu that the delivery of war matériel already in the pipeline for Saigon would be greatly accelerated.

Over the weekend, Weyand himself traveled partway up the coast,

* The order is composed of former French prostitutes who work with prostitutes in countries around the world. In Da Lat, the French nuns supported themselves with a pleasant little restaurant.

stopping in to see Consul General Moncrieff Spear and ARVN commanders in Nha Trang on Saturday.

By the time Thomas Polgar saw Weyand in his temporary offices at DAO on Tuesday morning, the Army Chief of Staff had come to the conclusion that President Thieu was still unaware of the seriousness of the military crisis. Further, Thieu's unrealistic assessment of the situation seemed to be reinforced by the ambassador, who still appeared not to have grasped the dramatic changes of the last three weeks.

Weyand had been the senior American officer in Vietnam in the early 1970s, had known Thieu for years and spoke Vietnamese. He wanted to see Thieu alone, one general spelling out the military realities for another. Martin vetoed the meeting.

The ambassador lived and ruled by laws. One of these was that no American saw Thieu unless the ambassador was present. But Polgar had an understanding first with Ellsworth Bunker and then with Martin that he could see Thieu without the ambassador on purely intelligence matters. It took a day to set it up, but on Wednesday, April 2, Polgar took advantage of the understanding to try to do what General Weyand would have done if he had been allowed to see Thieu alone.

He traveled to the palace with Ted Shackley, one of his predecessors as station chief in Saigon and now one of his Washington bosses. They drove into the palace grounds at a side gate and were taken up to the second-floor office of Laughing Boy Quang. After a few pleasantries, Thieu's fat national security adviser took the two CIA men through the long reception hall and not into the formal office where Thieu normally met with diplomats but into a spare room with a small conference table. Polgar guessed that it was probably the briefing room where Thieu met with his commanders. Then Quang left.

After more of the obligatory pleasantries, Thieu invited the Americans to join him at the conference table.

Often, as a matter of protocol, when Thieu met with foreigners he used an interpreter and spoke in Vietnamese. With Polgar and Shackley, he used his English, which was close to fluent.

Polgar had come to relay Weyand's private, candid view of the battlefield realities. He was surprised and finally irritated when Thieu launched into a detailed account of his strategy for the elections that were scheduled that fall. As the president spoke, Polgar noted how gaunt and haggard he appeared to be.

He would broaden his own political party, he said, and at the same time sanction a real opposition party. He put a chart showing how the parties would be organized, province by province, on the table. The next time, no one could accuse him of so intimidating the opposition that the election was a one-man affair, as it had been in 1971.

For years, the street running directly in front of the palace had been blocked to traffic, for the same reason that all air navigation charts showed a large rectangle around the palace into which no one was to fly. As Thieu rambled on about politics, Polgar thought idly that these interior rooms in the palace might be the only ones in Saigon from which one could not hear the rumble of trucks or the rising and dying *sprr-r-r-r-a-a-aats* of the unmuffled motorcycles and *cyclo-pousses*. Thieu's irrelevant ramblings were the only noise in what would otherwise have been a novel utter silence.

"Now for a little reality," Polgar thought, as he opened the file on the table in front of him.

"Yes, Mr. President," he said. "You are planning for the kind of political system we have always hoped to see here. But now, with your permission, I would like to review the military situation."

Polgar had nothing that Colonel Luong, the intelligence officer at the Joint General Staff, could not have given Thieu. Luong was a sober, realistic military intelligence man. But bad news is slow to travel upward, especially in Asia. So Polgar set out to review what Luong had shared with Bill Le Gro, his U.S. counterpart, as supplemented by what Frank Snepp and the other analysts of North Vietnamese intelligence in Polgar's office knew, region by region, division by division.

Polgar himself was sober and calm, as Weyand would have been in the hour the ambassador denied him. As he drew to a close, Thieu cradled his face in his fists. He had said nothing through the briefing. His expression was first bored, then seemingly dazed, abstracted; in the last few moments he was fully alert. The corners of his mouth had turned down.

"General Weyand wanted to do this himself," Polgar said. "Some . . . niceties . . . at the embassy prevented him from coming. You understand, Mr. President, how it is with this ambassador. I am acting on General Weyand's behalf."

"Yes," Thieu said. Then there was movement in his chest and shoulders, and he closed his eyes.

Polgar and Shackley looked at each other as Thieu pulled for breath. Polgar stole a glance, and saw the thin trickle of tears from the eyes to the fists, the cheeks quickly rubbed dry.

Shackley finished with a brave two-minute review of the effort the Administration was mounting in Congress for the supplemental aid. Thieu managed the closing pleasantries and it was over.

16

On the afternoon of Monday, March 31, I was on a plane making the ninety-minute hop to Bangkok. The bureau had footage so urgent that it had to be satellited from the Thai capital. Again I was a courier, and didn't even know what was on the film in the cans in the red mesh bag between my feet. Now the days were starting when life was lived in ten- and five-minute bites of time, moving from one small specific task to the next. All the little lulls in daily routine, when, in normal times, Arthur Lord would have told me what I was carrying, had disappeared.

A Thai just outside the customs area held aloft a sheet of paper reading:

DAVID BUTLER
NBC NEWS
Barry Kalb Is Waiting
Outside with a Car

The driver inched through strangled traffic to the TV studio from which the film would be transmitted. Kalb jumped out, instructing the man to take me to the Montien Hotel.

I had been in Bangkok briefly on a magazine assignment six months earlier. I knew only three cities in Asia—Saigon, Phnom Penh and Bangkok. And although I knew Bangkok and Phnom Penh hardly at all, I knew that Bangkok was very different from Saigon and Phnom Penh. As I walked through a park on that first visit and looked across a pond to a tapering thirty-story hotel called the Dusit Thani, and next to it the clean modernistic Southeast Asia headquarters building of IBM, I realized that not all the capitals in the region had had their economic development arrested in the early 1950s. There were U.S. servicemen in Bangkok, and plenty of policemen. But you didn't see Thai soldiers on the streets; you certainly didn't see the one-legged veterans that were on every crowded Saigon sidewalk.

The magazine article had been about the hordes of European men, especially Germans, who came to Bangkok for its wide-open night life. So I had spent most of my ten days and nights in Bangkok in bars, nightclubs and massage parlors. I was not much of an expert on the bars of Saigon. But I knew a few of them well enough to know that the atmosphere in the sex-oriented bars of Bangkok was easier, opener and less desperate than in Saigon. And the sound equipment was better.

Now, on this last night in March, I left the Montien Hotel and walked down a strip of bars on Patpong Road to the Mississippi Queen, which had the best sound system I had ever heard in Asia. American Air Force men and German tourists laughed with their arms around girls in miniskirts or bikinis and looked up at girls in bikinis go-go dancing to a mixture of soul music and reggae on platforms cantilevered over each end of the bar. I drank a beer called Singha, and bought a couple of drinks for a girl named Noi. She giggled as I tried to get the tone right. Above me, a girl was grinding her hips to "Proud Mary," riding her loosely twined hands in a great arc to and from her crotch.

In bars, listening to music, I thought I did my best thinking in bars, listening to music. And I loved the blaring, brilliant fidelity of the music in this place. But after less than an hour in the Mississippi Queen I got up, slipping pretty little Noi a few extra baht for wasting her time, and walked back to the hotel, ignoring the temptation to explore more of Bangkok. I felt that I had to distance myself from this vivid, exotic reality outside Vietnam in preparation for Saigon, where I knew the rooms of my life, and even had a little of the language— where there was, I thought, no danger at all.

I had an early flight, so I skipped breakfast and didn't buy the Bangkok *Post* until I got to Don Mouang airport, flipped it open after I had settled into my seat. Above the fold there were two photographs from the North Vietnamese news agency showing their troops entering Hue and rushing to the Citadel with their flag, those photos six days old now. And a map of South Vietnam with half the territory, sweeping up through the Central Highlands and encompassing all of Military Region 1, including Da Nang, blackened. Neither the photographs nor the map would appear in that day's Saigon *Post*. Nor would the main story, which ran under the banner "HORROR SCENES ALONG COAST" and the headline "S-VN TROOPS KILL, RAPE REFUGEES":

Off the coast of Da Nang, South Vietnam (AP, UPI)—South Vietnamese Marines shot about 25 people on the fantail of an American evacuation ship, boatloads of troops fought sea battles for lighters [landing craft], and troops shot their way aboard barges Saturday in frantic last-minute attempts to escape the fall of Da Nang.

The Marines later terrorized the ship, *Pioneer Contender*, just before it arrived at Nha Trang yesterday morning, forcing the US crew to barricade themselves in a cabin and killing, raping and looting other refugee passengers.

In the Da Nang evacuation panic, refugees who had paid their life savings, abandoned their families and everything they owned for a passage to safety died by the scores on the barges in the harbor waiting for ships to rescue them.

AP reporter Peter O'Loughlin alone saw 15 corpses and was told of hundreds dead on other barges.

In the city, according to those who escaped on Saturday night, anarchy prevailed. An estimated 1.5 million persons—one million of them refugees from other northern provinces—were abandoned by the officials, deserted by an army that refused to fight, and killed by North Vietnamese rockets.

Marauding troops who shed their uniforms but not their weapons went on the rampage, looting rice stores, robbing warehouses of tinned goods and soft drinks, and setting fire to buildings.

Overloaded lighters and small boats capsized in choppy seas as they headed out to evacuation ships. Hundreds drowned. Bloated bodies floated in the harbor.

Even a dog was seen swimming away from shore.

These were some of the incredible scenes of panic, fear and flight witnessed by O'Loughlin and crews of American ships over Easter weekend in Da Nang harbor. . . .

[Earlier, in Da Nang], up to 6,000 people were jammed in an area about as big as three tennis courts for up to four days without food, water, shelter or toilet facilities.

People died by the score and their possessions [were] looted by their fellow passengers.

O'Loughlin saw two men scavenging in the debris of an emptied barge, picking over the belongings of a dead woman before they boarded the evacuation ship *Pioneer Contender*.

In Nha Trang, South Vietnamese Marines fired at the helicopter of President Ford's personal photographer, David Kennerly, when he attempted to take pictures of the ship, the *Pioneer Contender*.

Passengers aboard the *Pioneer Contender* told tales of rape, looting and murder by the Marines.

They said about 8,000 persons were aboard the ship, about one third of whom were Marines and South Vietnamese soldiers.

Civilians said the Marines beat up refugees, stole money, raped some girls and women and killed those who protested.

Kennerly said he flew over the *Pioneer Contender* in an Air America helicopter, accompanied by the US consul general in Nha Trang, Moncrieff J. Spear.

As Kennerly took pictures of the ship, "the military people on the ship started shooting at us," said Kennerly, a Pulitzer prize-winner.

Kennerly, who has been Ford's personal photographer since the President took office, is on a fact-finding mission for Ford, along with Army Chief of Staff Gen. Frederick C. Weyand.

Weyand conferred in Saigon and briefly visited the Mekong delta yesterday and did not witness the shipboard incidents.

Refugees said they could not say how many persons aboard the ship were murdered by the Marines, considered one of the best fighting forces in Vietnam.

One witness said Marines robbed one man of US$4,500, then threw him overboard.

Another said a priest was beaten up by Marines when he tried to intervene.

At Cam Ranh, military police sealed off the port and tried to quell the Marines, but the rebellious troops managed to break out of the cordon and began commandeering vehicles to Nha Trang, about 20 miles to the north.

If drivers of the vehicles refused, the Marines blew out the tires with gunfire.

In Nha Trang, the first signs of panic hit the city yesterday and rumors began spreading wildly that communist forces were close and evacuation of Nha Trang was imminent.

Residents of the refugee-swollen city began looking for ways out, and police and military police cordoned off the airport. Air tickets to Saigon were virtually unobtainable.

US officials pruned the consulate staff to essential personnel only.

In Saigon, a US Embassy spokesman said about 10 members of the US mission in Vietnam had decided to send their families out of Saigon to safer Asian cities because of the deteriorating situation.

In the first few pages of the paper and especially on the editorial page there were other Vietnam stories. I forced myself to read the first two paragraphs of a story by Peter Arnett of the Associated Press:

SAIGON (AP)

The military slippage by the South Vietnamese government has been so unexpectedly widespread in recent weeks that informed Western and Vietnamese sources believe a major Communist assault against the capital of Saigon could not be adequately resisted.

These sources, who see the push against Saigon as inevitable, believe that President Nguyen Van Thieu's power base among senior military officers is being rapidly undermined, and that political changes could swiftly follow more Communist successes.

That was enough for now. I turned to a story on the back page that promised a Muhammad Ali-Joe Frazier title defense in Bangkok in the next few months. I read the first few lines, refolded the paper so that I came across the big ad below the fold on page one—line drawings of a lovely Asian woman and a good-looking Western man with the legends "The Garden of Onsen" and "Bangkok's Finest Massage Parlor"—and then put the paper on the empty seat next to me.

I reached into the pocket of my white short-sleeved shirt and jiggled out the first cigarette of the day, a sweet, strong cigarette from a blue-and-white pack identifying the contents as Samits, Thailand's version of Ruby Queens, which I must have bought last night in the Mississippi Queen, I really didn't know.

I pushed a button and ordered something, a coffee or a tea or a Bloody Mary, and picked myself up and moved to the window seat to look down at the light cloud cover scudding under us and thought that the first thing I had to do when I landed and got back into the only city I ever loved was to tell Peter O'Loughlin, a young convivial Australian, that that was a great line, the bit about the dog.

And I would have to have a minute or two with Arnett, who had been there forever.

"Peter thinks they're going to take it all," I thought. "That's crazy."
"Isn't it?"

Leaving work at eight o'clock that night, I hesitated at the mouth of the Eden Building. Loudspeakers that had gone up in the last few days blared scratchy government propaganda. The crowds on the sidewalk were thick and urgent, as if the loudspeakers were telling them to hurry. The men's white shirts glowed in the greenish night lighting. A girl in a red miniskirt and shiny black boots that reached over her knees veered close, looked dreamily into my face and darted her tongue in and out of her painted mouth, purple in that light, in mock and hate-filled seductiveness. I shook my head.

I was leaving work early. Most of my colleagues were trying to find out if the government had abandoned Nha Trang. Maybe it was the forty-five minutes at the Mississippi Queen the night before. I wanted to hear some music. I wanted to see Anh Tu* and the band again. Tu was the younger brother in an attractive clutch of brothers and sisters who made up the core of a pop-music band they called The Uptight. I was attracted to Tu in part because he had the best English in the group, and also in part because I thought Tu was the best musician, the one of them in the family who might conceivably make it in the States, or in Paris.

In the fall, Tu and his older brother had been arrested when they were close to obtaining fake papers that would have identified them as Chinese, providing them a much better chance of being allowed to bribe someone to give them exit visas. Tu had spent a few weeks in jail. Then, after the payment of a consideration raised by his family and by a young Belgian diplomat with a special interest in the family, Tu had been allowed to join the Army. There was a bit of irony here, since the family and the Belgian diplomat, Patrick Van der Velde, had been paying bribes for years to keep Tu out of the Army. But the Army was better than jail. And in fact, a little more money changing hands, Tu was sent to a relatively safe area west of Saigon, and was given occasional leaves so that he could come to Saigon to see his mother and to sing for a couple of nights with his sisters and older brother. (In fact, it wasn't all a function of bribery: La Anh Tu had reached a level of fame in South Vietnam. He and his family weren't as famous as the family that constituted CBC,† the GIs' favorite band, or Elvis Phuong; but there were cassette tapes all over the country with his face and name on them. Beyond that, anyone who took one look at Anh Tu knew instantly that he was built to sing pop music, not to carry a pack. On his infrequent patrols, fellow soldiers volunteered to carry his gear. When he was in training camp, his commanding officer was a fan, and Tu lived with him and his family on the base.)

The Pink Night Club was only half filled when I arrived. Vietnamese teen-agers mostly, just two or three tables of Americans with their Vietnamese girl friends. But I sensed a buzz of expectation. I had already stood and moved briefly to the corner of the bar to see that Tu's sisters and Van der Velde, the young Belgian, were seated at the band's table, next to the door to the dressing room behind the bar. I

* Pronounced Ahng Dtuh.
† CBC stood for *Con Ba Cu*—Mothers' Children. They played hard, psychedelic rock, and managed to relocate to Bangkok in 1973.

finished the very weak first Scotch, ordered a double and moved to the table. Van der Velde and the girls, who had so little English that I could not communicate with them, made room for me.

Duc Cang,* a strikingly handsome young man who had more or less taken Tu's place in the band, was off in another mournful ballad, the standard thing, a soldier pining for his loved one. Tu's older brother, a much sturdier young man who did a good Tom Jones imitation, and who had managed to keep singing almost every night by arranging to get himself assigned to the National Police band, still had not appeared.

Patreek, as Tu pronounced it, was the number-two man in the two-man Belgian Embassy. "I am the commercial attaché, and the military attaché, and the political attaché—all the attachés," Van der Velde had said when he and I first met, at the same table. "There are the two of us, the ambassador and me. And the ambassador cannot understand that I actually have friends here. My little brown friends, he calls them."

In the club, which was the only place I ever saw him, Van der Velde wore black pants and a ruffled white shirt. I was little traveled in Europe. I did not know that many European men looked this way: a little short, a little plump, a little delicate. Van der Velde was given to tossing off funny judgments in near-perfect English.

Patrick's story was that he was engaged to be married to Lan Anh, the youngest of the three sisters in the band, a pretty little girl who flailed away at the drums; but her mother objected. I tried to believe the story, knowing that in fact before he went into the Army Anh Tu had lived with the diplomat. Through the months when we were feeling each other out, Van der Velde and I spoke in code. Now Van der Velde spoke plainly.

In a quick, low whisper, he told me that Tu was being very stupid. "I didn't tell you. I haven't seen you these last few weeks. The same day that Thieu told the Army to leave the plateau—what a fool, to do it that way—Tu abandoned the Army. You understand? He quit. So stupid. Now he is staying with me. Okay, hiding with me; yes, I understand, very difficult for the police or the Army to come into my house, I am the diplomat. And Tu says that the same day he quit the Army many officers run away also. But really, this is stupid, what he is doing tonight; I tried to stop him."

Duc Cang broke into the pattering of applause at the end of a song and spoke urgently in Vietnamese, and the band led a burst of applause punctuated by shouts of pleasure. I listened for it but did not hear the name. Then, Duc Cang in English: "We have a special guest

* A pseudonym.

tonight, ladies and gentlemen. If you have to leave, please go out that way"—he pointed to the door I had entered through—"because we lock the Nguyen Hue door [the main entrance to the nightclub]. Now, our friend, our friend . . ."

Tu was making his way to the stage and the applause built to a crescendo and Duc Cang was able to keep from saying the name.

> I prayed that he would finish, but he just kept right on,
> Strumming my pain with his fingers,
> Singing my life with his words,
> Killing me softly with his song,
> Killing me softly with his song,
> Telling my whole life with his words,
> Killing me softly, with his song. . . .*

Remarkably, with the curfew at ten, the room almost filled in the half hour between eight-thirty and nine. Most of the customers were still young Vietnamese, but there were also tables of Americans I had never seen before: Marines with their bar girls, middle-aged USAID civilians, a few men alone at the bar whom I saw when I went to it for a new drink, including my friend Paul Schaberger.

Schaberger and I shook hands and grinned but didn't try to talk over the music and laughter. I wondered how the word had spread so quickly. It was as if the relatively small Saigon that knew the Pink Night Club, as it digested the news from Da Nang, suddenly knew that it had to go to the room, that the next ratcheting back of the curfew could kill the music altogether.

There was one bad moment. Tu and his sisters were singing "How Can I Tell Her About You?" and a big American started abusing a waiter. He wanted a table on the edge of the dance floor. "I *tole* Mouse I was coming tonight," the man said, loud, in the semidarkness. "He *swore* I could have that table. Now you ain't gonna put me back there in the corner, goddamnit! I been comin' to this f-----' club for five years. Ask Tu."

I shuddered and shut my eyes and finally the commotion died down. When I opened them, the Vietnamese teen-agers at the prized table had been displaced.

With the opening chords of "Chain Chain Chain," the room erupted in applause, whistles and rebel yells. As he usually did when he wasn't carrying the melody, Tu joined his sisters in the backup vocals. His voice was normally an upper-range tenor, controlled to sweetness. But when force was called for, it was there; and when it

* "Killing Me Softly with His Song," music by Charles Fox, lyrics by Norman Gimbel, copyright © 1972 by Charles Fox and Norman Gimbel.

came, there was always a shock that that reed of a body could blow so clear.

In only six weeks, I had forgotten the effect the music had on me. As the band moved through "You're So Vain" and "It Never Rains in California" and "A Rose in Spanish Harlem" and "Proud Mary," I tried once more to identify the spell it cast on me. Some of it, I knew, was simple homesickness. I yielded with the other Americans to the familiar music celebrated in an alien culture. "Gloria would call it cultural imperialism, of course," I thought, a nod to Gloria Emerson, *The New York Times* correspondent who had been one of my first Saigon tutors, and dismissed the thought with a very small smile: Would that all we had done for twenty years was teach them to imitate the Bee Gees.

No, it was something in the band. And not just Tu, but Tu with two of his sisters. Khanh Ha, the older girl, wore her hair just a little longer than Tu wore his. There was a curl to her smile that made her look French; in fact, if one had seen just the two of them together, Tu and Khanh Ha, one could guess that they were half or perhaps a quarter French, the girl getting more of the foreign genes than the boy. But Thuy An, the younger girl, whose smile was sweet and mischievous, could have been only Vietnamese.

The three of them danced as they sang, the girls coordinating their steps with each other more than they did with Tu, and when one of them missed a word or a beat, they glanced at Tu and at each other and brought their hands to their lips to hide giggles, for a moment under their Western dresses and the Western music blushing schoolgirls.

Khanh Ha's voice shaved the smokiness that colored Tu's except when Tu's was at its very clearest. Thuy An's lower, open voice completed the sound. Tung Giang,* the band's bass player and the manager of the club, was smart enough to mike the singers so the loud true harmony pushed against the chest even harder than the trumpets and the amplified guitars. But finally the effect flowed even more from the transparent joy in the tight movements and open faces of the three young musicians than from the music.

Tuan Ngoc,† Tu's tough-looking older brother, joined the band and finished the set with a near-perfect copy of "American Pie," good ole boys down on the levee, and the lights went on so suddenly at the height of the applause that I wondered if the place was being raided, cops or troops rushing in to grab Tu. But no one around me seemed

* Tung Zahng—and "Mouse," to most of his American friends, following his Vietnamese nickname, which was not insulting.
† Twahn Nyop.

alarmed and I looked at my watch and saw that it was two minutes before ten.

It was like the end of any other night in the Pink Night Club, but a little rushed, the lights coming on to reveal a shabby room with beer-stained carpeting, and then the wretched tape playing the original of one of the songs we had just heard in wildly exuberant imitation.

As Tu moved from the stage to the table, he laughed, touching friends and fans lightly on the shoulder, leaning to speak a word, the athlete after the win who had, in addition, gotten away with something.

Now everyone stood, preparing to leave. Van der Velde moved toward Tu, spoke his name with a note of authority and said they had to go. "I know," Tu said, but he wasn't finished with a friend.

I didn't need to speak to Tu. In that room, I was truly a voyeur, wanting only to sit there and watch them sing, turn over in my mind the joy they took in the music and letting some of it wash into myself.

But as it happened Paul Schaberger and I fell in behind the family and Van der Velde at the tail end of the crowd shuffling to the now unlocked Nguyen Hue exit. As I listened to Schaberger propose that we move to a nearby hotel rooftop bar that stayed open after hours, I took in Van der Velde's impatience to hustle Tu to the door, the singer's gradual disentanglement from fans and friends who hadn't seen him since Tet.

Then we were on the sidewalk and Van der Velde opened the back door of a limousine. "Tu. Let's go. Quick," he said.

Tu, who was all eyes, had finally spotted me. He seemed to want to say something. I told Schaberger to wait a minute and said, "It was great, Tu. Just like before. How are you?"

"I'm okay," Tu said, the postperformance energy almost drained away. "Patreek told you? I escaped the Army."

"Yeah, very dangerous to sing." Tu was one of the few young Vietnamese I knew who spoke with what sounded like a Jamaican lilt.

"Maybe I have to see you someday," Tu said. Apparently the thought had just occurred to him.

"You have the telephone number?" I asked.

"Tu, come on!"

"I think Patreek has it."

"Yes," I said, and watched him slip quickly into the big car. Tuan Ngoc and the sisters, including the little teen-aged drummer girl to whom Van der Velde was theoretically engaged, had sped off minutes before in one of the last taxis left on the boulevard. The limousine bottomed slightly as it pulled away from the curb in a low-throated roar.

. . .

"David, come on!" Schaberger called from fifteen yards down the sidewalk.

I liked Schaberger. He had been in Saigon for years, first with the Phoenix program and now with the Mission Warden Office, which was what the U.S. Embassy called what amounted to a unit of military police. Since there were no longer any active-duty U.S. troops in South Vietnam, there were no military police. But the embassy needed a corps of men to supervise the guards at American installations and homes of American officials, and to act in liaison with the South Vietnamese police, especially in cases that involved Americans. As Schaberger had told me when we first met, in the Pink Night Club, he normally spent the couple of hours after work—before he went home to his Vietnamese wife and her son, whom he had adopted, and the two big dogs he had brought over with him from Queens this tour, Bourbon and Whiskey—in the bars where girls drank with Americans for "tea," an expensive few ounces of Coca-Cola and perhaps a whiff of alcohol. ("I like those bars; hell, I came of age in them; but I'll tell you, David, I'm a happily married man. I don't screw around, and that's the truth.") But once in a while he dropped into the Pink Night, with mail from the States for Tu or more often for one of the sisters.

I caught up with him at the heavy glass doors of the Central Palace Hotel. A Chinese teen-ager in a natty hotel uniform unlocked the doors and led us to a bank of elevators. We rode to the penthouse bar and I watched, bemused, as for the second time in twenty minutes someone I knew worked a crowd.

Schaberger moved into the room, which was crowded with American men and Vietnamese women, as adroitly as any politician—bending over and over again to touch a shoulder, speak a word, flash the grin. We got a table with some pilots and there was talk of Da Nang and Phnom Penh. I found myself being challenged to fly into the Cambodian capital with a rice flight, one of the planes that shuttled into Phnom Penh with American-funded rice from Saigon, and accepted eagerly, exchanging phone numbers with the Continental Airways pilot.

Then I got up to find a men's room. I found it, started back to the table, and stopped instead at the bar to talk with George Esper.

The Associated Press bureau chief looked tired and alone.

"The universe has spun off its wheels," I said. "George Esper is not in his office reporting the fall of another province to the North Vietnamese."

"Ahh," Esper said. "*David* Butler, *NBC* News, *Sai*-Gon. Good to see you. 'The universe has spun off its wheels.' That would be a good lead. I wonder what they'd say in New York if I used it? Actually, I just gave them another province."

"Nha Trang?"

"Yeah, where you been?"

"Off the story again," I said. "I was in the Pink Night. Tu, the kid, the soldier, you know, the singer I like, he deserted a couple of weeks ago, and he decided to sing tonight, dumb really. Risky. Is Nha Trang really gone?"

"Yeah," Esper said. "I almost made it to the club. I heard Tu might be singing. I wanted to see Khanh Ha. I gotta talk to her. We don't know about Nha Trang, really. Looks like Phu bugged out first, then the Americans. Christ, it's fast. How's Tu?"

"Okay, I think," I said. "Same as ever on stage. Best stage presence I've ever seen, and I've seen both Baez and Jagger. Nobody else has that joy, that smile. But I talked to him for a second just now on the sidewalk. He's a little scared, I think."

"S - - -, he oughta be scared," Esper said. "I know you like him. Everybody likes Tu. I like his sister. Hey, bartender, can we get a couple of drinks over here?"

The efficient middle-aged bartender brought the drinks and we kept talking.

In the last thirty minutes I seen Anh Tu get rather quickly serious. Esper had been serious from the beginning.

"I'm not an old man, Dave," he said. "But I'm over forty. I've given most of my adult life to this place. What the hell does it all *mean?*"

"It's not as if it were unimportant work, George," I said.

"Yeah, I know," the bighearted Greek-American reporter said. "I'm not really thinking about me, I guess. Christ, we used to write for *days* about battles for little towns, for camps in the f - - - - -' jungle. Guys were *fighting*. Vietnamese and Americans. For f - - - - -' *weeks,* David. You remember."

"Not really," I said. "This is my first offensive."

"Qui Nhon and Nha Trang in one day," Esper said. "Jesus."

17

The communists finally entered Da Nang and restored order on Sunday, March 30. And in the next four days, the defenders of four important cities on the bulging coast of South Vietnam south of Da Nang abandoned their posts and fled south as if Da Nang were a contagion carried by the demobbed, bitter Marines and foot soldiers who made it out of the northern provinces.

As shells crashed around the province headquarters in Qui Nhon, the country's third-largest city, on the night of Monday, March 31, the commander of the ARVN 22d Division, a General Phan Dinh Niem, suffered a nervous collapse. A naval officer, Commodore Hoang Co Minh, was told to take control of the division. He circled offshore with contradictory orders streaming in to him from various commands. But he did not even know the correct frequency on which to contact whatever commanders of the 22d Division might still be at their posts. In fact, most of Qui Nhon's defenders that night were fighting not the communists but one another to get to the shore and escape.

At the nearby Phu Cat air base, nearly sixty aircraft, many of them flyable, were left for the enemy.

On Sunday, March 30, in Nha Trang, pathetic General Pham Van Phu prohibited his soldiers from moving without orders. On Tuesday,

April 1, he left his headquarters, got in a helicopter and hopped to the very nearby air base, from which he and a few senior officers flew to Saigon. As in Pleiku, Phu's chief of staff, Colonel Le Khac Ly, did not learn that Phu had left until after the fact.

That afternoon, Colonel George Jacobson, the ambassador's special assistant for field operations, ordered the Americans to pull out of Nha Trang. Consul General Moncrieff Spear, unlike Al Francis, had done little to prepare for a possible evacuation. He and the sizable number of official Americans in Nha Trang—many of them refugees from the northern provinces—had to cope with mobs both at the consulate and at the airfield. Marines fired in the air to keep soldiers from overtaking the American flights. The Americans also left behind more than a hundred Vietnamese consulate employees whom they had promised never to abandon.

Drunken, looting ARVN troops set fire to the central market and other points in the pretty seaside resort town. The communists were still many miles away, and did not occupy Nha Trang for another four days.

The same thing happened in Cam Ranh Bay two days later, on April 3. Commanders fled, defenses collapsed, and the city was taken over by the Marines, who shot one another and other troops and the terrified civilians as they tried to board vessels out or commandeered vehicles for the drive south.

On that same day, the panic reached the next town south, Phan Rang. But in Phan Rang, the threat was so remote that the next day a new advance headquarters, commanded by General Nguyen Vinh Nghi, was established in the city with an Airborne brigade and remnants of other divisions. Nghi's forces were to hold Phan Rang for another twelve days.

Late in the afternoon of Thursday, April 3, Captain Anh, the translator at the government's daily military press briefings, stood at an American military map in NBC's inner office. "They fought about two hours here," he said, pointing to Tuy Hoa, north of Nha Trang. He moved his hand down to Cam Ranh Bay: "They say they fought half an hour here." He swept the arm farther south down the coast, to Phan Rang and Phan Thiet: "And here, and here," he said, "they just run away now. It's so fast now, Butler. Too fast."

II

Early that week, Graham Martin gave one of his rare interviews. His correspondent was Garrick Utley, who had recently arrived to bolster NBC's coverage. John Swenson, the USIS officer with whom Martin preferred to deal, made the arrangements, and sat in on the interview. Martin spoke with evident sincerity about the prospects of holding a truncated South Vietnam, from Nha Trang south, living off the riches of the Mekong delta. Swenson thought the scenario was absurd.

III

Sometime in the middle of the week after the fall of Da Nang, Don Hays, the junior budget officer, discovered that a cable from Washington allowing embassy dependents to leave the country was being held in the communications center. Hays saw to it that the cable was in every in-box in the embassy the next morning. He also booked passage for his wife, who was nine months pregnant, and his four-year-old daughter on the next Pan Am flight out.

The ticket counter was jammed with Vietnamese waving fistfuls of piasters and dollars at the agents. Hays had to shoulder his wife and daughter through the mob into the waiting room. He thought he had been the first to act. But when he reached the lounge, he found both Denny Ellerman, the economics counselor, and Jim Devine, Martin's handpicked political-military counselor, waiting to put their wives on the same flight.

In the chaos of the boarding procedure, Hays found himself whisked onto the plane. He was tempted to stay on it. Instead, he kissed his wife goodbye and headed back into the city, wondering how long he would be a bachelor in Saigon.

IV

Immediately after the fall of Da Nang, Alan Carter's superiors at the Washington headquarters of the United States Information Agency cabled their man in Saigon with a request for an "atmospheric"—a report on the mood in Saigon.

It was not unusual for people in Washington, both inside and outside the United States Information Agency, to go to Carter for reporting they sensed they were not getting from the embassy. Indeed, on one of Carter's trips home during his brief tenure as USIS* chief in Saigon, Philip Habib, the Assistant Secretary of State for East Asia, had said: "You know, Alan, we'd like to hear from you once in a while." The animosity between Habib and Graham Martin was well enough known so that Carter understood that what Habib wanted were reports Martin had not cleared.

Alan Carter came to Saigon at the beginning of September 1974,

---

* In 1975, the agency was known as the United States Information Agency in Washington and as the United States Information Service abroad. The idea was to prevent confusion between USIA and CIA.

after a particularly successful posting in Tokyo. He was one of those men in the bureaucracy who at various stages had been the youngest ever chosen for a certain slot—the case, for example, when Edward R. Murrow picked him to head up the agency's television service. "Every organization has to have its house black, its house woman and its house maverick," Carter sometimes told the small groups of journalists he regularly invited to lunch at the USIS villa on Tu Xuong Street, a few blocks north of the palace, in the heart of the diplomatic quarter. "I'm the agency's house heretic—the guy they can point to and say, 'Hey, we're not all faceless apparatchiks here; we encourage dissent; look at Carter.' "

Between Tokyo and Saigon, Carter asked Martin when they were both in Washington if he really wanted him in Vietnam. "Sure," Martin said. "I'm surrounded by yes-men. I need someone who'll say no once in a while."

It didn't take long to discover that Graham Martin's interpretation of "once in a while" was, say, maybe once, five years from now. At two early meetings, Carter concurred when other participants were bold enough to suggest that the virtual state of war between the embassy and the American press corps might be working against the embassy's advantage. Each time, the ambassador moved quickly on to other business and then managed to say: "What we don't really need are newcomers telling us how to conduct our affairs."

The second cut came at one of the weekly gatherings of the senior staff called mission council meetings. As it broke up, the USIS chief caught up with Martin and said, "Mr. Ambassador, whether you like it or not I'm going to accompany you back to your office."

There he said: "If you're going to humiliate me at a mission council meeting, you may as well send me home. Because I obviously can't do my job without your support."

Martin tilted his head, fixed his eyes on Carter's and said, "Now, Alan, whatever would make you think I meant *you?*"

Shortly thereafter, Carter hosted the first of his series of lunches and dinners with the American journalists in Saigon. He was a solid, youthful-looking fifty-one years old, the possessor of a trim goatee and trim, mildly iconoclastic views. He also had a tempered liking for journalists, which is to say a genuine respect for the good ones and a keen realization of the damage the few bad ones could do. He was gregarious. He thought it was very much part of his job to repair the poisonous relations that existed between the embassy and the journalists. And so the small gatherings served a number of purposes.

After that first dinner, the ambassador called him to the embassy and asked for a detailed "memcon"—a memorandum of the conversation. He wanted the names of the participants along with what each had said—and what Carter had said in reply.

"Mr. Ambassador, you know that I can't do that," Carter said. "I can tell you now, standing here, that they had numerous complaints about their relationship with the embassy. And I can also tell you that I agreed with many of those complaints. That's my report."

Martin shook his head and spoke with what seemed to be some sadness. "Well, Alan," he said, "this just proves again that you're not really interested in getting on the team."

Carter's cable in reply to the request for a report on the mood of the city said that Saigon was possessed now of a "fear bordering on panic," and that it would not take much to plunge the city over the threshold and into chaos.

v

At about two in the morning on Friday, April 4, the phone in Dr. Tran Kim Tuyen's house rang. "They just came to arrest my husband!" a distraught friend said. Dr. Tuyen hung up and dressed. Before he was out of the house, the phone rang again. All over the city, it seemed, opposition legislators and journalists and lawyers were being rounded up. Dr. Tuyen spent the hours until dawn in the back garden of his house, ready to jump over the wall and try to go into hiding if the police came.

They didn't. In the morning, phone calls in and out revealed that the police had picked up about twenty-five people. At least half were closely involved in Tuyen's scheme for getting rid of Thieu. Many were arrested because of their contact with Tuyen. For a few days, it was a mystery why Dr. Tuyen was still free.

About a month before, an intermediary had arranged for Dr. Tuyen and his wife to be invited for dinner at the home of Nguyen Van Hao, the young deputy prime minister in charge of economic affairs. Hao's wife's first husband was a warlord who had been tracked down and killed under Diem. But they didn't talk about that. They talked about economics, and politics.

A few days after the roundup in the early hours of April 4, Nguyen Van Hao spoke with the go-between. "You can tell Dr. Tuyen that his name was first on the list," Hao said. "But I protested. I don't know most of the others. But I know Dr. Tuyen. And I know that we may need him one of these days."

VI

The first three days of April were almost routine for Meritt Stark and his wife. USAID was pushing to get dependents out of Vietnam, and when Ann, their twenty-year-old, boarded a commercial flight at Tan Son Nhut to act as an escort for orphans being flown to Seattle on April 1, they knew that she would not be coming back anytime soon. But in the six years that the family had lived in Asia, the absence or presence of various of the children for months at a time had in itself become routine.

Oddly, in those three days the most traumatic departure was that of Bruno, their Doberman pinscher. A few days earlier, Dorothy had seen an embassy directive to the effect that household pets could not accompany U.S. government dependents leaving Saigon. Obviously, the only way to get Bruno to the States was to send him on his own.

That task—finding a large enough traveling cage, getting a veterinarian to certify that Bruno was free of heartworm and otherwise fit for arrival in the U.S., and finally getting him out to the airport and onto the plane—took up most of Thursday, April 3. And that night Co Ba, the maid, who loved them all, cried at the loss of Bruno as she never had when any of the kids had left.

The days were routine enough so that on at least one of the evenings Meritt and Dorothy made what she thought of as their evening neighborhood rounds. This was a matter simply of leaving the apartment and following a familiar route in the few short streets, including their own, that radiated from a statue of an ancient Vietnamese naval hero in a little semicircular park on Ben Bach Dang, the riverfront road. As usual, neighborhood children waited for the *bac si** and his wife, trailed behind them as if the Americans were Pied Pipers. The children knew that they would be treated to a bowl of *pho* or a handful of fruit from a corner stall. And Meritt would quietly check the children for illness, sometimes spot a new one with one leg shorter than the other, a harelip that might be treatable at the Barsky Unit.†

Dorothy held her husband's hand, in part simply to keep from falling behind. As they passed a friendly dark little Franco-Vietnamese bar on the same street as their building, she remembered the night that Meritt had said urgently, "Walk ahead of me, darling." "Why?" "I think these guys behind us are about to jump us." At that moment the two Vietnamese women who ran the bar suddenly appeared in the twilight shouting a stream of curses. The would-be attackers fled.

* Doctor.
† The common name for an advanced plastic surgery hospital in the city, founded by an American plastic surgeon.

It was odd, she thought; here they were, an American couple in their mid- and late-fifties, neither of whom spoke much Vietnamese. And she was sure that they were not just safer but more at home, more part of the society, than they would be in any neighborhood in an American city except their own, in Denver.

Among the Starks' many friends in Saigon was the doctor in charge of the children's section at the city's main tuberculosis hospital, a Dr. Le. Dr. Le's wife had studied in the United States, and one of their two children, the boy, was born in the States and had a U.S. passport. The couple pleaded with the Starks to help them get a South Vietnamese government exit visa for the boy—whom they called Danny—and to get him out of the country.

Another project for Dorothy to apply herself to. But on the morning of Friday, April 4, she was suddenly fully engaged at one of her two jobs, teaching at the embassy's Phoenix school.

Shortly after she arrived at school that morning a notice came from the headmaster, at the upper form, which was in another building, saying that this was to be the last day of school. Dorothy was stunned. The school year wasn't scheduled to end until June. She had been teaching the day before, and was unaware of the memo Don Hays distributed authorizing the departure of all dependents.

On her own, Dorothy insisted that her students wait while she wrote out detailed reports for each of them, so that their teachers in the States would know where to place them.

Late in the morning, Meritt arrived at the school and told Dorothy that he had to make a run to the States. A large contingent of orphans was being shipped out on a big U.S. Air Force cargo plane and he had been asked to accompany the flight as medical director.

"Can't someone else go?" Dorothy Stark said.

"Well, they asked me to be the doctor on board. Also, we're very short of escorts. Do you suppose you could . . ."

"Meritt, they're closing the *school*, can you believe it? How can I possibly go? I've got to write notes for all the kids. How are their teachers ever going to know all the wonderful work they've been doing?"

Laurie arrived at the apartment at about the same time Dr. Stark did. It was the last day of school for the Mother Hubbard school as well. And as it happened, Laurie was due to leave Saigon as an escort on yet another orphan flight the next day. Her father asked if she could throw her things together and be ready to go in a couple of hours.

There were well over two hundred orphanages in South Vietnam. Dr. Stark knew. He had been in many of them. But the sudden rush in early April to speed the movement of orphans to the United States was not exactly a wholesale raid on the orphanages. The great majority of the children who were put on the flights passed through one of seven adoption agencies operating in Vietnam and had adopting parents waiting for them in the U.S.

Rosemary Taylor was the Saigon representative of one of the largest of the seven agencies, Friends for All Children, and was the prime mover behind what quickly was named Operation Babylift. Miss Taylor was normally a quiet, compassionate adoption-agency director. But in the very first days of April 1975, she fell momentarily under the spell of Ed Daly, the hard-talking, hard-drinking founder and president of World Airways. Daly was not done with rescuing Vietnamese. He talked both Miss Taylor and Dr. Phan Quang Dan, the deputy prime minister for social affairs, into accepting his offer to fly hundreds of orphans from Vietnam to the United States on his planes.

By now, the embassy was well sick of Ed Daly. When senior American officials realized that he had lined up both the adoption agencies and at least part of the Saigon government behind his latest scheme, they made Miss Taylor a counteroffer. If she would drop Daly, the U.S. government would allow her to put her orphans aboard U.S. military transport aircraft that were funneling war matériel into Saigon on an accelerated basis—the first concrete result of the Weyand mission—and returning to the Philippines empty. Miss Taylor was happy to oblige.

Several months earlier, Dr. Stark had accompanied a commercial airliner filled with orphans on a flight that began in Saigon and ended thirty-four hours later when the last child was delivered to its waiting parents at New York's LaGuardia airport. His most vivid memory of that trip centered on his hot, cramped feet at the end of it. So for the relatively short hop to the West Coast on which he was embarking on this first Friday in April, Dr. Stark put on a pair of light, well-vented sandals over his socks.

When she had finished writing out her reports at the embassy school and let the children go home, Dorothy Stark wondered what to do with the rest of her day. As she rode through Saigon's traffic in a hot little taxi to the apartment, for some reason she remembered a Vietnamese boy at the small Vietnamese school where she taught part-time saying to her a few days earlier: "You're going to lose the war."

"No," Dorothy had said. "We may not win. But we'll never leave you."

"What an odd conversation," Dorothy Stark thought. Then she remembered that she had packed one trunk and one cardboard box of things—documents, photographs, a few valuables—that really should be sent out of the country for safekeeping, now that everyone was talking about the departure of nonessential personnel. She decided that this would be a good afternoon to mail the things, from the APO facility at DAO, wherever that was.

At the apartment, Co Ba and Laurie were rushing to finish packing as many of Laurie's things as she could carry. A few of Laurie's friends from the Madame Curie School were there to see her off. There was time for only hurried goodbyes.

Dr. Stark and Laurie got in the USAID car, stopped by headquarters so he could pick up the travel orders that would get him on a military or commercial flight back into Vietnam, and drove out to the Friends for All Children facility near the airport where all the orphans were being assembled.

As the children were being loaded on the half-dozen buses that would take them to Tan Son Nhut, Dr. Stark was given a copy of a letter, in Vietnamese, from Deputy Prime Minister Dan to Prime Minister Tran Thien Khiem. The letter was dated April 2, and was in fact two days out of date. He was also given an admittedly crude translation of the letter done by someone connected with the adoption agencies. The Vietnamese version of the letter was to prove crucial in the next couple of hours. The English translation provides some sense of the cynicism that colored Operation Babylift:

> Subject: Immigration to U.S. of 1,400 orphans.
> DEAR MR. PRIME MINISTER,
> At present time, there are 1,400 orphans sponsored by the International Charity Association[s] living in Saigon, waiting for departure to foreign countries where foster parents are ready for them. Actually the Department of Public Health and the International Rescue Committee want to solve this problem immediately in order to concentrate to perform the other problems more important. Besides, the immigration of these orphans will initiate a shock in the world, especially the United States, and will be a profitable subject for the Republic of Vietnam.
> Right now, there are 2 Boeing 727[s] of World Airways, ready for them free. Mr. Daly, president of this airline company, is a political well-known person. The U.S. Embassy also want them out of Vietnam. Mr. Daly points out their immigration, plus the fact of million people leaving the sections occupied by Communists, will provide a good propaganda for Vietnam, especially including the TV and newspaper of America exploiting deeply this event.
> Therefore, please, Mr. Prime Minister, accept this proposition. The Department of Public Health will cooperate with USAID in order to

follow up and to control, and with the International Charity Association[s] to perform this task.

Sincerely,
DEPUTY PRIME MINISTER
DR. PHAN QUANG DAN

The children, all 243 of them, were eventually loaded onto half a dozen buses. With a colleague named Dr. Brown, Meritt Stark and Laurie led the caravan to the main gate at Tan Son Nhut airport. The guards there were reluctant to let the buses pass. Their commander was sent for; he read the letter from Dr. Dan to the prime minister and waved them in.

They drove directly to the huge cargo plane, which was still unloading its weapons and ordnance. George Jacobson, the embassy's veteran special assistant for field operations, was there, as was a sizable contingent from the Western press corps. It was a good story, especially for the cameras: weapons, ammunition and bombs off, orphans on. Only a few airport security guards seemed to care that the entire area was posted with signs strictly forbidding the taking of photographs.

As soon as they got to the plane, Dr. Stark and his daughter handed over their passports to immigration officials. A few minutes later, one of the officials asked for "Mrs. Stark." In his haste to pack, Dr. Stark had picked up his wife's passport. Dr. Brown offered to go back into Saigon with instructions about which drawer to look in.

The officials were appalled at the notion that close to 250 Vietnamese children were about to leave the country without a single exit visa among them. They kept the children cooped up in the hot buses for close to an hour until, again, someone arrived who was senior enough to declare that Dr. Dan's letter to the prime minister amounted to a *laissez-passer* for the entire group.

Finally the loading got under way. The smallest children, a few who were blind and others who wore braces or used crutches were passed from the cavernous cargo hold up a narrow metal ladder to the flight deck, where they were strapped in two to a seat. One hundred and sixty children made it to that top deck. The rest were placed on blankets in the cargo hold and strapped in under the restraints that were normally used to secure cargo. The children were hot and dehydrated. Several cried. Laurie Stark, who would be able to communicate with the mostly older children in the cargo hold, volunteered to travel there. Dr. Stark, anticipating that the most serious medical problems would come from the infants and the handicapped children on the flight deck, would ride with them.

The clamshell doors at the back of the huge transport were shut.

Now the only light in the hot flight deck where Dr. Stark, crew members and a few other escorts moved from seat to seat checking the children came from an open hatchway at the front. Dr. Stark still did not have his passport.

He moved to the front hatchway and saw the USAID car speeding toward the plane, climbed down, took the passport from Dr. Brown and scrambled back up into the plane.

The escorts crouched in the aisle and held tight to seat armrests for the takeoff. As the plane climbed, Dr. Stark stood to check on the children closest to him. As soon as they leveled off, he told himself, he would introduce himself to the men and women among the crew who had volunteered to help with the children and organize a system for feeding and changing the children.

About twelve minutes later, the plane shook with a huge explosion. "Surface-to-air missile," Dr. Stark thought immediately. There were no windows on the flight deck. He could only guess what had happened. In fact he was too busy to speculate much. Oxygen masks dropped from the ceiling, but there weren't nearly enough of them for all the children. He and the other adults moved from seat to seat holding the masks for a few seconds at a time over the small faces. Then a crew member appeared and announced that the rear cargo doors had blown out.

Would Laurie and the children have been sucked out of the plane? Dr. Stark kept working. He felt the plane bank into a long turn. As his ears began to ache, he knew they were losing altitude. Obviously, the pilot must be trying to make it back to Saigon. What would Laurie want him to do? As soon as he framed the question, the answer appeared: "You do what you have to do, Dad, and I'll do what I can do down here."

Dr. Stark had been on enough airplanes, especially through these last six years, to have a rough idea what was happening even though he could not see outside. The pilot was having difficulty controlling the descent. Every minute or two he gunned the engines, obviously trying to gain altitude.

They landed and the plane shuddered and roared, and then they were in the air again and they landed again, the plane buffeting and things flying and there was mud flying in the flight deck and they landed again, and again, and again, and then at last they ground to a halt.

Dr. Stark was unhurt. His first thought was to get to the emergency exits and lower the chutes that would be stored in the doors there.

He and crew members kicked open the doors. To Dr. Stark's astonishment, they were sitting in the mud of a rice field, the doors just above the water.

He glanced back to the broiling, oily flames that roared from the rest of the plane, a quarter of a mile or more behind them.

As he glanced back, he considered the possibilities—all the possibilities concerning Laurie, and the possibility that drifting flotsam from the fire would reach them, set this part of the wreckage on fire. After a few moments it was clear that this last was unlikely. So they worked methodically. A crew member with a broken leg stationed himself at one of the doors. Dr. Stark and an Air Force nurse who had a broken arm unbuckled the children and relayed them to the man at the door. At the beginning, in their haste, they were laying the terrified, mud-splattered children on the dikes of the paddy field, the concrete-hard dikes that had sheared off the bottom two-thirds of the huge plane. Air America and South Vietnamese helicopters arrived quickly. Eventually, they slowed the off-loading of the children so as not to get ahead of the helicopters. The children were better off in the plane than out on the dikes.

It took close to half an hour to get them all off. There was only one death on the flight deck, so far as Dr. Stark could see. Some kind soul had thought to put one little boy's pathetic belongings in a little bag tied around his neck.

When they were done, Dr. Stark walked the length of the flight deck, checking under seats. At the rear of the plane, some of the seats had tumbled forward. But even there there were no little bodies under seats.

Finally he lowered himself into the mud and set off for the wreckage behind him.

His intention was to make a complete circuit of the burning wreckage. There was at least the chance that Laurie had been thrown clear. But with each step his feet sank six or eight inches into the mud. And then his socks started oozing out of the holes of the sandals. Progress was slow, and the fire was hot.

When he had struggled about a third of the way around the fire, an Air America pilot he knew came up to him and said, "Dr. Stark, believe me, we're making a completely thorough search. There's really nothing you can do. You should go back."

His friend hailed a Vietnamese helicopter that was heading back to the base. Dr. Stark got on it, its only passenger. He was the last survivor to leave the crash site.

All the other survivors were flown to the Air America base at Tan Son Nhut, and were taken from there to the Seventh-Day Adventist

Hospital just outside the air base. But Dr. Stark was put down in the South Vietnamese part of the base. As it happened, there was a German television crew there, and they were about to depart for Saigon. They offered Dr. Stark a lift, which he accepted. And so it was that in the days—and even the years—that followed, many officials in the American community in Saigon never realized that Dr. Stark was on the Galaxy C-5A that crashed that afternoon.

VII

In the middle of the afternoon, Dorothy Stark called for an embassy car and had herself driven into Tan Son Nhut and found the line in the long corridors leading to the mailing office. To her astonishment, the line was a good fifty yards long.

She sat on the trunk, edging it forward every minute or so. And just as she was deciding that it was time to give up and go home, a man who had been working behind the counter in the APO office came out and said: "Is there a Mrs. Stark here? Calling Dorothy Stark!"

He escorted her into the office. She picked up a phone and spoke with an old friend, a woman who was the wife of a CIA analyst and who, with her husband, had been in Saigon forever.

"I've got something you should know," the friend said. "The plane Meritt was on has crashed."

The man who had brought her to the phone arranged transportation and took her to the Air America landing strip. The helicopters landed, one after another. People—Vietnamese and American, men and women—rushed to the helicopters with stretchers. Some of the children were so small that they could lay them sideways on the stretchers, heads at one pole, feet at the other. The air was filled with blowing dust. It would be hard to learn anything here. Everyone was being taken to the hospital. The helpful young man from DAO took Dorothy Stark to the hospital.

At the Seventh-Day Adventist Hospital, she found herself in a bathroom with a young man she assumed was a member of the crew of the plane. Years later, she couldn't remember if she was in a men's room or he was in a ladies' room.

"You were on the plane?" she said.

"Yes," the young man said, dabbing at facial cuts with toilet paper. "The doors opened. At the back. The doors blew out."

Dorothy Stark decided that he was in shock.

She went back out into the dirt courtyard with people and stretchers rushing through it, dusk settling in now. In the gathering twilight, she recognized a young woman on one of the stretchers. She knew the young woman, the daughter of one of the American oil executives in town; the woman was scheduled to go on this first big Air Force plane, with a child who had a family waiting for him in the States; they called the child Bien Hoa, all they knew about him, the place where he came from.

"Susan," Dorothy asked, walking with the stretcher, "did you see Laurie or Dr. Stark? This is Mrs. Stark, darling. Did you see either of them?"

Susan looked up, tried to focus, held out her hand, in which she gently held her ear.

"Oh, dear, Susan darling," Dorothy said. "You're going to be all right. Everything will be fine," and Susan was whisked into the hospital.

"Look at this one!" a young American woman shouted at an American radio correspondent who was pestering her for a quote. "I put him on that plane two hours ago! God! What now? What happens to him now?"

Now some of the journalists had somehow found out who she was. ("That's Dr. Stark's wife—he was on the plane.") They moved in.

"Please don't take my picture," she said, pulling her hands to her face.

They shot away—*click whirr click whirr click whirr* . . .

Then, mercifully, she found herself with a Korean doctor who worked with Eben Dustin, the embassy doctor; dear Dusty, who had turned his home into a clinic in the last few weeks, using all the doctors who had poured into Saigon from up-country; sweet Dusty, who had instantly solved that skin problem Sister Lawrence from Phuoc Long was having with her orphans when that other American doctor had said, "No, sorry, I really cannot get involved. . . ."

"Dr. Kim," Dorothy Stark said, "I can't find Meritt. He was on the plane. And one of my daughters too. . . ."

"I keep looking for Dr. Stark too," the man said.

"Get them to take me out to the plane," Dorothy Stark said.

"No," the Korean doctor said. "I ask too. We can't go out to the plane."

"Mrs. Stark?" Another young American. "Calling Mrs. Stark. Telephone for Mrs. Stark."

"Dorothy?" someone called.

"Yes?"

"Meritt's at the apartment."

"Thank you," Dorothy said. "Thank you for reaching me. Tell him I'll be there right away."

She lowered the phone to its cradle, thinking of the simple thing that had to be done next. Get a car to the apartment. Maybe the pleasant young man from DAO was still around. If not, Dusty's friend would find a car. Thinking above all, acknowledging above all, "Thank you, God, for this much: Meritt alive."

The corollary was hard: Meritt at the apartment, alone. Meritt would not leave Laurie. So Laurie was dead.

VIII

The crash shook the remaining American community, as well as many Vietnamese, even more deeply, in some ways, than all the losses that had gone before. What had gone before was war. What happened that afternoon was perceived by some Americans and Vietnamese as something else—something very much like a curse.

Years later, Dr. Stark communicated with the German television crew that picked him up that day, in an ultimately successful effort to get a copy of their footage. The correspondent wrote him: "I will never forget your face, that afternoon, Dr. Stark. You looked seventy years old." And later that night, Co Ba told Dorothy Stark that when the *bac si* arrived at the apartment, she didn't recognize him at first. She thought that for some reason an American black man had stumbled into the apartment.

That day at the airport, a Vietnamese government official told a correspondent for *The New York Times:* "It's good that the American people are taking the children. They are good souvenirs, like the ceramic elephants you like so much. It's too bad that some of them broke today, but don't worry, we have many more."

For months after he left Vietnam, Dr. Stark carried a folded piece of paper in his wallet, with brief notations about his final days. It eventually disintegrated, but this much was still legible nine years later:

March 31: Return from Nha Trang and Cam Ranh
April 1: Ann departs to Seattle with orphans
April 3: Put Bruno on the plane
April 4: Galaxy C-5A crash

One hundred and thirty-five of the three hundred and twenty-seven people on the plane died. Seventy-eight of the dead were orphans; the other fifty-seven were escorts and crew members. Most of the escorts were embassy and DAO female employees. They were needed as escorts; but that flight and the others like it in early April also served the secondary goal of getting them quietly out of Vietnam.

IX

A day or so after the crash, Graham Martin came across Alan Carter's cable earlier in the week on the mood in the city. (Martin saw virtually every official report that left Saigon, poring over cable traffic deep into the night, striving to assure as he had throughout his career that he— and ideally he alone—knew everything in his domain.)

He called Carter and exploded. He did not go so far as to explicitly blame Carter for the crash. But that was the implication. Now that "people in Saigon" were telling Washington that Saigon was on the verge of panic, Washington was bypassing him, Martin said. If they had asked his advice, he certainly would have told them not to put those orphans on a C-5A, with its notorious history of cargo-door blow-outs. And those children would still be alive today.

18

"All *available personnel, please come downstairs. All available per-sonnel, please come downstairs.*"

It was Sergeant of the Guard Babel on the Marine House sound system. There were just eight off-duty Marines in the house. Sergeant Babel told them that there had been a plane crash, people were hurt, they should get ready fast, cammies and no weapons. The eight, including Sergeant Robert L. Frain, got into their camouflage uniforms very fast and rode out to Tan Son Nhut in the unit's personnel carrier. At Tan Son Nhut they were met by an American with the International Red Cross and were helicoptered to the crash site. It was still full daylight, but they carried "beaters," outsized heavy flashlights that could stand free on the ground and could also be used as billy clubs.

There were already quite a few people there, including several nurses, Vietnamese and American. Most of them were working the side of the downed plane on which the helicopter had landed. One of the American nurses told Frain and the other Marines to go around on the other side of it and "start looking for bodies."

Sergeant Frain still did not know that the victims they were looking for were mostly children. He found out quickly. That same nurse had given him a stethoscope. But in all the hours of looking that afternoon and evening and through the night, Frain and his buddies happened to find no survivors. Others did. He would hear people calling out for doctors or nurses. All Frain found in the mud was bodies and limbs.

Others said later that it was a rice paddy, but Frain thought it was just marsh—stinking mud. He threw away his boots the next day, and his uniform stank of mud and death, but he didn't have another set of cammies and had to keep those.

It was weird the way the clothes were blown away. Some of the bodies were fully clothed. On some, one side was fully clothed, half a shirt and half a pair of pants, say, the other naked. Frain found a little girl with her dead face up wide-eyed to the sky, her body all belly down. He tossed aside a boomerang-shaped fragment of the aircraft and reached to a little arm protruding from the mud; tugged at it with the force required if it were attached to a little body; fell on his ass in the mud with the tiny arm in his horrified hand.

II

George Esper answered a phone in the AP office. He sat forward and grabbed so hard for a piece of paper that the first one sailplaned off the desk and drifted to the floor, and he rumpled the second one as he tucked the earpiece into his shoulder and groped with his other hand for a pencil.

"Where?" he said. "Is Neal still out there? Carl, is Neal back from the airport? Okay, where, exactly? The airport side of the river? Can you get to it by road?"

Carl Robinson shook his head to show that Neal Ulevich wasn't in the office. Esper said, "Wait a minute, wait a minute," into the phone and looked back to Robinson: "Get a photographer. The Galaxy crashed coming back into Tan Son Nhut. Have him hold while I get the location."

Climbing the back stairway to the sixth floor, I thought, "F - - - it. I could just go down to Bo Da's for a couple of hours and have a *coupe Jacques* and four or five *cafés filtres* and they wouldn't be able to get me."

NBC had a tipster in the control tower. Schiller and a recently arrived second radio stringer named Robert Wiener had left for the crash site three minutes before. Arthur Lord told me to go to the Seventh-Day Adventist Hospital, just outside the airport. "Do what you can there," he said, "and then go to General Smith's office at DAO. We think the pilot walked away from it and is already briefing Smith."

"How many survivors?" I asked.

"We don't know," Lord said. "Apparently it bounced across the river and then bellied into this rice field, shearing off the bottom. So those kids in the cargo hold wouldn't, uh, you know . . ." He wiggled his hand and looked down at a Telex Mr. Khi had brought him.

On the ride to the hospital, I tried to keep my eyes straight ahead over the shoulder of the burly motorcycle driver. I wanted to lean into the man's back and close my eyes. I hoped the Vietnamese moving with me along Cong Ly Street didn't know about the crash yet, but assumed they did.

Police held back a small crowd at the hospital gate. I lifted my press pass high and slipped into the compound. Phil McCombs of *The Washington Post* and a knot of other reporters appeared in the bobbing television floodlights around an ambulance. When I reached it, two young Americans were taking the last litter from it. A blanket covered four small forms laid out side by side, feet at one pole, heads at the other. A Vietnamese policeman opened the door for the litter bearers. Again I held up the press card and asked in Vietnamese if I could enter. The man shook his head.

Three more ambulances arrived in the next twenty minutes, and I didn't attempt to interview anybody or try again to get into the hospital. Photographers were shooting everything they could get now and that was right, that was their job. But there was nothing for me there.

I sat on a concrete bench in the darkness and lit a cigarette. Before I had finished it, Phil McCombs sat down beside me.

"I don't know what I'm doing here," McCombs said. "The way things have been going lately, I might as well still be working for the wires."

"I can't figure out the crowd at the gate," I said. "I thought orphans didn't have parents." McCombs flipped back through a pocket notebook, tapped a page and said, "Curious onlookers." I looked at his face. He had attempted a joke and then discovered he couldn't smile.

"I'm supposed to interview someone," I said. "You know—a survivor, or a doctor, or something."

"Yeah, so am I, that's the idea," McCombs said. "Color and quotes. Make 'em come alive." Now he did laugh. "Bring 'em back alive, David, right?" It was a short laugh. "S - - -," he said.

Half an hour later, a sergeant escorted me to General Homer Smith's suite of offices, and a colonel relayed my request to interview the pilot to the general and then appeared occasionally to assure me that they were working on it. Homer Smith himself emerged once and shook my hand. All of them were courteous. They offered me coffee, apologizing for the Coffee-mate.

Someone had hung three typically unsuccessful oil paintings on the walls, each with a legend: *The Farmers' Marketplace, The Fishermen,*

The Beggars. I leafed through *Naval Support in I Corps—1968,* and poured myself more coffee and stared down at the pages of *Pacific Architects and Engineers, Vietnam, 1963–1966* and *Tenth Awards Ceremony.*

An hour and a half later, the colonel said that he was sorry. CINCPAC * in Hawaii had finally said no. He would answer my questions as best he could, he said. The rear cargo door had blown off at twenty-three thousand feet. Off the record, he doubted that it was sabotage, but of course they would know better when they recovered the flight recorder. No, he was sorry, he was afraid he couldn't give me the pilot's name or rank. No, he wasn't sure how many children or adults or even crew members had been on board, let alone how many had survived.

With nothing else available, I took a motorized *cyclo-pousse* back to the office—the driver and his silence-rending engine behind and me perched on the plump plastic-covered settee, ready to be catapulted to a broken spine at the first hard bump or fast stop. I wished I had met the pilot, wondered briefly if the man would have been able to smile. No, he wouldn't smile. If he wasn't in shock he would be technical, correct. I thought with a touch of envy of all the people I knew who had decided years before that everything that issued from that labyrinth of offices called MACV and now DAO had to be evil. Then as the wind rushed through my hair and over my face I told the moral questions to go to hell. I had been lucky after all: I hadn't had to go to the crash site.

III

Doan Van Toai was beginning his fourth year as an officer in a private Saigon bank. He was twenty-nine, and had a round, open, pleasant face that was filling out from his student days. But he still looked and spoke very much like the student activist he had been in the 1960s. He was also a middle-level communist agent.

Toai was not fully committed. He certainly had never joined the Party, or even the National Liberation Front. And the services he provided what everyone called "the other side" were only flimsily clandestine. They didn't entail much risk beyond the chance of time in Nguyen Van Thieu's jails, where Toai had already been a frequent, if always short-time, guest. People would talk to him in his office at the bank—young people he had known since his student days, or older customers. And after a while, after sufficient political confidences had been exchanged, the man on the other side of the desk would say

* Commander in Chief Pacific.

something like, "Of course, I'm with the other side, Toai, you must have known that," and Toai would nod and accept his latest instructions.

What Toai provided as a result of these routine, almost offhand meetings were, in the beginning, reports on what he knew of the government's economic plans. After the Paris Peace Accords were signed in late January 1973, his assignment changed: Now he drew up plans for the reconstruction of the South after liberation. Toai and his leftist friends were happy with the agreement. They were sure it guaranteed a victory for the Viet Cong, which they did *not* envision as a take-over of the South by the North.

Toai never thought of himself as a traitor. Rather, the reports went a small way, he thought, to fulfilling his patriotic duty. Too small, he thought. All his life, he had had friends who disappeared. He envied them. For the first few days there would be some concern that they had been picked up by the police. But in fact none of the Saigon governments Toai hated so much routinely caused leftist students to disappear without a trace. They usually had lawyers. The friends Toai envied were the ones who went to join the heroes in the jungle.

Toai thought they were heroes. But something—which he sometimes thought of as cowardice—had kept him from joining them. He was a middle-class intellectual southern Vietnamese, which meant that he had grown up in a family of subtly calculated political loyalties, and that he had a healthy instinct for survival. It was no accident that he was both a comfortable banker and a spy for his government's enemies.

He thought of himself as a nationalist, working for an independent, neutral Vietnam. The guidelines that the Front gave him for his reports explicitly stated that the South needed an economic policy different from the North. Toai knew that the communists would dominate whatever government emerged in the South after liberation. But he thought that communist Vietnamese, even if they were northerners, would be more open to compromise and justice than the corrupt Thieu apparatus. And he was a Buddhist, which meant that he wanted reconciliation and an end to the fighting above all.

The day after the C-5A crash, Toai kept an appointment with one of his journalist friends for dinner in a Chinese restaurant off Tu Do Street.

"Did you listen to the BBC this afternoon?" Toai asked.

"No, I was filing."

"They said that President Ford has made an office—an officer—in charge of evacuation of Americans from Vietnam. Do you know about that?"

"No."

"If it's true," Toai said, "—it must be true, the BBC. It means it is the end." He whispered: "We win." But he did not smile.

Toai or the BBC misunderstood. President Ford was in the midst of an extended Easter golfing vacation in Palm Springs, California, on April 5. But the Associated Press Washington bureau did file a story that day quoting unnamed officials as saying that the government was studying plans for the evacuation of as many as a million people from South Vietnam.

IV

General Weyand and his party arrived back in the United States on that same Saturday. The party landed in Palm Springs and met with the President that afternoon.

Weyand was grim, but thought something might be salvaged. If Congress quickly voted not the $300 million in supplemental military aid that had been before it for months but new supplemental aid in the amount of $722 million, the South Vietnamese military might be able to stabilize the situation. They would not regain any of the lost territory, Weyand told Ford and his advisers, including Secretary of State Kissinger. But with the additional aid and the psychological boost it would give to the commanders and their troops, there was a good chance that they could form a strong defensive perimeter around Saigon and force the communists to negotiate.

Ford accepted Weyand's recommendation. Ignoring Kissinger's advice to blame the debacle in Vietnam on Congress, five days later he went before a joint session of the legislators and appealed for the $722 million for the Saigon military and an additional $250 million in economic and humanitarian aid for the regime.

The President asked Congress to act on the large request by April 19, just nine days away. He said that the money was meant not only to keep Saigon from military collapse, but also to buy time in which negotiations between Hanoi and Saigon might be arranged. Such negotiations, his aides had told reporters earlier in the day, would help facilitate the extraction from Vietnam of about 6,000 Americans and tens of thousands of Vietnamese—as many as 200,000, the aides said.

> Members of the Congress, my fellow Americans [Ford said], this moment of tragedy for Indochina is a time of trial for us. It is a time for national resolve.
>
> It has been said that the United States is overextended, that we have too many commitments too far from home, that we must examine what our truly vital interests are and shape our strategy to conform to them. I find no fault with this as a theory, but . . . we can-

not, in the meantime, abandon our friends while our adversaries support and encourage theirs. We cannot dismantle our defenses, our diplomacy or our intelligence capability while others increase and strengthen theirs. Let us put an end to self-inflicted wounds. Let us remember that our national unity is a most priceless asset. Let us deny our adversaries the satisfaction of using Vietnam to pit Americans against Americans. At this moment the United States must present to the world a united front.

As he spoke, two freshman Democrats, Toby Moffett of Connecticut and George Miller of California, stood up and walked out of the chamber. As far as Gerald Ford could remember, this had never before happened.

By the afternoon of Sunday, the sixth, David Kennerly's film had been flown to Washington, developed and flown back to Palm Springs. Late that afternoon, the young photographer sat with Ford as the President slowly turned over one black-and-white print after another of ships crammed with refugees from Da Nang, of buses filled with fleeing villagers in Nha Trang, of fleeing South Vietnamese soldiers, of children dying in Phnom Penh hospitals.

Ford shook his head sadly as he turned the prints.

"This is what's going on," Kennerly said. "Cambodia is gone. And I don't care what the generals tell you: They're bulls - - - - ing you if they say that Vietnam has got more than three or four weeks. There's no question about it. It's just not gonna last."

When Ford returned to the White House, he directed that blown-up prints of Kennerly photographs replace the scenic views and portraits of American life that normally hung in the corridors of the West Wing. And when White House staffers complained that the pictures were making it difficult for them to eat, the President told Kennerly: "Leave them up. Everyone should know what's going on over there."

That same Palm Springs weekend, according to President Ford's press spokesman Ron Nessen, he and Secretary of State Kissinger were riding together in a limousine to dinner with the Fords when Kissinger said softly: "Why don't these people [the South Vietnamese] die fast? The worst thing that could happen would be for them to linger on."

v

Pierre Brochand, the young French political and intelligence officer, was at the office early. The sound of a jet grew like the longest, smoothest, building roll of thunder he had ever heard. He knew something was wrong: Planes were forbidden over the heart of the city that centered on the Presidential Palace.

He picked out the plane, high to the south, coming in over the river, a flash of silver in the bright blue sky, a beautiful morning, watched it all the way through its dive to about two hundred meters, where it pulled into an upturn, slowing so greatly that the bombs dropped from it just like eggs—*Ka-boom!*—shaking the window in front of Brochand's face. The plane climbed back up to about a thousand meters, made another dive, dropped two more bombs and Brochand braced for it— But nothing. Two duds. Then the antiaircraft fire opened up and the plane fled northwest.

VI

Early in the morning of Tuesday, April 8, First Lieutenant Nguyen Thanh Trung of the South Vietnamese Air Force took off in his F-5E fighter-bomber from the air base at Bien Hoa on a routine bombing mission.

To this day, no one in the West knows whether Trung was a Communist Party member even before he received his flight training in the United States, or simply a disaffected young pilot whom the communists got to a few days or weeks before April 8. Hanoi claims that he was one of theirs all along. U.S. intelligence analysts are inclined to doubt it.

In any case, shortly after he and the rest of the squadron were airborne, Trung radioed his flight commander that he was having engine trouble and would have to return to Bien Hoa.

Instead, he headed straight for Saigon.

Coming from the south, over the river, he went into a steep dive on Doc Lap Palace, dropping two of his four bombs. They landed in the palace courtyard, so close to the bull's-eye that they killed a couple of gardeners but did not do serious damage to the palace buildings.

He turned in the sky and went into a second dive. But the second bombs were duds.

He still had his 20-mm. cannons and turned for the Nha Be fuel dumps west of the city. He strafed the Shell storage tanks there, setting some of them ablaze, and then flew northwest to the airfield at Phuoc Long, the isolated province the communists had captured in early January.

In twenty days exactly, Trung would return to Saigon, leading the squadron of captured American jets that bombed Tan Son Nhut airport and sent me scurrying for the cover of the Marines Statue.

VII

Dorothy Stark had just ordered up a car and was sipping a cup of coffee in the restaurant of the Combined Recreation Association at the rear of the American Embassy when Nguyen Thanh Trung made his passes over the palace and the antiaircraft fire shook the morning.

"Okay," she said to herself. "That's it. Wherever Meritt is he's going to be killed. First Laurie, now Meritt."

She stood up. And for the second time in her life she fainted.

Sometime later—she had no idea how long it was, probably just a matter of moments—she heard someone say, "Oh, my God, it's Dorothy Stark. Her husband was in the crash."

She pulled herself to her feet, got in the embassy car, and went home.

VIII

The United States Information Service compound and a subsidiary institution called the Vietnam-American Association were close enough to the palace so that the explosion of the two live bombs rattled the windows, and Lieutenant Nguyen Thanh Trung's dives and climbs were roars and whines in the sky.

Like virtually everyone else in Saigon, Alan Carter had no idea what was going on, except that what sounded like bombs had fallen nearby, and there was firing all around him and roars and whines in the sky. He ordered the gates to the compound closed and locked, and asked his senior American staffers, most of whom had been in Saigon longer than he had, if they had emergency stocks of medicine, water, food—and guns. They checked, and reported quickly: No, none of the above. There was a radio in the compound, but no one knew the emergency frequencies. They could use it to communicate with their colleagues at VAA, but that seemed to be the extent of its usefulness.

Carter called the embassy number for Hank Boudreau, the administrative officer. Boudreau was occupied, and Carter spoke with one of his deputies. "What's going on?" he asked.

"We don't know," the man said. "We're trying to find out."

"Should we try to get over there?" Carter asked. "Is it safe for us to move in the streets?"

"We don't know," the man said. "You'll have to use your own judgment on that."

"How the hell can I use my own judgment when I don't know what's going on?" Carter asked.

"Sorry about that," the voice on the phone said. "We just can't give you any advice till we have more information."

. . .

A twenty-four-hour curfew was announced immediately after the bombing. It was lifted a few hours later, in the middle of the afternoon. Thieu appeared on national television to announce that "thanks to the superior powers," he was unhurt.

At a meeting at the embassy the next morning, Carter exploded. "Listen, Wolf," he told Lehmann, "whether you like it or not, we're part of the mission. You've got to get Boudreau off his ass. I want emergency rations, and a radio that I can use in an emergency. And I could use some weapons."

"You're not going to be getting any guns, Alan," Lehmann said. But that afternoon, cases of food and a radio with instructions on emergency frequencies arrived at the compound.

IX

Thomas Polgar, the CIA station chief, was beginning to think that the ambassador was never going to catch up. Martin returned to Saigon just as Da Nang entered its final agony; and in those first few days, Polgar thought, the ambassador spoke and acted as if it were still February. Polgar knew Martin's reading habits. The ambassador was narrowing the gap; but even now, almost two weeks after his return, he was still three or four days behind the curve of events, Polgar thought.

One doubts very much whether Graham Martin ever laid eyes on the cable Polgar sent to headquarters on the day after the bombing.

THE RUDDERLESS-SHIP SYNDROME TO WHICH WE REFERRED IN EARLIER MESSAGES IS STILL VERY MUCH WITH US [POLGAR WROTE]. COS STILL HAS TO SPEND AN INORDINATE AMOUNT OF TIME ARGUING ABOUT THE VALIDITY OF INTELLIGENCE WHICH CONTAINS BAD NEWS, AND DEBATING NEED FOR ADMINISTRATIVE DECISIONS WHICH EMBASSY IS RELUCTANT TO MAKE FOR ONE REASON OR ANOTHER. THE AMBASSADOR IS SPENDING THE BULK OF HIS TIME TRYING TO GENERATE SUPPORT FOR INCREASING ECONOMIC AND MILITARY ASSISTANCE TO SOUTH VIETNAM, AND TO MAINTAIN[ING] ORDERLY ATTITUDES IN THE FACE OF WHAT IS CLEARLY A WORSENING SITUATION. THE GVN* HAS NOT MANAGED TO GATHER ITSELF FOR EFFECTIVE ACTION, WHILE THE COMMUNISTS ARE INCREASING PRESSURE. THE AMBASSADOR'S ENDEAVORS ARE HIGHLY COMMENDABLE AND ESSENTIAL TO STABILIZING THE SITUATION, BUT THERE ARE FACTORS OPERATING WHICH ARE LIKELY TO FORCE A TIMETABLE ON US WHICH CANNOT BE ALTERED BY ANY OF THE PROCESSES NOW UNDER WAY EITHER IN WASHINGTON OR IN SAIGON. BOTH COM-

* Government of (South) Vietnam.

MUNICATIONS AND HUMAN SOURCE INTELLIGENCE SUGGEST THAT THE NORTH VIETNAMESE HAVE MADE A DETERMINATION TO CONTINUE AND EXPAND MILITARY PRESSURE AIMED AT THE ISOLATION OF SAIGON, WITH THE ULTIMATE MILITARY OBJECTIVE BEING TOTAL VICTORY IN 1975.

COS IS WELL AWARE THAT HISTORY SELDOM MOVES ALONG THE LINE OF STRAIGHT-LINE PROJECTIONS. NEVERTHELESS, IT IS CERTAIN THAT WE ARE HEADING FOR A DEBACLE OF HISTORIC PROPORTIONS UNLESS THE NECESSARY CHANGES ARE EFFECTED IN TIME.

STATION FORWARDING TODAY SITUATION APPRAISAL WHICH CONCLUDES THAT HANOI IS DETERMINED TO MAXIMIZE PRESSURE ON GVN IN PREPARATION FOR A COMMUNIST RESOLUTION OF THE SITUATION BY JUNE 1975.

SAIGON MORALE AND DISCIPLINE CONTINUE TO DETERIORATE, WITH CRIME AND VENALITY ON RISE IN PUBLIC AND PRIVATE SECTORS. THE GVN HAS NOT BEEN ABLE TO ORGANIZE ITSELF TO COPE WITH SITUATION. IT REMAINS COS JUDGMENT THAT THE MILITARY SITUATION CANNOT BE STABILIZED WITHOUT DECISIVE AMERICAN MOVES. IF NO DECISIVE AMERICAN MOVES ARE MADE, THEN WE BELIEVE MAJOR AND USELESS BLOODSHED CAN BE AVOIDED ONLY IF THIEU STEPS DOWN AND A NATIONAL UNION GOVERNMENT OFFERS TO IMPLEMENT THE PARIS FORMULA AS DEFINED BY THE COMMUNISTS.

X

The Associated Press monitored Radio Hanoi, which reported on Thursday that Nguyen Thanh Trung was, he said, "highly indignant at the aggressive schemes of the United States and traitorous acts of the Nguyen Van Thieu clique, who were only concerned with making money for their families out of the blood of the people and soldiers."

Trung supposedly continued: "This is also the feeling of the majority of the Air Force as well as the Army in general and the people in the areas still under Thieu's control."

The broadcast added that after the attack on the palace Trung had flown to an air base "in the liberated area" and was a given "a very warm welcome." He was promoted from lieutenant to captain and awarded the Liberation Exploit Order, Second Class.

I turned to Esper from the clipboard and made the easy crack: "Looks like the Liberation Exploit Order, First Class is reserved for the guy who gets his man."

Esper was kind enough to smile.

XI

A few days after the fall of Da Nang, Ken Moorefield ran into Al Francis in a hallway on the third floor of the embassy. The former consul general in Da Nang was distraught. Over coffee in the CRA restaurant, he told Moorefield that he had just left the ambassador's office. "He cannot accept what happened," Francis said. "I told him the truth. I told him we were wiped out, overwhelmed, that it happened so fast we didn't know what hit us and couldn't plan for it. I told him about the chaos, the total breakdown in law and order in the last couple of days. We damned near didn't get out. And Martin cannot comprehend it. He either will not or cannot accept the reality of what happened up there. He doesn't want to hear about it. He thinks I'm sick or something. Making it up. I don't know. Jesus."

He took a breath to compose himself, and then managed a smile. "He told me I've got twenty-four hours to get out of the country."

Al Francis was one of the few Foreign Service Officers Moorefield had met who was not only competent (many were that) and decisive (many fewer) but, rarer still, a good manager. And like Moorefield himself, he was now a Graham Martin protégé fallen from grace.

"That's crazy," Moorefield told Francis. "After what you've been through, you should be working on the evacuation here. You're the natural choice. If he can't see that, you're right—he's running away from reality." He paused a moment. "What are you going to do?"

"Stick around for a while," Francis said. "Talk to some people."

Al Francis remained in Saigon for another couple of weeks. He explored what DAO was doing to get people out of the country and talked with the logical officers at the embassy: Colonel Jacobson; Steve Bray of the Mission Warden Office; Marvin Garrett, the embassy's security chief. Martin tolerated his presence. And acting on Wolf Lehmann's behalf, Francis made a critical breakthrough with the interior minister. He persuaded the official to allow a simple *laissez-passer* to substitute for an exit visa in the numerous cases of Vietnamese dependents of Americans desirous of leaving the country.

But Martin made sure that his senior lieutenants understood that he was of the opinion that Al Francis was on the verge of a nervous breakdown. Francis' wife, Mary, had not returned to Vietnam with him from their last home leave, and Al depended on her, Martin believed. Whatever experience he had picked up in the hasty evacuation from Da Nang was not transferable to an evacuation from Saigon, if it came to that. Da Nang fronted on the sea; Saigon did not. Further, from Da Nang there was still part of Vietnam to which to flee.

Eventually it became clear that Martin would not allow Francis to play a central role in embassy evacuation planning, a role that Francis wanted and was certain he could play. A mere three weeks earlier, he had been a rising star in the State Department, a tough young officer with an ambassadorship clearly in his future. In the middle of April, he got on a plane and left Vietnam for good.

XII

Donald Hays huddled with a secretary in the restaurant of the Combined Recreation Association quadrant of the embassy compound. He was telling her to get the hell out of Saigon. A few tables away, deputy chief of mission Wolfgang Lehmann was taking a break with Hank Boudreau, the embassy's administrative counselor and Hays's boss.

"Goddamnit, I'd like to find the defeatist who's telling all these secretaries to leave," Lehmann said, loud enough for those at the nearby tables to hear.

Hays cleared his throat, looked at his young acquaintance, and asked her if she had been at her desk when the guy hit the palace.

XIII

Dr. Stark picked up where Dorothy had left off in the round of visits to various offices to arrange for an exit visa for Danny, the son of their Vietnamese friends. The visa was finally granted late on the morning of Thursday, April 10, two days after the bombing of the palace—and an hour before the Starks were due at Tan Son Nhut for the flight home.

They made the plane. Starting with Tom, the Marine, the Starks had spent a cumulative total of more than twenty years in Vietnam. They left without Laurie, the feisty one, the antiwar activist who was starting to beat her father at tennis. But they took much more of Vietnam with them than the ten-year-old boy, who, as it happened, was reunited with his Vietnamese family in the States a few months later.

XIV

On Saturday, April 12, I paid a hundred dollars for a Honda 90, the first motorcycle I had ever owned, and taught myself to drive it on a course of streets around the house of the seller, out near Tan Son Nhut.

The seller was Charlie Benoit's American assistant. He told me that I was foolish to attempt to drive into the center of town with only an hour's practice, especially at dusk, the most dangerous hour of the day. But a stretch of Thong Nhut Boulevard in front of the American Embassy where, I was sure, I would be able to get the machine into fourth gear lured me. Gingerly at first, and then with greater confidence, I drove down Cach Mang, past the narrow side streets that led to Paul Schaberger's villa. Cach Mang became Cong Ly, and prettier, tree-crowded, and I picked up speed in front of Benoit's office. I was tempted to stop at each place to show off my new toy. But I'd had some trouble starting the thing; and I was more and more eager for the stretch of Thong Nhut.

Under the riding, some news from the office that I had heard—I knew that it had to do with Vietnam, but only indirectly—tugged at my consciousness.

I emerged from the leafy tunnel of Cong Ly into the bright lights of the great traffic circle around the darkened basilica. Still in third, leaning to make my first relatively high-speed turn, I remembered what it was: That morning, the Americans had abandoned Phnom Penh, the ambassador running for a chopper with the embassy flag, taking about one hundred and sixty Cambodians with them.*

* The 159 Cambodians were predominantly U.S. embassy staffers. Others had left earlier in the week. The total figure for the number of Cambodians who left that month was very low, mainly because officials in the Cambodian government resolved to stay.

19

The communists reached Xuan Loc,* a province capital just thirty-six miles east of Saigon on Highway 1, on April 9, the day of Thomas Polgar's "rudderless-ship" cable to Washington.

Xuan Loc was an uninspiring city of 100,000 people—before a huge barrage of communist artillery rained on it before dawn that day, causing most of its residents to flee west toward Saigon. If they were to stop the communists anywhere, the South Vietnamese military would have to stop them there, in Xuan Loc.

Don Harris had a full head of very well cut sandy hair. He stood at least three inches over six feet tall and dressed in handsome boots and khaki leisure suits. He was to tell me later that he was forty-one, but looked to be about thirty-three, and had been seconded from the NBC affiliate in Los Angeles. When he spoke, which was as seldom as possible, it was with a Georgia or Alabama accent that he managed to neuter for the cameras. On the day Harris arrived, I had nodded toward the Eden Building from the terrace of the Continental and told someone: "It's so bad up there now that they're sending in the Hollywood cowboys."

* Pronounced Suan Lawp.

But when Xuan Loc came under siege just after he arrived that week, every day Harris went out as far east on Highway 1 as he could get. I went with him on the first trip. In a little hamlet called Hung Nghia, a veteran German photographer took some shrapnel in the groin during a brief shower of mortar rounds. I considered the morning a waste. Except for the minor excitement of the attack, it had consisted of advancing to the last government artillery position, once again getting used to the way the sound of the guns pushed against my face and chest when they jumped in the dirt, and then finding myself idle in the dust and heat of the edges of the war zone.

I had done it before, on my first trips to Vietnam. There had never before been even the novelty of the surprisingly small burst of sound and light producing the small cry and then, several seconds later, the sight of blood. It was all so long-range and clumsily technological that I still wondered, that late in the game, if men ever killed each other face-to-face in Vietnam.

Harris asked quiet, informed questions of the other journalists, and after the few seconds when we all simply dived for cover, directed the filming of the aftermath of the mortar attack not with bravado but coolly and thoroughly.

As we rode back into the city, I said: "You did say that this was your first time out here."

"Yup," Harris said.

"Well you sure as s - - - covered some war."

"Middle East," Harris said.

"Which one?"

"Last couple."

Things were out of kilter. Long-held assumptions as well as first impressions had a higher than normal casualty rate. The traditional attack routes on Saigon were from the north and west. Where was the attack on Tay Ninh, on the Cambodian border? The communists kept nibbling away at Tay Ninh, as they'd nibbled away at it for months before Ban Me Thuot, nibbling just enough to tie up a couple of ARVN divisions. And here they were, coming in from the east.

On the morning of Sunday, April 13, Harris and I and about twenty other journalists climbed into the back of an ARVN two-and-a-half-ton truck at the press center on Tu Do Street. The trip to the air base at Bien Hoa, from which we would be helicoptered into Xuan Loc, should have taken forty-five minutes. Instead we crawled along back roads for two hours without reaching the base. With all the TV gear, there were few places to sit comfortably, and no way to get out of the sun. When we finally reached Bien Hoa and were climbing down from the back of the truck, Peter Arnett of the AP said, "Hey, Anh. What was the idea of the tour? To show us you've still got the suburbs of Saigon?" Arnett was a New Zealander who had covered the arrival of the first U.S. combat troops in Vietnam, the Marines who waded ashore in Da Nang to be garlanded with flowers by pretty Vietnamese girls in *ao dais.** In the intervening ten years and thirty-six days, his coverage of the war had won him the great respect of his peers, and a Pulitzer Prize.

Captain Anh, the young translator for Colonel Hien, the military spokesman, had made the trip in the relative comfort of the cab. He shook his head without answering, and checked our names against a list on a clipboard, as if some of us might have decided to abandon the project since he had checked us getting on—or as if we might have been infiltrated. He looked not only busy but embarrassed, and I entertained the possibility that neither Anh nor the driver actually knew the way to Bien Hoa. (It transpired later that the driver had been drunk.)

We headed for a collection of food stalls on a long concrete platform under a tin roof. The rough tables of the place were crowded with civilians, many of them with children and bundles of clothing in their laps. An hour later, we followed a company of ARVNs in full battle gear into the belly of a Chinook. I stood at a porthole for most of the flight. I followed Highway 1, trying to find Hung Nghia, but the terrain was all chalky and dead, seemingly uninhabited. We set down on the highway a few miles west of Xuan Loc and transferred to a waiting truck. The civilians and soldiers in clusters off the sides of the road hardly registered and were soon behind us.

We were taken first to a row of 155-mm. artillery pieces where General Le Minh Dao, the commander of the ARVN 18th Division, had set up his headquarters in the last rows of a rubber plantation. An expanse of rice field stretched from the plantation to a tree line, and beyond the trees we could just see the slightly lopsided spire of Xuan Loc's Catholic church.

The stand at Xuan Loc was supposed to be the turning point, the place where the ARVN finally stopped running. General Dao spoke passionately in Vietnamese at a chartboard propped on a tripod in the dirt, detailing the six communist attacks against the city in the last four days. I was surprised at how much of it I understood. Finally, at

* Ow zai, the traditional Vietnamese women's dress, and surely one of the most alluring garments in the world: a long-sleeved form-fitting top flowing to two long panels, front and back, that open and close with the breeze or any motion of the wearer, revealing loose black or white pantaloons beneath.

Don Harris' and others' requests, Dao switched to English. The North Vietnamese were fighting badly, General Dao said. His troops had chased after them. He grinned, jabbing the chart with his pointer. "I vow to hold Xuan Loc," he cried. "I don't care how many divisions the other side sends against me, I will knock them down." I was crouching to get it on tape and yet not to appear on CBS, the only crew filming at the moment.

Leon Daniel, a reporter for UPI, challenged the military to let us go into Xuan Loc itself. This wasn't on the agenda, but the foray was approved.

Back into the truck. "I think he's going to hold," I said.

Peter Arnett, who had a voice like a seal even in conversation, barked a laugh.

The truck entered the small city in a section where there had been little damage, and moved slowly down a broad avenue, stopping now and then so that an escort who had joined Captain Anh in the cab could pull back a roll of concertina wire. In twos or threes, some of the photographers left the truck. Then we passed a long, well-made school building. A lone girl in her student uniform was walking up the sloping concrete walk to its main entrance. She was the first civilian we had seen. Shortly beyond the school, the truck stopped and the rest of us got off and followed a colonel who led us along narrow streets to the center of the city. There was enough damage now to interest NBC's Korean camera crew. Some of the houses had been blown to rubble; all of them were marked with small-arms fire. We picked up a few civilians—scampering children mostly. The rubble and barbed wire slowed us, but the colonel walked briskly when he could, answering questions.

Then, quickly, we were at the main exhibits, in a corner of a very large square. I saw the bodies in front of the burned-out bus station just a few yards away from us, but first took in the sights as they were offered. A notebook, a few bleached flags and dozens of weapons, ranging from grenades and pistols up to mortar tubes, were laid out neatly on four large ponchos on a sidewalk. In the shade of a drugstore's black-and-green-striped drop awning, two boys lay on cots and a third squatted on the lip of the shop's floor. They wore the unmarked, loose-fitting pea-green uniforms of the North Vietnamese Army. The head of one of them was bandaged; the hair of the other two stood out thick and coarse. I looked very briefly into the eyes of the seated boy, who apparently had only an arm injury, and found neither fear nor contempt nor interest in the eyes. He could have been as young as fifteen or as old as eighteen. Like the other two, his features seemed slightly broader than those of most Vietnamese I had seen, and darker. The broadness could have been boyish fat, the color might have come from the sun.

The dead ones looked older than the wounded boys, if only because they were considerably larger, bloated to corpulent manhood. I certainly couldn't guess their ages from their faces, which were fat and black. Their blackened intestines swelled from rents in the dark-stained uniforms. The flies were thickest at the wounds and on the mucus and blood around their eyes and nostrils and mouths.

Colonel Le Xuan Hieu led us to his pleasant headquarters in the tree-shaded courtyard of an elementary school beyond the bus station and the Catholic church. I saw now that the spire of the church had been a tall rectangular plinth. Half-destroyed, it approached the more conventional steeple shape. Colonel Hieu's briefing was longer and not so excited as General Dao's, although he did manage to say in English at one point, "Now I kill seven hundred VC."

Late in the afternoon, when we had been taken to a few more positions and Captain Anh had determined that he'd picked up all of us, we returned to the stretch of Highway 1 where we had been dropped off. Sitting in the back of the truck or on the side of the road in the truck's shadow, I made no effort to talk to the others. I sensed an urgency about Anh and the cluster of journalists around him, but ignored it. Harris moved to the group around Anh and then, filming, to the clusters of people along the highway.

The first Chinook set down almost a hundred yards in front of the truck. The back hatch came down and reinforcements like those we had flown in with started climbing out of it. We began to move toward it, many of the journalists trotting but myself and some of the others walking. A crowd of civilians and several dozen soldiers swept through us. A shoulder of one of the ARVNs hit the back of my shoulder. As I spun away, the stock of the running man's M-16 slapped hard into my back. I moved to the side of the road, laughing as the realizations finally came, among them the fact that almost none of the men wore packs. They weren't troops anymore, they were refugees in uniforms.

Five or six teams of men carrying wounded on litters had also given up the chase. Some of them stood still, as if trying to decide whether they could set their burdens down in the dirt of the roadside. Others had turned and were walking off to softer ground.

I turned at the sound of Captain Anh's voice. He was trying to reassemble his charges. The Chinook had lifted before it had disgorged all its men and before the point of the mob had reached it. The big helicopter moved another hundred yards down the highway and descended again. It never firmly settled on the tarmac, but hovered with the hatch just off the road, the nose of the aircraft pointing up, like a fat fish depositing eggs on the seabed. This time the troops got out, but they had supplies as well. It took about a minute to get most of the crates onto the ground, and by that time the mob had reached its objective. One of the reinforcements shot in the air, which slowed the back half of the crowd. But forty or fifty men managed to clamber on board before the pilot slowly gained altitude, the hatch still down, two or three men having to choose to drop back to the road from heights of six to ten feet.

"Good show, mate," Peter Arnett barked at Captain Anh. "This is for those of us who missed Da Nang, right?"

The second helicopter in the lift landed a few minutes later. There had been time for radio communication. The fresh troops dropped out smartly and kept order until half a dozen litters were on board. I moved with Captain Anh and the other journalists in a pack behind the wounded, surrounded by refugees, wondering how I was going to behave. I glanced back and satisfied myself that I wasn't taking the place of someone who had been wounded. As I reached the hatch, the sun disappeared in the jam of bodies. Ahead were the legs of journalists and refugees already on the hatch. I was pushed from behind. I pushed no harder than anyone else, but I kept my elbows pointed a little off to the side, my hands in fists in front of my chest, my elbows stiff. Like the others who made it, I had to use the elbows to check the pressure behind me. I didn't jab anyone in the face. Like everyone around me, I communicated with small tough gestures and a stiffness throughout my body that I was close enough to get on and was not going to be stopped from doing so.

On the flight back to Bien Hoa, I reviewed the force I had used as if it were important that intellectual analysis not reveal any weakness in the emotional certainty that I had not panicked. The review was successful, but it was a test I hoped I wouldn't have to face again. I was also troubled by my uncertainty as to whether all of my colleagues had made it. (They hadn't, but the rest of them would come out on the next flight.) Most of all, I marveled at my ignorance. I had been to Hung Nghia. I'd read the morning and afternoon military releases and numerous AP stories about Xuan Loc through the last five days. And yet it was not until the rush for the first helicopter that I had finally realized that the helicopters were the only way out.

The NBC van was supposed to be waiting for us at Bien Hoa. When it was obvious that it would be late, Harris took the film and my tape and got on Captain Anh's truck; I volunteered to wait for the van with the crew's equipment. It was a long wait. With no more work in the afternoon sun ahead of me, I ordered a beer. The concessions in the long shed flowed into one another. Later, I had *pho* and coffee, and everything I ordered came from a different small businessman. Continuing the day's pattern, I finally realized that the families that filled the long benches of the place, many of them three-generation clusters with paper bags or sacks or baskets of fruit and clothes—the odd, pitiful light things people choose for flight—were refugees.

I made some of the children laugh, as I had learned to do from Charlie Benoit. The apartment on Tu Do was about thirteen miles away from where I sat. I looked around in the twilit, crowded shed and toyed with the idea that it really was getting pretty close now.

II

Early that afternoon, Pierre Brochand, the boyish-looking chief political operative at the French Embassy, approached Thomas Polgar at the poolside terrace of the Cercle Sportif and asked the CIA station chief if he could join him. "Of course," Polgar said.

Brochand began with a review of the military situation. "This business at Xuan Loc doesn't matter," he said. "The war is lost. It was lost at the moment of surprise at Ban Me Thuot. Da Nang was just confirmation that the North has a military victory—if they want it."

"Go on," Polgar said.

His government, Brochand said, had reason to think that the North Vietnamese might choose to forgo the military solution and accept a transitional, independent government in what he called Cochinchine. Why? First because they said so. Why not take them at their word, now, quickly? Second, it was rational for them to have a government in the South acceptable to the South Vietnamese people. Finally, most important and even more logical, Brochand said that the French thought Hanoi would make concessions to keep Western aid coming to the South.

Brochand went on to outline a solution that would install a neutralist peace government in Saigon as a bridge—over a period of at least months and perhaps years—to communist rule. Duong Van ("Big") Minh would be most acceptable to Hanoi as head of this new government, although several other figures both inside and outside the current regime might also do.

The alternatives were horrible, Brochand said. What the French feared most was another Da Nang in Saigon, a collapse of authority. If that happened, if there was what he called a "vacancy" in the functioning of the police and other public services—then the communists could simply wait at the gates to the city until the people called them in to restore order. "Believe me, Mr. Polgar," he said, "we know that that is a card they are considering. Of course, you would be gone by then. We are staying. Think what it would be like for us, with fifteen thousand French citizens here, and God knows how many Vietnamese with claims to citizenship."

He rose to leave. "Of course you know that the one man they will not accept is Thieu," he said. "That is the first obstacle."

"Yes," Polgar said. "Thank you for sharing your thoughts with us."

"De rien," Brochand said conventionally. Then: "No, it is not nothing. It is the only hope. Thieu must go, quickly. Forgive me for lecturing you, Mr. Polgar. But, you know, it did not have to come to this. There was a chance for peace in 1971, if you had permitted a real election. But no, you had to back Thieu. Stability was everything. No compromise, no risk. Well, the time for compromise is very past due. And it begins with getting rid of Thieu."

An hour later, Polgar called Frank Snepp, his analyst for North Vietnamese affairs, to his office. He directed Snepp to write a field appraisal concluding that Nguyen Van Thieu had become the chief obstacle to any hope for a negotiated settlement.

III

Late that night, about fifteen men crowded into the office of Marvin Garrett, the American Embassy's chief security officer. They included Garrett's three assistants; and Major James Kean, the commander of the embassy Marines, who in normal times was stationed in Hong Kong, where he oversaw all the embassy Marine units in the region; Steven Bray, the head of the Mission Warden Office; a couple of Seabees; and half a dozen young Foreign Service Officers, including Ken Moorefield and Donald Hays, both of them recent combat veterans.

Garrett, a short, trim man with a neat sandy beard and mustache, chaired the meeting. Without criticizing the ambassador directly, he told the group about the embassy's standing evacuation plan, which he himself had updated six months earlier. The group knew that the word from the top was that it was business as usual. Garrett said that he understood the ambassador's position, but added that he thought it was time to quietly go ahead with preliminary work to help assure the security of what he considered an inevitable evacuation.

He outlined a plan in which a number of sites around the city—the DAO compound, the embassy itself, and about a dozen buildings owned or rented by the embassy—would be used as helicopter pickup points. Various officers at the meeting were assigned to see that Americans in each of the outlying buildings were equipped with radios and ropes, and to reinforce the rooftop landing zones themselves if necessary. He emphasized that any work that had to be done should be done as quietly and inconspicuously as possible. Like the ambassador, he didn't want the people of Saigon to see the Americans preparing to run. He also didn't want the ambassador himself or his lieutenants to see what he was setting out to do.

As the meeting broke up, Don Hays, the young budget officer, said to someone: "You know, all this business about not doing anything to let the local employees know we're getting ready to bug out is kind of weird when we've been burning files for—what? ten days now? All eight stacks goin', the sky gray with smoke and ash, ash so thick on the swimming pool that no one uses it anymore. Seems to me the locals might have a clue already."

Hays had been assigned to improve security at the embassy. The next day, through channels, he sent a request for workers to heighten the fence around the compound and to change gates that opened out to open in. But functionaries in the embassy, out of deference to the ambassador, refused to cooperate. Hays got on the phone to his counterpart in the parallel USAID bureaucracy and got his work crew. Later in the week, as Hays was supervising the construction, Hank Boudreau—as the administrative counselor, Hays's boss—came out of the chancery and asked him what the hell was going on.

"Gee," Hays said disingenuously, "I thought you ordered this."

Boudreau humphed and walked away. The work continued.

IV

Captain Do Duc Cuong of the military security section of the now shattered and lost ARVN 1st Division spent most of the first half of that ghastly April moving south.

When the communist shelling of Cam Ranh began in earnest on April 5, Cuong decided to follow the people south. A little less than ten miles south of Cam Ranh, the column he was moving with skirted a battle between the communists pushing toward the coast from Ban Me Thuot and the Airborne brigade that had been split off there to fight. The paratroopers were holding out. They helped the people move south; and from that point on Cuong felt that he was back inside government lines. He walked, or more often rode in one military vehicle or another, for a week, covering the 150 miles from Cam Ranh to the small city of Ham Tan in Binh Tuy province, just 80 miles east of Saigon.

There was fighting close to Ham Tan. Cuong saw bodies again for the first time in a week.

He also found his superior, Colonel Nhon, who told Cuong that it was time for both of them to get to Saigon. Despite the fighting, here in Military Region 3, the military region around the capital, things functioned as they had not in Captain Cuong's world for nearly a month. The morning after he arrived in Ham Tan, Cuong and the colonel found seats on a plane for Saigon.

At house number 9 on Nguyen Binh Khiem Street, the headquarters of his service, the military service that did the dirty work, Captain Cuong waited for an hour, listening to a discussion between Colonel Nhon and Colonel Nhon's superior in which voices were raised. When Cuong was brought into the office, Colonel Nhon had calmed himself. He and the other officers told Cuong that the Army was trying to regroup the remnants of the regular forces from MR 1 at Vung Tau, the pretty little town forty miles southeast of Saigon that had been the capital's beach resort—when the level of fighting permitted excursions to the beach—ever since the French, who had called it Cap St. Jacques, first arrived.

They didn't order Cuong to Vung Tau, but told him what was happening there. He asked where he should go to get on a truck.

Cuong was in Vung Tau for five days, helping to clothe and feed and rearm what finally amounted to a thousand men, Cuong among them. He was no longer a security or intelligence officer but a uniformed infantry captain.

Captain Cuong gave himself a few hours off on some of those days to explore the city and neighboring villages, a vague plan forming in his mind.

v

Shortly after the tension between Jay Scarborough and the missionaries in the place they called Camp Sunshine came to a head—and was defused by Carolyn Miller—a camp official they had nicknamed "Bath Man" announced with obvious pleasure that Nha Trang had been liberated. Carolyn Miller's heart constricted as she thought of the three older children she and John had left at school there. She assumed that Wycliffe Bible Translators officials would have had enough warning to get Margie, Gordon and Nate out of Nha Trang before the fighting reached there. But the prisoners in Camp Sunshine had also been told that panic conditions in Da Nang had made evacuation so difficult that "hundreds of American military advisers in civilian clothing were left standing on the beach." For all she knew, this had happened in Nha Trang as well.

The Millers had left a will in Saigon stipulating that in the event of their deaths, Carolyn Miller's parents would become the children's guardians. Would their director in Saigon have assumed the worst—as the fate of other missionaries captured by the communists in earlier offensives might lead him to do—and sent the children on to their grandparents in upstate New York? Or were they still in Vietnam, or with the Wycliffe group in the Philippines?

Carolyn Miller headed for the latrine corner of the camp, to get away for a few minutes. She swallowed hard, and managed to hold back the tears, surrendering her fears to God.

One of the oddities of life as a prisoner, Carolyn Miller discovered, was that her ability to concentrate dissipated. While her husband was able to absorb himself day after day in a 1,500-page Bible dictionary, she seemed incapable of any prolonged effort. She added Psalm 139 to the twenty or so she had committed to memory as a child. But when she tried to read through the New Testament in Greek, she was able to get through only the first few chapters of Matthew. The same list-lessness affected most of the others. Scarborough, Struharik, Whitlock and Tolentino amused themselves with card games for a few days—but then lost interest.

Carolyn assumed that their weakened physical condition was one cause of the problem, but there were deeper sources of her malaise. For the first time in her life she had no responsibilities. Aside from seeing after LuAnne, there was really nothing she had to do between the wake-up gong in the morning and the bedtime gong at night. Bleakest of all was the sense of utter lack of control over their future. Their fates were entirely in the hands of others. Despair, she knew, was a sin, and she never gave in to it. But, unable to foresee the future, she found it almost impossible to prepare for it with projects of intellectual or spiritual self-improvement. It was all she could do to try to keep the three of them well.

On the last day of March—the day after Easter and their move to the new, drier shelter—Carolyn's own health broke, quickly. She came down with the same symptoms her husband had been suffering from for several days: fever, a sore throat and a headache. A few days later, John Miller was a bit better, but Carolyn could only barely manage to get herself to the latrine and back to the shelter, where she collapsed on her place on the floor.

Dick Phillips and Norm Johnson were suffering from milder forms of the same illness. Lillian Phillips several times appealed to the camp's North Vietnamese medic, but the man said he had nothing to offer.

When Carolyn Miller got up on the morning of April 3 for the trip to the latrine, waves of dizziness overcame her. She gripped one of the bamboo roof supports, thinking the blackness would recede as it had before, but it did not. Her head was ringing, and she felt her grip on the pole slipping. She sat down and crawled back to the corner where she and John and LuAnne slept.

Her husband reached out and put his cool hands on her cheeks.

"John, I don't think I'm going to make it."

"Don't get discouraged," he said softly. "I think you'll pull out of it in a few days."

"Honey, if they were to let us go today I'm too weak to go. And without proper food and medicine I think the only way to go is down. I'm not afraid to die. That really doesn't worry me at all. But I hate to think of leaving you and LuAnne here, and I hate to think I won't get to see the other kids again."

The medic still showed no concern. But he grudgingly surrendered three days' worth of antibiotics and vitamin injections, with a few old syringes and dull needles. As she rubbed a very sore hip that afternoon, Carolyn said, "I never thought I'd feel so thankful to get a shot!" She was able to make it to the latrine with John's help, and over the next few days a measure of strength returned.

Less than two weeks later, in the middle of April, LuAnne stirred restlessly in her sleep and threw her legs over her mother's hips. Only half awake herself, Carolyn reached to move the legs and then was suddenly wide awake. LuAnne was burning up.

It was two-thirty in the morning. John slipped out of the mosquito net for water and an aspirin, which LuAnne managed to get down without a protest, although it obviously hurt her to swallow. Carolyn lay with her at the foot of the net, so that her kicking wouldn't disturb Peter Whitlock inches away, and LuAnne began to speak, quietly and rapidly. Her story combined elements of two or three Bible stories with the bedtime fairy tale her mother had told her that evening. In the middle of the jumbled story, LuAnne fell asleep.

The fever broke within an hour. Through the next day, LuAnne did little but sleep. She could not eat, but took the aspirins they gave her. The camp medic seemed genuinely concerned about her, and asked one of the ARVN doctors to look after her. The medic even brought some precious tetracycline tablets for her.

Late in the afternoon, LuAnne leaned over the sleeping platform and vomited the little that was in her stomach, including the last pills she had taken.

The night was a repeat of the previous one. Toward morning, she called out, "Mommy! Nate's got a Coke!" Awake, she was amused by the dream. "I really thought Nate was here," she said. "He was drinking a Coke, and it looked so good I wanted some too."

The wake-up gong rang out at 5 A.M. as usual. LuAnne woke up and again retched over the platform.

Half an hour later, as the adults were folding away their mosquito nets and tarpaulins for the day, a guard arrived and announced urgently: "Get all your things together! You are being moved to another location!"

VI

By the middle of the month, the ambassador's health was starting to deteriorate. There was the seemingly endless round of meetings, large and small, during the day; the current urgent intelligence reports and cable traffic to attend to; and then the reading to be done at night, routinely until two or three in the morning. So it is not surprising that in a cable the ambassador wrote through the evening of April 15 in the subdued light of his large office on the third floor of an embassy in which, as he wrote, lights blinked off in office after office until the building was nearly dark and empty, he wandered. He returned over and over again to the idea that if the vote in Congress on the Administration's request for additional military aid to South Vietnam were to be negative, it would be better if the vote could be delayed. Nevertheless, the cable included a few of the tart observations and assertions that caused people in the mission as well as in Washington to read Graham Martin cables for entertainment.*

TO KISSINGER.

1. I REPORTED TO YOU THIEU'S COMMENT THAT IF IT WERE ABSO-LUTELY CLEAR THAT THE REQUEST FOR MILITARY AID—THE $722 MILLION SUPPLEMENTAL—WAS TO BE DEFEATED, IT WOULD BE HIGHLY PREFERABLE TO FIND SOME WAY TO DELAY THE FINAL VOTE. AL-THOUGH HE DID NOT SAY SO, IT SEEMS CLEAR THAT HE, AS WELL AS EVERYBODY ELSE, IS UNSURE OF WHAT COMES NEXT. SO FAR, GENERAL TOAN† IN MR 3 IS DOING A JOB ALL THE EXPERTS THOUGHT ABSO-LUTELY IMPOSSIBLE: HE HAS INFLICTED WELL OVER 2,000 KIAS IN PUSHING BACK THE ELEMENTS OF THREE NVA DIVISIONS FROM XUAN LOC. THE TOTAL COUNT NOW OF THE REGULAR FORCES RETRIEVED FROM MR 1 AND MR 2 IS CLIMBING TOWARD 60,000, OVER A QUARTER

---

* Throughout this book, cables have been edited, for space reasons only.
† The immensely fat general who had been relieved of the command of MR 2—the Central Highlands—in October for corruption. At the urging of Ambassador Martin, who didn't give a damn about the man's personal life but recognized a good commander when he saw one, Toan was rehabilitated as commander of MR 3 after the fall of Phuoc Long province in January.

OF THE REGULAR FORCE, AND THEY ARE EITHER BEING FED INTO EX-
ISTING DIVISIONS OR BEING RE-FORMED AT RATE ALSO DEEMED IMPOS-
SIBLE BY THE EXPERTS. MANY OF THE NVA TROOPS KILLED AND SOME
CAPTURED ARE IN THEIR MID-TEENS. ONE YESTERDAY SAID HE
"THOUGHT" HE WAS FOURTEEN. THERE IS THEREFORE A ROUGH EQUIV-
ALENCY IN NUMBERS, AND THE QUALITATIVE DECREASE IN THE FIGHT-
ING EFFICIENCY OF THE RVN* AS THEY ARE BEING RE-FORMED IS OFF-
SET IN PART AT LEAST BY THE INEXPERIENCE AND YOUTH ON THE
OTHER SIDE. THERE ARE OF COURSE MORE NVA DIVISIONS ON THE WAY
SOUTH. TOAN, HOWEVER, CAN NOW MASS TO HIT THE ENEMY, AN
ABILITY HE RELISHES AND HAS RARELY HAD BEFORE. BELOW SAIGON,
THE NVA 5TH IS ALSO GETTING MAULED AT BOTH ENDS. SO THE FORCES
THAT WERE PROGRAMMED FOR ATTACK ON SAIGON ARE NOT IN AS
GOOD SHAPE AS THEY WERE WHEN THE AMBITIOUS PLANS NOW SHOW-
ING UP IN OUR INTELLIGENCE WERE MADE. I AM DELIBERATELY LEAN-
ING OVER BACKWARD TO KEEP MYSELF A DISPASSIONATE OBSERVER
VIEWING VIETNAM AS IF FROM A SEAT ON THE MOON. I DO NOT FOR
ONE MOMENT UNDERESTIMATE THE SITUATION'S SERIOUSNESS. IF
THERE IS AN ADVERSE VOTE FROM WASHINGTON THIS WEEKEND, I DO
NOT THINK THAT THE RVNAF† WILL NECESSARILY FOLD. IT WILL NOT
BE ALL THAT PLEASANT, HOWEVER, TO BE AN AMERICAN IN SAIGON
UNTIL THE SHOCK [OF THE CONGRESSIONAL VOTE] WEARS OFF.

2. THE JUXTAPOSITION OF EAGLE PULL [THE U.S. EVACUATION
FROM PHNOM PENH THREE DAYS EARLIER] TO THE CRUCIAL VOTE, THE
[ADMIRAL NOEL] GAYLER REMARKS ABOUT HOW PERFECT [EAGLE
PULL] WAS AND HOW HE COULD DO IT AGAIN IN SAIGON IF NECESSARY,
THE LEAKS IN WASHINGTON, THE REMARKS BY JAVITS AND MUSKIE ON
FACE THE NATION AND MEET THE PRESS THAT THE PRESIDENT HAS AU-
THORITY TO USE A SMALL NUMBER OF MARINES TO EVACUATE AMERI-
CANS BUT WOULD NEED CONGRESSIONAL [AUTHORITY] BEFORE "TROOPS
COULD EVACUATE 200,000 VIETNAMESE THE ADMINISTRATION FEARS
WOULD BE PUNISHED BY THE VIET CONG FOR COOPERATING WITH THE
UNITED STATES," AND MUSKIE'S ECHO THAT HE "CAN SEE SOME DIFFI-
CULTIES WITH RESPECT TO EVACUATING SOUTH VIETNAMESE ON ANY
MASSIVE SCALE," ARE NOT PRECISELY CALCULATED TO MAKE MY JOB OF
GETTING US OUT OF HERE ANY EASIER. I AM NOT SURE THAT JAVITS' RE-
MARKS WERE NOT, IN ONE WAY, A BLESSING IN DISGUISE. IT MAY
PREVENT US FROM ENDING UP IN A VERY GHASTLY WAY WITH THE
MARINES OVERWHELMED BY AN RVNAF SO ANGERED AT OUR FINAL DE-
SERTION, AND THE VNAF SHOOTING DOWN OUR TRANSPORTS [SIC]. I HOPE
THEREFORE YOU KEEP CLEARLY IN MIND THAT THE DECISION WHETHER
FORCE WOULD BE FINALLY REQUIRED IS A VERY DELICATE ONE AND ONE
WHICH, ABOVE ALL, SHOULD NOT BE MADE BY THE MILITARY.

* Republic of Vietnam (i.e., South Vietnam).
† Republic of Vietnam armed forces.

3. THERE IS ONE CONTINGENCY HOWEVER WHERE I WOULD WANT IT. IF THERE BEGAN TO BE A BREAKDOWN IN INTERNAL ORDER IN SAIGON BEFORE THE BULK OF THE AMERICANS WERE OUT, I WILL ASK FOR IT QUICKLY. THERE ARE MANY REASONS WHY THIS WILL BE UNLIKELY, NOT THE LEAST OF WHICH WOULD BE THE DESIRE OF OUR PAL LE DUC THO TO BE INVITED INTO SAIGON. IF THE CONGRESS VOTE IS NEGATIVE IN THE END, THERE IS STILL NO NEED FOR IMMEDIATE PANIC. IN AN ASIAN WAY, THERE WILL AT LAST OCCUR A SITUATION WHICH HAS NOT EXISTED SINCE MY ARRIVAL: EITHER THE GENERALS OR THE COLONELS WILL FINALLY SCREW UP ENOUGH COHESION AND COURAGE TO POINT OUT TO THIEU THAT THE MANDATE OF HEAVEN HAS BEEN REMOVED. MY REMARKS ON THIS SCORE IN THE RECENT ISSUE OF TIME WERE CAREFULLY PHRASED. THEY HAVE ALREADY BEEN CORRECTLY INTERPRETED HERE THAT OUR SUPPORT HAS ALWAYS BEEN FOR THE GOVERNMENT, NEVER FOR THE MAN. . . . IT IS MY SENSE THAT THIEU UNDERSTANDS THIS ALSO, AND THE ATTACKS THAT WILL BE MADE UPON ME IN THE AMERICAN PRESS AS A DEVOTED SUPPORTER OF THIEU, AS THE INEVITABLE DISTORTIONS OCCUR IN THE PRESS HANDLING OF THE REMARKS WILL, IN FACT, EASE HIS DEPARTURE, SINCE AT THE END WE DID NOT KNIFE HIM IN THE BACK, WHICH WOULD HAVE BEEN EQUALLY RESENTED BY THE VIETNAMESE, WHO DETEST THIEU, AND OTHER ASIAN LEADERS, LIKE OUR FRIEND [SINGAPORE PRIME MINISTER] LEE KUAN YEW. . . .

4. SO THE PRESS ATTACKS WILL SERVE A USEFUL PURPOSE, AS I HAVE OFTEN MANAGED FOR THEM TO DO. THE RELATIVELY FEW PEOPLE ABOUT WHOSE OPINIONS I REALLY CARE WILL NOT CHANGE THEIR OPINION OF ME. EVEN THE SLY, ANONYMOUS INSERTIONS OF THE PERFUMED ICE PICK INTO THE KIDNEYS, IN THE FORM OF THE QUOTES FROM MY COLLEAGUES IN THE DEPARTMENT, ARE ONLY A PECULIAR FORM OF ACUPUNCTURE INDIGENOUS TO FOGGY BOTTOM AGAINST WHICH I WAS IMMUNIZED LONG AGO. THERE ARE ONLY TWO IMPORTANT CONSIDERATIONS I KEEP IN MIND: THE SAFETY OF THE PEOPLE UNDER MY CHARGE AND THE INTEGRITY OF U.S. POLICY. . . .

VII

Two weeks before, as the panic swept down the coast, government units and most of the population of Phan Rang, the next important town south of Cam Ranh, had fled, although there was no immediate threat from the communists. In fact, the following day a general named Nguyen Vinh Nghi, who had been fired five months earlier for corruption, established an advance headquarters for Military Region 3 in the small city.

His forces were finally overwhelmed on April 16. Nghi, one of his deputies and a CIA officer named James Lewis were all taken prisoner.

As I read of the real fall of Phan Rang that evening in the Associated Press office, I turned to George Esper and said, "This is kind of embarrassing. I think I reported the fall of Phan Rang a week or so ago."

"You did," Esper said. "We all did. Everyone bugged out. Then the military bugged back in when they realized there weren't any communists around."

"They're gettin' close," I said idly. "I was in Phan Rang just a few months ago."

"They're a lot closer than Phan Rang, David," Esper said.

"Yeah," I said. "Well, I guess I ought to do a spot. Who's this American—Lewis? The province rep?"

"Something like that," Esper said. "Our man in Phan Rang. Listen, there's another aspect of the story I'm working on. You can't go with it yet, but you might ask about it at the briefing tomorrow. Thieu's family is from Phan Rang. And it looks like maybe some ARVN decided to bulldoze the ancestral tombs on the way out of town."

"Thanks," I said. "I can't imagine Colonel Hien confirming that one, but I'll check at the embassy."

Mercifully, the call to New York went through quickly. I took the stairs back down to the AP office to ask Esper if he could join me on the terrace of the Continental for a drink.

"I wish I could, Dave," Esper said. "I wish we both could pack it up and go down to the Hotel Catinat and listen to Khanh Ha and the band."

"Someday," I said.

"You think so?"

"Sure. 'Fight fight, talk talk.' Thieu's gotta go. Then they'll talk."

"Maybe you're right," Esper said. "And maybe you and I will have another drink some night in the Pink Night Club. But I don't think we'll be listening to Khanh Ha."

The phone rang. Esper pushed a button, lifted the receiver and said, "Yeah?" I left.

Mercifully again, I had an hour before curfew. Less mercifully, I knew none of the few drinkers on the terrace of the Continental. But that night the memories were more pleasant than not.

Benoit and his girl friend, Tai, and I had reached the outskirts of Phan Rang late in the afternoon. Benoit turned inland, and we bumped across a dusty plain to a conical, lonely hill crowned with a Cham temple tower. "I've seen most of the other towers around here," Benoit explained, "but never this one. I think it's still active, not just a ruin." We left the Deux Chevaux at the base of the hill and started up the steep hillside path, reinforced every few paces with rock slabs shaped like railroad ties. A boy whose skull was marked with ringworm appeared out of the desolate landscape and informed us that he would be our guide.

At the summit we went directly to the one tower still standing. Through a tunneled entrance that either Benoit or I would have had trouble entering, we could see in the darkness relieved a little by three guttering candles a *mukta linga,* an eighteen-inch phallus that Benoit explained represented Siva. He spoke with the boy and determined that three old women kept the candles lit and changed the stiff red robe embroidered in gold that was draped around the shaft.

Tai, the daughter of a culture with many gods, was silent before the temple of this one. She seemed at first to want to enter the stuffy little tabernacle but settled for kneeling in front of it with her palms together and the tips of her fingers touching her forehead. Benoit and I peered into it like archeologists.

Charlie and I moved off to a ruined square antechamber, its roof and one of its walls crumbled into itself. It was overcast, and the low sun in the west gave no color to the white strip of sea on the horizon. The surrounding chalky fields had fallen into disuse. It was odd to have such a commanding view but not to see a village.

"The Vietnamese are so much like us," Benoit said. "As a city, rather than just a fishing village, Saigon isn't all that much older than San Francisco. The Chams were all along the central coast. They were driven south by the Vietnamese, and they made their last stand here, at the end of the seventeenth century. There are a few villages left. A French priest I know is trying to put together a dictionary. I read somewhere that the descendant of the last Cham queen is here somewhere. Maybe she's one of the old women who take care of the temple."

He descended into the foundation of another tower, sunk off the crown of the hill. Then he called to me.

Fresh writing covered part of one crumbling wall. "Some troops must have made camp here recently," Benoit said. "Do you want to hear some Vietnamese graffiti?"

"Of course," I said.

"This one's nice," Benoit said. " 'Marching with new comrades, I think of old school friends.' " He read several more without speaking, and then added: " 'Wait for me, mother and little sister.' " He looked at it for a moment and then added: "You can't tell if it's really his sister or his girl friend."

"Are they all poetic?" I asked.

"I haven't got a dirty one yet," Benoit said. "Some of them are just a name and a hometown and a date."

Tai had joined us now. She sat on the edge of the foundation with me, our potbellied guide between us, looking at the big bald American in the hole. "Here's one," Benoit said. He pointed to the carefully chipped ellipses and read, " 'Vietnam . . . I weep.' "

In the fading light, he repeated it in Vietnamese. The boy's eyes were bright with wonder.

20

On Thursday morning, there was news so terrible that President Thieu had to be told. Through this third week of April he had been increasingly inaccessible and irrational. He sometimes refused to take phone calls even from generals in the field. And with ever more reason to fear a coup or a repeat of the bombing of the palace, he moved from one to the other of his several homes in Saigon, or slept in the underground bomb shelter at the palace.

But this was different. In their inexorable push down the coast, the communists in the last two days had reached and occupied Phan Rang and Phan Thiet, the two southernmost coastal cities in Military Region 2. (Phan Rang and Phan Thiet were two of the coastal cities from which regular government defenders fled long before there was a communist attack.) All of MR 2 was now theirs. But the crushing news was that Marines and Rangers who had been sent to guard the Thieu family ancestral graves in a village outside Phan Rang as they fell back had bulldozed the tombs into the ground.

Aides with him said that when Thieu was given the news his face writhed in agony. He walked from the room as if in a trance, retreated to the basement bomb shelter and was not seen again for twenty-four hours.

II

Henry Kissinger knew how to preface a difficult order with a high compliment.

TO: MARTIN
SENSITIVE
EXCLUSIVELY EYES ONLY
WE HAVE JUST COMPLETED AN INTERAGENCY REVIEW OF THE STATE
OF PLAY IN SOUTH VIETNAM. YOU SHOULD KNOW THAT AT THE WSAG*
MEETING TODAY THERE WAS ALMOST NO SUPPORT FOR THE EVACUA-
TION OF VIETNAMESE, AND FOR THE USE OF AMERICAN FORCE TO HELP
PROTECT ANY EVACUATION. THE SENTIMENT OF OUR MILITARY, DOD
[CIVILIAN LEADERSHIP OF THE DEPARTMENT OF DEFENSE] AND CIA
COLLEAGUES WAS TO GET OUT FAST AND NOW.

IN ADDITION, AS I INDICATED IN MY MESSAGE TO YOU LAST NIGHT,
THE CONGRESSIONAL SITUATION IS FAST GETTING OUT OF HAND. OUR
TASK—YOURS AND MINE—IS TO PREVENT PANIC BOTH IN SAIGON AND
WASHINGTON, AND I KNOW THAT YOU RECOGNIZE THIS MORE CLEARLY
THAN ALMOST ANYONE IN THE UNITED STATES GOVERNMENT.

I APPRECIATE YOUR INDICATION THAT YOU CAN WILL MEET MY RE-
QUEST THAT WE REDUCE TO APPROXIMATELY 2,000 OFFICIAL AND NON-
OFFICIAL AMERICANS BY THE END OF NEXT WEEK, BUT MUST NOW, IN
LIGHT OF THE SITUATION, ASK THAT THIS SCHEDULE BE ADVANCED. IT
IS ESSENTIAL, DESPITE THE CONCERNS THAT YOU HAVE EXPRESSED AND
THAT I ACCEPT, FOR YOU TO SPEED UP THE MOVEMENT OF AMERICAN
CITIZENS OUT OF VIETNAM. WE MUST BE AT OR BELOW 2,000 OFFICIAL
AND UNOFFICIAL U.S. CITIZENS BY TUESDAY, APRIL 22. I ASK THAT YOU
MOVE IMMEDIATELY TO ACCOMPLISH THIS AND ASSURE YOU THAT WE
ARE PREPARED TO DO EVERYTHING WE CAN TO GIVE YOU ANY ADDI-
TIONAL ASSISTANCE YOU NEED. YOU WILL BE RECEIVING A FRONT-
CHANNEL MESSAGE TO THIS EFFECT, PLUS CERTAIN OTHER QUESTIONS
AND INSTRUCTIONS IN TANDEM WITH THIS MESSAGE. KISSINGER.

III

That cable ordering the ambassador to speed up the flow of Americans out of the country, and saying that there was no enthusiasm in Washington for the evacuation of any Vietnamese, arrived on Thursday, April 17, the same day that Thieu was told of the desecration of the ancestral graves. That evening, Alan Carter appeared on South Vietnam's television network for an interview carefully structured to allay Vietnamese fears that the Americans were abandoning them.

Graham Martin did not go so far as to script the entire interview

* Washington Special Action Group.

himself. But he created it, outlining the points to be covered and then editing it before sending Carter out to perform.

Carter's interlocutor was an official from the South Vietnamese Ministry of Information. The USIS chief's first task was to dispel a rumor that had circulated among informed circles in Saigon to the effect that if the U.S. Congress failed to pass the Ford Administration's request for emergency supplemental military aid by April 19—the day after tomorrow—all the Americans would be evacuated. The President had asked Congress to act by the nineteenth, Carter said. But there was nothing magical about the date. It was merely a requested date for congressional action. "In any event," Carter went on, "it should be remembered that the President has said he would ask Congress in our next fiscal year to appropriate $1.29 billion in military aid for Vietnam. . . .

"If you would visit Ambassador and Mrs. Martin's home," Carter added truthfully, "you would see that nothing whatsoever has been packed. The same is true of my house."

"Another rumor says that the American Consulate has been issuing passes to Vietnamese citizens for the purposes of evacuating them," the questioner said.

"This is still another rumor to which there is absolutely no truth," Carter said.

The man left the realm of rumor and asked about the patently real—all of Saigon could see them—long lines that snaked from the consular section of the embassy out along the sidewalk of Thong Nhut Boulevard.

"Well, we are really talking first about normal functions performed by American consulates," Carter said. "The filing of marriage papers, the reporting of births, the issuance of visas. I think it is obvious that present circumstances have created some nervousness in both the American and Vietnamese communities. It is true that some Americans have been leaving. I am sure many of you have noticed that some of your American friends have gone. But given the circumstances it is understandable that some Americans or their dependents would have wanted to leave somewhat earlier than they had originally planned. . . .

"It is logical that we should have reduced slowly over the past few weeks, and on a somewhat accelerated basis now, the number of nonessential Americans in the embassy. Even when we have completed this process, however, we will still be one of the largest U.S. embassies in the world."

Carter did not feel particularly used by the episode that night. The only outright falsehood was the denial that the Americans were getting any Vietnamese out of the country. And there was—he thought—such a thing as disinformation in a just cause, which was to prevent panic in Saigon. But what the ambassador had not told him was that he was planning to run the interview on three consecutive nights. And by the third night, planning was completed for the evacuation of several hundred Americans and several thousand Vietnamese a day.

IV

SENSITIVE
SECRET
SAIGON

Late that night, the ambassador sat alone in his third-floor office and tapped out the three words. He trusted Eva Kim, his secretary, as much as he trusted anyone. But now the time had arrived when the circle of trust must be drawn to the practical minimum: himself and the young man who would transmit these few thousand words to Washington, shred the paper they were written on and, the ambassador hoped, forget them.

TO KISSINGER FROM MARTIN

He reached for the text of the Alan Carter interview and began:

AT 8:30 P.M. TONIGHT AND AGAIN AT 9:30—AND AGAIN FOR THE NEXT TWO NIGHTS, I HOPE—ALAN CARTER APPEARED ON TV WITH GVN INFORMATION MINISTER WITH Q & A, TEXT OF WHICH FOLLOWS: . . .

He rolled a new sheet of paper into the typewriter and wrote a second paragraph about the other moves he had made in recent days to defuse the importance of the April 19 deadline for congressional action on the Administration's request for supplemental aid.

. . . IF THERE IS A NEGATIVE VOTE, I HOPE YOU AND THE PRESIDENT WILL CALMLY ANNOUNCE YOU ARE GOING ALL OUT TO WIN THE FIGHT FOR THE FISCAL YEAR 76 APPROPRIATION. AS UNREALISTIC AS THIS MAY SEEM, IT WILL HAVE GREAT EFFECT HERE. . . .
THERE IS ONE GREAT AND MOST IMPORTANT CAVEAT. THERE MUST BE NO PANIC IN WASHINGTON. THE ONE THING THAT WOULD SET OFF VIOLENCE WOULD BE A SUDDEN ORDER FOR AMERICAN EVACUATION. . . . THE ONE THING THAT COULD TRIGGER WHITE-HOT ANGER WITH INCALCULABLE RESULTS WOULD BE TO SEND IN THE MARINES OR HAVE ANY GREAT TALK ABOUT IT.
. . . THE ARVN CAN HOLD THE APPROACHES TO SAIGON FOR QUITE A WHILE, AND I STILL DOUBT THAT HANOI DESIRES A FRONTAL SMASH AT SAIGON, FOR A MULTITUDE OF REASONS. . . . MOST OF THE AMERICANS LIKELY TO PANIC HAVE ALREADY LEFT AND THE ONES WHO ARE

LEFT AFTER WE GET THE GREAT REMAINDER OUT IN THE NEXT FEW DAYS WILL BE COOL, TOUGH CHARACTERS.

I REPEAT ONCE AGAIN THE ONE THING THAT ALMOST SURELY WOULD TRIGGER VERY GREAT ANGER WOULD BE TO SEND IN AMERICAN ARMED FORCES NOW, EXCEPT A VERY FEW IN THE MOST UNOBTRUSIVE MANNER. THE REACTION, BITS AND PIECES OF WHICH I AM SENDING TO YOU, ALL CONFIRM THIS IS THE ONE THING WE MUST NOT DO. IT WILL BE UNIVERSALLY INTERPRETED AS A MOST CALLOUS BETRAYAL, LEAVING THE VIETNAMESE TO THEIR FATE WHILE WE SEND IN THE MARINES TO MAKE SURE WE GET ALL OF OURS OUT. IT WILL NOT BE BELIEVED WE CARE A TINKER'S DAMN WHAT HAPPENS TO THEM. AND FROM THAT DEEP FEELING, THE TINIEST INCIDENT COULD TRIGGER A HELL OF A MESS. AS IT IS, WE HAVE THE SYMPATHY OF MOST VIETNAMESE, WHO BELIEVE THE AMERICANS HERE HAVE, TOO, BEEN BETRAYED. ALSO, MANY OF THEM WANT TO GET OUT. TODAY I SENT OUT, QUITE ILLEGALLY, THE WIFE OF A SENIOR INTELLIGENCE OFFICIAL. HE WILL NEVER LEAVE HIMSELF, BUT WE WILL BE COMPLETELY INFORMED, AND HE HAS ALREADY USED HIS CONSIDERABLE INFLUENCE WITH SOME SENIOR COMMANDERS OF SOME OF THE BEST UNITS TO SEE THAT THE "REAL FRIENDS" OF VIETNAM GET OUT SAFELY. ALL THAT CAN SWITCH IMMEDIATELY IF SOME GOD-DAMNED FOOL PERSUADES ANY OF YOU IN SENIOR POSITIONS TO SEND IN THE MARINES UNTIL I SEND FOR THEM. I WILL NOT HESITATE IN THE SLIGHTEST TO DO SO IF PUBLIC ORDER BEGINS TO CRUMBLE.

Then the part of the cable requiring the deep secrecy:

IF THERE IS A NEGATIVE VOTE, THIEU WILL BE FINISHED. I AM SEEING BUI DIEM* TOMORROW. HE AND [TRAN VAN] DON, NOW MINISTER OF DEFENSE, ARE MOST EAGER TO GET THE NEGOTIATION PROCESS STARTED. . . . I SHALL STILL SAY THAT ANY CHANGE IS THEIR BUSINESS, BUT THAT IT SEEMS TO ME THAT THE ESSENTIAL PROCESS OF NEGOTIATIONS CANNOT BE STARTED WITH THIEU IN POWER. I SHALL THEN, UNLESS INSTRUCTED TO THE CONTRARY, GO TO THIEU AND TELL HIM THE SAME THING, MAKING IT ABSOLUTELY CRYSTAL CLEAR THAT I AM SPEAKING ONLY FOR MYSELF, THAT I AM SPEAKING AS A FRIEND WHO HAS ALWAYS TOLD HIM THE WHOLE TRUTH, AND THAT IT IS MY CONCLUSION, ARRIVED AT MOST RELUCTANTLY, THAT HIS PLACE IN HISTORY WOULD BE BETTER ASSURED, WITH THE RECORDING OF ALL THE TRULY SIGNIFICANT THINGS HE HAS ACTUALLY ACCOMPLISHED, IF HE DOES NOT, BY STAYING TOO LONG, BE REMEMBERED FOR FAILING TO PERMIT THE ATTEMPT TO BE MADE TO SAVE WHAT IS LEFT OF VIETNAM AS A REASONABLY FREE STATE. . . . I WILL SAY THAT IT IS MY DISPASSIONATE AND OBJECTIVE CONCLUSION THAT IF HE DOES NOT DO THIS, HIS GENERALS WILL FORCE HIM TO DEPART. I WOULD SAY THAT

* Former Saigon ambassador to Washington.

IT WOULD SEEM TO MOST OF THE WORLD A MUCH MORE HONORABLE WAY TO GO, IF HIS DEPARTURE WAS AT HIS OWN VOLITION, TELLING HIS COUNTRY HE DID SO TO PRESERVE THE LEGITIMACY OF THE CONSTITUTION AND THE SUCCESSOR ADMINISTRATION, WHICH WOULD HELP THEM NEGOTIATE FROM A GREATER POSITION OF STRENGTH TO PRESERVE A FREE VIETNAM. I WOULD SAY IT WOULD BE AN ACT WHICH COULD ONLY BE TAKEN BY A MAN OF GREAT COURAGE, WHO PLACED HIS COUNTRY'S INTEREST FIRST AND FOREMOST. I WOULD MAKE IT QUITE CLEAR SEVERAL TIMES THAT I WAS GIVING HIM ONLY MY PERSONAL ASSESSMENT OF THE SITUATION, THAT I HAD NOT BEEN INSTRUCTED TO DO SO EITHER BY THE PRESIDENT OR THE SECRETARY OF STATE, WHO, I ASSUMED, WOULD CONTINUE TO SUPPORT THE GOVERNMENT AND PEOPLE OF VIETNAM TO THE BEST OF THEIR ABILITY.

THIS IS BEING PERSONALLY TYPED. THERE WILL BE NO RECORD EXCEPT IN WASHINGTON. I BELIEVE THIEU WILL LISTEN TO ME. I KNOW HE BELIEVES THAT WHAT I SAY IS WHAT I BELIEVE TO BE THE TRUTH, AND HE KNOWS WHAT I HAVE TOLD HIM ALMOST ALWAYS TURNS OUT TO BE RIGHT.

IN THE MEANTIME, IT DOES SEEM TO ME THAT THERE SHOULD BE AT LEAST A SMALL PRICE FOR DÉTENTE, AND PERHAPS SOME WAY COULD BE FOUND TO MAKE THE SOVIET UNION AND CHINA BELIEVE IT WOULD BE TO THEIR ADVANTAGE IN THEIR FUTURE DEALINGS WITH US TO EXERCISE THE MOST MASSIVE RESTRAINT ON HANOI TO BACK AWAY FROM SAIGON AND RESUME THE NEGOTIATING TRACK.

OF ONE THING I AM CERTAIN, DEADLY CERTAIN. IF U.S. ARMED FORCES COME IN HERE IN FORCE UNDER THE PRESENT CIRCUMSTANCES, THEY WILL BE FIGHTING THE SOUTH VIETNAMESE ON THE WAY OUT. IF WE PLAY IT COOL, I CAN GET OUR PEOPLE OUT ALIVE IN A WAY THAT WILL NOT, REPEAT, NOT ADD A RATHER GHASTLY MISTAKE TO THE THOUSANDS THE AMERICANS HAVE ALREADY MADE IN AND ABOUT VIETNAM. WARM REGARDS.

V

The next day, Friday the eighteenth, was the day that Graham Martin got himself up in the most casual kind of disguise.

Ever since Nguyen Cao Ky had begun agitating for Thieu's ouster in the final week of March, the Americans had blocked him. Time after time, Ky would talk to Cao Van Vien or one of the other senior generals; the man would agree with him that Thieu had to go. But always the pattern was the same. After the conversation with Ky, someone from the embassy would meet with the general and say, "Don't do anything with Ky. Don't move against Thieu. We don't want a coup. If you play the game correctly, we will take care of you and your family for the rest of your life in the States."

Now, on Friday morning, Charlie Timmes, the CIA's contact man with all the senior generals, called Ky in the morning. Could he drop by Ky's villa at Tan Son Nhut that afternoon with a "high authority"? Of course, Ky said.

Martin dressed in a sports coat instead of his usual gray or blue suit, and pulled a cap over his forehead as Timmes drove onto the base in an old Volkswagen.

"You must be surprised to see a man like me at your house," Martin said by way of an opening. Ky took it as an insult—after all, he had been the prime minister of the country—but let it pass.

They spoke over tea for two hours. Ky was struck by the ambassador's physical weakness, especially his sunken, red-rimmed eyes. The flamboyant young flier was struck by Martin's weakness even as Martin, with consummate skill, toyed with him.

"This is a hypothetical question, of course, Marshal," Martin said. "But if you were able to form a new government, how would you treat President Thieu?"

Ky replied that even though he hated Thieu for what he had done to the country, he would let him go. "Actually," he added, "it is up to the people to judge Thieu. It wouldn't be my problem."

Martin asked if Ky had given any thought to who might serve in his new government. Ky named names.

There followed a lengthy discussion as to whether the Army would pull together and fight under new leadership. Ky of course maintained that it would. Timmes had brought along a map, which they spread on the floor. With a pencil, Ky outlined the obvious remaining territory to be held: on the coast, Phan Thiet if possible, but if it was too late for that, then certainly Vung Tau; the capital and its immediately surrounding provinces; Tay Ninh on the Cambodian border; and all of the delta.

Finally Martin rose to leave. "It's not easy, you know," he said. "Give me a few days. Then we'll see what we can arrange."

Ky was elated. He called together his staff and told them to hold the plans for a coup in abeyance. Martin had as much as assured him that the embassy would back him in a new government.

"I don't trust him," one of them said. "What if his only intention was to keep us from acting?"

"He said a few days," Ky said. "I'll give him a few days."

VI

General Nguyen Van Toan, the fat, corrupt—and competent—commander whom Graham Martin had urged Thieu to reinstate a few months earlier, that afternoon forced a meeting with Thieu, drawing him out of his bunker. That morning, Toan had made a helicopter tour of the battlefield to the east of Saigon. Four North Vietnamese divisions were less than thirty miles away now, chewing up whatever replacements Toan fed into Xuan Loc. Any day now, Toan realized, they could simply choose to bypass the city. And they were about to be joined by the three divisions hurtling down the coast.

Toan landed first at JGS headquarters next to the airport, and picked up General Cao Van Vien. The two flew to the palace and insisted on the meeting with the president, who ushered them personally into his office.

"Monsieur le Président," Toan said, *"la guerre est finie."*

Thieu listened ashen-faced as Toan spelled out the collapse of his forces to the east. There were no reserves, Toan said. There was nothing left to do but negotiate with the communists. And since the communists would never talk with Thieu, he must resign.

The president thanked the generals for their report and retired to consult with "Laughing Boy" Dang Van Quang and to resume his brooding.

VII

In Washington on Friday morning, Lionel Rosenblatt speed-read through a long, tendentious cable from Graham Martin and decided he must act, even if by acting he risked his career.

Sometimes impending disaster can be seen more clearly from afar than from the eye of the storm.

Intense, black-haired and thirty-one, Rosenblatt that April was a young man on the rise in the State Department with every reason to think that he had seen the last of Vietnam for a long time to come. He had served there as a district adviser in the late 1960s, with a special interest in PRUs—Provincial Reconnaissance Units, paramilitary teams that used the same sort of terrorist tactics against the communists that the communists used against the pro-Saigon forces.

Rosenblatt was still deeply involved in Vietnam, as an aide to Deputy Secretary of State Robert Ingersoll and a member of the interagency Washington Special Action Group—WSAG—monitoring the crisis in Southeast Asia. He was also the leading figure in a group of about a dozen young Foreign Service Officers from State, the United States Information Agency and the National Security Council who came to think, about the time of the fall of Da Nang, that it was all going down, the North had won, Martin was dreaming, and someone had pretty damned well do some much more detailed planning for an evacuation not only of the Americans but also of the tens of thousands of deeply committed—deeply compromised—Vietnamese who had allied themselves with the Americans in things like the Phoenix program and the Provincial Reconnaissance Units. They met in Rosenblatt's apartment and more often in the drab institutional expanse of the State Department cafeteria to plot ways to alert their superiors to the disaster forming in Saigon and especially to what they saw as Graham Martin's blindness.

Two days before, on Wednesday, Martin had sent a long, technical cable containing the text of a report to him from Rear Admiral Hugh Benton on the feasibility of getting "large numbers of people—U.S. citizens, third-country nationals and local nationals—out of Vietnam."

MSC stands for Military Sealift Command, and refers to the President's authority to appropriate commercial shipping for military purposes in time of war or other national emergency. Admiral Benton outlined several scenarios. The most ambitious envisioned using half of the MSC capability available in the waters off and around Vietnam for eight days—in combination with U.S. aircraft and U.S. Navy ships. Under this ideal, maximum evacuation, close to a million persons could be taken out of Vietnam.* Since in mid-April there were about six thousand Americans left in Vietnam, Admiral Benton was hypothetically considering the removal from Vietnam of one hell of a lot of Vietnamese.

The scenario did assume ideal conditions. "This concept of massive evacuation would only be practical assuming the following: No interference by either the NVA or the VC; full cooperation by the Government of Vietnam; reasonable degree of crowd control," Admiral Benton wrote.

Elsewhere in the report, Admiral Benton had noted: "Best chance of success requires maximum number of evacuation points. This should reduce crowding and panic at each point. Vung Tau is particularly desirable because of easy access to the sea and defendability."

A half paragraph written by Martin set off alarm signals in Rosenblatt's mind:

THIS MORNING, I MET WITH ADMIRAL BENTON, WHO HAD BEEN LOANED TO US BY ADMIRAL GAYLER, AND WITH ADMIRAL OBERG, NOW CINCPAC FLT REP SGN. . . .

. . . IN DISCUSSION, WE AGREED ON OPTION D. IT WOULD BE VASTLY PREFERABLE TO PROVIDE FOR THE GREAT MAJORITY OF OUR VIETNAMESE NATIONAL LOCAL EMPLOYEES AND THEIR FAMILIES, AND OTHER VIETNAMESE WE WOULD WISH TO TAKE OUT, TO BE EMBARKED FROM VUNG TAU RATHER THAN FROM THE SAIGON AREA, AND THAT THE PRIMARY RESPONSIBILITY OF GETTING TO VUNG TAU MUST BE THAT OF

* The figure was 921,200.

THE LOCAL NATIONALS INVOLVED, ALTHOUGH WE WOULD HELP AS MUCH AS WE CAN. THIS DECISION WAS INTENDED TO REDUCE TO AB- SOLUTE MINIMUM THE NUMBER OF U.S. ARMED COVERING FORCE WHICH MIGHT OTHERWISE BE NECESSARY. . . .

The next day, Rosenblatt sent a cable to Saigon saying that he and up to ten of his friends—all from his interagency lunchroom group— were eager to come to Vietnam to work on evacuation planning, free- ing Lacy Wright and the other embassy officers to go about their nor- mal business. (Wright had become a principal contact for Foreign Service Officers around the world who had friends or relatives in Viet- nam.) The offer was ignored.

Then, on Friday the eighteenth, Rosenblatt read the cable that prompted him to act. Martin was writing in response to a cable from Kissinger. Before sending the Kissinger cable in to the ambassador, his aide Brunson McKinley made two notes on it. Kissinger had written:

WE HAD A VERY SOBER INTERAGENCY MEETING TODAY TO REVIEW THE STATE OF OUR PLANNING ON THE EVACUATION OF AMERICANS AND VIETNAMESE IN LIGHT OF THE DETERIORATING SITUATION.

THERE IS STRONG DOMESTIC AND CONGRESSIONAL CONCERN THAT WE MUST PUT A HIGHER PRIORITY ON ENSURING THE SAFETY OF AMERI- CANS IN VIETNAM. THIS REQUIRES AN ACCELERATED DEPARTURE SCHEDULE AND DETAILED PLANS WHICH MATCH OUR POTENTIAL NEEDS TO OUR ASSETS AND IDENTIFIES OUR REQUIREMENTS AS PRECISELY AS POSSIBLE. . . .

THE ACCELERATED DEPARTURE OF AMERICANS SHOULD NOT JUST INCLUDE OFFICIAL PERSONNEL BUT ALSO SUCH NONOFFICIAL AMERI- CANS AS CAN BE INFLUENCED TO LEAVE. WE MUST BE AT OR BELOW THE LEVEL OF 2,000 BY TUESDAY APRIL 22 FOR ALL AMERICANS IN VIETNAM. ANY ASSETS THAT YOU NEED TO ACCOMPLISH THIS TASK WILL BE MADE AVAILABLE. . . . [In the margin here, McKinley wrote "1 magic wand."]

I WOULD APPRECIATE MORE DETAILS OF WHAT YOU HAVE IN MIND FOR EVACUATION OF VIETNAMESE. IS IT REALISTIC TO BELIEVE THAT CER- TAIN SOUTH VIETNAMESE FORCES COULD BE COUNTED ON TO HELP SECURE EVACUATION ZONES FOR MASS EVACUATION?

[MARTIN SHOULD CONSULT CLOSELY WITH PRESIDENT THIEU ABOUT GETTING VIETNAMESE OUT.] IT WILL BE NECESSARY TO WORK CLOSELY WITH [THIEU] IF WE ARE TO HAVE ANY CHANCE OF AVOID- ING A CHAOTIC SITUATION BROUGHT ABOUT BY OUR OWN MOVES. YOU MAY, AT YOUR DISCRETION, DISCUSS WITH HIM THE OPTIONS YOU HAVE PRESENTED TO US AND SEEK HIS VIEWS. HE SHOULD UNDERSTAND THAT WE DO NOT WANT TO PROCEED IN A SPIRIT OF PANIC. [McKinley's mar- ginal note: "We just can't help ourselves."]

WE ARE PARTICULARLY CONCERNED ABOUT THE SAFETY OF VIET-

NAMESE ASSOCIATED CLOSELY WITH US, INCLUDING OUR EMPLOYEES, AND RELATIVES OF AMERICAN CITIZENS AND RESIDENT ALIENS. WE WOULD LIKE TO KNOW WHETHER THIEU IS PREPARED TO ALLOW SOME OF THEM TO LEAVE NOW, BY BROADENING THE CATEGORIES OF VIET-NAMESE CITIZENS EXEMPTED FROM THE VIETNAMESE TRAVEL BAN. . . . WE NEED YOUR RESPONSE BY OPENING OF BUSINESS HERE ON FRIDAY IF POSSIBLE, BUT IN ANY EVENT NO LATER THAN CLOSE OF BUSINESS FRIDAY. KISSINGER.

Martin's reply was typically discursive and acerbic:

WE ARE GLAD TO KNOW THAT THE INTERAGENCY MEETING YESTERDAY WAS A SOBER ONE. IT SHOULD HAVE BEEN, BUT IT IS NECESSARY TO AVOID THE TENDENCY OF ALWAYS ASSUMING THE WORST CASE, WHICH WILL LEAD TO DECISIONS WHICH MAY ENDANGER THE SITUATION HERE. WE ALSO ASSUME THE WORST CASE AND PLAN FOR IT, BUT TO MAKE DECISIONS ON AUTOMATIC ASSUMPTION OF WORST CASE CAN AUTO-MATICALLY BRING IT ABOUT.

WITH THE LIFT AVAILABLE, WE WILL REDUCE THE AMERICAN COM-MUNITY HERE TO 2,000 BY TUESDAY. IN DOING SO, WE WILL CUT SOME CORNERS ON PROCEDURES. THERE WILL BE SOME CASES WHERE WE WILL SEND OUT SOME UNDOCUMENTED ALIENS, SOME OF WHOM HAVE BEEN REQUESTED BY SENIOR WASHINGTON PRINCIPALS, AND OTHERS WE DEEM IT NECESSARY TO INCLUDE IN ORDER TO KEEP THE FLOW OF AMERICANS GOING UNIMPEDED. . . .

WE HAVE NOTED THE COMMENTS ABOUT "THE PRESIDENT'S DETER-MINATION TO FULFILL HIS OBLIGATIONS FOR THE SAFETY OF AMERI-CANS AS WELL AS FOR THE PROTECTION OF VIETNAMESE WHO HAVE BEEN ASSOCIATED WITH US." AS EXPLAINED IN PARAGRAPH 3, SAIGON'S 5111 [THE CABLE CONTAINING ADMIRAL BENTON'S RECOMMENDATIONS, QUOTED EARLIER], WE DO NOT BELIEVE IT FEASIBLE TO TRY TO ASSUME RESPONSIBILITY TO LIFT ALL THE VIETNAMESE TO WHOM THE PRESI-DENT REFERS DIRECTLY FROM SAIGON. WE WILL INSTRUCT OUR OWN LOCAL EMPLOYEES TO MAKE THEIR WAY TO DESIGNATED SPOTS ON THE COAST WHERE THEY MAY BE EVACUATED. MANY MAY NOT MAKE IT, BUT WE DO OWE THOSE WHO DO THE CHANCE TO ESCAPE. . . .

I HAVE SET A TARGET OF 1,700 AMERICANS REMAINING HERE BY COB* TUESDAY APRIL 22 WASHINGTON TIME. WHILE THERE MAY BE SOME SLIGHT SLIPPAGE ON THAT GOAL, WE SHOULD BE UNDER THE 2,000 FIGURE SET IN YOUR CABLE. I WOULD HOPE TO REDUCE THAT CONSIDERABLY FURTHER IN THE FOLLOWING DAYS. MARTIN.

At Martin's last meeting in the White House, President Ford had asked him to put a figure to the number of Vietnamese for whom the United States would feel an obligation if the communists won the war.

* Close of business.

At least 100,000, Martin had said. Between 100,000 and 200,000. A few days later, following the panic in Da Nang, Ford had been asked the same question. "Upwards of two hundred thousand," he had said. So the ambassador was thinking in terms of very large numbers. It was clear to him on the eighteenth that the only way you could get anything like 200,000 Vietnamese out of Saigon was by inserting an American force so large that it would set off the panic he feared above all else. As he had written just days before, the Marines would be fighting the South Vietnamese on their way out in such a scenario. So he had Admiral Benton put figures to what he considered a reasonable scheme to get out hundreds of thousands of Vietnamese—a kind of MSC and U.S. Navy Dunkirk from Vung Tau.

But in Lionel Rosenblatt's mind, the import of the Wednesday and Friday cables from Saigon was clear. The ambassador was saying, in effect: As for the Vietnamese, screw 'em. They can make their way to Vung Tau and take their chances.

Under his guidance, Vietnamese had risked their lives to identify communists. Some had died. All of the surviving PRUs and the Phoenix cadres and their wives and children would be in grave peril in a communist Vietnam. Rosenblatt would be damned if that gray old man in the embassy would tell men he had enlisted in the struggle that they were abandoned by the U.S. government, hike out to Vung Tau and catch a boat if you can, good luck.

It took a few hours for the anger to build, a couple of days for the plan to form and be put into effect. On Sunday, Rosenblatt and Craig Johnstone, his ally on Kissinger's National Security staff, signed themselves out on annual leave and took off for Saigon.

VIII

Charlie Benoit, the young Ford Foundation representative, was normally a cautious, deliberate man in all matters, and certainly in anything touching on Tammy, his four-year-old daughter. On Friday afternoon, he suddenly gave in to impulse, and regretted it.

Benoit had known since the day after Tammy's mother attempted to go into hiding with her that they were in a house on an alley off one of the streets running from Saigon into Cholon. Until Friday afternoon, he made it a point not to be seen in the neighborhood, much as he longed for a glimpse of Tammy, whom he had not seen in five weeks.

At some point in those five weeks, he told me that as a rule things unfolded in Vietnam much more slowly than one anticipated. "I've seen just two major exceptions to the rule," he said, "Tet '68 and now this."

Benoit managed to keep working, although as the offensive rolled south there was little left to do except monitor the situation for Ford, report on the evacuation and contemplate the disposition of the foundation's assets in Vietnam.

He monitored the situation by noticing how many villas occupied by Americans had their household goods lined up on the lawns or in the driveways, waiting to be packed (even if the official American was still in Saigon); by checking with friends in the press corps; watching the ratcheting official and black-market devaluation of the piaster; reading the censored newspapers, English and Vietnamese. Above all, he formed a fairly accurate picture of what was happening from numerous conversations every day with his very wide circle of Vietnamese friends and acquaintances.

Increasingly, and then overwhelmingly, his attention focused on Tammy. In late March and even in early April, he spent many hours waiting in line at the American Embassy, trying to prove his paternity and secure a passport for her. Morning after morning, he would violate the curfew, driving slowly to the embassy between five and six, with his headlights on, so as to be at or near the head of the line when the consulate doors opened at nine. Sometimes his girl friend—beautiful, independent Tai—held the place for him. In that same period, Benoit wrote to his Massachusetts congressman to sponsor a private bill allowing Tammy to be paroled into the U.S.

Then Benoit in the course of getting a distraught acquaintance into the evacuation process at Tan Son Nhut discovered that Tammy wouldn't really need any papers at all. All he had to do was get her out there.

That discovery had come in the second week of April, when DAO in particular was getting a few hundred Vietnamese out every day. Shortly thereafter, Benoit through an intermediary sent a letter to Tammy's mother, and then called her directly, twice. His approaches were reasonable, he thought. He said that he had never intended to deny Tammy's mother custody—so long as he could share it. He offered to leave Vietnam with Tammy's mother, *her* mother and Tammy's two half-siblings—a party of six, including Benoit and Tammy.

But Tammy's mother was indeed rather irrational. She in fact very much wanted to leave Vietnam; that was clear from the intermediaries. But she apparently feared that she would lose control of Tammy in the United States, the laws of which she didn't know. And there was an element of spite. In any case, in those two phone calls Benoit was treated to verbal abuse rougher than anything he had ever before heard in Vietnam, scatological and sexual imprecations so rococo and vile his extraordinary command of the language couldn't quite process them.

So plans had to be made. His original plan was, in retrospect, bizarre. He would kidnap Tammy and hide her *in Saigon* so deeply that her mother could never find her. Then he would fly to Bangkok and call Tammy's mother to say that he and Tammy were in Bangkok. And then he would return to Saigon and put Tammy and her mother and the two children from a previous liaison on a plane out while he himself stayed.

It was bizarre only in retrospect. Benoit knew the war was rapidly drawing to a climax. He loved Vietnam deeply, and wanted to be there for what he would refer to later as "the end of a cycle." He did not really want to live in Boston or New York with Tammy—Tammy's mother ten miles away someplace with visiting rights. That is, he would accept that solution if the solution were forced on him; but what he really wanted was to witness the end of the cycle, and then to live in a Vietnam at peace with his daughter for as long as the communists allowed them to do so.

What was utterly clear in his mind was that Tammy's mother's unilateral control of their daughter had to cease. He deeply regretted the fact that it had come to a contest for physical possession of Tammy. But it was her mother who had upped the ante.

Benoit would guess later that it took no more than a couple of hundred dollars to set up the string of friends and petty thugs and bought-off cops who mounted a twenty-four-hour-a-day watch on the comings and goings of Tammy and her mother. They watched; and they always knew where Benoit was—usually somewhere nearby, sipping tea or beer in a restaurant or street stall on the fringes of the neighborhood where Tammy's mother hid or the neighborhood where she worked, usually but not always taking Tammy with her.

So Tammy's mother went about her rounds, working and shopping and trying to take her ease in the evening, with three or four or half a dozen men on Hondas or Vespas or in automobiles on her trail, Benoit sitting anxiously at a table somewhere just outside the net, awaiting his moment.

And late on Friday afternoon, Benoit broke. He found himself driving slowly past the mouth of the alley, compelled by the desire of a father for the sight of his only child.

He didn't see Tammy. Instead he saw Tammy's mother walking toward him.

Benoit did not know if she had seen him. He thought she probably had not seen his face but may well have recognized the Deux Chevaux. In any case, he had to assume that his current story—that he had already left Vietnam, a story relayed through the intermediaries—was blown.

It took about two minutes—a drive around the few blocks surrounding the hiding house—for that assumption to become cast in concrete. Benoit acted on the assumption. He drove down the alley, parked in front of the house and knocked on the door. Tammy and her mother remained upstairs. Benoit explained to the woman who owned the house—one of his principal intermediaries—that his flight to Bangkok had been delayed by a day. He wasn't gone today, but he would certainly be gone in the morning.

With the operative fiction blown, Benoit had the liberating realization that he had a good twelve hours in which he could be seen in public in Saigon. He drove to my Tu Do Street apartment and accepted my offer of as many Scotches or beers as he chose to drink.

IX

The instructions were coming fast and thick now. Only the day before, the ambassador had been told to get below two thousand by Tuesday. Now this:

DESPITE YOUR BEST EFFORTS AND MY OWN INSTINCTS, THE PERCEPTION IN WASHINGTON OF THE MILITARY SITUATION AROUND SAIGON, AND OF HANOI'S OWN INTENTIONS, HAS REACHED THE POINT WHERE I MUST ASK YOU TO REDUCE TOTAL AMERICAN PRESENCE TO THE LEVEL OF 1,100 BY COB TUESDAY. THIS IS THE NUMBER OF PEOPLE WHOM WE ESTIMATE CAN BE EVACUATED IN ONE HELO LIFT.

I GIVE YOU THIS INSTRUCTION RELUCTANTLY AND WITH NO LITTLE CONCERN OVER THE RISKS THAT THIS ACTION MAY ENTAIL.

NEVERTHELESS, IT IS CLEAR TO ME THAT UNLESS WE TAKE THIS ACTION NOW, OTHER AGENCIES WILL LOSE NO TIME IN LEAKING THAT YOU AND WE ARE DRAGGING OUR FEET. CONGRESS WILL THEN ALMOST CERTAINLY PROMPTLY DIRECT AN EVACUATION OF ALL, REPEAT ALL, AMERICANS.

I KNOW THAT THIS DECISION WILL COME AS A BLOW TO YOU. IT IS SO FOR ME. I CAN ASSURE YOU THAT ONCE WE REACH THIS LEVEL, I SHALL NOT PRESS YOU AGAIN FOR FURTHER REDUCTIONS EXCEPT ON THE DAY, GOD FORBID, IF AND WHEN YOU ARE INSTRUCTED COMPLETELY TO CLOSE DOWN THE MISSION. WARM REGARDS. KISSINGER.

21

Major General Homer Smith, the commander of the Defense Attaché's Office, had a surfeit of bosses. He reported not only to the Secretary of Defense and to Graham Martin, but also to Admiral Noel Gayler, the Commander in Chief for the Pacific, and to Lieutenant General John J. Burns, the commander of the U.S. Special Advisory Group in Thailand.

Gayler would command the naval units in an evacuation of any magnitude. Burns, in his capacity as commander of the U.S. Seventh Air Force, was the man in charge of most of the American military aircraft in the region, some of which were already ferrying people out of Saigon to the Philippines.

On Saturday, the nineteenth, Smith, Gayler and Burns with their aides descended on the embassy. Burns and Gayler had flown in from Thailand's Nakhon Phanom air base and from Honolulu respectively to study the evacuation planning once more—and to see that Graham Martin understood the heat they were getting from Washington about the importance of drawing down the number of Americans in Vietnam.

Soon after the fall of Da Nang—which is to say only days after his return with the Weyand mission—Martin had realized that his job was going to be a lot easier if he could reduce the number of nonofficial Americans in Saigon. A minority of these were businessmen, journalists, missionaries and employees of voluntary agencies. They accounted for a few hundred people who, with some exceptions, would leave when they were told to leave.

His greater problem was with a few thousand active or retired "contractors" who had created a way of life for themselves in Vietnam. A contractor was someone who hired on with an American company or the U.S. mission or (less often) with the Saigon government to perform some job or another—build roads, repair helicopters, modernize the country's telecommunications system.

Many but by no means all had first come to Vietnam with the military. Many drank a lot. Almost all of them had a deep sexual attraction to the place, which now, seven years after the height of the American involvement, in many cases meant legal or common-law wives, and children. In one cable that month, Martin referred to them as "lotus-eaters."

Martin had no legal authority to order such men to leave. Homer Smith suggested at several meetings earlier in the month that Martin ask Washington for that authority—the authority to order nonofficial Americans out of Vietnam. Martin chose not to ask for it. He was walking a tightrope, balancing his own desire to reduce the number of Americans in Saigon with his instinct to do nothing extraordinary that would signal the collapse of the American commitment to South Vietnam.

Five days before, the Attorney General—whose Justice Department included the Immigration and Naturalization Service—had grudgingly given the State Department authority to "parole" certain Vietnamese into the United States. In effect, the cable said that any American in South Vietnam who was legally married to a Vietnamese could take out her and her parents and her kid brothers and sisters. He couldn't take out her grandparents, or her eighteen-year-old brother. (In a handful of cases, the American was a woman married to a Vietnamese man.)

And that wasn't good enough for the contractors. In the same cable in which he called them lotus-eaters, Martin said, in effect: "They've been through it all before, and they think this one will blow over too. They're not going to leave until they can take out the full Asian family."

In the five days since the granting of the new parole authority, the numbers leaving from Tan Son Nhut continued at the same level that had obtained since DAO started moving people in the first week of the month: a few hundred every day.

Now, on this third Saturday in April, Homer Smith listened as

General Burns and the ambassador discussed the details of a possible last-ditch hard pull of Americans from Saigon. At the same time, he read.

In the earnest, professional conversation between Burns and Martin, it turned out that the figure of 1,100 Americans that had shown up in Kissinger's cable of the day before was predicated on the assumption that eight hundred Marines would have to be flown in from the Seventh Fleet to provide ground security. But Burns allowed that three hundred would suffice.

There is a symmetry to these things. Eagle Pull—the extraction of the American mission from Phnom Penh—was seven days behind them. And General Weyand had reported to President Ford on the findings of his mission precisely fourteen days before, the first Saturday in April, a glorious April Saturday morning in Palm Springs. One imagines Ford or Kissinger saying, in effect: "Well, let's give them a couple of weeks. If Congress hasn't acted on the supplemental by—what's the date today?—by the nineteenth—we better tell Martin to get down to the number we can get out in one helicopter lift."

While Burns and Martin talked numbers, Homer Smith was studying a cable that had arrived just hours before. Like the cable conveying the original parole authority, this one was filled with intimidating, restrictive Immigration and Naturalization Service language. Smith cut through it to two key provisions: The first parole had insisted that the American principal be physically present in Vietnam. This was now waived. Any American—hell, any *Vietnamese wife* of an American, anywhere in the world—could vouch for his or her in-laws or relatives.

And that led to the second provision. Smith's mind focused on the sudden new legal jargon about "sponsors."

"Every candidate for parole, including children of all ages," the cable read, "must appear in person at the embassy for screening, etc., etc. . . . Sponsor is responsible for the cost of transportation, care, maintenance and resettlement, etc., etc. . . ."

"Uh, General Burns, Mr. Ambassador," Smith said at the next pause in the discussion, "excuse me for interrupting. But if I read this latest parole authority correctly, we can start to move people out of here in large numbers."

"Yes?" Burns said.

"Well, I could be wrong," Smith said, "but it seems to me that this cable says that anyone in the States—any American anywhere, or his Vietnamese wife—can vouch for people here and the INS will let them in. They're talking about financial sponsors. And if you can sponsor people from the States, it seems to me that the contractors here—any American here—could sponsor anyone he wants, including his wife's grandparents and second cousins. All we have to do is create some sort of . . . I don't know, what would it be called? . . . an affidavit of support maybe, and any American in Saigon could get out just about anybody he wanted to."

He turned to Martin. "I really think this might solve the problem with the contractors, Mr. Ambassador."

After the meeting, Homer Smith typed out the affidavit of support he had just invented and gave it to Eva Kim, who retyped it and ran off numerous copies.

Later that day, Brent Scowcroft sent a follow-up message to the cable that did in fact through Homer Smith's insistence lead to a dramatic change in the complexion of the evacuation:

> 1. ONE THING LEFT OUT OF LAST CABLE WE SENT YOU (WHITE HOUSE 50728) WAS THAT HENRY SAID YOU CAN, AT YOUR OWN JUDGMENT, BEGIN TO MOVE OUT VIETNAMESE IN THE HIGH-RISK CATEGORY. HE DOES NOT WANT TO SECOND-GUESS YOU IN THIS AREA. YOU MUST BE THE JUDGE ON WHEN AND HOW FAST TO MOVE SUCH HIGH-RISK ELEMENTS AS CIA ASSETS AND SO FORTH.
>
> 2. THANK GOD YOU ARE OUT THERE. WARM REGARDS.

II

Thomas Polgar, the CIA station chief, was somewhat surprised when a Colonel Janos Toth, whose title was military attaché to the Hungarian political counselor, called on the morning of the nineteenth, that same Saturday morning when the brass were meeting with the ambassador, and asked for a meeting somewhere outside the embassy. Polgar invited him to lunch at his villa on Nguyen Dinh Chieu Street, a leafy retreat on the edges of the diplomatic quarter of the city.

They spoke in English. When coffee was served and the servants left them, Toth began. He was grave.

"Do you agree with me that the war is lost?" he asked.

"Yes," Polgar said.

"Do you also agree that when a country loses a war there are bound to be certain political consequences?"

"Yes," Polgar said.

"Okay," Toth said. "Obviously the consequences for South Vietnam and for your country cannot be favorable."

"Obviously," Polgar said.

"Now," Toth said, "I don't think anyone wants the destruction, the bloodshed and—I must be blunt—the humiliation of the United States that would result if there were a battle for Saigon. It is possible that the war can come to an end without all of that. I have been talking to my friends in the North about this. They agree."

Polgar took a deep breath. "Okay," he said. "What's the price?"

"That will have to be negotiated," Toth said. "But the other side does have certain prerequisites before they would enter negotiations."

"Go ahead," Polgar said.

"Okay," Toth said again. "First, Thieu has to resign, immediately and unconditionally. Second, the new government must contain certain elements in whom the North Vietnamese have confidence. It must be a government that is truly prepared to implement the Paris Peace Accords—as interpreted by the North Vietnamese. Finally, the United States must declare that henceforth it will be completely uninvolved in Vietnamese affairs, and the embassy here must be reduced to the size and role of a conventional embassy. All those military advisers, whether they are in uniform or in civilian clothes, must leave. You understand that I am using their words."

"Of course," Polgar said.

"I must emphasize two points," Toth said. "This is not the solution. These are the prerequisites that must be met before the other side will enter into the negotiations for a cease-fire and the final solution. And the conditions must be met quickly. They said to emphasize this. It is a matter of days, not weeks."

"I understand," Polgar said. He stood, and reached out his hand to his visitor. As they shook hands, he said: "Thank you very much, Colonel. You have performed a noble service. I must consult with Washington, of course. In the meantime, it would be extremely useful if you would ask your friends whom they would find acceptable for the new government of reconciliation."

"Yes, I will try," Toth said.

At the door, he said again, "They specifically said a matter of days, not weeks, Mr. Polgar."

"I understand," Polgar said.

III

Tammy's mother called the Ford Foundation office that afternoon. One of Benoit's assistants took the call. He clamped his hand securely over the mouthpiece as he asked Benoit softly if he wanted to speak with her.

It was possible of course that she had finally seen reason. "God," Benoit thought, "how simple it would be if she would just bring Tammy to me." He would get them all out, arranging in the Philippines, or Guam, or wherever they landed for them to travel on to his parents in Massachusetts; and he would fly back into Saigon to see the end. But he had blown it once. What could he tell her now if she was still hostile—that the flight had been delayed again? No, he must stick to the story.

He shook his head, and with his hand made the motion of a plane taking off. The assistant spoke into the phone: "I was sure he was gone. But I had to check. He left early this morning."

IV

Late that afternoon, the ambassador drafted a long cable for Washington. It ended with a touch of bitterness, and humor:

TO KISSINGER FROM MARTIN   REF WHITE HOUSE 50727
19 APRIL [1810 SAIGON TIME]   SAIGON 0715
    . . . YOU MIGHT CARE TO REVIEW TOM POLGAR'S CONVERSATION WITH COLONEL TOTH, HEAD OF THE HUNGARIAN MILITARY INTELLIGENCE DELEGATION, ALSO CHIEF OF STAFF OF HUNGARIAN ICCS MILITARY CONTINGENT. COLONEL TOTH OUTLINES, IN THE RECORD OF THIS MESSAGE, HANOI'S DESIDERATA MUCH MORE ACCURATELY THAN THE "INTENTIONS" YOU'VE BEEN GETTING RECENTLY FROM HANOI'S EXHORTATIONS TO ITS CADRE. I THINK IT IMPORTANT THIS MAY BE FOLLOWED UP IMMEDIATELY AND UNLESS INSTRUCTED TO THE CONTRARY BY TOMORROW, I INTEND TO ASK POLGAR TO RESUME CONTACT WITH COLONEL TOTH TO SAY THAT PERHAPS THERE COULD BE SOME MOVEMENT TOWARD THOSE CONDITIONS, BUT HE WANTED TO EXPLORE FURTHER WHAT THE OTHER SIDE MEANS BY HIS COMMENT "THAT THE UNITED STATES UNDERTAKE TO RESTRICT ITS ACTIVITIES IN VIETNAM TO NORMAL, TRADITIONAL EMBASSY FUNCTIONS." YOU COULD DO THIS OF COURSE IN MESSAGE TO LE DUC THO, BUT THIS WAY WOULD LEAVE YOU FREE TO FOLLOW UP THROUGH THAT CHANNEL LATER SHOULD THE RESPONSE INDICATE IT USEFUL TO DO SO.

    I WOULD AGREE WITH COLONEL TOTH'S CONCLUSION STATED IN PARAGRAPH 6 THAT AN EVACUATION OF SAIGON BY THE AMERICANS UNDER THE CIRCUMSTANCES IN WHICH EVACUATION WAS ACCOMPLISHED IN PHNOM PENH WOULD BE CONSIDERED A HUMILIATING ACT WHICH MAY HAVE LONG-TERM PSYCHOLOGICAL EFFECTS ON UNITED STATES FOREIGN POLICY.

    WHATEVER TOTH'S REAL MOTIVES MAY BE, THIS IS AN APPROACH WORTH FOLLOWING UP AT ONCE, AND IT DOES NOT INDICATE THE NEED FOR PANIC, AT LEAST JUST YET.

    I HAVE JUST FINISHED A DISCUSSION WITH ADMIRAL GAYLER, LT. GEN. BURNS, MAJ. GEN. SMITH. WE WENT OVER THE VARIOUS ALTERNATIVES AS THEY REALLY FIT THE ACTUAL REALITIES HERE. IN THE FIRST PLACE, GEN. BURNS SAID THAT THE NET NUMBER HE COULD TAKE OUT

IN HELO-LIFT WOULD BE 1,900, NOT THE 1,100 YOU MENTION, WHICH PRESUPPOSES A SECURITY FORCE OF 800 MARINES. THREE HUNDRED WOULD BE SUFFICIENT, LEAVING A ONE-CYCLE LIFT CAPACITY OF 1,600 OR TWO-CYCLE LIFT OF 3,500. THIS CAN BE VARIED OF COURSE ON DE-CISION OF SIZE OF SECURITY FORCE.

WE WENT OVER THE CURRENT INTELLIGENCE AND PUT THE WORST-CASE INTO A TIME-FRAME. AGAIN THE LOWEST ESTIMATE WAS TEN DAYS. AS I TOLD YOU YESTERDAY I ACCEPT THAT ESTIMATE. WE SHOULD WORK TO SHAVE THE TIME TO BE PREPARED FOR TOTAL EVACUATION AS MUCH AS POSSIBLE UNDER THAT ESTIMATE, BUT, SINCE THE AV-ERAGE ESTIMATE IS THAT WE WOULD HAVE MORE THAN THREE WEEKS' TIME, THERE IS STILL NO REASON TO PRECIPITATE THE PANIC THAT WOULD SERIOUSLY ENDANGER LIVES HERE. . . .

. . . AS IT NOW STANDS, IT SEEMS EVERYONE HAS COMPLETED THE CYA* OPERATION IN WASHINGTON. THE INTELLIGENCE COMMUNITY HAS DRAWN THE ABSOLUTELY WORST POSSIBLE CASE, WHICH IS UN-REALISTIC BUT WHICH PROTECTS THEM. THE MILITARY AND DOD HAVE ORDERED OUT ALL POSSIBLE AIRLIFTS SO THAT IF WORST CASE HAPPENS IT CAN BE SAID BY DEFENSE THEY DID THEIR PART AND IF ANYTHING HAPPENS TO AMERICANS IT COULDN'T HAVE BEEN THEIR FAULT. YOU HAVE GIVEN ME A DIRECTIVE WHICH IT IS ALMOST IMPOSSIBLE FOR ME TO FULFILL WITHOUT DESTROYING THE FRAGILE FABRIC WHICH STILL EXISTS.

THE ONLY ONE WHOSE ASS ISN'T COVERED IS ME. THAT HAS BEEN TRUE ALL ALONG. THERE IS NO WAY I CAN COME OUT OF THIS WITH-OUT CRITICISM, NO MATTER HOW UNJUSTIFIED IT MAY BE. THIS IS LUCKY IN A WAY, BECAUSE IT REMOVES THE SLIGHTEST INCENTIVE TO DO SOME DAMN FOOL THING JUST TO ESCAPE CRITICISM. . . . [W]HILE I AM DELIGHTED TO HAVE ALL THE FORCE POSSIBLE AVAIL-ABLE, AND ALL THE CONTINGENT AUTHORITY POSSIBLE AVAILABLE FOR ADMIRAL GAYLER, IT WILL NOT BE USED UNTIL AND UNLESS I CALL FOR IT. . . .

MAY I SHARE WITH YOU TODAY'S MORALE BOOSTER, WHICH JUST CAME TO ME FROM NVA COMMUNICATIONS INTERCEPTS. "UP TO EIGHTY PERCENT OF THE SIXTH COMPANY HAS CONJUNCTIVITIS, AND IT COULD SPREAD THROUGH THE ENTIRE SECOND BATTALION. SUGGEST A MEDIC BE SENT DOWN FOR IMMEDIATE TREATMENT."

The reply came in overnight and was on the top of the cables on the ambassador's desk in the morning:

KISSINGER TO MARTIN
MY ASS ISN'T COVERED. I CAN ASSURE YOU THAT I WILL BE HANGING SEVERAL YARDS HIGHER THAN YOU WHEN THIS IS ALL OVER. . . .
NOW THAT WE AGREE THAT THE NUMBER OF AMERICANS WILL BE

* Cover your ass.

REDUCED BY TUESDAY TO A SIZE WHICH CAN BE EVACUATED BY A
SINGLE HELICOPTER LIFT, THE EXACT NUMBERS ARE COMPLETELY
UP TO YOU. THAT HAVING BEEN DECIDED, I WILL STOP BUGGING YOU
ON NUMBERS, EXCEPT TO SAY THAT YOU SHOULD ENSURE THAT THE
EMBASSY REMAINS ABLE TO FUNCTION EFFECTIVELY. YOU SHOULD GO
AHEAD WITH YOUR DISCUSSION WITH THIEU, AND YOUR SOUNDINGS
RELATIVE TO HIS POSSIBLE RESIGNATION, HOWEVER THE MATTER OF
TIMING IS ALSO OF GREAT SIGNIFICANCE. WE THIS MORNING HAVE
MADE AN APPROACH TO THE SOVIET UNION. . . .

V

Finally even the ambassador realized that Thieu had to go.

Martin went to the palace on Sunday morning with Brunson
McKinley, the very correct young Foreign Service Officer who had
been briefly Al Francis' deputy in Da Nang; he was now the ambassador's personal assistant. Thieu might have been more comfortable
had the conversation been in French, in which Martin was fluent.
But following a lifelong practice for important meetings, Martin spoke
in English.

As Thomas Polgar and Ted Shackley had done eighteen days before, Martin began with a detailed review of the order of battle, as
compiled by Colonel Le Gro, the DAO intelligence officer, and by
the CIA. He said that if Hanoi should choose to move in for the kill,
it would be difficult for Saigon to last more than a month, even with
the most skillful and determined resistance.

"It would probably be more like three weeks," he said. "Now, I
assume that they want the city whole, not as a pile of rubble. But we
cannot escape the possibility that they will go for the military solution,
if there is no move toward negotiations. You can make the stand, of
course. You can have a siege of Saigon. But what's the point?"

Thieu was well beyond tears in front of Americans. "And the aid,
Mr. Ambassador?" he asked.

Martin said that the answer to that question was "obscure" to him.
They might very well get an additional $350 million from the com-
mittees, but even that was uncertain. . . . The aid might come. He
hoped very much that it would come. But it could not come in time
to change the military balance sheet he had just read.

"Mr. President," he said, "I will speak very frankly. Anyone sitting
in your chair, or one like it—in the Élysée, or the White House, or the
Kremlin, or in Peking—you all have one thing in common. You can
never be sure that you are getting the whole truth. Some of your advisers will shade reports for personal or bureaucratic advantage, others
for fear of hurting you, others because they are simply afraid of you,
others because they don't want to be the bearers of bad news. What-

ever the reasons, it is difficult at times for a man in your position to perceive things as they are.

"Mr. President, please understand that I speak as an individual only, not as the representative of the President or the Secretary of State, or even as the American ambassador. I am simply a man who has watched events in this part of the world for a very long time, and who for the past two years has worked very hard at trying to understand the interweaving of the fabric of Vietnamese affairs.

"The older I get, the more I know I don't know it all. Reasonable doubt is always present. But it is a very difficult time now. Perhaps my perceptions are as accurate as those of any Westerner.

"A few things are very clear to me. The military situation is very bad, and the people hold you responsible for it. The politicians—both your supporters and your enemies—do not believe that you can lead the country out of this crisis. I told you I would be frank."

"Yes," Thieu said.

"It seems that your generals are willing to fight, but believe that defense is hopeless unless there is a respite—the respite that would come with the beginning of the negotiating process.

"Mr. President, I have reason to believe that if you do not step down, the generals will ask you to do so."

Thieu listened closely. He asked whether his leaving would affect the votes in Congress. The ambassador said that he thought it might have changed a few votes—or even more—some months ago. But now it was a bargain whose day had passed.

"Really, the question now is what effect your resignation might have on the other side," Martin said. "Frankly, I don't think it is going to have much effect at all. They are not opposed to you per se. They are opposed to any strong leader. Really, all they want is a weak man."

He was musing out loud, and reminded himself of the mission. "It is a question of time," he said. "If the destruction of Saigon is to be avoided, if there is any hope at all for the survival of an independent South Vietnam—even as reason recognizes the dimness of that hope—things must happen quickly."

The ambassador thought it was his closing. But they talked for another twenty minutes about the future of Laos, that discussion initiated and pursued by Thieu. Then it did close. Martin reiterated that time was running very short, that events were moving too fast to ponder long and that if Thieu did not act soon those events might overrun him. Martin made it "absolutely plain that I was speaking purely personally and that I was not, as an individual, nor was Washington, suggesting that he resign."

"Thank you, Mr. Ambassador," the president said when he realized that the end was near. "I will of course do what is best for my country."

"I know that you shall," Martin said, and then the closing pleasantries.

VI

On Saturday, April 19, after he had closed down operations in My Tho, Mac Prosser returned briefly to Saigon and to his wife, Kay. Prosser was the senior Foreign Service Officer who had earlier closed out Da Lat; now he was seconded to the delta. There was a dinner party that night. Someone was leaving, so they emptied their freezer and sponsored a feast.

Prosser sat next to Frank Snepp, the CIA officer who analyzed North Vietnamese strategy and intentions, and who was also the agency's chief briefer. On a paper napkin, Snepp sketched out the disposition of forces around the capital and in the delta. As Prosser looked at the lines and Xs on the napkin—especially the ones indicating that Tan Son Nhut could soon become within range of the NVA's 122-mm. artillery—Prosser for the first time felt that the situation was irretrievable.

As they drove home from the party, Mac told Kay that it was probably time for her to leave.

VII

Corporal Charles McMahon, Jr., of the United States Marine Corps, began the last day of an unexpected home leave in Woburn, Massachusetts, on Sunday, April 20.

There had been a bureaucratic foul-up. Since the implementation of the Paris Peace Accords, even active-duty Marines assigned to Vietnam had to have passports to enter the country. But of the fourteen Vietnam-bound Marines who had finished the short "embassy school" course at Marine Corps headquarters in Arlington, Virginia, early that month, four did not have the passports among their folders of documents. As soon as he discovered he would be another ten days in the States, McMahon talked a buddy into lending him a big Ford pickup and headed north from Washington to home.

Charlie McMahon was a month short of his twenty-second birthday. He had been a Marine for a little more than two years, and thrived on it. Woburn was a blue-collar industrial town eighteen miles northwest of Boston. In the late 1960s and early 1970s, when Charlie McMahon was a teen-ager, the split among his classmates at Woburn High School was even sharper than in most other towns around the country. Woburn was a working-class town in the most liberal state in the Union. Woburn had its share of conscientious objectors, and of bright young kids who got into college and, after 1971, didn't have to worry about the draft or the war in Vietnam. It even had a few young men who would gladly give the finger to any departing Marine Corps recruiter. But most of Woburn's young people were as straight as their hardworking parents, and Charlie McMahon was the straightest of the straight.

He was an athlete, a quick six-footer with biceps like hams and a cocky grin that masked an inarticulate charm founded on an utter lack of guile. His body could do almost anything: swing itself onto the support structure of the basketball hoop at the gym and dance down the rafters; soar and twist from a rise at the bottom of the slope into the seat of a moving T-bar; somersault off a traffic-clogged bridge. And when his buddy George Holland asked, "Why'd you do *that*, Charlie," McMahon would invariably crack, "For the fans, George, for the fans." There were things he couldn't get the brain or the tongue to do. When the Woburn Boys Club gave him its "Boy of the Year" award in 1971 before a standing ovation of three hundred of his friends, Charlie couldn't bring himself to the microphone.

He was the kind of Marine who gained ten pounds at boot camp and wrote home complaining that they weren't giving him enough to eat.

When the Marines say they're looking for a few good men, what they mean is that they're looking for a few more Charlie McMahons.

McMahon enjoyed those unexpected nine days at home in the middle of April. On the first day home, after what was more a nap than a night's sleep, he set off with a few friends for a weekend of skiing at nearby Tenney Mountain, a mild mountain in easy range of a young Woburn boy who never got to Stowe, let alone Aspen. Back in Woburn, one night he put on his dress uniform and went to the Boys Club dinner dance. On all the other evenings, he and George Holland—who had joined the corps a few months after McMahon— and a few other friends would sit in the living room of the pink-and-white two-story house across from the Greek Orthodox church and watch Walter Cronkite. They watched the red blot closing south on the map and laughed with their Budweisers, and his buddies told Charlie it would be gone before he got there.

Charlie McMahon, Sr., a heavily tattooed former Marine who was even taller than Charlie Jr. and who worked the night shift at the American Gelatin factory in town, thought it would be over before Charlie left Woburn, and he would get orders to report elsewhere. But that call never came.

On the Sunday morning of Charlie Jr.'s last day at home, Charlie

Sr. left to get the *Globe* and read it over coffee at Dunkin' Donuts, as he did every Sunday. When his wife, Edna, got up an hour later, she found Charlie Jr. at the kitchen table.

"What are you going to do today, Charlie?" she asked as she poured herself her coffee and lit the day's first cigarette. She was the talkative one in the family, a woman of average height with short blond hair who took charge when there was a crisis.

"Nothin'," Charlie said. "Take it easy. I'll be driving all night."

They were quiet for a few moments. When Charlie spoke, he smiled to take the edge off his words, but it wasn't the full grin. "Ma, I want my flag to go to the Boys Club," he said.

"What are you talking about?" his mother said.

"You know—if I get blown away over there, I want my flag to go to the Boys Club."

"Stop talking such foolishness!"

"No, I'm serious, Ma. And I want you to take the twenty thousand dollars the Marines'll give you and buy a cottage up at Hampton."

Edna nodded. "Okay," she said, to finish it off.

He left at six, with a couple of roast lamb sandwiches for the long ride to Washington. Breaking a custom, he didn't want the family to see him off from the driveway. They waved from the kitchen window as he pulled out and gave a goodbye honk on the horn.

VIII

The consul general in Can Tho, in the Mekong delta, was Francis T. McNamara, whom everyone called either Mr. McNamara or Terry. McNamara was a short, decisive man with a jaunty walk and a round Irish face with black eyebrows and a small, pointed nose. He was the only one of the four consuls general at the end who was not a Graham Martin protégé. He had a running joke with Eva Kim about his inability to see the ambassador—whenever McNamara was in Saigon, Martin was either back in Washington or too overloaded with work to see him, it seemed—but there was no bad blood between the two men.[*] McNamara was one of the few independent subordinates in the mission whose independence didn't bother Martin.

The standing evacuation plan for the delta envisioned waves of helicopters swooping down to pick up people. McNamara never thought it would happen. There might well come a day when heli-

---

[*] Martin spent much more time pleading for aid on Capitol Hill than most ambassadors do. He was the point-man in the Administration's battle for aid for Vietnam, giving testimony that one would expect to come from Kissinger or Assistant Secretary of State Philip Habib.

copters would swoop down on Saigon to extract people, he knew, but if it came to that, there would be none to spare for Ca Mau, say, the remote capital of South Vietnam's southernmost province. And even if he could get everyone—American and Vietnamese—for whom he felt a responsibility to Can Tho, there definitely would not be enough choppers to get out the Vietnamese.

In fact, after reading the reports and seeing the pictures of the disorder in Da Nang and especially Nha Trang, McNamara decided that the one thing that could ensure rioting in Can Tho would be flight after flight of helicopters trying to land in the city.

In late March, McNamara totaled up all the Vietnamese who worked for the Americans in the delta and multiplied by his best guess at the size of the average Vietnamese immediate family. He came up with a total of five thousand.

He knew he was not going to get out five thousand Vietnamese. So he devised three categories. Category one included everyone who might well be in mortal danger in a communist Vietnam: these included almost everyone who worked for the United States Information Service and everyone else in high-visibility intelligence or political jobs. Category two included all employees with marketable skills in the United States, such as accomplished interpreters and English-language secretaries. Category three was everybody else—whom they would get to if various miracles came to pass.

McNamara of course informed Saigon of what he was doing, and his three categories became something of a standard throughout what was left of the mission.

He told his subordinates—the chiefs of USIS, USAID and the CIA, for example—in Can Tho that they would have the difficult task of separating their employees into the categories. He urged them to be tough. When he said immediate family, he meant it: spouses and children of the local employee. Subsequently, he made exceptions, allowing dependent minor siblings or parents of an unmarried employee onto the list.

Twenty to twenty-five percent of those employees in categories one and two made it clear that they had no interest in leaving Vietnam. But even given that factor, and the tightness of the system, McNamara knew by mid-April that he would have about five hundred Vietnamese to get out at the end.

He decided to get them out by water. Like those in Da Nang and Bien Hoa, the consulate in Can Tho was on a river. (From the fortifications of the embassy in Saigon to the placement of the consulates, the key U.S. installations in Vietnam all anticipated flight.) The open waters of the South China Sea were a fairly straight sixty-mile run down the Bassac River from the dock of the consulate bar/restaurant/club in Can Tho.

With consulate funds, McNamara bought a Vietnamese rice barge and a couple of motors for it. Then, through the good offices of a logistician with USAID in Saigon named Cliff Frink, he secured two LCMs—big steel-plated flat-bottomed landing craft.

From the beginning, most of his own people and especially the CIA contingent in Can Tho thought the idea was crazy. The CIA people told him that just before he arrived in Can Tho nine months earlier, one of their number had suffered a head wound on the river. McNamara was never clear about the details. The spooks had a couple of speedboats. He didn't know if the man had been hit on an operation or water-skiing. But he knew that the LCMs were very similar to those that had landed at Normandy, and he wasn't worried about small-arms fire.

McNamara was attracted to the element of surprise. The Bassac was more than a mile wide soon after you got downriver from Can Tho. Further, he was attracted to the idea of traveling by any means other than air. He thought that the Americans relied too heavily on the ubiquitous helicopters. In fact, in 1970, during his previous tour in Vietnam, he had driven from the delta to the DMZ, the first American to accomplish the feat, he thought, since the 1968 Tet offensive. He hadn't run into a single problem.

Stories like that earned McNamara the reputation for being a bit of a showboat.

In any case, the CIA officers in Can Tho decided among themselves that they weren't going to join Terry and his pirates in their adventure down the Bassac River.

On Monday, April 21, McNamara and young Cary Kassebaum, whom he'd taken on as an assistant, and a Vietnamese finance officer in the consulate flew to Saigon. The finance officer—a woman who as it happened was not going to leave—was to pick up large quantities of cash to pay off local employees. McNamara for his part wanted to tie up some loose ends of his evacuation plan.

He spoke to Colonel George Jacobson. "Terry," Jacobson said, "you're not going out by boat. It's too risky. We'll pull you out by chopper." Left unsaid was the understanding that a helicopter evacuation meant no Vietnamese.

McNamara said that if he got an order to that effect he would have to disobey it.

It was not a shouting match. It was a discussion of what was going to happen in the delta on the last day. In fact, it was Jacobson who suggested that McNamara take the problem to the ambassador.

McNamara walked down the corridor to the ambassador's suite. This time he got in.

"Jacobson says I can't take my people down the river," he said. "We all know that if that's the decision it means leaving my locals. I'm not going to do it, Mr. Ambassador. I've got about five hundred locals who deserve to get out, and I'm getting them out."

"Of *course* you can take the Vietnamese," Martin said. He got up and led McNamara to Wolf Lehmann's office, which adjoined the ambassador's outer office.

"What's this about McNamara being told he can't get his Vietnamese out of the delta?" he asked.

"Oh, no," Lehmann said. "No. That isn't right."

"Clear it up," Martin said.

McNamara reported back to Jacobson. "Okay," Jacobson said. "Fine. But don't be surprised if you get an order at the last minute telling you to pull out the Americans only."

22

The speculation started around two, with an announcement that there would be a ceremony at the palace at four. By three, George Esper was able to report that Thieu would resign.

Thieu rambled on for more than an hour. I started watching the speech in the NBC office. Then I trotted down to the AP, where, as I had guessed, the translation was coming faster, out of two type-writers.

When Thieu cried, I had to grin to keep tears from my own eyes. The same thing had happened when I had watched Hubert Humphrey concede defeat to Richard Nixon in 1968. My wife had been disgusted. "Christ, Jean," I had said that night, "he's a public man, crying in defeat. Who cares if he's a war criminal? And he isn't one anyway. Besides, he looks like my father."

Thieu said: "The three hundred million dollars that the Congress won't approve is what they used to spend to support their troops here for ten days."

And: "Today I resign to see if, after there is no more Mr. Thieu, negotiations will be satisfactory. If the communists agree to negotiate, the South agrees to negotiate. If so, it is lucky for the country and the entire population. And after Mr. Thieu leaves, if South Vietnam is immediately given sufficient aid to enable fighting by the armed forces of the Republic of Vietnam, then it is lucky for the country. My departure is worth the sacrifice. Then I would put the palms of my hands together and bow down."

And: "Kissinger did not see that the Paris Peace Accords led the South Vietnamese people to death. Everyone sees it and Kissinger does not see it. The superpowers have an interest between them. We have nothing to sacrifice, only this tiny land."

Reading, I had to blink repeatedly to block the tears even more so than I did when I looked at the screen, where Thieu smiled and cried at the same time.

In a ceremony following the speech, Vice President Tran Van Huong—who was seventy-one, asthmatic and half blind—became president. He vowed to fight on "until all the troops are dead or the country is lost."

II

Charlie Lahiguera, the political officer at the consulate in Bien Hoa who had told his friend in the Weyand mission that South Vietnam probably had until August, changed his mind quickly. Just a few days after he made the remark, he and the rest of South Vietnam saw some of the photographs of the chaos in Da Nang, the famous photograph of a burly American in Nha Trang smashing his fist into the face of a Vietnamese man trying to board an aircraft. (In general, as a result of censorship, everyone in South Vietnam saw many fewer of the most dramatic pictures than did anyone outside the country.)

Lahiguera fully expected that the Americans would have to fight their way out of Saigon as they had in Da Nang and Nha Trang.

He watched Thieu's resignation speech at the home of the CIA base chief in Bien Hoa, which lay at the opposite end of the dreary military town from his own residence. On the drive home, he had to pass through two or three military roadblocks. Lahiguera was a first-generation American, the son of a Spanish diplomat and a German woman. His mother's genes had prevailed; he was stocky at thirty-seven, with the square build and face of a German butcher. He could handle himself in a fair fight. But he was as edgy that night as he had ever been in Vietnam.

This was his second tour. The first, in the late 1960s, had been in Phuoc Long, the province northwest of Saigon on the Cambodian border that the communists captured in the first week of January. When there was no response from Washington to the fall of Phuoc Long, Lahiguera realized that the U.S. was now truly out of the fight for good.

On the drive home that night, Lahiguera thought it entirely likely that some of the ARVN soldiers would take Thieu's bitter tirade against the Americans to heart and act on it.

But he reached his home near the consulate without incident. And in the next day or two, several Vietnamese friends, civilian and military, told him that Thieu was blaming the Americans for his own failure. It was his stupid mistakes that were losing the war.

III

Late that night, after midnight, Don Hays got an urgent summons from Marvin Garrett to meet him in the CRA restaurant at the embassy. The call came in over the Motorola walkie-talkie Hays and some other officers had been issued in Garrett's quiet campaign to prepare for an evacuation.

The embassy was drawing its people closer to home base. Shortly after he got his wife and daughter out, Hays had moved into an apartment under Ken Moorefield's in a building they called the "Golden Ghetto" on Gia Long* Street. The building was only a few short blocks from the embassy, but Hays had to pass through two tense checkpoints in the otherwise deserted streets on the way.

Garrett was waiting for him with the men Garrett worked most closely with—his own assistants and a few Mission Warden officers and Seabees. He made the young budget officer an unmeasured triple or quadruple Scotch on the rocks and sat him down to a huge T-bone steak that had just been barbecued in the middle of the dimly lit room.

When Hays had started in on the unexpected feast, Garrett outlined his problem. "I think it's going up," he said. "Now listen: I got a chance to get some people out of here quick. Some of my Mission Warden contractors and my own locals, the ones who worked on security clearances. Sensitive types. Y'understand?"

"Yup," Hays said.

"Okay," Garrett said. "You understand the whole thing is sensitive. I got some space on a special flight. It's going to be quick, the next day or two. And I got to pay these people. It's legit. Severance pay, they got it coming. Can you work it out? Quietly?"

Hays took another bite of the steak, a swallow of Scotch. "I can give it a try," he said.

Every chit leading to cash had to be signed by two men, a budget officer and a disbursing officer. Hays's boss covered for him. The boss signed as the budget officer and Hays signed as the disbursing of-

---

* Pronounced Za Long.

ficer. Garrett's men were gone the next night, with money in their pockets to start them on their new lives.

IV

One week earlier, two hundred miles north of Saigon, in the place the Westerners called Camp Sunshine, the news that they were being moved again created a rush of activity—and hope. Norm Johnson especially thought they were about to be released. "Now that they've released the ICCS men and everyone knows we're being held, they've almost *got* to let us go," he said.

When Bath Man came into the compound to take the group out to a waiting truck, the Canadian missionary grabbed him in a bear hug and swung him around saying, "We're going home! We're going home!"

Carolyn Miller hoped he was right, but noticed that they were not the only prisoners being moved. The few ARVNs with small children in the camp, as well as the sick and wounded, were also being led to the truck.

A short man with tinted glasses and the carriage of an officer approached them. He looked at LuAnne Miller, who was in her father's arms, her head on his shoulder, sick and exhausted.

"She is ill?" he asked.

"Yes, she is very ill," Carolyn Miller answered.

"What is the matter with her?"

Carolyn lifted her head to indicate Lillian Phillips and Joan Johnson and said, "The nurses say she probably has infected tonsils and her chest is congested."

The man went to Lillian and asked her several questions. "Don't worry," he said. "A medic will accompany you. I will tell him to give her injections if she needs them on the way."

Then he motioned for Carolyn to ride with LuAnne in the cab of the truck, between the driver and a guard.

The other Westerners and about forty Vietnamese prisoners were crammed into the back of the truck. When it was clear that there wasn't room for all of them, the official with the glasses ordered Jay Scarborough and Norm Johnson off, saying they would go in the next truck. Scarborough intervened, easily. The official had arrived on the scene recently, and was by far the most congenial North Vietnamese they had dealt with. Even the ARVN prisoners liked and respected him. "That man has his wife with him," Scarborough said. "Better to take the Australian; he's a bachelor here."

The truck lurched along a little-traveled track through uninhabited country until about noon, and stopped at a crossroads. A sign on a tree pointed south to Loc Ninh, the communist stronghold north of Saigon. The soldier on Carolyn Miller's right got out to read smaller signs at this intersection of four roads and trails. Carolyn Miller knew that if they were going to be released they would turn south, toward Loc Ninh. The guard jumped back in and they turned left, north on the Ho Chi Minh Trail.

Jay Scarborough, Peter Whitlock and the two thousand ARVN prisoners waited two days back at Camp Sunshine for the additional trucks they had been told would take them north. Something went wrong. The trucks weren't coming after all. Camp Sunshine was dismantled and all of them—cadres, *bo dois*,* ARVN prisoners and the two Westerners—set off for what turned out to be a hundred-kilometer march due north.

Before they set off, one of the *bo dois* gave Scarborough a pair of the standard black Ho Chi Minh sandals they made from discarded tires. Whitlock would march in the leather shoes he was wearing on the morning of the capture.

At the start of the trek, Scarborough and Whitlock were in good physical condition, and walked with the cadres and the *bo dois* at the head of the column. They kept up throughout almost the entire march. But on the first day, Scarborough got a bite on his knee that swelled to a small cyst that was especially painful when they set out after their five-minute breaks. And at the end of the second day's march, when the sun blazed and they did a good twenty kilometers through the flat, ugly scrubland of far western Darlac province, Peter Whitlock plunged into a cold stream fully clothed.

They marched the next day. Whitlock tied his shoes, which had been soaked, as lightly as possible, but they hurt.

They rested through all of the fourth day at a stream. When they set out again on the next day, Whitlock told Scarborough he could not go on unless he cut off the front halves of the uppers of the shoes. The *bo dois,* for whom a pair of cheap dress shoes would take a month's pay, strenuously objected. They moved on, and it started to rain.

In the rain, Whitlock said, "Okay, Jay, this is it. Tell them that either I cut the f -----' shoes or I sit down here and die. They can bleeding well go on without me."

The ensuing discussion was heated. Scarborough was an extremely

---

* Cadre in this context means a Vietnamese Communist Party member in a position of authority, whether military or civilian. *Bo doi* was little used in South Vietnam, where communist partisans and fighters were referred to as Viet Cong, until after the war. Then *bo doi* took on its North Vietnamese meaning: North Vietnamese Army foot soldier.

polite, good-natured young man who liked Vietnamese. But he found himself saying in a raised voice: "Here's this guy, he comes to your country, which he knows nothing about. A couple of weeks after he arrives he's captured and taken off into the jungle. Now you've got us on a forced march in the damned jungle. Every day you tell us what terrific treatment you're giving us. Do you think he'd treat you the same way if you came to Australia?"

"He's a prisoner," the ranking *bo doi* said. "Everything he has belongs to the revolution. Someone else can use those shoes someday."

Whitlock let them argue. He squatted on the trail with a pocketknife he got from one of the other prisoners and hacked off the front of his shoes.

He was not shot. They marched on. By the time he straggled into a place the Westerners came to call Camp Wilderness, each toe was wrapped in a separate rag, all of them oozing blood and pus.

The next day, the cadre whom the Westerners would come to call Mr. Spectacles heard of the argument and called for Scarborough and the *bo doi*.

"You're both in the wrong," he said. "Apologize to each other." Scarborough and the soldier mumbled some words and shook hands.

They were on the trail for seven days, six of them marching. At night, Scarborough chatted with the North Vietnamese soldiers. They talked about food, and girls, and the watches and cameras they had bought on the conquered South Vietnamese economy, and their home villages.

It was impossible, Scarborough discovered, to have an intelligent discussion with the *bo dois* about politics. They had a single source of information—extracts from *Nhan Dan,* the North Vietnamese Army newspaper, which were read to them in the evenings by Radio Hanoi— and it was gospel, not to be argued about. Later Scarborough would recall only one conversation with them about ideas, and that muddily. It was probably a muddy conversation. They found out that he was a Christian of sorts, and brought up evolution to prove that Christianity was wrong. For some reason lost in the mists of western Darlac province, the *bo dois* as part of their argument wanted to make the point that Vietnamese were descended from Vietnamese monkeys, Khmers from Khmer monkeys. Scarborough then made the point, using the two languages' words for the numbers from one to ten, that the Khmer and Vietnamese *people* were related linguistically, to hell with the monkeys. Again, the relevance of this point to the larger argument about the truth of Christianity is lost. But it impressed the *bo dois.* "Yeah, older brother might be right," Scarborough's antagonist in the great shoe debate allowed.

(Terms of address were important. It was on the march that Scarborough heard one of the captured ARVN refer to a *bo doi* as "comrade." He was instantly reprimanded. Scarborough was also amused when the ARVN soldiers used a nickname for President Thieu that meant little brat.)

On the last night, as they sat around a campfire after the evening meal, Colonel Nhien, or Mr. Spectacles, asked Scarborough what his philosophy of life was.

Scarborough, the fallen-away Catholic, knew that Nhien carried a Vietnamese translation of the New Testament. He asked for it, looked at the cover, marveled at the reach of the Gideons, and looked in the index for I Corinthians. He turned so the light from the fire could illuminate the page.

" 'Now I will show you the way which surpasses all the others,' " he read softly, in Vietnamese. " 'If I speak with human tongues and angelic as well, but do not have love, I am a noisy gong, a clanging cymbal. If I have the gift of prophecy and, with full knowledge, comprehend all mysteries, if I have faith great enough to move mountains, but have not love, I am nothing. If I give everything I have to feed the poor and hand over my body to be burned, but have not love, I gain nothing.' " He glanced down: "Love is patient; love is kind. Love is not jealous, it does not put on airs. . . ." No, the first three verses are enough, he decided.

"That is my philosophy of life," he said, feeling slightly exposed. "No political or economic system on earth has any value if it is not built on love."

"It is my philosophy also," Colonel Nhien said.

As the two men spoke in the jungle, Thieu was resigning.

v

Through the most elaborately exclusive means by which words on paper can be electronically transmitted from one capital to another, Henry Kissinger on the day after Thieu resigned sent Graham Martin a cable that was to govern all that the ambassador did in the days remaining to him in Saigon. It was still not as secure as a Kissinger-to-Martin conversation on a scrambler. But the coding at the top of the message told the young communicator sitting at or standing watch over the machines in the communications center on the fourth floor of the embassy that he was duty-bound (a) not to read the text that followed, and (b) to deliver it by hand to the ambassador only.

If the aggressive young activists in the mission had known the contents of this cable, they might have been more forgiving of the ambassador's calm, his seeming inaction.

WE HAVE JUST RECEIVED A REPLY TO OUR INITIATIVE TO THE SOVIETS [KISSINGER WROTE], WHICH IS QUOTED BELOW. (I WANT YOU TO KNOW THAT IN SENDING YOU THE DETAILS OF MY NEGOTIATIONS, I AM DOING SOMETHING I HAVE NEVER DONE BEFORE.) I WOULD APPRECIATE YOUR INTERPRETATION OF THE SOVIET RESPONSE. IT IS MY JUDGMENT THAT WE WILL BE PERMITTED TO CONTINUE OUR EVACUATION, IN-CLUDING THE EVACUATION OF VIETNAMESE, UNIMPEDED. I ALSO TAKE THE RESPONSE TO INDICATE THAT THE PRG IS PREPARED TO UNDERTAKE NEGOTIATIONS IN THE TRIPARTITE FORMULATION. THE SOVIET REPLY INDICATES TO ME THAT YOUR JUDGMENT ABOUT THE TIME WE HAVE AVAILABLE IS CORRECT. WITH REGARD TO THE PRESIDENTIAL DIRECTIVE ABOUT FURTHER REDUCTIONS OF NONESSENTIAL NONGOVERNMENTAL PERSONNEL BY SUNDAY NIGHT, WE ARE ASSUMING FOR OUR OWN PLANNING THAT A FIGURE SOMEWHERE AROUND 800 WOULD BE SATIS-FACTORY. IF YOU ARE ABLE TO REDUCE BELOW THAT GENERAL FIGURE, THERE IS A GREAT DEAL TO BE SAID FOR TRICKLING AMERICANS OUT SLOWLY AFTER SUNDAY TO KEEP THE AIRLIFT GOING, AND THUS STAY WITHIN THE LITERAL TERMS OF THE SOVIET NOTE.* I WOULD APPRE-CIATE YOUR VIEWS.

TEXT FROM THE SOVIETS:

"AS IT HAS ALREADY BEEN SAID TO THE PRESIDENT IMMEDIATELY AFTER THE MESSAGE OF THE PRESIDENT OF APRIL 19 WAS RECEIVED BY L. I. BREZHNEV, WE TOOK APPROPRIATE STEPS TO GET IN TOUCH WITH THE VIETNAMESE SIDE IN THIS CONNECTION.

"AS A RESULT OF THOSE CONTACTS, NOW WE CAN INFORM THE PRESI-DENT ABOUT THE FOLLOWING: THE POSITION OF THE VIETNAMESE SIDE ON THE QUESTION OF EVACUATION OF AMERICAN CITIZENS FROM SOUTH VIETNAM IS DEFINITELY FAVORABLE. THE VIETNAMESE STATED THAT THEY HAVE NO INTENTIONS TO PUT ANY OBSTACLES IN THE COURSE OF MILITARY ACTIONS TO EVACUATION OF AMERICAN CITIZENS FROM SOUTH VIETNAM. AND THAT NOW, IN FACT, FAVORABLE CONDI-TIONS HAVE BEEN ESTABLISHED FOR SUCH AN EVACUATION.

"AT THE SAME TIME, IT WAS EMPHASIZED THAT IN THE STRUGGLE FOR ACHIEVING A POLITICAL SETTLEMENT, THE VIETNAMESE SIDE WILL PROCEED FROM THE PARIS AGREEMENT. WE ARE ALSO TOLD THAT THE VIETNAMESE DO NOT INTEND TO DAMAGE THE REPUTATION OF THE UNITED STATES.

"INFORMING THE PRESIDENT OF THE ABOVE IN A CONFIDENTIAL MANNER, L. I. BREZHNEV EXPRESSES HIS HOPE THAT THE PRESIDENT WILL DULY APPRECIATE SUCH A POSITION OF THE VIETNAMESE SIDE, AND WILL NOT ALLOW ANY ACTIONS ON THE UNITED STATES PART WHICH WOULD BE FRAUGHT WITH A NEW EXACERBATION OF THE SIT-UATION IN INDOCHINA."

---

* With this sentence, the Secretary of State earns a place on the very short list of high American officials who saw a clear obligation to evacuate as many Vietnamese as possible.

VI

With Thieu's resignation, the plan already forming in the subtle mind of Tran Kim Tuyen, the tiny former chief of the secret police, gelled. Of course Big Minh would become president. He must be convinced to accept Vu Van Mau—the leader of the opposition in the Senate—as his prime minister. But that combination would terrify the generals. Cao Van Vien especially had every reason to believe that with Big Minh in power his life would be in jeopardy, for reasons going back to the 1963 coup, and would flee. It was all going to be difficult. Big Minh had to be persuaded to name Vu Van Mau as prime minister, and the two of them would have to be persuaded to appoint Nguyen Cao Ky as minister of defense. Only then, with the two soft men at the top and Ky under them, was there a possibility of talking with the communists and at the same time maintaining some morale on the battlefield. Indeed, if Big Minh and Vu Van Mau brought in Ky, maybe even Cao Van Vien would stay and fight.

So: much had to be done, very quickly. Further, Dr. Tuyen felt a responsibility to many of those who had been arrested in the early-morning hours of April 4. As soon as Huong was sworn in, Tuyen had gone to see him to urge that his friends be released; they should have been out this morning, but were still in jail.

These were the considerations that were uppermost in Dr. Tuyen's thoughts late on that same Tuesday afternoon when, with no advance warning, a handsome young American arrived at his house.

"I have just come from Washington," the young man said. "I'm with the government." He mentioned a friend who had asked him to find Tuyen, and added: "Dr. Tuyen, if you wish to leave, we have space for you and your family on a plane waiting at Tan Son Nhut. But we must know in no more than an hour what your decision is. Here is the number where you can reach me. You must call within an hour. Or perhaps you can tell me now?"

"No," Dr. Tuyen said. "I must think. This is very strange. . . ."

"Dr. Tuyen, it is a difficult time," the American said. "Those seats are valuable. You must decide quickly. And if the answer is yes, I must ask you for two thousand dollars. You understand, so many people want to leave."

The request for money quickly tipped the scales. Just a few nights before, Dr. Tuyen had met in a quiet restaurant with his current CIA contact, Kohlmann, the man with the withered arm; Kohlmann had assured Tuyen again, as he had all along, that when the end was at hand he would see that Dr. Tuyen and his family got out.

"No," he said. "Thank you very much for coming. But we cannot leave now. Not in an hour."

"Okay," the American said, and left.

VII

Charlie Benoit took Thieu's resignation as a propitious sign. With the payment of considerably less than a hundred dollars, he had arranged for the police in the neighborhood where Tammy's mother was keeping her to conduct a house-to-house search that night. This was a relatively routine occurrence in Saigon. The police would be looking for deserters, outsiders—anyone staying in a house who was not on that building's "family card," which was kept at the station. And while Tammy's mother was taken to the station to add her name to the family list, other cops would bring Tammy to her father.

What struck Benoit as fortuitous about the Thieu resignation was that it meant an earlier curfew than usual, and he could move freely in it, claiming he had been caught out in it.

He didn't want to drive, and he wanted company for the wait. And so, by previous arrangement, after watching Thieu resign I drove Benoit to the rendezvous, Benoit yelling directions into my ear over the cries of the small Honda engine toiling under our combined weight.

At a narrow corner café, Benoit slid off the machine and said, "Park it fast and get inside."

Benoit had taken a table that gave him line of sight to a good piece of the sidewalk but hid him from a main avenue they had skirted. When I joined him, he half turned, furtively, and explained that Tammy and her mother were in an alley off the avenue.

A boy was waiting for the order. "You want to eat?" Benoit asked.

"Some *chao tom*," I said. "Half a dozen sticks is plenty. And beer." Benoit ordered the little skewers of shrimp paste, and two beers, and then propped his forehead on his fist for a few moments. Looking at him in that attitude, I was glad I had never played guard against him.

The beer came and Benoit poured. He sketched out the plan for what he called the "pickup." I didn't ask many questions. I was not at all sure that he was doing the right thing, but sensed that the last thing he needed at that point was moral advice.

As I had suspected might happen, a platter piled with *chao tom* arrived. "Don't worry," Benoit said. "I didn't think I'd have an appetite but I do."

Ten minutes later, a black, bulbous-fendered late-1940s Citroën screeched to the curb. The Yale football player jerked wild-eyed from the table and plunged into the white-upholstered seats and was gone. I got only a glimpse of what I thought were sunglassed thugs.

And for six years thereafter, I thought that Tammy was in the car. She wasn't. The cops told Benoit that the curfew complicated things. They would have to do it the next night.

They didn't have to. Early the next morning, before eight, Benoit had taken up his wait at a *pho* stall near the stalking ground. His men followed Tammy's mother as she traveled with Tammy and a teen-aged servant girl to an office building. Tammy's mother went into the building, leaving Tammy and the servant on the sidewalk, looking into shop windows. The little servant girl was not holding Tammy. Early in the planning, Benoit had decided that the one thing he must try to avoid unless it was absolutely necessary was a physical struggle with her mother for Tammy. He had instructed his accomplices accordingly.

Now one of them arrived, with no words, just a quick motion for Benoit to hop on his motorcycle. As they approached the building, Benoit took it all in: the second accomplice on this shift idling on his machine nearby, no sight of Tammy's mother, the servant girl and Tammy separated by a few feet, Tammy mercifully facing away from him.

He reached down and encircled her from the back and lifted her between himself and the driver as she screamed.

"Tammy, Tammy, don't cry," he said. "Everything's going to be okay. If you cry . . ." He and his bawling daughter were suddenly whipped back; for a horrible moment, Benoit thought it was all going to end in disaster. The driver had forgotten to downshift, was taking off in third. Benoit held Tammy tight with one arm, and even as they were lurching backward reached wildly with the other and his fingers just got a purchase on the forward curve of the driver's skinny torso and they were saved.

"It's okay," Benoit said. "Please don't cry, darling, or I'm going to cry too."

For most of two days Benoit stayed with his daughter in a safe house he had arranged before the kidnapping. Even that late into the game, Benoit still thought that he could stay in Saigon, with Tammy, and get her mother out. He went so far as to send the Ford Foundation driver to Tammy's mother with messages saying that he and Tammy had already left but he would return shortly to get her.

On one of his few excursions out, he got into Tan Son Nhut and for the first time realized that there was a new twist: You could get out your Vietnamese dependents but you yourself could stay on by convincing the American officials in charge of the evacuation process that you were "mission essential."

In any case, on another excursion out of the safe house, a young American whose advice Benoit normally ignored finally managed to talk some sense into him.

"Look, Charlie," he said. "You have two goals. One is to keep possession of Tammy—here or in Bangkok or in Massachusetts. The other is to see the end. You have to decide which is number one and which is number two. You're playing a game now that could very well leave you in Bangkok, Tammy in Saigon, and you with no way to get back in."

Charlie Benoit achingly wanted to see the end of what had changed him so much—formed all of his adult life. But getting Tammy to safety was primary. And Benoit finally acknowledged that maybe his panicky young friend might be right. Maybe it was a matter now not of months, as Benoit had thought, but of weeks—or even days.

On Thursday afternoon, a little more than forty-eight hours after the kidnapping, he took Tammy to Tan Son Nhut. There was a difficult interview with a snotty Foreign Service Officer—Tammy did indeed have no papers—and then they were lined up and finally, hours later, they were on a C-130, no seats, strapped down to the pallets. There must have been some problem with one of the engines, because they spent forty-five minutes taxiing in a tight circle. But they finally took off, Benoit's exhausted mind turning over scenarios for his quick return even as it held out the almost absurd possibility that this was it: He would never see Saigon again. (And he wouldn't.)

PART 4

APRIL 23–APRIL 28

"Evil days."

23

Wednesday

Ky was again actively considering a coup. Early in the afternoon of Wednesday, April 23, Duong Van Minh told one of his American contacts that he had heard rumors that the "northern generals"* were planning to eliminate him, Minh, possibly even before he became president.

Martin sent Charlie Timmes out to see Ky, and in fact when Timmes arrived unannounced at the air marshal's villa, Ky was meeting with four northern-born generals. The day before, Ky had flown in one of his helicopters to the roof of the Presidential Palace and met with the new president. Ky offered himself as a replacement for Cao Van Vien—Thieu's man—as chairman of the Joint General Staff.

Old Huong used a neat Asian excuse to put him off. He told Ky that it would not be right for a man who had been prime minister and vice president to serve in the subordinate position of chairman of the JGS. If Ky would wait a few days, Huong said, he would make him his special assistant for military affairs.

"It is not a question of a few days, Mr. President," Ky said. "The communists could be here in hours."

So that night and the next day, Ky was again trying to put together

* The numerous senior generals in the South who were northerners by birth.

the forces required for a successful seizure of power. And again the problem was that while commander after commander said he agreed that someone had to do something, they had all been warned by the Americans that their own futures in the United States were at stake if they joined with Ky.

Now, on Wednesday afternoon, Timmes was direct. "Is it true," he asked Ky, "that you and the northern generals are planning a coup?" Ky was formulating a reply when Timmes added: "I mean, a move against Big Minh?"

Ky was flabbergasted. He knew of course that the French were campaigning for Minh. "But why Minh?" he asked out loud. "Minh has been out of power for years." The import of Timmes' words was just sinking in. The French had won. They had brought the Americans around. They were going to dump Huong and put Big Minh in his place. "My God," he thought.

"Well, Marshal," Timmes was saying, "I think I ought to tell you that if you *do* make a move against Big Minh, Washington and Hanoi will blame you for anything that happens afterward."

"*Washington and Hanoi?*" Ky thought. "It has gone that far?"

"General Timmes," he said, "you are a military man. I am a military man. Maybe you do not know as much about Duong Van Minh as we do. I tell you, General, if you think that the communists, with all of their troops and their artillery and tanks waiting outside Saigon, are going to sit down and talk with a man like Duong Van Minh, you have made a big mistake. Why should they talk to Duong Van Minh? He is a *nothing* man! If you make him the president, I promise you that twenty-four hours later it is the end of South Vietnam."

Charlie Timmes quietly thanked Ky for his opinions, repeated the warning—his mission that afternoon—and left.

II

In the three weeks between the fall of Da Nang and the meeting on the nineteenth that led to the sudden jump in evacuees, the young activists in the embassy who thought the ambassador was dragging his heels asked themselves why there wasn't some small secret staff that at least thought through the simple logistics—the movement of people— for a full-scale evacuation.

There was. Early in April, two of Martin's closest aides—James Devine, his political-military counselor, and Shep Lowman, another political officer—approached Mel Chatman and Russell Mott and asked them to set up an embassy evacuation control center.

Chatman and Mott were the two USAID officers who had handled the logistics for much of the evacuation from Da Nang. They were given the services of a young CIA communicator named George Kistia-kowski.* Later the team was augmented by the addition of Robert Schwab, a free-lance adventurer.

The group operated out of a small communications room on the fourth floor of the embassy. They contacted DAO and found the buses they needed—standard American city buses painted GI olive-green with thick grillwork in the windows. They roamed through Saigon, finding safe houses: American offices or villas with high walls. And they charted the routes from the safe houses out to Tan Son Nhut.

Within the embassy, and in every U.S. agency that had its head-quarters outside the chancery—USIS, USAID, USAID hotels, CIA hotels like the Duc—they established a contact, a man who could be reached by radio or telephone twenty-four hours a day.

He had to be an American. Chatman liked and respected the Viet-namese enough to study them. But he knew that if Vietnamese were in the net it would break down. If the Vietnamese discovered the sys-tem before the moment when they themselves were to be picked up and taken to Tan Son Nhut, when he sent buses for three hundred people to one of the villas with high walls, six hundred Vietnamese would be waiting. The last thing Chatman (or Graham Martin) wanted in Saigon was six hundred Vietnamese fighting for three hun-dred seats in a bus convoy.

They moved some people before the nineteenth, including orphans and several hundred past and present employees of American news organizations in Saigon and their dependents. That airlift was insti-gated when a senior executive at Time Inc. approached Henry Kis-singer about Time's Vietnamese. The Secretary of State was disposed to do a favor for the media. At Kissinger's behest, Martin directed John Hogan,† his special assistant for press affairs, to cooperate with Brian Ellis, a CBS News producer who flew into Saigon and worked full time that month on this evacuation.

After the breakthrough meeting on the nineteenth, Chatman or Mott every night was given a list of the people to be moved the next day, agency by agency. Typically, they would be told to pick up fifty people from Lacy Wright's villa, a hundred at one of the numerous USAID facilities in Saigon, seventy-five from a villa or office they knew to belong to the CIA—usually six or seven pickup points in all,

* A pseudonym.
† Hogan was a gruff, convivial man who easily adapted himself to Martin's contempt for most of the Saigon press corps but also enjoyed having a drink or two with some of them. He had begun his career as a composer of Tin Pan Alley songs in the 1940s. Typically, USIS chief Alan Carter was cut out of this operation and did not know of the cooperation between Hogan and Ellis until he was told about it nine years later.

and often resulting in a convoy of eight to ten buses. (Chatman and Mott knew that the spooks were getting additional people out on late-night flights fed by their own transportation system from Saigon to the airport.)

They made the telephone and radio calls to their contacts, frequently stressing the need for secrecy. Mott and Schwab accompanied the convoys. Chatman usually remained back in the radio room.

Considering the fact that most of the runs were made in daylight, from a limited number of pickup points that quickly became known at least to those in the neighborhood, the system worked remarkably well. But one morning Mott radioed in to say that one bus had been rushed by a dozen or so people who were not on the manifest of the agency involved.

"Can you get everybody on who's supposed to get on?" Chatman asked quickly, thinking of the woman who had bowled past him onto the chopper at the USAID hotel in Da Nang.

"Yeah," Mott said.

"Load 'em fast and get outta there," Chatman said. "We'll just retire that pickup point for a couple of days."

For the past few years, Mel Chatman had made it a point to get to Saigon at least one day a month for a tutorial in Vietnamese antiques from a man named Vuong Hong. Mr. Sen was a former curator at the National Museum; in retirement, his collection of porcelain bowls and vases and other artifacts of Vietnamese culture rivaled that at the museum.

On Wednesday, the twenty-third, Chatman had a driver take him out to Gia Dinh, to the house of polished teak that Mr. Sen had had transferred plank by plank from the delta.

If Mr. Sen knew a word of English, he never betrayed that knowledge to Mel Chatman.

"Respected teacher," Chatman said, "I think you might now consider leaving Vietnam."

Mr. Sen looked the mandarin, with his elegant soft old clothes and wispy beard. "I am seventy-two years old, nephew," he said. He smiled. "If I am going to die, I shall die in the land of my ancestors."

Then he gave Chatman autographed copies of each of his several books on Vietnamese antiquities. Chatman knew the subtle formulas with which one constructed a modest speech that feinted and dodged around but never uttered the words "thank you," and made to leave.

The old mandarin, who well knew how sensitive Chatman was to Vietnamese sensibilities, nevertheless felt it necessary to give him a parting piece of advice. "It is a very dangerous time now for all Americans," he said. "Be careful in everything you do. Stay off the streets."

III

Don Hays's four-year-old daughter had been in kindergarten in Saigon. One of her teachers, like Hays's wife, was a New Zealander. The teacher was married to a bright Vietnamese engineer who worked for one of the major U.S. companies doing business in Vietnam. Because he was Vietnamese, the engineer was paid on the local wage scale; by Hays's standards, the couple, whom he and his wife saw socially from time to time, lived in poverty.

After the fall of Da Nang, the teacher went to her embassy to try to get her small family out of Vietnam. At first, her countrymen were adamant: There would be no visa for her husband, or passports for her two small children. Finally, after days of pleading and tears, they relented and issued passports to the children. She left with them, assuming that her husband's employers would see that he got out.

They would not. The man came to see Hays at the embassy. "What am I going to do?" he asked, close to tears himself. "The company says that if I appear at their office in Bangkok, they might be able to move me on to New Zealand. But they won't help me leave Vietnam, because I'm still the age for the Army. How can I get out?"

Hays produced a map of Tan Son Nhut and showed his friend where three planes were waiting to take out Australians and New Zealanders, most of them from the two embassies.

"Here's what I'd do," he said. "Find someone who's got a black Mercedes and then go and get yourself a couple of little Japanese flags, for the fenders. You know what the fenders are?"

"Sure," the man said.

"Right, so it looks like an embassy limousine. Get a black suit and a homburg"—he decided not to test the man's command of English again—"and when you're driving through the gate pull the hat down over your forehead. It's the only thing I can think of. It might work."

When two and then three days went by, and Hays knew the planes had left and he hadn't heard from the man again, he called his office and asked for him. He smiled when a secretary said Mr. Nguyen had not come to work for three days, maybe he leave Vietnam.

IV

Since the beginning of the offensive, I was gradually drawn back into the Americans' Saigon. In the last few days, the process had accelerated. I started eating with the rest of the press corps in the French restaurants in or near the Eden Building, because I could afford them and they were close and kept the beggars out. I finally gave up my Vietnamese lessons altogether. I was working all day, and the curfew meant the restaurant staffs wanted to start shutting down shortly after eight, so there wasn't time for the noon swims in the pool of the Hotel Catinat or the leisurely hour in the sidewalk bookstalls on Le Loi or the *café suas* in the Rex cafeteria that had once broken the day.

When I returned to the office after lunch on Wednesday, there was a message to call a Senator Hien. I called and the man asked calmly if we could meet. I said of course and gave him the address. When I hung up, I still didn't know who Hien was.

In the fall, when Anh Tu, the singer, still needed cash to remain posted close to Saigon, he once asked me for a hundred dollars. I didn't have it then. Now I was rich from the money I was making covering the fighting, making seven and eight hundred dollars a week. Tu had called the office that morning. He said nothing about money. They might be leaving soon, he said. He wanted to see me to say goodbye.

He arrived at the apartment just at six. I gave him what the Vietnamese called a Coca and made a Scotch and water for myself. We stood on the balcony overlooking an unfinished building and the eastern quarter of the city and beyond it the snaking river and the rice fields on the horizon.

All through the first three weeks of April there had been one bright, almost cool day after another. Now the weather was returning to form, hot and close through noon and then gray until occasional rain showers, no thunderstorms yet. A shower had just ended.

"When?" I asked.

"Maybe tomorrow. Tomorrow or the next day."

"How do you do it?"

"It's a secret," Tu said.

"Okay."

"You know my sister Ha—Khanh Ha?"

"I never can get the names straight," I said.

"Ha sings with me. Ha and Thuy. Ha is the older one. She has a boy friend at DAO. He is going to help us."

"Will everyone go? Can he get the whole family out?"

"Yes," Tu said. "We think so. I don't know. Maybe Tuan Ngoc has to find another way."

He looked worse than I had ever seen him. There was something almost cold in his face as he mentioned the possibility that his older brother might have to get out on his own. "At last," I thought, "the world is beginning to shut down his sweetness, to make him just another man."

I hardly knew La Anh Tu. I was one of his many fans. One day two years before, when I had taken my three-week vacation from *Playboy* in Saigon—the trip on which I had decided that I would return to Chicago and extricate myself from the magazine and come back to Saigon to live—I had actually interviewed Anh Tu, tape recorder and all.

"Remember when I was here a couple of years ago—the first time we met—and I interviewed you before the show one night?"

"Yes," Tu said tentatively, possibly out of politeness.

"How much time do you have tonight?"

Tu glanced at me. "I can stay a little while more," he said in his soft voice, a voice that spoke English with what sounded like a Caribbean lilt.

"That tape is back in Chicago," I said. "Let me tape again for a few minutes, until you have to go. Someday I will write about all of this."

Later, when the mosquitos started in on our ankles, we moved into the light of the apartment. I went to my bedroom and got a hundred-dollar bill I had thought to bring from the office safe. Then I went back to the living room.

Sometimes in those last days words went from the heart to the lips without the usual detours. "Nobody has what you have, Tu," I said. "Tuan Ngoc has a better voice, in a way, a stronger voice. But nobody has what you have on stage. I've seen Joan Baez and Mick Jagger in person. No one has what you have when you're singing with Thuy and Khanh Ha. You're going to be okay. I wish I could have done this in September, when you needed it, but I was broke then." I handed over the bill.

In that society, spoken thanks diminished the gift. But La Anh Tu was familiar with foreign customs, committed now to learning them in earnest.

"Thank you, David," he said softly.

Two months before, all thirty apartments in the building had been occupied. Now there were only two or three tenants left, and I was the only one on an upper story. When the elevator kicked on, as it just had, it could mean only that the servant had thrown the switch to carry a visitor to me.

I recognized Senator Hien immediately. He was in fact a former senator, a Catholic politician who had been my landlord for a few months in the fall, when I first left hotels. I was ninety percent sure that the man's teen-age son had once stolen five dollars from me. His wife was a classic Vietnamese *petite bourgeoisie*—than which there are few women on earth more *petite* or *bourgeoisie*. But Hien had pretty daughters, and I liked him for acting as a buffer between me and his wife. He knocked on the screen door and I invited him in and introduced him to Anh Tu.

The calmness of the phone call was gone. "Mr. Butler," he began, "you must help me."

I sat folded in a chair, elbows to knees, drawing the cold glass to my forehead; Tu in another chair; Senator Hien alone on the sofa pleading his case, leaning toward me. He reminded me of my father: his age of course and something too about his voice and body shape. I looked beyond him to the last light on the edge of the city and thought how hard it must be for him, what desperation it displayed, to come to this building and ask for help from an American twenty years younger than himself, in the presence of a stranger who could have been his son. But I would not send Tu away. I knew that the next time I saw him it would be in Paris or the United States and knew that there was a chance that I would never see him again at all.

I waited for the senator to suggest marriage to one of the daughters. It came and I was glad that was out and over with. With a play of my hands and head and mouth, I almost succeeded in preventing Hien from mentioning money. Then I made more drinks and the three of us went out on the balcony. I told Hien that I needed the names and ages and relationships of his family. Hien produced the list from his pocket.

"I can do almost nothing at all," I said. "I'm married in Chicago. The Americans have speeded everything up at Tan Son Nhut, but they're not letting you get married if you're already married in the States. You don't work for an American company. All I can do is give your list to a good man at the embassy. I've done it with others. It's a great long list now. The embassy says that when the evacuation comes they will try to get everyone out. I don't know what that means."

"I must go now," Tu said.

I went to the head of the stairs with him and told him that I thought he would probably do better in Paris than in the States. "Wherever you wind up," I said, "keep the family together and keep playing music."

"Okay," Tu said in his singsong voice, and was gone.

A few minutes later, I walked down the stairs with Senator Hien. I asked about another American who knew Hien—an American with much better connections than mine—and Hien said the man hadn't returned his calls. "Well, we're all very busy," I said. I told the senator both times when he asked that I was sure Mr. Carter at the embassy could not see him. But I said that I would talk to Mr. Carter personally about him, and made an appointment to see Hien the next day at his office, in the rear reaches of the shoe shop above which I had briefly lived, on Le Thanh Ton Street, a street of shoe shops.

That afternoon outside the AP office, I had run into Tung Giang—the young songwriter who played bass in The Uptight and managed the Pink Night Club. He had cut his hair and looked greenish-gray with anxiety. But he told me that he was keeping the Pink Night open, as a coffee shop and beer hall. I could come and stay even after curfew if I liked.

After Hien left, I got on the Honda and drove through the sweet rotting smells of the Saigon night to the club. Only three of the dozens of low tables in the place were occupied. The light was brighter than it had been when the room was the focus of my life in Saigon. Tung Giang had picked up a batch of aluminum beer steins someplace. The low bandstand, with the room's chairs and tables no longer oriented to it, was forlorn in its casual and unlit emptiness.

Tung Giang sent an orphan boy whom he and his very elderly father had adopted out to the sidewalk for a plate of pork and rice for me and we drank beer.

For more than a hundred years, Westerners had studied Vietnam. When I finished eating and turned on the Sony tape recorder I now carried everywhere and asked Tung Giang to give me the history of Vietnamese rock 'n' roll, I was merely saving something, continuing a long tradition.

Toward the end of the interview, I asked how all the young men avoided the draft.

"I think I am famous in Vietnam," Tung Giang said. "Because I have show on Vietnamese TV, I have tape, I make a lot of tape. And I have, you see"—he pointed to the wall behind the bar, above his old father at the cash register—"I have certificate from the government. Because I make rock festival in the zoo, every New Year. All money that we give to the military. Like, last year, we make—only one day, Sunday—we make seven million piasters [about $10,000]. For one day. And what I have? If I go in the street, I have long hair, policeman can catch me, put me in military. I didn't have any help from Vietnamese government. But only I have a certificate; that's all I have. But . . . I think: I don't have lucky. I try very hard. I work very hard. Nobody help me."

I had had enough beer so that on the four-block ride up Tu Do Street to the apartment building I didn't much care if a cop stopped me. I was drunk enough to play out the drunk arrogant American if I had to, and that night it still might have worked. But I didn't have to. I parked the thing and made my way up to the apartment (waking the poor servant girl again, as I did almost every night now) and fell into a deep sleep.

"A whiner," I thought before I slept. "But strong as me. Maybe stronger. Tough little Mouse."

24

Thursday

A young photographer who called himself Raymond Ly came to the apartment early on Thursday morning. I was taking a shower. Raymond called out that I must go right away to La Pagode, the café across the street. He came again before I had finished dressing and now was insistent that I get to La Pagode "immediately." I was irritated. I hardly knew the boy; and I was not at all used to being ordered about by Vietnamese.

I finished dressing without urgency and crossed Tu Do to the café. A man I didn't know waved me to his table. He said that he was Raymond Ly's older brother. Obviously he was looking for a way out of the country. What only gradually dawned on me was that the younger brother wasn't going to appear. "Go to La Pagode," he had said, not "Meet me at La Pagode." I assumed the photographer was off on a job. The idea that funny-looking Raymond Ly, who meandered from bureau to bureau with his long-billed baseball cap on backward, could be one of those who had decided they would no longer be seen with the Americans was too absurd to take seriously.

The brother had worked for RMK/BRJ* from 1965 to 1972, he said. Over the coffee and papaya, it emerged that—unfortunately, it wasn't his choice, he insisted—he had become the man in charge of building prisons.

"I didn't design them," he said. "I was just in charge of the construction. I'm not an architect. At Oklahoma State, I study construction, just construction."

Twenty minutes later, an official in the Ministry of Tourism stopped on the sidewalk, peered into the café as if looking for a friend and then came in and took a table, alone, a few tables away from me and the construction engineer. I had met the man from the Ministry of Tourism early on, when I had thought I might do an article on the government's sad efforts to attract visitors. The official had launched a campaign built around the slogan: "Vietnam—you've heard about it, now come see it." He was a youthful-looking forty, his thick hair in a pompadour, and his clothes and watch and rings elegant and studied without being flashy. He had told me that he had made two movies before he took the government job, and I had the idea that the job was an alternative to military service.

When I had finished making notes about Raymond Ly's brother and the man had left, the undersecretary in the Ministry of Tourism glided to the table. He persuaded me to follow him to his brother's office. I knew it was madness: I was being sought out now by people who barely knew me.

The meeting with Senator Hien the evening before had been good preparation for this morning. It now seemed almost normal that men older than myself should turn desperately to me for help. And they were so clearly desperate that I found it impossible to say, "I don't even know you. God, you have no idea how hopeless it is if you have to turn to *me* for help."

As I had with Raymond Ly's brother, I said to the tourism official and his brother, a businessman: "I have no right to give you advice. You know your country better than I do. But I don't think you're in danger. I think perhaps you would be better off in a peaceful Vietnam than in the United States."

"Our families," the older brother said.

"My family," Raymond Ly's brother had said. "It's for my children."

Finally making my way to the office at eleven, I remembered a conversation I had had with Mr. Khi in October, at the beginning of

---

* Raymond, Morrison-Knudson/Brown, Root & Jones. An Oklahoma- and Texas-based construction consortium that prospered greatly in the presidency of Lyndon Johnson, in part by building roads, airports and other facilities throughout Southeast Asia.

Father Thanh's anticorruption campaign. Mr. Khi had said: "If these people who are trying to bring down Thieu succeed, I will leave Vietnam, somehow. Not because I like Thieu. But I cannot live with the communists. I work for NBC for five years. Before that, I work for the Americans in Cam Ranh Bay, as an accountant. And they never forget, the communists. They would give me a job, I think. Maybe not a good job, but perhaps they would use what I know. If it were only me, I would stay and work for a better Vietnam. But my children, never. They would punish me through the children."

I was sure my memory was right, that Mr. Khi—who was part-Chinese, and had a ceramics exporting business on the side—had actually said that he would stay if it weren't for his family. In the elevator, I marveled at how successfully the communists had made their case. But it was academic now as far as Mr. Khi was concerned. His bags were already in the office, and he would flee with his wife and two children as soon as Arthur Lord gave the word.

The only news was that three American banks, including Chase Manhattan, where I kept a small piaster checking account, had locked their doors. The banks' headquarters in New York and San Francisco revealed that their American employees had left the week before. I was out a couple of hundred dollars. I was glad I had been so busy that the recent big checks were in the office safe.

I started a long letter to Alan Carter, the USIS chief:

DEAR ALAN,
Evil days. I beseech you, my friend, to do what you can with the following information.
1) Pham Tung Giang, who resides at the Hotel Catinat on Tu Do (phone 91920/1) is 28. He never had to join the Army because he is the sole support of his aged father. Since the Americans landed in Da Nang ten years ago, he has—often working with MACV's entertainment people—provided Americans here with the kind of music they wanted to hear. The girl he was going to marry next month succeeded in getting out last week. He is convinced that his long association with Americans puts him in clear danger.

Then I wrote about former Senator Hien, and about the men who had sought me out that morning. In the paragraph about Raymond Ly's brother, I wrote: "When he was with RMK/BRJ, he often invited American friends to his home for dinner. Women in the neighborhood are reminding him of that fact lately. I'm finally beginning to see what I suppose everyone else knows, that the other side has always had people everywhere, and they know everyone's associations."

The bureau's final cast—five correspondents, their crews, an assistant producer for Arthur Lord—was in place. As I wrote, a dozen people around me typed scripts, read magazines, chatted in four languages. Among the crews were a fat cameraman and his skinny sound man, both straight from the Paris bureau with minimal English. An intellectual who had taken to hanging around the office—another former senator, who had, at some time in the past, had some connection with NBC—was straining the Frenchmen's English: "If your child goes to school and he has a new sweater," he was saying, "the teacher asks him, 'Who gave you the sweater?' And the first time, of course, the child says, 'My father,' or, 'My mother . . . whatever.'

" 'No, no,' the teacher says. 'The Party gave it to you. And Uncle Ho.' Everything, *everything*, is from the Party and Uncle. All day long: the Party and Uncle."

I made myself a coffee in the dark little hallway that connected the larger room in which I and the other troops worked to the room that the bureau chief—or, as now, the producer—and Mr. Khi shared with the safe and the Telex machine. As I did off and on throughout the day, I walked to the Telex machine to see what instructions were coming from Hong Kong.

Arthur Lord looked up from a list and said to one of the office drivers: "This first woman on the list, the one who's thirty-eight. She's your wife, right?"

"Yes," the man said. He sat on the edge of a chair facing Lord's desk, leaning forward.

"And this next name, another woman, twenty-nine, who is she?"

"Oh," the driver said, "she's my wife also." I grinned. When Arthur Lord shouted "S - - -!" I let the laugh come.

A few days earlier I had had a happy reunion with Dennis Troute, the energetic young Dick Cavett look-alike who had hired me seven months earlier—and who had quit NBC, and Saigon, days before the attack on Ban Me Thuot. From Paris, Troute had asked the network to send him back in. When it became clear that it would not, he quickly lined up an assignment from *Harper's,* and returned to Saigon at its behest.*

Troute called to say that a group of journalists was having lunch at Ramuntcho's, the good French restaurant on the ground level of the Eden Building.

Besides Troute, I knew only one of the six or seven others, but they

* The assignment resulted in a powerful, dark, impressionistic article in the July 1975 issue called "Last Days in Saigon." The cover quote read: "Don't Look in Their Eyes."

made a place for me. The pushed-together tables were noisy with cross talk.

Someone had just that morning bought a paperback left over from the American period called *How to Survive in Vietnam*. The drawings in the book were funny, but the text was serious. Toward the end, the author gave eight rules for survival based on the word "survival." He had to strain to come up with two that began with V— although he did well with one: "Value living." The rule for A was "Act like those around you." I knew instinctively that that was good advice. But in a matter of days, I would regret that I had come upon it.

When it finally grew serious, over coffee, the talk centered on whether to stay or go if there was an American evacuation. Before that, through the final five or ten minutes of the meal, an Australian journalist named Neil Davis became the focus of the conversation.

Davis happened to be sitting in the center of one of the two rows of journalists. But as Davis gradually became the man the others fell silent for, and questioned, I realized that the others held him somewhat in awe.

I had never met him before, and in fact did not quite register his last name, although Troute had made quick introductions. Neil was about thirty, and solid, and blond.

Then at the end, everyone listening to him, he said: "F - - - it, mate, I got on the chopper out of Phnom Penh and that's the last time for me. No more running. It's f - - - - -' humiliating."

II

French Ambassador Jean-Marie Mérillon saw President Huong at least once and usually twice a day that week. At every meeting, he urged the old man to give way to Big Minh. At almost every meeting, the new president managed to work in the idea that history had apparently chosen him to play the role of Pétain in a Vichy South Vietnam. More than once, he also quoted from a poem by Sully-Prudhomme.

Russian horsemen approach the far bank of a river border between Russia and Poland. They call across the river to a Polish peasant, demanding to know if the river is shallow enough to ford. The peasant knows that it is, but saves Poland by denying it, and proving his denial by walking into the river and crouching ever lower until he drowns himself.

"Wretched stuff," Mérillon muttered to an aide after the second allusion. "He began his career as an *instructeur*, you know. That's just the sort of drivel he must have forced down the poor boys' throats. *Mon Dieu,* the absurdity of it all. A sick old Vietnamese schoolteacher quoting bad French poetry about Poles and Cossacks to the French ambassador while his country prepares to die."

III

Ken Moorefield was working as hard as he had worked since he had commanded troops in the field in Vietnam. It was different from combat—nothing compared to combat—but similar in the day-to-day sameness, the anxiety, the sense that the job could never get done. The job was simply overwhelming; they had started too late. Everybody who ought to get out couldn't get out. Damn Graham Martin for not starting earlier.

Moorefield had gone out to the DAO evacuation center on Saturday, the nineteenth, shortly after the meeting in the embassy that changed the scope of the evacuation. It quickly became evident how major the change was: Whereas through the first two and a half weeks of the month DAO personnel had been moving out a few hundred people every day, the new parole authority meant that DAO and Moorefield's contingent from the embassy could move several thousand people every day. (In both the earlier and the now greatly accelerated evacuation, the great majority of those leaving were Vietnamese.)

The military had set up their processing center in the DAO movie theater, which was right next to the headquarters buildings known as Pentagon East.

Theoretically, every Vietnamese had to have a *laissez-passer* from the Ministry of the Interior. At the beginning, Moorefield sent some dubious cases down to the local police precinct. But he discovered within twenty-four hours that it was going to be simply impossible to get proper South Vietnamese documentation. The normal payoff rate for exit visas shot up ten- and twentyfold. So he told McBride and Hays and the others in the main room to feed just enough Vietnamese to the Ministry of the Interior desk to keep the two or three officials there busy during the day. Those officials had absolute assurances that eventually they and their families would go, and issued visas to nearly all the people they saw. Like the Americans, they did screen out some draft-age males.

On day four of the operation, someone decided, both for security and logistics reasons, to move the evacuation center to a complex of buildings and sports facilities—the DAO post exchange, a gymnasium, a bowling alley, a swimming pool and tennis courts—known collectively for reasons lost to memory in a long war as Dodge City.

With the move to Dodge City, the Ministry of Interior men vetted themselves and their families out of Vietnam. The bureaucratic need for exit visas simply vanished.

At Dodge City, Moorefield established himself in an office off the large main room of the rickety old building on stilts where he and other Americans, military and civilian, did the final paper work. This was not a matter of bureaucratic game-playing. Moorefield handled the borderline cases—those that were in dispute or especially sensitive, or both. Many of the conversations required privacy.

One day a middle-aged man in civilian clothes was shown into the office. Moorefield knew him. He was one of Phu's deputy commanders in MR 2.

"I'm sorry, Colonel," Moorefield told him. "There's no way I can let you go out at this stage without jeopardizing the whole evacuation. You know as well as I do that we're evacuating dependents of Americans, not officers in an Army that's still fighting."

"They'll kill me, Mr. Moorefield," the colonel said. "I don't care about myself. It's for my family." He was crying.

He was a decent, competent officer, and MR 2 was lost after all. But the Vietnamese had inserted military intelligence people into the operation. They had already caught an ex-minister trying to leave. Moorefield told him to come back in a few days, maybe the rules would be different. He never saw the colonel again.

At the beginning, until the others from the embassy out in the larger room realized that Moorefield's decision in the cases of young women with half-American children would always be the same, he saw many of them. Usually they clutched a soiled letter two or three or five years old. The messages were remarkably similar. They all said in effect: I love you very much. I miss you, and hope we can be together again someday. Unfortunately, I have to take care of my family back here in the States. Here's some money, I hope it's enough for a while. . . .

It gave Moorefield great pleasure to let them all go to the U.S. He knew there were tens of thousands of others like them scattered around South Vietnam. Knowing that only a small fraction would, he wished all of them could find their way to Dodge City.

Over and over again they were faced with contractors or other Americans who had made it out of the highlands or MR 1 with their common-law wife and children—and other children who had been pressed on them by relatives or friends in their flight.

Moorefield made up some forms. "Nguyen Thi Ba is my lawful wife and the paper work was lost in our evacuation from _____," one of them read. Or: "Nguyen Van X is my lawfully adopted son and the paper work was lost due to _____." Five or six forms covered most of the possibilities.

Moorefield listened to the Americans' stories. Most of them were retired or active contract workers, but some were with the mission itself, or from the voluntary agencies, and there were even several journalists. The stories too were similar. "Look, I've been living with this woman for six years," the American would say. "We've got three kids already. I just never got around to marrying her." Or: "This one, Mai, is the daughter of my wife's cousin. Her parents were killed in the Tet offensive. We've been taking care of her ever since. It's like she's my own kid."

And if Moorefield believed the story, as he usually did, he had them fill out the form and chopped it with his consular stamp.

Two or three days after the operation got rolling, someone in the consulate downtown finally showed Moorefield the text of a cable that had come in on the fourteenth, with strict instructions as to who was to be included in the evacuation. The cable read in part:

. . . IN THE MEANTIME, WE HAVE SUCCEEDED IN OBTAINING AUTHORITY FOR A VERY LIMITED, REPEAT VERY LIMITED, PAROLE PROGRAM. THIS PAROLE PROGRAM DEALS ONLY WITH ALIEN RELATIVES PHYSICALLY PRESENT NOW IN VIETNAM OF U.S. CITIZENS ALSO PHYSICALLY PRESENT NOW IN VIETNAM. THE PURPOSE OF THE PROGRAM IS TO ELIMINATE ONE OF THE REASONS WHY SOME AMERICANS REFUSE TO LEAVE VIETNAM. IT WILL BE YOUR RESPONSIBILITY TO MONITOR SUCH PROGRAM AS CAREFULLY AS POSSIBLE AND YOU SHOULD MAKE AVAILABLE WHATEVER SECURITY FACILITIES NECESSARY TO SAY NO, REPEAT NO, TO THOSE WHO CAN'T QUALIFY. HERE ARE THE CRITERIA:

EVERY SUBJECT MUST BE PHYSICALLY, REPEAT PHYSICALLY, PRESENT IN VIETNAM AND MUST HAVE THE SPECIAL FAMILY RELATIONSHIP HEREAFTER DESCRIBED.

1) LAWFUL SPOUSE
2) CHILDREN
3) MOTHER OR FATHER OF U.S. CITIZEN
4) MOTHER OR FATHER OF ALIEN SPOUSE
5) MINOR UNMARRIED SIBLINGS OF ALIEN SPOUSE
6) MINOR UNMARRIED SIBLINGS OF AN AMERICAN CITIZEN

EACH SUBJECT MUST HAVE IN PHYSICAL POSSESSION ALL AVAILABLE DOCUMENTS NECESSARY TO ESTABLISH SUCH SPECIAL FAMILY RELATIONSHIP AND BASIS TO ESTABLISH THAT SUBJECT'S QUALIFICATION AS AN IMMIGRANT, UNDER THE INA,* WHEREVER APPLICABLE. FORM I-94 MUST BE FILLED OUT FOR EACH AND EVERY SUBJECT.

* Immigration and Naturalization Act.

Moorefield laughed as he read the cable. It was good of them to finally show him the rules. Too bad he'd been breaking them for the last three days.

The State Department's criteria on "immediate family" flew in the face of Vietnamese custom. In Vietnam—in Asia—the family is everyone under the same roof for whom the principal breadwinner is responsible. Ricewinner, of course. And of course they could be under several roofs.

Moorefield and his colleagues routinely saw "families" of twenty to thirty people, anchored to one bewildered (or shrewd) American. Years later, he would remember a case of a Chinese-Vietnamese family group consisting of a full fifty persons.

He had a real problem with these groups. Most of his immediate colleagues, and as far as he could determine most of the people in the mission, for some reason thought that they had until June—mid or late June, the date varied and was never exact—to get out of Vietnam. From April 19, Moorefield determined that he had ten days. So, from the beginning, even when a few planes late at night left half empty, Moorefield told himself that he was dealing with scarce resources: seats and time.

Believing that the process was not open-ended, he felt that giving seats to extended families of twenty to fifty people chewed up the seats for four or five or six tighter families.

Over and over again, he told the patriarch (or matriarch): "I cannot let a family of your size leave. It's not fair. You're going to have to leave some people behind. Leave behind a breadwinner or two—a couple of unmarried sons. Leave behind the most elderly. The unmarried sons will support them. Of course take out the ones most likely to get a job right away in the States."

Over and over again, the head of the family and his wife, or her husband—the small clutch of family decision makers in their forties and fifties—would say: "No, Mr. Moorefield, don't ask us to make those decisions. You make them for us."

And he did, day after day, ruthlessly, just as he told them he would, carving two economic entities out of the big family: one or more young men to stay behind to look after the old grandparents and old uncles and aunts, always making sure that a girl in her twenties with a good command of English and typing skills, or a young engineer exempted from the draft, went on to America with the late-middle-aged anchors of the family.

But they cried in the office. It wasn't combat, but it was working for a living, facing a family of thirty people and deciding after fifteen minutes that these twelve would stay behind, these eighteen go.

In combat, you had to play God, too. But you usually didn't have to look the guy in the eye.

IV

After the lunch at Ramuntcho's, I got on the Honda and drove to the compound of the United States Information Service. There was a short wait in the outer office, and then I was shown in to see Alan Carter, who was himself: glib and sensible, his features pleasant behind a trim gray beard. But harried. "Five minutes, David," he said. "That's all. It's been unbelievable."

I spoke to him first about Senator Hien, my former landlord. Carter said it was long past the time when he could see new people. "When I got home last night, about seven," he said, "there were a dozen of them waiting for me at the house. I think the last one left about eleven."

He accepted Mr. Hien's family list and my letter. As he showed me to the door, he complained mildly about demands some of the correspondents were making on the embassy. "Alan Dawson [the UPI bureau chief] called yesterday saying he wanted to start writing about the evacuation. We've been helping him get his own people out. And we haven't even started getting our own people out yet, the Vietnamese staff."

I nodded goodbye to the pretty girl on the long couch in the outer office and hoped her half-American baby girl would get her out, if that was what she wanted.

On this day and the next, I ran a few errands that in normal times I would have let slide. Without fully admitting it to myself, I was beginning to prepare for an end of some kind.

Leaving the USIS compound, I rode the few tree-shaded blocks in that pretty part of the capital north of the palace to the headquarters of Vietnam Press, the government news agency. There I picked up a copy of A Thousand Years of Vietnamese Poetry that Nguyen Ngoc Bich, the editor of the book and the director of the agency, had inscribed for me before he flew off to Washington in a last desperate bid to make the case for more aid to congressmen and, more frequently, to their staffers. The inscription read: "To Dave Butler—as a living proof that there are more things to link an American and a Vietnamese souls than 'the war.'"

I had a cup of coffee with some soldiers at a little stall in the parking area of the agency's villa, showing them the book and trying to explain to them what it was—Vietnamese poetry in English translation, published in America for Americans. "Three more months," I said to myself forlornly. "Three more months and I could pull off this conversation."

So little fighting was reported at the afternoon military briefing that I felt compelled to do a spot that raised two possibilities. Either the communists had taken so much so fast that they needed time now to consolidate their gains, or they had ordered a battlefield lull to allow the political process in Saigon to play itself out. I hoped the second possibility was true—that they really would be willing to talk to Big Minh, and the offensive would end and Saigon would return to normal. But as I trotted down the five flights of stairs from the office to the ground-level arcade of the Eden Building, I acknowledged that I hadn't the slightest idea what the communists' real intentions were.

I was on my way to the terrace of the Continental Palace Hotel. But as I turned to the blaring sunlight in the mouth of the arcade, I saw my doctor silhouetted in the sunlight.

"Here," Dr. Loan said, "here," taking me tightly by the elbow, a breach of etiquette, to turn me to the plate-glass front of an Indian's necktie shop. "Don't look at me," he said. "Look at the ties."

Through the last few weeks, Dr. Loan had been treating me for a rash. He would hurry through the examinations so that we could sit at his desk and talk politics.

Dr. Loan had fought with the Viet Minh for ten years but then had joined the wrong side and became close to Thieu. He had since fallen out of favor at the palace, but the communists might not take that opposition into account.

He was also the first and only Vietnamese for whom I actually arranged a face-to-face interview with Alan Carter. Now, as we played out the charade that we were a Vietnamese and a Westerner examining neckties in an Indian's shop, Dr. Loan thanked me for that service. But from the beginning there had been a tentativeness about Loan's plans.

"Have you decided to leave?" I asked.

"Now I am trying to do what your presidents talk about," Dr. Loan said. "I try to keep open my options."

"This is my day for comic melodrama," I thought. "Movie producers who create ad campaigns calling people to witness the death of a society, subtle North Vietnamese physicians still trying to keep open their options."

I was aware that the business about pretending to examine the neckties could be a scene in a bad thriller, but never before having lived through a bad thriller gave Dr. Loan and myself the benefit of the doubt, and we took it all seriously.

I knew of Dr. Loan through Garrick Utley, the first NBC bureau chief, who had returned to Saigon in the middle of the offensive for a brief stay. "Garrick Utley came and went so quickly this time," Dr. Loan was saying now. "He is the only one who knew what I did for NBC."

"The new boss up there is named Arthur Lord," I said. "He is a good man. Talk to him. Now he may have even more power than Alan Carter."

"Thank you, Mr. Butler," Dr. Loan said.

"It's nothing," I said in French, thinking it was all not nothing, but absurd.

v

Early Wednesday evening in New Orleans, President Ford stood before several thousand students in the field house of Tulane University to deliver a speech that had been scheduled months before.

The crucial two sentences had been inserted in the speech just that afternoon. "America can regain the sense of pride that existed before Vietnam," the President said. "But it cannot be achieved by refighting a war that is finished as far as America is concerned."

The students broke into a roar of approval at the word "finished" and drowned out the rest of the sentence.

In Can Tho, as they learned of the Ford speech on BBC broadcasts on Thursday, a VNAF major turned to the CIA officer he had been working with. In the final weeks, they had thrown up a new perimeter of fencing around the billets of the chopper pilots, and installed showers so that they wouldn't have to leave the base to go to their homes in the city—all in preparation for the city's final defense.

"Okay," the major said dryly. "No more gas. No more supplies for all our American equipment. If we'd known this was going to come nineteen years ago, we could have saved a lot of lives."

That same Thursday, David Sciacchitano and Averill Christian were in Saigon. Christian was the Can Tho consulate's administrative officer. For a month now, Sciacchitano had been acting full time as its consular officer, drawing people into Can Tho from the outlying provinces and moving them from there to Saigon.

They flew to Saigon early that morning on an Air America plane, walked through the Air America terminal and were met by a friend who drove them through Dodge City. The first surprise was when half the girls from Ben Xe Moi,* Can Tho's red-light district, waved gaily at them from their place in the waiting crowds. The second surprise was more general. They were amazed to discover both the scope and the rules of the evacuation.

Sciacchitano went up to the main processing center and talked to some of the Americans there. It quickly became clear to him that the whole system had nothing to do with the few pathetic busloads of local employees they had sent up from the delta. Everyone who left had to have a sponsor. Further inquiries and travel around the city revealed that the people they had sent up from Can Tho were all grouped in various USAID hotels, with promises that they would be seen to eventually.

Sciacchitano and Christian managed to get a few minutes with George Jacobson. He seemed to Sciacchitano to be divorced from reality. "Nothing's going to happen to your people," he said. "There's not going to be any bloodbath. We'll get you out. Stop worrying about the locals."

On his way back through Tan Son Nhut, Sciacchitano stopped at Dodge City and talked someone into giving him a hefty stack of the improvised forms that had suddenly become the tickets out of the country for thousands of Vietnamese. Back in Can Tho, he explained to Consul General Terry McNamara that whatever the plan might be in Saigon, the locals they had already sent there were clearly low on the totem pole. He also gave about half of his blank marriage, adoption and sponsorship forms to the number-two spook.

They were little more than half a day in Saigon. But the whole experience—the crowds at Dodge City, the meeting with Colonel Jacobson and the fact that nothing tangible was being done for the people they had sent up—caused both Sciacchitano and Christian to change their minds about McNamara's river evacuation. On the way back to Can Tho, the two officers discussed the idea that if they depended on Saigon at the end, even *they* might not get out.

VI

Richard Peters, the consul general, and Charlie Lahiguera, his deputy, closed the consulate in Bien Hoa without incident that day. In the previous weeks, every piece of paper in the consulate had either been shipped to Washington or burned. Even the teletype machines had been removed. There would be nothing for the communists to find.

They weren't completely certain that they were closing it. On the

* Pronounced Bahn Seh Muoi, and meaning bus stop new.

off chance that there would be negotiations leading to some sort of skeletal U.S. mission, they carefully locked the consulate buildings. And they left the flag flying.

Over the past few weeks, Lahiguera had had primary responsibility for evacuating all American citizens and their dependents, as well as those Vietnamese employees and their families who wished to leave. They were moved from the provinces surrounding Saigon that made up Military Region 3 into the capital itself. Then the Americans and their dependents, at least, were evacuated out of the country through Dodge City.

Lahiguera was extremely irritated with a nun from New Zealand who left once and then returned and had to be evacuated again. He was aware, as he told the nun, that there was a finite number of seats out of Vietnam. Now she had taken two of them.

As a rule, he had few problems with the Americans. A few missionaries chose not to leave, as did a young American who worked at the Bien Hoa mental hospital. And there were a few retired contractors who hung around for the bars and the girls and just couldn't face up to the fact that the party was over. But Lahiguera satisfied himself that every American in MR 3 was given ample warning and opportunity to evacuate himself and his Vietnamese dependents.

Evacuating the local employees was trickier. It wasn't clear until close to the end how many would be allowed to leave, and what the escape route would be. The consulate had a large USAID contingent. The Americans in that agency got it in their minds that the evacuation was to be by boat from Vung Tau, and went there with those of their employees who wanted to leave.

But in the last few days, word had come from Saigon that the local employees would be leaving by air, from Tan Son Nhut. Lahiguera relayed that news to the AID people in Vung Tau, and all of them, along with the other local employees of the consulate who wished to leave, were taken to the USAID 2 compound in Saigon.

At night, the dwindling core of Americans in Bien Hoa would repair to their small club/restaurant and sit around the piano, which one of them played. It was like the end of any long party. They drank and sang the tensions away. A ballad of the time called "Tomorrow Belongs to Us" was a favorite.

Finally, on Thursday, with the communists in easy striking range, it was time to go. Peters, Lahiguera, and the few other Americans, including several Marines, got into four vehicles with their walkie-talkies and drove off to Saigon. The flag flew, and the consulate buildings remained guarded by the mostly old men who made up the guard contingent. They had never been urged to leave, and didn't seem to want to.

Lahiguera and the other Americans were put up in an American-leased apartment building from which most of the tenants had left. If you didn't like what the previous tenant had left in his freezer, you got the keys for the apartment next door and checked that one. Lahiguera and his friends rummaged from apartment to apartment until they found shirts that fit, the makings of small bars from the stocks of their departed colleagues—who would surely prefer that they use all this detritus than that it be liberated. At times, it reminded Lahiguera of *On the Beach,* and all the other post-World War III movies where a handful of people are left in a deserted city.

VII

I read the Saigon *Post* on the terrace. For weeks, there had been brief exhortations to austerity and heroism in boxes of asterisks in the bottom corners of the front page. The message that day reflected the new circumstances, the emphasis on negotiations. "MILITARY AID WILL HASTEN THE END OF THE PRESENT CONFLICT," it said. "IT WILL BOOST THE POSITION OF SOUTH VIETNAM TO REACH A POLITICAL SETTLEMENT WITH THE OTHER SIDE." And the struggle to form a government that the communists might talk to had put the censors out of work; there were no white holes in the columns of print.

Recently the paper had carried a number of lengthy letters signed "An American in Vietnam," or "An American Who Loves Vietnam," or "Betrayed," in which the writers railed at Congress for refusing additional aid. They were so clumsily done that I assumed they were the ramblings of the drunken contract workers they appeared to be and not of the CIA. I had started to read the latest one ("To an American taxpayer who has spent half his adult life in Southeast Asia and the Far East and never as a military man—it appears the current situation in South Vietnam could be solved if Congress would give the Vietnamese the equipment to cut the head of the Frankenstein and bomb Hanoi and destroy KNOWN North Vietnamese supply, ammo and fuel depots in South Vietnam, Laos, Cambodia, North Vietnam . . .") when Dennis Troute joined me.

"Thank God," I said.

"What have you been up to?" Troute asked as he turned to signal a waiter. It was as if we hadn't seen each other for days.

"I spent most of the morning listening to Vietnamese I don't know telling me why they have to get out," I said.

"It's getting bad," Troute said. He opened my paper to the classified ads, pointed to one of them and said, "Did you see this one?"

"No," I said.

Fairly pretty high-school girl, 18, holder of the Baccalaureate degree, piano player, of well-to-do family, seeks adoption by or marriage with foreigner of American, French, British, German or other nationality who would take her abroad legally to enable her to continue her college studies outside Vietnam at her own expense.

Please telephone . . .

" 'Fairly pretty,' " I said. "God, it's sad. She's probably a raving beauty."

VIII

At eight-thirty that evening, Nguyen Van Hao went on television to tell people not to flee.

Hao was the bright young technocrat who had sounded out Denny Ellerman, the U.S. Embassy's recently arrived economics counselor, on Thieu's plan to truncate the country a few days after Thieu had decided on it.

"We must keep firm, be quiet and disciplined," he said. "No one should flee. As an example, I pledge that I and my family will stay."

IX

Dennis Troute pleaded work to turn down my invitation to join me in the Pink Night Club. I drove to it and stayed late.

Tung Giang was sure that Anh Tu and his family had made it into Tan Son Nhut and the evacuation process that afternoon. Again the orphan boy was sent out to buy a Vietnamese supper for me, and as we had the night before, Tung Giang and I drank beers from the aluminum steins and talked.

I putt-putted up Tu Do Street to my apartment at about midnight, and didn't see a single sign of life.

It was warm that night. I tossed cushions from the couch in the living room onto the balcony, wrapped myself in a sheet and a light blanket and lay down on the cushions. And every fifteen or twenty minutes for as long as I was awake, which seemed to be more than an hour (and even afterward, for there were periods of near wakefulness), I would hear the drone of a plane and look up and the shape would break black from the black roof. I tracked them in their eastward course across the bright night clouds, wondering with each if it was the one that held Tu and his family.

25

Friday

No matter how much work was crammed into the curfew-shortened
days, or, strangely, even how much drinking followed, I like everyone I knew was up very close to sunrise every day now, as if sleep
were a waste.

I had a favorite uncle who had served in Vietnam in the early
1950s, a young U.S. Air Force lieutenant in a liaison job with the
French Air Force. A few months before, the uncle had sent me
two copies of a *Life*-style magazine from the period called *Indochine
d'aujourd'hui*. Now, on Friday morning, I set out early for the half-
hour ride into Cholon. Traffic was still light, and the air on my face
fresh and a little chilly with the speed. The city was calm and bright
under a spring sky ringed with teasing clouds. I drove to the shop
of a man who bound books for Charlie Benoit. It was an excuse for
a ride on the Honda; and I knew that my uncle would be pleased to
have the magazines returned in hard covers.

I picked out a green cardboard binding and told the man that I
would return for the magazines on Monday or Tuesday. In building
traffic and the heat that came with the rising sun and slower progress,
I proceeded to Pasteur Street, parked the Honda in the gutter and

sat at a sidewalk stall for the morning's second breakfast: *café sua**
and a croissant and a *thom xay*—pineapple and crushed ice whipped
and frothed with sugar in an Osterizer.

The air had its morning smell, mixing coffee and the smells of
flowers and fruits, still a touch of freshness; but under it already a
cut of decaying fruit and vegetables, and the kerosene fumes. Later,
in the heat, the fumes and the rot would prevail.

Ten feet away, at the corner of Le Loi, a woman was setting out
her PX wares on a wooden tripod with narrow removable shelves. She
was about fifty, with the look of a once arrogant woman reduced by
circumstances to bitter resignation.

She had positioned the tripod so that it did not quite block passage
into the restaurant at the corner, and lined its shelves mostly with
American cigarettes and jars of Nescafé and Cheese Ritz. She also had
a single jar of Aqua Velva after-shave lotion. For a full three minutes,
as I sat sipping my coffee, she tried to determine how best to display
the pretty blue bottle, switching it now from a place near the Salems
up to the row of Nescafé, turning it this way and that, as a fussy
housewife after she has dusted will fret with a precious photograph
on a crowded mantel.

Ten minutes later, at one of the photo kiosks on Nguyen Hue
Boulevard, I dropped off a roll of black-and-white photos I had shot
on the trips out toward Xuan Loc with Don Harris. I told the man
that I would pick up the negatives and contact sheet on Monday.

II

God, it all happened so fast now.

The previous Saturday, April 19, Captain Do Duc Cuong and a
few hundred men were flown north from Vung Tau to Phan Thiet,
on the coast, which was coming under artillery fire.

Half an hour after they landed, Cuong was wounded, a three-inch
shard of shrapnel knifing through his boot an inch into his left foot.
Men in the company he had commanded so briefly carried him the
few kilometers back to the air base and left him on the tarmac. When
two hours had passed, and many planes and helicopters had taken off
without him, Cuong began to get concerned. He didn't know what
to do, because he couldn't walk and people were ignoring his calls for
attention. Finally, after a few rounds landed on the periphery of the
small base itself, a big red-haired American civilian squatted like a
Vietnamese next to him and said, "Hey, buddy, looks like you got
a problem. We better get you outta here." The American—something
he said led Cuong to think he was a helicopter mechanic—picked him

* Strong coffee lightened with sweetened condensed milk from a can.

up and carried him onto a white Air America plane crowded with a few Americans and many Vietnamese.

After the short flight to Bien Hoa, the American carried him for fifteen minutes from the flight line to the base hospital, stopping a couple of times along the way for Cuong to get directions.

Doctors pulled out the shrapnel and dressed the wound. The next morning Cuong discovered to his surprise that he could walk.

He walked out of the hospital and hitched a ride to number 9 Nguyen Binh Khiem Street. Now he didn't find Colonel Nhon, or any of the officers he had seen on the earlier visit. He didn't know if Colonel Nhon had run away, but obviously many officers had left. Nevertheless, Cuong found another colonel. He explained what had happened to him and asked where he should go next.

"Let me understand this correctly," the officer said. "You just came today from the hospital at Bien Hoa, and yesterday you were wounded in Phan Thiet."

"Yes," Cuong said.

The colonel looked at him oddly, as if Cuong might be lying. "You know that we lost Phan Thiet last night," he said.

"No, I didn't know," Cuong said. "It's happening too fast now."

"Yes," the colonel agreed. After a pause he asked if Cuong had any family in Saigon.

"My brother," Cuong said, "a wounded veteran. We are Quang Ngai people. I don't know where my parents are. And I have no money. Where can I go to get my pay?"

"People are running away," the colonel said. "They go to America. Did you know that?"

"The soldiers talk about it," Cuong said.

"Yes," the colonel said. "Your pay. The payroll office is all gone. No one to sign the forms. But you want to fight?"

"Yes," Cuong said.

"You can go to America."

"What?"

"You can go to America, maybe. I have some passes."

"Buffalo s - - -," Cuong said.

"Okay," the colonel said. "It's Sunday. Maybe some of the officers will come back tomorrow. Come back and see me tomorrow, here. Now, if I were you I would find my brother."

"Okay," Cuong said.

Cuong's older brother had lost an arm in a battle in the delta in 1964, and was retired on a small disability pension. He lived with his wife and children in two mean rooms on the northern outskirts of the city.

Cuong asked the colonel for 250 piasters so he could take a *cyclo-pousse* there. "Really a loan between us," the colonel said as he handed over the money.

"Yes," Cuong said, not knowing where he would get any money if the payroll office was really gone.

Cuong's father had in fact survived the night of November 5, 1963, and was at the brother's house. He had left Quang Ngai at the same time that Cuong left Hue, and they had traveled south in loose tandem without meeting.

"The situation is very bad now," Cuong's father said. Cuong agreed. But he told his father that of course the Army had to stand to defend Saigon and the delta.

His father had managed to accumulate some money over the years and to bring it south. Cuong took a bit of it in the morning, found the colonel, repaid him, and asked where he could go to fight.

"I found someone from MR 1 who knows you," the colonel said. Cuong asked, but it wasn't Colonel Nhon. "Obviously you were a good officer," the colonel went on. "But you know the kind of work we do, Captain Cuong. You know we are the first ones the communists will kill."

"Sure," Cuong said.

The colonel then produced a pass with a code number—E2—on it and the address of some villa near the American Embassy. If Cuong presented himself there tomorrow morning, the colonel explained, a bus would take him and others gathered at the villa to Tan Son Nhut. A day or two later, they would be flown to a place the colonel pronounced as Goo-am. "It's an island in the Pacific that belongs to the Americans," the colonel said. "You don't stay on the island, you go to America."

Cuong made a short speech. "All my father's life," he said, "he fought—first against the French and then against the communists. Now for eight years I've fought them too, to try to keep freedom for this part of the country. We don't go anywhere." He tore up the pass and turned to leave.

"Good luck," the colonel said.

At eight o'clock that evening, Cuong and his father and brother sat around a radio and listened to President Thieu resign.

"It's crazy," his father said. "Everyone signs the Paris agreement: America, France, the U.N. Now the communists pull it down. Why doesn't anyone help us?"

"What do we do now?" Cuong asked.

"We must become new people," his father said. "We find another place to live, in the countryside. We get new identification papers, a new family certificate."

Cuong knew just the place. The next day, he and his father traveled to an isolated, heavily Catholic village several miles west of Vung Tau. Two days later, for a low price, they bought the house of a police colonel. He would not be around to help them with the creation of the false papers, but advised them whom to approach.

Cuong spent one night in the new house and then took a bus and walked on foot back to the war. He joined three companies of Airborne soldiers and a few Marines—about eighty men—setting up a defense at a bridge northwest of Vung Tau. The group was commanded by an Airborne major. The major took orders from no one. He had given up on his commanders. All he wanted to do was position himself at a point the communists would have to pass and kill them.

When Cuong found them, he showed the major his military identification card. The major said, "Good," and told him where to get a weapon.

Cuong never knew his name.

It was Friday, April 25, the second day of a lull in the fighting that lasted almost until the end. Cuong spent the next four days quietly, patrolling the area, watching his new comrades string the bridge with explosives and forcing images from his mind.

III

At noon that Friday, Tung Giang came to the NBC office.

"I don't know what I can do," I said. "I don't know how to get people out."

"Talk to George," the young musician said.

I had talked to George Esper about Tung Giang the day before. Esper had said that he was doing what he could. "But tell him that if we get him out I can't give him any money. I can't guarantee him. He's going to be on his own. He asked me for two thousand dollars the other day. I don't have it, David. You don't know what this thing has done to me. I'm not only broke, I'm in the hole."

Esper had a temper. One night early in the offensive he went into a rage at the two Vietnamese left in the office about a missed shipment of film out of Tan Son Nhut. He bellowed, and tried to check it, and then bellowed again. He was very nearly out of control, I thought; I thought that Esper might die in front of me, that the muscles in his heart or the vessels in his head would explode with the pressure. But as the offensive built, as Esper stopped shaving for days at a time and the story was page one, urgent, bulletin, every day, all day long, as he continued to run the swollen office and at the same time moved out not only Vietnamese AP employees and their families but also personal friends and acquaintances from his years in Saigon, an extraordinary thing happened: He became calm, easy.

I looked at Tung Giang, picked up the phone and dialed. "George," I said, "I've got to talk to you for forty-five seconds, in your office." Despite the new calmness, I squinted, waiting for Esper to shout "F - - -!" in my ear. Instead, Esper said sure, come on down.

Esper wrote with everybody else in the bullpen, where he could hit every button on every phone: monitor the office; monitor all of non-communist Vietnam. Once in the battle for Quang Tri in 1972 he reached a Vietnamese commander in a tank on Route 1 for a quick field report. I lifted my chin to indicate that I wanted to talk in the bureau chief's private office.

"George," I said, "this is the last time I'll mention Tung Giang's name to you, I promise. He wants out. I don't blame him. The girl left last week. I can't do anything. What can I tell him?"

"Where is he now?" Esper asked.

"Upstairs."

"Tell him to wait," Esper said. "He just waits right there. We may do it today. But don't promise him anything."

"When?"

"Maybe an hour from now. Maybe five hours from now. Do you have any money?"

"I could give him twenty bucks," I said.

"Jesus," Esper said. "I don't know what they think they're going to do over there."

I went upstairs and told Tung Giang he had fifteen minutes to get whatever he needed. "I don't know if it's going to happen or not," I said. "George is working on something. He wants to help you. Go home and get what you can, one small bag, but be back here in fifteen minutes."

Fifteen minutes later I stood amid the dry dog turds in the open-air corridor outside the NBC office, Tung Giang approaching from one direction with a flat black Samsonite briefcase and Esper from the other.

Esper was rushed now but still calm. "Get him out to the airport," he said. "Go to the restaurant upstairs above the departure lounge. You know where I mean?"

"Yeah."

"Domestic departures. Get him there, and, Mouse, you just wait there. No matter how long it is, you just stay there."

"Okay," Tung Giang said gravely.

"How can I get him through the gate?" I asked. "I'm sorry, George, I don't know s - - - about all of this. You've been doing it for weeks."

"Take one of the cabs from the Caravelle," Esper said. "Tell the guards at the gate you're meeting an Air Vietnam flight. Tell them anything. Just get him in. I tell you, Dave, I can't do it myself right now."

Mr. Khi and Arthur Lord both told me that we wouldn't make it. I asked for documents I could wave at the guards. Khi gave me an out-of-date airport press pass. I told them that I had an open Air Vietnam ticket, Saigon to Phnom Penh, back in the apartment. They told me to get it.

Tung Giang came with me as we rode up to the apartment to get the air ticket, and then we walked quickly across the plaza between the National Assembly and the little park that contained the Marines Statue to the big cars in front of the Caravelle, the overpriced taxis I had never before had to take.

We got into a white '58 Chevy. A blue plastic plaque with BAO CHI and PRESS lettered in white on it was fixed to the lower right-hand corner of the windshield. It clattered to the floorboards before we got to the cathedral. The fat driver stuck it back in place as he maneuvered slowly through the traffic and it dropped off again on Pasteur Street. Tung Giang talked to the driver in quick, soft sentences with minutes for calculation between each question, a desperate, calm young man trying to anticipate his fate. The "press pass" fell again as we entered Cach Mang, with its rows of bars and massage parlors and cheap tailor shops leading to the airport, and I hunched low into the hot white-covered cushion of the back seat and cursed it.

Even in normal times, the main gate into Tan Son Nhut was a place of fear. It was a checkpoint, a cops' place. And it was a place where all but the privileged had to switch between whatever transportation they used to get there and the scooters inside the air base, a hustlers' place. That morning, the long, triangular piece of littered ground between the entry and exit roads, the space just forward of the billboard that read "THE NOBLE SACRIFICE OF ALLIED SOLDIERS WILL NEVER BE FORGOTTEN," was crowded with people. The driver eased over to the side of the entry road well short of the checkpoint. More back and forth, and then Tung Giang told me that the driver couldn't get through even if we put Tung Giang in the trunk.

"You mean the goddamn guy doesn't even have the papers to get an American journalist in?" I asked.

"Nothing," Tung Giang said.

"Tell him to try anyway," I said. "F - - - it."

We eased forward and a VNAF guard waved us over. I leaned out the window and said, "NBC. Come on, I come out here every day. I'm just picking up an American."

The guard shook his head and turned his back on us.

The driver moved thirty yards down the exit road and nosed into a tangle of cars and small trucks and people.

"I see a friend," Tung Giang said. He went off to talk to his friend, and I waited, leaning against the trunk of the car, convinced that I had failed.

Tung Giang came back and said he thought he could get in. I asked him how. "My friend," Tung Giang said.

I asked the driver again through Tung Giang if the man could get me in alone. No again. I gave the man less than he had received for a ride to the airport in at least a year and turned my back on him, moved away.

Tung Giang gave me his briefcase. "Okay," I said. "You know where the restaurant is, right? *Domestic Air Vietnam*, like you were taking a plane to My Tho. Or Da Nang, before. I don't see how the f - - - you're going to do it, but I'll get in somehow, and I'll wait there for five hours." I looked at my watch. "I'll wait until at least seven, okay?"

"Okay," Tung Giang said.

I was not at all sure that I could walk into the base. On either side of the open but guarded entrance road there were booths, one for THE RIDERS on the left and the other for THE WALKERS. Now the anger was building. I did what any American in Vietnam did when he was angry. I assumed a look that said, "Don't tread on me or I'll shoot you, you little motherf - - - - -," and did whatever I pleased. I walked down the middle of the entrance road, looking straight ahead and bored but a little angry. There were shouts behind me as soon as I crossed the plane of the gate. I picked up my pace a little. *"Right between the shoulder blades,"* I said to myself, and the shouts continued but then I was almost at the Hondas. I got on the closest one, exercising great will not to run the last few steps to it, the shouts dying off, I thought, but still concerned enough to whisper in the boy's ear as I straddled the pillion of the machine, "Air Vietnam, *di, di,* go, go, man, come on, *di, di* this f - - - - -' thing," using language that I had never before used with a Vietnamese, and the little Honda 50 putt-putted up past Pentagon East to the terminal.

I needed a beer. I was happy to be in an air-conditioned place where I could sit down and have a beer and look down to the planes on the apron, and study the tables of Vietnamese all around me and maybe have more than one beer, maybe have half a dozen. I had half an hour, I told myself, before I had to start believing that Tung Giang was not going to make it.

Several tables along one wall had been pushed together for a party of a dozen Vietnamese adults and about an equal number of children. I had never seen the refugee-crowded bowling alley at Dodge City, but had heard about it. I had not realized that some Vietnamese in the evacuation had access to the restaurant. These people were cheery, unhurried, waiting out their last hours in Saigon over beer and coffee and Cokes. After seeing the crowd at the gate, it was reassuring to discover that some corner of the escape process was possessed of order and ease. Anything normal was a relief from the general breakdown, in the same way that a touch of disorder had always been welcome in all the other ordered months of my life.

I watched the edge of the partition that screened the room from its entrance. Twice there were young men with Tung Giang's height and shape. The beer helped. I lost much of the agitation I had felt in the car.

After an hour, I went to the two phones at the cashier's station. It took half a dozen tries on one of them to figure out that it was never going to connect to a line off the base. As soon as I hung up either phone, someone would take it. And I had to call NBC to get the AP number. But finally I got through to the bureau and asked for Esper.

"He's gone," an American on the other end said.

"Well if he comes back, tell him that David Butler is in the restaurant, but he's alone. Tung Giang . . . tell him that I'm here alone and our friend is out at the gate trying to get in. He should look for our friend at the gate."

Tung Giang touched me on the shoulder.

"Correction, correction," I shouted into the phone. "We're both here now. Tell him that we're both here. There are two of us waiting for him in the restaurant."

Tung Giang had found the empty table with his briefcase and my camera case on a chair. There was an older man with him: late thirties, beefy, civilian clothes, and the look, furtive and arrogant at once, of a cop or a hustler. As we sat down, I shook Tung Giang's hand. The young musician smiled for the first time.

"Jesus, how did you do it?" I asked.

"My friend told me what to do," Tung Giang said. "This isn't my friend, but he's the one who helped me. I ought to give him some money."

"Yes," I said. "How much?"

"Maybe five thousand."

For the last few days, less than five dollars. I suggested that the stranger and I go to the men's room. The man followed a few steps behind me. I made the payoff and we returned to the table. The man finished half his beer and left.

Most of the guards, the men whom I had thought might just conceivably stop me with a shot, were on the right. There was a guard-house on the left as well. Tung Giang's friend told him to go there and to tell the officials that he was in the Air Force up north and had just reached Saigon and needed housing. Tung Giang watched the operation for most of an hour, saw that it was routine, and did as he was instructed. As soon as he got the first couple of sentences of the story out, the man I had given the five thousand piasters to suddenly materialized, and Tung Giang slipped onto the back of the Honda and they drove in.

It was an all-Vietnamese operation. All I had done was to give Tung Giang a taxi ride to the gate. But I was filled with enormous relief that Tung Giang was where Esper had told him to be, that the mission hadn't failed in my stage. I found myself uncharacteristically chain-smoking and drinking beer as if it were water.

Tung Giang needed something from the briefcase. He opened it, and said: "A shirt, a toothbrush, one picture."

I propped the Sony's microphone on an empty Coke bottle and we talked for a little more than an hour.

Then on the tape: "Chiang! Chiang!" Esper's pronunciation of Giang's name—and then, louder, a command: "Mouse! Mouse! Come along!"

Esper was standing just inside the partition near the top of the stairs, and looked bigger than ever. He was frantic to get Tung Giang's attention, but didn't move into the room; all the motion was in place.

Tung Giang rose as if a hand lifted him from the chair, but smoothly. I looked down at Giang's sunglasses on the table. "Okay, okay. See you later, my friend. Take your briefcase . . . and here, your glasses." Tung Giang turned back for the briefcase and glasses. I reached across the table to grab Giang's flimsy Windbreaker from the back of his chair and tossed that to him.

"Bye-bye, Giang, good luck."

One of the rules in the last couple of weeks was never to cry in front of Vietnamese. I broke it a couple of times. On the tape there's a few seconds of distant chatter, and ice clinking in glasses, and then I had put my head down on my arms.

Late in the afternoon, as I was crossing Tu Do from the Eden Building to the terrace of the Continental, I saw Esper in the AP car. Esper slowed, tried to edge to the curb, rolled down his window and shouted: "Did you give him the twenty bucks?"

"I forgot," I said. "I was taping him. Is he okay?" Esper had to move, horns blaring behind him. He smiled and made a gesture with his free hand of a plane taking off.

After the beers at the airport, I had several cups of coffee at the office and did a couple of spots. I decided I was sober. I would have a drink on the terrace and then go home and change for a cocktail party that evening.

As was my habit, I patted the pockets of my white pants just before I sat down. There was more metal than usual in the pocket where I kept my keys and change, and instantly I remembered. Tung Giang had given me a kind of custody of the Pink Night Club. I laid the new bunch of keys on the table and ordered the drink.

I had the drink and then walked down to what had so recently been the Pink Night Club and now was the Pink Night Café. Giang's old father at the cash register and I communicated in broken French. Two nights before, Tung Giang had told me with pride that his father years ago had been a train conductor in Cambodia, a French civil servant. He was seventy-two and toothless. I told him what I knew: Tung Giang was either at Tan Son Nhut waiting for a flight out or already gone. The man turned just slightly away from me: dry, soft sobbing of an old man.

An honest old man. The April rent for the club, which I knew had not been paid, was what Tung Giang had told me in the car it would be, the equivalent that week of about thirty dollars. I gave the man enough piasters for the rent and the insignificantly few piasters required to buy the next day's beer supply. I handed over the set of keys and said that I would try to drop in every night to see how things were going. Tung Giang's father thanked me gravely and I left.

As I walked up Tu Do to the apartment building, I knew that I was by no means the owner of the Pink Night Café, only its bankroller, to the tune of eight or ten dollars a night. But I was amused at the symmetry of events: In collapse, Saigon giving me rough control over the room that had drawn me back to her in the first place. And I thought lucidly: "The collapse will freeze, reverse. Old Huong has *got* to resign. They'll talk to Big Minh, make a deal. Then the night life will return and it will again be the Pink Night Club, and I'll make a deal with Tung Giang's father and the Pink Night Club will make me rich."

IV

That afternoon, Nguyen Cao Ky addressed a rally of about five thousand people in a small city called Ho Nai, northeast of Bien Hoa on Highway 1. The city, whose name was an anagram of Hanoi, had been settled by northern Catholics who had fled south in 1954. There seemed to be a Catholic church on every other block.

Ky raged against the communists, the government and especially those who were fleeing. He heaped scorn on those who had left, saying they were cowards who had run away even before the fight.

"Where will they get *nuoc mam** over there?" he asked, meaning in the United States. "What can they do over there to make a living except become servants for the rich people?"

The crowd roared its approval.

V

The day before, Russell Mott had asked Hai† in the bar she worked in on Ben Bach Dang, the river road, if she wanted to leave. Hai said she wasn't sure; she would have to ask her parents.

Mott was fond of Hai. She wasn't straight from the rice field, but neither was she a hardened pro. She was, as he placed it, less than halfway through the progression. Mott had known her for about two years. She was one of the most beautiful women he knew in a country where he found many women beautiful.

On Friday afternoon, Hai told him yes, she wanted to leave. She would go alone.

Then she handed Mott a card with three or four names on it. She pointed to the first one. Of all the Americans she had known, he had been the kindest to her, she said.

Hai's English was limited, and so of course they spoke in Vietnamese. Mott discovered that the man was probably about fifty. Mott supposed that he had been in Vietnam as a contractor with PA&E‡ or one of the other construction firms. Hai had a phone number. Mott recognized the area code.

They repaired to the apartment Mott was staying in that day, and he made the call. By the time the call went through, Mott figured it was about 4 A.M. in Vermont.

He introduced himself calmly, emphasizing his official status: "Mr. ———," he said, "I'm calling from Saigon. My name is Russell

---

* A fish sauce used ubiquitously in Vietnamese cooking. Most Westerners found the smell of the stuff to be rank. The taste was quite different: a kind of salty sweetness.
† A pseudonym.
‡ Pacific Architects and Engineers.

Mott. I'm with USAID, and I've been here since 1968. I'm working on the evacuation of Vietnamese. I want you to know that I have no ulterior motives at all in making this call."

He had obviously waked the man, who said very little, only a word now and then as Mott continued. Mott sensed that the man was either choking or beginning to cry.

By the time Mott finished, the man had composed himself. He said: "Mr. Mott, you cannot imagine what this means to me. My wife died six months ago. Nothing would make my life more complete than for Hai to come to me."

Mott told the man in Vermont that Hai would be at Clark air base in the Philippines in the next twenty-four to forty-eight hours. He gave the man her Vietnamese ID number—adding that the Americans would undoubtedly give her another number.

"I'll get her out," Mott said. "But then you've got to pick up the ball. Call the Red Cross—or Catholic Relief Services—in Washington."

"I understand," the man said. "Don't worry. I'll find her. God. Thank you, Mr. Mott."

VI

Two days after Thieu resigned, the new president sent word to Martin that he would like to see him.

Whether or not Thieu meant it to be so, President Huong explained to Martin that Thieu's continued presence in Vietnam was making it difficult for him, Huong, to make any progress toward negotiations with the communists. Could the ambassador do something about it?

Martin asked Charlie Timmes and Polgar to see what could be arranged. Polgar remembered a DC-6 that had been used by Ellsworth Bunker when he was ambassador and which now stood empty.

Like all the three- and four-star South Vietnamese generals, Thieu had a villa in the compound of the Joint General Staff. There were other fairly secure homes around Saigon in which he could stay, and the last line of a long cable from Martin to Kissinger that left Saigon in the early hours of Thursday, April 24, reads: "Thieu is in bed here tonight, and I hope I can be in mine for a while."

On the afternoon of Friday, the twenty-fifth, Charlie Timmes drove to the villa of Thieu's former prime minister, Tran Thien Khiem, at JGS. Khiem called Thieu—at the palace, Timmes thought. Then Timmes himself spoke to Thieu. Yes, he would be willing to leave (for Taipei) that evening, if the security arrangements were tight, Thieu said. Timmes assured him that they were. He and Polgar had arranged with General Nguyen Khac Binh—still the chief of the National Police and the head of the South Vietnamese counterpart to the

CIA—for a police colonel with command presence to be at the main gate into Tan Son Nhut. American drivers would pick up Thieu, if he wished, and the others in his party, and take them to Khiem's villa at dusk. After drinks, they would be taken to a waiting plane.

The details were worked out. Thieu traveled from the palace in his own gray Mercedes. A party of twenty-two, most of them generals and colonels with only a few wives among them, gathered at the villa between seven and seven-thirty. Over the drinks—Scotch the overwhelming favorite—Timmes and Polgar filled out *laissez-passers* on a parole authority that the ambassador had obtained from Kissinger that afternoon.

CIA analyst Frank Snepp and two of his colleagues had been recruited as drivers. As they waited in the villa's grounds, several burly men lugged obviously heavy, large suitcases to the three cars that would make the run to the plane. Snepp heard the clunk of metal against metal as the bags were hauled into the trunks.

At about eight-thirty, Thieu and his entourage emerged from the villa and squeezed themselves into the three limousines. The lead car—carrying Polgar and Khiem among others—and the tail car were especially crowded, because Thieu and Timmes, with just two of Thieu's personal aides, rode in the second car, which Snepp drove. Thieu sat in the middle of the rear seat, with Timmes on his left and one of the aides on his right.

It seemed to Snepp that the ten-minute ride lasted forever. After Polgar had proposed the mission that afternoon, Snepp and his fellow drivers had amused themselves with reminders of the fate that had befallen Ngo Dinh Diem and his brother after the 1963 coup: bloody assassination in an armored car personnel carrier on the orders of Duong Van Minh. It was fun to spook themselves, but the possibility of a sudden roadblock and shots ringing out was real enough so that at least two of them, Snepp and one of his friends, had side arms under their seats.

Timmes and Thieu reminisced about their first encounter over a campfire in 1961. At some point, Timmes introduced Thieu to Snepp, with a compliment about the young CIA man's talents. Thieu asked Snepp where he was from. When Snepp answered that he had been raised in Charlotte, North Carolina, Thieu replied, "Yes, I've been there."

Despite the precaution of the insertion of the tough senior colonel at the gate, Timmes advised Thieu to duck his head as they moved through it. But the convoy of three limousines with diplomatic plates was waved through. Inside the air base, they switched their main headlights off, and traveled by the illumination of dim blue police-type lights mounted beside the main lights.

Graham Martin had been driven alone—that is, his driver, but no Marine bodyguards—directly to the plane. When he got to it, its interior lights were all on. He climbed on board and told the crew to douse them.

In the darkness, the three cars nearly collided as they drew to a stop at the plane. Carrying only briefcases, Thieu and Khiem and the other senior men walked smartly up the ramp, to be welcomed by Graham Martin. The younger aides followed with the heavy luggage.

Somewhat strangely, given what he had said about the Americans in his resignation speech, Thieu was almost profuse in his thanks to Martin for arranging the flight.

"It was the least I could do," Martin said. "Goodbye. Good luck."

Martin and Polgar went directly from Tan Son Nhut to a cocktail party the Poles were holding at their villa in the ICCS compound, which lay at the head of Ly Thai To Boulevard in the western reaches of the capital's residential district.

For ten or fifteen minutes, Martin worked the reception as if he did it every night of the week. Then, easily, he arranged a few minutes alone with the Polish ambassador, Ryszard Fijalkowski.

As Martin had hoped he would, Fijalkowski after the pleasantries expressed alarm at the huge American armada gathering offshore.

"We are all working for negotiations, an end to the fighting, Mr. Ambassador," Fijalkowski said. "Why do you need so much power to be displayed there?"

"I'm very glad you asked, Mr. Ambassador," Martin said. "I also note that now our intelligence detects many surface-to-air missiles close to Saigon. I hope you will tell your friends in Hanoi that if they interfere with our evacuation they will discover very quickly, in Hanoi, why the fleet is there."

VII

That evening, I came as close to meeting my country's last ambassador to Vietnam as I was ever to come in Saigon. I too was invited to the Poles' reception.

The clouds that had seemed harmless when I had driven this way in the morning to have my uncle's magazines bound weren't harmless after all, and Saigon late that afternoon had one of its first downpours of the early monsoon season. No thunder and lightning, but the sudden sheets of cooling rain. It didn't start until I had almost reached the ICCS compound, and was quickly over.

A map at the entrance showed the location of the four delegations. Puttering along in first gear on wet gravel, I circled the villa the Indonesians had occupied until their pullout earlier that week. Indonesians, Iranians, Poles and Hungarians. As I pulled up to the Poles' villa, thankful that there was space for the Honda under the portico, I thought of the constant debugging that must have gone on in that leafy park.

The Polish delegation's press attaché was a good public-relations man. He enjoyed giving bottles of good Polish vodka to Western journalists; if they wanted to open the bottle and share some of it with him—or offered some of their own Scotch or PX Remy Martin to sip over a comradely chat—he was pleased to accept. It was his job.

When I got to him, he was having a drink with Peter Collins of CBS and a couple of other American correspondents. "I never thought it would happen this way," he was saying. "So fast."

"You must be pleased," I said with a smile. The nearest other Poles were ten feet away, talking among themselves.

"Oh, yes," the man said. "But I thought there would be more talking, not so much fighting. Of course the Thieu regime had to collapse. And now perhaps we will have the talking."

"Perhaps not," Collins said.

"Everything will change," the Pole said. He looked at the other Poles, considered—and took the risk: "Everything will change." Now the tone of wistfulness was clear. It was the limit of his courage, and a rather daring limit at that. He realized he'd reached it: "Here, you need another vodka," he told me cheerfully, back in role.

When Peter Collins and I both wandered out of the reception early, we had no reason to think that we were doing anything but cutting short our attendance at a fairly interesting cocktail party to attend to more urgent pursuits. There was little precedent for the fact that our ambassador was about to show up.

Collins had a good, deep radio and TV voice, and views on the struggle in Vietnam considerably more conservative than those of most of his colleagues. (A blond, well-spoken American in his late twenties who was a committed anticommunist and an advocate of American military might was something of a rarity among American journalists in Saigon in 1975.)

In the portico, I offered Collins a ride back to the center of town on the back of the Honda.

"Thanks. I've got a car," Collins said. "I always have a car now, did you hear?"

"No."

"They made me a staff correspondent. Yesterday."

"Beautiful," I said, and shook Collins' hand.

"Thanks," he said. "I'm not all that pleased that it took the fall of South Vietnam to get it. But what the hell."

The rain was over, the sun on the horizon. Drinking in the smells of the washed city, the bright pastels of its buildings and the shimmering bronzes and golds of the still-wet streets in the late twilight, my feeling that I belonged to the city and possessed it in turn reached its climax. Knowing that it was absurd, I felt as I rode through that resplendent dusk that everything lay open and known to me.

I wondered how many more days I would have when each day was sweeter, richer and more terrifying than the day before, until something broke the world back to routine. I tried—and almost succeeded—not to speculate about the end.

A glimpse of the end came clear to me. It would all end, somehow, and then I would drown myself in the richness of Saigon—as a spectator, no obligation to NBC or to any other American news organization. I half allowed a vague image of mindless midnight joy in a darkened hotel room above the Pink Night Club, no muffled rocket and artillery explosions disturbing the peace, myself the proprietor of the prosperous Pink Night Club, shuttered and dark beneath me in a quasi-communist, permissive Saigon, Vietnam's version of Hong Kong.

Then I was quickly in the Tu Do Street tunnel into the Hotel Catinat that led to the back door of the Pink Night Café, which I now sort of owned, and I gladly, easily, let the fantasy go.

26

Saturday and Sunday

This was the week that Nguyen Van Hao found himself speaking on the phone every day with Denny Ellerman about South Vietnam's remaining gold reserves.

Early in the month, shortly after the fall of Da Nang, the governor of the central bank studied the possibility of transferring the remaining reserves—sixteen tons, worth about $120 million—to the Bank of International Settlements, in Switzerland. (It is not uncommon for small countries to keep their gold reserves in Switzerland, or in the vaults of the Federal Reserve Bank in New York.) The idea was that the gold would serve as collateral for arms purchases in the event of a final cutoff of all military aid from the United States.

It was more a study of options than a firm plan. But word of the study leaked, and the instantaneous assumption in the streets and cafés of Saigon was that Thieu was trying to smuggle the gold out of the country for himself. At that point, the charter airlines and insurers to whom the Vietnamese were talking backed off.

The U.S. Embassy then weighed in with the idea that the gold could go to New York. It would go out on a military plane, which solved the problem of finding a carrier. But there was a delay of a week or ten days before the State Department was able to arrange insurance. And during that delay, Thieu resigned.

Nguyen Van Hao was bright enough to see that in the new political atmosphere, with the sudden emphasis on negotiations, shipping out the nation's gold reserves might not be such a good idea after all.

Eight years later, he would claim that Thieu never said anything to him about the gold, and that he did not know either from the Americans or from the governor of the central bank that the gold was to be used to finance arms purchases. During that week, he says, he continually asked Denny Ellerman why the *United States* was so eager that the gold leave the country.

"Because it might be destroyed if there is a battle for Saigon," Ellerman would say, according to Hao.

Ellerman, who was fond of Hao and his small family, remembers the week differently. He claims that in lining up the plane and the insurance, the embassy was merely trying to expedite a South Vietnamese initiative.

There seems little question but that Martin—who was badgering the State Department with cables proposing Saudi loans to South Vietnam—wanted the gold out. As for Hao, who now immersed himself in the details of the transaction, he quickly came to believe that if the gold was on deposit with the Federal Reserve Bank, the U.S. government would have control over how it could be used. And during that week he rapidly came under the influence of the French, which meant that he anticipated the transfer of power to Big Minh. Ellerman was caught in the middle.

On Thursday, a few hours before he went on television to plead with fellow officials not to flee, Hao met with President Huong. He argued that if they shipped out the gold and then power was transferred to Minh, Minh could accuse them of treason.

Huong agreed. Hao called Ellerman and informed him of the president's decision.

Ellerman reported to Ambassador Martin, who asked for and was granted a meeting with Huong.

Martin briefed Ellerman on Saturday morning, saying that Huong had told him the gold could go. And that same morning the last impediment to the shipment was removed. The State Department cabled the embassy in Saigon saying that it had arranged insurance in the amount of $60,240,000 for "the shipment"—the cable traffic about the gold tried to avoid using the word "gold"—but added that "the firm's limit will be valid only if shipment leaves Saigon by 7 A.M. Saigon time April 27," which was the next day.

The gold still sat in the basement of the central bank. But it was crated, and the U.S. Embassy had laid on tight security measures for its transfer from the bank to Tan Son Nhut. The plane in which it would leave stood by at Clark Air Force base in the Philippines. Ellerman called Hao, assuming they would make the final arrangements.

"There's some misunderstanding, Mr. Ellerman," Hao said. "I'll call you back in five minutes."

Hao called President Huong. "I'm sorry," the old man said, as if he was at fault. "But that isn't what I told the ambassador. I told him the gold should stay here."

Hao called Ellerman. "I'm sorry, Mr. Ellerman," he said. "There really *has* been a misunderstanding. I just checked with the president. He says that he told the ambassador he does *not* approve of the plan." (On these final calls, Ellerman's and Hao's memories dovetail.)

Ellerman was a straight-thinking embassy officer, a former Marine. Someone sure as hell was lying, but he would give the benefit of the doubt to his ambassador, to whom he quickly reported.

Martin was unfazed. "Okay, it's up to them," he said. "Tell them the plane is standing by at Clark and we'll keep it there another twenty-four hours if they change their minds."

II

Martin had more pressing things on his mind than the damned gold that Saturday. He was still trying to take advantage of the fact that the South Vietnamese controlled the seaport town of Vung Tau, southeast of the capital.

TO CINCPAC FROM AMBASSADOR, DRAFTED BY AMB G. MARTIN/EK

1. I HAVE THOROUGHLY LOOKED INTO THE PROPOSALS INFORMALLY PUT TO YOU BY GENERAL SMITH TO USE TWO C-130 AIRCRAFT FOR THE MOVEMENT OF 250 RVN MARINE CORPS DEPENDENTS FROM VUNG TAU ON 27 APRIL.

2. I HAVE APPROVED THIS PLAN AND WOULD LIKE IT CARRIED OUT WITH CONSIDERABLE PRECISION. THIS IS A PERSONAL REQUEST FROM GEN. LAM, COMMANDING GENERAL OF THE MARINE DIVISION. HE HAS COMPLETE CONTROL OF AIRFIELD AT VUNG TAU. THESE DEPENDENTS WILL BE COMPLETELY PACKAGED INTO TWO LOADS. PREMANIFESTED, THE PLANES CAN LAND, LOAD, AND DEPART WITH ABSOLUTE MINIMUM GROUND TIME. THE [SOUTH VIETNAMESE AIR FORCE] ARE NOT PRESENT. THE REFUGEES IN VUNG TAU HAVE NOT THEREFORE CONCENTRATED AT AIRFIELD. GEN. LAM CAN THEREFORE GUARANTEE COMPLETE SAFETY FOR OPERATIONS.

3. THERE IS A CONSIDERABLE POLITICAL STAKE IN DOING THIS JOB WELL, WITH PRECISION AND SPEED. IT WILL BOTH SET A PRECEDENT AND ALSO BE A TEST CASE OF POSSIBLE USE OF VUNG TAU IN FUTURE

IF I CAN FEEL CONFIDENT GEN. LAM CAN PROVIDE NECESSARY PRO-
TECTION.

4. THROUGH OTHER CHANNELS WE HAVE INCREASING EVIDENCE
THAT HANOI HAS GIVEN TACIT ACQUIESCENCE TO PERMITTING EVACUA-
TION OPERATIONS TO CONTINUE UNINTERRUPTED WHILE THE POLITI-
CAL EVOLUTION IS SAIGON CONTINUES IN WAY THEY DEEM FAVORABLE.
THEREFORE, ALTHOUGH THE UNDOUBTED CAPACITY EXISTS TO INTER-
DICT OR EVEN TAKE VUNG TAU, I THINK THERE IS A GOOD CHANCE THEY
WILL NOT USE THAT CAPACITY. THIS OPERATION, WHICH I AM CERTAIN
CAN BE DONE WITH COMPLETE SAFETY, WILL GIVE US ADDITIONAL EVI-
DENCE OF THEIR INTENTIONS AS WE SEE HOW THEY REACT AFTER THE
FACT.

5. UNLESS YOU SEE SOME OBJECTIONS NOT APPARENT TO US HERE,
WE WILL NOTIFY GENERAL LAM THAT WE WILL LOAD AT A PRECISE
HOUR AND PLAN TO BE IN AND OUT IN ABOUT THIRTY MINUTES.
MARTIN.

III

French Ambassador Mérillon and his aide Pierre Brochand were still
shuttling between Huong and Big Minh, but Brochand thought that
they might well be too late. He called Thomas Polgar in the middle of
the day on Saturday and confided his gloom. "They played around too
long," the French intelligence man said. "I think we might not even
get a negotiated surrender." This time Polgar, who was now fully committed to the Big Minh solution, argued with his counterpart, putting
positive interpretations on the latest communist statements. As Brochand put down the phone, he thought to himself, "Now Polgar is
more of a believer than I am in our own game."

IV

In that last full week, the week when Mérillon was meeting daily and
sometimes twice daily with President Huong, Nguyen Van Hao also
saw Huong frequently. At each meeting he urged the old schoolteacher
to press Mérillon to explain in detail why he was so sure that if power
was transferred to Big Minh the communists would negotiate.

"Mr. President," Hao said at one such meeting, "you must ask him
whom he is talking with on the other side. Of course they have the
embassy in Hanoi. Do they talk to anyone in the Politburo? Does he
talk to someone who can give us a guarantee?"

"He won't say about the communists," Huong said wearily. "But he
says that Giscard* is the guarantee."

That was the week that the politicians of Saigon were paralyzed.
Only the young activists around Big Minh, and a few plotters—such as

* Giscard d'Estaing, the president of France.

Tran Van Don, who was known to the French and even to many of his friends as André, and who was acting as Huong's minister of defense; and Tran Van Lam, who was the president of the Senate and constitutionally the next in line after Huong—and Nguyen Van Hao found the will to act.

On Saturday, President Huong told Hao: "If you insist on transferring power to Minh, all right. I will agree. But you must go to the National Assembly and find a constitutional way to do it."

V

Suddenly that day the abandoned consulate at Bien Hoa was no longer being guarded. The fifty men of the guard contingent materialized at the USAID 2 compound in Saigon demanding to be paid.

Richard Peters, the consul general, had been seconded off to Guam to help with the growing stream of refugees arriving there. Charlie Lahiguera was now the senior officer of the consulate, and he had a problem. His administrative officer had taken it upon himself to get on an airplane leaving Vietnam. (Lahiguera found out later that the man's wife had refused to leave the country unless he left too.)

Lahiguera at that time was not even sure where his administrative officer was. He certainly didn't know what the guards made each month, or when they had last been paid. Now they were here, and agitated. He thought that if they weren't satisfied they could very easily start a riot.

He had been working closely through the last few days with an officer from the erstwhile consulate in Da Nang named Paul Daly. Both of them were attempting to arrange for the evacuation of the local employees from their respective regions.

The two of them had been given enormous wads of piasters to use as bribes if they ran into trouble moving people from USAID 2 to Tan Son Nhut. As it happened, Lahiguera had had remarkably few problems at roadblocks, and hadn't had to use any of the money. He and Daly sat down and picked a figure at random that they guessed would satisfy the guards. They called in the local police to witness the payments, for which each man had to sign a receipt, and paid them off with the bribe money. After the first few men smiled at the sum and gladly signed the receipt, Lahiguera and Daly realized that that small crisis was defused.

VI

There is a vulgar military joke that turns on the image of a sailor swabbing the deck with a mop shoved up his ass. Martin had alluded to it in a cable to Washington earlier in the week. On Saturday, Scowcroft shot back: "Authorization for broom tied up in Vietnam supplemental. Suggest during interim that a modified shaft be used."

A more substantive cable arrived that day from Kissinger:

MY THINKING REGARDING THE POLITICAL EVOLUTION IN SAIGON IS THAT FOLLOWING THE FORMATION OF A MINH GOVERNMENT THERE WILL BE NEGOTIATIONS WHICH WILL RESULT MORE OR LESS RAPIDLY IN AN AGREEMENT ON A TRIPARTITE GOVERNMENT. THAT GOVERN-MENT WILL BE TWO-THIRDS COMMUNIST AND ONE-THIRD CON-TROLLED BY THEM [THE COMMUNISTS]. OUR PROBLEM AT THAT POINT WILL BE WHAT TO DO WITH THE EMBASSY.

AT SOME JUNCTURE, PERHAPS SOON, THE NORTH WILL DECIDE TO PREVENT THE FURTHER EVACUATION OF VIETNAMESE. WHEN THAT HAPPENS, I THINK WE SHOULD CUT DOWN TO VERY BARE-BONES OPERA-TION AT THE EMBASSY. THE QUESTION THEN WILL BE WHETHER OR NOT WE SHOULD PULL OUT ALTOGETHER OR MAINTAIN A TOKEN PRES-ENCE WITH A HANDFUL OF EMBASSY PERSONNEL. . . .

WHAT I WOULD LIKE IS MORE OF YOUR CONSIDERED JUDGMENT THAN YOU HAVE THUS FAR GIVEN ON THE PROBABLE EVOLUTION OF EVENTS, AND HOW WE SHOULD REACT TO THEM. I WANT IT BY BUSI-NESS MONDAY.

VII

Don Harris came to the Pink Night Club on Saturday evening, the only American who came to see me there through the few days when I knew it was open and told friends about it.

I was used to the toy tables and chairs, the flies in the beer rings. I was used too to the company of young Vietnamese. But Harris was way too big for the furniture, and obviously uncomfortable. After I tried to explain to him that he was sitting in the wreckage of some-thing beautiful, the eight of us at a table ran out of things to say to one another. (When there were six Vietnamese and one American, I could talk; at least I could practice the language. The second Ameri-can, with no Vietnamese at all, made it more difficult.)

Duc Cang, the young man who had taken La Anh Tu's place in the band when Tu was off in the Army, was not there, but a girl who may or may not have been Duc Cang's wife was, with a boy about four or five. The boy had a stick of gum in his hand. Harris reached across the table and asked for it, to make contact, and the boy burst into tears.

"It's not that he isn't used to Americans," I said. "I've seen him here, when it was a real nightclub. There's just too much emotion in the air, especially around him."

Harris gave the orphan boy who worked in the club way too many piasters to go out and buy a couple of packs of gum. He came back with the gum and gave Harris his change. Harris and the mother were able to get the child to take the gum and then he quieted down. Then Harris finished his beer and went back to his hotel to call his wife and son.

I joined him there an hour later. Harris had a pistol, and he had told me that he would give it to me when he left the country.

I knew nothing about guns. Harris showed me how it worked and asked me to oil it every couple of weeks. He wanted me to have it, but he also very definitely wanted to make sure that I got it out of Saigon. I hefted it. It felt heavy and balanced.

Harris had a big corner suite. His call to Los Angeles finally came through, and he stretched out on the bed. I made myself a Scotch and water from the refrigerator bar and stood on Harris' balcony looking down Nguyen Hue toward the river.

Harris talked for twenty minutes. Then I went in and sat in a heavy armchair. "Let me tell you about the boy at the club," I said. "His father is named Duc Cang. I don't think that he and the mother were ever married, actually. And there are four of them, four kids. They came to the club a lot, the mother and usually just one or two of the children. Duc Cang played the guitar and sang. He was good. He's an extraordinarily good-looking guy, for what that's worth. I was sure he was half-French, but he insisted he wasn't. Not that you have to be a Matisse to be beautiful. He just happens to have this perfectly straight nose, and good eyes. Anyway, twenty-six I suppose, something like that. Four kids. And he left last week. *Fini*, bye-bye. Alone."

After Los Angeles, Georgia or Alabama left Don Harris with an easy way of talking, and when he talked he made sense. He loved his thirteen-year-old son to distraction. He had told me that he had almost brought the boy with him to Saigon.

"Well," Harris said after a pause, "that singer friend of yours oughta be shot."

Then he told a story about the only time his daddy beat up one of his black tenant farmers, because the farmer was getting fat and the children had swollen bellies.

"I don't know," I said. "I think if she were my wife—or my common-law wife, or whatever she is—I'd have probably left her behind too. The children are a problem, though, aren't they? Morally."

"Yup," Harris said.

"Anyway, that's what I meant when I said the boy's got too much emotion running around in his world right now. The mother's trying to get out. Anything would have scared him."

"I want to go home and see my boy now," Harris said finally. "It ain't my war."

VIII

Shortly after midnight on Sunday, five communist 122-mm. rockets slammed into the capital. One scored a direct hit on the penthouse of the Majestic Hotel on the river.* Three others landed in a crowded, ramshackle neighborhood of Cholon. The rockets themselves and the fires they started killed at least twelve people. The rocket attack seemed to be a pointed message to the Saigon politicians to stop their squabbling.

In the last few weeks, an embassy Marine named Harbin who had left Saigon a few months earlier called his buddies and pleaded with them to look after his French-Vietnamese girl friend, a redhead with the same name as Charlie Benoit's daughter: Tammy.

After daybreak, Bobby Frain and Tim Creighton and a few of their buddies got in a Marine van and drove across the city to look for Harbin's girl, who lived in Cholon. In doing so, they were breaking strict instructions not to leave the embassy compound.

The top of Tammy's hooch was blown away. A girl of ten or twelve told them that they could take Tammy if they wanted her, she was upstairs, but she was dead.

IX

That morning, I joined Don Harris and a crew in the NBC van and headed northeast toward Bien Hao and Long Binh. Uncannily, for the first ten miles beyond the New Port bridge, only light traffic moved east with us and only a few military vehicles moved in the lanes headed toward Saigon. Some of the factories had shut down as their owners had fled. The air was clear, as I had never before seen it on that baneful industrialized corridor.

Harris had no attachments in Saigon and was focused entirely on the story to be reported. From the first day after his arrival a couple of weeks earlier, he had been better informed than I about the military situation. He never volunteered anything, but I learned from snatches of conversation among Harris and the crew about the rocket attack, which I had slept through. I also came to understand that we were heading out toward Bien Hao because it seemed likely that the North Vietnamese would cut the road to Vung Tau that day, and we might be filming refugees.†

* The penthouse was being remodeled; it was the room in which the Saigon politicians fantasized they would negotiate with the communists.
† The communists did cut the road to Vung Tau on Sunday. The operation to remove 250 South Vietnamese Marine dependents went smoothly, but the exercise was now pointless as a test of the possibility of getting any Vietnamese in Saigon out of the country through Vung Tau.

Then we came over a low rise. Even imperturbable Don Harris sounded a whistle of surprise. On the other side of the highway, halted at a barricade formed by ARVN trucks and a platoon of men, a column of trucks, buses, Japanese minibuses, tractors, oxcarts, motorcycles and bicycles hung with people and their possessions stretched as far as the eye could see. Harris told the driver to stop and the crew filmed the head of the column. The recently arrived French cameraman—who was middle-aged, bald and obviously strong—stood half in and half out of the van and panned as we drove.

When we reached the sprawling base at Long Binh, we turned onto Highway 15 and parked the van again. Harris and the crew went off for more footage of the refugee column, which they had filmed off and on for the last ten miles with no end in sight. I walked a hundred yards to the main gate into the base—hundreds of abandoned buildings on ten square miles of rolling dirt. The long headquarters building, its yellow paint faded to dust, stood at the summit of a long drive rising above the gate.

I remembered the girls who had waited at the gate there and the children who had sold Cokes to the truckloads of GIs. I wrote a spot that included the girls and the kids and the column of refugees moving past the abandoned base. It was too long, but I didn't care.

A town called Long Thanh was under attack ten miles down Highway 15. At a crossroads, an ARVN captain asked the driver if the foreigners were Americans. No, the driver said, they were all French. The officer said that was good, because if they were Americans someone might want to shoot them. Harris' French wasn't much better than mine. Few of the youngest ARVN troops spoke French, but many of the officers did. As we rode toward Long Thanh, the two of us practiced speaking English with a French accent, which amused the French cameraman and sound man and me more than it did Harris.

Five minutes later we reached the last government position, a small artillery battery. Fifty yards down the road were the twisted remains of three minibuses. A trickle of refugees walked toward us, many of them ARVN soldiers in or out of uniform, almost all of them with their weapons. Everyone slowed to look at the old man with the Ho Chi Minh beard, the woman with the infant and the child sprawled at her outflung hand, and the other dead on the soggy asphalt.

According to the men at the artillery position, the minibuses had been ambushed as they tried to move toward Saigon at dawn. I looked down at a man with a shredded chest. Then I walked back to the van and opened the back doors and sat in the shade. Because of the right-angle turn at Long Binh, it felt as if we were an hour away from the city. But I knew that in fact only about eighteen miles of rice fields and marshland lay between Long Thanh, a few miles up the road, and the capital.

X

Lionel Rosenblatt and Craig Johnstone—the two young bureaucrats who had convinced themselves that Graham Martin's plan for the Vietnamese was to let them make their way to Vung Tau, where the lucky ones would be picked up—were on the last Pan Am flight into Saigon, which arrived on Tuesday, the twenty-second. The other fifteen or twenty passengers on the plane were a largely mercenary bunch: One guy was hoping to buy some used warplanes cheap; another was picking up a minesweeper the U.S. Navy had left in the Saigon River.

The two conspirators knew from their first contacts with friends in the mission that Ambassador Martin had told his staff to have nothing to do with them. Rosenblatt shaved off his mustache as a weak hedge against being spotted if the rumor that Martin had the special police looking for them was true.

They operated out of a U.S.-leased hotel called the Regent out on Phan Thanh Gian Street, near Tan Son Nhut. The Regent consisted of three buildings that were connected only by catwalks on the top floors. Rosenblatt and Johnstone entered one building and made their way to another, in which they met their Vietnamese contacts.

For Rosenblatt, these were men who had worked for him in the Mekong delta in Provincial Reconnaissance Units, the counter-terrorist groups that themselves used many of the techniques of terror. Johnstone was interested in a different group.

In his years in Vietnam, he had worked with an outfit known as the Evaluations Branch of CORDS.* The section did independent studies of various American and Vietnamese programs and policies. Their evaluation of the impact of the South Korean troops in Vietnam led to the Koreans' departure. Similarly, their study of the Phoenix program led to its restructuring.

The group always included some antiwar Americans. The Vietnamese staffers were highly trained and skilled; many had formerly been with the Viet Minh. About two-thirds of the Vietnamese in the unit whom Johnstone contacted chose to stay. Some of them, he was sure, would continue to fight the communists in a resistance if the war was lost.

Rosenblatt and Johnstone each got about 200 Vietnamese into the evacuation. Then, on Sunday, the twenty-seventh, they left. They

* Civil Operations and Rural Development Support—the umbrella organization that married American support for rural development with the military effort.

didn't want to be accused of taking up two seats in the final evacuation.

A young Vietnamese man in the evaluations section was in Australia for training. His tiny teenaged wife could not decide whether to go or stay. Her mother wanted her to stay. But the girl finally decided to leave. Rosenblatt and Johnstone told her to meet them in front of the basilica at ten on Sunday morning. They waited until twenty minutes past the hour, and left without her.

Johnstone learned later that she had stopped on the way to the rendezvous to pick up a girl friend who also wanted to leave. The two of them arrived at the basilica at ten-thirty.

XI

Charlie Lahiguera was deeply unhappy over the fact that the flag at the consulate in Bien Hoa had flown over deserted buildings for nearly four full days now. That afternoon, he approached Wolf Lehmann with a request that he be allowed to fly up to the consulate and get it. Lehmann consented.

Two of the Marines who had been assigned to the consulate volunteered to accompany Lahiguera, who also found an Air America helicopter pilot willing to make the short flight.

The consulate and a general's house both faced the Dong Nai River, on opposite sides of a street. The landing pad was in the general's front yard, at the river's edge. A squad of ARVN soldiers with a machine gun stood between the home—from which the general had absconded—and the pad. The machine gun was aimed across the landing pad and out to the river.

As he and the two Marines hopped from the helicopter, Lahiguera gave the soldiers a friendly wave. He and the Marines strolled as nonchalantly as they could manage away from the pad and across the street to the consulate compound.

The consulate guards were still at their posts.

Lahiguera and the Marines closed the gate to the compound to give themselves some privacy. Then Lahiguera stood at attention while the guards ceremoniously lowered the colors. They folded the flag and handed it to Lahiguera.

The three of them then retraced their steps to the waiting helicopter. No one shot. No one spoke. Now the Americans had truly left Bien Hoa.

XII

One of the reasons for the delay in the Saigon politicians' death dance was the fact that old Huong bore a grudge against General Minh for having sided with Thieu against Huong in the 1971 elections. He would not accept the legislators' invitation to transfer power directly to Minh by presidential order. Instead, shortly before noon on Sunday, he told Tran Van Lam, the president of the Senate, that while he was ready to designate Minh as his successor, he insisted on submitting the recommendation to the National Assembly for its approval. The move was cagey: It forced the politicians to share responsibility for whatever might follow.

That afternoon, those senators and representatives who had not yet fled were rounded up and called to the National Assembly. They were briefed by the commander of the capital military district; by Tran Van Don, now minister of defense; and by General Cao Van Vien, the chairman of the Joint General Staff. The military reports were unrelievedly bleak.

Early in the afternoon, Nguyen Van Hao and Senate President Tran Van Lam broke away from the meeting and went to Big Minh's villa to ask him what he was going to do if the National Assembly transferred power to him. Big Minh as usual had no detailed plans. He said only: "I will tell you one thing for sure. When we have the power we will not capitulate."

Huong's last maneuver required a new National Assembly resolution. And so it was that Pierre Brochand found himself sitting not in the legislative chamber itself but on a stairway to the visitors' gallery with Peter Collins, the hawkish young CBS correspondent, writing the phrases that eventually resulted in the transfer of power. He handed them to Minh's Third Force lieutenant, Assemblyman Ly Qui Chung, who relayed them to the floor.

"This is mad," the French intelligence man said to Collins at one point. "I'm not supposed to be doing this."

At eight o'clock in the evening, Hao left Lam and the rest of them and went back to the villa to plead with Minh to come to the assembly building and spell out his program. Minh declined, on the grounds that it was a bad day on the Vietnamese horoscope. "But I am confident, Dr. Hao," he said, "that when the assembly acts and it is announced on the radio, when the other side knows, the guns will fall silent."

Hao returned to the National Assembly. About two-thirds of the full Assembly had gathered. Sitting as a single body, those 136 men and women finally, at 10 P.M., voted on the question: "Which of the deputies and senators agree that the president of the Republic of Vietnam transfer all the powers of the president to General Duong Van Minh in order to carry out the task of seeking ways and means to restore peace in South Vietnam?"

The weary and frightened legislators all voted in favor of the motion.

XIII

Around midnight on that Sunday, Graham Martin cabled the politicians' doings to Kissinger, adding:

> . . . IT IS QUITE PROBABLE THAT MOVES TO COMPLETE THE INTERDICTION OF ROADS MAY CONTINUE. AND IT MAY BE ALSO POSSIBLE A FEW MORE ROCKETS WILL BE LAUNCHED THIS EVENING. [BUT] IT IS THE UNANIMOUS OPINION OF THE SENIOR PERSONNEL HERE THAT THERE WILL BE NO DIRECT OR SERIOUS ATTACK ON SAIGON. I HAVE TALKED WITH ADMIRAL GAYLER. HE WAS PLACING HIS FORCES ON ONE-HOUR ALERT, A NECESSARY AND WELCOME PRECAUTION. HE SEEMS TO BE CONSIDERABLY CONCERNED OVER A MESSAGE WHICH WAS TRANSMITTED IN THE CLEAR CALLING FOR ARTILLERY FIRE ON TAN SON NHUT DURING THE NIGHT. EXPERIENCED COMMUNICATIONS ANALYSTS HERE CONCLUDE THAT "SINCE FOR THE PAST FIFTEEN YEARS NO SUCH MESSAGES HAVE BEEN TRANSMITTED IN THE CLEAR, THIS IS PART OF A PRESSURE OPERATION." IT WAS, IN FACT, USED BY TRAN VAN DON IN HIS BRIEFING OF THE ASSEMBLY. WE WILL THEREFORE CONTINUE WITH THE AIR OPERATION DURING THE EVENING. AS OF NOON [TODAY], WE [HAD] EVACUATED 35,245 PEOPLE [IN APRIL]. BY MORNING, THIS SHOULD HAVE REACHED CLOSE TO 40,000.
>
> I HAVE JUST BEEN INFORMED THAT MINH WILL MAKE A POLICY SPEECH ON THE OCCASION OF THE TRANSFER OF POWER AT THE PALACE AND WE WILL HOPE TO GET A COPY BEFORE THE ACTUAL DELIVERY. I HOPE YOU CAN KEEP YOUR COLLEAGUES TIED DOWN ANOTHER 48 HOURS. AFTER MINH'S SPEECH, WE WILL BE BETTER ABLE TO JUDGE WHAT THE NEAR- AND SHORT-RANGE FUTURE MAY BRING. WITH THE WARMEST REGARDS, MARTIN.

XIV

Late that same Sunday night, *Time* magazine's Pham Xuan An and a big blond American photographer named Dick Swanson sat in the *Time* bureau in the Continental Palace Hotel. The lights were low. An smoked as they talked.

Swanson had first come to Vietnam in 1966, as a *Life* photographer. He stayed five years, in the course of which he married a journalist named Germaine Loc. He had arrived back in Saigon that afternoon, alone, to try to get Germaine's mother and eleven other relatives out of the country.

He saw the family that afternoon. One of Germaine's sisters was married to a colonel, who was staying. She would use her clout as a colonel's wife to get all of them into Tan Son Nhut very early the next morning, and then Swanson would take over with the Americans. There was nothing he could do for them that night. He had dinner at Ramuntcho's with five friends from the height of the war. They reminisced a little, and talked about how many more weeks or days Saigon had to live.

After dinner, Swanson had some wine with friends in the interior terrace of the hotel, and in the room of one of them. Then he drifted to the bureau.

He and An started with small talk, about An's beloved dogs and caged birds. Then Swanson said that he honestly didn't know what he would do if he failed to get the family into the evacuation. "Obviously, I can leave anytime I want to," he said. "If things don't work out with the family, I don't know whether I'll get on a plane or not."

"You would be safe here," An said.

"Do you think Western journalists *should* stay?" Swanson asked.

"The good ones will."

Swanson let a silence grow. Then he said: "An, the war's over. Tomorrow, the next day, the day after that. Whenever. We've known each other for nine years now. You can tell me. Are you with them, the other side?"

"I'm a Vietnamese," An said. "I'm not concerned about the communists. I want to stay here."

Swanson smiled. "It's like when I ask Germaine if we have ice, back home, in Bethesda. Yes, she says. I go to the refrigerator and the ice-cube trays are filled with water. Germaine says, 'We have ice, it's just not frozen yet.'"

An smiled.

"Are you going to have problems with the communists?" Swanson asked.

"At a time like this, danger comes from several different directions," An said.

"Okay," Swanson said later, as he finally left for bed. "It's good to know that if I get stuck in Saigon one of my best friends here is a communist."

An smiled again.

XV

On Friday, the twenty-fifth—the day that George Esper and I and Tung Giang himself succeeded in getting Tung Giang into the evacuation—Tu and most of his family also went out to Tan Son Nhut. But their papers didn't work; they were turned back at the gate.

There were six of them: Tu and his mother, Tuan Ngoc and his wife, and the two youngest girls. Their ticket out was an American named Barry Falk,* who worked at two of the last clubs on the base, one for DAO and another for the ICCS delegation. Falk had asked Khanh Ha, the oldest sister, to stay until he left. She agreed to do so if he would get her family out.

That night, Falk refined his plans.

In the middle of the afternoon on Saturday, Tu and the others made their way to an unguarded, deserted cemetery inside the air base.

Barry Falk had access to a DAO car, with a Tan Son Nhut pass. He smuggled them into the operational part of the base in the trunk of the car, two at a time. Anh Tu curled up in the trunk with his mother.

Falk took them to Nguyen Cao Ky's villa, where they spent the night, the only guests of the former prime minister, whom they never saw. This was an arrangement between Ky and Falk. Ky had seen the band occasionally, but knew none of them.

The next day was Sunday, but Barry Falk still had to work. Remarkably, his clubs were still open. Tu, his mother and the rest of them on Falk's instructions spent the hours from eight in the morning until four in the afternoon in his DAO white Datsun, parked on the main street running past DAO. Falk brought them lunch.

Several times during the long day, Tu saw QC† drive out of the place where the people were getting on the airplanes with other Vietnamese in their jeeps. They drove into DAO, and were there for twenty minutes or more, and then took the Vietnamese back into the evacuation compound. Tu assumed that money changed hands between the coming and the going.

Late in the afternoon, Barry Falk drove them into the evacuation place. It was a big yard, full of people. Vietnamese whom he and Tuan Ngoc knew seemed to be working for the Americans, helping them, carrying lists on clipboards and calling out names, forming people into lines for the buses that would take them to the planes.

Anh Tu and Tuan Ngoc observed this game for a while, understood its rules, and themselves pretended to be workers. They volunteered to help process people for evacuation. And by volunteering, by playacting as monitors, they did in fact become part of what from the beginning had been an ad hoc process, depending on volunteers.

Finally, at about nine-thirty in the evening, Tu and his family boarded one of three buses heading for the next C-130.

A jeepful of QC followed those buses, screeched to a stop at the

---

* A pseudonym.
† Quan Canh, South Vietnamese military police.

open back hatchway of the plane. These buses clearly had at least two draft-age males on them.

Tu was terrified. "We get this close, and now they stop us," he thought.

Nobody drew any weapons. The Americans shouted at the QC, and waved their arms at the people on the bus, and then they all got off and walked quickly, but without running, into the blackness of the inside of the airplane, and the QC didn't do anything.

Everyone sat on the floor, very close. The Americans on the airplane gave them blankets.

Then, after sitting in the heat for many minutes, Tu whispering to his mother and his sisters and to Tuan Ngoc and his wife, and then falling quiet as the plane started to roll, the engines roared and they were in the sky over Saigon.

Tu was near the side of the airplane. He lifted himself to a little round window, looked down in the silence of the roaring engines at the lights of Saigon, shimmering Saigon swaying below him in a sea of black.

27

Monday

At eight o'clock, I sat down at the sidewalk coffee stall at the mouth of the alleyway separating my building from the unfinished one behind it. Street boys slept in the unfinished building, and over the months I had taken to bantering with them occasionally. The first night they gave me the light abuse you could expect from street boys seeing a figure in white appear across from them with a drink and a cigarette. But early on I had attached half a dozen Ruby Queens to an eraser and tossed the package to them and then it was friendly.

Before I'd gone to bed the night before, I had shouted to the figures in their ponchos across the way to join me at the coffee stall at eight. They always waited until dusk to climb up onto the roof. I had never seen any of their faces clearly. I thought now that perhaps it was too late in the morning, that they might have gone to wherever they spent their days. But over a ten-minute period five of them slipped out of the building like rats. They sat with me at the little aluminum folding table and had tea and greasy pastries. With boys who spoke almost no English, I was reminded how bad my Vietnamese was. I said: "Soon, I think, Vietnam will have peace." And: *"Toi o lai Sai-gon"* (I stay in Saigon).

In the office, I joked about the nightclub. I said that the old man had sold enough beer on Saturday to buy Sunday's supply, and as soon as General Minh was sworn in that afternoon and things started to get back to normal I was going to make my fortune at last.

I wrote three or four spots and drove to the radio station. While I was waiting for New York, an explosion shook the building. I knew they were close, that small advance units might be at the New Port bridge already. The people in the switching room wouldn't let me go up on the roof; they took me to a grimy window and pointed down to South Vietnamese troops in the courtyard, whom I hadn't noticed on the way in.

When you went to the fighting, you had an idea ahead of time what you were going to find. When the war comes to you, you don't know what's going on. From the window, I looked out at gray smoke reaching fifteen hundred or two thousand feet into the bright mid-morning sky, and its base was three miles away, at New Port. F-5s dove over the port. I did not know if the planes were friend or foe, if they had blown up an ammunition dump, or if the Viet Cong had, or if the smoke came from a fire that had nothing to do with the explosion. Finally it was my turn for the line, and I was through to New York, where it was close to midnight. I read the spots, and told the producer what I could see from the window.

I had forgotten that there were five hours a week, starting at midnight Sunday, New York time, when NBC radio had no one in the studios.

"My wife isn't going to like it," the producer said, "but I guess I better stay here as long as we can keep the line open. See what you can find out."

As I left the hot little room from which one made the calls and walked across the big equipment-crowded main switching room, I tried to picture the unknown man at the other end of the line in some studio far above the darkened Rockefeller Center skating rink.

The station manager told me that the operators at the domestic switchboards in the Postes, Télégraphes and Téléphone building next to the basilica were all going home. I went back to the little studio and reported that now civilians in Saigon were doing what they normally did when the war came to them: going home.

"My people want to go home too," the manager said.

I looked out the window and did one more spot. The station manager stayed with me as I did that spot. The voice in New York said he would stay overnight. I hung up and the manager asked to speak with me.

"For twelve years," he said, "I've helped Americans make their calls. Before JUSPAO,* they all had to come here: Garrick Utley, Peter Kalischer, Morley Safer. Many, many others. I hardly know you. I know you've been coming for the last few months. Ask at CBS. Ask at ABC. All the older men will know me. I helped everybody put their calls through. And I never took any money, even when it was *urgent.*"

He produced a *curriculum vitae*. It was done with obvious great care; single-spaced, crowded with detail. I saw that he had versions in French as well, all of them originals.

"They won't do anything to you," I said.

"My family," the man said.

I told him what I had told the ex-senator, my former landlord. I apologized for not being a bureau chief. And I said that it wasn't worth anything now, just words in the air, but I thanked him for all of the others down the years. I asked him to please do what he could to keep the lines open. I said that I or my colleague—"a man named Wiener, Robert Wiener"—would be back in a couple of hours.

"Some of my people have gone home already," the man said. "I can't force them to stay."

"I promise you that this afternoon I'll give this to Mr. Carter at the embassy," I said. "I don't know what good it will do."

"Talk to the other networks. Ask them about me."

"There's a man at CBS who's working on all the schemes to get people out," I said. "I'll talk to him. It's the best I can do."

There was a crowd in front of the PTT building, but when I reached the office the phones were working again. There were communist soldiers—a small group, most reports said—in the strutwork of the New Port bridge itself, and they had earlier set fire to a big PX warehouse in the port. But the city was apparently accepting these developments as minor. I always assumed that the people knew more than I did. Viet Cong at New Port, but not too many. No collapse yet.

I crossed the square to the Caravelle Hotel and climbed to the CBS offices on the second floor and for the first time met Brian Ellis. I told him about Mr. Huy† at the radio station.

"Can you do anything?" I asked. "Or should I call Alan Carter? That's what I've been doing with other people. I think it's pointless. But I don't have any other embassy connections."

"Call Carter," Ellis said.

* Joint United States Public Affairs Office—from which correspondents could call the U.S. during the years of heavy American involvement.
† A pseudonym. I have also attempted to disguise his position. I have no idea whether he ever got out.

I called Carter from the NBC office and then went back down Tu Do for Colonel Hien and Captain Anh's afternoon military briefing.

II

One of Ken Moorefield's closest friends in the embassy—an Annapolis graduate who had switched to the infantry to fight in Vietnam and then, like Moorefield, returned as a civilian—had left Saigon with his Vietnamese wife several months earlier. In the middle of the month, he telephoned and wrote from the States imploring Moorefield to see that his wife's parents and two other members of her family got out.

Moorefield promised to do what he could. But then he was caught up in the evacuation, and for the first few days could not get away from Dodge City until the curfew or later.

In the middle of the week he gave the address of his friend's in-laws to a former Special Forces officer at DAO. "I haven't had a chance to see these people," Moorefield said. He explained who they were to the man, another friend. "Do me a favor and go over to the house. If they're still in Saigon, explain who I am, although they probably already know my name from the girl. Tell them I haven't forgotten them and I'll try to help them as soon as I can get away from here."

Finally, on Sunday, when he realized that he actually had a couple of hours to himself, Moorefield wondered how to fill them. He remembered the family, and drove to the address. It was a nice villa. He discovered that the girl's father was a senior bank official.

As the man welcomed Moorefield into his home, he said casually: "Ah, we knew you would come eventually, Mr. Moorefield." Their suitcases stood in the entrance foyer.

The four of them qualified. They arrived in Dodge City in the middle of the afternoon on Monday, just before the storm. In his first meeting with them, and again when he spoke with the father on Monday afternoon, Moorefield never let on how stunned he was by their trust.

III

Captain Anh: . . . *Uh, no casualties in any of those actions have been reported yet.*

Also, in Bien Hoa province, early this morning, a number of enemy troops set up a blockade on Highway One five kilometers northeast of Di An . . . D, I, A, N. Government forces are now operating in that area in an attempt to lift the blockade.

Tay Ninh provincial capital, from oh seven hundred to oh nineteen hundred hours today was hit by forty rounds of artillery and rocket fire. Six civilians were killed and four others were wounded. Seventeen civilian homes were destroyed.

Hung Nghia provincial capital early this afternoon was hit by forty rounds of artillery and rocket fire. No casualties were reported yet.

In Dinh Tuong province, Ben Tranh district town this morning was hit by four rounds of one-twenty-two-millimeter rocket fire. Two civilians were killed and twenty-five others were wounded.

That's all we have. Are there any questions?

Me: *Can you describe the situation in the New Port area now?*

As usual, Captain Anh translates the questions into Vietnamese; Colonel Hien answers in Vietnamese; and Captain Anh translates again.

Captain Anh: *Colonel Hien answer that there is about one enemy squad still holding a blocking position on the other side of the river. I mean, beyond the New Port.*

Me: *How large a force?*

Captain Anh: *A squad.*

Me: *You mean that whole business this morning was just a squad of Viet Cong?*

Captain Anh: *Colonel Hien answer that there are bigger and bigger enemy units in other areas, farther from the New Port. But closest to the New Port is a blocking position manned by one enemy squad.*

Another correspondent: *What are the fires out there?*

Captain Anh: *Colonel Hien said that we do not have any specific report yet of what was on fire. Apparently the communist sapper blew up sort of a warehouse in that area.*

Me: *Are you moving troops from Bien Hoa down toward Saigon?*

Captain Anh: *Well, Colonel Hien say that our troops are trying to lift the enemy blockade on Highway One, which is about five kilometers northeast of Di An district town in Bien Hoa province, as we have just announced. Thank you.*

I did not believe *Time* and *Newsweek.* I did not accept the judgments of the new NBC correspondents—most of whom had covered the war before I ever set foot in Vietnam—who arrived and took one long look around and said it was all coming down. I didn't accept the judgment of Paul Schaberger, who was plotting to get Whiskey and Bourbon and his Vietnamese wife and son out well before Da Nang. But all through the offensive, when I kept thinking it was going to stabilize, that something would happen to lurch the nightmare in its tracks, it was Captain Anh's despair more than anything else that slowly taught me I was wrong.

As Anh walked from the podium and many of the other journalists rushed it to ask Colonel Hien the questions they did not want to ask in the briefing proper, I looked at Anh and the two of us walked to one of the room's grand French windows, windows that reached from the floor almost to the high ceiling. Quite unexpectedly, the windows were opaque with luminous, beating rain. Neither of us could have said who had signaled that he wanted to talk to the other.

"It's very bad now, Butler," Anh said.

"Captain, I don't know what you want to do," I said, eager that Captain Anh not articulate a request. "You've had this job for years. You know all the correspondents, the bureau chiefs. You have your own people in the Army. I don't know what you want to do, but if you needed my help at this point I could only say God help you."

IV

The CIA base chief in Can Tho was a big, florid, tennis-playing Irish-American named Jack Donleavy.* Both he and his deputy were veterans of the CIA's clandestine war in Laos. It was the belief of Terry McNamara, the consul general, that battles in Laos were frequently decided by which side shouted the loudest. He thought the two top spooks in his consulate were out of their depth in Vietnam, where some battles, at least, were decided by which side fought better.

The spooks were convinced that there were three NVA divisions north of Can Tho to pounce on the city at any time. McNamara and his political-military adviser—and the MR 4 commander, General Nguyen Khoa Nam—on the other hand believed that there were *no* enemy divisions close to Can Tho. And the prime objective of the NVA and Viet Cong units that did operate in the delta was to tie down the three ARVN divisions there, to keep them from coming to the relief of Saigon.

The spooks' intelligence network was compromised, McNamara thought; it was to the communists' advantage to try to persuade the Americans that they were stronger in the delta than was actually the case.

The CIA officials' assessment of the communist strengths and intentions governed all that they did. In late March, there had been a sudden rumor that the communists were going to attack My Tho, which lay between Saigon and Can Tho. The spooks there fled to Can Tho. When no attack materialized overnight, they returned to find their

* A pseudonym.

compound stripped by looters. They'd taken even the tennis rackets.

So the working relationship between the feisty consul general in Can Tho and his associates in the CIA was not what it should have been. The conflict came to a head over the evacuation.

That weekend, George Randall, the CIA officer who would soon hear a panicky Marine calling, "They're coming up the stairs!" was in Saigon attempting to insert fifty of the agency's Vietnamese employees from the delta, with their dependents, into the evacuation at Tan Son Nhut. He was not having a great deal of luck. He discovered on his second day in Saigon that his fifty names were actually moving *down* what seemed to be the master list rather than up, as mission employees closer to the evacuation were inserting their dentists and cooks and maids onto the list.

On Sunday, he got a call from Donleavy in Can Tho. "We're on our own down here," the base chief said. "We've got to start moving people. All I need is coordinates for a ship."

For the last week or so, two and sometimes three Air America helicopters had been assigned full time to Can Tho. By mutual agreement between McNamara and the commander of the Can Tho air base, the choppers overnighted at an American residential compound they called Palm Springs, where they had to cut down a few palm trees to accommodate them, and in the consulate parking lot. (The air-base commander had told McNamara that he could not guarantee the discipline of his troops if the Americans tried to evacuate anyone from the base.)

Randall sought out Rear Admiral Hugh Benton, who was the senior CINCPAC officer in Saigon, Admiral Gayler's man on the ground. Benton told Randall, in effect: You're the first guy who's given me a straight request. Where do you want the ship and when do you want it? To Randall's surprise, apparently a Navy ship could be positioned close to the mouth of the Bassac River and begin receiving evacuees not in a matter of days but of hours.

Randall tried to call Donleavy from DAO. When he failed to get through, he headed for the embassy.

But Admiral Benton did get through to George Jacobson to tell him what he was doing. Jacobson called McNamara and together they decided to ground the Air America choppers in Can Tho. It was premature to start flying people to the fleet.

The order stayed in effect for about twenty-four hours. Then McNamara met with Donleavy and arranged a compromise. The spooks could start flying people wherever they wanted to, McNamara said. But they were to use pickup points outside the city, and change them frequently, and fly low. And when they had their people out, they were to put the choppers at McNamara's disposal.

Finally, on the last day, whenever it came, the CIA contingent—which amounted to about eighteen Americans, roughly half of the mission—was to join the downriver evacuation. Donleavy seemed to acquiesce in all of this.

V

When the rain had eased, I went back to the apartment and packed a suitcase.

Three generations of the landlord's family lived in the big apartment on the first floor of my building. The business was done by the women. My contacts were with a pretty young woman of about twenty-five. One night earlier in the week she asked me if I could help them get out of the country. I sat with her in the living room. Her husband stayed in a bedroom. She got up to consult with him once while she and I talked. Strangely, I had the impression that the woman did not want to leave Vietnam but the husband did. I didn't give it much thought, but wondered if the man was a military officer or government official who stayed out of sight because he feared that the omniscient American journalist would recognize him.

"My sister-in-law is coming from Geneva," the pretty young woman had said that evening. "We'll decide then."

The sister-in-law arrived from Geneva and decided that the first order of business was to get the American out of the building. The woman I liked told me on Sunday, with patently sincere apologies.

I put the essentials in a suitcase and let the family know through the maid that I would be back for the rest of my things the next day. Then, without the slightest idea that I was starting to make the final mistakes, I trundled the suitcase and the Honda to a high-rise hotel on Nguyen Hue Boulevard called the Central Palace, a place without character someone had thrown up for the Americans. Arthur Lord had been urging me for weeks to get out of the apartment and move to the hotel, where he and Harris and all the other NBC people were staying.

The first leg of that short journey took me past the terrace of the Continental Palace Hotel, in which I had stayed for the first few days of my three times in Vietnam, a place I loved. Why it did not even occur to me to check into the Continental would remain a mystery to me years later. But in a crisis—and even I by now understood that a crisis was at least approaching—one tends to reach for security.

At the desk of the Central Palace, the boy asked me which side of the hotel I wanted to be in *"pour les rockets."*

"I want a view of the river," I said, not out of bravado (that was the direction from which the rocket attacks I always slept through came) but because of the simple compulsion to live in sight of water. The young Chinese boy smiled. Years later, I could still see the smile. I wasn't one of them, but I had a few friends here and there around the world who lived for that smile, the nod of respect to danger shrugged away.

I got the view of the river, but discovered that the door to the narrow balcony was locked. The girl who was attending me had no key, and she said it was the same for all the other rooms, which I knew to be untrue from having stood on Don Harris' large curved balcony.

I asked for a beer and she brought two of them, both as warm as the afternoon, and didn't have a bottle opener. We finally found an opener at the floor station. I drank one of the beers, cursing under my breath, and took a bath.

I stopped in the lobby because now a second storm seemed to be lowering over the city. Idly, with two or three other Westerners I didn't know and a few of the hotel staff, I watched the televised ceremony in which Big Minh became the third president of the Republic of Vietnam in eight days.

VI

At the palace, the first warm, humid gusts of a new storm stirred the white damask curtains of the slightly open tall French windows in the reception room where power would be transferred. The ceremony that followed was an entirely Vietnamese affair. There was of course a large contingent of foreign journalists. But no representatives from the French or American embassies, the embassies that in varying degrees had worked to bring this moment to pass, were present.

According to rank, senior officials of the Thieu and Huong governments who had not yet fled Vietnam were seated in the first rows. Mingled with them and behind them were close associates of Big Minh, senior Buddhist and Catholic prelates, and the dignitaries of Saigon, all in conservative suits and ties or military uniforms or clerical garb.

Two flags of the republic, yellow with three horizontal red stripes, stood on either side of the podium.

Tran Van Huong spoke first. Through the thick dark glasses that seemed to hide half his face, he read a brief speech. At its conclusion, he turned to Big Minh and said: "Your responsibilities are great, General." Then, supported by an aide and his cane, the bent old man shuffled to his seat.

Minh did not rise. A young soldier appeared in the glare of the television lights and removed the flags. He removed the republic's coat of arms from the podium, and another soldier replaced it with a plaque showing the five petals of a blue-and-white flower enclosing the Chinese yin and yang, images of peace and conciliation.

There was a murmur in the room, and outside a roll of thunder and the crack of lightning in the wet heat.

Big Minh approached the podium slowly, gravely.

"I can make you no promises," he said. "In the days ahead we will have nothing but difficulties, terrible difficulties. The positions to be taken are grave and important, our position is a difficult one.

"I have thought for some time that the use of force is not a good solution for us," he said. At that moment, many in the room thought that Minh was going to surrender, or sue for peace. But then he went on.

"The order to our soldiers is to stay where they are, to defend their positions, to defend with all their strength the territory remaining to us.

"I accept the responsibility for seeking to arrive at a cease-fire, at negotiations, at peace on the basis of the Paris Accords. I am ready to accept any proposal in this direction."

He spoke slowly, from a prepared text. Then he folded the speech and put it away and spoke with great and evident gravity from his heart.

"Citizens, brothers, patriots!" he said. "In these difficult hours I can only beg of you one thing: Be courageous, do not abandon the country, do not run away. The tombs of our ancestors are here, this is our land, it is here that we all belong."

The room applauded emotionally. Minh then introduced Nguyen Van Huyen, the Catholic speaker of the Assembly, as his vice president, and Vu Van Mau, the leader of the Buddhist opposition to Thieu, as his prime minister-designate. Huyen would be in charge of the negotiations with their brothers on the other side, he said.

It was over at ten minutes before six. What remained of Saigon's elite in their hot Westernized garb made for the after-storm freshness outside.

VII

It was the first thunderstorm of the monsoon season: First the hot gusts of wind boiling up dirt and debris from the streets; then rolling thunder and the crack of lightning like the discharge of a big artillery piece four feet from your ear, and blowing curtains of rain; and now, at six-fifteen, low golden light on the washed pastels of the old French buildings, and a welcome coolness.

The storm died almost as suddenly as it had come, and then the ceremony at the palace was over. In its final minutes, Don Harris had passed through the lobby. He and I exchanged a few words. Both of us were heading to the office. But I did not offer Harris a ride on my Honda. I did not yet fully trust myself to carry passengers, and the Eden Building was only a long block away anyway.

I retrieved the Honda from the garage and caught up with Harris halfway down the stall-crowded block, sidewalks so crowded with stalls and their big umbrellas or low-slung ponchos and flies that Harris had to walk in the gutter. As I slowed to Harris' pace beside me, I remembered a literary allusion—or was it actually something my Uncle Bill had said?—about the long decades in Saigon when Vietnamese stepped into the gutter at the approach of a Frenchman.

"See you there," I said, and toed the machine into second gear, cautiously twisting my right wrist for speed.

And it was during that movement of my fist that Saigon exploded.

For a wild moment, I thought that the machine under me was exploding between my legs. I braced my back and buttocks for a fall as I bumped over the curb and the low protective hoops around the small plot of grass and concrete that held the massive, pockmarked Marines Statue, skidded the motorcycle to a stop, crouched at the rear base of the statue and dug in my shoulder bag for my tape recorder.

> *I'm at the Marines. . . . Five, four, three, two, one. . . . I'm at the Marines Statue in downtown Saigon. It is twenty minutes after six, Saigon time. President Minh has just been inaugurated. For some reason, there is antiaircraft fire and the sound of small-arms fire right here in the heart of the city. I'm not certain where it's coming from. It seems to be coming from the area of the Presidential Palace. The palace is closely guarded. I have no idea why troops there would be firing in the air at this time. People are running in the streets. Yes, there's a plane in the air. And we have antiaircraft . . . [Bap bap bap bap bap bap bap bap] This is heavy fire now, tracers rising from positions on all sides of me, streaking up from behind the buildings. We are half an hour after a thunderstorm. The sky is gray and sparrows are wheeling. Sparrows are wheeling in the sky, and the tracers, the red tracers, arc through them. It's extraordinary. The war has come to Saigon. [Bap bap bap bap bap bap bap bap] . . .*

PART 5

APRIL 29—MAY 6

. . . a doorway of brilliant sunlight
at the end of what seemed like a long tunnel.

28

April 29—0400 hours

The pilot of the plane that was almost fully loaded was an Air Force captain named Arthur Mallano. He looked out of his cockpit and saw the crew of the second C-130 lowering its ramp to begin to receive passengers. At the same time he saw what he thought was lightning in the sky, and said to his copilot, "Gee, that thunderstorm is getting closer. It's moving toward the field, fast."

Then the flashes were not only white, but red and blue and green, and Mallano realized that they were rockets and mortars, raining on the field and with great accuracy.

Within the first minute, they hit a fuel truck and the control tower and the Air America flight line. A rocket landed just under one of the wings of the third C-130 and exploded. Its crew scrambled from it and up into the waiting hold of the second C-130.

No more than thirty seconds before the attack began, a Marine major named Roger Delligatti spoke briefly with Darwin Judge and Charlie McMahon, the two corporals manning an isolated position between Dodge City and DAO headquarters. One of the first rockets was a freak direct hit on the two young Marines, who died instantly.

Another early round knocked a wall off the building in which Homer Smith and his wife and twelve other people—most of them high-ranking officers—were sleeping. All fourteen were knocked out of their beds. None was hurt.

Either the first or second round to reach the gym shot straight through the roof of a men's room. Don Hays was sleeping against the outer wall of the room. The incoming round woke him but did not kill him: It was a dud.

Yet another of the very first rounds landed on the roof of the gym, sending sheets of the roof flying and wounding several of the 1,500 Vietnamese inside. They surged away from the round, even as the Vietnamese outside tried to surge in. "They're bug-f - - - - -," Don Hays said to himself. "Just like a jar full of lightning bugs."

The gym caught fire. But the Defense Attaché's Office was still functioning. There were still several hundred American civilian and military men on the base, and hundreds of DAO Vietnamese employees. The DAO fire squad arrived and put out the fire.

The crew of Mallano's plane took on their string of 180 evacuees and another 80 from the string lined up for the second plane, but now half the runway was gone, Mallano figured. "Get the last of them on," Mallano shouted back to his loadmaster. "We're going!"

As he rolled, rockets were landing all around him, left and right, front and rear. He considered getting airborne fast by taking off from the taxiway, but then remembered the antiaircraft emplacement at the end. He'd seen it earlier that day. "I'll just get this mother airborne and we'll be right over the sonofabitch," Mallano said to himself.

He turned onto the runway and pushed the throttles to the wall. As they rolled, rolling away from the antiaircraft position, the rockets still raining down around them, the C-130 that had been disabled when the round landed under its wing exploded. Mallano thought the crew was still in the plane.

Now the South Vietnamese Air Force began its own evacuation in earnest. Men fought and killed each other to board their own C-130s and smaller aircraft. People were pushed off C-130 ramps as they taxied. One took off on an abandoned north-south runway, barely clearing the abandoned control tower for the older field. A C-7 tried to take off on one engine. It spun off the runway into the grass infield and burst into flames. It looked from a distance as if most of the passengers got out, but no one bothered to check.

With first light, VNAF F-5s and A-37s, its fighter-bombers, were fired up. They took off not to fight but to flee to U Tapao and other air bases in Thailand. Many jettisoned their external fuel tanks and ordnance on the active runway.

At dawn, at least forty vehicles and several hundred Vietnamese, most of them military men, blocked the runway in their attempt to board two of the last C-130s.

All was not cowardice and flight. From the start of the attack, a twin-boomed AC-119 gunship was in the air, shooting off flares and blasting away at communist positions around Tan Son Nhut. It was joined by two small A-1s, which cruised the perimeter of the base, low and slow, "trolling" for gunners at communist emplacements to reveal themselves.

At dawn, the AC-119 landed to refuel and rearm. Half an hour later, at seven, it finally caught the SA-7* missile it had been inviting for the last three hours. It spun lazily to a fiery crash just east of the air base.

II

With the first rockets, Nguyen Cao Ky got up, dressed and headed for one of his helicopters with a couple of other pilots and a navigator. It was impossible to scramble any planes from the shelled and littered runways of Tan Son Nhut. But Ky contacted the air base at Can Tho, in the delta, and they loaded up four A-1s with 750-pound bombs. For the next few hours, Ky acted as a forward air controller.

Code names were pointless. When the A-1s reached Saigon, Ky said: "This is Marshal Ky. The biggest rocket position is over at Phu Lam, near the radio transmitter. Go in and destroy it."

He guided them to two other positions on Highway 1. When the largest rocket batteries had been destroyed, the A-1s headed back to Can Tho.

Ky was getting low on fuel. He set down at Nha Be, outside the city, where there was a huge Shell aviation-fuel depot. Dozens of planes and helicopters were lined up for gas. Most of the pilots had lost contact with their commands, and looked to Ky for guidance. He squatted with the young men in a semicircle before him. He told those who had run out of ammunition to refuel and fly back to Can Tho. Those who still were armed should spend those rockets and bombs and bullets on the enemy and then they too should head back to the delta.

Then Ky flew back to VNAF headquarters at Tan Son Nhut. He found the entire command—consisting of about thirty generals, colonels and majors—in the office of General Tran Van Minh, the Air

---

* A surface-to-air missile.

Force commander. Included in the group were most of the remaining Army generals.

Minh told Ky that the Americans had ordered all F-5s to be evacuated to Thailand or the Philippines. Now he and the rest of them were waiting for the Americans to take them over to DAO and get them out.

Ky went back to his villa with his lieutenants. Mai and the children had left for Guam just twenty-four hours earlier, on the morning of the twenty-eighth. The men had a bachelors' breakfast and discussed what to do next.

III

There would be rocket and mortar and artillery fire on Tan Son Nhut off and on all day. The heaviest concentration was from four-thirty until eight in the morning, when the base took about forty rounds an hour. After the initial barrage, the fire became more and more concentrated on the flight line and on fuel and ammo storage depots. Few if any rounds landed directly on DAO or Dodge City after the nightmarish first half hour of it.

Nevertheless, with the Vietnamese milling about on the verge of panic and rockets and other rounds landing every sixty or ninety seconds somewhere nearby, Don Hays figured he was in for a long spell as a prisoner of war.

Ken Moorefield slept fitfully for a few hours after his midnight return from the mass feeding and the tour of the perimeter at Dodge City. He awoke with a bang when a rocket landed somewhere nearby. As he dressed and tossed the final articles into the getaway bag he had packed hours before, he heard the deeper rumble of artillery shells exploding somewhere in the distance, north maybe.

He lived on the top floor of his embassy-leased building, three blocks away from the embassy. The top floor was not the place to be when they were rocketing the city. Moorefield went to a friend's apartment on a lower floor. It was a little after four in the morning. He and the friend and other visitors sat on the balcony until dawn, watching the rockets land in an arc from Cholon to the west up toward the airport.

From traffic on the walkie-talkie they quickly understood that Tan Son Nhut was coming under a heavy barrage of rocket and artillery fire. Two Marines dead.

A Mission Warden officer and one of Marvin Garrett's security people who were also in the building both had vehicles. Shortly after sunrise, they said they were going out to the airport to take a look around. Moorefield joined them.

It was seven-thirty. As they passed the billboard that read "THE NOBLE SACRIFICE OF ALLIED SOLDIERS WILL NEVER BE FORGOTTEN," a couple of rockets whooshed overhead too close for comfort. The two-vehicle convoy pulled to a stop and the three Americans huddled in a ditch until things quieted.

IV

Bobby Frain took the call from Sergeant Stringer out at DAO. Sergeant Stringer was a little flaky, which was why he was out at DAO. The assumption among the embassy Marines was that the action would be at the embassy, not out there.

"Two of your men have been killed, Frain," Stringer said.

"You've only *got* two of my men," Frain said, throttling as he almost always succeeded in doing the urge to succumb to the ubiquitous profanity.

Frain couldn't believe it. Judge and McMahon were the only reinforcements the unit had gotten, and they hardly qualified as reinforcements, since the unit was still short of the number its table of organization called for. He couldn't believe that two green men had been put at the same important position, alone. Because he couldn't believe it—wanted so badly *not* to believe it—he got a vehicle and rushed out to Tan Son Nhut in the darkness.

Vietnamese paratroopers about a quarter of a mile in front of the gate, right at the billboard about the "noble sacrifice of allied soldiers," stopped the car. Frain waved some passes and took off, running the gate. He wasn't real concerned, the car was plastered with embassy tags. He just wanted to find out that Stringer was wrong.

Stringer was right and nobody had done anything; they couldn't even find any f -----' body bags at first.

It was bad. They must have taken just about a direct hit. A rocket, not a mortar, Frain could tell from the way the remains were deployed in the cool dawn light.

Finally someone found a couple of body bags and they got the remains to the Seventh-Day Adventist Hospital just outside the base, and delivered them to the morgue there.

V

From the roof of the Central Palace Hotel in downtown Saigon, it seemed that the first of the close-in shells landed east of Tan Son Nhut, out near the marsh and rice fields where the C-5A had crashed. They zeroed in quickly on Tan Son Nhut. Now they were easier to feel. The shapes of the fireballs were distinct, and the crumpling push in the air came just ten or fifteen seconds after the light of the fire-balls.

A still photographer named Matthew Naythons had been with us all night. Naythons had a black mustache and sharp features. When things were slow on the war front, he practiced medicine in California. When things heated up somewhere, he grabbed his cameras and made good money as a photojournalist, for *Time* and others.

After sunrise, we all came more alive. Aaron Fears, the NBC cameraman, checked light-meter readings with Naythons and made occasional entries in a diary he was keeping in a pocket tape recorder.

At seven-thirty, Naythons was taking a break, sitting with his back against the wall around the roof. Fears kicked him lightly, and Naythons rose with a single motion. Fears was locked in on a C-119 that was about three thousand feet up and close, over the radio station beyond the American embassy. Smoke was streaming from it and it arced slowly, gracefully. It crashed out near Tan Son Nhut—far enough away so that no explosion reached the hotel roof, giving the whole episode a remote dreamy character.

Arthur Lord was still out there, with his walkie-talkie. A few minutes after the C-119 crash, a bubble of fire blossomed at the airport. Don Harris pointed to it; Aaron Fears bent to his camera on its tripod and shot for a few seconds and then we heard the noise. Harris held the walkie-talkie to his ear and Arthur Lord said, "Jesus, that one was close. Over by Air America, I think." From the office, Jack Critchfield said, "Base to Lord, base to Lord: You're still up against a wall, right?"

Arthur Lord answered with a small laugh: "You bet your sweet bippy I am, base."

VI

The rocketing of Tan Son Nhut at 4 A.M. woke Thomas Polgar as well. As usual, he had two officers on duty overnight at the embassy. Polgar called them from his bedroom. They reported that Marines on the embassy roof thought that Tan Son Nhut was coming under artillery fire.

"Okay, this is going to be a tough day," he told the officer on the other end of the line. "I'll be in soon. For now, the best thing you can do is start making up packets of thousand-dollar bills."

As Polgar showered and dressed, his household staff was up, making his breakfast. He packed an airline bag with his camera, his passport, his checkbook and his last bank statement. But when he left the residence—number 7 Nguyen Dinh Chieu Street, eight minutes from the embassy—shortly before five, he did not take Love, his dog. He did not expect to be leaving Saigon that day.

Martin arrived at the embassy shortly before six. For about half an hour, he and Polgar were alone in Martin's office. The ambassador's several illnesses—principally bronchitis and pneumonia—had left him with almost no voice. He listened to Polgar's quick briefing and then called DAO. Later his voice grew stronger. But in the first calls that morning, Polgar acted as an intermediary, listening on an extension and then relaying Martin's whispered questions and replies.

By seven, Homer Smith in the underground operations center at DAO had determined from U.S. Air Force officers who had gone to the flight line and the runways that they were littered with jettisoned ordnance and wing tanks. Much of the Vietnamese Air Force had already scrambled, on orders from Eric Von Marbod, the visiting Assistant Secretary of Defense, who had stayed on since arriving with the Weyand mission.

Admiral Gayler called from CINCPAC in Hawaii to ask what was going on. Martin relayed what Gayler almost certainly already knew from earlier calls and cable traffic between Hawaii and DAO. A few minutes later, Kissinger called from Washington. Again, Polgar relayed Martin's factual report on conditions at Tan Son Nhut. Neither Gayler nor Kissinger was yet talking about what was referred to in the standing evacuation plan as Option 4: the full-scale helicopter evacuation of Saigon.* The morning's first calls were tightly focused on the conditions of the runways at Tan Son Nhut.

VII

At seven-thirty, one of Big Minh's young lieutenants delivered a note from the new president to the embassy. It was immediately translated and rushed to Martin's attention:

> DEAR MR. AMBASSADOR:
> I respectfully request that you give an order for the personnel of the Defense Attaché's Office to leave Viet Nam within twenty-four hours beginning April 29, 1975, in order that the question of peace for Viet Nam can be settled early.
> [signed April 28 by Duong Van Minh]

Without a moment's hesitation, the ambassador called in Eva Kim and dictated the following reply:

> DEAR MR. PRESIDENT:
> I have just received your note dated the 28th of April requesting that I immediately give an order for the personnel of the Defense

---

* Option 4 was the last and least desirable of the options in an evacuation plan that had first been called "Talon Vise" and, when that code name was compromised, "Frequent Wind." The first three options all included the use of fixed-wing aircraft.

Attaché's Office (DAO) to leave Vietnam within twenty-four hours. This is to inform your Excellency that I have issued orders as you have requested.

I trust your Excellency will instruct the armed forces of the Government to cooperate in every way possible in facilitating the safe removal of the personnel of the DAO.

I also express the hope that your Excellency may intervene with the other side to permit the safe and orderly departure of the Defense Attaché and his staff.

Sincerely yours,
GRAHAM MARTIN,
American Ambassador

With the original typed and signed and sent off to be delivered by hand to Big Minh, the ambassador got around to informing Henry Kissinger that he had just ordered Homer Smith and all other American military men in Vietnam save the Marines out of the country.

He began the cable with the two notes. Then:

IN VIEW OF THE ABOVE, I REPEAT MY REQUEST TO PERMIT ME AND ABOUT 20 OF MY STAFF TO REMAIN BEHIND, AT LEAST FOR A DAY OR TWO, TO AT LEAST GIVE SOME DIGNITY TO OUR DEPARTURE, [AND] TO FACILITATE AN ORDERLY DISPOSITION OF OUR EXTENSIVE PROPERTIES HERE.

I CAN KEEP TWO AIR AMERICA HELICOPTERS AND WE CAN DEPART AT A MOMENT'S NOTICE. I DO SERIOUSLY RECOMMEND THIS COURSE AND HOPE FOR YOUR PROMPT APPROVAL.

I WOULD INTEND IN EITHER CASE TO ASK THE FRENCH EMBASSY TO ASSUME NORMAL CARETAKER RESPONSIBILITIES. THERE IS NO OTHER EMBASSY LEFT. IN ANY EVENT, PRESIDENT MINH'S REQUEST WILL PERMIT THE ANNOUNCEMENT OF [OUR] DEPARTURE TO BE BY REQUEST, NOT FROM OUR PANIC.

VIII

The rocketing of Tan Son Nhut also woke Wolf Lehmann. The embassy duty officer called between four-fifteen and four-twenty. Two Marines dead, he said, but not much damage. Maybe something on the Air America flight line. Lehmann got up, showered and dressed in a coat and tie. There was chatter down in the grounds of the villa, which stood behind high walls. U.S. mission guards and their families were already gathering for that day's evacuation.

In a roomy old briefcase, Lehmann crammed binoculars, a camera, one set of underwear, a couple of pairs of socks and a lightweight safari suit, along with his passport and other essential papers. He was less sanguine than Polgar, and as he packed he considered the possibility that he might be in for a stretch in a prisoner-of-war camp.

His cook, Mr. Tu, had rustled up the usual breakfast of bacon and eggs. Mr. Tu knew it was the end. "I'm not going to leave, master," he said. "But could I remind you to leave me some money? I work for the Americans twenty years now." Lehmann replied that he would get his severance pay to him later in the day if it came to that.

Lehmann's driver's family were among the people to be evacuated from the villa that day. But the driver and a guard accompanied him on the short run to the embassy.

At eight-fifteen, Lehmann was deeply immersed in discussions about the planning that had gone forward in the last few hours, and the drafting of messages for the ambassador. He did not attend the small meeting in Martin's office.

Nine years later, records of that meeting are sketchy. And because it is nine years later, memories are dim. It seems certain that those in attendance included Martin, Polgar, Colonel Jacobson, Alan Carter and either two or three military officers. It is likely but less certain that Brunson McKinley, Marvin Garrett and a few other officers were present.

The discussion covered considerable ground, even including Polgar's latest contacts with the Hungarians. But it focused on conditions at Tan Son Nhut. The plan that had emerged from the midnight meeting* counted on sixty C-130 sorties during the day—enough sorties to remove ten thousand people from Vietnam.

Colonel Jacobson called Homer Smith. Smith said that he was convinced that the runways were unusable. Minutes before, at 8:10, he had dispatched Air America helicopters and bus convoys to begin the air and surface extraction of American and Vietnamese DAO employees from rooftops and pickup points around Saigon to the air base.

Martin was not convinced that the runways were unusable. He knew from personal experience that aircraft had operated out of bases that were under direct artillery attack. Hell, he knew it from reading about Khe Sanh.

He announced that he would take a look at the runways himself, and told Polgar and Jacobson to get him a helicopter. It quickly transpired that there were no Air America choppers available. Some of them had been crippled in the rocketing. And the others were shuttling Polgar's CIA people from Can Tho in the delta to the Seventh Fleet.

* At which Alan Carter had shouted at Shep Lowman, and Denny Ellerman had been bemused by the grizzled old bushwhackers—in Chapter Three.

"Fine," Martin said, with a glare at Polgar and then a self-possessed grin. His strength was returning minute by minute as the adrenaline began to take over. "Better to go by road anyway. I can get a look at conditions in the city."

"Sir, that would be a big mistake," Jacobson said. "We have reports of numerous Viet Cong around the airport. I strongly urge you to wait until we can get a chopper."

"Well, we all make mistakes, don't we, Jake?" Martin said. "Someone call my car. I'm going."

IX

Shortly before that meeting got under way, General Tran Van Minh and his thirty colleagues got tired of waiting. They walked from VNAF headquarters to the DAO compound. They were armed, and demanded to be included in the evacuation.

General Smith was in the underground "readiness room"—the crisis command center—when he was informed of the visitors' demand. He turned to Lieutenant Colonel Richard Mitchell, who was the assistant air attaché and had coordinated the evacuations of the VNAF dependents through the month.

"Go out and disarm them, Dick," Smith said. "If any of them refuse, tell them I'll have them shot."

Mitchell was a long-faced veteran, grizzled now after the weeks of long days. "Just me?" he asked.

Homer Smith smiled.

Mitchell approached the group, spoke his piece slowly and clearly. He reached out his hand, and General Minh handed over his pistol. All the others followed suit.

Ky was still out, and Truong, a few others. But the group basically comprised what was left of the high command of the South Vietnamese armed forces. Until it was time to get them out, the Americans kept them under guard and under wraps in an intelligence briefing room.

X

A thoroughly engaging leftist Italian journalist named Tiziano Terzani, who had covered Vietnam for years, was expelled shortly after the attack on Ban Me Thuot. The head of the press section in Thieu's Ministry of Information informed him that his latest article in the German newsweekly *Der Spiegel,* Terzani's principal employer, had insulted Thieu and "thrown mud on the Republic of Vietnam."

It was Terzani's second expulsion in two years. This one angered him more than the first had. *Giai phong**—liberation—was imminent, and the venal bastards were trying to keep him from witnessing it.

On Sunday, April 27, Terzani took a chance and boarded an Air Vietnam plane in Singapore, one of the last commercial flights into Saigon. The gamble paid off. So many of the customs police at Tan Son Nhut had already left the country that he slipped through the net.

Now, at 9:15 on the morning of Tuesday, April 29, Terzani was gathered with other journalists in a corridor of the Continental Palace Hotel. All of them had been up since shortly after four. Early on, one of them had discovered that with a simple FM transistor radio they could monitor the Americans' walkie-talkie traffic. And now at 9:15 they heard Colonel Jacobson telling someone who identified himself as "Whiskey Joe": "Pay close attention. Tell the ambassador to proceed toward Tan Son Nhut with extreme caution."

Half a dozen of the journalists gathered in the corridor of the Continental were Americans. Was the ambassador *leaving*, sneaking out of the country without telling them?

XI

The ambassador's car was adaptable, a black armor-plated Chevrolet sedan. The armor plating didn't show. The stanchions for the small fender flags were retractable. Flags flying, it was a modestly respectable American limousine. Retracted, it was just another car. On the run to Tan Son Nhut that morning, the flag stanchions were retracted.

But he was the American ambassador to Vietnam after all. Colonel Jacobson and Marvin Garrett, who would suffer the bureaucratic equivalent of being shot at dawn if Graham Martin was killed on his run to Tan Son Nhut, saw to it that Marines rode shotgun in embassy vehicles fore and aft of the ambassador's Chevy. And Jacobson alerted Whiskey Joe and everyone else on the net to safeguard the passage of this small convoy.

Nevertheless, there was a delay of a full twenty minutes at the main gate into Tan Son Nhut. Martin sat silent in the back seat of the Chevy, Marines at his immediate left and right, Marines all around him, casually considering the two or three hundred most important facets of the ten thousand facets of the problem now before him: How to extract every American and approximately ten thousand Vietnamese from Saigon in a way that would grace the leaving with a final touch of dignity—a grace stroke the historians almost certainly would not discover for years, if ever.

"Whatever happens, they'll attack," he thought. "The perfumed ice pick to the kidneys from my friends in the Department . . . the

* Pronounced zy fong.

sledgehammer blows from the idiot leftist press. Damn this delay."

The men with radios and guns who commanded people finally solved the problem at the main gate into Tan Son Nhut, and the ambassador was driven the hundred yards to the main entrance of the Defense Attaché's Office.

In the readiness room, Smith had the Air Force colonel who was most familiar with the condition of the runways give Martin a quick briefing. Colonel William Le Gro, Smith's intelligence officer, was with them, as was Le Gro's counterpart, Colonel Le Van Luong, the intelligence chief of the Joint General Staff.

As had been the case all morning, Martin was unimpressed by accounts of litter on or damage to the runways. When he was told about the troops milling about on the field, he asked Colonel Luong to call someone at JGS so that he and Smith could talk to him about restoring order.

Luong made the call. And there was no answer. Even the switchboard operators had left. Smith then told the ambassador that he had General Minh and most of the rest of the South Vietnamese command confined to a room in this building. Now Martin was concerned. But he still resisted surrendering the lift capacity of the C-130s.

From the secure phone in Homer Smith's office, he spoke to both Brent Scowcroft and Henry Kissinger. General Smith left him alone in the office for the call.

Martin emerged from the office and walked with Smith back down to the readiness room. On the way, he said that Washington had agreed to continue with the fixed-wing lift if order could be restored on the runways.

"But, Mr. Ambassador . . ."

"If we can't, okay, but let's try." Then he moved on to the most important point. He told Smith that both of them were going to be under enormous pressure all day, from Schlesinger, and the Joint Chiefs, and CINCPAC, to yank the Americans and leave the Vietnamese. He said that he had thousands of high-risk Vietnamese lined up and ready to go, and they had to get out just as many of them as possible. The United States owed a moral obligation to them. If we failed them, Martin said, it would be one last ghastly mistake capping the thousands of mistakes the United States had made in Vietnam. And it would be a failure with unforeseeable impact on relations between the United States and the two other superpowers. He was as forceful as Smith had ever seen him, repeating the key ideas several times.

. . .

On the ride back to the embassy, touches of lawlessness flashed past the ambassador's windows. A few truckloads of armed men half in and half out of uniform careened around the still largely empty streets, and there seemed to be fewer police on duty than just forty-five minutes earlier.

Now a crowd was gathering at the embassy. Some Vietnamese pounded on the ambassador's car as it moved through them and into the gate at the rear of the compound.

Martin was quickly told that while he was at Tan Son Nhut, Prime Minister-designate Vu Van Mau had gone on the radio to make public the government's order that all American military officials must leave the country in the next twenty-four hours.

In the first fifteen minutes back in the office, poring through cables and again talking to Washington, Martin made time to call Homer Smith twice. In the first call, he reported that he had a message from the White House confirming the decision to stay with a fixed-wing evacuation for as long as possible. In the second, he again reiterated what he was now calling "my order" that great numbers of Vietnamese be included in whatever evacuation took place.

Between those two calls, at about 10:40, Homer Smith called Admiral Gayler in Honolulu. Smith reiterated his belief that there was "no way" they could continue to land C-130s. Gayler had been of the same belief for hours. He told Smith that he was now going to tell the Joint Chiefs that they had to go to Option 4.

Out of deference, Smith called Martin. "Mr. Ambassador," he said, "CINCPAC is at this moment recommending to the Joint Chiefs that we go to Option Four. I thought you should know."

"It's not their decision," Martin said. "Homer, are you absolutely certain we can't get any more planes in there?"

"Yes, Mr. Ambassador, I am."

"Well, you're probably right—for the wrong reasons. We could get them in, but we couldn't control the boarding."

"I agree with that, sir," Smith said. "I've been saying that all morning, too."

"Okay," Martin said.

At 10:48, from the secure scrambler phone in his office, with no one else in the room, Martin called Kissinger. He told the Secretary of State it was time to go to Option 4.

James Devine, the ambassador's political-military counselor, entered the office just as Martin was cradling the phone.

Martin was standing, but stooped slightly with chest pain. As usual, the eyes peering out from under the brows held Devine's, who had approached close to hear his words.

"Kissinger," Martin said, nodding at the telephone. "I told him it's Option Four."

Devine walked out through the small group gathered in the outer office and into Wolfgang Lehmann's office. "Option Four," he said. "Graham just got off the phone to Kissinger."

Lehmann got up and walked into the ambassador's office.

"I'm told the decision is made to go," he said.

"Yes," Martin said. "That's it."

Lehmann walked out into the group in the outer office and repeated what they had already learned from Devine. He turned to Hank Boudreau, the administrative counselor, and finally gave the order: "Okay, Hank," he said. "Now you can tell 'em to take down the damned tree."

29

Charlie Timmes' driver didn't show up for work that day. After break-fast, the old soldier drove himself to the embassy. Then, at about nine, he went to see Big Minh, who was still holding council at his villa rather than at the palace.

Aides and old friends came and went in the living room, which was crowded with orchids and outsized aquariums, the quarters of a man who would have brought the whole outdoors into his house if he could. Vu Van Mau was there, and Tran Van Lam, and Mai Huu Xuan, who would surely be chief of police and national security adviser if Minh succeeded in forming a government.*

Timmes found the new president of the republic cheerful and hope-ful. Nevertheless, he thought it his duty to ask Minh if he or his fam-ily had any interest in leaving the country.

* Timmes would tell colleagues whom he thought would know the allusion that when Xuan was chief of police for Saigon in the early years of the Ngo Dinh Diem regime, he was the Baron Scarpia of the city. Diem later shunted him into a minor post. Acting on Big Minh's orders, Xuan was in charge of the small military convoy— an armored personnel carrier and four jeeps—that picked up Diem and his brother at the Catholic church in Cholon where they sought sanctuary after the 1963 coup. The brothers were assassinated in the APC when the convoy stopped at a railroad crossing in its progress from Cholon to military headquarters in Saigon. The men who actually wielded the guns and knives were believed to be a major who was a tank commander and Minh's personal bodyguard.

"Absolutely not," Minh said. "We are here."

Timmes then assured Minh that his government could count on continued American aid. And he advised Minh that, like Eisenhower at the end of World War II, he should offer to meet his adversaries on neutral ground.

As Timmes left, Jean-Marie Mérillon and Pierre Brochand arrived. Even though Brochand had done as much as anyone in Saigon to arrange Minh's ascension to power, the young French diplomat was struck by the appurtenances of power around Minh: "Thieu's" Mercedes-Benz with the national flags on the fenders in the driveway, even two small helicopters on the apron of the compound. He did not find Minh either cheerful or hopeful; rather, he thought the general had little idea what would come next. As his ambassador and Minh spoke, Brochand stared idly at a great golden fish undulating almost imperceptibly in a tank on a shelf above Minh's head.

Mérillon and Minh spoke in French. Without using the word "surrender," the ambassador urged Minh to declare a unilateral cease-fire.

"No," Minh said. "I ask your advice as to what we can do next, for the negotiations. But not that. I am a French general. Your military code does not permit me to surrender under these conditions."

"I don't understand," Mérillon said. "Forgive me, I am not a military man."

"There are circumstances in which one is permitted to surrender," Minh said. "A garrison under siege, other conditions. But not when the battle is joined."

"Saigon will be under siege in a matter of days if not hours," Mérillon said.

"No," Minh said. "We are all going to die together."

"*Non, mon général,*" Mérillon said. "I am not going to die. In a few weeks, I will be with my wife and son in Paris. *You* are going to die. Or you are going to be a prisoner. Now you must choose. And I urge you not to die. Because if you do, much of this city will die with you."

II

Minutes after the decision to go to Option 4 was made, George Jacobson called Terry McNamara in Can Tho on the special circuit that ran to one phone in the consul general's residence, another in the consulate, and said: "This is it. We're leaving. Go out by chopper. Take only the Americans."

"Jake, listen," McNamara said. "The choppers are out on operations . . ." Then the line went dead.

For the next half hour, McNamara tried a variety of ingenious ways of re-establishing contact, including attempts to patch through on radio networks through Thailand and the Philippines. Finally he picked up the phone with the special circuit that had failed earlier. To his surprise, he heard a couple of rings and Jacobson answered.

McNamara knew that some Air America choppers had been lost in the bombing raid and the rocket attack on Tan Son Nhut. He guessed that the three in the delta—which the spooks had been flying all morning—would be needed in Saigon.

"Jake," he said, "I imagine you'd like to have these aircraft available to you in Saigon."

"We certainly would," Jacobson said.

"Well, our friends have got them out on operations right now," McNamara said. "When they get back here, if you insist on us flying out to the fleet in them, we'll have to refuel 'em. By hand. As you know, we can't use the air base. Then there's the time in the air to the fleet, and I imagine they'd have to be refueled again out there. The way I see it, if we go out that way you aren't going to get these things until late in the afternoon. Now if you'll just give me permission to load my people on these boats—which are all set to go—I can tell our friends in the agency to order those pilots right back to Saigon the moment they put down. You can have 'em in an hour or less."

Jacobson said something to the effect of okay, and good luck.

McNamara issued orders, fast. The spooks had one of the two LCMs, tied up upriver at Palm Springs. It was, supposedly, understood that they were all going out together.

"I've got the authority from Jacobson," McNamara told Jack Donleavy, the CIA base chief. "He needs those choppers in Saigon. As soon as you can contact the pilots, you tell them that their *orders* are to return to Saigon as soon as they get back here from shuttling your people around. Round up the rest of your people and get them on the boat. We'll join up at noon in midriver."

"Yeah," Donleavy said. Then he and his deputy bolted for their offices on the second floor of the consulate building.

McNamara was in the courtyard a few minutes later when Donleavy came down the stairs, hauling a gray mail sack behind him. McNamara assumed the bag was stuffed with gold bars.

Donleavy's driver was sitting in a white government sedan in the parking lot. Donleavy got to it as fast as he could, dragging the sack behind him, yanked open the door, grabbed the driver by the shoulder and pulled him out into the heat. Then he threw the bag in the back seat, he and the deputy jumped in, Donleavy gunned the machine into reverse, spinning the steering wheel, and they hot-rubbered out of the compound.

A few minutes later, a phone rang. David Sciacchitano answered it. It was a Vietnamese employee in one of the remote delta provinces. For some reason he had not been brought into Can Tho. Now he asked desperately: "What's the plan? What am I supposed to do?"

McNamara had put them all under strict orders not to tell anyone who would not be getting on the boats that they were leaving.

"I don't know," Sciacchitano said. "I'll have to check with some people. Call back after lunch." He hung up, knowing that there would be no one left to answer the phones after lunch. He pictured the man waiting, out in the boondocks, listening to the phone ring over and over again in Can Tho.

III

At about 8 A.M., the Vietnamese—now numbering a little more than 2,700—and the handful of Americans with them in Dodge City started to take sporadic small-arms fire from frustrated, bitter ARVN troops holed up in billets three or four hundred yards away. It continued off and on throughout the morning and early afternoon, two or three isolated shots every twenty minutes or so, forcing everyone in Dodge City to try to stay under some sort of cover.

In the middle of the morning, two Vietnamese whom Hays knew— a young man and woman—decided that they would take their chances with the communists after all. Hays argued with them briefly. When it was clear that their minds were made up, he escorted them to the gate into the Dodge City compound. He suggested a route, snaking from one building to another and through some of them, to the main gate into Tan Son Nhut. The only danger, Hays figured, was on the base.

He had about two hundred dollars in piasters in his pockets. He gave half to the young man and half to the woman. Two U.S. Marines prone and alert in a ditch there near the gate looked up at him as if he were crazy.

At about eleven in the morning, an Army medic told Hays: "We're all leaving—all the Americans."

Hays approached an Air Force lieutenant colonel who was the senior officer in Dodge City at that point. "Yup, we're all leaving, Mr. Hays," the colonel said. "And if you don't realize what that means for these people"—he swept his eyes across the Vietnamese, most of them huddled under the raised buildings—"that's your problem."

Hays had been working with half a dozen other American civilians, including a priest and the manager of an ICCS restaurant, a big man who could have been Broderick Crawford's identical twin. They stayed in the gym, while Hays was usually out with the Vietnamese. His voice choked with tears and anger as he told them that the choppers would be coming soon and the military intended to leave the Vietnamese behind. The others cried too. They were all exhausted.

Hays returned to the colonel. "Look, Colonel," he said, "these people worked for the embassy. We've been telling them for weeks that we'll get them out."

The colonel said that he and three others would be staying until the last helicopters. They would try to get some of the Vietnamese out. And Hays could stay with them if he wished.

IV

The shelling of Tan Son Nhut had diminished but not entirely ceased. There was still almost no one in the streets. The small group of somewhat groggy journalists on the roof of the Central Palace Hotel had lost the room boys and waiters during the night, but they came up again after dawn. The journalists sent down for coffee and croissants and orange juice. The boys remained friendly, but said that the hotel might close that day.

I went back to my apartment to throw the remaining important belongings into a cardboard box. One of the maids for the family that owned the building came up to the seventh floor with me. It was obvious that I was going to leave some books and magazines and clothing behind, and I told the maid that she could have them. But it confused me when she started stacking the books in piles before I had chosen the two or three I wanted to put in the box, and I asked her to wait outside until I finished. Suddenly washed with exhaustion and shame, I cried as I threw things into the box, trying not to cry, cursing the humiliation. I quit for a minute and went out onto the big balcony with its strong breezes and said "F - - - it" over and over again until I was back in near control of myself.

Then I changed into an old pair of Levis that had always been too heavy to wear in Saigon, and a blue T-shirt, sailing clothes.

Several members of the family that owned the building were in the lobby. I asked if they wanted me to pay the April utilities bill; the woman I liked shook her head no. I spent what seemed like long minutes twisting keys off a ring, handing them over to the maid. I told her I was going to give her the motorcycle as well. I said that if anybody in her family could use it that was fine, but I didn't want her to sell it. "It's going to be all over in the next few days, I think," I said. "If I can stay, and if things get back to normal, I'll come back for it."

From the shadows at the top of the stairs, the sister-in-law let it be known that she wanted the Honda out too.

So I strapped the box on the back of the machine and lumbered out onto Tu Do with it. There, as I walked the motorcycle on a long diagonal across the deserted street, I saw Dennis Troute crossing directly from Givral's to the Continental. I didn't have an arm free with which to wave. The two of us glanced at each other briefly but did not speak. It was as if something might have changed us overnight. Perhaps in this new reality we did not know each other after all. Even years later, everything that happened to me through the next few hours came back in memory as if it were more dream than reality.

v

Out at Dodge City, Ken Moorefield checked with the banker who had been so calmly certain that Moorefield would come to get him. He and his small family were still calm. Instinctively, Moorefield felt that his duties at the evacuation center were over. This would be the day the Americans left Saigon. What was his role now? he asked himself.

He walked to DAO and proceeded to the operations center. Everyone was talking about the final roundup, from throughout the city, of the remaining DAO employees—Americans and Vietnamese. Moorefield realized quickly that some of the officers involved, especially the recently arrived Marines, did not have a good grasp of the city. They had maps showing the various pickup points but were still debating routes.

"Listen," Moorefield said, "I know the city pretty well. If you give me some support I can guide the buses around."

"Fine."

Moorefield got in a DAO staff car with a Marine captain and civilians who would act as drivers and they proceeded to the motor pool, where the situation was normal: all f - - - - - up. None of the buses were fully gassed, and it quickly became evident that they didn't have enough drivers. Then there was another small shower of mortar rounds. Back into the ditch. In the ditch, Moorefield asked a Vietnamese man who happened to be taking cover there if he knew how to drive a bus. The man seemed reluctant to get involved—until Moorefield told him that he could get him out of Vietnam if he was willing to drive a bus for a few hours.

Eventually they arranged two convoys of three buses each, jeeps fore and aft on each convoy, and headed into the city.

They ran into trouble right away, as they emerged from the main gate of the air base, with what sounded to Moorefield like a shell from a 122-mm. artillery piece landing about fifty yards to the left of them, followed seconds later by one about the same distance off to the right. Moorefield figured they were being bracketed, and that the communists had no intention of letting them evacuate anyone. He and the others again pulled to a halt and crouched in a roadside ditch until the shelling stopped.

Except for that incident, the first run—to half a dozen pickup points around the city, mostly close to downtown, and then back out to Tan Son Nhut—was clean. Traffic was beginning to build, but police were doing what they could to keep order. At the same time, Moorefield for the first time noticed armed, uniformed officers in private cars looking for a way out. And he shuddered when he saw a few trucks, here and there, filled with armed troops dressed in a ragtag mix of uniforms and civilian clothes. If they were going to fight anyone, Moorefield knew from the way they were dressed and the looks on their faces, it would be fellow South Vietnamese—or Americans.

VI

At about ten-thirty, Nguyen Cao Ky climbed into his helicopter once again and made the very short hop from the VNAF air base on Tan Son Nhut to the adjacent compound of the Joint General Staff. The compound was littered and almost deserted. Ky climbed to the office of the JGS chairman and found General Dong Van Khuyen, who had been the chief of staff, acting as commander. Khuyen told Ky that Cao Van Vien had been flown out of Vietnam by the Americans the day before.*

Ky called various commands around Saigon, including the Marine and the Airborne divisions. Everywhere there was either no answer or the confused, bitter voices of colonels or majors deserted by their superiors.

Ky asked a young soldier to get him a cup of coffee, anything to drink. "There is nothing ready, Marshal," the soldier said.

Ky was there for about an hour. At eleven-thirty, he saw that the skies over the airport and the city were filling with Air America choppers.

At noon, a Lieutenant Colonel Hung, who was a very good F-5 instructor-pilot and a member of Ky's entourage, said: "I think it is time for you to leave too, Marshal. It's too late." They had heard small-arms fire nearby and assumed the communists were on the edge of the base.

* One of Tran Van Huong's last acts as president was to accept Vien's resignation.

"Okay," Ky said.

As Ky emerged from the headquarters building, General Ngo Quang Truong, the former commander of what had been Military Region 1, came out of a ground-floor office. Truong saluted Ky.

"What are you doing here?" Ky asked.

"I don't know," Truong said. "I was assigned this office and I've been sitting here waiting for orders."

"Has your family left?" Ky asked.

Oh, yes, Truong said, they had left several days before.

"Okay," Ky said. "Come with me."

Truong and the dozen Air Force officers in Ky's entourage piled into his helicopter. He did not return to the villa, but flew south over the city toward the sea.

It never occurred to him to fly to Can Tho to continue the resistance. The sky was filled with planes, some of them from Can Tho asking him on the distress emergency frequency to which they were all tuned what they should do. "Fly to the fleet, find a carrier and land on it," Ky told them. "Or if you have the range, fly to Thailand."

Off the coast, thousands of boats of every description were sailing toward the great American fleet. Ky did not know where the fleet was. He would claim later with evident sincerity that he had never prepared for this moment. From the moment Hung said that he thought it was time for them to leave, Ky acted, he said, like a robot, or as if it were all a dream.

The aircraft carrier USS *Midway* picked up Ky's own distress signals and guided him in.

As it happened, the admiral commanding the *Midway* was someone Ky had once decorated for heroism in Vietnam. The man was waiting for him on deck. He shook Ky's hand and asked, "How are you?"

Ky could say nothing. The admiral took him to his quarters and left him there alone for twenty minutes. Ky cried like a baby.

Ky and his group were to be transferred to the USS *Blue Ridge*, the fleet's command-and-communications ship. Before they boarded the American helicopters that would take them there, Ky walked to his own helicopter, undid the holster around his waist and laid it with its pistol on the seat. He was sure they would be disarmed somewhere along the line and decided to avoid the indignity.

VII

As soon as I walked into the NBC office, Jack Critchfield—Arthur Lord's assistant and now replacement as producer—told me that the embassy had called insisting that the bureau get down to an "absolute minimum" number of Americans.

"You're going, right?" Critchfield added.

"Uh, no," I said.

"Jesus," Critchfield said.

Bob Wiener had come in to help with NBC's radio coverage earlier in the month. Now Wiener and I told each other with considerable pique on both sides that each was going to stay. Somebody from Swedish broadcasting was using the radio booth. I told Wiener that I would take over the line to New York when the Swede left, and Wiener went back to the Caravelle, where he was staying.

I made a coffee and idly watched the frenzy in the office. Mr. Khi was still there, still working the phones, when he had had every reason to believe twenty-four hours before that at this moment he would have joined his family in a comfortable hotel in Hong Kong. He was again scheduled to go out now in what at ten o'clock in the morning was being called an accelerated withdrawal.

I got on the phone to New York, wiping the handset across the T-shirt, and told them what I could about what was happening. Don Harris called from the roof of the Central Palace Hotel; I held the walkie-talkie up to a microphone and adjusted the sound level.

Then I simply kept the line open. I asked the voice in Rockefeller Center to call my parents in the Boston suburbs and tell them I was safe. Fifteen minutes later the man reported that that had been done, and my mother sounded fine.

I was not thinking about leaving. I was operating in small, finite bites of time. *"Someone else is talking to New York now, thank God; I can make a cup of coffee. Khi's busy and screwed-up, can't ask him to carry the suitcase to Hong Kong for me."*

A recently arrived American radio correspondent named Jim Laurie and Neil Davis, the Australian cameraman and correspondent whom I had half met at Ramuntcho's five long days ago, were in the inner office with Critchfield. I took my coffee and wandered into that office. I hadn't even sat down when the call came. It was Wiener, on the walkie-talkie, and it was a few minutes after eleven. Brian Ellis at the CBS bureau in the Caravelle was the coordinator for the three networks' evacuation plans. "This is it," Wiener said. "The whole thing. The full pullout. Ellis just got a call from the embassy. Everybody goes."

For the next three or four years, I told myself and others that when I joined the evacuation I thought that every American journalist in Saigon was leaving. Then, when I was able to begin to write about it,

I remembered Jim Laurie, who went on to a distinguished career as a television correspondent.

Critchfield got up and walked to Laurie and gave him the keys to the bureau and the combination to the safe, talking about whom he and Davis would have available to drive them around the city and to take care of the equipment. (Of the large NBC staff, only a couple of drivers, an electronics handyman and the office maid were staying.)

I went into the radio booth and stayed on with New York for another thirty minutes. I told them what had happened, cryptically, telling them that it wasn't for broadcast. Finally, as Critchfield and the others who were leaving started to pick up their luggage, I said: "Okay, I'm going to get off the line now. But Jim Laurie and Neil Davis are still here. They'll be in in a minute. Hang on even if you get silence for five minutes or so. The rest of us are taking a trip. We'll be talking to you from some other place in a day or two. You understand, right?"

"Right," the producer in New York said. "Bon voyage."

I gave Jim Laurie the keys to the Honda, told him where it was, and for some unfathomable reason asked him politely and earnestly not to sell it.

It barely occurred to me to ask Laurie and Davis if they could use me; when it did, barely, I understood instantly from the urgency that possessed them, an urgency that dismissed those of us who were leaving, and dismissed complicated entreaties about a damned Honda 90 (all this unspoken), that the answer would be no. I didn't know them and they didn't know me.

It did not occur to me at all to go one flight down and ask Esper if anyone from the AP was staying. Ever since Dennis Troute had hired me in the fall, I had not passed a day in Saigon without checking in at the AP at least twice, and more often three or four times.

Until that morning. I stopped thinking of possibilities, thought only, and this with great clarity, about what I had to do—check the desk drawer, say goodbye to the office maid, pick up the beautiful suitcase my wife had given me when I left Chicago—in order to be part of the evacuation.

I got in the NBC van and the driver pulled it around to the Central Palace Hotel. Shouting at one another to speed it up, the other five NBC Westerners retrieved their luggage from their rooms and paid off what were in some cases huge hotel bills. I had paid for my single night when I checked in. I threw some clothes and the most important papers in the suitcase, and kissed off everything else in the cardboard box.

We proceeded to a bus pickup point at the Grall Hospital, not far from the Eden Building. We waited in the sun, and finally, without too much shoving, boarded the bus. I filed in behind Malcolm Browne of *The New York Times,* who for some reason was wearing a World War II-vintage German helmet.

The bus sat there for a few minutes. I looked out the window and saw Peter Arnett.

"Isn't Arnett going?" I asked the reporter next to me.

"Yeah, yeah, everybody's going," the man answered.

"But, Jesus," I said, "all he's carrying is a camera. And he's shooting."

The grimy windows of the bus were meshed with heavy-duty chicken wire.

We meandered from one pickup point to another for an hour. Then we stopped for half an hour in the sun. I was standing in the aisle among a jumble of suitcases. I finally had to ask Malcolm Browne if he could rearrange his duffel bag so I could sit on it. Robert Shaplen of *The New Yorker* sat in the heat and kept as quiet as he could while tears rolled down his cheeks. And slowly, as the caravan of buses made its rounds and then turned onto the road out to Tan Son Nhut, the people of Saigon realized what was going on and the curfew finally broke.

VIII

As noon approached in Can Tho, it was clear to David Sciacchitano that they were going to miss some people. In the last few weeks, he had issued U.S. passports to the half-American children of two women. The husband of one of the women was working in Singapore. Sciacchitano had kept expecting him to show up. He never had. In any case, the women and children could go. Both women lived close to the consulate. And neither was at home. Sciacchitano assumed they were out shopping. Likewise, none of the staffers, all of them local, were at the nearby headquarters of the USIS-sponsored Vietnam-American Association. Apparently, they were all off at lunch.

A Greek-American with DAO and one of the spooks set off downriver in a small boat on which they had mounted an M-60. A few minutes later, they reappeared, passing upriver and telling McNamara and the others who were gathering on the dock behind the Americans' club/restaurant that they were going back to check on the group at Palm Springs.

Like almost the entire CIA contingent of sixteen to eighteen Americans, they were not seen again until McNamara's group reached the open seas. The spooks simply took off, out to the fleet.

The LCM on which they had said they would leave appeared around the bend of the river, loaded with Vietnamese.

McNamara's deputy, Hank Cushing, and the Marine NCOIC* in Can Tho, whose name was Boyette S. Hasty, decided to make one last check of the consulate building itself, which was about a mile upriver from the club. There they found the CIA's American communicator going about the task of destroying files and gear. If Cushing and Hasty hadn't happened upon him, he would have almost certainly been left behind. Cushing and Hasty pitched in with the destruction, and then the three of them sped back to the club.

When it was clear that they were going, the Vietnamese crew of the LCM at the club disappeared. McNamara assumed that they simply didn't want to go and would make their way back to Saigon, where they had come from. So McNamara and his colleagues had to quickly teach themselves how to pilot the ship.

Sometime in the last few days, the Marines had stitched a gold star and the letters "COMMODORE, CAN THO YACHT CLUB" to a blue baseball cap. They presented it to McNamara, and he wore it gladly: Anything to break the tension. The effort was not entirely successful. A USAID officer whose name appears nowhere in this account was distraught at having to leave his Vietnamese male lover. In his anxiety, he gunned the engines of the ship and rammed it into a mudbank; another Vietnamese, not his friend, had to jump fast to avoid being crushed. There were a few moments of high anxiety. The tide was running out. But at half past noon they freed the ship and cast off.

It was a flotilla of three ships, the two LCMs and the rice barge. On board were about 20 Americans and 298 Vietnamese. The Vietnamese included a number of draft-age males who had worked for the Americans, as well as a handful of police and Army officers who had shed their uniforms.

* Noncommissioned officer in charge.

30

Minutes after the decision to go to Option 4 was made, Wolfgang Lehmann called Alan Carter and told him to come to the embassy right away for an important meeting.

Carter made his way through about 150 Vietnamese in the USIS compound and got in the office car with its driver. They inched through the throng at the gate and drove the half mile to the embassy.

On the third floor of the embassy, Carter found the few remaining secretaries and numerous junior officers furiously destroying files. Lehmann, he was told, was tied up in a meeting. When Carter finally found him, Lehmann said: "This is it. We're all leaving."

"For Christ's sake," Carter said. "I've got three Americans over there, Wolf, and a hundred and fifty Vietnamese. I've been telling them for *days* that we'll get them all out."

"Get the Americans over here," Lehmann said, and started to turn away.

"How the hell do I do that, Wolf?" Carter asked. "I've sent my driver away. God*damn* the way this show is being run!"

"Well, get an embassy car then," Lehmann said. "But do it fast. You're scheduled to go out on one of the first choppers."

Alan Carter did not know how to get an embassy car. But at that moment Lacy Wright, who had overheard the exchange, said, "Take it easy, Alan. I've got a car. I can run over there and get the Americans."

"But what about the Vietnamese?"

"There's a lot going on," Lacy said. "Get in touch with Mission Warden—they might be able to do something."

Wright called the USIS compound to alert the Americans that he was coming for them. They in turn calmly reassured the more than 150 Vietnamese with them that buses would be coming for them soon, and made their way to the front gate. The embassy car pulled up and they slipped in, as if it were all routine.

II

Shortly after eleven, the ambassador called the Marines in his personal security unit into his office and assigned them various duties. Three were to round up the Special Police* and their families and bring them to a safe haven for evacuation. A Sergeant Paul Gozgit was to go to the residence, pick up Mrs. Martin, and accompany her on her flight from the embassy to the Seventh Fleet.

Sergeant Gozgit did as instructed, escorting Mrs. Martin and the Martins' poodle, Nit Noy,† from the residence to the embassy.

III

About an hour after they cast off from Can Tho, McNamara's ships were approached by Vietnamese naval ships that fired across the bow of the lead LCM, the one with the Americans.

The MR 4 commander, General Nguyen Khoa Nam, who was not running away—and that day had already shot at least one of his subordinates who made the attempt—had sent orders for McNamara's flotilla to return to Can Tho. His assumption was that the three boats were carrying officers who had demobbed themselves.

There was a standoff, McNamara and Hank Cushing on their LCM talking with the senior naval officer, who was accompanied by a short, stern-looking Army officer.

The commander of the MR 4 riverine forces was a Commodore Dang Cao Thang. Thang was staying. But McNamara had inserted his small family into the Saigon evacuation the week before. Now he announced that he was not going to turn around until Commodore Thang had been sent for.

* In this case, Special Police means the small unit of Vietnamese police who worked with the embassy Marines to protect Martin and Lehmann.
† Thai for little; pronounced Neat Noy. Thai for very little is *nit nit noy noy*.

IV

Early in the afternoon, the following cable landed on the ambassador's desk:

TO: GRAHAM MARTIN
FROM: KISSINGER
REF: SAIGON 758
    WE HAVE STUDIED YOUR REQUEST TO KEEP SMALL STAFF BEHIND AND THE PRESIDENT INSISTS ON TOTAL EVACUATION. WARM REGARDS.

Up until that moment Martin had hardly contemplated his own departure. When he got out of bed that morning, he thought he would be staying on, as the American representative at negotiations between Big Minh and the communists.

Now Martin realized that it was time to get some things from the residence. And there were classified papers there as well; they would have to be destroyed.

He told Sergeants Colin Broussard and James Daisey what he was going to do. Broussard checked with Major Kean, who had flown in from Hong Kong. Kean strongly advised against letting the ambassador himself leave the compound.

Fifteen minutes later, Martin and the two Marines were in the ambassador's principal car. But when they eased open the gate at the back of the compound, Vietnamese swarmed over it. Martin realized they wouldn't get out this way. Broussard, who was driving, drew back quickly in reverse and the Marines at the gate secured it.

Martin returned to his office and made a phone call. At three-thirty, he told Broussard and Daisey: "We're going for a little walk."

They walked through the CRA compound to a door that had been recently created in the wall separating the Americans from the French. They were greeted by Mérillon. Then Martin and the two young Marines walked from the French embassy to the residence. The crowd hardly noticed the small party.

At the residence, Martin emptied the safe, which contained among other things biographical sketches of numerous Vietnamese. He gave these and everything else in the house that he didn't want the communists to find to the Marines, who took them out on the back patio and blasted them to smithereens with a thermite grenade.

As he arrived at the residence, Martin had noticed a small crowd of Vietnamese at the abandoned New Zealand Embassy across the street. They were, he sensed, on the verge of breaking into it.

He had just told Mérillon that he was leaving. Mérillon of course agreed to attempt to act as caretaker for American property, including this house. On the chance that the French would be able to perform that role, the ambassador decided to pack a trunk with some valuables, including the extensive collection of antique maps he and Dorothy had acquired in the years in Paris. He also intended to place in that trunk a thirteenth-century Sukhothai platter that his SEATO* colleagues had presented to him when he left Thailand. But as he was climbing the stairs with it, he stumbled and fell forward. The platter shattered.

The older cook—the one who smoked opium—had no interest in leaving Vietnam. Three or four other servants did want to leave. Martin told the houseboy to stay with him. He told the others that he would send someone for them soon.

The ambassador had a back-up car at the residence. He, the houseboy, Broussard, Daisey and three other Marines who had been guarding the house through the day got into the back-up car and drove back to the French Embassy.

According to Mérillon, the last meeting between the two ambassadors had an air of theatricality about it, Martin playing the role of the American ambassador who had done the best he could and now had been ordered to leave his post, Mérillon himself playing the gallant ally who would stay behind. Beyond that, eight and nine years later, neither man was willing or able to recall much in detail. There was certainly no rancor between them. Despite the wide differences between their two governments over Indochina policy through the last quarter century, in the final days Mérillon and Martin shared one supreme objective: no Da Nang in Saigon. And as of that moment they had succeeded.

One of the Marines with Martin was a tall, serious young black man. And he was nervous as hell when it became clear that it was going to be difficult to carry Mérillon's going-away present to Martin— a foot-tall head of the Lord Buddha—and his M-16 at the same time. After trying various ways to cradle the two exquisitely contradictory objects, he gave up and handed the weapon to one of his buddies and the party slipped through the door in the wall to what was still U.S. territory.

In his office, Martin told Broussard and Daisey: "Boys, I owe you a fifth of Scotch."

v

Now Martin was finally willing to let Dorothy leave, something Wolf Lehmann and Colonel Jacobson had been trying to arrange for hours.

* Southeast Asia Treaty Organization, soon to become defunct.

She would be flown out to the fleet in an Air America helicopter with her Marine escort and the wives of two other senior embassy officials.

George Jacobson accompanied the women to the rooftop helicopter pad. Sometime in the last ten days, Jacobson had called what he thought were all of the Air America chopper pilots to the embassy for a briefing on the fleet's location and radio frequencies. Now, on the roof, he double-checked. And these two guys had never heard of any briefing.

Jacobson let them go. Then he spent forty-five minutes of god-awful anxiety until they radioed word that they had found the fleet and the women were fine.

Oddly, Dorothy had left Nit Noy with the ambassador, who leashed the dog to a chair in the office.

VI

Graham Martin had been led to believe that helicopters would be landing in Saigon one hour after he made the decision to go to Option 4. In fact the first three Marine Corps CH-53s did not arrive at Tan Son Nhut until twelve minutes after three in the afternoon.* They put down in a landing zone close to DAO headquarters, disgorged the first elements of what would be an 840-man ground security force from the fleet, took on evacuees who had been lined up in the corridors of Pentagon East and lifted off.

As they flew southwest over barracks for ARVN dependents, they took more than a hundred rounds of M-16 and M-79 grenade fire. That was the first fire to come from that direction. There was of course a constant flow of radio traffic between DAO and the helicopters, and among the helicopter crews themselves. Subsequent sorties found routes out of Tan Son Nhut that avoided the fire from the ARVNs. As to the communists, the pilots knew from a light that glowed red in the cockpit from the time they crossed the beach on the way in until they crossed it on the way out that surface-to-air missiles were constantly locked on them. They were never fired on by the communists.

During the long hours in the sun between word at 11 A.M. that the final pull was on and the arrival of the first choppers at three, Hays moved among the 1,500 Vietnamese gathered around the swimming pool and under the nearby buildings. (The remaining thousand or so Vietnamese were in and around the gym.) Having no idea whether or not he was lying, he assured them over and over again that they would not be left behind. No one had eaten since the night before.

---

* The delay was due primarily to what the Navy calls "cross-decking" operations. The Marines who made up the ground security force were not berthed on the ships from which the helicopters took off, and had to be ferried to those helicopter carriers.

Finally an Air Force colonel who was one of the senior DAO officers arrived with a jeep loaded with C rations and baby food, which Hays distributed. There were at least two births among those 2,700 Vietnamese that day. In one case, people crowded around the woman in labor in a failed attempt to keep the Americans from discovering what was happening.

There were three landing zones at Tan Son Nhut that afternoon and early evening: the one very close to a corner of Pentagon East where the first choppers landed; another east of the first in a baseball field; and the third in a parking lot right in front of the office building on stilts that was the Dodge City final processing center.

When the first helicopters set down there, in Dodge City, at almost exactly four, Don Hays was awed. The Marines spilled out in full battle gear and ran, crouching, to perfect positions to guard against the threats that faced them. Some of their officers may well have served in Vietnam, but certainly none of the grunts had. And it went off with the precision of a maneuver that had been practiced over and over again on some bizarre replica of Dodge City someplace. It went off, Hays thought, like a movie.

Things happened quickly. The same damned Air Force lieutenant colonel who had been giving him a hard time since eleven now gave him a direct order that he was to be on the next—the second—sortie. "Hays," he said, "I don't want any bulls - - -. You round up forty-five of your people now, and you get 'em over there for the next chopper."

"Colonel, if I leave, you're going to have chaos on your hands here."

"You're on the next chopper," the colonel said and stomped off.

As calmly as he could, all the time reassuring others, Hays selected about twelve men and women whom he personally knew to be embassy employees, all with relatively small families, arranging it so that it came out to exactly forty-five. As the second sortie approached, he ran with them from the swimming pool to the landing zone, a distance of about seventy-five yards. They were fired on, from the north—the damned Airborne. The seventy-five yards felt like a mile.

Don Hays wasn't about to get on a chopper until he was forced to.

Someone in charge of loading took over his forty-five people. Hays ran over to another colonel, this one from the Marines who had just landed. Before Hays could say anything, the colonel said: "You from the State Department?"

"Yeah."

"Good. What's the situation?"

Hays explained about the sniper fire from the Airborne billets. The colonel consulted with a Marine major, who sent a platoon into the area. Within half an hour, they had rounded up and disarmed close to thirty ARVN troops. They tied them together and kept them under guard.

The Marines especially were deferential to Hays. A lieutenant said, "Sir, you just tell me what to do and I'll do it." (Within hours, Hays would learn that the Marines for some reason thought that he and the few other civilian Americans were from the CIA.)

Hays asked a few quick questions and realized that the Marines were planning on flying more than enough sorties to accommodate his 2,700. The same colonel who had sent the unit in to shut off the sniper fire now approached and said: "Mr. Hays, we've got a bunch of Vietnamese over there at the swimming pool. Who are they?"

"They're all embassy employees and their families," Hays said. "Every Vietnamese here in this compound. There are a little less than three thousand of them. We've been tellin' them for a month that we were going to get them out, sir. They were all lined up to go on the fixed-wing last night when the s - - - hit the fan."

"Okay," the colonel said. "Get to work. We can get about— Well, let's see. They're small enough, aren't they? Form 'em up in groups of ninety. We'll see how that works."

VII

The bus carrying me and the other journalists was one of the few that got into Tan Son Nhut without much incident. As it moved from the main gate toward the Defense Attaché's Office, we saw a downed or abandoned VNAF helicopter in the grass, lying on one skid, its rotor blades spinning lazily. And as we sprinted from the bus into the sunlight and then quickly through one of the doors into the sprawling American office building, a rocket or a mortar round landed about forty or fifty yards away. I never did figure out the difference in sound between an incoming rocket and a mortar. I hadn't seen that much war. Some sort of pop registered off in the distance.

Then we joined a queue that snaked through the corridors of that complex of buildings that was aptly nicknamed Pentagon East. I shuffled the suitcase and the little Olivetti Lettera 32 along as one does in a conventional queue at an airport check-in counter, turning many corners, always to be faced with another long corridor lit with dim fluorescent lighting.

Hank Dorrity, the owner of a classy hamburger joint downtown called the Viet-My,* was helping the official Americans keep order. Later, I would find out that Dorrity had taken over the provisioning of the Combined Recreation Association restaurant in the embassy

---

* The Vietnam-America.

compound in the last week or ten days of the crisis, at no profit to himself.

Just before I turned the final corner, a big Marine came down the line shouting: "No luggage, no luggage at all. Just bodies, no luggage."

Goodbye Olivetti. Goodbye beautiful suitcase.

Then I turned the corner. I was one of a block of fifty who had been formed up for the next chopper, and already the ones in the front were running. We ran through a doorway of brilliant sunlight at the end of what seemed like a long tunnel.

Marines were prone in the grass of a baseball field, cocked and sharp-eyed in the sunlight.

31

The convoy that got me into Tan Son Nhut turned around, went back into the city and loaded up again at various pickup points. But this time when they arrived back at the main gate into the air base, the ARVN security platoon there simply was not going to let the buses into the base. The platoon was led by a young lieutenant, and the soldiers locked and loaded on Moorefield and the Marine officer with him in the lead jeep.

The moment embedded itself in Moorefield's consciousness. Saigon and six busloads of evacuees lay behind him. Ahead was the line of armed men and beyond and above them in the bright-blue cloud-puffed sky of another beautiful Saigon afternoon scuttling Air America choppers and VNAF aircraft of every size, the VNAF aircraft all taking off.

"You turn around," the young lieutenant said for the fifth or sixth time. Moorefield sensed that the U.S. Marine officer next to him in the jeep was about to reach for his pistol. "Let's get out of here," he said.

They moved from the access road to the one leading out. In the process, Moorefield's jeep fell behind the first three buses. And they were no sooner out of the long triangular apron with its apex at the gate when they ran into more trouble.

Just past the Seventh-Day Adventist Hospital there was an evacua-ation pickup point close to what had been a bachelor officers' quarters in a high-rise apartment building. As they took on more people there, nearly filling the buses to capacity, armed police infuriated that the buses were blocking traffic shouted wildly at them.

Moorefield jumped out of the jeep and ran to the white DAO Chevrolet at the head of the column, leaving his getaway bag in the jeep. Sometime during the afternoon the jeep was cut off from the column. Moorefield never saw the bag again.

II

Lacy Wright got Ken Jackson and the two other Americans from the USIS compound into the embassy shortly after noon. The USIS officials gathered with Carter in an office on the third floor and tried to figure out how to rescue the Vietnamese they had just abandoned.

They called the compound and told the Vietnamese to sit tight, they were doing all they could. Then they called the Mission Warden people, who told them they had no spare buses.

Brunson McKinley and others had set up an ad hoc evacuation control center in a bullpen of secretaries' desks outside the ambassador's outer office. As he wandered into the area about two, Carter for the first time heard that there were barges on the river.

"What barges?" he shouted at McKinley. "You sons of bitches aren't telling us anything!"

Carter found out as much as he could about the barges. As usual, he didn't get the right information. He left the bullpen believing that the barges would leave between two-thirty and three. There was no way, he decided, that his people could make it from the USIS compound to the docks in time. He never told the Vietnamese about the barges.

Instead, he called back to the compound and suggested to the leaders that they leave as quietly as possible from the compound and make their way inconspicuously, in small groups, to his villa. He would see if he could get buses to them there.

The first Marine Corps helicopters arrived at the embassy at about four. Wolf Lehmann was now insistent that Carter and his American staffers be on them.

Carter was carrying an attaché case and nothing else. He joined a slow queue up the stairwell to the roof.

Then, on the roof, he decided that he could not leave yet. "Go," he shouted to Jackson and the others. They went. Carter moved against the queue back down to the third floor.

There were two telephone lines into the USIS compound, the normal Saigon PTT line and an embassy line. From John Hogan's office, Carter tried both numbers over and over again, working against frequent busy signals. But whenever either line was clear and he heard the rings at the other end, there was no answer. And he never succeeded in getting through to the phone at his villa.

Later, Carter learned that about twenty of the people in the compound he had administered had made it to his villa. They called the embassy at about four, as he was making his way down from the roof. A Marine told them that Carter had left. Slowly, over the next few hours, the twenty then slipped out of the villa and into the new Vietnam.

III

Moorefield had a walkie-talkie, but communication with the embassy was spotty. But at two-thirty or three he got an urgent message to proceed to Shep Lowman's villa. With Lacy Wright, Lowman had been primarily responsible for the evacuation of politically compromised "high-risk" Vietnamese. Following the midnight meeting at the embassy and again at dawn, Lowman had made a telephone canvass of the names at the top of his list. Now more than a hundred people were at the villa.

But Moorefield's buses were full. He and Lowman conferred in the tree-shaded street that ran past the villa's high walls. "Shep, I don't have room for any of them," Moorefield said. "And if I try to squeeze one on, you'll have a riot on your hands. I'll try to come back."

Lowman said nothing; he looked stricken.

Moorefield never made it back. And the great majority of the men and women—pro-American intellectuals, politicians, agents—and their families that made up the hundred people with Lowman were left behind.

On the way to Lowman's villa, Moorefield got a call from Jim Devine ordering him to pick up the household staff at the ambassador's residence. This wasn't part of the plan, to the extent that there was any plan. But Moorefield had lived in the residence for a month when he first arrived in Saigon, and was happy to oblige. Further, there was, oddly, a gas truck at the residence, and some of his vehicles were running low. He made the stop, picked up a couple of servants and their families, and topped off the tanks.

IV

In the middle of the afternoon, two huge sandbagged* barges were tugged down the Saigon River to the docks at Khanh Hoi. At least eight thousand Vietnamese, including everyone waiting at the USIS compound, the hundred high-risk people at Shep Lowman's villa and the several groups of CIA employees gathered at various facilities around Saigon, could have made it out of Vietnam if their American employers had waited just a few more hours before retreating to the embassy.

The possibility that thirty to forty thousand Vietnamese would be evacuated from Khanh Hoi was moot from the moment it became clear that the only Marines they were to get from the fleet would be tied down first at DAO and then at the embassy. But the barges were immense. If people could get to them on their own, without Marine protection, all they had to do was step from the docks onto them. There was no government presence, American or Vietnamese, to stop them.

But by midafternoon, most American officials of all agencies were in the embassy. The communications network that had served Mott and Chatman so well through the past weeks—all those contact people who so definitely had to be American—had collapsed back into the embassy.

Chatman got to Khanh Hoi shortly after the barges pulled in. When he saw how enormous they were, he called Kistiakowski, the communicator back on the fourth floor, and said: "George, we've got these two huge barges here. Call everyone and tell 'em that if they got any people who are still looking for a ride, we got the space. All they gotta do is get down here to Khanh Hoi."

But Kistiakowski had no one to call. They were all in the embassy. And when Americans called the outlying agencies or the safe houses where their Vietnamese waited to urge them to get to the docks, many of the Vietnamese chose not to do so. They had been promised buses. A curfew was theoretically still in effect, and some of the Vietnamese apparently did not realize the extent to which the curfew had disintegrated, beginning at just about noon. In case after case, Vietnamese decided alone and collectively that if there were no Americans to shepherd them to the docks, they would not risk the trip.

Of course Ken Moorefield and the two bus convoys were still prowling the streets of Saigon. In fact, near the river, three of the buses headed

---

* The five-foot-high walls of sandbags around the edges of the barges were good protection for the run downriver, but were not put on the barges with this evacuation in mind. Until the Khmer Rouge victory in Cambodia, the barges were used to ferry military equipment up the Mekong River to Phnom Penh, and were routinely fired upon from the riverbanks.

for the docks. But Moorefield himself never heard about the barges until he got himself into the embassy later in the afternoon.

The decision not to tell Moorefield about the docks came from the top. The man at the top and his lieutenants still held their supreme goal in mind: no Da Nang in Saigon. The barges were for the Special Police and other cops, and no one else. It was ruthless, and it worked. The barges eventually left almost half empty, with whoever knew about them or heard about them that day on board, and thousands of Vietnamese who could have been on them never found out about them and were left behind. But it worked. Chaos did not descend on Saigon and Martin got all his Americans out.

It was brutally unfair to thousands of Vietnamese who had loyally followed the U.S. government. But it held off the chaos to the last possible moment, and may well have saved American lives. And Graham Martin was American to the depths of his being.

v

At the docks, hundreds of people milled about, many of them armed. These were Vietnamese who would stay in Vietnam. Here and there in all the other cities that had been abandoned or had fallen to the communists in the previous seven weeks, some people chose to stay behind. But that afternoon at the docks of Khanh Hoi was the only time in the final offensive when hundreds of Vietnamese had easy access to escape and ignored it.

Twice Chatman saw cowboys* make vicious grabs for the watches on the wrists of American bus drivers entering the dock area with a short-sleeved arm crooked in the driver's window. He marveled that men entrusted with a reasonably important role in the physical evacuation of Saigon were unaware of what most Americans learned in their first day or two in-country: Don't stick your arm out of a moving vehicle in a crowd.

Many Vietnamese arrived in their own cars. As soon as they got out of the cars with their luggage and moved for the barges, men moved to strip the vehicles. Mechanics all over the southern neighborhoods of Saigon soon heard that there were carburetors up for grabs on the docks of Khanh Hoi. Eventually, you didn't get a carburetor unless you had a weapon. (The men with the weapons for some reason did not organize themselves to relieve people heading for the barges of the dollars and taels of gold the great majority of them were carrying. Here in Saigon, looting was permitted but armed extortion was not.)

* The American and Vietnamese term for teen-agers and young men, usually long-haired, with mischief on their minds.

The late afternoon was also punctuated by occasional shots ringing out from a nearby rice warehouse that was being looted.

"Same same Quang Ngai, same same Da Nang," Chatman thought. Almost everyone running around at a trot, and, here and there, a few other figures, older men especially, who stood in a kind of stunned trance. He knew they were stunned by the madness of seeing their world collapse, one manifestation of which was seeing so many Vietnamese running at one time. (Vietnamese are no slower than any other people, and quicker than many of their neighbors. But in the tropics, it's simply too hot to run.)

When it wasn't hot anymore and there were long shadows, no one was left who wanted to get on the barges. Mott was on board. So were all of the Vietnamese in the small cell that had run the bus convoys for the last few weeks. George Jacobson, back at the embassy, had radioed Chatman that he wanted him to stay—he might have something for him to do later.

The American captain of the tugboat had a radio. Earlier, he had told Chatman: "I've got eight to ten thousand now and could take another eight thousand."

He was ten or fifteen feet above Chatman and so could see more of the crowd than Chatman could. Now, at dusk, he was getting concerned about some rowdiness at the back of it. "I think it's time to get out of here," he told Chatman.

"Well, I don't know why, but I don't have any more people for you," Chatman said.

"Good luck, partner," the captain said. He throttled his engines, and the barges inched away from the docks of Khanh Hoi, a little more than half full.

VI

From a pickup point near the river, Moorefield and his three buses headed back to the Grall Hospital.

The apartment building he had lived in was across the street, and his maid spotted him. She rushed to him, distraught. "What am I going to do?" she asked as she held his arms. She was the wife of a policeman, with eight children. Moorefield hadn't seen her for a week, not because she stopped coming to the apartment but because he was never there during the day. "They're breaking into the apartments!" she cried.

Moorefield gave her all the piasters he had, and the keys to the apartment, including keys that would unlock drawers. "Take anything you want," he said.

Two or three times during the day, he had driven near the embassy. He knew that he was never going to get his three buses through that mob. His radio now was of no use at all, and he needed instructions. He left the car and headed on foot for the nearby Brink Building.*

Moorefield walked into the courtyard of the building and found that a somber, fearful crowd of about a hundred and fifty Vietnamese filled the courtyard and the small lobby and other public rooms on the ground floor of the place.

He didn't conduct a survey. They looked like room boys and bartenders and waitresses. But there was a healthy representation as well of the hard-faced men in their forties and fifties who could have been Phoenix cadres or PRUs five or ten years ago. They were a remarkably disciplined group. No one rushed him.

Moorefield asked a few questions. They had been instructed by various American friends over the last few days to gather here. But he was the first American they had seen since noon.

He found an office behind the front desk from which he could call the embassy without being overheard by the Vietnamese. Miraculously, he got through to Eva Kim.

"Eva," Moorefield said, "I got about a hundred and fifty people here at the Brinks. All employees. They've all been told to come here, over the last few days. What am I supposed to tell them to do?"

Eva Kim put him on hold for a long sixty seconds. When she came back, the basic message was that there was no help in sight.

"Jesus," Moorefield said to himself.

He walked slowly through the lobby and out into the late-afternoon glow, mumbling colloquial English—"Stand fast, stand fast"—to the polite men who dared to ask questions, never looking them in their eyes.

Then he was free of them, and none of them chased after him, and he double-timed it back to the convoy, trotting as much out of eagerness to distance himself from those faces as to get on with the job.

Now people were crowding around the buses, shoving to get on. Hours before, the passengers had discovered that the grilled-over windows could be forced down six inches to provide a little air. People were

---

* The Brinks, as everyone called it, towered over the Continental Palace Hotel next door on the same block, immediately north of the National Assembly Building. It housed American officers during the war, and, after the Paris Accords, embassy and DAO personnel. There was a half-decent restaurant and bar on the penthouse floor. I happened to know from my Uncle Bill that it was actually the Brink Building, named after one of the first American generals to serve in Vietnam, in the early 1950s. At the end of his tour, General Brink returned to Washington and shortly thereafter put a bullet through his temple in his Pentagon office.

now pressing infants through the windows, trying to force the American driver to make a decision: "My baby's on the bus, you must take me."

Moorefield shouldered his way to the door of the first bus and stood spread-eagle in it, trying to keep order. He was infuriated that a clutch of Western journalists stood back from the melee, clicking away.

"Why the hell don't you guys do something to help?" he called out.

"No one told us what to do," one of them answered.

When order had been restored and the final loading finished, Moorefield headed back to the DAO car. He was surprised to find it empty. The Marine captain who had been driving it was gone, but he had left the keys in the ignition.

Moorefield started the car and threaded north, assuming the buses would follow.

Perhaps they did. More likely the Marine captain or one of the three bus drivers finally heard about the barges and headed for the river. In any case, when Moorefield got to the embassy, the only place he knew of to go now, he had lost them.

As daylight faded, Moorefield tried for a minute or two to raise someone in the convoy on his walkie-talkie, already anticipating the surety of the embassy across the street, beyond a thick crowd of panicky Vietnamese through whom he would have to make his way.

The car was almost out of gas. Moorefield reviewed the events of the day dispassionately but at very high speed. "I think I've played out my hand," he said to himself, and let himself out of the car. He started toward the crowd.

Ken Moorefield had acquitted himself much better than most Americans had that day in Saigon. But he lingered on the fringes of the crowd in his approach to the gates of his embassy, plotting his entry. And when someone he took to be a journalist approached and asked him who he was he found himself suddenly brazenly denying his identity.

"I'm a journalist too," he said. "Canadian. I just got in last week." He didn't want the Vietnamese to know that he was a U.S. government official. He needed time to think. A black moment, not for him, a hero, but for us.

Eventually, Moorefield eased his way to part of the wall where the crowd was thin, and called to a Marine on the wall. That Marine found an embassy Marine who knew Moorefield. They cracked a gate and three or four of them marched smartly out at port arms (the weapon crossed neatly across the full-muscled chest) and Ken slipped in.

VII

Eight Marines, including Sergeant Bobby Frain and two of his buddies, Walt Sweeney and Tim Creighton, were standing shoulder to shoulder at the back gate on Hong Thap Tu, the only gate anyone got in through now. There was an American TV camera crew in the crowd. A young Vietnamese threw the bolt on his M-1, aiming at the Marines. The cameraman, who was almost directly between the Vietnamese and the Marines, filmed the man and wheeled to film his targets; twisted to turn back to the Vietnamese with the live weapon. Both Creighton and Sweeney—a six-foot-four-inch black—started yelling. Frain yelled louder. "Okay! Sweeney! Creighton! The three of us will get him! The rest of you guys just stand tall!"

They charged over the cameraman and Sweeney got the rifle and Frain tackled the Vietnamese at the same moment. Creighton turned and picked up the camera, held it high over his head, and smashed it to the pavement close to the cameraman's head.

VIII

It was a long wait dead in the river in the midafternoon sun until Commodore Thang of the MR 4 riverine forces reached Terry McNamara's ships on the Bassac River, a good hour and a half.

Thang came alongside the consul general's LCM and said, in Vietnamese, loud enough for all to hear: "I have orders from General Nam to take you back to Can Tho. He's afraid that you have officers or enlisted men, or draft-age males, on board. Do you?"

David Whitten, McNamara's young political-military officer, acted as interpreter.

"No," McNamara said. "Everyone here worked for the consulate. As you can see, they are mostly women and children."

"Okay," Thang said. "I'll take your word for it. I don't have to enforce this order. You may proceed."

The sailors on the ships that had stopped the Americans and their charges had been quiet, even sullen, through most of the confrontation. But now one of them realized that his elderly father was on one of the LCMs. The old man knelt to accept his son's embrace. At that moment, the tension disappeared.

The engines they had rigged to the rice barge failed early, and the barge had been taking on water as McNamara towed it downriver. He knew it would be useless—dangerous in fact—in the open sea. So they transferred the people on that boat to the LCMs, cut it free, and gave it to the sailors who had stopped them, as a gift.

The river widened ahead, but there were numerous islands, some of them very large, that would force them close to shore. Commodore Thang took a map the Americans had and traced the safest channels.

Thang had had some training at Annapolis. He stood erect, gave McNamara a smart salute, and said: "I wish you Godspeed."

IX

Dr. Tran Kim Tuyen stood at a window of the *Time* magazine office on the second floor of the Continental Palace Hotel as close to despair as he had been since the communists had jailed him for two weeks nearly thirty years before. It was late in the afternoon. As he looked down on Tu Do Street, he saw civilians and military men in their underwear running in confusion. He and the others in the bureau— Pham Xuan An and the other Vietnamese *Time* staffers, a few others— for the last half hour had been largely quiet, lost in their thoughts. The phones rang only occasionally now. And in the silence all they could hear was the rushing of feet on the street and the rising and falling blattering of the helicopters. It had been a terrible day; and unless something happened soon, there would be worse terrors to come.

Jackie and the children had left with papers from the British Embassy on Thursday. They said that Dr. Tuyen was too well known to get out the same way. He didn't care. Kohlmann, his CIA contact, would get him out if it came to that. Dr. Tuyen thought there was still time—plenty of time, if the right figures could be persuaded to join Big Minh's government. But with the bombing of Tan Son Nhut and the curfew it brought, all the scheming died.

When he awoke that morning, a nephew, an ARVN major who was staying in the house, told him that the communists were at the New Port bridge.

Tuyen could get through to no one from the phone at his house, and so went next door to the house of an American who had worked for Esso. The man had left two weeks before, but his maid let Tuyen use the phone. He called the British and American and French embassies, and journalist friends, and all the phones were still busy. As he hurried out to Cong Ly Street, he realized that for the first time in years there were no police watching his house.

Finally he got through to the Continental. He asked for Robert Shaplen, the *New Yorker* correspondent. Shaplen told him that of course he—Tuyen—must try to get out; but just then Shaplen was very busy, he had to go to the embassy. "Come here about eleven," he said.

Dr. Tuyen was even more frightened to travel the streets in a curfew than most Saigonese. But his nephew, who was extremely eager that one of Dr. Tuyen's contacts could get him and his family out as well, drove him to the hotel. Shaplen was just coming out to join a group of about thirty other journalists assembled on the sidewalk when Dr. Tuyen got out of his car.

Shaplen towered over the little doctor. At first, he seemed ready to take Tuyen with him. He explained that he and his friends were going to walk the few blocks to the Grall Hospital, where a bus would pick them up and take them out to Tan Son Nhut. But then he had second thoughts. The bus was supposed to be for foreign journalists only. Maybe when they got to Tan Son Nhut, the military would throw Tuyen off.

Using the phone at the reception counter, Shaplen tried for ten minutes to reach someone at the embassy who could authorize him to take Tuyen with him. But he couldn't get through, and the other journalists began to get impatient.

Shaplen had been in and out of Vietnam for thirty years. Now he was distraught. He gave Dr. Tuyen the keys to the big front room that he always stayed in when he was in Saigon. "Don't go back to your house," he said. "Stay in the room. Try to get out. And here, I won't need these anymore." He handed over about fifty thousand piasters. A month before, the thick packet of bills would have been worth almost a hundred dollars. But in the last couple of days the black-market rate had soared to close to five thousand piasters to the dollar. The other journalists were already moving away. Shaplen looked in Tuyen's eyes for a moment and said, "Good luck, Dr. Tuyen." Then he reached down to his bags.

Dr. Tuyen's nephew drove him back to the house, where Tuyen gave most of Shaplen's piasters and the other Vietnamese money in the house to his two servants. He packed a small case with papers, a few piasters and twenty U.S. dollars. Then he returned to the hotel. He went directly to the *Time* office.

Cao Giao,* an old intellectual with a wispy beard who worked for Terzani, the Italian journalist, was in the office. "Why do you have to leave?" he asked Tuyen. "There is nothing to be afraid of." But Cao Giao was the only Vietnamese or American Dr. Tuyen spoke to that day who did not seem to realize that the director of President Diem's secret police and the Vietnamese co-architect with the Americans of its first counterpart to the CIA might be in mortal danger in a communist Vietnam.

Tuyen asked Pham Xuan An if he was leaving. "No," An said. "*Time* got my wife and children out. But I cannot leave now. Of course you must go."

---

* Pronounced Cow Zow.

Twice during the afternoon, Tuyen asked An to drive him to the embassy. Each time he saw friends in the crowd. And after even the first trip, around two, when the crowd was not yet too large, it was clear that there was no way Dr. Tuyen could fight his way to a gate and identify himself to the Americans. It was after that first trip that he gave the keys to the car to his waiting nephew and told the man to return to pick up his family and try to make his way into the embassy on his own. "Perhaps you are young and strong enough," he said.

Back in the office, they called around the city. Usually the phones were busy, the lines jammed. Often when they reached the home of a civilian government official or a ranking military man, there was either no answer or the servants reported that their masters had left.

Around three, they reached Bui Tuong Huan, who was a friend of Dr. Tuyen's. Huan's house was across the street from Tuyen's. And Huan was a truthful friend of Thich Tri Quang; a minister of education under Ky; then the deputy leader of the Vu Van Mau group; and now for half a day defense minister-designate of Big Minh. "I must tell you the truth," Huan told Dr. Tuyen. "I have just come from the palace. All is finished. We can do nothing. You must try to escape from Saigon as soon as possible."

Dr. Tuyen: "And you?"

Huan: "Now I am minister of defense; it is different for me. My wife and children left already. I would if I could. . . ."

Tuyen asked An to take him to the embassy again. Now it was close to four. People tried to climb over the walls and the barbed wire on top of the walls, but the Marines and the guards pushed them down. Now it was truly impossible for Dr. Tuyen.

Back in the office, Tuyen was desperate. Shaplen had left. Who else was there? He could not reach Kohlmann, the CIA man with the withered arm.

An said: "If you don't get out, don't go back to your house anymore. You can come temporarily to stay in my house."

At such a moment, a Vietnamese cannot say thank you. In the face of a gift so large, there are no words. Dr. Tuyen moved to the window. He looked down at the running figures in the street, listened to the sound of the helicopters, and thought of his wife and children in Singapore, wondering if he would ever see them again.

The phone rang. An spoke briefly in English, which Dr. Tuyen understood almost not at all. Then in Vietnamese to Tuyen: "It's Dan Southerland. He called for news, but this is your chance."

Dr. Tuyen had known young Dan Southerland, first of UPI and now the correspondent for something with the great long name *Chris-*

tian Science Monitor, for years. They spoke in French. Southerland instantly saw the gravity of the situation. "I will try to see the ambassador now," he said. "Hang up, and try to keep the phone free."

"Yes," Dr. Tuyen said.

Then they waited, no one using the phone, cutting the incoming calls short. They waited. What if Southerland cannot get through? It was a miracle that any of the operators at PTT were still working, that the automatic system hadn't been cut. They waited, glancing frequently at the silent telephones, Dr. Tuyen moving sometimes to the window.

They waited in near perfect silence a full thirty minutes. Then Southerland called back. He had spoken to the ambassador. If Dr. Tuyen could get into the embassy, of course the ambassador would see that he got out. But they could not send anyone to get him; it was too late for that. If Tuyen could not get into the embassy, he must get to number 18 Gia Long Street, an apartment building for the Americans next to the Alliance Française.

"If you can't come here, go there quickly," Southerland said. "Very soon, the last helicopter will be there. Tran Van Don is there, with twenty or thirty other people."

Tuyen grabbed his little cardboard case and hurried after An down the wide dim red-carpeted hallway and stairway into the dusk. They got into An's car and careened around the corner onto Tu Do, up Tu Do two blocks, another right onto Gia Long and pulled to a stop at the American apartment building just as the Nhung guard was yanking down the roll-down gate flush to the sidewalk that cut the driveway from the city. An jerked the car to a stop, jumped from it, got to the gate when its bottom edge was eighteen inches from the pavement, held it.

"By order of the ambassador, this man must get in!" he shouted. The Nhung guard, as small as Tuyen, was startled. With his left hand, An pushed the gate up another two feet, shooing little Tuyen in under the gate with his right.

Tuyen knew he must hurry, knew too that he must turn to say goodbye to the tall, handsome southerner who knew the Americans so much better than he did and who had now tried to save him.

"Run," An said, the tears thick on his cheeks. "Go."

Tuyen could say nothing. He cried. And then he turned and ran to the building, to the elevators. And of course they were dead, and he ran up the eight flights to the roof, stubby fifty-year-old legs and stout fifty-year-old heart pumping, and he made it. On the last two or three flights of stairs, he thought the body would give out. It did not. The little body throttled up the dim unknown stairwell and then he was in the understood reality of an American rooftop an hour after sunset on the last day of the war, Tran Van Don far above him, so far above Dr. Tuyen could only wave hello.

There is a famous picture from the last day of that war, stick figures on a rooftop stairway to a helicopter. Dr. Tuyen is the figure at the bottom of the staircase. The great machine shuddered and started to lift and Dr. Tuyen couldn't reach the iron mouth of the thing and André Tran Van Don reached down to him and hauled him and his little briefcase with the piasters and the dollars and the pajamas onto it.

X

About half an hour after McNamara left Commodore Thang and the naval ships, as the LCMs were approaching the dangerous stretch where they would have to sail close to the riverbank, something—either a rocket or a recoilless rifle round—just missed them—*boom whoooo-o-o-o-s-s-s-s-sh blam!*—as it slammed into the opposite bank.

It was just aft, and just a little high. And just the one round. Some of the Marines stood at the back of McNamara's LCM and fired into the greenery. (Others had no interest in firing at all.)

Sciacchitano wanted to join them. One of the gun positions had been his, until Hank Cushing had insisted that only the Marines should concentrate on security. But then the Browning automatic rifle that Sciacchitano had manned earlier jammed on the first or second round, and the Marine didn't know how to clear it. Sciacchitano did. He rushed to the tail of the boat, grabbed the weapon, got it cleared and emptied a thirty-round clip into the spot from which the shell had come.

This wasn't sport, or a gesture. Sciacchitano didn't like being shot at, and was pissed off.

Later, without making much of it, he would wonder if he and those few Marines were the last Americans to fire shots in anger in Vietnam.

There was never any doubt in Sciacchitano's mind that the shot came from an NVA or a Viet Cong. And there was still a good stretch of the dangerous part of the river to go. But soon after the one shot, the skies darkened and heavy rain fell all during their passage through the tight part. Even the communists didn't particularly like sitting around in the rain.

When the rain stopped and the residual fog burned off, David Whitten, McNamara's political officer, stood transfixed as the great wall of green, rich in the lowering sunlight, flowed close and stately past the ships.

He tried to imagine what the Vietnamese were feeling at that moment, watching their world disappear, and failed.

XI

Doan Van Toai, the former student activist, spent most of the day riding around the city visiting friends. The ordinary people he saw on the streets looked frightened. The leftist friends with whom he spoke reassured one another that there would be no atrocities, that the coming peace must be better than life under Thieu. Perhaps the communists would not use their full abilities; but they were ready, they said, to accept hard work to rebuild the country. One of the men Toai spoke to was the chairman of the Vietnamese American University Alumni Association. He had advised the members of the group to stay in Vietnam, and most of them had. They knew the weather, the food, the unceasing homesickness like a sack of rice on the back—there to be picked up in the morning and not to be laid down until bed every night—in America.

"I have never been in the government, or in the Army," Toai said several times during the day. "I can live with them."

He stayed away from the crowd at the American Embassy and went to bed early, sure he had made the right choice.

XII

Off and on during the afternoon and early evening, Graham Martin moved from the desk with its cable traffic to the windows. He looked down on the people in the two courtyards, and quickly understood the system Marv Garrett and the military had put in place. He looked at the Marines on the walls and knew what was going on there as well. Decent American kids were not smashing their rifle butts or the heels of their boots at the desperate Vietnamese trying to climb their way over the walls and through the concertina wire. The Vietnamese were getting in. It wasn't a steady flow but neither was it a trickle.

Every twenty or thirty minutes after the helicopters finally started arriving, a message arrived from one of the multiple command posts overseeing the evacuation asking how many people remained to be extracted. And even though the choppers were steadily moving people out, every time Martin asked for a new estimate of the number of people in the embassy and the courtyards it came back at just about two thousand.

XIII

Late in the afternoon, John Hogan was down at some gate vouching for the identity of an American journalist trying to talk or claw his way into the compound. The phone rang and Alan Carter answered it.

Alan Dawson, the UPI bureau chief, said that a very distraught Miss Thai Quoc Quang from Carter's staff was in his office and wanted to know what she was supposed to do. And for that matter, Dawson added, he'd like to know if there was any chance that he and his people would get out.

Carter was deeply demoralized by his failures during the day. More, he was filled with bitter anger at this culmination of Martin's misuse of him. The anger and shame unmanned him. He told Dawson that he didn't know what to suggest, and would have John Hogan call him as soon as he returned.

Hogan returned a few minutes later and called Dawson. "At this point, all I can tell you to do is get your people to the gate into the consular section, Alan," he said.

Dawson and the other UPI staffers, and Miss Quang of USIS, chose not to try to fight their way through that mob.

XIV

Ken Moorefield spent his first hour inside the embassy compound in a state of slightly dazed relief. For the first time in eight hours, Vietnamese were not screaming at him to let them onto buses. And the knowledge slowly grew in him that for the first time in nine days he had no responsibility at all for the evacuation. In fact, he had no responsibility for anything. In his own body, he felt the truth of the cliché of a weight being lifted from his shoulders.

It was late in the afternoon, and there were perhaps two thousand people—mostly Vietnamese—in the compound. The landing zone in the parking lot had been cleared hours before, but the Marine helicopters were still extracting people from DAO and none had yet set down at the embassy.

An hour of idleness was enough for Moorefield. He made a tour of the compound, saw the system in place—at its heart, the strictly controlled access from the Combined Recreation Association compound into the parking-lot landing zone—and started looking for things to do.

Someone anticipated that they would need more light in the CRA compound. Moorefield climbed onto the wall that separated the French and American embassies and helped string a light.

Finally, at five, the first Marine choppers arrived. They took out evacuees, and over the next three hours transferred 130 Marines from DAO to the embassy.

At dusk, Moorefield found himself on another wall, the one that separated the embassy compound from a police station on the northeast corner of the same block. The police there had been assured weeks before that they would be included in the evacuation, and now were starting to demand that the embassy make good on the pledge.

In a minor example of the balancing act that characterized everything Graham Martin masterminded that month, Moorefield and the Marines with him on the wall, which had been reinforced with a roll of concertina wire, hauled up some of the policemen and their families, at the same time insisting that others stay on duty. It was important, of course, that there not be an open breach into the compound there. And it was important that the police maintain control of their own facility. But the time for starting to make good on the promises to that group had come.

As the small contingent of embassy Marines was reinforced by the men from the fleet who had spent the day at DAO, Moorefield was no longer needed on the walls. He made another tour of the compound. The desperation of the Vietnamese at the gates was searingly painful. A middle-aged woman at the gate into the part of the compound that held the long, low consulate building was weeping, and crying out over and over: "I've got a passport, I've got a passport!"

The Marines had learned hours ago that while the crowd would part to allow a Westerner in, hauling up a Vietnamese invited chaos.

Earlier, at another gate, Moorefield had seen a young woman—she could have been nineteen, or twenty-five—with tears streaming down her face who called out with unfakable anguish that her parents were already in the compound, how could they keep her from her parents? As far as Moorefield knew, that woman also did not get in. On the walls and at the gates, it was hard to look anyone in the eye.

After dark, there was a loud explosion on Thong Nhut, in front of the embassy. Moorefield had the impression that someone had dropped a match into the gas tank of a car parked across the street. The crowd was more tense than it had been during the late afternoon. Obviously, it would now include desperate and bitter ARVN troops; it might well include communist agents provocateurs. Most of the gates were of open grillwork. It occurred to Moorefield that the darkness invited an anonymous shot from the crowd. In the penultimate quasi-military act of his years in Vietnam, he went from gate to gate advising the Marines that they might be safer if they stood off to the sides, behind the protection of the concrete walls.

xv

Mel Chatman drove himself in a Scout from Khanh Hoi to the embassy. He parked the Scout on the street, knowing it would be stripped or hot-wired and taken soon. Then, like Moorefield—like many Americans that day—he forced his way to the front of the crowd at a side gate and the Marines satisfied themselves that he was one of theirs, and inched open the gate and let him in.

He helped man the phones and the radios in the small communications center on the fourth floor through the next six hours. Early on, a contractor called from a hotel downtown, demanding that the embassy send a car for him. "What the hell are you still *doing* here?" Chatman said. "We've been trying to get you guys out of here for the last three weeks. It's too late for cars. Get yourself to the embassy and talk your way in."

Then someone radioed from Tan Son Nhut. Chatman thought the man's name was Behr, but he wasn't at all sure about that. "Behr" was nearly inarticulate in his rage.

Trying to filter out the expletives and insults, Chatman got the picture: The man and an American colleague and a couple of Vietnamese with them, all of them on current contract with the embassy having to do with running a restaurant or a club or something, had spent the afternoon at the NCO club at Tan Son Nhut, waiting for helicopters that never came. Early in the evening, they set the club on fire to draw the helicopters to them. Still no choppers. And their damned embassy vehicle wouldn't start. Even as he yelled, his buddy and the Vietnamese were pushing the vehicle away from the burning club. *"And there's a f-----' tank firing at somebody maybe a hundred meters from here, you dumb f---s, there's tanks all over the place, and fires, how the f--- could you leave us out here?"*

Jim Devine, Martin's political-military counselor, wandered into the communications room during the harangue. He took Chatman's radio and said, "Hey, calm down, buddy. From where you're at, can you see the gate into Dodge City over there?"

A much calmer voice came back: "Yeah, we can see it. You've got to forgive my friend. He's a little shook up. We're in a pretty bad situation out here."

"I understand," Devine said. "Leave the car—or keep pushing it if it offers any protection. Get yourselves over to Dodge City. There are still Marines there. You'll be okay if you can just make it to the gate."

"Okay," the calm voice said. They didn't call back.

XVI

Out at Dodge City, Hays had tried to get the family groups that included the newborn infants and the ill and the very elderly on the first choppers. As it happened, it didn't much matter. The Marines gave him a free hand, and by nightfall they had evacuated all but a couple of hundred people.

Despite the earlier arrests, some firing continued throughout the afternoon. And between seven-thirty and eight a couple of snipers appeared on the roof of the bowling alley. For a few minutes, they moved to the edge of the roof, only head and shoulders and weapon visible, and took potshots into the small crowd below. Hays assumed that they were not aiming to kill, but only venting their rage. He feared that they might be drunk and in their drunkenness manage to kill someone accidentally.

An Air Force man at the pool picked up a carbine and shot one of them, a clean hit to the head. The other didn't show himself again.

It was like a bizarre Western, made more bizarre by the sight of Marines lugging IBM Selectric typewriters from the processing center into the choppers, and by the rain that started to fall in the early darkness.

Then the military decided they wouldn't land any more helicopters in Dodge City. The only Westerners left were Hays, the Air Force man, the Marines and a couple of civilians Hays didn't know.

Hays snaked the remaining Vietnamese through a cluster of trailers that had served as officers' living quarters to the DAO movie theater, which had become the final DAO evacuation staging area. On the way, he passed through the baseball field, with its ring of prone, alert Marines. Someone had set fire to an old wooden barracks, to give the helicopter pilots a beacon.

Over the next hour, his last Vietnamese were loaded and gone. Someone told Hays it was his turn. In the hours of loading people under the wind blast from the choppers, he had lost his shirt and even his shoes. He climbed onto a helicopter with a camera bag, a revolver, and his State Department ID.

As they headed east, he looked down. Long Binh was in flames and other fires formed a dotted ring around the city. Shirtless and barefoot, Hays pictured himself as a tough young Airborne sergeant operating out of Long Binh, in another world.

He was a tall, sturdy American with pleasant features under a hairline receding in wings. On the USS *Midway*, someone asked him if he was Vietnamese.

32

"Now it is starting," Mérillon thought; "Da Nang is coming to Saigon."

With the crumping of not-so-distant artillery in their skulls and the *whomp-whomp-whomp* of American helicopters above them, the French temporarily lost heart. There was no good news, or bad news, no news at all, from the sister mission in Hanoi. Maybe the Viets had cut it off. Neither Mérillon nor Brochand saw a way to get out to Camp Davis;* how could they if Minh himself could not?

One of Minh's young aides, one of the most eager of the young Buddhist politicians, got through to Brochand late in the afternoon. He was in tears. "My wife wants us to leave," he sobbed. "It is all over. The communists will stop at nothing. They want everything. And I can*not* go. You know I cannot go, Monsieur Brochand."

"Yes," Brochand said.

Then the ambassador called for him. They discussed the breakdown in communications with the other side, the few reports they had of fighting around the city, the looting.

---

* The compound inside Tan Son Nhut that housed the communist delegations to the various bodies called for in the Paris Accords.

They speculated about why Big Minh had the helicopters standing by at the villa. Was he going to flee after all? Or would he fly to the delta and try to command a resistance from there?

Mérillon decided that it was not his place to do what must come next. He was careful in his instructions to his young aide.

Brochand made the call from the ambassador's office. He told Big Minh that he was speaking not as a French diplomat but as a friend. *"Monsieur le président,"* he said, "it seems that everything we hoped for has died. Apparently they are going to take Saigon. It is futile, useless, to resist. It will end in nothing but terrible destruction and disorder and needless loss of life. I strongly urge you to call on your soldiers to lay down their arms."*

Brochand was swept with a kind of embarrassment as he heard himself saying the words. He was twenty-five years younger than Duong Van Minh, whom he admired as a patriot trying to play out the last act of a terrible drama with dignity. Again, Brochand felt that he was playing a role far above his official station. He also told himself that it was his duty to give this advice, the only advice that could save the city.

Big Minh thanked the young diplomat formally for the advice, without indicating whether he would follow it.

Early that evening, shortly after Brochand's call to Big Minh, the disorder that was building in the city reached into Mérillon's staff. In thick Parisian accents, two of his Marines refused point-blank to go out into the streets to reach the men at the top of the list of notables and tell them to go to the first stage of alert. "Too dangerous," they said. "Too much high shooting." It wasn't their job.

Mérillon had seen the same sort of thing when he was ambassador to Jordan during a period of unrest. A crisis brings out the best in many people; others become very tense, aggressive. Understanding the syndrome helped him control himself. But he was furious at the insubordination.

The Marines won. Mérillon's cultural affairs minister counseled him to calm himself, to let it pass. Mérillon calmed himself with one of his aspirinated bourbon and Cokes. Then he announced that for the

* Mérillon's fervor to prevent a siege of Saigon had among its sources an interesting historical and personal impetus. During the German occupation of Paris in World War II, Mérillon's father was an official of the French Red Cross. The Swedish consul general in Paris, Raoul Nordling, was an occasional guest at the Mérillon home when the man who would become the last French ambassador to Saigon was in his late teens. Nordling played a key role in persuading the German generals in Paris to disobey Hitler's orders to raze the city before it was liberated. In the final days in Saigon, Mérillon saw his role as somewhat analogous to that of Nordling.

first time in three nights he was going to go across the garden to the residence and have a proper dinner.

When he got to "the first house in Saigon," Ah Don, the huge old Chinese head butler, who had been with the French since 1940, asked if Monsieur would like his bath. Yes.

An hour later, refreshed, the ambassador sat down to an exquisite dinner. As usual, Ah Don took a sip of the first bottle of wine. And as happened once a month or so, he turned to one of the two other butlers and rejected the bottle in disgust.

The ambassador was able to smile. But he wondered how long it would last. He wondered if the man who came once a week to see to the orchids, bringing fresh ones and throwing out those whose day had passed, would come that week.

II

In the grounds of the embassy next door the military and the embassy security officers were in full control, carefully feeding chopperloads of evacuees through the gate between the CRA compound and the landing zone in the inner courtyard. Every twenty minutes or so, a chopper made the difficult descent out of the blackness, a blinding Cyclopean eye on the nose of the beast flicked on for the final twenty or thirty yards of the maneuver.

Ken Moorefield watched two landings, marveling at the pilots' skill. Then he went back into the embassy, to which he had repaired off and on over the last few hours.

He wandered into the office of a CIA analyst who had been something of a fellow plotter against Graham Martin. Someone somewhere in the building was still monitoring NVA troop movements. But Moorefield's friend and the CIA colleagues with him were taking a last break from the war, over drinks. After a few minutes of desultory conversation, his friend said: "I don't think you ought to stay here, Ken."

"Right," Moorefield said.

He went down one floor to the ambassador's outer office. The word there was that the Old Man's health was failing fast.

A phone rang, and Moorefield picked it up. "My God," the woman on the other end of the line said, "I'm a Vietnamese, but I got my American citizenship in 1973. I've got three kids. What can I do?"

"I . . . I don't know what you can do," Moorefield said. "I'm sorry." He hung up.

He didn't want to have to take any more calls. So he went down and sat on the few steps leading up to the rear entrance into the embassy lobby, and watched the pilots work. It was tough enough coming in. Getting out, they moved straight up, overloaded, straining, inching up as if lifted by the hand of God, and then slipped back over the garden of the French Embassy, clearing all the nearby buildings save for the American Embassy building itself, and that gave them room to make a quick nose-down forward run to pick up the speed that would allow them to climb up into the night.

In the long minutes between landings, from far above came the faint rumble of invisible fighter-bombers flying cover.

Vehicles of the (Vietnamese) embassy fire squad and other cars were arranged in a circle around the landing zone with their lights on. Those lights crisscrossed under the greenish light of the embassy's normal outdoor lighting, augmented over the last few weeks in anticipation of this night. Especially after a sortie, dust hung in the glow.

George McArthur emerged from the embassy and stood surveying the scene, a drink in hand. On the few other occasions when Moorefield had seen the correspondent, McArthur had been working. Now he stood there, thin and casually well dressed as usual, and obviously now, like Moorefield himself, a spectator.

III

No American ambassador to Saigon had a worse relationship with the resident American press corps than did Graham Martin. None of his predecessors held the journalists in quite the same black contempt that Martin did. Martin himself had briefly been the Washington correspondent for a small string of southern newspapers, and he felt some of the bitterness of a man who believes that a fraternity to which he once belonged has fallen from grace. More than that, he remembered his years in Europe and even Bangkok, when there were still correspondents he could trust, men who believed that their work should of course further their government's policies when those policies were sound—as they damned well were whenever he was in charge.

In Saigon it was war, with the special enemies being the young correspondents of *The New York Times*.

There were a few exceptions to this poisonous state of affairs. Martin could unbend a little with Keyes Beech of the Chicago *Sun-Times*; Bob Shaplen of *The New Yorker*; a few other older correspondents, like Joe Alsop, who would occasionally drop in. And Martin enjoyed the company of George McArthur of the Los Angeles *Times*. McArthur was from Thomasville, Georgia. Like Martin, he was tall, thin and distinguished-looking. He was in his early fifties, ten years younger than Martin, and so qualified (barely) for inclusion in that generation that remembered the ideals and gentlemanly rules of World War II. The man of affairs from Thomasville, North Carolina, often invited the man of affairs from Thomasville, Georgia, and Eva Kim, who was McArthur's lady friend, to the residence for movies.

Two months before, the friendship had seemed to break. After the last movie, on March 1, the night before he returned to Washington with the last congressional delegation, the ambassador had played a favorite theme one time too many for McArthur.

"The one thing that will never happen is that the South Vietnamese will lose the struggle on the battlefield," he had said. As politely as possible, McArthur told the ambassador that he thought he was full of s - - -.

There had been no invitations to Eva and George to come see the movies at the ambassador's residence in the month since his return.

But at about nine that last evening, after his breath of air on the back steps, McArthur walked up to the third floor and things changed. Eva was there in the outer office of course, and soon young Moorefield, and Walter Burke, the consul general, and a CIA secretary, and Lacy Wright, a few others. And there was booze in paper cups, anything you wanted.

Suddenly Ambassador Martin (who was not drinking) emerged from his office and greeted McArthur as if they were the best of friends. He shook the correspondent's hand and invited him into the office.

McArthur sensed that Martin had something he wanted to say. But when he saw Nit Noy leashed to the leg of a chair, he remembered Eva saying that she thought the ambassador was going to leave the dog.

"Mr. Ambassador," McArthur said, "would you like me to take Nit Noy out with me?"

"Why, thank you, George," Martin said. "Dorothy would appreciate that." Then, as McArthur untied the little dog, the ambassador began a litany of complaints against Polgar. If the CIA man hadn't been seeing to his own assets that morning—not that he did very well by his people after all—there might have been an Air America chopper available for him when he wanted to go out to the airport. This wasn't a matter of perquisites; if he'd had the chopper he would have been able to get a better look at the runways. "Then I find out a few days ago that he's running his own little negotiations with the communists, through Malcolm Browne [of *The New York Times*]. I tell you, George, that might have cost us an extra day. I was counting on having today to finish up the fixed-wing evacuation."

There was more. In the last few days, the CIA had been flying some of its KIPs—its Vietnamese assets—to an airstrip in eastern Thailand. They didn't realize until they made the first run that the base had never been finished; it was just a great long concrete slab in the countryside. And the ambassador's guess was that the Thais were not going to be too happy about this sudden breach of their sovereignty.

Someone must have gotten word to Polgar. He appeared in the doorway at the moment when Martin was complaining about the effect on embassy morale of Polgar's shipping out his household goods earlier in the month. The ambassador finished the sentence, but it was clear that the interview now must come to a close. There was going to be a pissing match when it was all over, McArthur thought, but it wasn't going to come this night. He left the two of them together.

Polgar left the office, and a few minutes later the ambassador emerged again. McArthur was perched on the edge of Eva Kim's desk.

"Miss Kim, I don't think I'll have any more dictation tonight," Martin said. "Why don't you leave?"

"Yes, sir," Eva said. Then she and George and Nit Noy moved off to the column of people snaking through the corridors and stairwell to the roof.

IV

By nine o'clock in the evening, there was truly nothing more Alan Carter could do. For hours, no one had answered the phone at the USIS compound and he had not been able to get the phone at the villa to ring. He had checked, off and on, but never found Miss Quang in the crowd pressing against the gate into the consular section.

So, hours after he had been ordered out of the country, for the second time that day he joined a line of people snaking to the roof. He chatted with George McArthur and Eva Kim, who were close to him in the line, Carter throttling his bitterness, jokes about Nit Noy. They went out on the same chopper, Carter and George and Eva and the dog.

The anger built on the short flight to the fleet. When they landed on the USS *Okinawa,* one of the first Americans from the mission Carter saw was Shep Lowman.

"Someday," Carter said to Lowman, his tone of voice making it clear that he did not think Lowman himself was primarily responsible, "someone will nail the sons of bitches who f - - - - - this thing up."

V

[9:41 P.M., SAIGON TIME]   SCOWCROFT TO MARTIN.
   UNDERSTAND THERE ARE STILL ABOUT 400 AMERICANS IN EMBASSY COMPOUND. YOU SHOULD ENSURE THAT ALL, REPEAT ALL, AMERICANS ARE EVACUATED IN THIS OPERATION ASAP. WARM REGARDS.

Now the ambassador was angry. He walked out of the office and asked Jim Devine to come with him up to the communications room on the fourth floor. There he scratched out a message on a yellow legal pad.

The larger Chinooks—the CH-53s—landed in the parking-lot landing zone. The pad on the roof could support only the smaller model, the CH-46. The normal (American) capacity of the bigger aircraft was fifty. But Martin knew that, even with the luggage, the Marines were cramming sixty to seventy people, most of them Vietnamese, onto the 53s.

Devine typed the message, and handed it to the communicator:

[10:00 P.M.] FLASH WHITE HOUSE FOR BRENT SCOWCROFT.

PERHAPS YOU CAN TELL ME HOW TO MAKE SOME OF THESE AMERICANS ABANDON THEIR HALF-VIETNAMESE CHILDREN, OR HOW THE PRESIDENT WOULD LOOK IF HE ORDERED THIS.

FOR MORE THAN 50 MINUTES THERE HAVE BEEN NO CH-53S HERE. AND ONLY ONE CH-46.

COMMANDER SEVENTH FLEET MESSAGED ME ABOUT HOUR AND HALF AGO, SAYING HE WOULD LIKE TO STAND DOWN ABOUT 2300 HOURS AND RESUME 0800 TOMORROW MORNING.

I REPLIED THAT I DAMNED WELL DIDN'T WANT TO SPEND ANOTHER NIGHT HERE.

FOUR HOURS AGO, I TOLD NOEL [GAYLER] THE NUMBER OF SORTIES WE NEED. NOW THE NUMBER IS 30 CH-53 SORTIES. I DON'T REALLY MIND GIVING DAO COMPLETE PRIORITY—THEY WERE MORE EXPOSED THAN WE WERE HERE. I NEED 30 CH-53 SORTIES DAMNED QUICK AND I HAVE RECEIVED NOTHING BUT SILENCE SINCE I ASKED FOR THEM. AM WELL AWARE OF THE DANGER HERE TOMORROW AND I WANT TO GET OUT TONIGHT. BUT I DAMN WELL NEED AT LEAST 30 CH-53S OR THE EQUIVALENT TO DO THAT. DO YOU THINK YOU CAN GET PRESIDENT TO ORDER CINCPAC TO FINISH JOB QUICKLY? I REPEAT I NEED 30 CH-53S AND I NEED THEM NOW. WARM REGARDS. SECRET.

Eleven minutes later, there was a message from Dean Brown, a distinguished former ambassador who had been called out of retirement a few weeks earlier to head up an interagency task force on the evacuation and the planning for the resettlement of thousands of Vietnamese in the United States.

FOR MARTIN FROM BROWN

IBM HEADQUARTERS REPORTS ITS PERSONNEL STILL IN SAIGON AND IS MOST DISTURBED. DO WHAT YOU CAN.

If IBM's Vietnamese employees and their families had been included in the evacuation, it would have been through the instigation of Denny Ellerman, Martin's economics counselor. Ellerman had joined the queue snaking up to the roof at about nine. Martin tossed the cable aside and wrote out another message, reformulating for Admiral Gayler in Honolulu what he had just told Scowcroft.

[10:15 P.M.] FOR CINCPAC FROM MARTIN

I NEED 30 CH-53 SORTIES TO GET US OUT OF HERE. I DON'T REALLY MIND GIVING DAO COMPLETE PRIORITY—THEY WERE EXPOSED. BUT THAT LIFT WAS FINISHED AT 1900 SAIGON TIME. I THOUGHT WE WOULD GET THAT CAPACITY ADDED HERE, BUT THIS HAS NOT HAPPENED.

I REPEAT I NEED 30 CH-53 SORTIES AND I NEED THEM NOW, AND I HAVE JUST ASKED SCOWCROFT TO SO INFORM THE PRESIDENT. I DON'T WANT TO SPEND THE NIGHT HERE, BUT I CAN'T COME OUT UNTIL THE 29TH OR 30TH SORTIE. SO PLEASE GET THEM MOVING. WARM REGARDS.

Gayler answered within minutes that he had Martin's latest message and "you will have already seen the response by the chopper crews"—that is, additional helicopters should have already started landing. That was not good enough for Martin.

[10:20 P.M.] SAIGON TO FLASH WHITE HOUSE

AMONG AMERICANS HERE IS FATHER MCVEIGH, HEAD OF CATHOLIC RELIEF SERVICES, WHO WILL NOT LEAVE WITHOUT HIS VIETNAMESE STAFF, WHO HE KNOWS WILL BE PERSECUTED ON BASIS OF WHAT HAS HAPPENED IN MRS 1 AND 2.

HOW WILL PRESIDENT EXPLAIN TO BISHOP SWANSTROM,* US HEAD OF CRS, OR FR. MCVEIGH'S GREAT AND GOOD FRIEND CARDINAL COOKE, WHY I LEFT HIM? I REPEAT I NEED 30 SORTIES TONIGHT. PLEASE GET THEM FOR ME. WARM REGARDS, MARTIN. SECRET.

The ambassador was sick, and tired. He needed a break. He and Devine repaired to the third floor.

The ambassador was so sick that he felt no temptation for a drink. If the temptation had appeared, he would have throttled it: He was still working. But he wasn't a spoilsport.

Someone had found a framed map of Hanoi in an office. Not without a touch of malice, Martin removed a photograph of Henry Kissinger that had hung near Eva Kim's desk and replaced it with the map. "May as well let them feel at home," he said, and went into his office, where there were pills, and a private bathroom.

Twenty minutes later, he and Devine were back in the communications room.

* Bishop Edward Swanstrom, executive director of Catholic Relief Services.

FROM SCOWCROFT, SITUATION ROOM, TO MARTIN, AMERICAN EMBASSY, SAIGON

DEFENSE PROMISES 30 CH-53S ON THE WAY.

Then at 11:06 P.M., a message from President Ford's chief of staff:

TO MARTIN FROM [DON] RUMSFELD

I UNDERSTAND THAT 154 IBM EMPLOYEES, INCLUDING THEIR FAM-ILIES, ARE STILL AWAITING REMOVAL FROM SAIGON. I FURTHER UNDER-STAND THAT THEY ARE NOW STANDING IN FRONT OF THE IBM BUILDING AWAITING INSTRUCTIONS WHERE THEY SHOULD GO FOR EVACUATION. I ASK THAT YOU DO YOUR UTMOST TO SEE THAT THEY ARE EVACUATED WITH THE CURRENT HELICOPTER LIFT.

"S - - -," Martin said.

VI

At about eleven-thirty, urgent orders came from inside the embassy that all Americans except the Marines on the walls and gates were to get into the building and take cover. People squatted against the cor-ridor walls. The rumor was that there had been a communications in-tercept indicating that the embassy would be shelled at midnight.

Midnight came and went. Twenty minutes later, by a tacit consen-sus, people started moving normally within the embassy, and felt free again to leave it.

Moorefield set out on a deliberately nostalgic tour of the embassy, collecting memories. He moved from office to office, especially on the third floor, surveying the debris. Some offices looked as if they had been visited by a small tornado.

In the office of a friend from the political section who had already left, he found a can of pipe tobacco, and decided to borrow it. In a pile of rubble on the floor, he also found a commentary on Clausewitz' *On War* and appropriated that as well.

During that slow, reflective survey of the dying embassy, he ran into Thomas Polgar. "This wouldn't have happened if they hadn't cut off our ability to support the GVN," the CIA man said. Moorefield was unprepared for a post-mortem. He mumbled a kind of agreement and moved on.

Shortly before two in the morning, a Marine on the rooftop helipad fell from the pad to the roof itself, suffering a serious skull injury. He was medevac-ed out on the next helicopter. Moorefield went up to the roof to take his place.

Very soon after he got there, the Marines withdrew from the CRA compound and sealed it off. Several hundred people remained in preformed helicopter loads in the landing zone itself, but the CRA compound was quickly violated by the mob around the embassy.

Between two and five-thirty, when Moorefield finally left the roof, the chopper sorties were painfully slow. Moorefield knew from their faces that the pilots and crews were exhausted. Two had already died at sea, flying in from the fleet to Saigon, the last two American military men to die in events directly related to Vietnam.* And Moorefield knew that many of the helicopters were down for emergency maintenance. The helicopters arrived—on the roof and down in the parking lot, until that operation ended at about three-thirty—at forty-five-minute intervals, sometimes alone, more often in strings of two or three.

VII

While the midnight scare was in effect, Ambassador Martin was still hectoring Admiral Gayler in Honolulu and Scowcroft in the Situation Room at the White House.

[11:45 P.M.] TO: FLASH WHITE HOUSE FOR GENERAL SCOWCROFT

SINCE MY LAST MESSAGE NINETEEN, REPEAT 19, CH-46S HAVE COME AND GONE. THEY CARRY ABOUT TWO-FIFTHS OF CH-53 CAPACITY. I NEEDED THIRTY CH-53 SORTIES CAPACITY. I STILL DO. CAN'T YOU GET SOMEONE TO TELL US WHAT IS GOING ON? WARM REGARDS.

And at precisely midnight:

FROM MARTIN FOR ADMIRAL GAYLER

INFORM GENERAL BROWN, BRENT SCOWCROFT

THERE IS NOW ANOTHER LULL. NOTHING IN LAST TWENTY MINUTES. WE NEEDED THE CAPACITY, REPEAT CAPACITY, OF 30 CH-53 SORTIES TO GET US OUT OF HERE. AS I RECALL, A CH-46 HAS ABOUT TWO-FIFTHS THE CAPACITY OF A CH-53.

WE STILL NEED THE CAPACITY, REPEAT CAPACITY, OF THE THIRTY CH-53 SORTIES REQUESTED IN MY PREVIOUS MESSAGE. IT NOW SEEMS I WILL SPEND PART OF APRIL 30 HERE—A VERY SMALL PART I HOPE.

BUT I SURE DON'T WANT TO SPEND MAY DAY HERE. WARM REGARDS.

At 12:15, Scowcroft informed the ambassador that the evacuation of the last Marines from DAO was under way and the six Chinook-53s would be made available to the embassy.

One more message clattered over the wires:

---

* The 58,022 names on the black marble slabs of the Vietnam Memorial on the Mall in Washington are arranged chronologically, the names of those who died on a given day then listed in alphabetical order. The names of a helicopter pilot and gunner who died when they ditched at sea that night appear with those of Darwin Judge and Charles McMahon, Jr. They are followed by the names of the forty-one men who lost their lives in the rescue of the *Mayagüez* off Cambodia in mid-May.

FROM CTF [COMMANDER OF THE TASK FORCE, OUT ON THE FLEET]
TO AMEMBASSY SAIGON
EXTRACTION OF GROUND SECURITY FORCE FROM DAO COMPOUND COM-
PLETE.

Then there was a break in communications. They would be restored
later, but through roundabout routes, including voice messages on the
Marines' radio net. But at 12:16, the embassy lost the use of the satellite dish that had been installed at DAO in the first days of April. The
satellite dish, along with the entire DAO headquarters building, at
that moment was crumpling in upon itself from the barrels of thermite
and other explosives with which the Marines had laced the compound
during the night.

With that, Martin and Devine again went back down to the third
floor.

VIII

That morning, Homer Smith had sent an Air Force colonel named
John Madison, accompanied by two other officers and three sergeants,
from DAO to the embassy. If Martin had succeeded in convincing
Washington that there was a role for a drastically reduced embassy,
Madison and his colleagues would have stayed on as the U.S. military
representatives at one of the various "teams" or "parties" envisioned in
the Paris Peace Accords.

Even before word came in the early afternoon that absolutely all
official Americans would be leaving, Colonel Madison and his men
found themselves involved in crowd control and other aspects of the
evacuation from the compound. What all of them did that day was in
fact ad hoc. Even at dawn that morning, the evacuation plan called for
extracting only 100 to 150 people from the embassy. As it was, eventually about two thousand people were flown from the parking lot or
the roof to the fleet.

Toward the end of the long lull in helicopter arrivals at the embassy
that straddled midnight—a lull caused by the diversion of all choppers
to Tan Son Nhut for the removal of the last Marines at DAO—a rumor swept the crowd around the swimming pool that after midnight
the communists would begin shooting down helicopters. The crowd
panicked and surged against the chain-link fence that separated it
from the parking lot.

Colonel Madison was there, with an Army captain named Stuart
Herrington. Speaking in Vietnamese through a battery-driven bullhorn, both of them assured the crowd, as they had been doing all day

and night, that they would all get out. In fact, the panic did not die away until two other Americans joined them and shoved the lead elements of the crowd away from the gate.

In the midst of this small but dangerous melee, a middle-aged American contractor clutched his chest and fell to the ground.

Madison and the Marines managed to haul the man through the gate into the parking lot without letting loose a flood of people. He was put on the first helicopter to come in after DAO was finally shut down, but died of heart failure on the forty-five-minute flight to the fleet.

IX

Shortly after midnight, Martin asked for another head count.

If he had waited just another half hour to do so, 420 people who had as much right as anyone who was evacuated from the embassy that day and night almost certainly would have made it out. The mission had stranded others all over Saigon. But if the ambassador had not asked for that one census at around midnight, he would have been able to say later that at least they cleared the compound.

The figures he got were estimates, and they were wrong. Martin told the fleet that he had 726 people to go—about 500 Vietnamese, 173 Marines and 53 other Americans.

But once the helicopters started landing again, Colonel Madison and the Marines moved virtually everyone left in the CRA compound through the gate, and this time they actually counted heads as the people moved through. (One family decided they didn't want to go to America after all. They stayed behind, and began rummaging among the abandoned luggage for valuables.)

The figure Martin should have been given was not 726 but 1,100.

The 1,100 were overwhelmingly Vietnamese. But that figure also included a handful of nonofficial Americans; a Vietnamese-speaking German priest, who had been helpful through the long day; and a group of about a dozen Korean diplomats who had missed their own embassy's hurried evacuation that morning.*

Among the Vietnamese was the contingent from the embassy's fire brigade. Their families had left, but they had stayed behind on the strength of constant reassurances by the Americans that they would make sure they got out.

Colonel Madison got word to Martin that he finally had an abso-

* Among them was Brigadier General Rhee Dai Yong, a former deputy commander of South Korea's expeditionary force in Vietnam and also a former deputy head of the Korean CIA.

lutely firm count for the number of people in the parking lot: 1,100—and there would be no more. (Nearly 700 of the 1,100 would in fact be lifted out in the next few hours.)

Working the Marines' radio net, Martin reached the fleet and reported the new count.

It was too late. Commanders with the fleet, in Honolulu and in Washington now thought that Martin was playing with them. It was a repeat of the afternoon and early evening, when they had been steadily removing people from the compound and whenever they called for a new estimate of those remaining the figure hovered around two thousand. Martin was holding back Americans to evacuate a bottomless well of Vietnamese.

With the advent of Daylight Savings Time in the United States three nights earlier, Washington was now a neat twelve hours behind Saigon. At two o'clock that morning in Saigon, it was two in the afternoon in Washington, and Henry Kissinger was telling reporters that the evacuation was going very smoothly. He would talk to them again at four. And when he talked to them at four, Kissinger damned well wanted to be able to tell them that there were no more Americans in Saigon.

At about 3:15 A.M. in Saigon, the pilot of one of the Chinook-46s landing on the roof passed a piece of paper with a handwritten message scrawled on it. The words "no more" were underlined with two bold strokes:

From CINCPAC to Saigon
I have been directed to send you the following message from the President: "On the basis of the reported total of 726 evacuees, CINCPAC is authorized to send 19 helicopters and no more. The President expects Ambassador Martin to be on the last helicopter."
FYI: The Secretary of Defense wishes the last lift no later than 0345 Hotel [Saigon time] and we will do our best to meet [that deadline at this] end.
FYI: Please acknowledge this presidential message.

Martin acknowledged receipt of the message. If they were lucky, nineteen choppers might be enough—although it would have been helpful of them to tell him how many of the nineteen were the big ones.

Maybe a breath of air would be good for him. The ambassador rode down to the lobby and walked out into the parking lot. He asked Colonel Madison to get him a new count of the remaining people there.

Minutes later, Colonel Madison pressed a button on his walkie-talkie and raised Wolf Lehmann. He told Lehmann to tell the ambassador that he had 420 people, preformed in six sticks of seventy people each. All the American civilians were gone, Madison said, but he still had the Korean diplomats, the German priest and the embassy firemen.

Lehmann's first response sent a shock through Colonel Madison. The deputy chief of mission said that, judging from the traffic on the Marines' radio net, they might get no more CH-53s into the parking lot. All they would get from here on out were the choppers on the roof, and they would take out only Americans.

"*Jesus,*" Madison said. "I've been telling these people for *hours* that we'll get them out. Give the ambassador the numbers. Tell him who they are. Tell him this is the honest-to-God end of it."

Lehmann did as Madison had asked, and two or three minutes later called back to say that the ambassador thought they could get the additional six heavy Chinooks. A minute or two later, Brunson McKinley appeared in the parking lot with the same message.

Colonel Madison and Captain Herrington circulated among the 420 assuring them once again that they would all get out.

X

Pierre Brochand thought it was like a scene from Dante's *Inferno.* When the American Marines withdrew to the smaller perimeter, looters breached the gate to their swimming pool and restaurant compound. There were fires. As it happened, the extra fuel tanks the French had stockpiled were lined up against the wall that separated the two embassies. Brochand got ten young Vietnamese staffers to move them to the middle of the compound, on a path through the flower gardens.

And still the big helicopters kept coming. The smaller ones were plucking people from the roof. It was the big ones that came down to the ground. The eerie light of flares and smoke from the flares and whatever else was burning over there—documents, money, Brochand supposed, the fires set by the looters—drifted into the French compound. It was dangerous. Sometimes the big helicopters could not make the landing on the first try. They would rear back to try again, hovering just above the Frenchman's hair. Brochand would be glad when this hellish night ended.

XI

From Moorefield's vantage on the roof, the last hours of the last picture show were Felliniesque. Below him, people lined the corridors and stairwells of the embassy to the roof. And in the parking lot, with its four or five hundred people waiting for evacuation, order prevailed.

But next door in the CRA compound a macabre carnival was under way. The bottom of the rancid swimming pool—people had been pissing in it all day—was littered with handguns. Its surface was covered with papers and the big-flaked ash of the documents and U.S. currency that Marines were burning in barrels on the roof. Old mama-sans in white blouses and black silk pajama pants were looting the restaurant. Drunks were playing bumper cars with the embassy vehicles that had been abandoned there. And at some point deep in the night, while the mob disported in the CRA compound, someone he couldn't see out on Thong Nhut in front of the embassy had a bullhorn and was leading what Moorefield assumed to be an anti-American rally.

XII

Wolfgang Lehmann had read the Marines' radio traffic correctly. Deep in the bend of the night, helicopter crews now truly overextended and Henry Kissinger's 4 P.M. Washington-time news conference rapidly approaching, Ford and Kissinger and Defense Secretary Schlesinger and Noel Gayler in Honolulu and Air Force General John Burns in Thailand called Martin's bluff.

At three-thirty in the morning Saigon time the C-130 circling high over Saigon as the communications-and-control plane transmitted this message, in the clear, to all aircraft in the area: "The following message is from the President of the United States and should be passed on by the first helicopter in contact with Ambassador Martin. Only twenty-one lifts remain. Americans only will be transported. Ambassador Martin will board the first available helicopter and that helicopter will broadcast 'Tiger, Tiger, Tiger,' once it is airborne and en route."

Major Kean picked up the message directly from the fleet on his Marine Corps network. He marched down to the third floor and told the ambassador that he would go on the next chopper.

"Well, there's a little more to be done, Major," Martin drawled. "Wolf, let's go upstairs."

Through slow land links, teletype messages were still getting through from Saigon to Washington. Martin scrawled out the last message on the legal pad at 4:15 A.M. Lehmann typed it and handed it to the communicator.

FLASH MARTIN TO SCOWCROFT
PLAN TO CLOSE MISSION AT ABOUT 0430 30 APRIL LOCAL TIME. DUE TO NECESSITY TO DESTROY COMMO GEAR, THIS IS THE LAST MESSAGE FROM EMBASSY SAIGON.

As Martin and Lehmann left, the young men got to work with their sledgehammers and thermite grenades.

Major Kean went up to the roof. He was excited as he spoke to Moorefield and Sergeant Bobby Frain and the other Marines on the roof. "They've just broadcast a message in the clear from the President," Kean said. "We're only going to get twenty-one more lifts. And from here on out, it will be Americans only."

Kean was a burly five feet eleven. In uniform, he looked like the kind of officer the corps might use on a recruiting poster. That night he was in civilian clothes, including a short-sleeved shirt. Moorefield was struck by the way Kean was obviously caught up in the drama of the moment. But why not? How often does a military officer get to relay a direct order from the President of the United States?

XIII

Ambassador Martin went into the office and put a few last-minute things into his briefcase.

When he came out, the others were standing. "Okay," he said. "Let's go."

The Marines were left, and a few military officers from other branches. And Ken Moorefield and Marvin Garrett would stay for another hour. But now the rest of the remaining American bureaucrats made their way to the roof.

They emerged from the stairwell onto the roof at 4:40 A.M.

"Hello, Ken."

"Mr. Ambassador."

Thus the exchange between Graham Martin and the young veteran Martin had brought with him twenty-one months before as a favor to his only surviving son. Twenty-one months earlier, Moorefield had gently, lightly—a hand on the elbow—helped Martin from the plane, one of the fleet of them from out there at Andrews. Graham Martin left Saigon as he had come to it, and as he had always come and left, on aircraft controlled by the Commander in Chief.

Two minutes later, a CH-46 with the words "Lady Ace 09" painted on its flank settled onto the roof.

The pilot jumped from it and approached Moorefield. Strapped to his thigh was a knee pad with the scrawled notation: "Ambassador, presidential order for helo (20) limits, only Americans plus crews will be carried. The ambassador should get on *Lady Ace 09*, the aircraft that passed this message. LA/09."

Over the roar of the blades, the pilot repeated the message.

Moorefield trotted to Martin. "Mr. Ambassador, they say you have to take this helicopter," he shouted. "Presidential order."

The ambassador looked at Moorefield quizzically, glanced over his shoulder at Lehmann and Polgar and the rest of them. It occurred to Moorefield that maybe Martin thought he meant they were saying he had to fly out alone. "I mean you first," he said.

Then Martin gave Moorefield a look that said, "Let's go." Moorefield touched his elbow and the two of them bent and walked into the rotor wash.

At the lip into the bay of the helicopter, only because he knew the ambassador was sick, Moorefield slipped his hands into the armpits of his gray-suited ambassador, lifted and gave a slight shove.

XIV

Major Kean descended to the courtyard and motioned for Colonel Madison to come to him. He told the Air Force officer that "by presidential order" there would be no more choppers in the parking lot and the ones on the roof would take only Americans.

Madison was devastated. "Let me talk to Lehmann, or the ambassador," he said.

"You can't," Kean said, gesturing with the aerial of his radio. "They just left."

There was nothing Madison could do. Kean was quietly moving some of his Marines into the embassy lobby. Madison spoke to Captain Herrington and the few other men with him. With nothing left to say to any of the 420 would-be evacuees, and without looking in their faces, Madison and his men slowly, one after the other, slipped back to the embassy.

XV

As it happened, *Lady Ace 09* was almost full, with the very last of the Marines extracted from DAO. In addition to Martin, there was room only for Polgar, Colonel Jacobson and John Hogan. Wolfgang Lehmann and five other senior embassy officers* waited another thirty-five minutes for the next chopper.

During those thirty-five minutes, it occurred to Wolfgang Lehmann that with the ambassador's departure he was now the President's representative in Saigon. He could go down to the ambassador's office on the third floor and change the whole goddamned thing, call up Big Minh and order a defense of Saigon.

---

* Josiah Bennett, political counselor; Hank Boudreau, administrative counselor; James Devine and Brunson McKinley, special assistants to the ambassador; and Jay Blowers, from the political-military section.

In his mind, it was not entirely a fancy. He would let the others go and leave with the last Marines, if it came to that, as, he knew, it certainly would.

"Okay, Wolf," he said to himself. "You're fifty-six years old, the Marines have got a job to do, this isn't the moment for any goddamned grandstanding. It's time to get the hell out of here."

XVI

The chopper that extracted Lehmann and the five other embassy officers landed at five-twenty and left with almost all of the remaining Mission Warden officers. Another followed, quickly. Ken Moorefield saw Marvin Garrett, the embassy security officer, and Steve Bray, the Mission Warden chief, get on with a few other civilians—their senior staff. John Madison, the Air Force colonel who had represented the United States on the Four-Party Joint Military Team, and who had worked with Major Kean to keep order in the embassy compound through the long day and night, also got on that helicopter, with his five men.

Now, if you didn't count the 420 or more Asians waiting patiently in the parking lot below, the only ones left were Kean and several chopperloads of Marines. And the chopper with Garrett, Bray and Madison and their people was half empty.

"Time to go," Ken Moorefield said to himself at five-thirty on the morning of April 30, looking at the last of the men hustling into the belly of the CH-46.

He ran for it, lightly, easily, not caring much whether he made it, clutching the critique of Clausewitz in his hand.

When they lifted above Saigon, it was still night. Moorefield gazed down at fires at Tan Son Nhut, fires consuming Bien Hoa.

About thirty minutes later they crossed the coastline, near Vung Tau, and it was starting to be day. Hundreds of boats of all sizes were beating out to sea, to the fleet.

In that helicopter, half filled with men who had worked hard through the last few weeks and days and hours, no one spoke.

Moorefield relished the silence, the calm. He had done what he could. Now there was nothing left to do. His heart was washed with an unaccustomed peace.

XVII

As the last Chinook-53 lifted from the parking-lot landing zone, Major Kean shouted: "That's it! Frain! Now!" Bobby Frain and the four embassy Marines left in the parking lot bolted for the back entrance to the embassy, pulled its doors shut behind them and slammed down a steel bar across them. With Major Kean and a few other Marines, they ran across the lobby to the stairwell behind post number two, yanked down the steel barrier rolled into the top of the doorway there and started up the stairs.

There were still more than a hundred Marines, along with a few Army officers, in the building. As the tail end of the column moved to the roof, they drew down more barriers to the stairwell and locked the elevator doors on the top floor. The last line of defense was a flimsy door at the top of the short, narrow, turning staircase to the roof. They jammed a wall locker between that door, which had a pane of glass in it, and an air-conditioning unit that, along with several other pieces of heavy machinery as well as the door itself, was under the raised helicopter pad.

By the time Frain and Master Sergeant Valdez and Major Kean got to the roof, the ground-force Marines were leaving in a steady, quick stream of CH-46s. Frain and some of his buddies pressed Browning automatic rifles and valued handguns on the pilots. "Y'ain't going to forget us, right?" Frain shouted at one pilot. The pilot grinned and gave a thumbs-up signal.

With the last few sorties, men below with M-1s started taking potshots at the helicopters, and there were mortar pops nearby, although the Marines on the embassy roof couldn't tell what the targets of the mortars were: the compound beneath them or the building itself or the helicopters. Then, as the last of the ground-force Marines were loaded and borne away, what sounded like an explosion in the compound or the first floor of the embassy ripped the night. Cautiously, some of the remaining Marines leaned over the low wall that encircled the roof and reported that the small fire truck that had stood by all night—in case there was a fire, and to provide illumination for the landing zone—had been rammed through the back doors of the embassy. Whether the truck was commandeered by looters or driven by the men who stood with it during the night, assured that they would be taken out, no one on the roof knew.

It took only a couple of choppers to get almost all of the embassy Marines out. Frain saw to it that all of his men were on one of them. When the second one left, there were only eleven men on the roof—Major Kean, Master Sergeant Valdez, Sergeant Frain and eight others.

Far to the east, out beyond the great U.S. armada offshore, a little light began to mark the horizon. Not quite perceptibly, one of those gradual things one can gauge only by putting it out of consciousness for a few minutes at a time, that quarter of the sky was banded with whitish gray and then the richest naval blue and then pink and then salmon and bronze—ribbons in the sky—and then the molten bulge of gold you couldn't look at; and silence. Nearby, punctuations of violence. The muffled sounds of men beneath them, working their way up. But silence in the sky eastward. It would be broken any moment, of course; but it was not broken this moment, had not been broken for moment upon moment, adding up, when you stopped to think about it every few minutes, by many minutes.

Toward the end, they had made a real point of making sure that every pilot knew there were still men left.

"They know, they gotta know," Major Kean said. "Didn't any of you give a signal to that last guy?" The ten looked at one another. Major Kean shielded his eyes with his hand and looked off to the east.

Someone had left behind a comset—a radio backpack with a long antenna. They diddled with it, broadcasting in the clear, no radio lingo. But they all knew its range was line of sight, and the static hiss in the receiving mode was so unremittingly even and gray that it was clear to all of them that they didn't have line of sight to the fleet. They kept at it, of course; never could tell who would be flying recon off Vung Tau or someplace, looking for stragglers.

An arm smashed through the window of the door under the helipad. Frain got to it fast and pulled the arm into the broken glass, and it was yanked back with a cry and the force of a snapped snake thick as a man's arm, even a small man. That is, Frain, who was a big man, meant to arrest the arm and could not.

More arms reached through the broken window. So they kept a man there to grab the arms and jam them into the glass.

Major Kean was calm. He discussed tactics with Valdez and whomever else was not standing guard at the door. It was kind of hard to believe that the fleet commanders had forgotten them, but maybe they had; it was a big, tricky operation after all. He told them what had to be done next if in fact a chopper didn't arrive in the next hour, say, glancing at his watch, straight up seven o'clock in the morning, full daylight: "Obviously, we gotta deploy down the rocket shield, and then make our way to water," he said. Then he told them how he thought they should do that, inviting suggestions, from Valdez especially.

Then they waited, jerking arms into shards of glass.

This is how we left Vietnam.

At 7:49 on the morning of April 30, 1975, specks appeared in the southeastern sky. Before 7:51, they were identifiable as one Chinook-46 escorted by six nimble Cobra gunships, which looked and maneuvered as much like dragonflies as any machine man had ever devised.

And then the eleven Marines left on the roof of what had been the

American Embassy in Saigon unloaded canister after canister of tear-gas grenades over the front, back and sides of the building onto the heads of the Vietnamese below. Over the back, from which came the major threat, they put a hand grenade in a box of tear-gas canisters.

They did it for their own protection. But they forgot that a settling helicopter sucks up air. So the last official Americans out of Vietnam—the eleven Marines and the crew of the CH-46, including the pilot—all flew blind out of Saigon.*

* Besides Major Kean and Sergeant Frain, the last nine off the roof were: Sergeant Philip A. Babel, Corporal Stephen Q. Bauer, Sergeant Terry J. Bennington, Corporal Duane R. Gevers, Corporal David E. Norman, Gunnery Sergeant Robert W. Schlager, Sergeant Steven T. Schuller, Staff Sergeant Michael K. Sullivan, Master Sergeant Juan J. Valdez, Noncommissioned Officer in Charge.

33

On the last day of the war, Neil Davis—the Australian cameraman who was suddenly the NBC correspondent in Saigon—awoke at dawn. As usual, he walked directly from his bed to the tall French windows of his room in the Continental Palace. The city was unusually still. In the plaza beneath him—the expanse of asphalt marked by the two foreigners' hotels, the National Assembly Building and the small park that held the brutal Marines Statue—nothing moved. What struck Davis most was that for the first time in the eleven years he had been coming to Saigon there were no police in the plaza or on the streets. Over a breakfast of croissants and thick black coffee in the hotel's open-air courtyard, he told a colleague: "You know, I never liked some of the things the bastards did, but it's a little disconcerting to have none of them around."

II

At dawn, the fear and panic of the last few days had quieted to an almost perfect stillness of anticipation. The nearly deserted streets and the muted, soft-colored buildings of the capital lay naked under the high cover of thin but unbroken cloud like a vast stage.

Doan Van Toai was one of the few Saigonese to venture out into this strange world of virtually no traffic, and no police at all. He walked the few blocks to the palace, found it quiet and made his way home, stopping in the only open shop along the way for his morning bowl of *pho*.

He spent the morning playing with the boys, explaining to the oldest that this was a holiday, and talking quietly about the future with his wife.

In all his years of opposition, Toai had come to hate the government radio. He fiddled with the shortwave band, but the BBC and VOA were broadcasting news twelve or more hours old, mostly about the evacuation, as if Vietnam itself had ceased to exist. But the phones still worked, and Toai was alerted shortly after nine that the government radio had announced that there would be an "important announcement" in a few minutes.

III

Tear gas, tongues of fire, and acrid gray and pink smoke from burning carpeting, furniture and classified documents rose from the small openings in the rocket shield that encased the U.S. Embassy. ARVN soldiers in a house nearby fired in rage at the low, slow-moving helicopter. But it swerved, unhit, climbed, accelerated. In less than a minute, it was a soundless speck.

Neil Davis was filming from the street. By his watch, it was 7:55 A.M.

The looting that followed was casual—friendly, Davis thought. Everything that could be carried—office furniture, typewriters, air conditioners, signed photographs of presidents—was carted off.

Davis climbed through the gutted embassy to the roof with NBC's driver. As he surveyed the scene below—the streets still largely deserted except for the small crowd around the embassy—he noticed an ARVN soldier attempting to hot-wire the driver's car, which he leased to the bureau. The Australian and the driver jogged down to the street and spoke to the man, telling him that there were plenty of abandoned vehicles around, but this one belonged to a Vietnamese who was staying. The soldier apologized and walked off.

Shortly thereafter, a rumor swept through the crowd that the Marines had left timed dynamite charges in the basement. Most of the looters left. A few remained, as did knots of people in the grounds, on the stairwells and on the rooftop pad itself, waiting for helicopters that would never come.

IV

The night before, Big Minh had sent three emissaries to the communists' delegation at Camp Davis to plead with them to spell out what they wanted of him.

The communists listened to the three. Then they politely but firmly informed them that "for their own safety" they would not be allowed to leave the compound that night. They offered their guests bananas, and the security of the bunkers they had dug under their sleeping quarters if the Americans or their puppets decided to bomb Tan Son Nhut.

Now, a little after eight in the morning, Big Minh was huddled with Vu Van Mau and a few other aides at the prime minister's office, an old French colonial mansion on Thong Nhut Boulevard halfway between the U.S. Embassy and the zoo. An officer joined them with word that the American evacuation was complete.

Ly Qui Chung, the young crew-cut legislator who would have been Minh's minister of information if the government had lasted long enough to be sworn in, said: "It's time to make the announcement."

Just an hour earlier, Chung had driven to Camp Davis, spoken with the communists and returned with a repetition of their final offer. They didn't use the word "surrender." Their formulation instead called for "the dissolution of the puppet military and police." There would be no more negotiations, and no guarantee to Big Minh or anyone else of a position in the new government. But the safety of Minh and his associates would be assured. Chung was convinced it was time to surrender.

Big Minh was undecided. As a general, he knew that Saigon's situation was hopeless. But the communists had always insisted that they would not take Saigon by force.

For years, the communists had made just two demands. These were that all U.S. military officers, in or out of uniform, leave the country; and that a "peace-loving" administration with no ties to Nguyen Van Thieu—which Minh understood to mean the government he was trying to form—be established. Four days before, when it became clear that the first two conditions were going to be met, they had added this third condition, the abolition of the armed forces and the police.

Minh sent Chung back to Camp Davis for one more clarification of what they wanted.

While Chung was gone, both Minh and Vu Van Mau—who through his years of opposition to Thieu was the An Quang pagoda's chief political operative—spoke on the telephone with Thich Tri Quang.

Tri Quang told the new president and his old friend the prime minister-designate that his contacts in the National Liberation Front now no longer had any idea what Hanoi's true intentions were. Like Chung, Tri Quang urged surrender.

Chung returned from Camp Davis with the same final offer, in blunter language. Big Minh was to go on the radio and call on his soldiers to lay down their arms. If he did so, there would be no battle for Saigon.

Minh sent Chung back to Camp Davis once more, this time with word that he would speak on the radio within the hour. It was a few minutes before nine. At nine, Radio Saigon announced: "Citizens, stand by. The president will shortly deliver an important speech."

It took Minh a little longer than an hour to write and record the announcement, which was brief and to the point. An aide took it to the nearby radio station, where there was only a skeleton crew, but enough to play it.

> I believe firmly in reconciliation among all Vietnamese [Minh said]. To avoid needless bloodshed, I ask the soldiers of the Republic to put an end to all hostilities. Be calm and remain where you are now. To save the lives of the people, do not open fire.
>
> I also call on our brothers, the soldiers of the Provisional Revolutionary Government, not to open fire, because we are waiting here to meet with their representatives to discuss the orderly turnover of the reins of government, both civilian and military, without causing senseless bloodshed to the people.

The first broadcast came at ten-twenty. It was repeated not only on the radio network but also on the system of loudspeakers in the streets and squares of Saigon. As it was played, the streets began to empty of looters.

V

Captain Do Duc Cuong and the rest of the ad hoc command staff of the three companies of men waiting at the bridge northwest of Vung Tau listened to the announcement on a bulky military radio. The day before, as they listened to the mad chatter on the radio of the Americans and their own leaders running away, they had taken a few artillery rounds. But they still had seen no communist tanks or troops.

The Airborne major who commanded the free-lance band of resisters waited until Minh's voice was followed by martial music. The major lay on a slight incline above the riverbank, the radio propped against a tree fifteen yards in front of his boots, a very easy target. As the shot echoed away and the stillness prepared to rush in to replace the music, Cuong and the others cheered.

VI

Doan Van Toai listened to the surrender announcement, pleased that it would turn out as all his conversations with people close to Minh had led him to expect: No battle for Saigon.

For another hour, when friends called suggesting that they go to the palace, or to the old student center on Duy Tan Street, closed for months by Thieu, Toai said, "I'm going to wait a little longer. If you see them come in, call me again."

VII

Nguyen Van Hao had found Big Minh and Vu Van Mau with their aides at the prime minister's office shortly after the speech was first broadcast. He urged them to repair to Doc Lap Palace, the seat of the presidency.

At the palace, Hao called his wife and told her to take care of the children in case he never returned. Later he spoke briefly with Jean-Louis Arnaud when Arnaud emerged from a meeting with Minh.

"What is going to happen?" Arnaud asked.

"I have no idea," Hao said. "I am still alive, that's all I know."

"What do you think the future will be like?" Of course they were speaking in French.

"I think it will be rosy," Hao said. "I hope it won't be red."

Big Minh's wife—Madame Minh to these French-educated Vietnamese—along with other relatives and friends of the new president were gathered, with their luggage, in a room in the living quarters of the palace. Hao gradually understood that a ship that belonged to a commercial bank had been standing by as late as just an hour earlier to extract Big Minh from Saigon. But finally the ship's captain decided it was time to leave.

One of the passengers on that ship was General Mai Huu Xuan—the man Charlie Timmes referred to as the Baron Scarpia of Saigon under President Diem. Big Minh had the intelligence and charity to insist that his friend Xuan not stay until the end.

VIII

At about eleven, on an impulse, Neil Davis decided to see if he could get into the palace. The main front gate was closed, but the correspondent directed his small, quiet driver to the back, which was open and unguarded. Davis left the car and driver at one side of the palace building and walked around to the broad front steps. As he started up the stairs, a young civil servant with his jacket over his arm, who was leaving the building in some haste, stopped and asked Davis if he wanted to see the president.

The thought that he might have an interview with Big Minh hadn't occurred to Davis. He said, "Well, yes," and the young man said, "Okay, he's up there on the second floor."

Davis climbed the wide, carpeted marble stairway from the large entrance foyer to the second floor of the palace with his camera on his shoulder and his eyes down. As he reached the last couple of steps, he raised his head. Big Minh was standing six feet away, alone.

He was dressed in a dark-tan safari suit, and was unshaven and red-eyed. Davis was certain that the new president had not slept that night. He was almost as certain that he had recently been weeping.

"Oh, Mr. President," Davis said, not in commiseration but in the tone of voice with which one says, "Oh, fancy meeting you here." The two men had known each other for years. They shook hands. And then Davis' mind went almost blank as he wondered what one said to a president, and a general, who had just surrendered after thirty years of war. Finally he asked, "What are you doing?"

"I'm waiting for the other side," Minh answered.

"Are they going to come here?"

"Yes, very soon."

Davis now could think of no way to carry the conversation forward. He initiated a parting handshake. Minh turned and walked toward the president's office down a long, open passageway colonnaded with marble columns along the front of the building. Davis filmed the retreating figure, thinking it was one of the saddest shots of his career.

IX

Perhaps the encounter with Neil Davis gave Big Minh the idea. In any case, shortly after the Australian left him, the new president told Ly Qui Chung to call Jean-Louis Arnaud and invite him to the palace.

Arnaud was struck by how deserted the place was. There were no soldiers, and few aides. It took him at least five minutes from his entrance at the side gate to finally find the little group around Minh on the second floor of the palace. In the phone call, Ly Qui Chung had referred to Minh as *"le général"* rather than *"le président,"* so Arnaud followed suit.

"Thank you for calling for me, General," he said. "How are you?"

"I am fine," Minh said. "As you see, I am waiting here for our brothers from the other side. I do not know if they will come today or tomorrow."

Arnaud was struck, as Neil Davis had been, by Minh's exhaustion: the tiny untended whiskers, the gray pouches under the eyes. He tried to fight against slipping into the realization that he was present at a historical moment. But he acknowledged Minh's high gravity; and as all the quiet dinners at Minh's villa over the years ran before his mind's eye, he admonished himself not to let it come to tears.

"Tell Monsieur Mérillon that you have seen me doing what the French government has asked me to do," Minh said. *"Je suis ici."*

"I understand, General," Arnaud said.

The phone rang. Ly Qui Chung answered it. After he hung up, he spoke first in Vietnamese to Minh, then in French to Arnaud: "The others are crossing the New Port bridge. They will be here soon."

Arnaud knew immediately that he must leave. He didn't want to be trapped in the palace—not because he feared for his safety there but because he was a wire man. Clearly, he had just had the last interview with the president of the Republic of Vietnam. He had to file.

They were of a size, the general and the journalist. As they embraced in the French manner, Arnaud felt the tears welling. His hands still lightly on Minh's shoulders as he leaned back from the embrace, Arnaud saw that Minh too had been taken by the moment. His expression conveyed no embarrassment for the tears, as if it were permitted of a French general to cry soundlessly when the moment of defeat was at hand.

"Good luck, *mon général*," Arnaud said, and left.

x

Out on the front lawn of the palace, Neil Davis for the first time noticed a group of about fifty ARVN soldiers sitting in the shade of one of the numerous trees on the grounds, their weapons neatly stacked beside them. A young captain detached himself from the group, approached the correspondent and spoke to him—in French, the first time Davis had heard a Vietnamese junior officer use that language in years.

They spoke for a few moments about nothing in particular. Then they saw, through the trees, a tank moving along the side street next to the palace, the tank moving in the direction of the basilica and, beyond it, the American Embassy. As Davis and the captain looked on, a great lick of flame flashed from its cannon, followed an instant later by "this great bloody *wham!*" The shot had no target. In fact, it ran the risk of blowing up a tank in the column it had outstripped.

"Christ, what's that?" Davis asked.

"That's a communist tank," the captain said calmly.

Davis couldn't believe it. He was one of the best journalists in Saigon, even when it was full of journalists. He knew, intellectually, that this was the day the communists would enter the city. But the speed of the advance, and, more, a resistance born not of fear but of the experience of his years in Indochina to the thought that they were actually *here,* gave the next hour or so the quality of a dream.

"Come on, don't be silly," he said to the captain. "It's a coup or something." Davis thought that a desperate coup attempt, or simply a vengeful assault on the palace by bitter troops opposed to the surrender, was in fact rather likely.

"No, it's a communist tank," the officer said. "Look."

The tank was turning the corner to approach the main gate. Through a break in the trees, Davis now could see it clearly, and there was no question as to what it was: a Russian T-54 tank with a soldier sitting on its nose waving the biggest Viet Cong flag Davis had ever seen.

"Well, thank you—and good luck," he said to the captain.

"Good luck to you," the officer said. He walked casually back to his men. He was to surrender less than a minute later.

Davis walked across the lawn to within thirty yards of the main gate—gates, really: an elaborate affair of four wrought-iron gates closing on sandstone pillars. The tank rammed one set of the gates, and the top half of its stone centerpiece exploded in a billow of dust. It backed up a few yards, roared forward again, smashing through the last obstacle, the gates torn from their hinges, and kept coming.

The man with the flag leaped from the tank and ran past Davis to the palace. At the same time, a second man who had been perched on the tank ran directly toward Davis and his driver, who had bravely rejoined the only Westerner in the palace grounds. The communist soldier was carrying an American M-79, an ugly weapon that fires grenades from under its thick barrel.

Davis knew that this was the crucial moment. He looked like an American. Worse, he was carrying this black thing on his shoulder that might very well look like a weapon to someone who presumably had just come from years in the jungle.

The tank was rumbling past him, but he could hear the man shouting "Stop!"—and something else. Davis had a fair command of the language. He finally understood over the din that the man was telling him to put his hands up. His camera weighed about sixteen pounds, and he had been working hard for many weeks; but he managed to lift the camera with one arm and raise the other. Then he said his well-rehearsed piece: "Welcome to Saigon, comrade. I have been waiting to film the liberation."

"You're an American," the man shot back.

"No, comrade," Davis said. "I promise you that I am an Australian, and I am here to film the liberation."

The soldier's bright gaze shifted beyond Davis, who believed now that he was going to live, unless the man's finger slipped. It did not. The man moved away. Davis turned and filmed him taking the captain's surrender.

. . .

Tank 844 was quickly joined by others from its column, which had proceeded up Thong Nhut Boulevard past the American Embassy and around the basilica. (A member of the crew of 844 told Davis later that in their haste to be first they missed their goal by a block and drove past the palace. They had had to stop and ask someone on the street where it was, which was why they approached it from the wrong direction.)

The tanks formed a semicircle facing the palace, and for a moment Davis thought they were going to blow it away. The lawn was filling with infantry as well as the tank crews. And then, as both the man from tank 844 and a second soldier with a Viet Cong flag appeared simultaneously on the balcony of the palace, the air was filled with the sound of hundreds of weapons being fired into the sky. The two figures waved the flags so that they crisscrossed, as if they were flashing a semaphore signal of the end of the war.

XI

The two men waving the flags were Pham Duy Do and Pham Huy Nghe, a sapper team. They ran one of the flags up the flagpole there on the balcony, and then ran back into the palace, searching the rooms.

On the second floor, they pulled aside a curtain that hung across a conference room on the north end of the building and found Minh and his entourage.

Do pointed his AK rifle and said: "You've been surrounded. If anyone has a weapon, throw it down and surrender."

No one moved. No one said a word.

Do ordered Nghe to stand guard at the door and went out to find his political superiors. And just as a few Vietnamese photographers were bold enough to appear by the young Nghe's side, he said: "Who is Duong Van Minh? Duong Van Minh must come forward and kneel down!"

Nguyen Van Hao's heart seemed to miss a beat. This was his moment of greatest danger. Because if Big Minh did it, Hao knew that he could not. The photographers were there. The pictures would go all over the world, and Hao had friends everywhere, in Vietnam, and Europe, and the United States. He knew, as certainly as he knew his name, that he would force the soldier to kill him before he would allow such a photograph to be taken.

Fortunately, Do at that moment reappeared with four political officers, among them a man who identified himself only as Tung. Big Minh and the others rose.

"Put that down," Tung said to Nghe. "This is the time for politics, not guns."

"We have been waiting for you so that we can turn over the government," Big Minh said.

"You have nothing left to turn over," Tung said, spitting out the words contemptuously. "You can only surrender unconditionally. I invite you to come to the radio station to announce an unconditional surrender."

At about the same time, Le Duc Tho, Pham Hung and Generals Van Tien Dung and Tran Van Tra in their command base north of the city were bent over a large map of Saigon and its environs. The red arrows had reached their objectives. Suddenly a cadre gleefully brought in a tape recorder and placed it on the table: The men who had won the war listened to Big Minh's first surrender speech.

The four men hugged one another, kissing lightly on the cheeks in the French manner. Tran Van Tra's eyes filled with tears. He felt as if his soul were translucent, that all the pain and suffering had sunk to the bottom and drained out of it.

XII

Very soon after the tanks roared past the French Embassy, at noon sharp, Pierre Brochand had himself driven around the city. The scene was not exactly ugly but deeply disconcerting. People came out on the streets, going nowhere, in civilian clothes, many of them carrying weapons. Some people lined up along Thong Nhut to watch the tanks come in, but Brochand saw no scenes of joy.

The city was tense, and very quiet. Brochand felt a profound physical malaise, as if he might be sick. Now, in these hours: the death of a society, something one might see once in a lifetime, if that.

Then, rather quickly, as the *bo dois* emerged from their leaf-covered tanks and trucks, Brochand's sickness or fear or whatever it was began to drain away. They were so young, the conquerors, so friendly and naïve. So small.

XIII

The palace was open to the conquerors. Neil Davis climbed the few stairs from the lawn to the entrance foyer and filmed the hundreds of *bo dois* who stood in knots, staring at the opulent furniture and chandeliers.

He found one youngster alone.

Davis was a strong six-footer with an easy way with people. He towered over the young soldier. When he lowered his camera and reached to shake hands with the boy, the boy followed suit.

"Where are you from?" Davis asked.

"Hanoi," the soldier said, meaning North Vietnam. It was the same answer the others Davis had talked to had given him. Like most of the rest of them, this one looked as if he came from the countryside. He also looked to be fifteen at the most.

"How old are you?"

"Seventeen or eighteen," the boy said. "I'm not sure."

Then Davis asked him his name. He wondered later why he had done so, because this was the only one of the *bo dois* he asked for a name that afternoon.

The youngster looked beyond Davis for a few seconds, calculating. Would he be believed? Would he be laughed at? Finally he looked back at the correspondent and said softly but clearly, "My name is Nguyen Van Thieu."

Davis didn't laugh. He thought for a moment and said: "You do know who lived here before."

"Yes," the boy said. "It's a fairly common name, you know."

XIV

Just after the surrender speech was broadcast, George Esper and Matt Franjola of the Associated Press approached a lieutenant colonel of the South Vietnamese police who stood under the muzzle of the point man in the Marines Statue. Esper began an interview. But after a few confused replies, the man handed Esper his police identification card. Esper failed to note his name; he was arrested by the man's eyes, which were filled with despair.

"*Fini, fini,*" the colonel said. He fingered his holstered pistol. For a moment, Esper thought the man might shoot him. Instead he did a sharp about-face, saluted the ugly figures towering above him, raised the pistol to his own head and fired.

The man fell spread-eagled on his back. He died moments later in the arms of Franjola, who was helping to take him to a hospital.

XV

A few blocks away at the palace, a North Vietnamese soldier who might have been sixteen was assigned to stand guard in the center of a large circular carpet in the first-floor foyer. Dragons chased one another around the border of the red-and-gold rug. Nayan Chanda, the Indian correspondent from the *Far Eastern Economic Review*, watched as the boy, in his baggy green trousers, slipped out of his Ho Chi

Minh sandals and edged toward the center of the carpet with his AK-47, wriggling his toes into the plush.

Later, Chanda saw a *bo doi* hunched up against a wall of the basilica, his back to the crowd in the long park that led to the palace. He looked for all the world as if he were urinating, but stood in the position for so long that Chanda went to investigate.

The young soldier huddled over his compass and a crude map of the city, trying to figure out where he was.

XVI

When Doan Van Toai heard the long fusillade of firing in the direction of the palace, he assumed that it was a victory volley rather than fighting and called his closest friend from the old days of student activism.

He met his friend at the palace around one in the afternoon. The excitement was largely over, although whenever a group of bold Saigon youngsters got into conversation with a group of *bo dois* on the expanse of lawn in front of the palace, the growing, curious crowd drifted to the talk. The sudden ubiquitousness of the term *"bo doi"* was an omen. In theory, whenever a unit of whatever origin crossed into the South, it became part of the Liberation Army—Viet Cong. But the troops on the lawn in front of the palace referred to themselves as *bo dois*—regular foot soldiers in the North Vietnamese Army—which they clearly were.

Northern Vietnamese in general are slightly taller and paler than their southern compatriots. The paleness of these troops derived from a mix of genetics, weather and the fact that many of them had spent months or years in the forest, traveling often at night. Many of them were short; they were still growing. Their baggy gray-green fatigues exaggerated their slightness, and their pith helmets seemed primitive, anachronisms of the resistance against the French. It was commonplace to remark on how young they were—most seemed to be between seventeen and nineteen, but some could have been sixteen—but Toai had anticipated that. Instead he thought, "My God, they are just ordinary people."

Toai and his friend walked down Thong Nhut Boulevard past the American Embassy—the looters were gone but it still smoldered, the abandoned filing cabinets and broken television sets giving it an air of ugly dereliction—and a few blocks farther on to the radio station.

The station was guarded by a handful of *bo dois*. Toai explained that the two of them were "with the revolution." He was prepared to produce names of contacts to support this tenuous assertion, but the youngsters didn't seem to care. One of them who might have been their leader said, "Okay, you can go in." Toai thought his brown-black eyes looked dead.

The cage elevator running up the center of the old concrete plinth had never much worked even when people were around to run things. Toai slapped the button on the off chance, and then climbed the four flights of stairs to the broadcast studios.

Two technicians who had been called by Ly Qui Chung to play the surrender announcement had stayed on, playing tapes of what patriotic music they could find that was not identified with the Thieu regime. They looked eagerly to Toai for leadership. "I'm not a cadre," he said. "Keep playing the same music." But he acted. He called Trinh Cong Son, a composer whose conciliatory songs had been banned for many years but were still performed clandestinely, and were available on cassettes. Toai asked him to come to the station with his tapes.

Shortly after they started broadcasting Trinh Cong Son's songs and the other banned music he'd had at home, a stream of politicians, journalists, and representatives of the array of religious, cultural and economic associations in Saigon made the climb to the studios with statements of support for the new regime, which had yet to announce itself. "Toai, you must read this on the air, it's important."

"I'm not in charge," Toai told them. "I'll keep your announcement. When the cadres come I'll give it to them."

It did not occur to Toai that for the two hours before a small group of cadres did arrive he could have broadcast whatever he wished. But he did type out an order, which he was bold enough to call "Directive Number 1." In the walk from his apartment building to the palace and on to the station, he had been appalled at the abandoned weapons in the streets. Anyone could pick them up—cowboys, gangsters. Children could be hurt. Directive Number 1 called on all citizens to gather up the weapons in their neighborhoods and take them to one of the locations Toai had listed including the campus of the Buddhist university, the headquarters of the student union, and the palace itself.

Finally four men in their thirties and forties wearing the same uniforms as the *bo dois* but without pith helmets and with one or more ball-point pens in their shirt pockets arrived. Toai said, "Welcome, comrades," and introduced himself, his friend and the composer. He was quite sure that the youngest of them was someone he had known years ago, in his first years at the university. In any case, the man did nothing to acknowledge that he recognized Toai. And none of them acted as if they knew the name Trinh Cong Son.

"People have brought statements of support for the new government," Toai explained. "And I wrote out an appeal for the people to gather up the weapons in the streets. But we haven't broadcast anything but the music."

The man whom Toai took to be their leader—the eldest, three pens—was reading Toai's directive. "Good," he said flatly, and flipped to the first of the statements of support. That didn't interest him. He looked around and asked, "How does all this work?"

Toai said that the technicians could show them. "Good," the cadre said. After an awkward moment, Toai and his friends made their way down into the first evening of a liberated Saigon.

There was a nominal curfew, but Toai stayed out until after midnight, seeking out friends in the quiet crowds that moved around the palace and the blocks south of it toward the river. These few blocks had always been the most French, or American, in Saigon. Tonight they were wholly Vietnamese, and there was a restrained holiday feeling in the wonderfully quiet air. At the mouth of an alley on Nguyen Hue Boulevard that widened into what had always been a dirty open-air beer-drinking place, Toai stopped to listen for a moment to the first loud voices of the night: thinly disguised southern accents crudely praising the liberation. He glanced into the dim light as he passed, and marveled at the daring arrogance of the sunburned, short-haired young men in cheap working-class clothes within. One of them wore only a white short-sleeved shirt and his Jockey briefs, as if he couldn't be bothered to find pants after shedding his uniform.

"Why is it so quiet?" Toai asked the friend who had been with him since early afternoon.

"Everyone whispers," the friend said. "We still don't know what we're supposed to do."

"No, something else," Toai said.

"No traffic."

"No," Toai said. Then he realized. He raised his eyes toward the airport, then off to the east. "Listen," he said. "No more airplanes. No more artillery. No more thunder. The sky is quiet."

A few minutes later a voice on the radio in the nearest shop broke into a patriotic march to announce that the Saigon-Gia Dinh Military Management Committee would now begin issuing announcements. The first was Toai's Directive Number 1. Another officially changed the name of Saigon to Ho Chi Minh City, although the name of the committee was not changed for days. Then some of the statements of support for the new government Toai had been given that afternoon were read.

. . .

Toai was not a drinking man. But by midnight he had had two and a half bottles of beer. The relief he had felt when he had realized that the war was actually over was rapidly giving way to an unanticipated, subtle fear. Before the end, when he had tried to imagine what it would be like if he was wrong about the communists, he had allowed himself brief images of military tyranny, the bloodbath that the Americans talked about. It had never occurred to him that the liberators would be stupid, or overwhelmed.

Toai and his friend invited small groups of *bo dois* to join them in *pho* shops. The soldiers slurped at the soup hungrily, and seemed not to know how to spice it or to separate the thin medallions of beef. Their eyes were very tired. They were reluctant to talk about politics, at least in groups. They were, Toai thought, like robots.

Three times during the long evening, he and his friend were alone with a *bo doi*. One said: "We never knew it was like this." Another said: "How could an army from a city like this not fight for it?" And the third: "Why did you let us win? It will be terrible now. We can never understand a society like this."

XVII

Many people, foreigners and Vietnamese, sought asylum at the French Embassy that day, although their numbers tapered off after noon. Mérillon and his staff did everything possible to discourage them. The ambassador himself spoke to a small group of Hmong guards from the American Embassy, tiny primitive men in gray uniforms and red berets. He said that he would grant their request if they insisted, but it was pointless. Surely the communists would quickly learn the identity of everyone in the embassy, and he would not be able to protect them indefinitely. They would do better to try some other way to see to their safety.

That night, for the first time in Mérillon's years in Saigon, there was a complete silence, no distant artillery. And also for the first time his residence was not bathed in light from the huge embassy next door, now gutted and dead.

Then, in the middle of the night: *Blam . . . blam . . . blam. . . .* Half a dozen pistol cracks in the silence.

Someone had eliminated the pathetic guards. Mérillon never found out whether they had stayed close to their posts in fulfillment of their duties or to await deliverance from the sky.

34

At four-thirty or five in the morning on April 30, word reached the press center aboard the USS *Okinawa* that the ambassador was on his way in. I went up top and watched the chopper arrive. I hit the play and record buttons on my Sony, on the off chance that Martin would say something. And there was so much electronics on that ship that the Sony ceased to function as a tape recorder and became a radio receiver, picking up the signals emanating from the *Okinawa*.

Graham Martin was in no mood to talk to the press. He lowered himself from the *Lady Ace 09* and walked around the back of it, hoping to avoid the reporters that way. No luck. Someone from a TV crew shoved a microphone in front of his face and said: "Mr. Ambassador, how do you feel?"

"Hungry," Martin said.

He was given something to eat and was then looked at by the ship's doctor, who ordered medicine that put Martin into a deep sleep for most of the day.

II

The press center was poisoned with the presence and spirit of a rat-faced, slight, red-bearded Navy public affairs officer. On Wednesday morning, he circulated a story that the communists had entered Saigon and rounded up and shot every Western journalist who stayed behind.

Now I was exhausted. I hadn't shaved for several days. All my friends were in the press center, but to see them I had to put up with the vicious little creep.

Early in the afternoon on Wednesday, there was a commotion in the small room with the teletype machine. I went to it.

"SAIGON (AP)—North Vietnamese and Viet Cong troops today peacefully entered Saigon," I read, in an AP story with George Esper's byline.

As it happened, nobody in the last twenty-four hours had told me that Esper had stayed. (With Peter Arnett; with most of the UPI Americans; with many others.)

"Communists enter Saigon peacefully," I said to myself. "George stayed. I could have slept on a cot in the office. He would have given me piasters or dollars against the NBC checks."

I turned away from the chattering, accusing machine. I knew that for the rest of my life I would calculate the proportions of reason and cowardice in my behavior on the morning of April 29, 1975. At the moment, I was pegging cowardice at approximately seventy-five percent. Above all, I was suffused with a dry, suffocating humiliation.

III

Seldom, if ever, has a victorious army entered the enemy capital with the discipline shown by the forces that occupied Saigon that week. The harsh turnings of the economic and political screws would come later, and would be harsh indeed. But it must be said that no one has ever claimed, let alone documented, a single instance of theft, rape or other mistreatment on the part of the occupying forces.

And seldom, perhaps, have the citizens of a vanquished regime felt so superior to their conquerers. More than once, Nayan Chanda, the Indian correspondent who had stayed on in Saigon, saw *bo dois* clustered around a glass of water into which one of them had immersed a "waterproof" watch. The cheap digital watches were a marvel in the first place. And, marveling that the things would keep running (as they would, for a few minutes or hours) underwater, the *bo dois* bought thousands of them.

The sophisticated Saigonese raised their eyebrows at the way the *bo dois* walked hand in hand on the sidewalks, pushing from their collective memory the fact that this display of innocent friendship was common in all of Southeast Asia fifty years earlier—still common in rural Thailand and North Vietnam. The French and the Americans had taught them the sneer.

A bar girl named Mai Linh set up a little soft-drink and beer stall on the sidewalk near Nayan Chanda's apartment building at the foot of Tu Do Street. Chanda was an earnest young Indian family man. He didn't know Mai Linh in her days as a bar girl, but took to chatting with her in the days after "liberation."

She had paid three thousand dollars to an American to get her out. He had absconded.

One day a group of *bo dois* ordered two Cokes, which they shared. Then they discovered that they didn't have enough piasters to pay for them. They left, promising to make good. Mai Linh didn't care. She thought they would be like normal soldiers, and come back soon and get drunk on beer. Instead they returned the next day with a small bag of rice to pay for the Cokes, thanking her for her trust and addressing her as "sister."

Mai Linh was disgusted. "Ho Chi Minh talk sweet," she told Chanda, "but don't like f - - -."

The *bo dois* and their officers and their political cadres had to have places to live. They moved into the villas and apartments abandoned by the foreigners and their puppets, and into homes and apartments still occupied by Saigonese. And the story about the toilet bowls has been repeated so often, by so many Saigonese who subsequently left, that it must have some substance of truth.

The *bo dois* scrape up enough money to buy some fish or vegetables at the market. They put their purchases in the toilet bowl. Out of curiosity, they flush the toilet. The fish and the vegetables disappear. And the *bo dois* are outraged at this imperialistic booby trap.

Early on, there *were* reports of looting and extortion by the *bo dois*. In every instance, the culprits were Saigon cowboys dressed up in the baggy uniforms of the conquerors, the city slickers out to capitalize on their fellow citizens' fear of the country cousin/conquerors.

Saigon's rip-off of the country cousins lasted three weeks. Then directives went out. And there was a series of quick "people's courts" for cowboys who snatched a purse on a sidewalk, the cowboy dead on the asphalt fifteen minutes after the purse snatching, for cowboys who pretended to be liberation fighters, and the crime rate in Ho Chi Minh City fell off to just about zero.

It was about that time that Saigonese stopped making public fun of the *bo dois*.

IV

Within hours after Darwin Judge and Charles McMahon died, Marine officers arrived at their parents' homes with the news. Then, on Thursday, the first day of May, Edna McMahon sat at her kitchen table in Woburn and read a letter from Saigon.

From: Marine Security Guard, American Embassy, Saigon, RVN, 24 April, 1975

Mr. C. McMahon:

Your son, Cpl. C. McMahon, has just arrived in Saigon, Vietnam, for duty as a Marine Security Guard with the American Embassy here. As Noncommissioned Officer in Charge of the Marine Security Guard Detachment, let me assure you that although he is new here, he appears to be the type of Marine that will make an important contribution during his tour of duty, and his efforts in helping to create among the people of Saigon, RVN, and all Vietnam a favorable impression of the Marine Corps and of the American people, will be a source of pride to you.

Juan J. Valdez

Master Sergeant, U.S. Marine Corps

A few days later, it was worse. The letter was handwritten on lightly lined Marine Corps notepaper.

Hi Mom,   April 26

How's everything at home? We got here Thursday afternoon. Did you get my postcard?

This will be the only letter I'll be able to write for a while, so don't get all upset if you don't hear from me.

All my gear is on its way home by mail. I don't know how long it will take to get there. I don't even know if it's been mailed out yet. But you have to pay the postage on it. They wouldn't let us pay here.

They may stop outgoing and incoming mail any day, so don't worry if your letters don't get here. . . .

After this duty, I think they may send us home for a while. Well I have to go now. Say hi to everybody for me.

Love, Charlie

I'll try to write when I have time and don't worry Ma!!!!

IV

Less than an hour after the Airborne major blew away the radio at the bridge northwest of Vung Tau, Do Duc Cuong and his band finally saw enemy tanks, four of them, leading a heavy column. For the few minutes after the bridge was blown, while the tanks and the trucks behind them edged along the opposite bank like dumb timid water buffaloes, Cuong at his good position behind a cluster of boulders felt almost like a hero. But then one and then another of the tanks nosed gently into the water, and Cuong realized quickly that it was all idiocy and waste. The river, which had looked so black, was shallow enough for the tanks to ford.

The Airborne major rose from a shallow inadequate bunker at the foot of the broken bridge and cried to his men that they had to destroy all the tanks before they died. He didn't make it. They stopped the first two with rocket-propelled grenades, but the other two kept coming, the rounds from their casually sweeping 100-mm. turrets sprouting blossoms of dirt in the riverbank and catching the major and throwing him up in the air and back, arms outflung, hand-held grenade launcher flipping end over end in the air, other rounds *thwock-thwock-thwocking* into the cluster of boulders from which Cuong was scrambling away, backward on all fours, suddenly absolutely certain that he did not want to die.

Of the eighty, ten got away. But Cuong was still not done with war. There was resistance at the Army training center in Vung Tau, and from a hill crowned with a radar dish at the edge of the sea. Cuong went to the training center to tell them the communist position, and then walked to the hill among the thousands of people who had come to Vung Tau looking for boats.

Cuong spent that night and the daylight hours of the next day, May 1, on the hill, where more than a hundred men holed up in positions protected by boulders and trees from which they could survey the plain below. Cuong watched the column advance on the town. He was pleased, in a numb way centered not on himself but on the major, that the column was led by only two tanks. But that night and even during the bright next day the faces kept coming back more clearly and persistently than ever. There were faces of communists he or his men had had to interrogate harshly, the stubborn ones. In defense, his mind threw up the faces of his sisters and brother from the night of November 5, 1963, faces that hadn't come to him that way for years. He saw the smiling, terrified face and bald skull of the man who had given him the cigarettes and money, the black head and dark-green ballooned-out clothes moving away so fast in the ship's wake; the bulging eyes of the dead children on the quays at Cam Ranh; the smoothing mask of the old priest.

As the sun began its slide into the western lands, drawing out the shadows of everything on the plain—trees, houses, tanks—to long knives pointed at the hill, Captain Cuong stood and walked around to the darkened side of the hill facing the blood-dark sea. He said nothing to the clutch of men he left, or the few he passed. Before the trees gave way to shrub, he opened his right hand, heard the M-16 fall.

Below the shrubs, boulders fell to the sea. Cuong knew that advance parties of communists were everywhere, but he moved from boulder to boulder unafraid. All along the shore, people still moved in hopes of finding a fishing boat. There were many more people than communists. Now Cuong would become what he had been as a child, just one of the people. Slowly, cautiously, he let a bud of relief appear in his breast.

v

Jay Scarborough and John and Carolyn Miller and the other Westerners captured in Ban Me Thuot learned from Radio Hanoi that the Americans had fled, Saigon was liberated and thirty years of war had ended. There was no special announcement by the camp authorities. And if they were jubilant, they did not show it in front of their captives. In the final days of the war, "Liberate the South," the anthem of the revolution, was played almost continuously on the radio. With the victory, the authorities fixed a loudspeaker to a tree, and for several days a tape describing the Liberation Army's triumphant entry into Saigon was played over and over again.

May Day was of course a holiday in communist Vietnam, which is to say all of Vietnam that May Day, save for patches held here and there by desperate men.

In the camp, ARVN prisoners had a day of rest from their work assignments, and joined with their captors in volleyball, tugs-of-war and Chinese chess played with men moving in squares marked out in the dirt. The prisoners were given pieces of salt-pork fat, and the guards had a feast that included meat and eggs. One of them brought a big plate of the prized food for LuAnne Miller and the few Vietnamese children in the camp, all of whom played with her. Carolyn Miller was delighted. LuAnne had been feverish and nauseated at night off and on ever since their arrival two weeks before in this place the Westerners had named Camp Wilderness.

Although she worried about LuAnne's health, Carolyn Miller was more comfortable in Camp Wilderness than at any time since their capture. Here the Western men for the first time were given real work details. Along with the Vietnamese, they quickly built two outhouses, complete with thatched roofs and walls. The women's was set on the edge of a huge bomb crater. As she picked her way to it for the first time, Carolyn realized that with the addition of this single facility, Camp Wilderness was a great improvement over Camp Sunshine.

"You know," Struharik said one night early on, "if we ever get out of here I'll be looking for a job. I don't think there's going to be a real big demand for American experts on Darlac province. Maybe I can make it on the outside as an outhouse builder."

Through the night after the May Day celebrations, LuAnne had stomach pains and diarrhea. She complained that her legs ached. Her tonsils were swollen, and during the night her temperature rose to 104.6°. Her parents bathed her with wet towels through the night to try to keep the fever under control.

In the morning, Carolyn Miller and Lillian Phillips tried as they had before to get medicine from the camp medic. When he insisted that he had nothing for LuAnne, Lillian Phillips told him that she had seen him giving sulfa tablets to an ARVN prisoner. "I don't have any more," he answered curtly.

There were a few tetracycline pills in the emergency kit a friend had given Paul Struharik. Not knowing what lay ahead, the Millers were very reluctant to ask for the pills. But Lillian Phillips decided that LuAnne's condition constituted an emergency. She asked Struharik for them.

Over the next couple of days, LuAnne's fever receded. But the diarrhea continued and she began to vomit again, once bringing up bloody mucus and another time one of the precious pills.

Then an ARVN doctor named Ly who was housed in the same long shelter with the Westerners suggested boiling rice and giving LuAnne the boiled water. It would be easy to digest, he said, and might help the diarrhea.

LuAnne had lost so much weight that her pants slipped from her waist. She was lethargic, and had to be carried to and from the latrine.

Then, in that first week in May, an ARVN captain died. The prisoners discussed the death in muted voices. Apparently the man had been sick for weeks, but no one thought it was serious. The consensus was that he had died of *trung gio*—which translates as "poisonous wind" and covers a variety of complaints. In order to release the wind, parts of the torso must be scraped with a spoon or similar object. Westerners who spent any time in Vietnam were familiar with the belief, because one could not be three or four days in the country without seeing someone with the broad red welts of the cure, if that's what it is, on the backs and abdomens of bare-chested cyclo-peddlers or farmers.

Dr. Ly thought that exhaustion and malnutrition had undoubtedly contributed to the man's death. Whatever its cause, the captain's death may have saved LuAnne Miller's life.

The day after the captain died, Dr. Ly was called to a small building that had been recently constructed near the fence. It served as a clinic and a meeting and interrogation room. Even after the Millers crawled under their mosquito net, they could hear a heated discussion coming from the new clinic.

In the morning they learned that changes were to be made in the camp medical system. Dr. Ly had been asked to sign the captain's death certificate. He had resisted doing so, since he had been allowed no voice in the man's treatment. The authorities yielded: He and the other trained medical personnel among the prisoners were to see to it that all prisoners with health problems were reported to the authorities. And while the North Vietnamese medic retained a veto power, Dr. Ly and his colleagues could advise him on treatment.

With this change, little LuAnne as well as the Canadian missionary, Norm Johnson—who suffered from symptoms similar to Lu-Anne's—were given injections of antibiotics. They both responded well to the treatment, although LuAnne's cries at the first couple of injections brought even some of the guards rushing to find out what was the matter.

When LuAnne submitted calmly to the third shot, her mother rewarded her with half a stick of gum she was still carrying in her purse. LuAnne had learned well by now about economies of scarcity, and of sharing. She ran off to share bits of the gum with her Aunt Betty and Aunt Lil.

May 6 was Carolyn Miller's birthday. The morning began routinely, but all the Westerners were aware of the significance of the day—they needed little excuse to break the monotony of their confinement—and after their late-morning meal, Carolyn was presented with an unusual "birthday cake." The day before, she and Peter Whitlock, who was exempt from work duties because of his damaged feet and generally weakened condition, had discovered a way to make a paste from mashed boiled manioc that could be coaxed into sticking together and baked on an old sheet of tin Whitlock had found and scoured. Yesterday they had added salty fish powder to the mixture. This morning, in some of the patties, Whitlock substituted for the fish powder some of a hoard of sugar they had been given at Camp Sunshine.

After that treat, with the noon sun reaching into the cleared patch in the middle of the camp, Carolyn Miller gathered up a little hand towel and the clothes she would change into and left with the other women for their river bath.

When they reached the bamboo-and-thatch guardhouse at the gate that led to the stream, they politely asked permission to go on, as usual. As usual, the guard gave it. But this morning, as they were moving off he called them back and said: "If you want to go a little bit farther up to the left, you would have more privacy."

"Thank you, brother," Carolyn Miller said, surprised at the sudden kindness. When she and the other women in the last few weeks had unexpectedly come across nude men in the stream, they had always averted their eyes. The men had done the same with them, and there had never been a lewd or suggestive remark. But with permission to roam farther along the stream, they found a site that afforded them complete privacy. For the first time since their capture, Carolyn Miller and the other women could undress openly, not behind a bush, with no fear that a man might suddenly appear. As she luxuriated in the cool water, Carolyn Miller realized how much she had missed the privilege of privacy.

She had no idea where three of her children were. The child with her was recovering from her sickness—but only God knew what lay in store for the three of them in Camp Wilderness. Easily, without pain or tears, she yielded their fates to God's grace, and thanked him for this birthday gift of unhurried, untroubled cleansing in His waters.

VI

On that same first day of May when the Westerners captured in Ban Me Thuot were onlookers at the subdued, childlike celebrations in Camp Wilderness, Doan Van Toai went to the student center on Duy Tan Street in Saigon. He helped lead the university students' participation in the campaign to restore order to the city. The students acted on their own, guided by the steady stream of directives now issuing from the radio. They organized squads of high school students to direct traffic and mimeographed copies of the Military Management Committee's orders as well as their own Patriotic Students Association communiqué welcoming the liberators. And they sent out older students to enforce the committee's decree closing all bars, massage parlors, dance halls and other places where "American-type activities" took place.

On Saturday, May 3, in response to another directive, Toai returned to his office at the Nam Bo bank, which had reopened for its staff but not for its depositors. But on Friday, May 2, the first day the interprovincial buses ran again, Toai made his way down to the quiet little coast town of Rach Gia in far southwestern Vietnam, near the Cambodian border. He had been there once before, and treated himself to the small barbecued birds—eaten whole, beaks, claws and all—that were the area's specialty.

He spent the few hours at midday allowed by the long trip back and forth making quiet inquiries about the possibilities of buying a fishing boat.

Doan Van Toai gave up on the revolution on the first night of liberation, at the moment the third man had confirmed what Toai had come to feel all day, with growing dread: That the northerners who had won the war were incapable not of controlling but of understanding or making peace with the South.

VII

Finally, late in the afternoon on May 1, the ambassador was strong enough to take a breath of the immense bright clean breezy air on the deck of the USS *Okinawa*. Two or three of his closest assistants attended him. As it happened, a junior embassy staffer was also nearby.

Thomas Polgar strode up to the small group around the ambassador. As usual, Polgar was brisk and enthusiastic. Grinning, he said to Martin, "Well, we got out everyone we had to."

Martin hoarded his expletives. The junior embassy staffer was shocked when the handsome gray Old Man said, "The f - - - you did," turned and walked away.

VIII

In the middle of the morning on Saturday, May 3, helicopters of the Seventh Fleet transferred about a hundred Korean, Japanese and Western journalists from various ships to the USS *Blue Ridge*, the fleet's command-and-communications ship. Ambassador Martin and the other officials on the *Okinawa* were also transferred to the *Blue Ridge*. Just as on the *Okinawa*, a press center had been prepared on the *Blue Ridge*. A few hours after we had accustomed ourselves to the new environment, Thomas Polgar wandered into the press center and sat on a couch. At first, he spoke in his quiet, accented English only with the older men in the press corps: George McArthur, Robert Shaplen and Keyes Beech. But of course word of the conversation spread, and the couch was soon mobbed.

Word also spread to the ambassador. About ten minutes after Polgar had started talking, Graham Martin wandered into the room and made his way to the couch. He was still pale, still sick and under the influence of his medications. He was also, for a change, dressed almost casually, wearing a jacket but no tie, and he was munching an apple.

Polgar made room for Martin on the couch. One of the few quotes from the ambassador that made it out of that impromptu press conference was: "The verdict of history will be that we did not have to leave Vietnam in the way we did. If we had done what we said we would do in the first year after the Paris agreement, if we had kept the commitments . . ." His voice trailed off.

The reason that there were so few quotes from the meeting was that soon after Martin joined it, Keyes Beech of the Chicago *Sun-Times* mounted what turned into a harangue. "I was on your side most of the time, Graham," he said. "You know that. And the one thing I want to know from you is why the f - - - I had to fight my way over that wall on Tuesday!"

With that, the ambassador excused himself. Polgar followed suit a few minutes later.

A few hours after the brief conference in the press room, a ship's officer handed Graham Martin a one-line cable:

I THINK IT ADVISABLE THAT YOU AVOID ALL PUBLIC COMMENT UNTIL YOU HAVE MADE YOUR REPORT TO THE PRESIDENT—KISSINGER.

IX

Big Minh, Vu Van Mau, former speaker of the National Assembly Nguyen Van Huyen (whom Minh had named as his vice president-designate) and Nguyen Van Hao were kept two and a half days at the palace. They were largely confined to the small palace infirmary.

The other three quickly distanced themselves from Hao, who was the only one of them from the Thieu government. Vu Van Mau and Big Minh made numerous calls to Thich Tri Quang. And the three wrote letters to various communist acquaintances asking for leniency— for the three of them. Vu Van Mau wrote to General Vo Nguyen Giap, the mastermind of the French defeat at Dien Bien Phu thirty years earlier and now Hanoi's minister of defense. "We were classmates," the letter said. "We should be friends again."

The room contained three cots and a surgical trolley. For a Vietnamese—as for most Asians and indeed for some Westerners, one supposes—the idea of spending the night on a surgical trolley seemed to be tempting the fates. But Hao was considerably younger than the other three. And he assumed that his fate—the fate of a loser—was pretty well sealed. On the first evening, when the moment came, he volunteered to sleep on the trolley. The others were visibly relieved.

Hao had plenty of time to think. One of the things that occurred to him—it hadn't struck him at the time—was that he had been seated in the first row of chairs at Big Minh's inaugural speech on that terrible afternoon (could it have been only three days ago?) when the skies blackened and roared, followed so quickly by the attack on Tan Son Nhut. He was in the first row because *there were no foreigners at the ceremony.* Was it possible? Yes! They inaugurated a new president— the president the French and even the Americans wanted—and there was no one present from either embassy! Or from any other embassy. Even the Hungarians and Poles weren't there—but of course that was because the Poles had already left and the Hungarians were preparing to leave, which Hao knew. Hao's next thought, which he did not share with his fellow guests in the infirmary, was seemingly contradictory, but in fact the absence of the French and the Americans at the ceremony proved its truth: "That week, the week between Thieu and Minh, the communists were right," Hao said to himself. "That week, we were truly the puppets of the foreigners."

They were released on Saturday morning, following a ceremony to which the remaining foreign journalists in Saigon were invited.

Nguyen Van Hao had a joyous reunion with his wife and three small children.

The next day, two representatives from the Military Management Committee that had taken over the administration of the city called at Dr. Hao's house. Hao thought it entirely likely that he was to be arrested. Instead, they asked him if he would be willing to advise the committee on economic affairs.

Hao felt a door opening, others closing silently in the dark. It was a risk. What should he do, for the people?

"Yes," he said.

IX

The three strung-together messages were handed to the ambassador on the *Blue Ridge.*

PRESIDENT FORD TO AMBASSADOR MARTIN:

I WANT TO EXPRESS MY DEEP APPRECIATION TO YOU AND YOUR EN-
TIRE STAFF FOR THE SUCCESSFUL EVACUATION OF AMERICANS AND
VIETNAMESE FROM SAIGON. THE TIRELESS DEDICATION OF YOUR MIS-
SION AND ITS SKILLFUL PERFORMANCE UNDER THE MOST SEVERE PRES-
SURE WAS VITAL TO THE ACCOMPLISHMENT OF THIS MOST DIFFICULT
AND DELICATE OPERATION. PLEASE ACCEPT AS WELL MY SINCERE PER-
SONAL COMPLIMENTS. YOUR COURAGE AND STEADINESS AT THIS CRITI-
CAL PERIOD ENABLED US TO EVACUATE OUR OWN CITIZENS AND A VERY

LARGE NUMBER OF ENDANGERED VIETNAMESE. I HOPE YOU WILL CON-
VEY TO YOUR ENTIRE STAFF MY DEEP GRATITUDE AND THAT OF THE
AMERICAN PEOPLE FOR A JOB WELL DONE. SINCERELY.

TO GRAHAM MARTIN
FROM HENRY KISSINGER

I'M SURE YOU KNOW HOW DEEPLY I FEEL ABOUT YOUR PERFOR-
MANCE UNDER THE MOST TRYING CIRCUMSTANCES. MY HEARTFELT
THANKS. WARM REGARDS.

PS: WOULD APPRECIATE INFORMATION ABOUT YOUR ONWARD TRAVEL
PLANS TO PASS ON TO MEMBERS OF YOUR FAMILY.

GRAHAM, YOU WERE SUPERB. BRENT.

X

The journalists were on the *Blue Ridge* for one night only. Then it
transpired that the *Okinawa* was going to be the first ship of the fleet
to reach port in the Philippines. The Navy graciously ferried all the
journalists back to the *Okinawa*.

Naval ships are claustrophobic by design. When you add a few
hundred Vietnamese and American refugees to any of them, the contrast between life below decks, where almost all the living and working is done, and the vastness of the sky and the freshness of the air
on deck is intensified. Like most of the other correspondents, I made
frequent trips up top. Also like most of them, I never stayed up very
long. It was oddly lonely and boring up there.

But one day on deck there was a Marine who wanted to talk to me.
It reminded me of those few months I spent in Vietnam when there
were U.S. troops. Every group of servicemen seemed to include one
cocky one who dared to approach the reporter. This boy was short,
and he really did look no more than sixteen, in part as a result of an
active case of acne that he picked at as we talked at the rail. He told
me that America had really f - - - - - up in Vietnam, the military had
to fight the war with one arm tied behind its back. Everything would
have been different if we'd been allowed to invade the North. "Never
should get in a f - - - - -' war if you ain't prepared to win it," the Marine said.

I listened earnestly. "Lot of guys have thought that way over the
years," I allowed. Then, after a few moments had passed: "How long
were you on the ground in there?"

"Eighteen hours," the boy said. "Out at the airport, you know?"

"Right."

The boy stared out at the horizon. "Yup," he added. "A real bad
f - - - -up. But I'll tell you, some of these chicks—some of these Vietnamese chicks—they're really all right."

Now I allowed myself a laugh. "Lot of guys have thought that way too down the years," I said.

All five nights on the ships were bad. On the worst of them, I gave up on sleep after midnight and got back into my filthy clothes with no idea where I would go. Phil McCombs of *The Washington Post* was just getting ready for bed, after writing a story. He listened to me speak a few confused sentences and suggested we go someplace for a cup of coffee.

We found some finally in the officers' mess. I did not really need someone to talk to, although it was good of McCombs to think so. I needed a place to sit and drink coffee where I couldn't hear the violence and vulgarity of the movies on the closed-circuit television sets or the groans of a man in the sick bay.

We were joined by a couple of senior pilots, and McCombs talked post-Vietnam U.S. Pacific strategy with them. It seemed odd to me that people kept working. Even I had done a few silly spots about one thing or another at the beginning, but not for several days now.

One of the four women journalists on board—three from the evacuation, one who had come out from Manila—let me know that she had some marijuana in the big stateroom a ranking officer had had to vacate for them. I told McCombs I'd see him in the morning.

"This stuff is from Cambodia, and pretty strong," the woman said as she led me to the stateroom.

About an hour later, I made my way back to the sick bay overflow, two decks down and the length of the ship, in my bare feet. Some of the passageways were lit with what looked like infrared light. I surprised only one officer with my slow, grinning progress.

I knew I could not get back into my bunk, the third off the floor in a tier of four. So I collapsed on a larger one in the next tier. I was muddily aware that it had been appropriated by George McArthur, but it was two o'clock in the morning and the bunk was empty and the drug was starting to affect me badly.

At first it was only visual, all the images color cartoons, and all of them streaming out of themselves in smooth replication, proving the existence of essences within things. I would say "Yes, of course" to myself as an image—muscular, legless soldiers bobbing naked in the swimming pool of the Hotel Catinat, say—would yield to a concept— the ineffable mystery of the evil in men's hearts—and that to another, all of them in satisfying correspondence.

Then it turned aural as well. My mind took up the vibration of the ship's propellers under us, took up the spaced cries of the Vietnamese in the sick bay beyond, separated from us by a sheet—*ayeeyow* . . .

ayeeyow . . . *ayeeyow*—controlled, soft, repeated over and over and over again in time with the groaning of the ship.

And all the sounds, in my mind, turned into the sound of my wife crying. Knowing it was nonsense, but terrified and desolate, I was sure that my wife was crying at that moment in Chicago and that the universe had picked up her sobbing and bent it over the round of the earth to let the pulsing of the ship and the groaning of the Vietnamese man project and amplify it into a soul that in that hour, lying on that cot, only through an act of will succeeded in holding on to itself and prevailing over its shame.

Epilogue

Here is what has happened to some of the people in this book.

Either with the Seventh Fleet or in the Philippines, Graham Martin was given medicine that effectively stripped his immune system and landed him in a hospital in Bethesda, Maryland, for several months. He also was treated for a variety of lung diseases, and finally quit smoking.

Martin retired from the State Department in early 1977, telling Frank Snepp that his colleagues hadn't even bothered to throw a farewell luncheon for him.

In late 1984, the ambassador and his wife were living quietly in North Carolina.

Wycliffe Bible Translators staffers flew Carolyn and John Miller's three older children from Nha Trang to Saigon before the communists reached Nha Trang, and from Saigon to the Philippines before April 29.

The Millers and the other Westerners (and Ike Tolentino) captured in Ban Me Thuot were eventually taken north to Hanoi and held in the "Hanoi Hilton" compound that had held most of the American prisoners of war. They were released in November 1975, eight months after their capture.

In late 1984, Jay Scarborough was a lawyer with an investment banking firm in New York City.

The Millers were continuing their mission as Bible translators in Sabah, Malaysia.

The Vietnamese man who was captured with his family in Paul Struharik's house in Ban Me Thuot had reason for his fear: He was a senior local employee of the CIA. His name was Phong. With senior officers, he was culled from the run-of-the-mill prisoners early.

In 1980, Struharik received a letter from him. He said that he had jumped from the jeep in which he was being driven through Nha Trang, and escaped. He went underground, eventually finding his wife and children and then making it to Malaysia—where he had just arrived—on a fishing boat.

Struharik informed Phong's superiors at the CIA, assuming that they would quickly secure his release. A few weeks later, his contacts at the agency notified him that Phong and his family were on one of the boats that the Malaysians towed out to sea and sank.

Don Harris was one of two NBC journalists killed in the opening stage of the massacre and mass suicide in Jonestown, Guyana, in November 1978.

The remains of Corporals Charles McMahon, Jr., and Darwin Judge were returned to their families in early March 1976, more than ten months after they were killed. The McMahons believe that Senator Edward M. Kennedy and his staff were instrumental in getting the authorities in Vietnam to find and release the remains, which had been buried in plots next to the Seventh-Day Adventist Hospital.

The Vietnamese engineer whom Don Hays advised to slip into Tan Son Nhut as a Japanese diplomat did make it, but not without incident. Guards at the main gate into the air base fired into the air as his rented limousine slowed almost to a stop and accelerated into the base. The engineer got himself onto one of the Australian flights and deplaned in Bangkok. His American employers there told him that he had to return to Saigon; they would see that he was eventually evacuated. He chose not to take them up on the offer. Eventually he found a sympathetic junior officer at the New Zealand Embassy in Bangkok who issued him a temporary passport on the formal pledge that he surrender it to a colleague of the diplomat who would meet the plane in Auckland, which the engineer did. When Don Hays visited Auckland after the war, the man showed him the homburg he had worn during the escape.

Dr. Tran Kim Tuyen's nephew, the ARVN major who served as his driver on the morning of April 29, succeeded in getting into the embassy and getting out.

Either a seemingly innocuous shrapnel wound that Sergeant Robert L. Frain received in the summer of 1974 or some other infection he picked up in Vietnam led to a disease that in mid-1983 had cost him most of his lower intestine and liver and part of his stomach. Because of that physical condition, Sergeant Frain was receiving full disability pay.

Approximately one hundred and fifty of the children on the Galaxy C-5A that crashed on April 4 survived and were quickly sent on to the United States. (The precise number is uncertain by a factor of a child or two; there was no manifest.)

The adopting parents of some of the children sued Lockheed and the U.S. government on the basis that the sudden loss of pressure and the crash had caused brain damage in or done grave psychological harm to the children. Fifty cases were settled for an average of $325,000 per child in 1982. And in 1984 Lockheed and the government reached a settlement with lawyers for many of the other children amounting to $17.8 million.

Dr. Meritt Stark and his wife, Dorothy, in late 1984 were living in a small southern city where Dr. Stark, despite being sixty-eight, was the medical director of a state hospital for the mentally retarded.

After all the years of bribes, first to keep Tu out of the Army and then to keep him and his brother out of jail, when Tu and his family arrived on Guam their total fortune was the hundred dollars I had given him. But they still had fans in America, and after a few months (during which Tu worked as a security guard in New York), most of the family—including the father, who left separately—resettled in southern California. Tu and three of his sisters—including Khanh Ha, whom they have made the central attraction—are the heart of the band they still call The Uptight.

Nguyen Van Hao's advice to the communists—don't rush to collectivize the southern rice farmer; encourage private enterprise; reach out a hand to the United States—went largely ignored for seven years. In 1980, his wife and two eldest children, both boys, were allowed to leave for France. Two years later, Dr. Hao and his two younger children, both girls, were also allowed to leave. Initially—for two years—the State Department denied Hao a visa to join his wife and four children in Houston, citing a provision in the immigration law that bars "former communists, anarchists and subversives." It took two years of vigorous lobbying by Ellsworth Bunker and others before Dr. Hao was granted immigrant status and allowed to join his family.

Through an intermediary, Mel Chatman happened to make contact after the war, in the States, with the family of the young ARVN officer

on the ship off Da Nang who had told him that he would not run.
He didn't. As far as the family knew at that time, in 1979, he was still
in "re-education."

Pham Xuan An, the *Time* correspondent who helped Dr. Tran Kim
Tuyen escape on April 29, had already sent his wife and children out
of the country. A few weeks after the end of the war, he asked them to
return and they were allowed to do so.

He may have vague duties in the branch of the foreign ministry in Ho
Chi Minh City. Cao Giao, the wispily bearded intellectual who could
not understand why everyone was running away, himself finally succeeded in emigrating to Belgium in 1984. Cao Giao confirms the widespread belief among Vietnamese exiles that An was in the service of
the communists throughout the war and now has the rank of colonel
in the Vietnamese Army. Dr. Nguyen Van Hao, on the other hand,
still refuses to believe that An is a communist. Before Hao was allowed
to leave Vietnam in 1982, he and An often sat over tea complaining
about the stupidities of the new regime.

In late 1984, Dr. Tuyen and Jackie were running a neat, comfortable
bed-and-breakfast in England.

A couple of years after the end of the war, Russell Mott made very
discreet inquiries through the Red Cross to find out how "Hai" was
doing. If she was living alone, or with a Vietnamese family, he would
have contacted her, in hopes of re-establishing a relationship. Word
came back that she was in Vermont, and happy there. Mott dropped it.

As for Mott himself, he became first a psychologist, and then a professional photographer, and lives in the Southwest.

Liz Montagne, the secretary in Da Nang, fulfilled her ambitions. In
1984 she was made a Foreign Service Officer and took up her first posting abroad, in Vientiane, Laos—the only capital in communist Indochina with an American mission.

In the fall of 1984, Ken Moorefield became an economics counselor in
the U.S. embassy in Lima. Earlier, he had been the director of the
Vietnam Veterans Leadership Project, which encouraged successful
Vietnam vets to help those who weren't doing so well.

Jean-Marie Mérillon stayed on in Saigon for a few months after the
end of the war. His position was somewhat ambiguous, as reflected in

the fact that the communists continued to address him as "Ambassador"—but not as "the French Ambassador." As far as the communists were concerned, there was one French Ambassador in Vietnam, and he was in Hanoi.

Sometime after the crisis at the end, Mérillon became a teetotaler. He also resumed a distinguished career in the French foreign service, and in the summer of 1983 was ambassador to NATO.

Even under a new, assumed identity, Captain Do Duc Cuong had to spend a year in "re-education." He escaped in a fishing boat with his wife and son in 1979. (A daughter was to follow in another boat. She was lost.)

Cuong was resettled in South Dakota, where he worked for a year sweeping out a supermarket overnight. During the year, he saved enough money to resettle in southern California. There he talked his way into a job with an electronics firm. After the successful job interview, he stayed up all night reading about the new technology he had somehow convinced his employers he already understood. Since then, he has had one promotion after another.

Doan Van Toai was arrested in June 1975, after a heated argument at the bank with its new communist officials about the correct economic policies for the South. He was held until November 1977, and was released after an uncle who was a colonel in the NVA intervened on his behalf.

Through a ruse (and a subsequent payment of a bribe), he was allowed to leave Vietnam within weeks of his release from prison.

The ruse involved his prison release papers. Officials didn't know how to classify him—as a student leader, a revolutionary or a banker. He left prison with a slip of paper handwritten by a senior official saying only that Toai had successfully completed his "re-education" and should be allowed to join his wife.

The man didn't realize that Toai's wife was in Paris. And the officials who rather quickly issued Toai a passport and an exit visa were not willing to test the authority or knowledge of the man who drew up the prison release.

The day after he arrived in Paris, Toai called a press conference and started talking about the "Vietnamese Gulag," which became the title of his first book.

In 1984, he was living in California and continuing to publish books and articles about Vietnam.

. . .

Duong Van Minh was allowed to leave Vietnam for France in 1982. One assumes that the French government pressed for his release. In any case, he left Vietnam very quietly, and has not spoken for publication since settling in France, which may well be the result of an understanding among himself, Hanoi and Paris.

Early in April, President Thieu arrested General Pham Van Phu, the former commander in the highlands, along with the commander at Phuoc Long, which fell in January, and Phu's subordinate with responsibility for the defense of Nha Trang. Thieu would have liked to jail General Ngo Quang Truong, the MR 1 commander, as well, but upon his arrival in Saigon, Truong checked himself into a military hospital.

At the end of the month, Phu succeeded in inserting some of his family into the evacuation. He stayed behind, and put a bullet through his brain on April 30.

That evening, General Le Van Hung, the deputy commander in the Mekong delta, made a short, moving speech to his staff and then killed himself in his bedroom. (Two of his children later walked across Cambodia to Thailand. His wife lived as a hunted woman in Saigon for several years, but eventually escaped in a fishing boat.)

On the morning of May 1, Hung's superior, MR 4 commander General Nguyen Khoa Nam, also killed himself.

Expatriate nationalist Vietnamese generally feel that Phu died in disgrace but that Hung and Nam should be honored as heroes who died rather than surrender—or run.

After enormous losses on both sides, the communists eventually bypassed Xuan Loc. General Le Minh Dao, the commander of the 18th ARVN Division, stayed in Vietnam and presented himself to the new authorities. In 1984, he was either still in "re-education" or, as rumor had it, had died in the summer of 1984 in one of the camps in the North where the senior officials were held.

"Laughing Boy" Dang Van Quang settled in Quebec.

Nguyen Cao Ky settled in southern California and owned a liquor store. He filed for bankruptcy in 1984.

Nguyen Van Thieu in 1984 was living in a London suburb.

Nguyen Tu, the journalist whose dispatches from the Convoy of Tears so demoralized Saigon, had numerous opportunities to leave Vietnam in the closing days of the war but missed them all. He died in Chi Hoa, Saigon's main prison, in late 1975.

Charles Benoit learned later that the last telephone call from Tammy's mother, which he refused, was a peace offering. She had seen reason, and was willing to bring Tammy to Benoit and leave with them. In late 1984, she was still in Saigon. Benoit was working for a small computer peripherals company in New Hampshire. Beautiful Tammy had lost all of her Vietnamese; her father of course was still fluent.

Sources

What follows is a partial listing of people who spoke to me for publication. The list is partial because I interviewed dozens of people who, as it turned out, contributed no specific scene, sentence, noun, quotation. To any of those people who read this book and say to themselves, "He used nothing I gave him," let me say that in the last two years I have not had a single conversation with anyone about events in Vietnam in March and April 1975 that did not in some way deepen my understanding. "No one knows all of Brooklyn," a cabdriver once told Thomas Wolfe. It is a truism that no one knows everything that happened in the nine weeks about which I have written. It came down to choices. I chose the 250-odd scenes that constitute the book. I do apologize to the several dozen people—most of them Vietnamese, and many of them Vietnamese in California, whom I interviewed early in the process—whose stories have gone untold here.

In most cases, interested readers or scholars will be able to make a good guess as to who is the principal source for each scene. It is almost always the person from whose point of view the scene is written. Having said that, I should add that I have tried to achieve the journalistic ideal of having at least two sources for each assertion.

For convenience, I will split the list of interview subjects in two: Westerners (more accurately, non-Vietnamese) and Vietnamese.

Westerners, in alphabetical order, omitting military ranks, other titles, and middle initials:

Jean-Louis Arnaud, Keyes Beech, Charles Benoit, Pierre Brochand, James Bullington, Ellsworth Bunker, Alan Carter, Nayan Chanda, Mel Chatman, Neil Davis, James Devine, Denny Ellerman, John Finney, Robert Frain, Marvin Garrett, Don Hays, George Jacobson, Craig Johnstone, Cary Kassebaum, David Kennerly, Charles Lahiguera, William Le Gro, Wolfgang Lehmann, Mike Marriott, Graham Martin, George McArthur, Charles and Edna McMahon, Terry McNamara, Jean-Marie Mérillon, Liz Montagne, Ken Moorefield, Russell Mott, John Murray, Thomas Polgar, Lamar Prosser, Lionel Rosenblatt, Jay Scarborough, Paul Schaberger, David Sciacchitano, Gerald Scott, Homer Smith, Meritt and Dorothy Stark, Paul Struharik, Dick and Germaine Swanson, John Swenson, Charles Timmes, David Whitten, Lacy and Jackie Wright.

Though I spoke to at least a hundred Vietnamese, I can list only those few upon whose stories I have obviously relied. I list them alphabetically by given, not family, name:

Do Duc Cuong, Nguyen Van Hao, Nguyen Cao Ky, Doan Van Toai, La Anh Tu, Tran Kim Tuyen, Nguyen Hung Vuong.

I quote directly from two books:

Our Great Spring Victory, General Van Tien Dung. Monthly Review Press, New York and London, 1977.

Captured!, Carolyn Paine Miller. Christian Herald Books, Chappaqua, N.Y., 1977. In fact, I quote no passages from *Captured!*, only dialogue. The unspoken prayer on page 95 is invented, modeled on numerous other prayers in Mrs. Miller's book.

Some of the material on Corporal Charles McMahon's character, and on his last home leave, is based on "The Last Casualty," by Donovan Moore, an article in the December 1976 issue of *Boston* magazine.

The rest of the core library of reference materials consisted of:

55 Days: The Fall of South Vietnam, Alan Dawson. Prentice-Hall, Englewood Cliffs, N.J., 1977.

A Time to Heal, Gerald R. Ford. Harper & Row, New York, 1979.

The Fall of South Vietnam: Statements by Vietnamese Military and Civilian Leaders, Stephen T. Hosmer, Konrad Kellen and Brian M. Jenkins. Crane Russak, New York, 1980.

Without Honor: Defeat in Vietnam and Cambodia, Arnold R. Isaacs. Johns Hopkins University Press, Baltimore and London, 1983.

Shooter, David Hume Kennerly. Newsweek Books, New York, 1979.

Twenty Years and Twenty Days, Nguyen Cao Ky. Stein and Day, New York, 1976.

Vietnam from Cease-fire to Capitulation, William E. Le Gro. U.S. Army Center of Military History, Washington, D.C., 1981.

The Vietnam-Cambodia Emergency, 1975. Pt. 3, "Vietnam Evacuation: Testimony of Ambassador Graham A. Martin," January 27, 1976. (Testimony before the International Relations Committee of the House of Representatives.)

Decent Interval, Frank Snepp. Random House, New York, 1977.

Last Flight from Saigon, Thomas G. Tobin, Arthur E. Laehr, John F. Hilgenberg. U.S. Air Force Southeast Asia Monograph Series, Vol. IV, Monograph 6, Washington, D.C., 1978.

Southeast Asia Report, No. 1247: Vietnam: History of the Bulwark B2 Theater, Vol. 5, *Concluding the 30-Years War,* Tran Van Tra. Joint Publications Research Service, Arlington, Va., 1983.

The Final Collapse, Cao Van Vien. U.S. Army Center of Military History, Washington, D.C., 1983.

Index

About the Author

David Butler was born in Massachusetts. He has worked as an editor at *Playboy* and *Newsweek,* and made three trips to Vietnam during the war. He was in Saigon reporting for NBC radio from mid-1974 until the helicopter evacuation on April 29, 1975. When not in the United States, he lives in Asia.

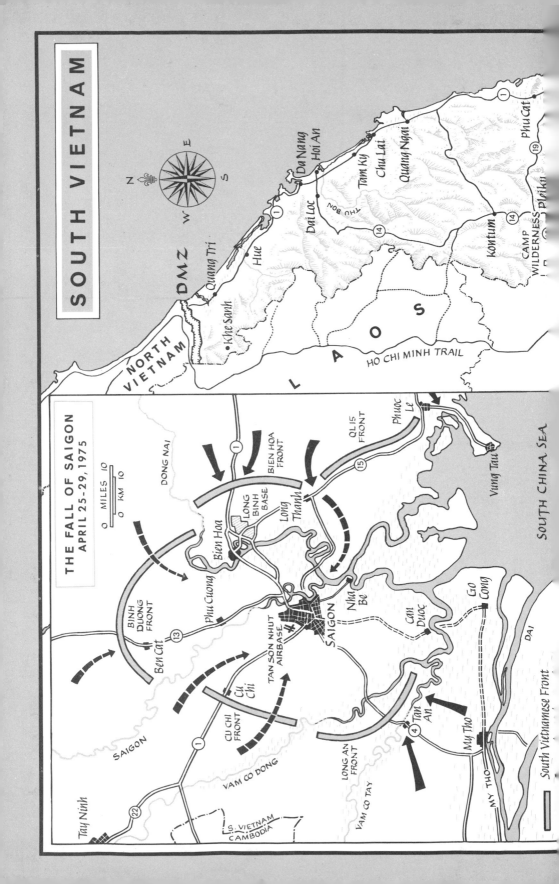

SOUTH VIETNAM

THE FALL OF SAIGON
APRIL 25-29, 1975

0 MILES 10
0 KM 10

NORTH VIETNAM

DMZ

Quang Tri

Khe Sanh

Hue

Da Nang
Hoi An

Dai Loc

Tam Ky

Chu Lai

Quang Ngai

Phu Cat

Kontum

CAMP WILDERNESS

Pleiku

LAOS

HO CHI MINH TRAIL

Tay Ninh

S. VIETNAM
CAMBODIA

VAM CO DONG

SAIGON

CU CHI FRONT

Cu Chi

TAN SON NHUT AIRBASE

BINH DUONG FRONT

Ben Cat

Phu Cuong

Bien Hoa

DONG NAI

LONG BINH BASE

BIEN HOA FRONT

Long Thanh

QL 15 FRONT

Phuoc Le

Vung Tau

SOUTH CHINA SEA

Nha Be

Cam Duoc

Go Cong

DAI

LONG AN FRONT

Tan An

My Tho

MY THO

VAM CO TAY

South Vietnamese Front